TOLERATION

TOLERATION

AN ELUSIVE VIRTUE

Edited by
David Heyd

PRINCETON UNIVERSITY PRESS   PRINCETON, NEW JERSEY

Copyright © 1996 by Princeton University Press
Published by Princeton University Press, 41 William Street,
Princeton, New Jersey 08540
In the United Kingdom: Princeton University Press,
Chichester, West Sussex

All Rights Reserved

Library of Congress Cataloging-in-Publication Data

Toleration : an elusive virtue / edited by David Heyd.
p. cm.

Includes bibliographical references and index.
ISBN 0-691-04371-X
ISBN 0-691-04370-1 (pbk.)
1.Toleration.   I. Heyd, David.
BJ1431.T64 1996
179'.9—dc20 95-34037 CIP

This book has been composed in Sabon

Princeton University Press books are printed
on acid-free paper and meet the guidelines
for permanence and durability of the Committee
on Production Guidelines for Book Longevity
of the Council on Library Resources

Second printing, and first paperback printing,1998

http://pup.princeton.edu

Printed in the United States of America

10 9 8 7 6 5 4 3 2

Contents

Preface

THIS VOLUME contains papers delivered in the Tenth Jerusalem Philosophical Encounter held in Jerusalem in January 1992 under the auspices of the S. H. Bergman Center for Philosophical Studies at The Hebrew University. I am grateful to Yirmiyahu Yovel, the founder and general editor of the Jerusalem Philosophical Encounters, and to Ruth Gavison and Igor Primoratz for their assistance in planning this conference on toleration.

Will Kymlicka's article was first published in *Analyse und Kritik* (vol. 14/1, 1993). Joshua Cohen's article was originally published in *Philosophy and Public Affairs* (vol. 22/3, 1993). I am grateful to Princeton University Press and to the editors of both journals for their kind permission to reprint these articles.

One article is sadly missing from this collection. Judith Shklar was in the process of writing a paper for the conference in Jerusalem when she died suddenly and prematurely. In the abstract, which she wrote just a few weeks before her death, Shklar wrote,

> Because toleration emerged as a vital issue in political theory as part of the upheavals of the Reformation, it was some time before arguments in its favor lost their originally religious character. The question of what meaning and worth toleration has within a pluralistic and skeptical context is far from clear, but it might be helpful if one looked at the demands of tolerant personal conduct apart from toleration as a political practice. By keeping the two apart from one another, one might gain a better view of the actual intellectual and political issues that confront us here and now.

Typical of Shklar's acute sensitivity to the philosophical zeitgeist, these words, written long before the conference, can now serve as a motto to this collection of essays. The problematic status of the idea of toleration in a pluralistic society and the tension between its public use as a political practice and the private manifestation as a personal virtue are indeed the two major lines of discussion running through most of the articles.

Judith Shklar was a staunch defender of liberalism, a person of rare intellectual integrity, a sharp and relentless interlocutor, but above all a warm and generous friend. This collection of essays is fondly dedicated to her memory.

List of Contributors

JOSHUA COHEN, Department of Philosophy, Massachusetts Institute of Technology

GEORGE P. FLETCHER, School of Law, Columbia University

GORDON GRAHAM, Department of Moral Philosophy, University of St. Andrews

MOSHE HALBERTAL, Department of Philosophy, The Hebrew University of Jerusalem

ALON HAREL, Faculty of Law, The Hebrew University of Jerusalem

BARBARA HERMAN, Department of Philosophy, University of California–Los Angeles

DAVID HEYD, Department of Philosophy, The Hebrew University of Jerusalem

JOHN HORTON, Department of Politics, Keele University

WILL KYMLICKA, Department of Philosophy, University of Ottawa

AVISHAI MARGALIT, Department of Philosophy, The Hebrew University of Jerusalem

DAVID A. J. RICHARDS, Faculty of Law, New York University

T. M. SCANLON, Department of Philosophy, Harvard University

BERNARD WILLIAMS, Corpus Christi College, Oxford

TOLERATION

Introduction

I

Tolerance is a philosophically elusive concept.[1] Indeed, in the liberal
ethos of the last three centuries, it has been hailed as one of the fundamental ethical and political values, and it still occupies a powerful position in
contemporary legal and political rhetoric. However, our firm belief in the
value of tolerance is not matched by analogous theoretical certitude. Perhaps the best indication of the shaky grounds on which the philosophical
discussion of tolerance rests is the intriguing lack of agreement on paradigm cases. In the theory of rights, virtue, and duty, people who radically
disagree about the analysis and justification of these concepts can still
appeal to a commonly shared repertory of examples. But with tolerance,
it seems that we can find hardly a single concrete case that would be
universally agreed to be a typical object of discussion.

Courage and habeas corpus are standard cases of virtue and rights,
respectively. But would we agree on defining the attitude of restraint toward neo-Nazi groups as tolerance, or, alternatively, would we describe
as tolerance the way the heterosexual majority treats homosexuals? I suspect that today, despite the long and respectable history of the idea of
religious toleration, only a few Catholics or Protestants would describe
the way they feel about each other in terms of tolerance. And beyond the
derivative use we make of the concept of tolerance in everyday language,
it is doubtful whether the attitude of conservative parents toward their
children's styles in music and fashion can be taken as a genuine case of
toleration, that is, as exemplifying the deep moral value associated with
the concept.

The threat of indeterminacy seems to arise from two opposite directions: absolutism and pluralism. There are, on the one hand, cases in
which the firm commitment to a moral truth restricts the scope of application of the concept of toleration. For instance, any mode of restraint in
the attitude to anti-Turkish incitement by German skinheads would
hardly be considered "tolerance," because the object of the restraint is
patently immoral. In other words, some actions are straightforwardly
"intolerable," and any conciliatory attitude toward them could at best be
based on *pragmatic* considerations (of fear or the need for compromise),

but never on the idea of tolerance. On the other hand, there are cases in which the belief in moral pluralism calls for the acceptance of ways of life (or beliefs) different from my own, either because I acknowledge their legitimacy or because I simply do not care about them. Refraining from a hostile reaction to members of other religions, or from persecuting homosexuals, is accordingly hardly to be considered as displaying tolerance under contemporary pluralistic conceptions.

So it seems that the idea of toleration has undergone a gradual process of compression between the demand not to tolerate the immoral (absolutism) and the requirement to accept the legitimacy of the morally different (pluralism). On the theoretical level, this means that toleration in the strict sense must be clearly distinguished from <u>pragmatic compromise</u> with the otherwise "intolerable" as well as from <u>moral indifference</u>. That is to say, the concept of toleration must be narrowed down in its philosophical use so as to refer strictly to cases in which restraint in the response to another's belief or action is based on some specifically *moral* grounds (thus excluding both compromise and indifference). But what are the typical examples for such a narrowed-down idea of toleration?

The history of the idea of tolerance provides us with good examples, from religious toleration in Locke to the modern toleration of minorities, such as Jews, African Americans, homosexuals, and so on. But these are typically historically outdated examples, because today we would expect people to abstain from hostile behavior toward all these groups, not as a matter of toleration but as a matter of the rights of others or the recognition of the value of their ways of life, or because it is simply "none of our business" to interfere with the beliefs and most of the actions of other human beings.

Classical liberalism, such as Locke's or Mill's, rested on the principle of tolerance more than does today's form of liberalism, which is closer to skeptical pluralism. Locke's argument for tolerance was based on the counterproductiveness of the compulsion of religious beliefs; Mill's was based on the value of personal autonomy. The shift from these views to the modern conception, which rests on easy acceptance of the heterogeneity of values and ways of life, pushes the concept of tolerance dangerously close to that of indifference. And even if this moral development is welcomed by the moral pluralist, it must be clear that much of the original intrinsic value of tolerance is put under threat.

It is accordingly fair to say, as a generalization, that side by side with the growing use of ideas of toleration in public discourse and political debate, there is also an increasing awareness in philosophical theory of the tensions and difficulties involved in the definition and justification of the concept of toleration. The present collection of articles attests to this skeptical trend: in emphasizing the shifting locus of toleration in the historical evolution of the idea; in the narrowing down of its scope in the attempt to supply the necessary and sufficient conditions defining it; in the normative difficulty in defending it from the challenges of intolerant ideas and groups; or, in general, in navigating between the Scylla of some minimal commitment to the defence of moral ideals and the fight against evil and injustice and the Charybdis of the indifferent acceptance of an overly "liberal" pluralism.

Bernard Williams's paper sets this skeptical scene for the whole collection in a masterly way. Toleration, according to Williams, is paradoxical, because it is both necessary and impossible. That is, pluralism and conflict of values call for toleration, but toleration is required only for what seems to be intolerable! The attitude of tolerance should be clearly distinguished from both indifference and Hobbesian compromise, particularly if we wish to regard it as a personal virtue rather than merely a political arrangement.

The distinction between tolerance and indifference is an important constituent in any theoretical attempt to delineate the contours of the former. But, as Williams points out, the borderline between the two is constantly shifting in the history of moral and political value. In seventeenth-century England, people's religious practices were hardly treated as lying beyond the legitimate concern of their fellow citizens. In nineteenth-century England, people were rarely indifferent to their neighbors' sexual practices. But in present-day England, most people do not feel very strongly about either the religious faith or the sexual preferences of others. One could even generalize and say that the scope of indifference is growing in the field of value judgment, and that liberalism today means less the toleration of other ways of life than the cool acceptance of the very plurality and heterogeneity of lifestyles. If that is the case, toleration might prove in the future to have been "an interim value," that is, an attitude that characterized political morality between the age of absolutism, in which every deviation from the only truth was suppressed, and the age of pluralism, in which nothing is considered a deviation.

It is an interesting feature in the analysis of toleration that the narrower its definition the more paradoxical it becomes. Thus, the virtue of tolerating the intolerable would not be paradoxical if the object of toleration were not "really" or genuinely intolerable. But John Horton, who in many respects shares Williams's skepticism, adds to the definition of toleration the condition that its object be not only thought to be morally wrong, but *justifiably* thought so. The homophobe's restraint toward homosexual behavior cannot, accordingly, be defined as a case of toleration, because there are no good reasons to object to the behavior in the first place. The same applies to restraint in interracial relations and attitudes. Horton's strict definition of toleration excludes two types of phenomena:

those that are so bad or wrong that they must not be tolerated and those there is no objective reason to reject and that hence should be fully accepted or even respected. This leaves only a narrow space for toleration, namely, the scope of beliefs and actions justifiably disapproved of yet not to the extent of being "intolerable." Abortion could be an example. But one could speculate that in the future even this deeply contested issue will become a matter of indifferent acceptance by liberals.

A possible solution of the paradox of toleration lies in metaethical relativism, that is, in an attempt to deny the objectivist assumptions on which Williams's and Horton's definitions of toleration rest. Thus, if no commitment in matters of values can be justified, we are called on in the name of a second-order principle to restrain ourselves in our attitude to views and practices different from our own. However, as Gordon Graham argues, the very point of toleration is that, contrary to conventional wisdom, it must be distinguished from moral pluralism and relativism. Thus, relativism, on the one hand, can lead to a Nietzschean intolerant model of power relations, whereas objectivism, on the other, as in the case of Mill and Popper, might positively require a tolerant attitude. It is Graham's conviction that toleration and objectivism in morals go hand in hand: there can be no progress in our study of moral truth without an unrestrained flow of ideas and beliefs, and the value of this tolerant attitude to ideas and beliefs does not make sense unless the existence of a right answer in moral issues is assumed.

The starting point of Barbara Herman's paper follows the line of Graham's concern with the threat of pluralism. Deep pluralism is dangerous to social stability as well as to "engaged moral judgment." Like Williams and Horton, Herman recognizes the tension between toleration as a form of restraint in the response to the beliefs and actions of the other and the moral disapproval of these beliefs and actions. The first step she takes in attempting a solution to the paradox is to distinguish between the political, that is, public, character of the tolerant restraint and the moral, that is, private, character of the negative judgment of the belief or action in question. But Herman observes the danger of suppressing the other under the guise of toleration, that is to say, legitimizing the negative judgment by the political ideal of tolerance (like letting the minority express its grievances but not really listening to it).

Herman proposes a Kantian analysis of moral judgment, which would both save objectivism in ethics and be sufficiently context-sensitive to satisfy modern pluralistic views. The key lies in the idea of "a community of moral judgment" in which competing value systems are discussed in a shared deliberative field under second-order regulative principles. One of these principles is toleration, whose particular virtue is that of allowing for a community of moral judgment more inclusive than the one based on

*Later
Rawls*

a common value system shared by all members. However, Herman warns
that toleration cannot be taken as adequate for creating a pluralistic society, because it is only a negative (political) principle, lacking the positive,
affective mutual engagement called for by a stable society. Toleration in
itself cannot secure the understanding of other points of view. The ultimate solution to the problem of the Kingdom of Ends in Herman's interpretation is moral rather than merely political, that is, the creation of a
maximal set of compossible ends.

So far the idea of toleration has been discussed in traditional, individualistic terms. Indeed, the history of toleration is closely associated with
the rise of the individual as the locus of natural rights and personal autonomy. However, the inception of the ideal of toleration is no less related to
the Wars of Religion and the call for restraint in the attitude to people
belonging to other religious _groups_. Will Kymlicka takes seriously the
tension between the two levels of the alleged right to be tolerated: personal liberty on the one hand, and the rights of a group to maintain its
collective identity on the other. The millet system of the Ottoman Empire
and the status of Native American tribes and the Amish in America are
examples of the toleration of others _as_ groups. The trouble, as Kymlicka
shows, is that with all its moral merits, group toleration can involve sacrificing individual rights, particularly by giving the group immunity from
external interference (e.g., by the state) in the way it deals with the internal "deviations" of individuals. According to Kymlicka, Rawls's late
"political liberalism" is not rich enough to support a conception of toleration in which individuals are left with the autonomy to form their own
lives, especially when this involves changing deep group affiliation (religion, tribal life, etc.). Yet Kymlicka warns against forcing the ideas of
liberalism on nonliberal groups and calls for a solution of compromise,
leaving them with some living space of autonomy in running their own
collective affairs.

In an interesting critical examination of Kymlicka's views, Moshe
Halbertal challenges the deep-rooted association of toleration with autonomy. His main thesis is that autonomy, in the sense of the ability to
rationally _choose_ to revise one's ends and identity, is not a necessary condition of individual freedom of the sort toleration is meant to protect.
Moreover, if toleration is justified in terms of autonomy, there is the risk
of imposing a particular conception of the good (autonomy, in our case)
on individuals who do not value it. The weakness of a justification of
toleration by appeal to autonomy is especially manifest in the sphere of
education: kibbutz education and Jewish Orthodox education inculcate
particular values, which do not include autonomy, and Halbertal insists
that there is nothing intolerant about these forms of education that would
justify public interference. In other words, society is not entitled to force

communities (kibbutz, the Amish) to bring up "rational choosers" (a goal Halbertal suspects is conceptually incoherent anyway). Political toleration is thus extended to communities in a truly pluralistic society (which, unlike the millet system, is not based on the asymmetrical relations of power between the dominant culture and the minority groups).

Harel's article also shows sensitivity to the shortcomings of traditional liberal theory that advocates toleration on purely individualistic grounds. Harel, like Kymlicka, argues that the individual has strong communal interests. Some of these come under the concept of "exclusionary interests," that is, "interests of members of the community in reinforcing their separateness from a larger social body"; others are entitled "inclusionary interests," because they refer to "the interests members of a community have in becoming an integral part of a broader society." Orthodox Jews' condemnation of homosexual practices is an instance of the former; women's demand to suppress pornography and the struggle of Blacks to curb racist hate speech are examples of the latter. Harel's central claim is that the liberal idea of toleration is challenged from both sides, that is to say, Orthodox Jews demand toleration of their intolerant attitudes to others, and women demand an intolerant interference in the freedom of expression of the producers of pornography. As Harel notes, the two types of challenges are also mutually exclusive; that is, the appeal to the right to maintain a particularistic, separate communal identity within the larger society is incompatible with the appeal to the egalitarian principle as the basis of social membership. Thus, we may add that the paradox of tolerance seems to be unsolvable, because there are good reasons both for tolerating certain forms of intolerant practices and for not tolerating them.

A different perspective on the toleration of groups is suggested by Richards. He draws an analogy between the role of the idea of toleration in interfaith relations and interracial relations. Racial discrimination, like religious persecution, is based on the corruption of conscience and the violation of rights. Toleration was motivated, says Richards, by an attitude of political skepticism about enforceable political epistemologies in both spheres. Accordingly, the abolitionists should be seen as the most principled advocates of the idea of toleration in the nineteenth century, as were Bayle and Locke in the seventeenth. The kind of sectarianism that made slavery possible is challenged in the name of "public reason," the same Kantian idea to which Barbara Herman also appeals.

The theoretical difficulties in adopting a genuinely tolerant attitude are particularly manifest in religious contexts, in which the stakes are especially high, as Locke and all his followers were sharply aware. Although one could appeal to pragmatic, political, and "epistemic" arguments to justify a tolerant attitude to individual members of other religious faiths, a true acceptance of competing religions cannot be justified on the theological level, especially when monotheistic religions are considered. In Avishai Margalit's words, "a religion based on constitutive, redemptive, revealed truths cannot ascribe value to a religion that contradicts these truths." Through a detailed analysis of Lessing's *Three Rings*, Margalit reaches a conclusion that denies the possibility of religious pluralism and leaves little space for religious tolerance. Unlike the context of science and the growth of knowledge (so central to Mill's argument for toleration), religious belief—being a matter of revelation—cannot attach any value to error, and hence the traditional liberal justification for toleration cannot be applied in the relations of one monotheistic religion with its competitors.

The three main spheres in which the principle of toleration has been operative are religion, sex, and expression. George Fletcher analyzes the "instability" of the notion of toleration in its indeterminate range between the "ceiling" of harm (which calls for intervention) and the "floor" of disregard (things that are "none of my business"). This analysis is reminiscent of Williams's skeptical view of toleration, but Fletcher adds that the grounds for toleration vary in the three aforementioned spheres. In religious matters, there is the internal dimension of personal conviction that makes intervention counterproductive; in the case of freedom of expression, there is the danger of a "slippery slope," which calls for tolerating phenomena like flag burning or denying the Holocaust; and in the case of sexual behavior, immunity from intolerant interference is called for by the value of privacy and the high price of intervention. Again, all these arguments for toleration cast doubt on its allegedly "intrinsic" value, or its justification as an independent virtue.

It is also Joshua Cohen's claim that the protection of free speech is not freestanding or absolute. It is true that the special weight of freedom of expression together with the tendency of governments to curb it for unjustified reasons lend support to a strong protection and lead to the toleration even of "hate speech." But this protection raises the dilemma faced by American universities that try to restrict forms of speech that are directly offensive to minority groups within the campuses. Cohen carefully and systematically analyzes the basis for the principle of free expression and its limits, taking into account the kinds of interests promoted by free speech, the price of its restriction, and some fundamental background facts (like the sensitivity of human beings to offensive speech and the temptation of those who have the power to curb it).

Finally, and still in line with the qualified and suspicious approach to the idea of toleration, Scanlon's article highlights the *risks* of a tolerant attitude for members of a society who are not indifferent to the way their society develops. I may adopt a tolerant attitude toward an individual

fellow citizen, but that does not mean that I forgo my right to resist the
wider influence that person's kind of lifestyle has on the society in which
we all live. Thus, the protection from religious coercion provided by the
First Amendment does not fully satisfy my interests as a secular citizen
living in a society that in my mind is over-religious. In other words, under
the umbrella of the right to be tolerated, certain groups in society may
lead it to undesirable changes in its identity and character. Like Kymlicka,
Scanlon sharpens our awareness of the tension between toleration as an
ideal for individual human beings taken "in abstraction" and the deep
and legitimate interest of members of the community to take part in "the
informal politics of social life" and help mold it in a certain way.
Scanlon's powerfully illustrative analogy is to our attitude to members of
our family and close community, in which we do not typically show a
tolerant acceptance of behavior of which we strongly disapprove.
Scanlon concludes that this inner tension in the ideal of toleration requires a compromise or accommodation, which in its very nature lacks
stability or determinacy.

Thus, an overview of the varied collection of papers in this volume
points to a common suspicion of the sweeping liberal support for the
principle of toleration, not only because the line between the duty to tolerate and the requirement to oppose the intolerable is not always clear,
but because the concept of tolerance itself is problematic, or even paradoxical. The thread that persistently runs through all the papers is that
beyond the strong moral commitment of liberal citizens in modern pluralistic societies to the ideal of toleration there is a deep theoretical doubt
concerning the likelihood of providing it with a stable philosophical
ground.

II

In the remaining pages of this introduction, I try to propose an analysis of
the concept of toleration that attempts to give an account of its elusive-
ness. The concept of toleration I discuss is the strict or narrow one,
namely, that which is distinguished from other types of restraint, like
indifference or pragmatic compromise. This implies that the following
comments cannot be expected to apply to the whole variety of everyday
uses of the concept of toleration but only to the typical or paradigmatic ones. It focuses primarily on the ethical, rather than the political,
context, that is, on toleration as a virtue of individuals relating to other
individuals.

Furthermore, we should keep in mind that the indeterminacy of the
concept of toleration is due to its being "compressed" between two
spheres: phenomena that by no means should be tolerated (like cruelty

and murder) and phenomena that should not be objected to in the first place (like gender or racial identity). The remaining sphere left for this narrow (but morally valuable) concept of tolerance consists of beliefs and actions that are justifiably (and maybe morally) disapproved of and yet are said to be immune from negative interference. The duality of conflicting reasons for rejecting and accepting certain beliefs and actions creates the so-called paradox of toleration, which is obviously more pointed in the case of morally objectionable phenomena. One way to solve the paradox is (as suggested by Horton) to distinguish between the two types of conflicting reasons and then show, in each case, the grounds for appealing to one set of reasons rather than to the other.

The conception I wish to outline can be called "perceptual." It treats toleration as involving a perceptual shift: from beliefs to the subject holding them, or from actions to their agent. The model of two sets of reasons implies that the reasons for disapproval and those for restraint are *balanced* against each other by some sort of a weighting procedure. The perceptual model, on the other hand, treats the two sets of reasons as qualitatively distinct and irreducible to any common ground. The virtue of tolerance consists in a switch of perspective, a transformation of attitude, based not on the assessment of which reasons are overriding but on ignoring one type of reason altogether by focusing on the other. Thus, to be tolerant one must be able to suspend one's judgment of the object, to turn one's view away from it, to treat it as irrelevant, for the sake of a generically different perspective. It is a kind of a Gestalt switch, which, like the rabbit-duck case, involves on the one hand a choice, sometimes an intentional effort, and on the other hand an "image" that is always exclusive of its competing image at any given time.

The essential element in this perceptual shift might be called "personalization." When opinions and beliefs, actions and practices, are judged on their merit, they are considered impersonally, that is, in abstraction from the subjects holding, choosing, or acting on them. Opinions and practices can be judged for their validity, truth, and value irrespective of the way they have been adopted, chosen, and followed. But opinions and actions do not float subjectless in the air; they can also be viewed as held with integrity, chosen freely, or followed authentically. This personal dimension introduces a categorically different kind of judgment, to which tolerance belongs. The intimate relation as well as the distinction between beliefs and believers, actions and agents, has been the cornerstone of all theories of toleration from Locke, through Kant and Mill, to Rawls, Dworkin, and Raz.

Some contexts typically require an impersonal judgment of beliefs and practices, that is, in abstraction from the person holding them. Obvious examples are the evaluation of scientific beliefs or of legal rules. In these contexts, ad hominem considerations are rightly thought of as fallacies.

But in the sphere of interpersonal relations, particularly when actual interference in another's life is considered, the personal index of beliefs and
actions becomes highly relevant; it is never strictly with beliefs or actions
that we are interfering, but with individuals and their lives. Tolerance is
a virtue that can thus be viewed as the symmetrical counterpart of the
virtue of unbiased scientific neutrality (or the blindfolded goddess of justice, forced to ignore the identity of the accused). Both consist of a capacity to adopt a partial perspective in order to achieve a certain goal: the
truths of propositions, independent of the persons believing in them, on
the one hand; respect for persons, independent of their beliefs, on the
other. Note that respect is a moral attitude to others that typically disre-
gards most actions and opinions of the object of respect. Toleration is
thus a sub-category of respect, involving restraint.[2]

I call toleration a perceptual virtue, because it involves a shift of attention rather than an overall judgment. Tolerant people overcome the drive
to interfere in the life of another not because they come to believe that the
reasons for restraint are weightier than the reasons for disapproval, but
because the attention is shifted from the object of disapproval to the hu-
manity or the moral standing of the subject before them. This is a feat of
abstraction analogous to the opposite abstraction of ideas from the
human minds behind them. It consists of the capacity to ignore, or rather
suspend or "bracket," a set of considerations, which do not thereby lose
any of their original force. Toleration is a perceptual virtue, because it
makes one perceive the other as more than merely the subject of certain
beliefs or the agent of a particular action. The nature of this "abstracted
subject or agent" might be constituted by the very power of choice (as in
Millian theories of autonomy), the rational nucleus of the personality (as
in Kantian conceptions of autonomy), or the relation of the particular
belief or action to a wide system of beliefs or a biography (forming an
integrated whole, or a way of life). In any case, it presupposes a distinction between some sort of a core of the human personality and a periphery of particular beliefs and actions. It treats beliefs and practices not as
isolated entities but as belonging to a personal cognitive system or to a
form of life. This is exactly why the tolerating attitude is closely associated with "understanding" the other, that is, the capacity to anchor the
action or belief in its personal background of motives, intentions, or other
beliefs in the same cognitive system.

The inspiration for the perceptual model presented here is, of course,
John McDowell's work in ethics, as well as Iris Murdoch's ideas about
the role of attention in moral judgment. McDowell argues that virtuous
action is not an ability to follow rules or the inculcation of particular
desires but a perceptual capacity to view situations in a certain light as
constituting reasons for action. This, of course, does not mean that

McDowell would be willing to analyze toleration on these lines, especially because it is doubtful (as Williams has shown) whether toleration can be treated as an ordinary virtue at all. Above all, it should be noted that my perceptual analysis of toleration does not share the "silencing element" in McDowell's analysis of virtue: whereas in the mind of the virtuous person the "correct" perception of the situation silences all other alternative perceptions, making the person irreversibly blind to them, the Gestalt switch of the tolerant person is not exclusive, does not make the other set of reasons irrelevant in the mind of the person, and is reversible.[3] One important implication for this difference between my proposal and McDowell's conception of virtue is that toleration calls for *reasons*, that is to say, the switch to the personalized perspective must itself be rationally motivated, because the competing (negative) judgment of the belief or action does not completely lose its original (independent) force. The tolerator must therefore appeal to *second-order* reasons, such as the intrinsic value of autonomy, human respect, the overall value of the whole way of life of which the particular (wrong) belief or action are but a part (as in Harel's view), and so on.

Furthermore, because it is a rational choice of the tolerator to make the perceptual shift in one direction, so it might be rational to make the shift on another occasion in the other direction. In some contexts, we should ignore the individual agent and focus our attention on the action and the reasons for curbing it. This might be called for either when the actions or beliefs in question are particularly harmful or offensive (murder, hate speech) or when they are in some sense not genuinely the agent's (irresponsible behavior of children or mentally retarded adults). Again, unlike the case of virtue, which in McDowell's conception is "absolute," toleration has limits, and these can be rationally debated in terms of the weight of second-order reasons of various kinds.[4]

The traditional, "balancing" account of toleration can at most appeal to the overriding force of the reasons for restraint over the reasons for interfering in the wrong belief or practice. But this is an ad hoc explanation, which considers the relative weight of particular reasons in each case. The perceptual model, by appealing to a second-order reason, provides a *general form* for the tolerant option and is thus theoretically superior in being more systematic in the justification of toleration. The general superiority of the personalized perspective lies in the intrinsic value of individual integrity and the priority of the unique subject-agent to the impersonal content or validity of the beliefs and actions held by her. The values of autonomy, respect, authenticity, integrity, and interpersonal recognition and acceptance are indicative of this priority. These values are particularly conspicuous in the practical realm of agency (rather than the cognitive realm of belief), because they condition the very possibility

of cohesive communal or social coexistence. The Gestalt switch of toleration is grounded in the charitable way we want to treat people who are
not too distant (to whom we feel indifferent) or too close (whom we wish
to change or mold). Toleration is consequently seen to be also a specifically social virtue, that is, a virtue that not only presupposes but also
promotes the social cohesion of a community.

I cannot develop this extremely schematic idea for the analysis of toleration here. I will, however, make a few remarks as to the way it could be
deployed to help account for some of the issues raised by the discussion
of toleration. Take first the distinction between mere restraint and genuine tolerance. Restraint in itself is a psychological capacity: patience, the
ability to check and control one's emotions and actions. It is a typically
affective or conative concept, which might be a prerequisite for tolerance.
Tolerance, however, is, in the strict sense, the attitude of someone who
ideally would not even have to exercise restraint, because the perception
of the tolerated party as a rational or autonomous human being would
completely overshadow the motives for the initial objection to the beliefs
or practices in question. Like the virtue of innocence, that is, the disposition not to see defects in people, tolerance is a matter of perception, even
though it can certainly be assisted by a patient temper. We could say that
restraint and patience are the condition of the ability to make the perspectival shift, but tolerance is the disposition, the character tendency (and
hence virtue), of choosing to actually make this shift. The general nature
of the tolerant disposition accords with the general form of the second-
order reason for showing restraint toward an otherwise objectionable
practice.

According to the perceptual conception, only human beings are,
strictly speaking, the objects of toleration. We do not tolerate opinions
and beliefs, or even actions and practices, only the subjects holding disliked beliefs and the agents of detested actions. As I have suggested, toleration consists exactly in the shift from the perspective of judging beliefs
and actions impersonally to that focusing on persons. Only human beings
can be the object of restraint based on respect, which is required by the
idea of tolerance. This could also explain why we usually refer to traits of
character or psychological dispositions, rather than particular acts, as the
objects of tolerance. The former are conceptually closer to the way we
identify and refer to individual agents.

In his article, Horton raises the intriguing question of inculcating the
virtue of tolerance in the process of education. How can we bring up
children to become tolerant of others without weakening their commitment to their cherished beliefs and preferences? How can we expect people to grow up to have a sharply defined political or religious profile, a
well-defined aesthetic and moral personality, and yet be tolerant of in-

compatible sets of beliefs and values? If we adopt the perceptual model, this difficulty looks slightly less menacing. Training children to look at people without regard to some of their convictions and behavior might *really* not be easy, but it is fully compatible with implanting strong personal convictions and principles. I would even chance the generalization that young people tend to be less tolerant because they are less disposed to separate opinions from their subjects, actions from their agents. (Incidentally, it seems that they are equally more liable to the symmetrical fallacy in the cognitive sphere, namely, ad hominem judgment.) On the other hand, the perceptual analysis of toleration is compatible with Scanlon's claim (to which Halbertal would probably agree) that we show tolerance primarily to other individuals in our society whom we conceive of as independent of substantive values, rather than to our close relatives (e.g., children) whose moral character we try to mold.

Like Graham's thesis in his article, though for a different reason, the perceptual view frees tolerance from its dependence on relativism and multiculturalism. Toleration of the practices and beliefs of other peoples and cultures involves recognizing the intrinsic value of the human beings who are committed to certain cognitive systems or who autonomously choose and follow certain systems of rules and values. It does not require any weakening of certainty, confidence, or commitment to our own beliefs and values. Ignoring this rather trivial truth often leads modern liberal cultures to believe that open-mindedness and toleration are promoted by inculcating agnostic attitudes or loosening moral and cognitive attachments.

The perceptual account also interprets the idea of "being judgmental": it amounts to the tendency to conflate the judgments we apply to beliefs and actions with those we apply to their subjects and agents. In other words, being judgmental with regard to beliefs and practices in the abstract is a desirable attitude; being judgmental toward human beings is not always a virtue, because we should sometimes respond to them not through their beliefs but through the way those beliefs have been adopted or cohere with other beliefs in a whole system held by a particular human mind. This point coheres with the forgiving attitude or the "understanding" associated with tolerance, as noted above.

Approaching tolerance in perceptual terms also explains why governments cannot strictly be said to be tolerant. Tolerance is not only shown exclusively *to* people but also exclusively *by* people. Only human minds can make the perspectival shift that changes the criteria of relevance or salience of two competing sets of valid considerations. Governments or states cannot literally be said to be patient, to restrain themselves, to "suffer" (in Hebrew, the word for tolerance and the word for patience are derived from the same root, denoting burden or suffering). The state has no views, no likes and dislikes, which it has to suspend so as to honor people's autonomy or liberty. One may therefore speak only of the *neutrality* of the state, precisely in its having no concern whatsoever with the particular beliefs and lifestyles of its citizens. But neutrality is an abstract principle, like equality before the law, or the equal claim of individuals as citizens to be respected. Satisfying the requirements of this principle does not involve any kind of tolerance in the narrow moral sense.

It has often been said that although people are happy not to be persecuted, they do not like to be tolerated, because toleration is only partial acceptance, the acceptance of the right of a person to lead a certain life or to entertain certain beliefs; it does not extend to the acceptance of the practices and beliefs themselves. It seems to me that the asymmetry between the tolerator and the tolerated on this matter can be explained by the fact that the subjects of the beliefs or the agents of the practices in question find it harder to make the perspectival shift made by the tolerator, because they identify with their beliefs and practices in a much stronger way. The abstraction of agency from actual actions is harder for the agent than for the spectator. Thus, we do not usually apply the concept of tolerance reflexively; that is, we do not say that people tolerate themselves. Moreover, from the first-person point of view, such an abstraction usually has no point or function. It even creates a sense of alienation of subjects from their own beliefs and actions. But from the point of view of the second- or third-person perspective, there is an obvious social benefit to be gained by such a separation.

The lesson of many of the papers in this volume is that there is a distinction between genuine toleration (e.g., in religious affairs, sexual practices, and free expression, as noted by Fletcher) and "toleration" in the purely descriptive sense (e.g., racial toleration, in the sense used by Richards with regard to the abolitionists). The perceptual conception, however, explains why we tend to place some value also on restraint in relation to members of another race, even beyond the obvious value of avoiding racial persecution. My hypothesis is that if the restraint is based on moral grounds, then not only would these lead one to see members of the other race as deserving of human respect irrespective of their color, but eventually this perception would lead to a change in the initial objection or dislike. It is hard to imagine *morally* relevant reasons for restraining oneself from acting on the basis of racial prejudice without at the same time undermining the force of these very prejudices. This could have important implications for educational techniques for fighting racial prejudices. These would consist of a three-stage process: first, abstaining from acting against members of the other race (mere restraint); second, *seeing* them differently, that is, providing the morally relevant reasons for the restraint (toleration); third, abandoning the initial opposition or disapproval, thus making toleration (that is, the *shift* in perception) altogether superfluous (full acceptance). Richards's historical perspective attests to this very process in the passage from persecution and discrimination to racial equality via racial toleration.

The perceptual account does justice to the specifically moral dimension of tolerance, its being more than a simple psychological restraint or a behavioral disposition. It takes seriously Horton's conclusion that "not everyone who rightly restrains themselves from acting so as to interfere with conduct to which they object, acts tolerantly," but it does not see it as "most surprising" or a "hint of another paradox of toleration." By giving an account of the relation between the two sets of conflicting considerations, the perceptual view offers a framework for dissolving the original paradox of toleration. Nevertheless, the range of phenomena to which the narrow concept of toleration applies remains elusive and indeterminate. This is due to the dependence of the definition of the scope of toleration (indeed its very possibility) on general but changing moral theories concerning its purported objects.

Notes

1. In this volume, "tolerance" and "toleration" are used interchangeably.

2. Forgiveness is similar to respect in abstracting a certain idea of the subject from the action that deserves a negative response (like resentment or punishment). Hagit Benbaji has suggested to me the interesting possibility of solving the paradox of toleration by treating it as supererogatory. Indeed, the analogy between toleration and forgiveness might support this original proposal. Both forgiveness and the tolerant attitude are meritorious in going beyond the call of duty; that is to say, they are particularly valuable without being obligatory. The initial hostile response in both cases is justified; that is, the tolerated practice as well as the forgiven act remain in themselves "wrong." See my *Supererogation* (Cambridge: Cambridge University Press, 1982), ch. 7.

3. See J. McDowell, "Virtue and Reason," *Monist* 62 (1979): 331–50, particularly p. 335.

4. I am much indebted to John Horton and Yitzhak Benbaji for their detailed and illuminating comments on the limits of the analogy with McDowell's conception of virtue.

1

Toleration: An Impossible Virtue?

BERNARD WILLIAMS

THE DIFFICULTY with toleration is that it seems to be at once necessary and impossible. It is necessary where different groups have conflicting beliefs—moral, political, or religious—and realize that there is no alternative to their living together, that is to say, no alternative except armed conflict, which will not resolve their disagreements and will impose continuous suffering. These are the circumstances in which toleration is necessary. Yet in those same circumstances it may well seem impossible.

If violence and the breakdown of social cooperation are threatened in these circumstances, it is because people find others' beliefs or ways of life deeply unacceptable. In matters of religion, for instance (which, historically, was the first area in which the idea of toleration was used), the need for toleration arises because one of the groups, at least, thinks that the other is blasphemously, disastrously, obscenely wrong. The members of one group may think that the members of the other group need to be helped toward the truth, or that third parties need to be protected against the bad opinions. Most important—and most relevant for the dilemmas of liberal societies—they may think that the leaders or elders of the other group are keeping the young and perhaps the women from enlightenment and liberation. They see it as not merely in the general interest but in the interest of some in the other group that the true religion (as they believe it to be) should prevail. It is because the disagreement goes this deep that the parties to it think that they cannot accept the existence of each other. We need to tolerate other people and their ways of life only in situations that make it very difficult to do so. Toleration, we may say, is required only for the intolerable. That is its basic problem.

We may think of toleration as an attitude that a more powerful group, or a majority, has (or fails to have) toward a less powerful group or a minority. In a country where there are many Christians and few Muslims, there may be a question whether the Christians tolerate the Muslims; the Muslims do not get the choice, so to speak, whether to tolerate the Christians or not. If the proportions of Christians and Muslims are reversed, so will be the direction of toleration. This is how we usually think of toleration, and it is natural to do so, because discussions of toleration have often been discussions of what laws should exist—in particular, laws permitting or forbidding various kinds of religious practice—and the laws have been determined by the attitudes of the more powerful group. But more basically, toleration is a matter of the attitudes of any group to another and does not concern only the relations of the more powerful to the less powerful. It is certainly not just a question of what laws there should be. A group or a creed can rightly be said to be "intolerant" if it would like to suppress or drive out others even if, as a matter of fact, it has no power to do so. The problems of toleration are to be found first at the level of human relations and of the attitude of one way of life toward another. It is not only a question of how the power of the state is to be used, though of course it supports and feeds a problem about that, a problem of political philosophy. However, we should be careful about making the assumption that what underlies a practice or an attitude of toleration must be a personal virtue of toleration. All toleration involves difficulties, but it is the virtue that especially threatens to involve conceptual impossibility.

A practice of toleration means only that one group as a matter of fact puts up with the existence of the other, differing, group. A tolerant attitude (toward this group) is any disposition or outlook that encourages them to do so: it is more likely to be identified as an attitude of toleration if it applies more generally, in their relations to other groups, and in their views of other groups' relations to each other. One possible basis of such an attitude—but only one—is a virtue of toleration, which emphasises the moral good involved in putting up with beliefs one finds offensive. I am going to suggest that this virtue, while it is not (as it may seem) impossible, does have to take a very specific form, which limits the range of people who can possess it. Because of this, it is a serious mistake to think that this virtue is the only, or perhaps the most important, attitude on which to ground practices of toleration.

If there is to be a question of toleration, it is necessary that there should be something to be tolerated; there has to be some belief or practice or way of life that one group thinks (however fanatically or unreasonably) wrong, mistaken, or undesirable. If one group simply hates another, as with a clan vendetta or cases of sheer racism, it is not really toleration that is needed: the people involved need rather to lose their hatred, their prejudice, or their implacable memories. If we are asking people to be tolerant, we are asking for something more complicated than this. They will indeed have to lose something, their desire to suppress or drive out the rival belief; but they will also keep something, their commitment to their own beliefs, which is what gave them that desire in the first place. There is a tension here between one's own commitments, and the acceptance that other people may have other, perhaps quite distasteful commitments: the tension that is typical of toleration, and which makes it so difficult. (In practice, of course, there is often a very thin or vague boundary between mere tribalism or clan loyalty and differences in outlook or conviction.)

Just because it involves some tension between commitment to one's own outlook and putting up with the other's, the attitude of toleration is supposed to be more than mere weariness or indifference. After the European Wars of Religion in the sixteenth and seventeenth centuries had raged for years, people began to think that it must be better for the different Christian churches to coexist. Various attitudes went with this development. Some people became skeptical about the distinctive claims of any church and began to think that there was no truth, or at least no truth discoverable by human beings, about the validity of one church's creed as opposed to another's. Other people began to think that the struggles had helped them to understand God's purposes better: He did not mind how people worshiped, so long as they did so in good faith within certain broad Christian limits. (In more recent times, a similar ecumenical spirit has extended beyond the boundaries of Christianity.)

These two lines of thought, in a certain sense, went in opposite directions. One of them, the skeptical, claimed that there was less to be known about God's designs than the warring parties, each with its particular fanaticism, had supposed. The other line of thought, the broad church view, claimed to have a better insight into God's designs than the warring parties had. But in their relation to the battles of faith, the two lines of thought did nevertheless end up in the same position, with the idea that precise questions of Christian belief did not matter as much as people had supposed, that less was at stake. This leads to toleration as a matter of political *practice*, and that is an extremely important result; but as an attitude, it is less than toleration. If you do not care all that much what anyone believes, you do not need the attitude of toleration, any more than you do with regard to other people's tastes in food.

In many matters, attitudes that are more tolerant in practice do arise for this reason, that people cease to think that a certain kind of behavior is a matter for disapproval or negative judgment at all. This is what is happening, in many parts of the world, with regard to kinds of sexual behavior that were previously discouraged and, in some cases, legally punished. An extramarital relationship or a homosexual ménage may arouse no hostile comment or reaction, as such things did in the past. But once again, though this is toleration as a matter of practice, the attitude it relies on is indifference rather than, strictly speaking, toleration. Indeed, if I and others in the neighborhood said that we were *tolerating* the homosexual relations of the couple next door, our attitude would be thought to be less than liberal.

There are no doubt many conflicts and areas of intolerance for which the solution should indeed be found in this direction, in the increase of indifference. Matters of sexual and social behavior which in smaller and more traditional societies are of great public concern, will come to seem more a private matter, raising in themselves no question of right or wrong. The slide toward indifference may also provide, as it did in Europe, the only solution to some religious disputes. Not all religions, of course, have any desire to convert, let alone coerce, others. They no doubt have some opinion or other (perhaps of the "broad church" type) about the state of truth or error of those who do not share their faith, but at any rate they are content to leave those other people alone. Other creeds, however, are less willing to allow error, as they see it, to flourish, and it may be that with them there is no solution except that which Europe earlier discovered (in religion, at least, if not in politics), a decline in enthusiasm. It is important that a decline in enthusiasm need not take the form of a movement's merely running out of steam. As some Christian sects discovered, a religion can have its own resources for rethinking its relations to others. One relevant idea, which had considerable influence in Europe, is that an expansive religion really wants people to believe in it, but it must recognize that this is not a result that can be achieved by force. The most that force can achieve is acquiescence and outer conformity. As Hegel said of the slave's master, the fanatic is always disappointed: what he wanted was acknowledgment, but all he can get is conformity.

Skepticism, indifference, or broad church views are not the only source of what I am calling toleration as a practice. It can also be secured in a Hobbesian equilibrium, under which the acceptance of one group by the other is the best that either of them can get. This is not, of course, in itself a principled solution, as opposed to the skeptical outlook, which is, in its own way, principled. The Hobbesian solution is also notoriously unstable. A sect that could, just about, enforce conformity might be deterred by the thought of what things would be like if the other party took over. But for this to be a Hobbesian thought, as opposed to a role-reversal argument that, for instance, refers to rights, some instability must be in the offing. The parties who are conscious of such a situation are likely to go in for preemptive strikes, and this is all the more so if they reflect that even if they can hope only for acquiescence and outer conformity in one generation, they can conceivably hope for more in later generations. As a matter of fact, in the modern world, the imposition by force of political creeds and ideologies has not been very effective over time. One lesson that was already obvious in the year 1984 was the falsity in this respect of Orwell's *1984*. However, the imposition of ideology over time has certainly worked in the past, and the qualification in the previous statement, "in the modern world," is extremely important. (This is something I come back to at the end of this paper.)

So far, then, toleration as a *value* has barely emerged from the argument. We can have practices of toleration underlaid by skepticism or indifference or, again, by an understood balance of power. Toleration as a value seems to demand more than this. It has been thought by many that this can be expressed in a certain political philosophy, a certain conception of the state.

To some degree, it is possible for people to belong to communities bound together by shared convictions—religious convictions, for instance—and for toleration to be sustained by a distinction between those communities and the state. The state is not identified with any set of such beliefs and does not enforce any of them; equally, it does not allow any of the groups to impose its beliefs on the others, though each of them can of course advocate what it believes. In the United States, for instance, there is a wide consensus that supports the Constitution in allowing no law that enforces or even encourages any particular religion. There are many religious groups, and no doubt many of them have deep convictions, but most of them do not want the state to suppress others or to allow any of them to suppress others.

Many people have hoped that this can serve as a general model of the way in which a modern society can resolve the tensions of toleration. On the one hand, there are deeply held and differing convictions about moral or religious matters, held by various groups within the society. On the other hand, there is a supposedly impartial state, which affirms the rights of all citizens to equal consideration, including an equal right to form and express their convictions. This is the model of *liberal pluralism*. It can be seen as enacting toleration. It expresses toleration's peculiar combination of conviction and acceptance, by finding a home for people's various convictions in groups or communities less than the state, while the acceptance of diversity is located in the structure of the state itself.

This implies the presence of toleration as more than a mere practice. But how exactly does it identify toleration as a value? Does it identify toleration as a virtue? This turns on the question of the qualities that such a system demands of its citizens. The citizens must have at least a shared belief in the system itself. The model of a society that is held together by a framework of rights and an aspiration toward equal respect, rather than by a shared body of more specific substantive convictions, demands an ideal of citizenship that will be adequate to bear such a weight. The most impressive version of this ideal is perhaps that offered by the tradition of liberal philosophy flowing from Kant, which identifies the dignity of the human being with autonomy. Free persons are those who make their own lives and determine their own convictions, and power must be used to make this possible, not to frustrate it by imposing a given set of convictions.

This is not a purely negative or skeptical ideal. If it were, it could not even hope to have the power to bind together into one society people with strongly differing convictions. Nor could it provide the motive power that all tolerant societies need in order to fight the intolerant when other means fail. This is an ideal associated with many contemporary liberal thinkers, such as Rawls, Nagel, and Dworkin.

Under the philosophy of liberal pluralism, toleration does emerge as a principled doctrine, and it does require of its citizens a belief in a value: perhaps not so much in the value of toleration itself as in a certain more fundamental value, that of autonomy. Because this value is taken to be understood and shared, this account of the role of toleration in liberal pluralism implies a picture of justification. It should provide an argument that could be accepted by those who do find prima facie intolerable certain outlooks that obtain in the society, and which liberalism refuses to deploy the power of the state to suppress. As Nagel has well put it, "Liberalism purports to be a view that justifies religious toleration not only to religious skeptics but to the devout, and sexual toleration not only to libertines but to those who believe extramarital sex is sinful. It distinguishes between the values a person can appeal to in conducting his own life and those he can appeal to in justifying the exercise of political power."[1] No one, including Nagel himself, believes that this will be possible in every case. There must be, on any showing, limits to the extent to which the liberal state can be disengaged on matters of ethical disagreement. There are some questions, such as that of abortion, on which the state will fail to be neutral whatever it does. Its laws may draw distinctions between different circumstances of abortion, but in the end it cannot escape the fact that some people will believe with the deepest conviction that a certain class of acts should be permitted, while other people will believe with equal conviction that those acts should be forbidden. Equally intractable questions will arise with regard to education, where the autonomy of some fundamentalist religious groups, for instance, to bring up their children in their own beliefs will be seen by liberals as standing in conflict with the autonomy of those children to choose what beliefs they will have. (Such problems may be expressed in terms of group rights.) No society can avoid collective and substantive choices on matters of this kind, and in that sense, on those issues, there are limits to toleration, even if people continue to respect one another's opinions.

The fact that there will be some cases that will be impossible in such a way does not necessarily wreck liberal toleration, unless there are too many of them. There is no argument of principle to show that if *A* thinks a certain practice wrong and *B* thinks that practice right, *A* has to think that the state should suppress that practice or that *B* has to think that the state should promote that practice. These are considerations at different levels. Nevertheless, there is a famous argument to the effect that the liberal ideal is in principle impossible. Some critics of liberalism claim that the liberal pluralist state, as the supposed enactment of toleration, does not really exist. What is happening, they say, is that the state is subtly enforcing one set of principles (roughly in favor of individual choice—at least, consumer choice—social cooperation, and business efficiency) while the convictions that people previously held deeply, on matters of religion or sexual behavior or the significance of cultural experience, dwindle into private tastes. On this showing, liberalism will come close to being "just another sectarian doctrine": the phrase that Rawls used precisely in explaining what liberalism had to avoid being.

What is the critic's justification for saying that the liberal state is "subtly enforcing" one set of attitudes rather than another? Nagel distinguishes sharply between *enforcing* something like individualism, on the one hand, and the practices of liberal toleration, on the other, though he honestly and correctly admits that the educational practices, for instance, of the liberal state are not "equal in their effects." This is an important distinction, and it can make some significant difference in practice. Being proselytized or coerced by militant individualism is not the same thing as merely seeing one's traditional religious surroundings eroded by a modern liberal society. The liberal's opponents must concede that there is something in the distinction, but this does not mean that they will be convinced by the use that the liberal makes of it, because it is not a distinction that is neutral in its inspiration. It is asymmetrically skewed in the liberal direction. This is because it makes a lot out of a difference of procedure, whereas what matters to a nonliberal believer is the difference of outcome. I doubt whether we can find an argument of principle that satisfies the purest and strongest aims of the value of liberal toleration, in the sense that it does not rely on skepticism or on the contingencies of power, and also could in principle explain to rational people whose deepest convictions were not in favor of individual autonomy and related values that they should think a state better that let their values decay in preference to enforcing them.

If toleration as a practice is to be defended in terms of its being a value, then it will have to appeal to substantive opinions about the good, in particular the good of individual autonomy, and these opinions will extend to the value and the meaning of personal characteristics and virtues associated with toleration, just as they will to the political activities of imposing or refusing to impose various substantive outlooks. This is not to say that the substantive values of individual autonomy are misguided or baseless. The point is that these values, like others, may be rejected, and to the extent that toleration rests on those values, then toleration will also be rejected. The practice of toleration cannot be based on a value such as individual autonomy and also hope to escape from substantive disagreements about the good. This really is a contradiction, because it is only a substantive view of goods such as autonomy that could yield the value that is expressed by the practices of toleration.

In the light of this, we can now better understand the impossibility or extreme difficulty that was seemingly presented by the personal virtue or attitude of toleration. It appeared impossible because it seemingly required someone to think that a certain belief or practice was thoroughly wrong or bad, and at the same time that there was some intrinsic good to be found in its being allowed to flourish. This does not involve a contradiction if the other good is found not in that belief's continuing but in the other believer's autonomy. People can coherently think that a certain outlook or attitude is deeply wrong and that the flourishing of such an attitude should be tolerated if they also hold another substantive value in favor of the autonomy or independence of other believers. The exercise of toleration as a virtue, then, and in that sense the belief in it as itself a value, does not necessarily involve a contradiction, though in a given situation it may involve that familiar thing, a conflict of goods. However, we cannot combine this account of liberal toleration with the idea that it rises above the battle of values. The account gives rise to the familiar problem that others may not share the liberal view of these various goods; in particular, the people whom the liberal is particularly required to tolerate are precisely those who are unlikely to share the liberal's view of the good of autonomy, which is the basis of the toleration, to the extent that this expresses a value. The liberal has not, in this representation of toleration, given them a reason to value toleration if they do not share his or her other values.

Granted this, it is as well that, as we saw earlier, the practice of toleration does not necessarily rest on any such value at all. It may be supported by Hobbesian considerations about what is possible or desirable in the matter of enforcement, or again by indifference based on skepticism about the issues involved in the disagreement; though with indifference and skepticism, of course, the point will be reached at which nobody is interested enough in the disagreements for there to be anything to put up with, and toleration will not be necessary.

It is important, too, that the demands on toleration do not arise in contexts in which there are no other values or virtues. Appeals to the misery and cruelty and manifest stupidity involved in intolerance may, in favorable circumstances, have some effect with those who are not dedicated to toleration as an intrinsic value or to the respect for autonomy that underlies toleration as a virtue. As a virtue, it provides a special kind of foundation for the practice of toleration, and one that is specially Kantian, not only in its affinities but in what it demands: its worth lies partly in its difficulty, in its requirement that one should rise not only above one's own desires but above one's desire to secure the fullest expression of one's own values.

It may be that the best hopes for toleration as a practice lie not so much in this virtue and its demand that one combine the pure spirit of toleration with one's detestation of what has to be tolerated. Hope may lie rather in modernity itself and in its principal creation, international commercial society. It is still possible to think that the structures of this international order will encourage skepticism about religious and other claims to exclusivity and about the motives of those who impose such claims. Indeed, it can help to encourage restraint within religions themselves. When such skepticism is set against the manifest harms generated by intolerance, there is a basis for the practice of toleration, a basis that is allied to liberalism but is less ambitious than the pure value of liberal toleration, which rests on the belief in autonomy. It is close to a tradition that can be traced to Montesquieu and to Constant, which the late Judith Shklar called "the liberalism of fear."[2]

It is a good question whether toleration is a temporary problem. Perhaps toleration will prove to have been an interim value, serving a period between a past when no one had heard of it and a future in which no one will need it. At the present moment, in fact, the idea that intolerant outlooks will sink away from the world seems incredible: such outlooks are notably asserting themselves. If they are successful enough, there will once more be not much room for toleration; it will be the tolerant who, hopelessly, will be asking to be tolerated. More probably, we can expect in the medium term some situation in which there will be a standoff between liberal toleration and intolerant outlooks of various kinds. However, as I implied earlier, one thing that the modern international order does make less likely is the self-contained enforcement of opinion in one society over a long time. It will be harder than in the past for a cultural environment of fanatical belief to coincide for a considerable length of time with a center of state power, remaining shielded from external influences. Liberalism and its opponents will probably coexist on closer terms than across tightly controlled national boundaries.

In those circumstances, toleration and its awkward practices are likely to remain both necessary and in some degree possible. If so, it will be all the clearer—clearer than it is if one concentrates on the very special case of the United States—that the practice of toleration has to be sustained not so much by a pure principle resting on a value of autonomy as by a wider and more mixed range of resources. Those resources include an active skepticism against fanaticism and the pretensions of its advocates; conviction about the manifest evils of toleration's absence; and, quite certainly, power, to provide Hobbesian reminders to the more extreme groups that they will have to settle for coexistence.

Notes

* A shorter version of this paper has been published in the *UNESCO Courier*. June 1992.

1. Thomas Nagel, *Equality and Partiality* (Oxford: Oxford University Press, 1991), p. 156.

2. See her article with that title in *Liberalism and the Moral Life*, ed. Nancy L. Rosenblum (Cambridge: Harvard University Press, 1989).

2

Toleration as a Virtue

JOHN HORTON

IT IS WIDELY agreed that the core of the concept of toleration is the refusal, where one has the power to do so, to prohibit or seriously interfere with conduct that one finds objectionable.[1] Inevitably there is some vagueness to the concept that permits disagreements about both its interpretation and its application. For instance, how serious must interference with the disapproved conduct be for it to be incompatible with toleration? If, for example, the sale of pornographic magazines is restricted to specialty shops because some people object to them, should we regard this as a tolerant or intolerant response to the sale of pornography? It falls short of prohibition, yet it knowingly makes the sale and purchase of pornography more difficult. In large part, an answer to this question will depend on the reasons motivating the restriction, but, in any case, toleration is often a matter of degree.[2] There is no precise line that can be drawn dividing tolerance from intolerance, which is not to deny that we can identify clear instances of both.

In this respect, toleration is no different from any other moderately complex concept that features in moral and political discourse. However, it also gives rise to deeper perplexities, some of which are specific to toleration, for example, the so-called paradox of toleration. This can be stated in different ways, but one formulation of it is provided by Susan Mendus, who writes, "[N]ormally we count toleration as a virtue in individuals and a duty in societies. However, where toleration is based on moral disapproval, it implies that the thing tolerated is wrong and ought not to exist. The question which then arises is why . . . it should be thought good to tolerate."[3] Much of the philosophical discussion of toleration has been concerned to address just this question. So, in an oblique way, does this paper. However, it is not my intention to provide an answer to it or to seek to resolve or dissolve the paradox.[4] Indeed very little will be said about what is good about toleration. What I shall do is pursue certain questions about the conceptual structure of toleration with a view to bringing out some difficulties in identifying and characterizing a distinct virtue of tolerance or toleration.[5] The purpose of bringing out these difficulties is not to deny, or even call into question, that there is a distinct virtue of toleration. Rather it is to show that giving an adequate account of toleration is much less straightforward than might be thought; that such an account must be placed in some substantive moral context (though no attempt is made to provide such a context); and that the core concept of toleration with which I began stands in need of some refinement. Not surprisingly, perhaps, it is the first of these contentions of which I am most confident. In this respect, my main ambition is the modest one of seeking to show the complexity of the conceptual structure of toleration. In consequence, it will be argued that apparently unproblematic appeals to the virtue of tolerance are less straightforward than they appear, and that in some contexts in which such appeals seem to be most necessary they may yet be morally inappropriate.

The discussion will inevitably be highly selective. It seeks to draw attention to some neglected features of the conceptual structure of toleration and to explore some of their implications. Other significant features will be ignored. For instance, there will be no consideration of the requirement that the exercise of tolerance presupposes the power to interfere with others' conduct. It will be assumed, however, that one can appropriately speak of a disposition to be tolerant in the absence of the power to interfere. Such a disposition can be identified (in principle at least) counterfactually. Hence, very roughly, the tolerant person would not interfere *if* he or she had the power to do so, correspondingly, the intolerant person would interfere *if* he or she had the power to do so. Furthermore, no systematic attempt will be made to distinguish the kinds of entities that can be the objects of toleration: people, actions, beliefs, and so on. Such distinctions are important, and could be important in some respects to the subsequent argument, but they are not its focus.

The conceptual issue with which I begin concerns the question of whether toleration is only appropriately invoked when there is disapproval (where disapproval is understood as expressing a moral objection to what is tolerated) or whether it also extends to cases in which the objection takes a nonmoral form, such as dislike or distaste. The more restricted view is adopted by Peter Nicholson, who defines toleration as "the virtue of refraining from exercising one's power to interfere with others' opinion or action although that deviates from one's own over something important and although one morally disapproves of it."[6] It seems at first sight that Baroness Warnock is surely correct when she responds that Nicholson's definition renders

> the idea of toleration considerably narrower than the normal idea. Often one would think oneself tolerant if one refrained from criticizing something that one disliked, hated or regarded with varying degrees of distaste. I am tolerant

if one of my daughter's boy-friends wears sandals with his suits or a stock with his tweed coat, and I not only make no mention of this outrage, but actually express myself pleased when they announce their intention of getting married.[7]

The kind of undramatic examples Warnock cites seem to be the stuff of toleration in our everyday lives. Why then does Nicholson adopt the narrower view?

He argues that a distinction between dislike and disapproval is essential if a specifically moral ideal of toleration is to be identified. Nicholson allows that it is quite permissible to include dislike if toleration is employed as a descriptive term, perhaps in the context of a historical or sociological study. But the situation is different if we are trying to characterize a distinctively *moral* ideal of toleration. In this context, Nicholson writes, "Toleration is a matter of moral choice, and our tastes or inclinations are irrelevant. No doubt people's prejudices, their contingent feelings of liking or disliking, have to be taken into account when one is trying to explain why they are tolerant or not; but such feelings are not morally grounded, and cannot be the ground of a moral position."[8] It is this account of morality to which Warnock strongly objects. In fact she has two objections, but here the concern is only with the one that she herself regards as much the more fundamental:

> I simply do not believe that a distinction can be drawn, as Nicholson seeks to draw it, between the moral and the non-moral, resting on the presumption that the moral is rational, or subject to argument, the non-moral a matter of feeling or sentiment. So far is this from being true that the concept of morality itself would wither away and become lost in the concept of expediency if strong feelings or sentiment were not involved in the judgement that something is morally right or wrong. This *fact* (for such I take it to be) is of the greatest importance when we come to consider the limits of toleration. For when the question arises, "can this be tolerated?" or "ought it to be tolerated?", part of the answer must come from the strong feelings that are aroused by "this," whatever "this" may be. The ordinary meaning of the term "intolerable," may be used as evidence here. The intolerable is the unbearable. And we may simply feel, believe, conclude without reason, that something is unbearable, and must be stopped.[9]

In short, for Warnock there can be no sharp distinction between dislike and disapproval, and she argues that sentiment and feeling must be more closely connected with moral judgment than Nicholson's account allows.

I have quoted at some length from this disagreement between Nicholson and Warnock because I believe it raises issues of some importance for the task of trying to characterize a coherent ideal or, what is perhaps not quite the same thing, a virtue of toleration.[10] This, it will be claimed, is a rather more difficult task than has sometimes been appreciated. Certainly the issues are both more important and more difficult than Warnock's conciliatory conclusion might suggest. In the end, she is content to resolve her disagreement with Nicholson by distinguishing

> a strong and a weak sense of the word "toleration." In the weak sense, I am tolerant if I put up with, do not forbid, things which it is within my power to forbid, although I dislike them or feel that they are distasteful. In the strong sense I am tolerant only if I put up with things which it is within my power to prevent, even though I hold them to be immoral. The distinction between the strong and the weak senses can be roughly maintained even if we hold that sentiment or feeling must enter into the judgement that something is immoral. All I maintain is that no sharp line can be drawn between what I dislike and what I disapprove of. The edges between strong and weak sense may therefore be blurred.[11]

Although such a distinction is no doubt useful for some purposes, it seems to me that it largely evades the problems which really lie at the heart of this debate between her and Nicholson. These problems have to do with the particular character of toleration and the need to circumscribe it in such a way that it can be understood to be a specifically *moral* virtue. These difficulties also do much to explain why toleration is often viewed with suspicion or even rejected, especially by those who are the objects of toleration. I try to bring out some of these difficulties by first considering an important reason why Nicholson might be led to embrace an apparently implausibly narrow view of toleration. I approach matters in this way because I agree with Warnock that no very sharp distinction between morality and sentiment along the lines of Nicholson's account is satisfactory. Yet I also want to suggest that he is led toward that account by a most relevant consideration to which Warnock fails to attend.

Nicholson's underlying worry, I believe, is that if we interpret the moral value of toleration in a weak or wide sense, to include dislike, then we could be driven to regard as virtuous conduct that which is not. Take, for example, racial tolerance. If I am intensely prejudiced against a particular racial group but am able to restrain myself from discriminating against its members, then it might be appropriate, in the weak sense, to say that I am tolerant. I have strong feelings against this group but restrain myself, we shall suppose, on morally relevant grounds from acting on them.[12] But do I exhibit the moral virtue of toleration? In favor of a positive answer to this question is the practically important point that it is better that I show restraint than not. In this respect, my behavior is morally better than it would be if I acted in a repressively discriminatory way against members of the group. However, to regard such restraint as straightforwardly virtuous also seems to imply that my racial prejudices are in some way either acceptable or their wrongness entirely irrelevant in judging whether or not I am tolerant. By focusing exclusively on the restraint and its justification, and ignoring the nature or grounds of the objection to what is tolerated, the weak or wide sense of toleration seems, in this kind of case, to pass over something important.

Toleration always involves two sets of considerations: reasons for showing restraint toward that which is regarded as objectionable; and reasons (or sentiments) that make something objectionable—the considerations that make it appropriate to countenance prohibition or interference in the first place. Both sets of reasons are relevant to judgments about toleration, and both can be disputed and rejected. From their own point of view, racialists can regard themselves as exemplars of tolerance. So far as they are concerned, they are showing admirable and praiseworthy restraint in the face of that which they hate and despise. But does their point of view have to be accepted? Must we concur that they are indeed tolerant? Joseph Raz appears to think that we should when he writes, "Toleration is a distinctive moral virtue only if it curbs desires, inclinations, and convictions which are thought by the tolerant person to be in themselves desirable. Typically a person is tolerant if and only if he suppresses a desire to cause to another a harm or hurt which he thinks the other deserves."[13] Yet though this is a necessary condition, it is not sufficient. Interestingly, a little later, Raz himself writes that a person can be tolerant only "if the intolerant inclination is in itself worthwhile or desirable."[14] Notice the shift in perspective: initially it was enough that the tolerant person should think his inclination to be intolerant is desirable, but the second statement does not assume that the agent's own judgment about this matter is necessarily authoritative.

In fact there is no reason why we must accept people's own perspective on the validity of their objections to something. If, as Raz contends, a person can be tolerant only if the objection (or intolerant inclination) is itself worthwhile or desirable, then *we* do not have to accept that people are tolerant simply because they do not act intolerantly toward something *they* think is objectionable. Certainly, we cannot dispense with the agent's perspective, because only if the agent does have some objection to what is tolerated will it make sense to speak of that person as showing tolerance. However, it does not follow that this perspective is beyond criticism; such criticism can take the form of denying that the agent is behaving tolerantly, though we can accept that such a person (mistakenly) thinks that he or she is being tolerant. My claim here, I should make clear, is not that there is some completely objective, impersonal or impartial perspective on toleration, only that the agent's own perspective or judgment, though indispensable, is not necessarily compelling.

It is perhaps worth noting at this stage that this claim about the relevance of the nature or basis of the objection to what is tolerated does not precisely map onto the earlier distinction between dislike and disapproval. In some cases, it remains appropriate, as Warnock argues, to see tolerance of what is merely disliked as a straightforwardly moral virtue. The most obvious instances would be those in which people have a right to impose their likes or dislikes but choose not to. Warnock's examples are (sometimes ambiguously or disputably) of this sort. If I dislike people smoking in my house but permit them to do so, then I might be acting tolerantly. I would be within my rights to refuse people permission to smoke in my home—the house is mine and I have to live in it—even if it were agreed that there is nothing immoral about smoking. (Admittedly, this example is complicated by the alleged harms of passive smoking, but the general point, I hope, is clear. In any case, it seems to me that people often use claims about passive smoking simply to legitimize imposing their own preferences.) Dislike and disapproval, therefore, may interrelate in a variety of ways that undermine any attempt to base the concept of toleration on a simple distinction between them.

Allowing that Nicholson's strong sense of toleration is too narrow, however, the difficulty we have identified with the weak sense remains. We need some restriction on the objections that people can have for their restraint in not acting on these objections, if such restraint is to express a genuinely *moral* virtue. This is, of course, a different point from the more commonly remarked one that toleration must observe limits, that is, that there are some things that should not be tolerated and hence it is no virtue to tolerate them. (In any normal context, to describe someone as tolerant of, say, rape or murder does not constitute praise for being virtuous but is an ironical form of moral criticism or a joke in poor taste.) The claim here, however, is not that there are some things it is wrong to tolerate because they should not be permitted (which is of course true), but that there are some things it is inappropriate to tolerate because it is wrong or unreasonable to object to them in the first place. There are, so to speak, two directions from which toleration can cease to be a virtue: on the one hand, some things should not be tolerated, because they should not be permitted; on the other, some things should not be objected to, hence are not the appropriate objects of toleration.

So far, it might seem that I have been making heavy weather of a fairly simple point. Yet its implications, both practical and theoretical, are wider than they might at first appear. For example, there is a common tendency to speak of promoting religious and racial tolerance as if these were pretty much the same sort of thing. They are not. Tolerance can sometimes be an appropriate and important virtue in the context of conflicting religious beliefs.[15] Tolerance can allow the possibility of peaceful and harmonius coexistence without compromising the integrity of reasonably held and valuable convictions. Typically, the case of race is different. It is not tolerance toward different races that we generally wish to promote but the recognition of the intrinsic moral irrelevance of racial differences.[16] In the case of religion, we will sometimes recognize that the motivation to prohibit or interfere might have merit or is not entirely unreasonable, though we also believe that it is better not acted on. Hence toleration will be desirable. By contrast, in the case of race, we believe the objection, and hence the motivation to interfere or prohibit, to be itself unreasonable or without merit, hence the question of acting on it should not even arise.[17]

One hardheaded response to this would be to grant that the question of toleration should not arise in such a context but to note nonetheless that it clearly does. In a world of casual and commonplace racism, let alone such repulsive phenomena as ethnic cleansing, toleration is very much to the point, if less than an ideal. This response has obvious and undeniable power, and it would be foolish to deny, for example, that if racial prejudice cannot be eliminated then it is at least better that racial discrimination be controlled. If one cannot get people to change their minds, then their restraining their inclinations to oppress or coerce is still a real benefit. So it is, but how does this bear on toleration? The implication of the argument advanced so far is that such behavior does not manifest the virtue of tolerance, though it is obviously preferable to intolerance, and it is perhaps linguistically unexceptional to describe it as "tolerant." What needs to be stressed, whether or not they are both called 'toleration,' is that the logic and moral status of these two kinds of cases is quite different. So, too, are their implications for individual action and public policy.

To begin with a conceptual point, it is a rarely remarked feature of the core concept of toleration—the refusal, when one has the power to do so, to prohibit or seriously interfere with conduct that one finds objectionable—that it admits of two ways in which a person can become more tolerant. The first, and obvious, route is by people's restrictively interfering less with conduct that is objectionable. People become more tolerant by allowing others to act in ways that are found objectionable than by preventing them from, or punishing them for, so acting. However, it is important to note that, on this account, a person does not become more tolerant by finding less conduct objectionable: if a person approves of, or is indifferent toward, an action or practice, then the question of tolerating it does not arise. Moreover, the second route by which a person can become more tolerant is, paradoxically, through *increasing* the range of conduct that is found objectionable, so long, of course, as the person does not act so as to restrain the objectionable conduct.[18] Suppose, for example, that Jane disapproves of homosexuality; she is tolerant of it if she does not seek to prohibit it or otherwise disadvantage homosexuals in consequence of their homosexuality. By contrast, if she is indifferent toward homosexuality, then, on the standard view, she is neither tolerant nor intolerant of it. However, if subsequently she comes to disapprove of it, she might also become tolerant of it, provided she does not translate this disapproval into restrictive behavior. In short, in terms of the core concept or standard account of toleration, it would seem that not only does one not become more tolerant by ceasing to object to some conduct, one could become increasingly tolerant by disapproving or disliking more conduct, so long as such objections are not the basis of restrictive action toward that conduct.

I do not mention this strongly counterintuitive implication of the core concept of toleration because I think it describes a very credible mental process. The idea of people consciously adopting more-comprehensive standards of disapproval in order to become more tolerant of what they now disapprove of does not possess much psychological plausibility. It would be a mistake, however, to dismiss the point as a mere oddity. It does show, in this instance in an admittedly rather abstract and artificial manner, how focusing too narrowly on the connection between toleration and the negative evaluation of what is tolerated, without enquiring further into the nature and basis of that negative evaluation, gives rise to potentially unacceptable conclusions. They might not be unacceptable if one wishes to employ the concept of toleration in an exclusively descriptive sense. On this interpretation, toleration would be simply a matter of not acting in ways that restrain behavior that is negatively valued. (In fact, I have serious doubts about the coherence of an *exclusively* descriptive concept of toleration, but because these doubts are not my concern here, I will allow that it is an intelligible possibility.) The point is that such an interpretation would not identify a virtue, and this is not only for the obvious reason that some things should be restricted or prohibited but also because there are some things to which it is wrong or unreasonable to have any objection, and to which toleration is therefore a morally inappropriate response.

This point can help us understand one very common reaction to being tolerated. Generally, to be the object of tolerance is a welcome improvement on being the object of intolerance, but typically people do not wish themselves or their actions to be the object of either. Only when people themselves accept that what they are doing is in some respect objectionable is toleration likely to satisfy them. Otherwise, they do not want to be subject to the negative valuation that tolerance necessarily seems to carry with it.[19] Hence the frequently observed pattern that what begins, when people are faced with intolerance, as a demand for toleration becomes transformed into a demand for more than *mere* toleration, once intolerance is no longer a threat. The demand for more than mere tolerance is the demand that what one is or does no longer be the object of the negative valuation that is an essential ingredient of toleration.

Another issue that these reflections on the concept of toleration help to illuminate is the relationship between it and liberalism (in some of its forms). I take it to be uncontroversial that liberalism, at least historically, is the political theory that has particularly championed the merits of toleration. Yet nonliberals have often felt that there is something specious about this claim, that liberalism is really only tolerant of those things to which liberals have no objection.[20] Roughly, what these critics claim is that what liberals effectively advocate is that others should be tolerant toward actions and practices to which liberals do not object, but that liberals are under no corresponding duty to be tolerant of actions and practices that conflict with the values of liberalism.[21] For instance, Susan Mendus argues of autonomy-based liberalism that it must "construe the toleration of non-autonomy valuing sub-groups as a necessary evil, not a genuine good."[22] On this view, she writes, "Toleration becomes not a virtue, but merely a temporary expedient against the day when all are autonomous."[23] In consequence, for Mendus, the *ideal* of liberal toleration is much narrower than liberals are inclined to admit.

There is, however, another direction from which to question the claims of liberalism to be specially tolerant. For example, if we take neutrality toward competing conceptions of the good as central to liberalism, then it might reasonably be asked whether liberalism is properly described as *tolerant* even toward those conceptions it permits? Here the thought is not the familiar one that complete neutrality, however it is interpreted, is either incoherent or impossible, but simply that because liberalism professes to be neutral toward a range of conceptions of the good—that is it has no objection to them—it cannot therefore be tolerant of them. At least this seems to be the case if liberal neutrality implies indifference, a refusal to judge, the lifestyles it permits. In short, if it is only possible to be tolerant toward what is in some respect negatively valued, the very capaciousness of liberal neutrality could present conceptual difficulties to characterizing it as tolerant. Whereas the first charge against liberalism was that it is less tolerant than it pretends because it is less permissive, the second charge is that it is less tolerant (though not therefore intolerant) precisely because it is so permissive. These charges are to some extent directed at different forms of liberalism, but, taken together, they suggest that it might be surprisingly difficult to vindicate liberalism's claims to be especially *tolerant*: liberalism inclines toward either intolerance or indifference.

One area in which these reflections on toleration are of practical relevance is education. It clearly matters for the moral education of children whether they should be encouraged to be tolerant toward something or whether they should be discouraged from having any objection to it. Some of the confusions concerning multicultural education seem to relate to this issue. In their desire to protect minority cultures from abuse and vilification, some of the more enthusiastic advocates of multiculturalism appear to have dispensed altogether with the idea of judging the practices and values of other cultures.[24] No doubt they are right to try to combat ignorant and ingrained ethnocentrism by encouraging a less complacent response to children's negative attitudes to alien cultures and beliefs. It would be wrong to leave such prejudices and ignorance in place and encourage children simply to put up with that which, on whatever basis, they happen to dislike or disapprove. In this respect, merely to encourage children to be tolerant would be inadequate.

However, some element of judgment of the merits or reasonableness of alien cultures and beliefs cannot but be involved. Critics of the more extreme forms of multiculturalism are surely correct that any serious attachment to values implies that at least some things that conflict with those values must be judged wrong or inferior. Proponents of multicultural education themselves typically reject racism, for example. Toleration, as we have seen, does not require that one accept *any* negative evaluation of others' culture or beliefs and settle only for encouraging restraint in acting on that negative evaluation. We are not faced with a straightforward choice between a complete refusal to criticize the practices and beliefs of other cultures ("multiculturalism") and simply accepting whatever prejudices or antipathies children might possess so long as they do not act on them ("toleration"). Neither of these options is defensible. What we need to recognize is that any inculcation of the virtue of toleration (and any coherent form of multiculturalism) must attend to questions about what it is reasonable to object to, as well as about which of those things that are objectionable should be tolerated and which should not.

The argument so far has been that any attempt to characterize toleration as a virtue is beset by important difficulties of interpretation. In particular, it seems that what was earlier identified as the core concept of toleration needs to be both circumscribed and also perhaps enlarged. It needs to be circumscribed because, for restraint to manifest the virtue of tolerance, the objection to the conduct or practice that is being tolerated must itself not be unreasonable or without value. (Of course, what is being tolerated should not itself be intolerable.) More tentatively, however, it might also be suggested that our understanding of toleration should be enlarged, because the process by which indefensible objections are jettisoned should itself be regarded as part of the process of becoming more tolerant.[25] The virtue of tolerance should include more than for-bearance in not acting restrictively toward those who act objectionably; it should also include not having an excessive and inappropriate range of objections. The tolerant person is not a narrow-minded bigot who shows restraint; he or she is not someone with a vast array of prejudices about others' conduct but who nonetheless heriocally restrains him- or herself from acting restrictively toward them. The restraint involved in toleration is not exclusively of action but also of judgment. The tolerant person is not too judgmental toward others. In becoming less judgmental, a person becomes more tolerant.

This extension of the concept to include narrowing the range of what is considered objectionable is no doubt controversial. It does not easily fit with the core concept of toleration. Yet it is not altogether incongruent with many ordinary uses of tolerance. In describing a person as tolerant, this may be taken to include the idea that such a person is not excessively judgmental, not too narrow-minded, not inappropriately moralistic. Some will persist in the view that this is an illicit, if not uncommon, stretching of the term, which both gives rise to confusion and deprives toleration of its distinctive character. Nor do I want to imply that this objection is without any basis. Restraint of judgment and restraint of action are different, and these differences are worth some philosophical attention. However, such differences are perhaps not sufficient to pre-clude both kinds of restraint being accommodated within the virtue of toleration. Both can be plausibly viewed as constitutive qualities of a tol-erant person.

The claim that it is appropriate to speak of a virtue of tolerance only where the objection to the conduct or practice tolerated is not itself unrea-sonable or without value is also worth elaborating. The restraint dis-played in acting tolerantly will only be virtuous, on this account, if the restraint itself is appropriate. As we have seen, it can be inappropriate in one of two ways. The most obvious and widely recognized way is when what is being permitted should properly be prevented. The second way is more oblique but no less important. Here restraint is inappropriate be-cause it should not be necessary. One should not need to restrain one's desire to seriously impede some action or practice, because one should not have that desire in the first place. For example, if we think that racial prejudice is unreasonable and without value, it is not enough for Joe, who believes that all Black people are inferior, to be described as exhibiting the virtue of toleration merely because he shows restraint in acting on that belief.

It might seem at this point that a crucial component in characterizing toleration has been passed over, namely, a person's reasons for showing restraint. Surely it will be urged it is only when restraint is for certain kinds of reasons that we can speak of toleration.[26] For example, one is not genuinely tolerant of others' behavior if the only reason one does not prevent it is because one is too idle to do so. Indeed the criticism might be made of what was said just now—about Joe, the man who believes all Black people are inferior—that if his reason for showing restraint is that he recognizes it would be wrong to try to impose these beliefs on others, then is he not indeed a paradigm example of a tolerant person? Of course, people's reasons for showing restraint are crucial to identifying their conduct as being tolerant. (It is partly for this reason that I have serious doubts about a purely descriptive concept of toleration.) However, without going into what these reasons might be, I want to deny that having a morally good reason for showing restraint is of itself sufficient to make a person tolerant. For this reason, I do not agree that we are required to accept that Joe is genuinely tolerant, even though he restrains himself from acting on this belief for what we all might agree are morally good reasons. Some kinds of beliefs, whether or not acted on, might be incompatible with the virtue of tolerance.

One argument against this account is likely to be that the emphasis it places on the reasonableness or merits of an objection seems crucially to undermine the relevance of toleration to many situations in which it is most practically pressing. After all, it will be said, tolerance is a virtue that we both need and recognize without sharing the relevant beliefs of the person exhibiting tolerance. For instance, one can recognize that people who believe abortion is wrong show tolerance toward it if they do not seek to make it illegal, though one does not share their belief in the immorality of abortion. What is crucial in such cases is, I want to suggest, recognizing that the objection has some value or is reasonable. To do this, one does not need to share or endorse the belief. Because a belief in the wrongness of abortion is usually connected with beliefs about the value of life, it is not difficult to see value in the view that abortion is wrong even if one does not share it. Hence one can appreciate how a concern for the value of life could reasonably issue in a belief about the wrongness of abortion, how it makes such a belief far from contemptible though one thinks it misguided or wrong. In this respect, the antiabortionist is significantly different from the racialist.

No doubt many cases will be less straightforward than that of the antiabortionist, and in some the perceived value of the objection will be opaque or so slight that we are very uncertain about the appropriateness of characterizing any restraint as "tolerant." It is no part of my argument to deny that there will be disputes, disagreements, or hard cases: all this argument claims is that for anyone for whom toleration is a virtue, some objections will have value but not be shared, and other objections will be held to be unreasonable and without any value. The space within which objections are seen as having value or as not demonstrably unreasonable but are not shared is one important area where the virtue of tolerance has its place. Of course it is not the only area, for one must also recognize that toleration has a place with respect to conduct the agent finds objectionable. Otherwise, toleration would not be a virtue that one could possess or practice oneself; it could only be recognized in others. However, when one can see no reason for, or value in, the objection, and especially when the objection itself seems contemptible or disgusting, then there is no place for the virtue of tolerance.

Inevitably, much more needs to be said about many of the issues that have been raised by this argument. In particular, further elaboration is needed of what is involved in seeing the beliefs or commitments of others, which one does not share, as reasonable or having value. It would also be illuminating to compare tolerance with other virtues, such as courage and temperance. However, these issues cannot be pursued here.

What must be made explicit, though, is that in using these examples, I have made many assumptions about what sorts of objections are acceptable or reasonable, assumptions that have not been justified. However, the purpose of my argument is not to outline some background theory or, as I would prefer to say, specific moral context, which gives substance to the virtue of toleration; it is only to show that some such theory or context is presupposed by, or implicit in, any explanation of what is to count as an instance of the virtue of tolerance. (Tolerance is one of what Bernard Williams has called our "thick" ethical concepts.[27]) Nor is it probable that there will be only one such theory or context. Most accounts of the value of toleration will share some very general features in common—perhaps to do with the idea of respect for persons—but they may also have distinctive features. Tolerance could, for example, have a different significance for a certain sort of Christian than for a secular liberal: the former's account of the value of tolerance is likely to make reference to concepts, such as God's will or the example of Christ, that will have no part in the latter's account. It is unlikely that we will all have precisely the same reasons to regard toleration as a virtue. Insofar as our reasons differ, so, too, in all probability will our understanding of what exactly toleration requires, what things it is reasonable or right to object to and when it is morally appropriate to desist from trying to prevent others from doing them. Though this would require much further argument, I am not persuaded there is any one uniquely rational perspective, any Archimedean point, any view from nowhere, from which the reasonableness or rightness of a specific substantive conception of the virtue of tolerance can be established.[28] Tolerance is not a virtue that stands altogether outside the moral and political conflicts it often seeks to mediate. However, the attempt to substantiate these claims would take us into difficult and complex areas of moral philosophy and cannot be pursued here.

What I have sought to show is that identifying and characterizing a distinctive virtue of tolerance is both more complex and beset by more difficulties than might at first be appreciated. In particular, I have argued that no account of toleration as a virtue can ignore some assessment of the worth of the objection to the conduct or practice that is tolerated. Moreover, I have suggested that eliminating misplaced objections might also be seen as part of the value of tolerance. Both these claims, however, leave me slightly uneasy: neither is entirely in harmony with the core concept of toleration with which I began. Nonetheless, I believe that both are defensible and that perhaps the most surprising conclusion to which the argument of this paper has led is that not all who rightly restrain themselves from acting so as to interfere with conduct to which they object act tolerantly. It almost seems natural to say that though such people resist acting intolerantly, they do not necessarily manifest the virtue of tolerance. Do we have here the hint of another paradox of toleration?[29]

Notes

1. See, for example, Preston King, *Toleration* (London: Allen and Unwin, 1976), p. 22; Carl Kordig, "Concepts of Toleration," *Journal of Value Inquiry* 16 (1982): 59; D. D. Raphael, "The Intolerable," in *Justifying Toleration: Conceptual and Historical Perspectives*, ed. Susan Mendus (Cambridge: Cambridge University Press, 1988), p. 139; and John Horton, "Toleration," in *The Blackwell Encyclopaedia of Political Thought*, ed. David Miller et al. (Oxford: Blackwell, 1987), p. 521.

2. See Igor Primorac, "On Tolerance in Morals," *Philosophical Studies* 31 (1986–87): 72–73.

3. Susan Mendus, *Toleration and the Limits of Liberalism* (London: Macmillan, 1989), pp. 18–19.

4. I have discussed this and some other alleged paradoxes of toleration in "Three (Apparent) Paradoxes of Toleration," *Synthesis Philosophica* 9 (1994).

5. No systematic distinction will be made, as is sometimes attempted, between tolerance and toleration. See, for example, Bernard Crick, "Toleration and Tolerance in Theory and Practice," *Government and Opposition* 6 (1971).

6. Peter Nicholson, "Toleration as a Moral Ideal," in *Aspects of Toleration: Philosophical Studies*, ed. John Horton and Susan Mendus (London: Methuen, 1985), p. 162.

7. Baroness Warnock, "The Limits of Toleration," in *On Toleration*, ed. Susan Mendus and David Edwards (Oxford: Oxford University Press, 1987), p. 125.

8. Nicholson, pp. 160–61.

9. Warnock, p. 126.

10. In the ensuing discussion, I principally have in mind tolerance as an attribute of the character of individuals. It is unclear to me how far this emphasis unduly influences (or distorts) that discussion.

11. Warnock, pp. 126–27.

12. I shall assume here and subsequently that the reasons for showing restraint are moral rather than merely prudential. However, I shall not be concerned with the question of what these reasons might be.

13. Joseph Raz, "Autonomy, Toleration and the Harm Principle," in *Justifying Toleration*, p. 162.

14. Ibid., p. 163.

15. This assumes that a religious belief is accepted as having value even by those who do not subscribe to it. This is not without difficulties of its own. For a useful discussion of religious toleration, see Jay Newman, *Foundations of Religious Tolerance* (Toronto: University of Toronto Press, 1982).

16. Intrinsically morally irrelevant because there could be legitimate extrinsic reasons—the legacy of past discrimination, for example—that make them relevant in some circumstances.

17. Of course, speaking of race and religion in this very general and undifferentiated way obscures many complexities and fails to make numerous qualifications that would be a necessary feature of any fuller discussion of racial and religious toleration.

18. There is perhaps an interesting analogy here with accounts of freedom that allow one to increase one's freedom by reducing one's desires. See, for example, Tim Gray, *Freedom* (London: Macmillan, 1991), pp. 70–71.

19. Of course, in view of my earlier remarks, I do not mean to imply that the perspective of the tolerated must be accepted; typically it will not be by the tolerator.

20. See, for example, Alasdair MacIntyre, *Whose Justice? Which Rationality?* (London: Duckworth, 1988), pp. 335–36.

21. For an interesting attempt to defend liberalism against this charge see Thomas Nagel, *Equality and Partiality* (Oxford: Oxford University Press, 1991), ch. 14.

22. Mendus, *Toleration and the Limits of Liberalism*, p. 144.

23. Ibid., p. 108.

24. For a discussion of this issue, see Peter Gardner, "Propositional Attitudes and Multicultural Education, or Believing Others Are Mistaken," in *Toleration: Philosophy and Practice*, ed. John Horton and Peter Nicholson (Aldershot: Avebury, 1992).

25. This view is advanced in Peter Gardner, "Tolerance and Education," in *Liberalism, Multiculturalism and Toleration*, ed. John Horton (London: Macmillan, 1993).

26. See Joseph Raz, *The Morality of Freedom* (Oxford: Oxford University Press, 1986), p. 403.

27. Bernard Williams, *Ethics and the Limits of Philosophy* (London: Fontana, 1985), pp. 140–41.

28. For a discussion of this point in the context of the debate in the U.K. engendered by the publication of Salman Rushdie's novel, *The Satanic Verses*, see Glen Newey, "Fatwa and Fiction: Censorship and Toleration," in *Liberalism, Multiculturalism and Toleration*.

29. I am very grateful for their comments on an earlier draft of this paper to members of the Political Theory Workshop at the University of York, and in particular to David Heyd, Susan Mendus, and Peter Nicholson.

3

Tolerance, Pluralism, and Relativism

GORDON GRAHAM

WHAT IS the connection between a belief in toleration, the fact of pluralism, and the metaethical thesis of relativism? It is commonly supposed that in some way or other these three go together and stand allied in opposition to moral absolutism, metaethical objectivism, and a failure to recognize cultural incommensurability. But what *precisely* are the connections here? Implicit in much moral argument, it seems to me, is the following picture.

On one side, the fact of pluralism supports the contentions of the relativist, and because relativism holds that unconditional truth cannot be ascribed to any one moral or political view, relativism in turn provides support for toleration; if no one belief or set of beliefs is superior to any other in terms of truth, all must be accorded equal respect.[1] Conversely, an objectivist metaethics implies the endorsement of just one set of proscriptions and prescriptions as true, which are thus regarded as absolutely forbidden or required. This in turn legitimizes suppressing other erroneous views. Thus a belief in toleration requires us to subscribe to relativism; conversely, the rejection of relativism licenses suppressing moral variation on the general ground that "error has no rights."

In this essay I argue that none of these connections holds and that, contrary to common belief, it is subscription to objectivism that sits best with a belief in toleration. We begin with objectivity and absolutism.

I

Is an objectivist in ethics committed to moral absolutism? By moral absolutism I mean the belief that there are some action types that ought never to be performed, irrespective of context or consequence. Just what these actions are will vary, of course, according to specific moral codes. Some, like Kant, might hold that it is always and everywhere wrong to lie, a view that is unlikely to attract very widespread support nowadays, but equally absolutist is the view that it is always and everywhere wrong to have sexual congress with children, a view more likely to resonate with the modern moral consciousness. A consequentialist will hold, by contrast, that we can always imagine circumstances in which the consequences of not performing such an act are so horrific that any consistent ethics must license its performance. Consequentialism is thus highly flexible and commends itself to many in large part just because of the unattractive inflexibility of absolutism. But whatever is to be said about the respective merits of each side of this comparison, it is not hard to see that the arguments to be adduced here are different from the arguments that rage between objectivist and relativist. The best-known form of consequentialism is utilitarianism, but utilitarian ethics is as objectivist as any ethics can be. Because it holds that the rightness or wrongness of an action is a function of the happiness it produces or fails to produce, and because consequences for happiness are in principle empirically determinable, whether an action is right or wrong is, for utilitarianism, a question of empirical truth and falsehood. If there are difficulties with the notion of happiness, the same point can be made about the variety of utilitarianism that operates with preference satisfaction; what the relevant preferences are and whether they are satisfied or not are empirically determinable questions. But if this is correct, it follows that objectivism does not imply absolutism, because utilitarianism combines objectivism and the rejection of absolutism.

There are, it is true, complications here. A question arises as to whether the judgment that an action is right or wrong is to be based on estimated likely consequences or on a retrospective assessment of actual consequences. This is a very important issue but, depending on what we say about the estimation of probabilities, it need not affect the general point about separating absolutism and objectivism. Whether we are talking about actual or likely consequences, the determination of right and wrong can still be construed as an empirical question.

A further and more troubling question arises over whether utilitarian ethics is empirical (and hence objectivist), or for that matter consequentialist, all the way down, so to speak. What about its fundamental principle, "The best action is that which maximizes happiness"; does this admit of truth or falsity? David O. Brink has argued that an objectivist construal of utilitarianism is not only possible but attractive, and he calls on naturalism and coherentism to sustain this view.[2] In doing so, he is arguing against the persuasive lines of thought developed by Williams, Nagel, and Taylor, part of whose object is to argue against the impartialism that this seems to imply. But even if we side with them and accept their reservations, the main point I am making is again unaffected. It is not the fact, if it is one, that at bottom utilitarianism must rest on a subjective commitment that makes it nonabsolutist, but the fact that its basic principle characterizes a *class* of actions and not an action *type*.

This conclusion rests on a slightly contentious interpretation of "absolutism."[3] But clearly the labels we use are not a matter of fundamental importance. We can even say, if we like, that utilitarianism is absolutist with respect to this one fundamental principle (meaning by absolutism here that it admits of no qualification), but, unlike Kantian deontology, it still allows for the correctness of any specific course of action. Of course, "those that maximize the best consequences" picks out a kind of action, as does 'those that take five minutes to complete,' but there is still a distinction to be drawn between types of action and classes of action, otherwise the dispute between deontologists could not even be stated. In terms of this distinction and my use of the term, consequentialism is nonabsolutist. In short, whether we hold that utilitarianism is an objectivist ethics through and through, the contrast with absolutism as I have characterized it still holds.

If this is correct, the first connection in the familiar picture I am examining fails; although they commonly go together, there is no necessary link between absolutism and objectivism.

II

Equally specious is any supposed connection between relativism and toleration. Indeed, as Nietzsche's writings demonstrate, even radical subjectivism need not issue in toleration. Nietzsche believes realism and arguably objectivism in ethics to be an illusion, but this leads him not to the conclusion that all moral views are worthy of equal respect, but that in matters of the moral will might is right (though not, of course, *objectively* right). If there is no truth, what other mark of discrimination or superiority can there be but the brute assertion of a heroic will? Thus Nietzsche supposes, with Thrasymachus in *the Republic*, that in matters of value justice cannot be more than the assertion of the will of the stronger, or perhaps, in view of the possible variations in interpretation that Nietzsche's deliberately suggestive rather than systematic thought allows, we should follow Thomas Hurka in rejecting the straightforwardly egoistic account and say that perfection lies in the assertion of the heroic will.[4] Against this background, it seems implausible to expect either the Nietzschean Übermensch or the Thrasymachean ruler to be models of toleration. It is true that in places Nietzsche seems to suggest that the true Übermensch will be so supremely confident in his own will that he can afford to tolerate the wills and beliefs of lesser beings. Indeed, at least on occasion, tolerance might be thought to be the very mark of his strength of will. But it is evident that this is not a logical requirement. There is nothing inconsistent in an expression of dominant will through the suppression of others, and the fact that this is a more natural reading of superiority might explain the ease with which connections have been forged between Nietzsche's philosophy and the creeds of Nazism.

In similar fashion, accepting cultural relativism could result in intolerance. Mussolini (or Gentile) believed that war, not truth or reason, was the adjudicator between cultures. This view is not familiar among, or likely to commend itself to, many modern cultural relativists, but it is nonetheless consistent. Respect in the sense of toleration is only one attitude among many that can accompany the perception of cultural incommensurability, and truth is not the only criterion by which cultures can be judged. Those who hold that there is no truth in these matters might still regard some cultures as admirable and others as contemptible, and to be defended or suppressed for these reasons. Whether we take a subjectivist or relativist reading of "admirable" and "contemptible" here is of no significance. Slav culture might appear contemptible only to those of an Aryan culture, but that is still the way they see it. Brink makes this point effectively:

> [N]either noncognitivism nor relativism seems to have any special commitment to tolerance. If no one moral judgement is more correct than another, how can it be that I should be tolerant? Someone with well informed and consistent attitudes might be intolerant, and neither the noncognitivist nor the relativist can complain that his attitude is mistaken (although, of course, many noncognitivists and relativists will hold different attitudes and may express them in his presence). Thus, one person's intolerance is no less justified than the tolerance of others, on these antirealist claims, and the acceptance of these antirealist claims provides no reason for the intolerant person to change his attitude.[5]

Conversely, it is clear that objectivism as such requires no accompanying intolerance. Being true of objectivism, this is obviously true of moral objectivism also, but it is perhaps easier to make the point in other spheres. Take, for instance, mathematics. The practice of mathematics encourages criticism and dispute at the higher levels. The interpretation of mathematics, like the interpretation of morality, admits of disagreement between realists and intuitionists, but whichever side we take it is clear that we must give some account of the possibility of criticism, dispute, and resolution, because these are facts about the practice we are seeking to understand. A thoroughgoing realist about mathematics can consistently hold that there is a transcendent truth in these matters but that proof and refutation of the sort identified by intuitionism are the sole methods of arriving at it. Realism can also hold that dispute and disagreement must, in the interests of truth, be tolerated, even that it must be encouraged. Similarly, those, like Popper, who take a falsificationist view of natural science might think that progress toward the truth depends on conjecture and refutation, and so commitment to the practice of scientific investigation, if it does not depend on tolerating any and every view, nonetheless depends on tolerating many views that are held to be erroneous.

So, too, with morality. We could hold, as Mill did, that tolerating the public expression of what we believe to be error is an ineliminable part of the public process of arriving at what we hold to be the truth. This is a point to which I will return, but it is worth observing here perhaps that this sort of endorsement of toleration is more than the recognition that error has rights. Whether error has rights or not, if the possibility of error is a necessary accompaniment to the possibility of achieving truth, then the pursuit of truth has, so to speak, a self-interested motive in tolerating expressions of error.

III

It seems then that objectivism and toleration not only are consistent but can go together, even that they must go together. There are two ways we might read this: that a belief in objectivism is intelligible only alongside a belief in toleration, or that a belief in the virtues of toleration is intelligible only against a background of objectivism. We have seen some support for both contentions, it seems to me, but the brief argument I have adduced might not be regarded as a very strong one, because the parallels among science, mathematics, and morality I have been using are contentious. Indeed, to some it is a very superficial one, because a closer look at the facts reveals more differences than similarities. Famously, this is the view of J. L. Mackie in *Ethics: Inventing Right and Wrong*, where he says,

> [I]t is not the mere existence of disagreement that tells against the objectivity of values. Disagreement on questions in history or biography or cosmology does not show that there are no objective issues in these fields for investigators to disagree about. But such scientific disagreement results from speculative inferences or explanatory hypotheses based on inadequate evidence, and it is hardly plausible to interpret moral disagreement in the same way. Disagreement about moral codes seems to reflect people's adherence to and participation in differ-

ent ways of life. The causal connection seems to be mainly that way round: it is that people approve of monogamy because they participate in a monogamous way of life rather than that they participate in a monogamous way of life because they approve of monogamy. . . .

. . . In short, the argument from relativity has some force simply because the actual variations in the moral codes are more readily explained by the hypothesis that they reflect ways of life than that they express perceptions, most of them seriously inadequate and badly distorted.[6]

This argument has been widely rehearsed in favor of subjectivism or some related thesis that right and wrong are invented rather than discovered. And yet it seems to me a very weak one. To begin with, Mackie supposes that the extent of moral disagreement is more striking than disagreement in other spheres. This can be contested on the grounds that like is not being compared with like; Peter Railton makes this point. Accepting, with Mackie, that " 'the phenomenon of moral disagreement' refers not to a philosophical thesis about the impossibility of rational resolution in ethics but to the actual character and extent of moral disagreement," he says,

It is for various reasons easy to overstate the extent and depth of moral disagreement. Points of moral disagreement tend to make for social conflict, which is more conspicuous than humdrum social peace. And though we sometimes call virtually any social norms "moral," this does not mean that we really consider these norms to be serious competitors for moral standing in our communities. If, in any area of inquiry, including empirical science, we were to survey not only all serious competitors, but also all views which cannot be refuted, or whose proponents could not be convinced on non-question-begging grounds to share our view, we would find that area riven with deep and irremediable disagreement.[7]

But Mackie does not rely solely on the simple *observation* of moral disagreement. The heart of his argument also rests on the *explanation* of this "fact." Let us suppose that he is correct in his ambitious sociological generalization about the nature and genesis of moral belief. What is explained by this generalization, if anything is, is the state of moral consciousness on the part of the members of a culture. But unless we straightforwardly invoke the genetic fallacy, which mistakenly tries to reason about the truth and falsehood of beliefs on the basis of their causal origin, there is not much to be drawn from the truth of this generalization. Indeed, an objectivist might argue that it is precisely a tendency on the part of human beings to base their beliefs uncritically on received practices that explains the widespread existence of moral error and distortion. But so long as we can point to a long-term underlying convergence between cultures, which plausibly we can, we can continue to hold that the facts of moral variation are wholly consistent with a realistic objectivism.

This point needs some amplification perhaps. It is true that there is considerable variation between moral and religious practices over place and time. Let us suppose that, as in most other spheres, the first efforts of humans in morality and religion are fumbling and that among human beings there is indeed a fundamental uncritical conservatism. If so, we will expect the widespread existence of entrenched, but rationally indefensible positions. But so long as we can detect emergent norms that slowly command universal assent, as we can in the rejection of human sacrifice and slavery, for instance, we will have explained all the facts that Mackie seeks to explain without recourse to the metaethical thesis that morality is a matter of human invention.

Mackie himself observes that the existence of moral reformers is another fact that metaethics must accommodate. He suggests that we can understand moral reform as the pursuit of greater consistency among the elements of a morality. But this can at best be only part of the story. Why should the pursuit of greater consistency carry any force if it is not a part of a general endeavor to make our beliefs and practices conform with universal, that is nonrelativistic, standards of rationality? A simple account of moral reformers is that they apply the methods of reason all moral agents ought to apply, but which few do. It is, admittedly, a further step to claim that these methods of reason result in the apprehension of universally valid truth, but whether this is really required for metaethical objectivism is a matter to which I will return.

Before moving on, however, it might be valuable to take stock. I have argued that though the ideas of pluralism, relativism, and toleration are commonly thought to be associated in some way, this is not so. If and when they are, this is a purely contingent matter, and, as far as the beliefs and concepts these ideas invoke are concerned, there are no necessary links between them. Conversely, metaethical objectivism is a position quite distinct from moral absolutism and can in fact be quite intimately connected with toleration. The parallel with mathematics and science suggests this, but it is a parallel that many writers, including John Mackie, have rejected. But Mackie's argument from relativity, I have claimed, is a very weak one, and there is more to be said for the thesis that moral variation is to be explained as the outcome of distorted perceptions that are uncritically held than he allows.

This argument from relativity is not the only one Mackie employs. Equally well known is his 'argument from queerness,' according to which the postulation of moral and evaluative properties generally is the postulation of properties of a very peculiar kind, properties that, unlike the properties history and science deal with, would have to have the unerring ability to motivate. This is generally known as an argument, but it seems to me more in the way of an expression of puzzlement and assertion. But something more of an argument with a similar conclusion is to be found in Gilbert Harman's *Nature of Morality*:

> [O]bservation plays a role in science that it does not seem to play in ethics. The difference is that you need to make assumptions about certain physical facts to explain the occurrence of the observations that support a scientific theory, but you do not seem to make assumptions about any moral facts to explain the occurrence of so-called moral observations. . . . In the moral case, it would seem that you need only make assumptions about the psychology or moral sensibility of the person making the moral observation. In the scientific case, theory is tested against the world. . . .
>
> The observation of an event can provide observational evidence for or against a scientific theory in the sense that the truth of that observation can be relevant to a reasonable explanation of why that observation was made. A moral observation does not seem, in the same sense, to be observational evidence for or against any moral theory, since the truth or falsity of the moral observation seems to be completely irrelevant to any reasonable explanation of why that observation was made.[8]

Harman considers as a separate question whether there is a parallel between ethics and mathematics, but he concludes that modern mathematics and physics cannot be separated and that the difference between moral theories and observational theories still stands.

In explaining the observations that support a physical theory, scientists typically appeal to mathematical principles. On the other hand, one never seems to need to appeal in this way to moral principles. Because an observation is evidence for what best explains it, and because mathematics often figures in the explanations of scientific observations, there is indirect observational evidence for mathematics.[9]

Harman's contentions about the testability of moral claims have been the subject of extended discussion, especially between him and Nicholas Sturgeon, and it is instructive to see just how hard it is to state precisely the "obvious" distinction that Harman is invoking.[10] However, let us suppose that what he claims is broadly correct, that moral beliefs and principles are not rooted in empirical observation, that their "truth" does not figure in causal explanations of behavior except by way of some sort of reductionism, and that what people commonly refer to as "moral observations" can be given a wholly emotivist interpretation. A parallel with science and mathematics relevant to the concerns of this essay might nevertheless remain. Rawls has made the method of "reflective equilibrium" a familiar one in moral philosophy. This is the method by which moral principles are tested against considered moral judgments and mutual adjustments are made to both judgments and principles until an equilibrium between the two is arrived at. It is well known, however, that in invoking this method in ethics Rawls is merely deploying a device that Goodman earlier detected at work in both science and logic, which is to say, the pursuit of consistency between general principles of logic and particular judgments of validity.[11] And the pursuit of such consistency is, arguably, a requirement of rationality. The fact that the general statements we operate with are not empirical hypotheses and our particular judgments are not observation statements could mean, as emotivists allege, that moral beliefs cannot be "tested against the world," but it does not follow that there are not other methods of testing them, or that these other methods are any less applications of rationality.[12]

It has been pointed out by many writers, however, that the method of equilibrium cannot be guaranteed to produce just one right answer in any matter under dispute, and even that it is consistent with there being indefinitely many equally good answers. Obviously, if and when this is the case, the pursuit of reflective equilibrium is powerless as a method of rationally resolving disputes. But equally obviously, whether this is true or not is a matter that will vary according to the particular case and context. There is no reason to believe a priori that the method will never produce good resolutions. Moreover, there is no requirement on those who employ it to employ it alone. Indeed, it is hard to see how it could be used anywhere to any effect entirely on its own.

Consider, for instance, the examination of a historical hypothesis. The proposition that the Holocaust never took place requires criticism and refutation by reference to all the existing evidence, the significance of which is a matter of judgment. To begin with, there can be disagreement about what is to be regarded as "all the evidence,"and in the second place, because every piece of evidence *can* be declared the result of misidentification, faulty memory, or deliberate falsification, the pursuit of consistency on its own cannot result in refutation. Nor can the true claim that observational evidence is in play be made to rescue it, for notoriously in history every piece of evidence requires interpretation. But in this particular case, consistency can be preserved only by more and more improbable "explainings away." Past a certain point, such improbabilities and the concerted effort to make them fit together will be declared as "unreasonable" not because they introduce inconsistencies or involve false observations but because without such declarations, reasoning can accomplish nothing.

If this is correct, Harman's claims about the role of observation in science and in ethics are not entirely to the point. Unless there is some other ground, we must conclude that reason is no more or less powerful in ethics than in science or history. Of course, it will be claimed by many that the difference is this: the fundamental principles of ethics are culture-relative or subjective. But such a claim can hardly be brought to the defence of Mackie or Harman, because this was the conclusion their arguments were supposed to show.

IV

So far we have seen no good reason to accept the contention that moral thinking is radically different from the sort of thinking that goes on in history or science. All thought must operate with standards of reasonableness that cannot be wholly accommodated by standards of accurate observation and valid deduction, so to point to the fact that moral reasoning does not seem to involve the first of these directly is not to locate as radical a difference as might be supposed.

For all that, many people still share Mackie's puzzlement over the "queerness" of moral properties. This puzzlement arises, it will be recalled, from the suggestion that mere perceptible properties can motivate. The puzzlement need not generate a problem for moral objectivism, however, if we first acknowledge, with Mackie, that it is a mistake to construe values in general and moral values in particular as "part of the fabric of the universe." Objectivism can take other forms than Platonic-style ontology, and abandoning the ontology does not prevent us from thinking of evaluative considerations as deriving from objectively defensible principles of practical reason. Indeed, although the relations between metaphysics and epistemology are complex, it does seem possible to give a purely epistemological (as opposed to ontological) reading of all the metaethical positions with which we have been concerned. The heart of at least one dispute in this area is that, at some point or other, the power of reason to decide on questions of right and wrong runs out. Relativists and subjectivists can be construed as disagreeing about where this point is, but both contend, against realists and objectivists, that there is some such point. We might thus characterize the four positions as follows:

1. Subjectivism holds that for no evaluative question is there a right answer, or even a better answer. People might in fact agree on some evaluative matters, but this agreement is at most intersubjective. At any and every point, irresolvable subjective differences can arise.

2. Relativism holds that for some evaluative questions there is no right answer. At the level of particular judgments between people operating within some shared framework, we can apply the notions of correct and incorrect. But when evaluative disputes arise, or seem to arise, between conceptual frameworks, they are rationally irresolvable. These conceptual frameworks, it might

be worth noting, need not define distinct cultures. Gallie's well-known claims about essentially contested concepts, such as socialism or Christianity, make him a relativist in my sense, even though neither socialism nor Christianity can be regarded as a distinct and discrete culture.

3. Realism holds, aside from its ontological claims, that for all evaluative questions there is a right answer. In any particular case, we could fail to find it, but whether we do or not there is in every case a transcendent truth of the matter.

4. Objectivism holds that for any evaluative question there is in principle the possibility of a right answer. There is no class or level of evaluative dispute that the exercise of reason cannot in principle resolve.

These labels—subjectivism, relativism, and so on—are used here for convenience. I do not mean to suggest that the characterizations capture all the variations that have gone by these names or even that they capture those most frequently so called. Indeed, some writers, notably Geoffrey Sayre-McCord, expressly distinguish among these terms in ways that mark out the various positions rather differently.[13] But in my view, nothing much turns on labels, and, defined as I have defined them, they do represent a spectrum on which to place metaethical theories according to the degree to which they extend the scope of reason. Given its place on *this* spectrum, it seems to me, there is scope to defend objectivism in something like the way that Kant defends the postulation of human freedom.

The issue of freedom versus determinism, it will be recalled, is one of Kant's antinomies. Determinism seems the inescapable implication if human beings are regarded as bodies subject to physical laws; regarded as rationally choosing agents, on the other hand, they appear to be free of causal determination. In the final section of *The Groundwork to the Metaphysic of Morals*, Kant allows that he cannot offer a rational resolution of this antinomy. But he also argues that, from the point of view of practical reason, such a resolution is not needed, because the postulation of freedom of the will is an inescapable presupposition of deliberation. That is to say, even if we accept the *metaphysical* thesis of determinism, faced with alternative courses of action, we still have to go through a process of deliberation and choice. The thesis of determinism, we might say, is quite worthless from the point of view of human beings as deliberative choosers.

It seems to me that we can similarly represent the relativist/objectivist dispute as a contest between rival postulations and adjudicate between them in the following way: on which principle can we sensibly engage in the practice of reasoning through dialectic and deliberation? By reasoning here, I mean something rather general, not the application of formalizable systems of induction and deduction but merely the taking of thought with a view to arriving at a better view or opinion. Clearly, subjectivism as characterized renders such reasoning about matters of value otiose; if we can say at the outset that there are no better or worse answers in this case, we cannot sensibly deliberate about finding them. Of course, as the emotivists observed, this does not mean that there is nothing to *say*; expression and propagation of opinion is still a possibility. But it does mean that what we say to each other is not part of a reflective discovery but of a moral shouting match. In the terminology Kant uses in the *Critique of Judgement*, quarreling is possible but disputing is not. On the subjectivist view, then, any attempt at deliberation is misguided. But as communicating agents, we still have to decide what to say, and this in turn raises the question of what it would be best to say. From the point of view of the deliberator, therefore, the a priori claim that there are never any right answers is of as little interest or use as a belief in metaphysical determinism is to someone faced with a dinner menu.

On the relativist view, by contrast, there are some right answers to be found by reflection. What relativism does not tell us, however, except in abstract terms ("at the boundaries of conceptual schemes," say), is just where the power of reason runs out. Once we actually engage in deliberative reflection, therefore, relativism, even if true, never actually gives us reason to stop. If we can go on to deliberate fruitfully, the relevant boundaries have not been reached, and if we cannot, as yet, relativism gives us no reason to suppose that we never will. Once more, whether relativism is true or false it cannot figure in the practical postulates of the deliberating agent.

Neither can realism. Even if there are indeed transcendentally true answers to all evaluative questions, this, too, is an a priori assertion of no interest from the deliberative point whose concern is not to know whether there is an answer or not, but whether it can be found.

To all three, the response of the deliberative reasoner must be the same: None gives any good reason to engage in reasoning other than openmindedly, without assuming that there is, or is not, an answer that deliberative reasoning can bring us to. This just is the presupposition of objectivism as I characterized it, the belief that for any evaluative question there could be a right answer and that we always have reason to try and find it.

V

I have been arguing that the practice of practical deliberation and social dialectic gives us reason, as reasoners, to accept objectivism, understood as an epistemological rather than an ontological account of evaluation, in preference to other metaethics. Objectivism as I have characterized it can alone adequately account for practical reason from the point of view of practical reason itself. However, even if this is accepted, the connection with toleration might remain obscure. As I noted earlier, there are two possibilities here: it might be claimed that a belief in objectivism implies a belief in toleration, or that a belief in the virtue of toleration requires subscription to objectivism. The first of these, it seems to me, is too strong, so let us consider the second.

Brink remarks, "There is no special affinity between realism and intolerance or antirealism and intolerance. If anything, the appropriate sort of commitment to tolerance seems to pressupose the truth of moral realism."[14] His use of the term "realism" differs from mine, but the thought is largely the same, so the task here is to dispel, or at least abate, the uncertainty implied in the "if anything." Why should I tolerate, still less *believe* in tolerating, the opinions of others when I hold their opinions to be false or erroneous? One obvious answer, the answer that historically lies at the heart of the belief in religious toleration, is voluntarism, the claim that a large measure of the value that attaches to religious and moral belief arises from individuals coming to believe and accept moral and religious truths *for themselves*. Belief that is induced or coerced is not worth having, on one's own part or on the part of fellow believers. This is an argument that Luther uses and, more famously after him, Locke.[15] But rather obviously, the intelligibility of this defence arises from there *being* religious truth and error and from there actually being different ways of the mind's arriving at it. If all such beliefs are subjective or in the end relative to time and place, all that can matter is convergence and conformity for some other end—social cohesion or the maintenance of public order. It does not matter whether this is brought about by coercion or propaganda; no value attaches to voluntarism. If so, it is in this way that the connection between objectivism and toleration is to be made; the justification of toleration lies in voluntarism, and voluntarism is intelligible only on the presumption of objectivism.

What about the other way around? Cannot a belief in objectivism be consistent with an attitude of intolerance? The short answer is "yes," clearly, because there is no logical incompatibility between the belief that one's own beliefs are true and intolerance of those that conflict with them. Yet there is still something to be said, along the lines that Mill follows in *On Liberty*. If we think that the emergence of truth requires a process of conjecture and refutation and further think, as Mill does, that the validity of moral, religious, and philosophical doctrines requires the constant challenge presented by false competitors, we will have to allow social space for *some* false conjectures. Only by doing so will our grasp of the truth and that of others remain "lively," Mill thinks; more important, only by allowing the possibility of tolerated false conjectures can we reasonably look for the avoidance of error and the emergence of new truths, because "The fatal tendency of mankind to leave off thinking about a thing when it is no longer doubtful, is the cause of half their errors."[16]

Mill's argument has often been vilified but does have some force, in my view. However, we should note in the first place that the necessity of tolerated error for the emergence of new knowledge is an empirical claim about the consequences of certain contingent conditions; it has long been held that God can reveal truths to us independently of any of our inquiries and if so, there is no logical necessity that knowledge of the truth be the outcome of inquiry. Whether this renders Mill's argument less compelling in the world as we know it, of course, is another matter. More important, even where we can show that toleration is a necessary concomitant of the emergence of truth and understanding, just what degree of toleration concern with the truth requires is uncertain.

First, even if true, the contention that acquiring knowledge requires tolerating error does not imply that all beliefs must be tolerated. Consistent with it is the view that beliefs that are so easily shown to be false or foolish that they never count as serious conjectures need not be tolerated. Thus, the attitude of the Christian believers in toleration to the "conjectures" of Nazism about financial conspiracy among the Jews, or the incoherencies of modern-day American witchcraft ("wickism"), can be quite different from their attitudes to the "conjectures" of Islam or Judaism consistent with Mill's argument and with a belief in objectivism. Here there is an easy parallel with other spheres, one alluded to by Railton in the passage quoted above: though medical progress requires the toleration of false conjectures, many "folk" remedies need be given no hearing, though which these are is a different and more difficult question.

Second, if the defence of toleration for the sake of truth rests on a consequentialist argument about contingent conditions, it admits of trade-offs. That is to say, the emergence of truth and its perpetual validation are not the only social values we might hold. Others, such as protecting public order or social cohesion, could on occasion figure more prominently. Locke recognizes this in the *Letter on Toleration,* for, in the interest of public order, he thinks that toleration should stop short of atheism, just as a modern-day state might reasonably hold that certain varieties of Islamic fundamentalism ought not to be accorded the freedom and respect of other religious views. Whether this is a weakness in the argument for toleration, however, is uncertain, for it is hard to see that any social principles can be maintained that do not admit of any trade-offs.

There remains a final objection to be considered. It is parallel to one that has frequently been brought against Kant's defence of freedom, namely, that the argument presupposes what it is supposed to show. Kant's defence of freedom assumes that we are, in one respect at least, rational agents. But the "fact" of our rational agency is dependent on the falsehood of metaphysical determinism. If determinism is true, then rational agency is an illusion and there is no point of view from which Kant's transcendental argument can be made. Similarly, the argument I have mounted in favor of objectivism appeals to the "fact" that there is a practice of deliberative reason. But if radical subjectivism is true, this is false and any appearance to the contrary an illusion. How is this objection to be countered?

Commentators have found Kant's argument plausible to varying degrees, but in my view there is an incontestable truth in the claim that the point of view of action is inescapable for us as human beings. Even if it is an illusion, it is one we have no choice but to indulge, and, given the undecidability of the metaphysical question, given, that is to say, that it really is an antinomy, this gives us reason to make our own behavior intelligible by the presupposition of freedom. In a similar fashion, the possibility of deliberation is an ever-present one for us. Deliberation arises from a socially sustained pressure to produce reasons for our beliefs and desires. Given this fact, whether or not it is based on some grand delusion, there is pressure to give reasons for the reason giving. It is this that generates the argument I have deployed. Certainly, the argument as I have set it out amounts to less than an a priori proof, but given the general absence of such proofs in this area, it might nonetheless be the best that we can hope for.

VI

I have been arguing, contrary to common opinion, that we can forge more satisfactory connections between toleration and objectivism than with any of its rival metaethics. The connection that takes us from a belief in the value of toleration to a subscription to objectivism as I have construed it is traceable and substantial; the connection from the plausibility of objectivism to the merits of toleration is less so. But sufficient has been said, I hope, to throw doubt on associations and dichotomies whose apparent strength lies in their being largely unquestioned.[17]

Notes

1. This view is expressly endorsed by David Wong in *Moral Relativity* (Berkeley: University of California Press, 1984), chap. 12.
2. David O. Brink, *Moral Realism and the Foundations of Ethics* (Cambridge and New York: Cambridge University Press, 1989), chap. 8.

3. For an alternative definition, see Gilbert Harman "What is Moral Relativism?" in *Values and Morals*, ed. A. I. Goldman and Jaegwon Kim (Dordrecht: D. Reidel, 1978), pp. 143–61.

4. Thomas Hurka, *Perfectionism* (Oxford and New York: Oxford University Press, 1993), chap. 6.

5. Brink, p. 93

6. J. L. Mackie, *Ethics: Inventing Right and Wrong* (Harmondsworth: Penguin Books, 1977), pp. 36–37.

7. Peter Railton, "What the Non-Cognitivist Helps Us to See, the Naturalist Must Help Us to Explain," in *Reality, Representation and Projection*, ed. Haldane and Wright (New York: Oxford University Press, 1993), pp. 281–82.

8. Gilbert Harman, *The Nature of Morality* (New York: Oxford University Press, 1977), pp. 6–7.

9. Ibid., p. 10.

10. See especially Gilbert Harman, "Moral Explanations of Natural Facts—Can Moral Claims Be Tested against Moral Reality?" and the reply by Nicholas L. Sturgeon in *Spindel Conference 1986: Moral Realism, The Southern Journal of Philosophy*, ed. Norman Gillespie, vol. 24, supplement.

11. Nelson Goodman, *Fact, Fiction and Forecast*, 3d ed. (Indiana: Hackett, 1979).

12. It should be noted here that Harman, somewhat oddly perhaps, regards theories of practical reason as reductionist in his sense (see note 10 above). But even if this is so, they might still satisfactorily illustrate the possibility of objective rationality.

13. See Sayre-McCord, "The Many Moral Realisms," in *Spindel Conference 1986*, pp. 1–23. On Sayre-McCord's account, for example, subjectivism can attribute truth values to moral judgments, which my version of subjectivism cannot do.

14. Brink, p. 94.

15. See, for instance, "Secular Authority," in *Martin Luther: Selections from His Writings*, ed. John Dillenberger (New York: Anchor Books, 1961), pp. 363–402.

16. J. S. Mill, *On Liberty*, in *Three Essays* (Oxford and New York: Oxford University Press, 1975), p. 54.

17. I am grateful to my colleague Dr. Berys Gaut for many helpful comments on this essay.

4

Pluralism and the Community of Moral Judgment

BARBARA HERMAN

IT IS NOW widely acknowledged that social pluralism—the presence in a society of distinct traditions and ways of life—vastly complicates the project of liberal political thought.[1] The permanent presence of different and often competing systems of value challenges the ideal of civic culture on which liberal principle depends. Conceptions of equal citizenship or of universal human rights can be seen to have protected deep-reaching structures of inequality and domination that are damaging to women and other subordinate groups. The complementary separation of public and private intended to secure a univocal sphere of civic culture paid insufficient attention to the fact that the values governing people's daily lives are not ones they are willing to cabin off from decisions that affect the culture in which their lives take place. It was certainly a vain hope that the effects of continuing religious division would spend themselves in a private sphere of worship, a fact we see played out in the present struggle over gay rights and abortion. About the only thing one can confidently say is that there is no easy bridge between the need to secure uniform principles of reasonable public agreement and the social consequences of deep pluralism.

The hard questions that come with acknowledging the fact of social pluralism are not restricted to liberal political theory. If the elements of pluralism are deep—if persons of different ethnic and religious commitments, different races, men and women, bring different structures of value to bear on the problems of their lives and shared institutions—then this should affect our understanding of the norms and conditions of morality as well.

In much moral philosophy, however, the significance of social pluralism is seen in its potential for introducing ultimate moral disagreement: a challenge to morality's claim to objectivity. I believe that this characteristic response is mistaken in its view of the nature of the moral challenge deep pluralism poses. To explore this claim, I want to examine the much less attended to and prior question of moral judgment: the practical task of engagement with actions and practices embedded in distinct or opposing systems of value. There are very good reasons to begin here: an impoverished account of moral judgment not only is inadequate to the moral complexity of ordinary life, it also impedes our understanding of the theoretical issues pluralism introduces. One of the things I try to show is that a primary route to the standard epistemological worry depends on a certain obliviousness to what an adequate account of moral judgment involves.

I

In moral theory influenced by liberal values, toleration is sometimes offered as a reasonable strategy of response to a wide range of moral disagreements in circumstances of pluralism. Its value is defended as both pragmatic and instrumental: it does not require resolving all moral disagreements, and it enables other liberal values, such as autonomy, pursuit of truth, and privacy. It also supports an argument for a sphere of legal and social noninterference that, apart from contested issues of harm, requires formal neutrality (a public suspension of moral judgment). But toleration is not a morally or politically neutral response to pluralism insofar as it permits continued private moral hostility toward the values and activities that are the objects of toleration. If, for example, we are to be tolerant of diversity in private consensual sexual conduct, our tolerance is compatible with private disdain for, or abhorrence of, some of the tolerated activity. This can have (and has had) profoundly negative consequences for recognizing legitimate political claims for equality and civil rights. Moreover, widespread disdain for certain sexual preferences can create a moral culture of oppression.[2] The dynamic of toleration and oppression, although hardly inevitable, is, I believe, sustained by the morally minimal and instrumental nature of liberal toleration.[3]

It is useful in this regard to mark two general features of liberal toleration. First, the object of toleration has negative value to the tolerator: one tolerates what one dislikes or disapproves of. What I tolerate, I need not mind—indeed I might want—that it cease to be. Second, toleration is not in itself chosen as a good; one comes to it as the result of balancing competing considerations. One accedes to the continued existence of something one objects to either because its continued existence contributes to something else one values or because the costs of interfering with it are too high. Someone who exemplifies the virtue of toleration thus need not approve of, be interested in, or be willing to have much to do with the objects of her toleration. It is a laissez-faire virtue. If I must tolerate the public speech of minority groups because suppression of speech is politically dangerous over the long run, I do not have to listen. If we may not prevent groups with special histories and traditions from continuing objectionable practices, we do not have to live with them among us. (Though we might not be able to pass restrictive zoning, we can move.)

It is a condition of liberal toleration that the objected-to differences (in ways of life, activities) not be harmful, or not harmful to interests that must be protected. But whether a practice or set of values is harmful has to be to some extent an open question in circumstances of pluralism. An action may be benign in one social context and not in another; the harmfulness of an action may arise from its contingent and local support of objectionable values. A generalizable claim of "no harm" requires that we can show that an action or practice cannot harm regardless of social context. Where circumstances of pluralism obtain, then, to investigate any claim about harm not only must we be able to locate the fit of the questioned action or practice in its own sphere of value, we must be able to judge whether the action or practice contributes to a system of value that is itself morally possible, that is, one that does not generate impermissible actions or support practices inconsistent with persons' moral standing. Determinations of harm can therefore require the possibility of context-sensitive, cross-group moral judgment. Of course it is not enough to show that an action or practice harms someone to justify interference with it. The harm involved must be grave or impermissible or one that persons have a right not to receive. Such determinations also require a high level of contextually sensitive engagement with the object of judgment.

The demand for context-sensitive judgment leads to an awkward impasse. In conditions of deep social pluralism, the moral attitudes liberal toleration permits (and that are part of the values it supports) are inhospitable to the conditions on judgment necessary for justifying toleration. In encouraging a partition between moral attitudes and moral judgment, liberal toleration can be, in a practical sense, self-defeating.[4]

To understand the scope of this problem, we will need a fuller characterization of what engaged moral judgment involves. Much of what I want to say about moral judgment in the circumstances of pluralism is quite general in its import. But because a more theoretically informed guide is sometimes necessary, I develop the account of engaged moral judgment within a Kantian framework. Traditional interpretive misgivings notwithstanding, I believe the Kantian framework provides the reasoned balance between objectivity of judgment and sensitivity to the particular necessary to acknowledge pluralism without succumbing to across-the-board relativism.[5]

II

First, what are the facts of social pluralism to which moral judgment might need to attend? Consider some possibilities. Membership in a group or class of persons could be morally relevant to one's moral standing, claims, or obligations.[6] The fact that there are such groups may in turn alter the moral terrain of others who interact with them, directly or via participation in shared social institutions. Persons who belong to a group may identify themselves or be partly constituted by a cluster of distinct (or distinctly arranged) values. This will show in matters of character, dispositions, vulnerabilities, and conceptions of the good life. Acting with and toward persons so identified may require different sorts of knowledge and sensitivities than are required when one is "at home." And last, membership in a group may be a practically necessary means for identifying morally relevant facts that apply to a person, especially when the facts are a function of the group's history.[7] There might be other relevant facts; these facts might be inadequately described. But some such set of facts must be what is claimed to obtain if the occurrence of social pluralism is significant for moral judgment. Let us assume, then, that the moral relevance of social pluralism is manifested in these ways.

It would seem that any moral theory that had the resources even to acknowledge such parochial values would run the risk of inviting practical failure: different agents in different cultures (or subcultures) arriving at different conclusions (about themselves, about how they should regard and act toward others) in what seem to be relevantly similar circumstances, on valid grounds that are inaccessible to each other. In the face of this, one might well think that the best strategy is to develop some most widely acceptable neutral notion of impermissible harm, and about other moral matters, accept that we are limited to our own point of view. That this can look to be the only available response depends on holding onto a model of moral judgment that regards local values as fixed objects of local judgment. One of the reasons for employing a Kantian model of moral judgment is that it can acknowledge the distinct claim of local values without regarding them as fixed.

Kantian moral judgment attends to agents' maxims: the subjective principles that express actions in the form a rational agent wills them. Maxims thus represent the subjective justification of agents' choices, including their sense of means-ends fit, consistency with other ends, and judgments of permissibility or obligatoriness. The full relevance to agents of their perceived context of action—their different connections and commitments—is thus reflected in their maxims and available for moral assessment. So choices that are justified in ethnic or racial terms will have maxims whose content reflects those specific value commitments. If the fact that I am a woman or an ethnic European enters my understanding of, and so my reason for, acting in a particular way, my maxim will include these facts. It is an essential part of Kantian moral judgment to provide a method for assessing such maxims, since they contain agents' sincerely proffered justifications.[8] And surely *some* of the facts agents appeal to can make a difference in moral judgment. Being a member of a historically oppressed race might justify some actions or claims that being of Polish extraction cannot (and, perhaps, vice versa). It is because it has resources to register such possibilities that the Kantian model of moral judgment is well suited to the circumstances of pluralism.

The more comprehensive the claims of a way of life are, the more pervasive its values will be in agents' maxims. Consider the possible diversity of willings involved in child-rearing practices, recreation, conjugal relations, and caring for the homeless. Something as ordinary as choices in clothes can be dictated by slavishness to fashion, whim, religious discipline, or cultural identification. Quite precise facts about cultural commitments, pride, and the connection to personal taste need to be understood in order to determine the rationality—or even to appreciate the sense—of a given choice.

It is no different for maxims with explicitly moral content. Acts of beneficence or charity will be differently understood depending on an agent's view of the resources to be distributed. If wealth is regarded as deserved private possession, charity may be more personal (giving what is one's own) than if one views possessions as common goods held in trust for all (giving as a required redistribution). An account of moral judgment that could not register these differences in willing would plainly be inadequate.

Thinking about Kant here one might object: if we have obligations to the poor (or to those in need), then what morality requires is that we give what is necessary, and do that according to a conception that we are doing what morality requires (this is the motive of duty in its reason-giving form). Anything else in one's maxim of beneficence diminishes its moral content or purity. On this picture, there is *one* correct maxim of beneficence for all agents in comparable circumstances of giving. But this is a picture we have reason not to accept. What is necessary, indeed what counts as giving, cannot be determined independently of context.

We act from the motive of duty in circumstances of need by acknowledging the claim of need as a presumptive (conditionally sufficient) reason for action. The motive of duty, however, does not exhaust the value texture of our action and choices. If I view my level of wealth as a contingent feature of class and good fortune, and have a conception of wealth as joint social product, I can act as morality requires, fully acknowledging the claim of need as a sufficient reason for action, while acting on a maxim of trusteeship. Much of moral importance would be lost if this maxim of giving could not be distinguished from an act of giving *as charity*.

Kant himself adds to the duty to aid the further requirement that acts of charity be performed in ways that do not demean their recipients.[9] His point is not that we should give aid *and* act respectfully—that we should do two things—but that the aid given should be conceived of, and expressed in, a respectful way. This is a moral, not a conceptual point. And it is a moral point that can have far-reaching moral consequences. The further requirement on acts of charity might give reasons to favor an institution with a conception of property as trusteeship insofar as it supports a moral climate of ownership that avoids both arrogance and servility.

The importance of particular contexts and a morally complete conception of an action is not limited to circumstances that involve institutions. Moral judgment in general requires a fuller conception of action than what might be deemed sufficient to capture a singular performance. One of the things one wants (or ought to want) from a moral theory is an account of moral judgment and deliberation that can underwrite agents' confidence in each other's moral practice. Knowledge that someone has done or intends to do, the right thing is obviously important, but it is often also shallow knowledge. We may in addition need to know what the action meant to someone, how it fit with other things she is doing—questions that have implications about how she would "go on." This is often the case because circumstances of action are not in automatic one-to-one correspondence with judgment. The decision to act in the requisite way, even if correct, may not provide closure. Where resources are limited, an act of charity can strain other obligations. Or the act of charity itself can promote dependency. Some possible effects of an action can and should be anticipated. But some of an action's effects arise from the unexpected (and unexpectable) actions, reactions, and decisions of others. It is a substantive requirement on an agent's maxim that in acting she recognize and where possible anticipate likely outcomes. She must also act with and from the recognition that it is only in rare circumstances (and, perhaps, philosophical discussions) that a single action is a sufficient response to a complex moral situation.[10]

Further, the moral adequacy of an action can depend on the structure and content of the maxims of other persons. That I act from a maxim of beneficence does not guarantee that I act beneficently. If the recipient of my good will is insulted by what I would do, and if this response is at all reasonable, then my action has failed to be the kind of action I willed. This is not a challenge to my moral worth; it calls into question the efficacy of my agency. What makes this of special concern is the possibility that the efficacy of my agency may depend on factors over which I have no complete control and into which I have no automatic insight.

It is a normal feature of action and willing to be concerned with the conditions of effective agency. I do not will as I should when I ignore my own limits of skill and resources. Likewise, my maxims of action must be formed on the basis of some knowledge of how others act and react. If I had no idea about how another agent understands or reacts, the possible maxims of interaction I could responsibly adopt would be minimal. Much of this we take for granted, because we assume that others are like us: needing food when hungry and help when injured, being susceptible to guilt and shame, being responsive to disrespect, and so on. To a very large extent, we are warranted in this assumption: others *are* pretty much like us. But even in the normal range of cases, we are attentive to relevant differences. We do not treat children as we do adults; we recognize that gross physical or psychological differences can alter what counts as morally significant need. But because we tend to live among others whose similarities to ourselves we take for granted, and because patterns of action become routine, most of us are rarely challenged—in our private lives, anyway—to acknowledge differences that are deep or make us uncomfortable.

Recent lessons about gender and race in the workplace and at universities warn of ways this ordinary fact can support culpable complacency. When apparently sincere and decent people infer from the removal of formal, institutional discrimination that the barriers to the advancement of women and persons of color have been removed, it becomes easy to regard remaining complaints of discrimination as matters of insensitivity or delicate feelings, residues to be dissolved over time, aided by the accumulated effects of good intentions. One of the lessons of pluralism—of moral claims based in facts about groups and their relations—has to be sensitivity to the *moral* fault in such attitudes. Facts about institutions that favor white men, as well as facts about women and racial minorities that make them especially vulnerable to informal barriers, need to be acknowledged in maxims of action in relevant contexts. Educational practices and policies that have the effect of disabling women or racial minorities are not morally neutral.

The possibility of such moral complexity enjoins moral agents to develop a morally tuned sensitivity to the effects of their sincerely intended actions and to the interplay between what they intend and the social or institutional contexts in which they act. There must be intelligent anticipation about failure and subsequent response built into the initial maxims of claim and response. This cannot be restricted to some after-the-fact check. It is rather a morally required feature of judgment and deliberation—of agents' maxims—the effects of which will show in the way agents respond to morally complex circumstances and context-specific claims.

Special burdens of moral judgment are present whenever social circumstances are such that first-order sincerity is morally insufficient. This fact is perspicuous in, though hardly unique to, complex institutional settings. A labor negotiator's maxim with respect to wage claims includes more than a precalculated scale of offer and counteroffer. It presupposes a shared understanding of responsive action based on the institutional facts of good-faith bargaining, including the conditions for strikes, lock-outs, and so on. Part of the work of responsible labor organizing is to educate union members about the structure of collective bargaining. Wildcat strikes, for example, often provide more direct expression of workers' claims. But they can be inappropriate, arguably morally inap-propriate, where there exist fair procedures for settling labor and wage disputes.

The same kind of sensitivity and responsibility for the actions of others is plainly not required of agents in all circumstances. Members of a pro-foundly egalitarian, ethnically and racially homogeneous society would, for the most part, be able to rely on their first-order sincere intentions. The absence of traditions of persecution and dominance, plus public knowledge of the adequacy of institutions, create a context of delibera-tion and action in which each may be confident of what others' intentions are and of what they will do if the effects of their actions are untoward. Justified public confidence (in a well-ordered society) allows for a certain shallowness of agents' maxims.

III

In complex social circumstances, especially ones involving inequalities of power, in which differences in history (or class or race) produce compet-ing systems of local value, if agents on both sides of an issue are to include in their maxims claims (or responses to claims) that express local values, there must be principles that provide deliberative guidance. Their task is twofold: to reconcile the content of local maxims with objective moral principles and to provide resources for presenting differences that allow for moral conversation and real disagreement. A moral conception is defi-cient to the extent that it restricts agents to negotiated agreements from within their separate spheres of value. The preservation of mutual opacity forces terms of agreement that track power and trading advantage.[11] Fair procedural constraints on negotiation can eliminate abuse, but they can-not be relied on to be adequately responsive to relevant local claims. The procedural ideal of a level playing field implicitly assumes the irrelevance of differences—that differences, if ineliminable, need only to be balanced or handicapped. This misses the point in those cases in which it is ac-knowledgment of the significance of difference, or of a claim based on difference, that is the issue. Treating pregnancy as a disability is a good example of this mistake.

To move different systems of local value to a position where disagree-ments can be resolved through some other means than advantage-negotiation, a moral theory either must provide rules of value translation, so that disputes can be resolved through single-scale balancing or weighing, or it must establish mediating regulative principles that, although neutral, do not efface relevant differences when applied. I think there are many reasons to avoid rules of value translation, chief among them being the difficulty of establishing commensurability. But the deciding advantage of mediating regulative principles is that they better fit the issue at hand. If difference is potentially of the essence of a local value claim, value translation would be self-defeating in a practical sense when agents advancing local value claims have good reason to want their claims acknowledged, as far as possible, in their own terms.

Although the point of regulative principles is to secure fair placement of local value claims in a shared deliberative framework, this often involves costs. Again, the conditions of good-faith collective bargaining provide an instructive example. They demand a certain level of respect for organized labor, on the one side, and recognizing the claims for the necessity of profit and capital accumulation, on the other. Claims that all corporate profits are the illegitimate expropriation of the value created by labor power cannot be encompassed by the regulative principles of collective bargaining. Excluded on the same grounds is the presumption that a fair wage is measured by the price labor can get for itself in an open world labor market. This does not imply that each side must view the other in a sympathetic way. Accusations of greed, stubbornness, and misplaced class solidarity are within bounds as appropriate, and can be part of the process of constructing common ground. It is where the conditions of good-faith collective bargaining do not obtain, where they are not yet established or have broken down, that there may be no alternative to unmediated assertions of local value and advantage-driven settlements.

The effect of regulative principles in mediating local value claims is to constitute a community of moral judgment. Membership in such a community is a necessary condition for the various forms of moral colloquy: agreement in moral judgment, disagreement, even shared confusion. I do not mean to suggest that each person is necessarily a member of only one such community or that a single community of moral judgment can encompass all the relevant moral value claims of its members. I do want to suggest that all moral judgment in fact takes place within the framework of a community of moral judgment. The rules of salience that identify which features of our circumstances require moral attention, as well as the regulative principles that set the deliberative framework, are social rules acquired through participation in a moral community. Even the most basic moral facts—what counts as a harm that sets a moral claim, what counts as conditions for a valid agreement—are functions of social practice.[12]

It is reasonable to suppose that every valid moral conception will have a standard of harm and rules for agreement, and it may be that, given the kinds of beings that we are, certain harms will always establish a claim and certain conditions always invalidate agreement. But, as I noted earlier, general standards do not exhaust the array of reasonable claims and conditions. A culture or group might find nonphysical pain difficult to accept as real injury, and so not a candidate for harm. Another might hold that no pain is worthy of attention until it is named by its professional medical establishment. For them, incapacitating sadness or sorrow might not have moral standing until it is medically indexed as "depression." In such a culture, energy must be expended to influence medical institutions in order to make socially credible the moral standing of certain phenomena.[13] This may seem to us perverse and even abusive. And it may be. But although it might be wrong to allow the medical establishment the power to stipulate what is morally real—what has moral standing—some such institutional mediation of suffering, and so harm, is inevitable. Pain does not speak until it is a social fact, and it is *as* a social fact that it enters moral colloquy.

The general point is this. Neither agents' moral circumstances nor their obligations can be understood without locating them within a social setting. This is not in any way an aberration or something that ideal moral theory might avoid. Even universal grounds of obligation will have local instantiation. But to note the social bases of moral facts is not yet to see the way that regulative principles constitute a community of moral judgment. The question is thus not about the fact or role of a community of judgment, but about what impact the fact of pluralism has on its structure.

IV

Regulative principles constitute a community of moral judgment by creating what I call a shared deliberative field. An agent's deliberative field is the normative space constructed by the principles she accepts—usually, an ordered array of moral and nonmoral principles. What she values or wants is judged to be reason giving insofar as it satisfies the ordered principles and fits with other values or wants already present in the field. On a Kantian account, the ordered set of principles of practical rationality constrain the whole. (This does not imply that other principles and values, aesthetic ones, for example, cannot also have global scope.)

One role of regulative principles is as gatekeepers to the deliberative field. This is a general feature of practical reasoning. Without some developed conception of prudence or well-being, desires and interests cannot even raise deliberative questions. Consider the way pain gives rise to reasons. Its normally central status in a deliberative field derives from the fact that pain is typically a sign of injury or damage. If pain did not have this role, it is not clear that we would have reason (or the same reason) to prevent its occurrence. Formally, it is no different with desire. That I want something is not in itself a reason for me—or for anyone else—to act to procure it. Desire becomes potentially reason supporting through connection with permissible ends and values that refine the structure of an agent's deliberative field. Some desires (for some persons) have no deliberative place (a recovering alcoholic's desire to drink, for example).[14] It is because it goes without saying (or thinking) that eating is a good thing that the desire to eat can be taken to be reason giving. But this is misleading, of course, for once it is in the deliberative field, the desire to eat now supports a reason to eat *now* only if there is time, if I have not just eaten, if there are not more pressing things to do, and so on.

Not all positions in the deliberative field are equal, some interests weigh more than others, some trump some (or all) others. Principles of prudence may indicate that where a course of action is life-threatening, its avoidance has other-things-equal priority over the immediate end it promotes. But other things may not be equal: the loss of the immediate end may be of greater significance than the avoidance of the threat to life (or even to the loss of life). There are issues of balancing and weighing here. By contrast, principles of morality (Kantian ones, anyway) require a different kind of reckoning. That one's principle (maxim) of action involves disregard for the moral status of another person condemns acting on that maxim, regardless of the value of the end so acting would promote.

The practical principles that structure the deliberative field not only permit local interpretation, they require it. Even Kantian respect for persons (ourselves and others) as rational agents is empty if we cannot introduce, under interpretation, local experiences. In a culture that values individual autonomy, the pain of separation from a parent might be a stage of growth, not a sign of injury, and so does not provide a justifying reason to keep a child at home. In a different culture, one that values strong intergenerational bonds, it might be that the pain of separation indicates the absence of an important developmental stage, and so gives a good reason to resist institutional pressure for early schooling. Assuming that both developmental paths are normal, we cannot be respectful of the growing child or the concerned adult unless we know how these matters are worked out.

The interpreted principles of the deliberative field construct a sensibility that gives practical sense to our experiences. Essential to the nature of this sensibility is that it is shared. In part this is because the interpretations of practical principles must be taught; normal development is otherwise not possible. Children must learn how and in what sense their feelings and experiences have practical significance. They learn to value some feelings and to discount others. These values must be socially available, both in the sense that people around them hold and act on them and in the sense that circumstances permit their acquisition.

It is not just the role of socialization that explains why the sensibility must be a shared one. There are also social determinants of judgment in the usual sense: particular institutions of contract and property bring objects and the potential for relying on agreements into the moral sphere. Their mediation of our conceptions of what we can effectively desire and do is an integral part of moral deliberation and judgment. They explain why, if we live among persons, membership in civil society is both not optional and partly constitutive of a community of moral judgment.

Kant is quite explicit: The moral point of such institutions is not to compensate for our own and others' deficiencies (of goodness, strength, capacity to trust, etc.); they arise as the necessary social framework in which human beings can exercise and express their rational natures as free and equal persons.[15] Kant argues that, given the conditions of human life, there are things we each must be able to do that are not morally possible absent certain coercive political institutions. Our need to have exclusive use of things introduces a moral requirement for (and so justification of) a coercive political institution of property; our need to rely on (have a moral interest in) the fulfillment of commitments calls for the institution of contract. The needs reflect conditions for effective human agency; the move to civil institutions is necessary, because we cannot have what we need without enforceable rights against each other, without legitimate coercive force.

In neither of these cases, however, is the content of the justified coercive institution fully determined by its justifying argument. Kant's argument for an institution of property is not an argument for any particular system of property, private or communal. It is an argument to the conditions of intelligibility of the moral idea of property or right. The argument is not, however, neutral with regard to all systems of property. If property is justified as the necessary condition for effective rational agency, no institution of property that excludes some persons or groups of persons from ownership can be justified.

The Kantian deliberative framework is thereby able to conjoin contingent local institutions and principles of judgment in a way that preserves local value without sacrificing objectivity. The condition of moral legitimacy of coercive institutions—that they make possible the expression of free rational agency—makes it the case that even though moral judgments may make sense only within a particular culture, when they are expressions of legitimate institutions, local moral judgments can be fully objective. If this shows that objectivity does not require universality, it also explains why objectivity may not be the cure for moral disagreement.

The legitimate institutions of civil society add essential components to the shared sensibility that both identifies what is morally salient in a wide sphere of circumstances of action and gauges its standing in moral judgment.[16] As articulated, these institutions give the social world many of its moral features. Living in a twentieth-century capitalist democracy, I will directly *see* manufactured objects of a certain size or kind, such as tennis rackets or sports cars, as having the property of being privately owned, just as I directly see these objects as having a certain color. Although there is no necessity to this arrangement of possession (sports cars might have been like the famous white bicycles of Amsterdam in the 1960s were said to be—universally available for use), what is necessary is that such objects be *some* kind of property, under some kind of legal constraint.

In similar fashion, the community of moral judgment determines the relevant properties of morally salient desires and attitudes. Some desires have no standing at all: their satisfaction is not good, their frustration not in itself to be regretted. Sadistic desires, for example. The principles that exclude other desires may or may not be local. Desires to dominate other persons, to possess them materially or sexually, have no right of entry in any Kantian agent's deliberative field. What could be more of a local matter is determining when these are the desires in question. Is someone's emphatic solicitude reasonable parental care or a possessive wish to prolong dependency? The answer might not be available through scrutiny of psychological states alone. Correct identification of an agent's intentions can require interpretation through local institutions. When it is that control over another's choices expresses impermissible possessiveness may be a function of a community's conception of what an adult is. This is not to say that every conception of an adult is morally acceptable, only that more than one may be, and that the threshold for autonomous choice (or autonomous choice in some spheres) may be a region in which there is permissible variation.

V

That the terms and moral properties necessary for moral judgment have their origins in a community of moral judgment is not a view specific to Kantian ethics. What Kantian ethics adds to this is the claim that local values can support objective moral judgments only insofar as they are mediated by moral principle (the categorical imperative). Local value has moral standing insofar as it does or can express the value of rational agency. A given institution—of, say, property or family life—satisfies this role if it makes the expression of rational agency in action possible (for those within the orbit of the institution), and when the connection to the conditions of rational agency is or can be an essential part of the available cultural understanding of the institution (its structure and requirements). We might say that local values that satisfy this condition support translation or reconfiguration in the terms of moral principles. Values that cannot accept translation have no legitimate deliberative place.

Thus "family values" that support spousal rape (or other forms of abuse) would be condemned: there is no possible translation of these values into terms that accept or express the regulative priority of support for rational agency. Other local values that are not condemned might not have the standing in the deliberative field that they claim in their own terms. For example, some ethnic and religious traditions, in addition to specific practices, make claims of ultimate authority over their members' ways of life and sometimes even their beliefs. The translation of local value may leave religious or ethnic practices unperturbed while rejecting the authority of the tradition that supports them. There is room for only one supremely regulative value in the Kantian deliberative field.

Because the location of local values in a structured deliberative field cuts them off, to some degree, from their original source of authority, they will be regarded as *possible* sources of value, subject to regulative principle and constraints of fit. Local community values are thus treated, in a formal sense only, on a par with desires and interests. They provide sources for reasons: they are not reason giving on their own. This is not to say that all possible sources of value are reduced to mere interests, competing with each other and with interests in general for normative space. Much of the interior structuring of a life that religion or ethnicity may provide can be preserved. But this is not because there is something special about local values. Complex personal ends—career choices, attachments, political commitments, and the like—all provide substructures in the deliberative field that guide choice and perception. What makes this possible is the indeterminateness of shape of the deliberative field. Kantian morality does not designate a morally (or rationally) preferred way of life. The great variety of human interests and traditions, coupled with the fact that choices to pursue certain kinds of activities tend to preclude the pursuit of others, suggests that, from the point of view of rational agency, there cannot be only one way to live.

Not just normative authority but also the content of local values can be affected by their relocation in the Kantian deliberative field. It is a constitutive principle of the deliberative field that no maxim of action may be inconsistent with the principle of respect for persons. This normative constraint not only rules out certain kinds of actions that local value supports, it requires the transformation of local values concerning the kinds of reasons they provide. If it is a rule in my community that women's place is in the home, the practice of female homemaking may survive, but not as something women must see as their morally ordained place.

In general, where practices survive and where the values that support them gain entry into the deliberative field, they will be to a greater or lesser extent transformed along the dimensions of authority, content, and value-based reasons. This might in some cases undermine a local value; it will in other cases affect what counts as satisfaction of a value.

Although this is not the place to try to say what sorts of local values could survive translation to the terms of the Kantian deliberative field, or what they would look like if they could, some projection is possible. For example, it is not clear whether Kantian notions of autonomy permit vesting any person or group with ultimate deliberative authority, whether fathers, councils of elders, or experts. What I think we can say is that *if* deliberative authority is permissible, it must be justified by reasons that are consistent with deliberative norms: deference to expertise that cannot be easily shared, the necessity of efficient and final decision making in emergencies, and so on. Claims of authority are subject to deliberation-relative justification, and thus permanently open to rebuttal. A certain kind of critical practice is therefore necessary to maintain the legitimacy of authority. So, for example, to the extent that modern medicine relies on the obscurity of unnecessary Latin and the absence of generally accessible medical education, its authority is morally suspect.

Ways of life whose constitutive values resist transformation by moral principle can nonetheless contain virtues we admire. The courage and grace of a warrior class, the exquisite taste encouraged by great wealth or a hereditary nobility, or the self-sacrificial passion for justice in a revolutionary vanguard are unlikely to be present in a deliberative framework structured by Kantian principle. But the fact that, from the moral point of view, we cannot endorse everything in which we can see some good is not in itself an argument against the authority of moral principle.

VI

The range of differences that can be included in a single community of moral judgment is a function of the requirements for ongoing moral colloquy. Although neither consistency with moral principle (the values of rational agency) nor openness to reconfiguration in moral terms is sufficient to guarantee that two local values can be in the same community of moral judgment, there is reason to think that many encounters between initially incompatible systems of value need not conclude in mutual opacity and exclusion. The Kantian account, as I have reconstructed it, resists a kind of value stasis in judgment that encourages systems of value to remain disengaged from one another.

There is again an analogous deliberative problem for an individual. One can regard interests and commitments as making separate claims for deliberative attention and priority. Sometimes competing interests cannot be adjusted to each other: devotion to a fast-track corporate career conflicts with the desire to be a committed and available parent. Although a choice has to be made, its terms need not be dictated from the fixed perspective of either interest. If interests are denied authority independent of their place in a deliberative field, the exclusionary claim of a given interest is subject to reexamination, and it can be reestablished on different terms. There is nothing compelling in the picture that describes the choice to move to a different career track or a different model of successful parenting as choice to gain one thing at the expense of another. This is to accept the idea that our interests have some independent standing in our lives, some autonomous claim to expression. One could equally view one's life as involving in an essential way the development and mutual adjustment of a variety of interests. One does not know at any given point exactly how things will go, what one might come to care about, or how what one cares about might change as one comes to care about other things.[17] Practical rationality is a permanent task.

The point of the analogy is to underscore the conditional status of the interests and values that constitute a life or a community at a given time. Interests and values are to be adjusted to principles of practical rationality as well as to each other. The analogy breaks down over what drives each system toward higher degrees of unity and integration. One can exaggerate the unifying effect of being a person as a single locus of activity—we are all too able to adopt and pursue conflicting projects—but there is clearly something in the idea of a prudential need to live one life that is absent from the circumstances of multiple communities of moral judgment.

Kant argued that where "a multitude of persons" live in such a way that they "affect one another," they are under moral necessity to enter together into civil society.[18] This is because the absence of common institutions of property and contract, with enforceable rights, is an impermissible hindrance to the effective expression of human rational agency. I think it can be argued that we are similarly obliged to enter and sustain a community of moral judgment not to secure enforceable rights but to bring about the conditions for moral development and colloquy: the conditions necessary to secure what Kant calls the "public use of reason." This provides the moral impetus to unity in circumstances of pluralism. It also explains the inappropriateness of tolerance as a first moral response to pluralism. Because toleration is at issue only where people can affect one another, where the conditions for toleration obtain, there is already in place a prior moral requirement to a more inclusive community of moral judgment.

While the moral necessity of civil society justifies coercing entry, the community of moral judgment cannot be brought about by compulsion. The obligation to enter and sustain a community of judgment sets agents a task of understanding and accommodation: a constraint on maxims. It is the practical expression in judgment of the kingdom of ends as a cosmopolitan ideal.

VII

Suppose one faces a community of moral judgment different from one's own, where, by definition, one is in moral disagreement either with the community's justifying reasons or with the outcomes of its sincere moral judgments.[19] In circumstances governed by the model of liberal toleration, I maintain a position of judging outsider, attempting to assess in my own terms whether the area of disagreement meets the conditions warranting intervention. If it does not, having made my critical judgment, there is only the private matter of attitude, continued proximity, and so on. That is why toleration can be a matter of public policy.

If instead I act under the obligation to extend the community of moral judgment, my task is both more complex and more demanding. Because one needs to determine the possibility of moral colloquy, the task of judgment requires substantial engagement with the values in question, not just to determine consistency with moral principle but to consider the potential areas of mutual adjustment that may be necessary to make the community of moral judgment more inclusive. It can be difficult, for example, to determine whether one is facing a distinct community of judgment or whether moral deviance is masking itself as difference. Different questions arise depending on whether the focus of judgment is a subgroup within a pluralistic society or, as Kant imagined, groups encountered through travel and commerce.

Judgment that uses the conditions of moral colloquy to determine local legitimacy of ways of life must take care that difference per se is not read as grounds for exclusion. Correct judgment depends on the particular facts and norms of the institution or practice in question. Although, we might conjecture, the value of polygamous marriage as it functioned in the historical community of Latter Day Saints could not be mediated by Kantian principle (because of its institutionalized subordination of women), nothing follows from this about other patterns of multiple-spouse marriage. The issue is not the pattern of marriage per se but the moral meaning that comes with its mode of spousal relation.

Imagine two communities demanding local control over education, one seeing it as a necessary means for preserving its language and customs, the other wanting to protect its children from exposure to material that displays other systems of value in a favorable or even neutral light. Both demands might be in conflict with the dominant culture's value of uniform public, liberal education. In the United States, this sort of issue is usually discussed as it raises constitutional questions about the separation of church and state. But it is also, and perhaps first, a moral issue. The values involved and the practices they support are different in morally significant ways. Partial separation from the standard pattern of civic socialization in order to preserve a cultural identity need not threaten the conditions of moral colloquy. By contrast, because the proposed instantiation of the values of the second community promotes parochial intolerance, their case for preserving cultural identity (in this way) does not carry moral weight. This is not because their practice will lead to wrongful interference with others, it might not. Education to intolerance undermines the conditions for participation in an inclusive community of moral judgment.

The fact that a community would not survive the loss or change of a condemned value neither alters the terms of inclusion nor gives reason to shift to a model of toleration. Communities as such do not have rights of survival. However, where local values can be successfully mediated and the conditions for public dialogue and reasoning secured, a community's interest in preserving local value—in preserving itself—would seem to be determinative. The legitimate interests of the larger community are limited to the satisfaction of the membership conditions in the community of moral judgment. But this description concedes too much to the dominant group. The conditions of comembership in a community of moral judgment demand positive engagement with non-majority systems of local value. The issue is not whether one can put up with ways of life one does not like, or whether other values one has are promoted by noninterference. That is the question of toleration. Rather, one needs to know that, and on what terms, there is a possible community of moral judgment. And this may require changes in one's own values. Not all values will satisfy the terms of entry, and not all values that survive will do so unchanged. If there are costs of entry to a community of moral judgment—costs to the local values themselves—it cannot be that the dominant community always decides who pays. Engaged moral judgment requires an openness in both communities to the point and role of value differences and a willingness to modify local values (even if at some cost to the continuity of community tradition) in order to achieve mutual accommodation.

In short, the obligation to inclusion does not leave everything as it would have been absent the fact of pluralism.[20] In conditions of pluralism, parochialism is not acceptable. If we follow Kant, parochialism is a violation of our duty to enter and maintain (if necessary, to create) a cosmopolitan moral community.[21]

Notes

1. In recent essays, John Rawls talks about "the permanent fact of pluralism." He does not have in mind social and ethnic diversity as such, but rather the probable fact that philosophical argument will not demonstrate the truth of any single comprehensive conception of the good. That is why he thinks that the strongest available justification of principles of justice is found in an "overlapping consensus." The pluralism of views he has in mind coexists with deep social homogeneity. In this essay, the pluralism at issue is social, ethnic, and racial diversity in the familiar sense.

2. There is in this a reason to be cautious about the move from moral relativism to a social-contractarian resolution of disagreement. This accepts too easily the need for a political solution to a moral problem. (Gilbert Harman is tempted this way in his "Moral Relativism Defended," *Philosophical Review* 84 [1975]:3–22.)

3. That oppression might follow on toleration may also reflect a power asymmetry. The weak are not normally in a position to tolerate the strong. Nietzsche's *Genealogy of Morals* provides a delicate exploration of the complex strategies and attitudes involved in reversing this.

4. It is not much of an objection to claim that the conditions of judgment do not have to be satisfied by each agent because what is and is not to be tolerated is a public or political decision. We would have to give up a great deal to accept that persons who are required to tolerate or permitted to interfere could not know or appreciate the supporting moral reasons.

5. Before continuing, I should note that Kant's explicit discussions of toleration do not indicate that he saw any connection with the problems posed by social pluralism. (Kant's extended discussions of toleration are to be found in the essays "What Is Enlightenment?" and "Theory and Practice." The best treatment of Kant on toleration is Onora O'Neill, "The Public Use of Reason," in her *Constructions of Reason* [Cambridge: Cambridge University Press, 1989].) On religious toleration, Kant is consistently liberal—with a twist. The lack of certainty about all religious claims makes hatred and persecution of other religions groundless. Further, because religions are historically embedded and limited practices, it is only insofar as they express (independent) morality that their tenets are normative at all.

Kant does have striking views about political toleration, especially about the necessity of free speech as the public use of reason. He holds that "[r]eason depends on this freedom for its very existence. For reason has no dictatorial authority; its verdict is simply the agreement of free citizens, of whom each one must be permitted to express, without let or hindrance, his objections or even his veto." (*Critique of Pure Reason* A738/B766, trans. N. K. Smith [London: Macmillan, 1933]). Nothing follows directly from this understanding of toleration that connects with the moral effects of social pluralism. What can be drawn on is the ideal of public reason: a formal, normative construction of the space of moral judgment that can provide room for the expression of distinct values in conformity with the standard of practical reason.

6. Because the topic is social pluralism, I am not considering the special problems for moral judgment posed by nonhuman groups.

7. The contrast I have in mind is with cases in which knowledge of group identity is merely convenient for identifying something to which we have or could have independent access (e.g., susceptibility to a genetic disorder).

8. There are general arguments that support this assumption in chapter 7 of my *Practice of Moral Judgment* (Cambridge, Mass.: Harvard University Press, 1993).

9. Kant, *The Doctrine of Virtue*, 452, pt. 2 of Immanuel Kant, *The Metaphysics of Morals*, ed. M. Gregor (Cambridge: Cambridge University Press, 1991).

10. Because the required nature and degree of such further response is not a matter of individual choice, an adequate moral theory must have resources to develop such standards. And they need to be *developed*, for what counts as adequate preparation in one situation could be woefully unsuited to another. This can be an especially acute matter when the context of action involves agents with different or culturally diverse conceptions of what is at issue.

11. This is Harman's picture, I believe. It is what Rawls's original position blocks through constraints on information, justified by the goal of constructing principles on which all could reasonably agree. The Kantian alternative I am sketching takes the task to be one of elaborating the moral structures required for deliberation and conscientious action in circumstances of pluralism supported by complex social and cultural differences.

12. This does not mean that persons from different backgrounds and cultures cannot have fruitful moral debate. A shared moral root (religion, for example) makes overlapping principles possible. Powerful transcultural communities are created by international commerce and some deep similarities in forms of oppression. I have doubts, though, about how deep or wide-ranging such moral colloquy can be.

13. This can work in both directions. For example, the attempt to make sexual orientation a medical or biological fact can be seen as part of a morally questionable program to create inflexible sexual categories.

14. This is the reverse of the usual reason-desire connection. It is usually argued that there are no reasons without supporting desires. The claim here is that the presence of a desire does not by itself support reasons.

15. Kant, *Doctrine of Right*, 245ff, pt. 1 of Immanuel Kant, *The Metaphysics of Morals*.

16. Thus although it is the principle of manipulation of agency in Kant's famous maxim of deceitful promising that makes such promising impermissible, what makes it a maxim of deceitful promising is a function of the prevailing

institutions of promise and contract. This is not a deep point. Whether an expression of future intentions in a context of possible cooperative activity constitutes a commitment depends on conventions; it does not follow from the internal
logic of the utterance. In similar fashion, the terms of legitimate possession, and
so of misappropriation, are social, not natural.

17. That this is a normal fact does not exonerate those institutions that force
such adjustments when they are not necessary.

18. Kant, "Perpetual Peace," 358, in *Kant's Political Writings*, ed. Hans Reiss
(Cambridge: Cambridge University Press, 1970). *The Doctrine of Right*, 252–55.

19. To simplify matters, I am ignoring the fact that it is from within a group
that one encounters other communities of judgment.

20. It is possible that there are no a priori limits to the modifications in values
that might be required. But the losses involved should not be exaggerated, and the
potential benefits not ignored. It will be the task of a subsequent essay to explore
this claim.

21. There is no guarantee, of course, that such efforts will succeed. Failure of
the project of inclusion could have various sources. Systems of value might not
be able to survive proximity: their encounter can lead to one (or both of their)
demise. There need be no fault here. The conditions of comembership do not
guarantee sustained coexistence. Further, attempts at inclusion can fail if defining
social institutions are incompatible. Some institutions are more generous than
others. Within the system of liberal property, for example, it is permissible to have
a range of private arrangements that express different values: families, private
corporate entities, and utopian communities can operate within the dominant
system according to their own rules of possession. To be sure, private arrangements exist on the sufferance of the public, and there must be recognized authority to resolve system-based conflicts. It is a suggestive thought that those institutions are best that can accept the greatest range of normalized variants.

5

Two Models of Pluralism and Tolerance

WILL KYMLICKA

1. The Lessons of the Reformation

In his most recent work, John Rawls argues that "we must draw the obvious lessons of our political history since the Reformation and the Wars of Religion," namely, that we must recognize and accommodate "the plurality of conflicting, and indeed incommensurable, conceptions of the good affirmed by the members of existing democratic societies" (Rawls 1987:13; 1985:225, 249).[1] In the sixteenth century, Catholics and Protestants each sought to use the state to support their conception of true faith and to oppose the other. After innumerable wars and civil strife, both faiths learned that only the oppressive (and futile) use of force could ensure adherence to a single comprehensive religious doctrine. Both faiths now accept that "a practicable political conception for a constitutional regime cannot rest on a shared devotion to the Catholic or Protestant faith" (Rawls 1987:5).

According to Rawls, this development of religious tolerance was one of the historical roots of liberalism. Liberals have simply extended the principle of tolerance to other controversial questions about the "meaning, value and purpose of human life" (Rawls 1987:4; 1985:249). Unless oppressive state force is employed to prevent it, the members of a democratic society will invariably endorse different views about the highest ends in life, just as they endorse different religious views. Some will view civic participation or communal cooperation as our highest end, others will view individual accomplishment as the greatest good. Any conception of justice that hopes to serve as the basis of political legitimacy, therefore, "must be one that widely different and even irreconcilable comprehensive doctrines can endorse" (Rawls 1989:235). Hence liberal "neutrality" on questions of the good accepts and extends the lessons of the Reformation.[2]

In this paper, I want to raise some questions about this "obvious lesson" of the Reformation, or rather about Rawls's interpretation of it. I accept the need for religious tolerance. But there is more than one form of religious toleration. In the context of Western democracies, tolerance took a very distinctive form, namely, the idea of individual freedom of conscience. It is now a basic individual right to worship freely, to propagate one's religion, to change one's religion, or indeed to renounce religion altogether. To restrict an individual's exercise of these liberties is seen as a violation of a fundamental human right. Rawls views this as the most natural form of religious toleration. Indeed, as we will see, he often writes as if it is the only form of toleration. He simply equates "the principle of toleration" with the idea of individual freedom of conscience.

In this paper, I want to consider a second model of toleration, which is based on group rights rather than individual liberty. In both models, religious communities are protected from oppression, but in very different ways. The Rawlsian model protects each religious community by separating church from state. It removes religion from the public agenda, leaving adherents of the competing doctrines free to pursue their beliefs in private churches. In the group-rights model, on the other hand, church and state are closely linked. Each religious community is granted official status and a substantial measure of self-government. In the "millet system" of the Ottoman Empire, for example, Muslims, Christians, and Jews were all recognized as self-governing units (or "millets") within the empire.

There are a number of important differences between these two models. For the purposes of this paper, the most significant is that the group-rights model need not recognize any principle of *individual* freedom of conscience. Because each religious community is self-governing, there is no external obstacle to basing this self-government on religious principles, including the enforcement of religious orthodoxy. Hence there may be little or no scope for individual dissent within each religious community, and little or no freedom to change one's faith. In the millet system, for example, the Muslims did not try to suppress the Jews, and vice versa, but they did suppress heretics within their own community. Heresy (questioning the orthodox interpretation of Muslim doctrine) and apostasy (abandoning one's religious faith) were punishable crimes within the Muslim community. Restrictions on individual freedom of conscience also existed in the Jewish and Christian communities. The millet system was, in effect, a federation of theocracies.

My aim is not to defend this second model. On the contrary, like Rawls, I believe that the liberal system of individual liberty is a more appropriate response to pluralism. My aim, rather, is to see what sorts of reasons liberals can give to defend their commitment to individual liberty. The "obvious lesson" of the Wars of Religion is that diverse religions need to tolerate each other. It is less obvious why we must tolerate dissent within a religious (or ethnic) community.

Rawls has not, I think, adequately addressed this question. In fact, I believe that Rawls's recent work has obscured the basis for this liberal commitment to individual liberty. Hence, after spelling out some of the details of the group-rights model (section 2), I will turn to Rawls's recent work, particularly his claim that liberals should defend their views on "political" and not "comprehensive" grounds (sections 3 and 4). I will argue that liberals must give a more comprehensive defense of liberal values if they are to adequately defend individual liberty. I will conclude with some suggestions about how liberal democratic regimes should deal with minorities who reject liberal ideals (section 5).

2. The Group-Rights Model and the Ottoman Millet System

This section will consider the group-rights model, focusing in particular on the Ottoman millet system. The Ottoman Turks were Muslims who conquered much of the Middle East, North Africa, Greece, and eastern Europe during the fourteenth and fifteenth centuries, thereby acquiring many Jewish and Christian subjects. For various theological and strategic reasons, the Ottomans allowed these minorities not only the freedom to practice their religion, but a more general freedom to govern themselves in purely internal matters, with their own legal codes and courts. For about five centuries, between 1456 and the collapse of the empire during World War I, three non-Muslim minorities had official recognition as self-governing communities (or "millets")—the Greek Orthodox, the Armenian Orthodox, and the Jews—each of which was further subdivided into various local administrative units, usually based on ethnicity and language. Each millet was headed by the relevant church leader (the chief rabbi and the two Orthodox patriarchs).

The legal traditions and practices of each community, particularly in matters of family status, were respected and enforced through the empire. However, although they were free to run their internal affairs, their relations with the ruling Muslims were tightly regulated. For example, non-Muslims could not proselytize, they could build new churches only under license, and they were required to wear distinctive dress so that they could be recognized. There were limits on intermarriage, and they had to pay special taxes, in lieu of military service. But within these limits, "they were to enjoy complete self-government, obeying their own laws and customs." Their collective freedom of worship was guaranteed, together with their possession of churches and monasteries, and they could run their own schools.[3]

Although the millet system was generally humane and tolerant of group differences, it was not a liberal society, for it did not tolerate individual dissent within its constituent communities. It was, rather, a deeply conservative, theocratic, and patriarchal society, antithetical to the ideals of personal liberty endorsed by liberals from Locke to Kant and Mill. The various millets differed in the extent of their enforcement of religious orthodoxy. There were many periods during the five-hundred-year history of the millets in which liberal reformers within each community pushed for constitutional restrictions on the power of the millet's leaders. And in the second half of the nineteenth century, some of the millets adopted liberal constitutions. (Hence, the idea of according special rights of self-government to minority communities need not be illiberal, if this communal self-government respects the civil rights of its members).[4] But, in general, there were significant restrictions on the freedom of individuals in the Ottoman Empire to question or reject church doctrine. The Ottomans accepted the principle of tolerance, where that is "understood to indicate the willingness of a dominant religion to coexist with others" (Braude and Lewis 1982:3), but did not accept the quite separate principle of individual freedom of conscience.

This system of toleration is, in one sense, the opposite of that in the West, because it unites, rather than separates, church and state. It is interesting to note that the two systems had similar historical origins. The Ottoman restrictions on the building and location of non-Muslim churches were similar to the system of "licensed coexistence" established under the Edict of Nantes (1598). Under that edict, which ended the Wars of Religion, Protestants in France could build new churches only in certain locations, and only with a state license.[5] In the West, however, state-licensed coexistence between Protestants and Catholics gradually evolved into a system of individual freedom of conscience. This never occurred in the Ottoman Empire. As noted above, there were some liberal reformers who questioned the legitimacy of theocratic rule. Some Jews and Christians in the Ottoman Empire had extensive contact with the West. They brought back Enlightenment ideas of freedom and reason and, like liberals in the West, challenged the rule of "obscurantist" religious leaders who maintained power by keeping the people fearful and ignorant.[6] These reformers wanted to secularize, liberalize, and democratize the millet system and use it as the basis for national self-government by the various national groups in the empire. The Ottoman rulers actually sided with these liberal reformers in 1856 and demanded that the non-Muslim millets adopt new and more democratic constitutions.[7] However, unlike in the West, liberal reformers were a small minority, and the patriarchs were able to maintain their hold on the reins of power, albeit with ever-decreasing relevance.

The influence of Western ideas was just one of many external influences that ultimately combined to undermine the millet system (along with economic competition, military force, and diplomatic meddling). But its internal dynamics were remarkably stable. As Braude and Lewis note, "For nearly half a millennium, the Ottomans ruled an empire as diverse as any in history. Remarkably, this polyethnic and multireligious society worked. Muslims, Christians, and Jews worshipped and studied side by side, enriching their distinct cultures" (Braude and Lewis 1982:1).[8]

The millet system, therefore, offers a viable alternative form of religious tolerance to Rawlsian liberalism. It does not deny the obvious lesson of the Wars of Religion, that is, that religions need to coexist. Indeed, the existence of the millets probably saved the Ottoman Empire from undergoing these wars. In fact, this is arguably the more natural form of religious tolerance. The historical record suggests that "in practice, religions have usually felt most violently intolerant not of other religions but of dissenters within their own ranks" (Elton 1984a:xiii). This was true of paganism in antiquity (Garnsey 1984:24) and of leading figures in the English Reformation, such as Thomas More (Elton 1984b:174–75, 182–83).

The Ottoman millet system is the most developed form of the group-rights model of religious tolerance. But variations on that model can be found in many other times and places, including many contemporary liberal democracies. Consider the following three cases:

1. American Indian tribes have a legally recognized right to self-government. As part of this self-government, tribal governments are not subject to the U.S. Bill of Rights. Some tribes have established a theocratic government that discriminates against those members who do not share the tribal religion. For example, the Pueblo deny housing benefits to those members of the community who have converted to Protestantism (Weston 1981).

2. Both Canada and the United States exempt a number of long-standing religious sects (e.g., Mennonites, Doukhobours, Amish, Hutterites) from laws regarding the mandatory education of children. Members of these sects can withdraw their children from schools before the legal age of sixteen and are not required to teach the usual school curriculum. Parents worry that if their children received this broader education, they would be tempted to leave the sect and join the wider society (Janzen 1990:chaps. 5–7).

3. Britain has recently received a considerable number of Muslim immigrants from its former protectorates and colonies. Some traditional practices in Muslim countries violate current British law, including coercive arranged marriages and various forms of sexual discrimination. Some Muslim leaders have called for a milletlike system in Britain, which would allow Muslims to govern themselves according to their own laws regarding education and family status.[9]

In each of these cases, an ethnic or religious group has sought the legal power to restrict the liberty of its own members, so as to preserve its traditional religious practices. These groups are seeking to establish or maintain a system of group rights that protects communal practices not only from external oppression but also from internal dissent, and this often requires exemption from the constitutional or legislative requirements of the larger society.

This demand for group rights is often phrased in terms of tolerance. But it is not the sort of tolerance Rawls has in mind. These groups do not want the state to protect each individual's right to freely express, question, and revise her religious beliefs. On the contrary, this is precisely what they object to. What they want is the power to restrict the religious freedom of their own members, and they want the exercise of this power to be exempted from the usual requirement to respect individual rights.

Hence, the idea of group rights is a pressing issue in many democracies. Yet Rawls never considers this model of tolerance. He talks about "the principle of tolerance" (e.g., Rawls 1987:18; 1985:225) as if there were just one, which he equates with the idea of freedom of conscience. Indeed, he often writes as if respect for individual rights is the only way to accommodate pluralism. Consider his claim that the liberal commitment to individual rights was accepted "as providing the only alternative to endless and destructive civil strife" (Rawls 1987:18). Or his claim that parties in his "original position" would see the fact of pluralism as sufficient grounds for adopting a principle of individual rights: "[W]e need only suppose in the first stage that the parties assume the fact of pluralism to obtain, that is, that a plurality of comprehensive doctrines exists in society. The parties must then protect against the possibility that the person each party represents may be a member of a religious, ethnic, or other minority. *This suffices for the argument for the equal basic liberties to get going*" (Rawls 1989:251, my emphasis; cf. Rawls 1982b:25–26). Indeed, Rawls sometimes writes as if a religiously diverse society had never existed before the birth of liberalism: "[T]he success of liberal institutions may come as a discovery of a new social possibility: the possibility of a reasonably harmonious and stable pluralist society. Before the successful and peaceful practice of toleration in societies with liberal political institutions there was no way of knowing of that possibility. It can easily seem more natural to believe, as the centuries' long practice of intolerance appeared to confirm, that social unity and concord requires agreement on a general and comprehensive religious, philosophical or moral doctrine" (Rawls 1987:23). But the "successful and peaceful practice of toleration" existed in the Ottoman Empire long before England's Toleration Act.

Even if we endorse Rawls's liberal conception of tolerance, the millet system is a useful reminder that individual rights are not the only way to accommodate religious pluralism.

3. Individual Rights and Autonomy

The millet system is clearly incompatible with Rawls's theory of justice, because it restricts one of the basic liberties Rawls ascribes to each person.[10] But how can he defend individual liberty as a superior response to pluralism than group rights?

Most liberals would object to the millet system on the grounds that it makes it difficult or impossible for people to question or revise their religious commitments. It does not impose religious views on people, in the sense that there is no forced conversion. But nor does it allow people to judge for themselves what parts of their traditional religious faith are worthy of their continued allegiance, and why. They can only follow inherited customs and practices uncritically.

One way to express this objection is to say that the millet system restricts individual autonomy. It limits individuals' ability and freedom to judge the value of inherited practices and to thereby form and revise their own conception of the good. Many liberals explicitly appeal to this idea of autonomy as the basis for their defense of individual rights. Consider the following passage from J. S. Mill's *On Liberty*:

> [I]t would be absurd to pretend that people ought to live as if nothing had been known in the world before they came into it; as if experience had as yet done nothing towards showing that one mode of existence, or of conduct, is preferable to another. Nobody denies that people should be so taught and trained in youth as to know and benefit by the ascertained results of human experience. *But it is the privilege and proper condition of a human being, arrived at the maturity of his faculties, to use and interpret experience in his own way. It is for him to find out what part of recorded experience is properly applicable to his own circumstances and character.* (Mill 1982:122, my emphasis)

For Mill and other liberals, a basic argument for civil rights is that they help ensure that individuals can make informed judgments about the inherited practices of the community. For example, mandatory education ensures that children acquire the capacity to envisage alternative ways of life and rationally assess them. Freedom of speech and association (including the freedom to proselytize or dissent from church orthodoxy) ensures that people can raise questions and seek answers about the worth of the different ways of life available to them. Because the millet system restricts these civil rights, it harms a basic interest of people, by leaving them unable to rationally assess the worthiness of their current ends and to revise their ends accordingly.

I call this the "Millian" or "autonomy" argument for civil rights, that is, the view that we have a basic interest in being able to rationally assess and revise our current ends. These labels might be misleading, because Mill never used the term "autonomy," and this is only one of his arguments for civil rights. Moreover, there are other conceptions of autonomy present in the liberal tradition. However, I believe that this particular conception of autonomy—Buchanan calls it the "rational revisability" conception of autonomy—is central to Mill's defense of individual rights, and to many other liberal theorists.[11]

In his earlier work, Rawls seems to endorse the Millian argument. He says that members of a liberal society have the capacity "to form, to revise, and rationally to pursue" a conception of the good. It is important to note that Rawls explicitly mentions the capacity to *revise* one's conception of the good, alongside the capacity to pursue one's *existing* conception. Indeed, he suggests that the latter "is in essential respects subordinate" to the former. Exercising our capacity to form and revise a conception of the good is a "highest-order interest," in the sense of being "supremely regulative and effective." People's interest in advancing their existing conception of the good, on the other hand, is simply a "higher-order interest." Although it is of course important to be able to pursue one's existing conception of the good, the capacity to evaluate and revise that conception is needed to ensure that it is worthy of one's continued allegiance (Rawls 1980:525–28).

Hence people have a highest-order interest in standing back from their current ends and assessing their worthiness: "As free persons, citizens recognize one another as having the moral power to have a conception of the good. This means that they do not view themselves as inevitably tied to the pursuit of the particular conception of the good and its final ends which they espouse at any given time. Instead, as citizens, they are regarded as, in general, capable of revising and changing this conception on reasonable and rational grounds. Thus it is held to be permissible for citizens to stand apart from conceptions of the good and to survey and assess their various final ends" (Rawls 1980:544). This capacity to survey and assess our ends is in fact one of the two fundamental "moral powers" (along with the capacity for a sense of justice) that define Rawls's "conception of the person." And, like Mill, Rawls defends civil liberties in terms of their contribution to the realizing and exercising of this moral power (Rawls 1980:526; cf. 1989:254; 1982a:165).

Some communitarians deny that we can "stand apart" from (some of) our final ends. According to Michael Sandel, some of our final ends are "constitutive" ends, in the sense that they define our sense of personal identity (Sandel 1982:150–65; cf. MacIntyre 1981:chap. 15; Bell 1993:24–54). It makes no sense, on his view, to say that my final ends might not be worthy of my allegiance, for these ends define who I am. Whereas Rawls claims that individuals "do not regard themselves as inevitably bound to, or identical with, the pursuit of any particular complex of fundamental interests that they may have at any given moment" (Rawls 1974:641), Sandel responds that we are in fact "identical with" at least some of our final ends. Because these ends are constitutive of people's identity, there is no reason why the state should not reinforce people's allegiance to those ends.

This communitarian conception of the self as defined by constitutive ends is one possible basis for the group-rights approach to tolerance.[12] Sandel himself rarely discusses the question of group rights, and he often qualifies his idea of constitutive ends in a way that suggests that people can, after all, stand back and assess even their most deeply held ends.[13] Hence he and other contemporary communitarians might well object to the sorts of individual restrictions imposed by some group-rights systems.[14]

However, a milletlike system can be seen as a sort of hypercommunitarianism. It assumes that people's religious affiliation is so profoundly constitutive of who they are that their overriding interest is in protecting and advancing that identity, and that they have no interest in being able to stand back and assess that identity. Hence the millet system limits people's ability to revise their fundamental ends and prevents others from trying to promote such revision.

This is perhaps most obvious in the prohibition on proselytization and apostasy. If we assume that religious ends are constitutive of people's identity, then proselytization is at best futile and at worst an inherently harmful attempt to tempt people away from their true identity. This is indeed one reason why systems of group rights often seek to limit or prohibit proselytization or its secular equivalents (e.g., the attempts of the Amish to prevent their children from learning about the outside world in schools).

The liberal model, on the other hand, gives people access to information about other ways of life (through proselytization), indeed requires people to learn about these options (through mandatory education), and allows people to radically revise their ends (apostasy is not a crime). These aspects of a liberal society only make sense, I think, on the assumption that we have an interest not only in pursuing our existing conception of the good but also in being able to assess and potentially revise that conception. The liberal model assumes that revising one's ends is both possible and sometimes desirable. It assumes that people's current ends are not always worthy of their continued allegiance, and that exposure to other ways of life helps people make informed judgments about what is truly worthwhile.

4. Comprehensive versus Political Liberalism

In his earlier work, Rawls clearly endorses the Millian view that we have a basic interest in assessing and potentially revising our existing ends. In his more recent work, however, Rawls seems to want to avoid appealing to this conception of autonomy, which he now sees as "sectarian," in the sense that it is an ideal that is "not generally, or perhaps even widely, shared in a democratic society" (Rawls 1987:24; 1985:246). He wants to find an alternative basis for defending civil rights, one which can be accepted even by those who reject the conception of the person implicit in the Millian argument.

His proposal is not to reject the autonomy argument entirely but rather to restrict its scope. In particular, he wants to continue appealing to it in *political* contexts, while avoiding it in other contexts. The idea that we can form and revise our conception of the good is, he now says, strictly a "political conception" of the person, adopted solely for the purposes of determining our public rights and responsibilities. It is not, he insists, intended as a general account of the relationship between the self and its ends applicable to all areas of life, or as an accurate portrayal of our deepest self-understandings. On the contrary, in private life it is quite possible and likely that our personal identity is bound to particular ends in such a way as to preclude rational revision. As he puts it,

> It is essential to stress that citizens in their personal affairs, or in the internal life of associations to which they belong, may regard their final ends and attachments in a way very different from the way the political conception involves. Citizens may have, and normally do have at any given time, affections, devotions, and loyalties that they believe they would not, and indeed could and should not, stand apart from and objectively evaluate from the standpoint of their purely rational good. They may regard it as simply unthinkable to view themselves apart from certain religious, philosophical and moral convictions, or from certain enduring attachments and loyalties. These convictions and attachments are part of what we may call their "nonpublic identity." (Rawls 1985:241)

So Rawls no longer assumes that people's religious commitments are revisable or autonomously affirmed. He accepts that these ends might be so constitutive of our identity that we cannot stand back from them and subject them to assessment and revision. However, in political contexts, we ignore the possible existence of such constitutive ends. As *citizens*, we continue to see ourselves as having a "highest-order interest" in our capacity for autonomy, even though as *private individuals* we might not see ourselves as having or valuing that capacity. Rawls's conception of the person, based on the two moral powers of justice and autonomy, continues to provide the language of public justification in which people discuss their rights and responsibilities as citizens, although it may not describe their "nonpublic identity" (Rawls 1980:545).

Hence Rawls distinguishes his "political liberalism" from the "comprehensive liberalism" of Mill. As we have seen, Mill thinks that people should exercise autonomy in both public and private contexts. Mill's argument that people should be able to assess the worth of inherited social practices applies to all areas of life, not just political life. Indeed, he was mostly concerned about the way people blindly followed popular culture and social customs in their everyday personal affairs. Hence Mill's liberalism is based on an ideal of rational reflection that applies to human action generally and that is intended "to inform our thought and conduct as a whole" (Rawls 1987:6).

Rawls worries that many people do not accept Mill's idea of autonomy as a principle governing human thought and action generally. However, he thinks that such people can nonetheless accept the idea of autonomy if it is restricted to political contexts, leaving them free to view their nonpublic identities in quite different ways. People can accept his political conception "without being committed in other parts of their life to comprehensive moral ideals often associated with liberalism, for example, the ideals of autonomy and individuality" (Rawls 1985:245).

Is this a coherent position? The problem is to explain why anyone would accept the ideal of autonomy in political contexts without also accepting it more generally. If the members of a religious community see their religious ends as constitutive, so that they have no ability to stand back and assess these ends, why would they accept a political conception of the person which assumes that they do have that ability (and indeed a highest-order interest in exercising that ability)?

One answer Rawls might give is that everyone can accept his political conception, because those who do not generally value the capacity for autonomy can simply refrain from exercising it in private life. Although a liberal society allows rational assessment and revision of one's ends, it does not compel it. Hence, he might argue, even if this view of autonomy conflicts with a religious minority's self-understanding, there is no cost to accepting it for political purposes.

But there is a cost to nonliberal minorities from accepting Rawls's political conception of the person, namely, it precludes any system of group rights that limits the right of individuals to revise their conceptions of the good. For example, it precludes a religious minority from prohibiting apostasy and proselytization or from preventing their children learning about other ways of life. The minority might view these civil liberties as harmful. But if, for the purposes of political debate, they accept the assumption that people have a highest-order interest in exercising their capacity to form and revise a conception of the good, then they have no way to express their belief in the harm of allowing proselytization and apostasy.

Consider the Canadian case of *Hofer v. Hofer*, which dealt with the powers of the Hutterite Church over its members. The Hutterites live in large agricultural communities, called colonies, within which there is no private property. Two residents of a Hutterite colony, who had been members of the colony from birth, were expelled for apostasy. They demanded their share of the colony's assets, which they had helped create with their years of labor. When the colony refused, the two ex-members sued in court. They objected to the fact that they had "no right at any time in their lives to leave the colony without abandoning everything, even the clothes on their backs" (Janzen 1990:67). The Hutterites defended this practice on the grounds that freedom of religion protects a congregation's ability to live in accordance with its religious doctrine, even if this limits individual freedom.

The Canadian Supreme Court accepted this Hutterite claim. But it is far from clear that the Hutterite claim can be defended, or even expressed, within the language of Rawls's "political liberalism." As Justice Pigeon noted in dissent, the usual liberal notion of freedom of religion "includes the right of each individual to change his religion at will." Hence churches "cannot make rules having the effect of depriving their members of this fundamental freedom." The proper scope of religious authority is therefore "limited to what is consistent with freedom of religion as properly understood, that is freedom for the individual not only to adopt a religion but also to abandon it at will." Justice Pigeon thought that it was "as nearly impossible as can be" for people in a Hutterite colony to reject its religious teachings, because of the high cost of changing their religion, and so they were effectively deprived of freedom of religion.[15]

Justice Pigeon's view, it seems to me, is most consistent with Rawls's "political liberalism." Pigeon is assuming, as Rawls says we should for the purposes of political argument and legal rights, that people have a basic interest in their capacity to form and revise their conception of the good. Hence, he concludes, the power of religious communities over their own members must be such that individuals can freely and effectively exercise that capacity. The power of religious authorities clearly cannot be such as to make it effectively impossible to exercise that capacity. Were the Hutterites to accept Rawls's conception of the person, then they, too, would have to accept the view that freedom of religion must be interpreted in terms of an individual's capacity to form and revise her religious beliefs.[16]

Hence Rawls's strategy of endorsing autonomy only in political contexts, rather than as a general value, does not succeed. Accepting the value of autonomy for political purposes inevitably enables its exercise more generally, an implication that will be favored only by those who endorse autonomy as a general value.[17] Rawls has yet to explain why people who reject his conception of the person in private life should endorse it as a political good.[18] Rawls might be right that "Within different contexts we can assume diverse points of view toward our person without contradiction so long as these points of view cohere together when circumstances require" (Rawls 1980:545). But he has not shown that these points of view do cohere. On the contrary, they clearly conflict on issues of intragroup dissent, such as proselytization, apostasy, and mandatory education.[19]

Why has Rawls not seen this conflict? Perhaps because he thinks that his political conception is the only one that can protect religious minorities from the intolerance of the majority. Recall his claim that the fact of pluralism is sufficient ground for endorsing individual rights: "[W]e need only suppose in the first stage that the parties assume the fact of pluralism to obtain, that is, that a plurality of comprehensive doctrines exists in society. The parties must then protect against the possibility that the person each party represents may be a member of a religious, ethnic, or other minority. This suffices for the argument for the equal basic liberties to get going" (Rawls 1989:251). Rawls here implies that the only viable way to prevent persecution between groups is to allow freedom of conscience for individuals. But this is a mistake; one can ensure tolerance *between* groups without protecting tolerance of individual dissent *within* each group. A system of group rights ensures the former without ensuring the latter. If we want to defend civil rights for individuals, therefore, we must go beyond the need for group tolerance and give some account of the value of endowing individuals with the freedom to form and revise their final ends.

Rawls is mistaken, therefore, to suppose that he can avoid appealing to the general value of individual autonomy without undermining his argument for the priority of civil rights.[20] The mere fact of *social plurality*, disconnected from any assumption of *individual autonomy*, cannot by itself defend the full range of liberal freedoms.[21] If people's private identity really is tied to certain ends, such that they have no interest or ability to question and revise them, then group rights might be a superior response to pluralism. If individuals are incapable of revising their inherited religious commitments, or if it is not important to enable individuals to exercise that capacity, then the millet system might best protect and advance those constitutive ends.

This is hardly a novel conclusion. On the contrary, this is what defenders of group rights have often argued. They believe that once we drop the assumption that autonomy is a general value, then religious and ethnic groups should be allowed to protect their members' constitutive ends by restricting certain individual rights (Kukathas 1992; McDonald 1991).

If liberals wish to defend individual freedom of conscience, they must reject the idea that people's ends are beyond rational revision. At one point, Rawls seems to do just this. He notes that some people think of themselves as being incapable of questioning or revising their ends, but he suggests that this may be inaccurate: "[O]ur conceptions of the good may and often do change over time, usually slowly but sometimes rather suddenly," even for those people who think of themselves as having constitutive ends. For example, "On the road to Damascus Saul of Tarsus becomes Paul the Apostle" (Rawls 1985:242).

This is an important point. No matter how confident we are about our ends at a particular moment, new circumstances or experiences can arise, often in unpredictable ways, that cause us to reevaluate them. This is the beginning of an argument for why people should be free to stand back and assess their ends. But Rawls makes no attempt to elaborate on it. He does not explain why it is important for people to be able to make these kinds of changes, or how this capacity should be legally and socially encouraged (e.g., through education or freedom to proselytize).

5. The Issue of Nonliberal Minorities

Why is Rawls so reluctant to affirm the Millian argument and explicitly endorse autonomy as a general human interest? What is wrong with Mill's "comprehensive" liberalism? The problem, Rawls says, is that not everyone accepts this ideal of autonomy, and so appealing to it in political life would be "sectarian": "As comprehensive moral ideals, autonomy and individuality are unsuited for a political conception of justice. As found in Kant and J. S. Mill, these comprehensive ideals, despite their very great importance in liberal thought, are extended too far when presented as the only appropriate foundation for a constitutional regime. So understood, liberalism becomes but another sectarian doctrine" (Rawls 1985:246). Mill's defense of civil rights rests "in large part on ideals and values that are not generally, or perhaps even widely, shared in a democratic society," and hence "cannot secure sufficient agreement" (Rawls 1987:6, 24).

This is a legitimate point, but Rawls overstates it and draws the wrong conclusion from it. The idea that we have an interest in being able to assess and revise our inherited conceptions of the good is very widely shared in Western democratic societies.[22] There are some insulated minorities who reject this ideal, including some indigenous groups (the Pueblo) and religious sects (the Amish and the Mennonites). These groups pose a challenge for liberal democracies, because they often demand group rights that conflict with individual civil rights. We cannot simply ignore this demand or ignore the fact that they reject the idea of autonomy.

But Rawls's strategy is no solution to the questions raised by the existence of nonliberal minorities. His solution is to continue to enforce individual rights, but to do so on the basis of a "political" rather than a "comprehensive" liberalism. This obviously does not satisfy the demands of nonliberal minorities. They want group rights that take precedence over individual rights. Rawls's political liberalism is as hostile to that demand as Mill's comprehensive liberalism. The fact that Rawls's theory is less comprehensive does not make it more sympathetic to the demands of nonliberal minorities.[23]

How then should a liberal state treat nonliberal minorities? To begin with, we need to distinguish two very different questions that Rawls conflates: First, what kind of provision for religious and ethnic minorities is consistent with liberal principles? Second, should liberals impose their views on communities that do not accept liberal principles? The first is a question of *identifying* a defensible liberal theory of tolerance; the second is a question of *imposing* that liberal theory.

With respect to the first question, I believe that the most defensible liberal theory is based on the value of autonomy, and that any form of group rights that restricts the civil rights of group members is therefore inconsistent with liberal principles of freedom and equality. The millet system, or the Pueblo theocracy, is therefore seriously deficient from a liberal point of view.

That does not mean that liberals can impose those principles on groups that do not share them. There are a number of further steps that are required before we can answer the question of imposing liberalism. Once we know what an appropriate liberal conception of minority rights is, we can then determine how much it coincides with, or differs from, the wishes of a particular minority. Once we have determined the extent of any disagreements, then we are faced with the question of intervening in order to promote liberal ideals. This in turn will depend on many factors, including the severity of rights violations within the minority community, the degree of consensus in the community on the legitimacy of restricting individual rights, the ability of dissenting group members to leave the community if they so desire, the existence of historical agreements with the minority community (e.g., treaties with American Indian tribes;

historical promises made to immigrant groups), the nature of the proposed intervention, and so forth.[24]

The question of imposing liberalism comes, therefore, a number of steps after the question of identifying a liberal theory. In many cases, there will be little room for coercive intervention. Relations between majority and minority groups should be determined by peaceful negotiation, not force (as with international relations). This means searching for some basis of agreement. If two groups do not share basic principles and cannot be persuaded to adopt the other's principles, then they will have to come to some kind of accommodation. In cases in which the minority rejects liberal values, then the resulting agreement might well involve recognizing group rights. And, as noted above, contemporary liberal societies do in fact recognize some milletlike structures, for example, education exemptions for the Amish, theocratic government for the Pueblo Indians.[25] But this is a compromise of, not the instantiation of, liberal principles, because it violates a fundamental liberal principle of freedom of conscience. Hence liberal reformers inside the group would seek to promote their liberal ideas through reason or example, and liberals outside would lend their support to any efforts the community makes to liberalize.

Rawls seems to conflate these two questions of identifying and imposing a liberal theory of justice. His "political" conception of liberalism is not, I think, an adequate answer to either question. It does not adequately *identify* a defensible liberal theory, because he leaves it entirely unclear why citizens (but not private individuals) have a highest-order interest in their capacity to form and revise a conception of the good. It does not adequately answer the question of *imposing* liberalism, because it would enforce liberal rights in minority communities that might have a strong social consensus in favor of group rights, and a strong historical claim to them as well.

Rawls is right to worry about the existence of ethnic and religious minorities that reject the value of autonomy, but his response is misguided. In the face of such minorities, Rawls has become less willing to defend comprehensive liberalism but is still willing to impose liberal political institutions. A more appropriate response, I believe, is to continue defending comprehensive liberalism based on autonomy as a general value, but become more cautious about imposing the full set of liberal political institutions on nonliberal minorities.

6. Conclusion

I have described two models of religious tolerance: a liberal model based on individual liberty, and a hypercommunitarian model based on group rights. Both recognize the need for different religious communities to coexist, and hence are consistent with the fact of religious pluralism in modern societies.[26] However, they disagree fundamentally on the role of individual freedom within religious communities. The group-rights model allows each group to limit the religious liberties of its own members so as to protect the constitutive ends and practices of the community from internal dissent. The liberal model insists that each individual has a right to freedom of conscience, including the right to question and revise her religious beliefs, and so allows for proselytization, heresy, and apostasy.

Rawls has consistently endorsed the liberal model, and his theory of justice precludes any system of group rights that limits freedom of conscience. But his justification for this preference has become increasingly obscure. In his earlier work, he seemed to defend the liberal model on the ground that people have a basic interest in their capacity to form and revise their conceptions of the good, so as to ensure that these conceptions are worthy of their continued allegiance. This autonomy argument is a familiar liberal argument for civil rights. Indeed, liberals are often defined as those who support toleration because it is necessary for the promotion of autonomy.[27]

In his more recent writings, however, Rawls wants to avoid this autonomy argument, which he views as "sectarian" and insensitive to the views of certain religious and ethnic minorities. His solution is to abandon any form of liberalism that relies on a "comprehensive" ideal, such as autonomy, and rely instead on a "political" conception of the person as free and equal. But this strategy, I have argued, does not work. It simply leaves it unclear why a liberal state should assign priority to civil rights, without in fact being any more sympathetic to the demands of nonliberal minorities. A more appropriate response, I believe, is to continue to defend comprehensive liberalism, but to recognize that there are limits to our ability to implement and impose liberal principles on groups that have not endorsed those principles.

Notes

* This is a lightly revised version of a paper that first appeared in *Analyse und Kritik*, vol. 14/1, pp. 33–56. I would like to thank Sue Donaldson and Wayne Norman for helpful comments on an earlier draft, and Brian Anderson for invaluable research assistance.

1. By Rawls's "recent" writings, I mean his post-1985 articles, in which he emphasizes the distinction between "political" and "metaphysical" or "comprehensive" conceptions of liberalism (Rawls 1985, 1987, 1988, 1989). These articles have now been collected in Rawls 1993.

2. The term "neutrality" has a number of different meanings, and so talking about liberal neutrality often creates confusion. The sense in which a liberal state

is "neutral" with respect to competing conceptions of the good is a very specific one: the state does not justify its actions on the grounds that some ways of life are intrinsically more valuable than others. The *justification* of state policy, therefore, is neutral between rival conceptions of the good. This does not mean that the *consequences* of state policy are neutral, in the sense of equally helping or hindering each way of life. On the contrary, how well a way of life fares in a liberal society depends on its ability to gain or maintain sufficient adherents, and those that are unable to do so will wither away in a liberal society, while others flourish. A liberal state allows these non-neutral consequences of individual freedom of choice and association to occur. It does not, however, try to preempt this process by developing a public ranking of the intrinsic value of different ways of life, which it then uses to influence individuals' choices. For further discussion of the difference between "justificatory" and "consequential" neutrality, see Kymlicka 1989b. For Rawls's discussion of neutrality, see Rawls 1988:260, 265.

3. For a helpful introduction to the millet system, see Runciman 1970:27–35; and Braude and Lewis 1982:1–34.

4. It is important to distinguish two kinds of group rights that can be attributed to minority communities: rights of the group *against the larger society*, and rights of the group *against its own members*. I believe that in the case of minority cultures, the former are consistent with liberal views of freedom and equality if they protect a vulnerable minority from the impact of majority economic or political decisions. Such intergroup rights can include land claims, language rights, guaranteed representation in political institutions, veto power over certain kinds of policies, etc. For a liberal defense of these rights, see Kymlicka 1989a:chaps. 7–10. This paper, however, will focus on the latter kind of group right, which I believe is generally inconsistent with liberalism. For the rest of this paper, therefore, I will use the term "group right" to refer to rights of groups against their own members. I discuss the distinction between these two kinds of group rights in Kymlicka 1994 and Kymlicka 1995:chap. 3.

5. Another historical parallel is that both systems combined toleration of religious worship with discrimination in terms of public office. In the millet system, the non-Muslim communities gained freedom of worship in the 1400s but only achieved full legal equality in 1856. This parallels the growth of toleration in Britain, which adopted the Toleration Act in 1689, but which imposed some legal disabilities on Catholics and Jews until 1829 and 1846 respectively.

6. Davison discusses these challenges to clerical rule, inspired by Western liberalism, in Davison 1982:332. The impact of the "corrosive notions of the European Enlightenment" on the millet system is also discussed in Braude and Lewis 1982:18–19, 30–31; and Karpat 1982:159–63.

7. For example, the Protestant millet, established in 1850, was "lay controlled, democratic, and on Anglo-Saxon lines" (Davison 1982:329). On the more general attempts to liberalize the millets in the 1850s, see Braude and Lewis 1982:22–23.

8. On the foreign influences that conspired to undermine the millet system, see Braude and Lewis 1982:28–30.

9. For a discussion of the British Muslim case, see Poulter 1987; Parekh 1990; and my exchange with Tariq Modood (Modood 1993).

10. Rawls's first principle of justice states that "[e]ach person has an equal right to the most extensive system of equal basic liberties compatible with a similar scheme of liberty for all." First on the list of basic liberties, Rawls says, are freedom of thought and liberty of conscience.

11. Buchanan 1975. It is important to distinguish this conception of autonomy from others that have been defended within (or attributed to) the liberal tradition. Some people think that the exercise of autonomy is intrinsically valuable, because it reflects our rational nature (this view is ascribed to Kant). Others believe that nonconformist individuality is intrinsically valuable (this view is often ascribed to Mill). What I am calling the Millian conception of autonomy, however, is simply the claim that autonomy enables us to assess and learn what is good in life, and why. It presupposes that we have an essential interest in revising those of our current beliefs about value that are mistaken. I discuss these different conceptions of autonomy and their role in contemporary liberal thought in 1989a:chap. 4. See also Norman 1990.

12. This is anachronistic in the case of the millet system, which was based on Muslim theology not a more general communitarian conception of the person. Indeed, the Muslims did allow for certain kinds of voluntary revisions of religious ends (Braude and Lewis 1982:4).

13. He does briefly discuss the case of the Amish and defends the group's right to make it difficult for their children to learn about other ways of life (Sandel 1990). He argues that freedom of conscience should be understood as freedom to pursue one's constitutive ends, not as an "unencumbered" freedom to choose one's religion. People's religious affiliation, he claims, is so profoundly constitutive of who they are that their overriding interest is in protecting that identity, and they have no comparable interest in being able to stand back and assess that identity. Hence he defends the right of the Amish to withdraw their children from school before the legal age of sixteen, to ensure that the children do not learn about the outside world, and so are not tempted to stray from their true identity.

14. However, once these qualifications are added in, it is no longer clear how Sandel's conception of the person differs from the Rawlsian one he claims to be criticizing (see Kymlicka 1989a:chap. 2). D'Entreves argues that communitarians are committed to tolerance because they believe in a conception of the person "that critically evaluates his/her beliefs and desires, that reflects upon his/her needs and motives, and that judges the worth of his/her preferences" (D'Entreves 1990:83). This sounds very much like the Millian/Rawlsian conception of the person that communitarians claim to reject.

15. *Hofer v. Hofer et al.* (1970), 13 DLR (3d) 1, cited in Janzen 1990:65–67.

16. Rawls does emphasize that the point of protecting civil rights is not to *maximize* the development and exercise of the capacity to form and revise a conception of the good. As he rightly notes, it would be "absurd" to try to maximize "the number of deliberate affirmations of a conception of the good." Rather, "these liberties and their priority are to guarantee equally for all citizens the social conditions essential for the adequate development and the full and informed exercise of these powers" (1982b:47–49). It seems clear, however, that the Hutterites do not provide the social conditions essential for the "full and informed" exercise of autonomy.

17. Indeed, the connection between the political and the private is not only causal but conceptual. Rawls accepts that exercising autonomy in the political sphere might causally promote its exercise in private life. But he insists that this is a contingent and unintended effect and that his political conception of the person concerns only the way "that the moral powers [of autonomy and a sense of justice] are exercised in political life and in basic institutions as citizens endeavour to maintain them and to use them to conduct public business" (Rawls 1988:272n28). What does it mean to exercise our capacity for autonomy "in political life"? The capacity for autonomy is quite different in this respect from the capacity for a sense of justice, although Rawls treats them together in this passage. The capacity for a sense of justice is exercised by "assessing the justice and effectiveness of laws and social policies," and hence is primarily concerned with, and exercised in, political life. The capacity to form and revise a conception of the good, on the other hand, is primarily concerned with what Rawls calls our "nonpublic identity," with our comprehensive, rather than our political, identity. As Rawls himself puts it, "liberty of conscience and freedom of association enable us to develop and exercise our moral powers in forming, revising, and rationally pursuing our conceptions of the good that belong to our comprehensive doctrines, and affirming them as such" (Rawls 1989:254). Hence, the capacity for justice is about evaluating *public* policies and institutions, whereas the capacity to form/revise a conception of the good is about evaluating the comprehensive religious and moral doctrines that define our *private* identity. But then what does it mean to say that the exercise of this latter capacity can be restricted to political life, without its impinging on our private identity? Because the capacity involved just is the capacity to form and revise our comprehensive ends, it seems that any exercise of it necessarily involves our private identity.

18. Rawls does briefly suggest another argument for endorsing liberal freedoms over group rights, namely, that only the former is consistent with the idea of "citizenship." He says that a society "in which basic rights and recognized claims depend on religious affiliation, social class, and so on . . . may not have a conception of citizenship at all; for this conception, as we are using it, goes with the conception of society as a fair system of cooperation for mutual advantage between free and equal persons" (Rawls 1989:241). There is some truth to Rawls's claim here. There was only a very weak sense of shared citizenship in the millet system, and the same is true in other systems of group rights (e.g., amongst the Amish). People's identity as citizen is less important, in these systems, than their identity as a member of the group. But so long as the system is stable, why is this a problem? A defender of group tolerance would respond that the sense of citizenship should be molded to fit people's religious identity, not vice versa.

Rawls suggests that a strong sense of shared citizenship is needed to ensure the political virtues of "reasonableness and a sense of fairness, a spirit of compromise and a readiness to meet others halfway" (Rawls 1987:21). But I see no reason why these virtues cannot exist in the group-rights model. Indeed, the history of the millet system suggests that the creation of a shared sense of citizenship can threaten these virtues. In the Ottoman Empire, compromise between groups was traditionally ensured by the system of self-government that accorded equal status to each group and limited mutual interference. In the mid–eighteenth century, however, the Ottomans tried to promote a sense of shared citizenship that cut across religious and ethnic boundaries, so that everyone's political rights and identity were based on a common relationship to the Ottoman state rather than membership in a particular millet. As Karpat notes, the result was disastrous: "Once the corporate status of the millet and the segregation of the various groups ended, the relative position of the religious and ethnic groups in the Ottoman Empire toward each other began to be decided on the basis of their numerical strength. Hence they were transformed into minorities and majorities. It was obvious that sooner or later the views of the majority would prevail and its cultural characteristics and aspirations would become the features of the government itself" (Karpat 1982:163). A similar process occurred when indigenous peoples in North America were accorded citizenship (often against their will), and so became a numerical minority within the larger body of citizens, rather than a separate, self-governing people. Rawls suggests that a sense of shared citizenship is needed to deal with the danger that majorities will treat minorities unfairly. But the Ottoman experience suggests that the notion of shared citizenship might have created that danger in the first place, by transforming self-governing groups into majorities and minorities.

19. It is worth noting that Rawls's example of an "overlapping consensus" on his political conception of the person does not include any groups that reject the idea of rational revisability in private life. His example involves three doctrines: a theological conception of true faith that demands freedom of conscience; a comprehensive liberal conception of the person as autonomous; and a self-standing, liberal political conception of society as a system of cooperation between free and equal citizens (Rawls 1985:250; 1987:9).

20. The assumption that we can assess and revise our ends is also needed, I believe, to justify Rawls's claim that people "are regarded as capable of taking responsibility for their ends," in the sense that they "are thought to be capable of adjusting their aims and aspirations in the light of what they can reasonably expect to provide for" (Rawls 1985:243). Because people can adjust their aims, Rawls claims, we have no obligation to subsidize those with expensive tastes. I discuss this aspect of Rawls's theory in Kymlicka 1990:73–77.

21. Rawls's belief that social plurality can defend individual liberty, even in the absence of individual revisability, is made most explicit in "The Basic Liberties and Their Priority" (1982b). In that article, Rawls distinguishes two arguments for freedom of conscience. On the first argument, conceptions of the good are "regarded as *given and firmly rooted*; and since there is a plurality of such conceptions, each, as it were, non-negotiable, the parties recognize that behind the veil of ignorance the principles of justice which guarantee equal liberty of conscience are the only principles which they can adopt." On this view, freedom of conscience protects religious minorities. Without freedom of conscience, people could find, once they drop the veil of ignorance, that they "belong to a minority faith and may suffer accordingly." On the second argument, conceptions of the good are "seen as *subject to revision* in accordance with deliberative reason, which is part of the capacity for a conception of the good." On this view, freedom of conscience protects individuals who wish to change their faith, because there "is no guarantee that all aspects of our present way of life are the most rational for

us and not in need of at least minor if not major revision" (Rawls 1982b:25–29, my emphasis). Rawls thinks that these two arguments "support the same conclusion" (1982b:29), i.e., that recognizing the *plurality* of conceptions of the good within society has the same implications for individual liberty as affirming the *revisability* of each individual's conception of the good. But they do not support the same conclusion on such issues as proselytization, which is an essential liberty on the second argument but a futile and disruptive nuisance on the first argument.

22. See Nickel 1990:214. Rawls's fear that the Millian conception of autonomy is not widely shared depends on conflating this conception of autonomy with the other, more controversial, conceptions discussed in note 11 above. It is important to note that although Mill's conception is "general," in applying to all areas of life, it is not "comprehensive," because it does not define a set of final ends or intrinsic goods to be pursued by each individual. Rather, it concerns the process by which we deliberate and assess our final ends.

23. The only case of group rights that Rawls discusses concerns the demands of some traditional religious groups (e.g., the Amish) for exemption from mandatory education. Rawls argues that his political liberalism is more sympathetic to this demand than Mill's comprehensive liberalism. Whereas comprehensive liberalism "may lead to requirements designed to foster the values of autonomy and individuality as ideas to govern much if not all of life," political liberalism "has a different aim and requires far less," because it is only concerned with promoting a liberal ideal of *citizenship* ("the state's concern with [children's] education lies in their role as future citizens"). As a result, Rawls says, political liberalism "honors, as far as it can, the claims of those who wish to withdraw from the modern world in accordance with the injunctions of their religion, provided only that they acknowledge the principles of the political conception of justice and appreciate its political ideals of person and society" (Rawls 1988:267–68). However, it is doubtful that political liberalism meets the demands of groups like the Amish. For one thing, as we have seen, the distinction between political and comprehensive liberalism is unstable, because accepting the value of autonomy for political purposes has unavoidable implications for private life (see note 17). Moreover, it is clear that many religious communities would object to political liberalism on its own terms, as a theory of citizenship. Mennonites and Hutterites in Canada have objected to some of the materials they are required to teach their children, because these materials promote an ideal of citizenship that is in conflict with their religious ideals of person and society. Whereas the government talked about preparing children for the rights and duties of citizenship, Mennonites saw "a different purpose of education . . . to prepare their children for life in their communities." Similarly, the Hutterites are "concerned not primarily with the potential for rationality but with, as they see it, the need for obedience. They argue that education should reorient the individual's self-regard and nurture a desire to abide by the will of the community." These groups do not see political liberalism as honoring their claims, and, as result, they have sought exemption from the sort of education that Rawls's "political liberalism" insists on. See Janzen 1990:143 (Hutterites) and 97 (Mennonites).

24. The ability to leave the community is a very important proviso. However, unlike some commentators (Svensson 1979:437; Kukathas 1992:133), I do not

think that the ability of individual members to exit is sufficient to justify internal restrictions, any more than racial segregation in the American South was made legitimate by the fact that individual Blacks could move north (although many defenders of segregation made this argument).

For further discussion, see Kymlicka 1992:144–45, from which I have taken the following paragraph; and Kymlicka 1995:chap. 8.

25. However, we rarely grant such rights to immigrant communities. This suggests there is a morally relevant difference between national minorities and immigrant groups. I discuss this in Kymlicka 1991; and 1995:chap. 2.

26. The group-rights approach cannot be used to accommodate all facets of modern-day pluralism. It presupposes that pluralism takes the form of identifiable groups, each with a relatively high degree of self-identification and the potential for some kind of organizational and leadership structure. Without these features, self-government is not likely. Hence the group-rights model seems most feasible in cases of ethnic and religious pluralism. Other forms of pluralism arising from competing conceptions of the good (e.g., diverse sexual lifestyles) require other modes of tolerance. However, as Rawls notes, religious and ethnic conflicts are the most divisive and destabilizing. It is only when pluralism does take this form—cohesive groups capable of collective action—that pluralism becomes genuinely destabilizing. Hence, it is particularly important to assess the different models of tolerance that are feasible in these cases.

27. "The autonomy argument is sometimes referred to as the characteristically liberal argument for toleration" (Mendus 1989:56).

Bibliography

Bell, Daniel. 1993. *Communitarianism and Its Critics*. Oxford: Oxford University Press.

Braude, Benjamin, and Bernard Lewis. 1982. "Introduction." In *Christians and Jews in the Ottoman Empire: The Functioning of a Plural Society*, ed. Braude and Lewis, pp. 1–34. New York: Holmes and Meier.

Buchanan, Allen. 1975. "Revisability and Rational Choice." *Canadian Journal of Philosophy* 5:395–408.

Davison, Roderic. 1982. "The Millets as Agents of Change in the Nineteenth-Century Ottoman Empire." In *Christians and Jews in the Ottoman Empire: The Functioning of a Plural Society*, ed. B. Braude and B. Lewis, pp. 319–37. New York: Holmes and Meier.

D'Entreves, Maurizio Passerin. 1990. "Communitarianism and the Question of Tolerance." *Journal of Social Philosophy* 21/1:77–91.

Elton, G. R. 1984a. "Introduction." In *Persecution and Toleration*. Vol. 21 of *Studies in Church History*, ed. W. J. Shiels, pp. xiii–xv. Published for the Ecclesiastical History Society. Oxford: Basil Blackwell.

Elton, G. R. 1984b. "Persecution and Toleration in the English Reformation." In *Persecution and Toleration*. Vol. 21 of *Studies in Church History*, ed. W. J. Shiels, pp. 163–87. Published for the Ecclesiastical History Society. Oxford: Basil Blackwell.

Garnsey, Peter. 1984. "Religious Tolerance in Classical Antiquity." In *Persecution and Toleration*. Vol. 21 of *Studies in Church History*, ed. W. J. Shiels, pp. 1–27. Published for the Ecclesiastical History Society. Oxford: Basil Blackwell.

Janzen, William. 1990. *Limits of Liberty: The Experiences of Mennonite, Hutterite, and Doukhobour Communities in Canada*. Toronto: University of Toronto Press.

Karpat, Kemal. 1982. "Millets and Nationality: The Roots of the Incongruity of Nation and State in the Post-Ottoman Era." In *Christians and Jews in the Ottoman Empire: The Functioning of a Plural Society*, ed. B. Braude and B. Lewis, pp. 141–69. New York: Holmes and Meier.

Kukathas, Chandran. 1992. "Are There Any Cultural Rights?" *Political Theory* 20/1: 105–39.

Kymlicka, Will. 1989a. *Liberalism, Community, and Culture*. Oxford: Oxford University Press.

Kymlicka, Will. 1989b. "Liberal Individualism and Liberal Neutrality." *Ethics* 99/4: 883–905.

Kymlicka, Will. 1990. *Contemporary Political Philosophy: An Introduction*. Oxford: Oxford University Press.

Kymlicka, Will. 1991. "Liberalism and the Politicization of Ethnicity." *Canadian Journal of Law and Jurisprudence* 4/2: 239–56.

Kymlicka, Will. 1992. "The Rights of Minority Cultures: Reply to Kukathas." *Political Theory* 20/1:140–46.

Kymlicka, Will. 1994. "Individual Rights and Community Rights." In *Group Rights*, ed. Judith Baker. Toronto: University of Toronto Press.

Kymlicka, Will. 1995. *Multicultural Citizenship: A Liberal Theory of Minority Rights*. Oxford: Oxford University Press.

MacIntyre, Alasdair. 1981. *After Virtue: A Study in Moral Theory*. London: Duckworth.

McDonald, Michael. 1991. "Should Communities Have Rights? Reflections on Liberal Individualism." *Canadian Journal of Law and Jurisprudence* 4/2:217–37.

Mendus, Susan. 1989. *Toleration and the Limits of Liberalism*. Atlantic Highlands, N.J.: Humanities Press.

Mill, J. S. 1982. *On Liberty*, ed. G. Himmelfarb. Harmondsworth, Eng.: Penguin.

Modood, Tariq. 1993. "Kymlicka on British Muslims." *Analyse und Kritik* 15/1:87–91.

Nickel, James. 1990. "Rawls on Political Community and Principles of Justice." *Law and Philosophy* 9:205–16.

Norman, W. J. 1990. "The Revisionist Challenge: Can the Liberal Do without 'Liberty'?" *Canadian Journal of Law and Jurisprudence* 3/1:29–49.

Parekh, Bhikhu. 1990. "The Rushdie Affair: Research Agenda for Political Philosophy." *Political Studies* 38:695–709.

Poulter, Sebastian. 1987. "Ethnic Minority Customs, English Law, and Human Rights." *International and Comparative Law Quarterly* 36/3:589–615.

Rawls, John. 1971. *A Theory of Justice*. London: Oxford University Press.

Rawls, John. 1974. "Reply to Alexander and Musgrave." *Quarterly Journal of Economics* 88/4:633–55.

Rawls, John. 1980. "Kantian Constructivism in Moral Theory." *Journal of Philosophy* 77/9:515–72.

Rawls, John. 1982a. "Social Unity and Primary Goods." In *Utilitarianism and Beyond*, ed. A. Sen and B. Williams, pp. 159–85. Cambridge: Cambridge University Press.

Rawls, John. 1982b. "The Basic Liberties and Their Priority." In *The Tanner Lectures on Human Values*, vol. 3, ed. S. McMurrin, pp. 1–87. Salt Lake City: University of Utah Press.

Rawls, John. 1985. "Justice as Fairness: Political not Metaphysical." *Philosophy and Public Affairs* 14/3; 223–51.

Rawls, John. 1987. "The Idea of an Overlapping Consensus." *Oxford Journal of Legal Studies* 7/1:1–25.

Rawls, John. 1988. "The Priority of Right and Ideas of the Good." *Philosophy and Public Affairs* 17/4:251–76.

Rawls, John. 1989. "The Domain of the Political and Overlapping Consensus." *New York University Law Review* 64/2:233–55.

Rawls, John. 1993. *Political Liberalism*. New York: Columbia University Press.

Runciman, Steven. 1970. *The Orthodox Churches and the Secular State*. Auckland: Auckland University Press.

Sandel, Michael. 1982. *Liberalism and the Limits of Justice*. Cambridge: Cambridge University Press.

Sandel, Michael. 1990. "Freedom of Conscience or Freedom of Choice." In *Articles of Faith, Articles of Peace*, ed. James Hunter and O. Guinness. Washington: Brookings Institute.

Svensson, Frances. 1979. "Liberal Democracy and Group Rights: The Legacy of Individualism and Its Impact on American Indian Tribes." *Political Studies* 27/3:421–39.

Weston, William. 1981. "Freedom of Religion and the American Indian." In *The American Indian: Past and Present*, ed. R. Nichols. 2d ed. New York: Wiley.

Autonomy, Toleration, and Group Rights:
A Response to Will Kymlicka

MOSHE HALBERTAL

KYMLICKA'S main purpose is to establish a necessary connection between toleration of individuals and the possibility and value of autonomy. This principal thesis is preceded by an interesting historical observation drawn from the political arrangements in the Ottoman Empire, which leads Kymlicka to offer a distinction between group pluralism and individual freedom. In the Ottoman Empire and its millet system, religious freedom was granted to groups rather than individuals. Members of the Greek Orthodox community, Jews, and Armenians were autonomous in all matters of religious life and were thus tolerated by their Muslim rulers. However, these three communities did not tolerate individual dissent within themselves, and each minority group had the legal right to impose on its members its own particular way of life. Hence, according to Kymlicka, Rawls is wrong in claiming that religious toleration and pluralism began in the wake of Protestantism; in the form of group toleration, in fact, religious pluralism was practiced long before Protestantism and the religious wars of Europe.

This argument, though, is not merely historical. Kymlicka claims that Rawls was mistaken not only concerning the history of toleration. According to Kymlicka, Rawls's mistake is rooted in a philosophical error that equates pluralism with individual freedom of conscience. The Ottoman experience, he contends, teaches us that religious toleration of groups is possible without practicing individual freedom of conscience. This observation leads Kymlicka to the second and central point of his argument. He argues that the move from group pluralism, such as that found in the Ottoman millet system, to individual freedom must be supported by the value of individual autonomy. According to Kymlicka, Rawls's reluctance (in his later work) to base pluralism on the possibility and value of individual autonomy limits the application of pluralism to groups alone. On this point, Kymlicka and Rawls radically differ. According to Kymlicka, the principle of "autonomy" is necessary for the defense of individual freedom, whereas according to Rawls, the support of toleration based exclusively on autonomy ties pluralism to an excessively narrow conception of the "good life" and is therefore an obstacle to his attempt to provide a maximally broad consensus for toleration within a political structure.

This essay focuses on the problem of whether autonomy is a necessary condition for individual freedom. I contend that toleration can be more successfully defended without appeal to the possibility of autonomy or to its value. I also attempt to defend an even more cogent argument that basing individual freedom on the notion of autonomy could lead to imposing a particular conception of the good life on individuals who do not perceive autonomy as valuable. This second argument also reveals differences between Kymlicka's view and my own regarding the scope and nature of group rights within a framework of individual freedom.

Before entering the problem of the relationship between individual freedom and autonomy and its implications for group rights, I will address Kymlicka's historical argument and clarify Rawls's conception of pluralism. The millet system was not an attempt to build a consensus among believers of radically different religious worldviews concerning the nature of a pluralistic society. In the Ottoman experience, the dominant power, that is, the Muslims, granted weaker minorities self-rule in religious matters. Rawls would not consider such an arrangement to be a genuine case of religious toleration, not only because it does not involve individual freedoms but because it was done in a framework of extreme asymmetry of power. Rawls is searching for a case in which radically different communities are involved in shaping a shared political structure. In such a case, according to Rawls, the fact of pluralism would force all the groups to liberal neutrality, because they would avoid giving priority to a particular conception of the good life in shaping the basic structure of society and its norms. It seems that such a scenario is very far from the millet system and indeed is unprecedented before the Reformation. The asymmetry of power in the millet system is itself a violation of pluralism in its most basic form. In the Ottoman Empire, unequal distribution of power was also based on religious affiliation. Minorities were discriminated against regarding equal access to political power, merely because they belonged to other faith communities.

The context of asymmetry of power in the millet system also seems to defy toleration, even in the religious realm. This context does not allow us to attribute to any party genuine pluralism (even group pluralism). The weaker parties had no choice but to be tolerant of the other parties, whereas the stronger and dominant party did not share government with others and was not involved in shaping a common pluralistic political structure. It did, though, grant the weak minorities some privileges. Toleration, in its political manifestation as an attempt to shape a common political structure shared by radically diverse groups, is thus a relatively modern phenomenon.

It is important to stress that Rawls himself is not interested in providing another argument for toleration, namely, liberal neutrality. The Rawlsian idea of toleration as represented in the original position is that (1) people are granted rights independent of their conception of the good life, and (2) the constitutional framework of society is shaped in such a way that it enables different justifications of itself from different angles, that is, overlapping consensus. Neither condition of toleration exists within the millet system even on the group level. Rights are not granted even to groups within the millet system independent of their view of the good life. The constitutional framework of the Ottoman Empire can be justified only in terms of the Muslim dominant group. Thus, the problem with religious toleration in the millet model is not only its limited scope but its practice in a context of asymmetry of power. Let us turn now to the connection between toleration and autonomy and its implications for group rights.

Kymlicka's argument for toleration from autonomy proceeds in this way: (1) Individuals are capable of reflecting on their way of life, to assess it rationally and revise it. (2) It is in individuals' basic interest to be able to revise their life according to what they perceive as rational, thus avoiding staying in what they consider an unworthy form of life. (3) Therefore, only within a tolerant society can such a vital interest be secured. According to Kymlicka, "If liberals wish to defend individual freedom of conscience, they must reject the idea that people's ends are beyond rational revision."[1] Autonomy is thus necessary for the defence of individual freedom. The practice of toleration toward individuals rests on the fact that people are capable of free and rational revision of their ends, and preserving this capability is of extreme value. It is no accident that Kymlicka devotes part of his argument to debate views that, according to his reading, claim that conceptions of the good are constitutive of an individual's identity and are therefore not revisable.[2] It seems to Kymlicka that Rawls held such a view in his later work or at least wished to accommodate his earlier work to such a possibility, and thus undermined the very basis for toleration. Kymlicka quotes with approval another statement in which Rawls seems to agree that an individual is capable of revising a constitutive good: " '[O]ur conceptions of the good may and often do change over time, usually slowly but sometimes rather suddenly,' even for those people who think of themselves as having constitutive ends. For example, 'On the road to Damascus Saul of Tarsus becomes Paul the Apostle'" (p. 94). In order to examine Kymlicka's notion of autonomy, I consider Paul's conversion seriously, because it is a paradigmatic case for both Rawls and Kymlicka, exemplifying the autonomous capability of individuals to revise their conception of the good. I think that Paul's case is in fact an interesting counterexample to a notion of individual autonomy.

For the sake of argument, let us deny autonomy in light of four arguments, while using Paul's conversion as a paradigm for a nonautonomous revision of the concept of the good: (1) An individual who changes his or her way of life is no longer the same self. (2) An individual cannot change goals freely. (3) Such a change is never a result of rational assessment, but a leap of faith. (4) There is no value in presenting a person with different conceptions of the good so that he or she may assess them rationally and freely and choose between them. Paul himself, I think, would have described his own experience in terms closely related to the following four points. First, after the conversion on the road to Damascus, Paul was no longer Saul. Paul was not a self who revised his way of life, but rather a self that was transformed by a conversion to an alternate way of life. Saul thus became Paul, a totally different individual, who might describe conversion in terms of birth rather than revision. Second, Paul did not initiate his own conversion; significantly, it was forced on him, happening to him rather than by him. Third, Paul's conversion was not motivated by a change in his conception of the good born out of rational assessment of options; it was a leap of faith rather than an argument. And fourth, Paul would not consider it important to expose himself to various ideas of the good and continually assess them. From his perspective, his conversion was final. If we agree with Paul on these four points, thus denying autonomy, are we free to coerce him into paganism or back to Judaism? According to Kymlicka, the answer is yes, because "If liberals wish to defend individual freedom of conscience, they must reject the idea that people's ends are beyond rational revision" (p. 94). In my opinion, even if we deny the possibility of rational assessment and autonomous revision of ends of life, toleration ought to be practiced. Paul's right to his Christian way of life was not dependent on the fact that he achieved it through free and rational assessment (which he did not), nor on the possibility that in the future he might assess his own Christian way of life as mistaken. It is rooted in the fact that his present state is of enormous importance to him, because that state shapes his identity, and forcing him out of it means destroying his individuality and violating what for him is perhaps the most important and meaningful aspect of his being. I will call this argument for toleration the harm argument, because it is based on the enormous harm done to others by robbing them of the possibility of continuing a way of life that harbors great meaning for them as individuals. In this respect, the right to one's way of life is comparable to property rights or to rights over one's own body—rights that do not need any support from the fact or value of autonomy.

Kymlicka's emphasis on the possibility of revision as the main good protected by toleration results in a paradox. Toleration, according to Kymlicka, is geared toward enabling people to revise their way of life, rather than protect their right to the lifestyle they now lead, regardless of whether they are capable of revising it or whether they have reached it through a rational assessment of a previous way of life. To escape such a paradox, Kymlicka could reformulate his position, claiming that what is important for people in their lives are only those goals and forms of life they acquire through a rational assessment of their previous given life. According to such a formulation, people consider those goals alone as fully theirs, and therefore only coercion that is directed to such goals can be considered a crime. But this option seems to be mistaken as well. A great deal of our identity is not a product of choice and, needless to say, not of rational choice. National identity is one example. It is central and extremely important to many individuals, but usually people do not offer a rational argument about why they should remain English rather than becoming, say, French (I do not want to argue that it is not possible to find rational reasons for dissociating from a certain national identity. Regretfully there are too many examples for this). The ways of life that matter to people are charged with elements dear to them, goals and values they identify with and believe in, which were not necessarily adopted through a process of rational revision.

The argument I would like to offer in support of toleration as an alternative to autonomy recognizes that individual forms of life and goals are extremely important to people, they cherish them and are willing to endure great suffering in their defense. Preventing people from practicing their way of life, in cases that involve no denial of the same right to other individuals, is as wrong as violating their property rights or their bodily self-ownership.

Such an alternative to the argument of autonomy has two merits. One relates to the Rawlsian program. Rawls would hold that such an argument for toleration is preferable, because it does not rest on contested assumptions of the possibility and value of personal autonomy, and such an argument thus allows for a broader consensus. But I think that independent of the Rawlsian concern for overlapping consensus, this argument accords with the intuition that the basic wrong that coercion produces is not failing to allow for revision of one's ends but forcing people away from what is important and central in their life, thus causing tremendous pain and harm.

One of the interesting implications of Kymlicka's argument is related to the problem of group pluralism and its connection to individual freedom. Kymlicka considers other contemporary examples of group rights in order to distinguish between them and individual freedom and to stress the importance of autonomy. His first example is the American Indian tribes, who have a legally recognized right to self-government. Some of them discriminate against members who do not share the tribal religion. The Pueblo, for instance, deny housing benefits to those members of the community who have converted to Protestantism. This is indeed a violation of individual freedom, done in an attempt to prevent a group tradition from collapsing from within. It is a violation of the principle of toleration, because it is an attempt to force the converts to Protestantism away from their way of life. Thus, according to the harm argument for toleration, such a practice should be prohibited, not only because penalizing converts to Protestantism restricts the possibility for those who adhere to the Pueblo tradition to revise their religion but because for those already converted, being Protestant is of enormous importance. The argument for autonomy is not the only justification, in such a case, for restricting group rights in order to give room to individual freedom.

The second case Kymlicka mentions is more problematic, and there the difference between the harm argument and the autonomy argument becomes clear: "Both Canada and the United States exempt a number of long-standing religious sects (e.g., Mennonites, Doukhobours, Amish, Hutterites) from laws regarding the mandatory education of children. Members of these sects can withdraw their children from schools before the legal age of sixteen and are not required to teach the usual school curriculum. Parents worry that if their children received this broader education, they would be tempted to leave the sect and join the wider society" (p. 85). It seems to me that in this example the harm argument for toleration and the autonomy argument collide. According to the autonomy argument, the benefit of toleration consists in the possibility of revising one's way of life. Education, therefore, should be aimed at presenting options and producing a chooser, that is, a person who has the skills to make informed and rational judgments about different goals and forms of life: "[M]andatory education ensures that children acquire the capacity to envisage alternative ways of life and rationally assess them" (p. 87). The practice of education in the Amish community negates this notion of education and, according to the autonomy argument, is intolerant. An alternative approach views education as concerned primarily with transmitting a particular tradition and developing a strong commitment to that particular way of life. Such a conception might be accompanied by deliberately attempting to negate certain alternative ways of life, either by teaching them and claiming that they are false or by excluding them altogether from the curriculum. I know of no mandatory education system that does not contain dominant elements of this conception of education. Most public education in modern nation-states is geared toward educating loyal citizens. Emphasis is therefore put on the students' acquaintance with the particular history and culture of their community. Other alternatives naturally are omitted; sometimes, when the situation involves rival communities, those alternatives are intentionally blocked. I doubt whether educating a chooser is a serious educational concept, but even if it is, in its pure form it does not exist in any mandatory educational system known to me.

More overtly ideological conceptions of education do exist. Their aim is to foster loyalty to particular ways of life with stronger commitments than citizenship in a nation-state. In Israel there are two paradigmatic examples of such a conception of education. The first is kibbutz education, which aims at transmitting a socialist way of life, and one of its goals is to ensure the continuity of the kibbutz as a viable social ideal. The other trend is the Orthodox community and its autonomous educational system, which is directed toward ensuring a continuation of the Jewish religious tradition. Adherents to both forms of life feel in some respect besieged, trying to compete with the temptations of urban capitalistic life and secular ideology, and both present those alternatives as false and decadent; sometimes they do not present them at all. It is no accident that until the sixties graduates of the kibbutz education system who wanted to leave the kibbutz and integrate into urban Israeli society had to complete matriculation examinations on their own if they wanted to be admitted to a university. The same is true of yeshiva education in the ultra-Orthodox community, where secular studies are minimal and the main aim of the institution is to perpetuate the traditional form of Torah study. I do not think there is anything intolerant in the practices of these communities. At this point, though, the autonomy argument for toleration and the harm argument part ways. Kymlicka, in accordance with the autonomy argument for toleration, claims that such a conception of education is intolerant and, therefore, should in principle be prohibited. In contrast, the harm argument for toleration obligates a community not to force or penalize individuals who actually choose an alternative way of life. But the value of toleration does not obligate a community to pose that alternative to students and present it as a legitimate option for choice. In case they opted for such an alternative through their own efforts (because in a pluralistic community those alternatives do exist), no one is entitled to alienate them from that choice. Forcing a yeshiva or a kibbutz school or the Amish community to produce a chooser rather than a member loyal to a particular community, in the name of the value of autonomy, is intolerant toward those communities. Such communities must be entitled to shape their own form of education as long as they do not violate the principle of toleration in its harm justification.

Autonomy as the ground for toleration seems to me wrong for two reasons. First, it rests on a questionable metaphysical assumption concerning rational revisability of ways of life, an assumption that often does not capture the nature of "big decisions," as in Paul's case. In extreme cases of conversion, the possibility of rational revision is questionable, but we definitely want to include those cases within the realm of toleration. The other reason does not question the possibility of autonomy but rather the results of structuring toleration on the value of autonomy. In such cases, toleration would collide with conceptions of education that do not aim at producing a "chooser" but rather at transmitting a particular way of life. Those educational practices and institutions seem legitimate as long as they do not force members and students to adhere to a particular form of life without their consent. Toleration based on the harm argument applies to decisions and views that deny the possibility of autonomy. It also enables the operation of institutions and practices that do not recognize the value of autonomy as inherent in their conception of education. As applied to education, the principle of toleration should not delegitimize the very idea of transmitting cultural values; rather, it ought to set the limits to the means that are used in the process of transmission. The principle of toleration, therefore, excludes any use of force or penalty directed at members who dissent from the community's views. It does not obligate a community to present its younger or older members with alternative ways of life or develop in them the skills for assessment.

Notes

1. See W. Kymlicka, in this volume, p. 94.
2. I think, in opposition to Kymlicka, that the claim that notions of the good are constitutive of someone's identity does not entail that he or she cannot in principle revise them. The constitutive argument rejects a certain view of *how* such revision is accomplished and not *whether* it is possible to accomplish such a revision. The model of revision rejected by the constitutive argument is that a person can retreat from certain ends to his or her inner self, which is the "choosing self," and from that point of view opt for another way of life. Revision, according to the constitutive argument, is tied inherently to one's former way of life. In that sense, although Paul made a radical revision of his life on the road to Damascus, it is no accident that he converted to Christianity, which he was at the time trying to combat. In that respect, it does not make any sense for Paul to retreat to his "inner self" and then choose, for example, to become a Zoroastrian unless a story can be told concerning how such a choice is tied to his former life.

7

The Boundaries of Justifiable Tolerance: A Liberal Perspective

ALON HAREL

1. Introduction

It is often claimed that tolerance is a major virtue of liberal societies. Tolerance is praised as a means by which pluralism can be reinforced, the options available to individuals can be expanded, and hence their ability to pursue their own chosen projects and pursuits can be promoted.

The supposed value of tolerance is challenged, however, by two independent claims. First, religious or ethnic minorities holding intolerant views and practices persistently claim that they should be allowed to advocate intolerance as well as express it in their practices. Second, women and minorities demand the suppression of forms of speech or practices that seem to them to threaten their full integration in society. These two types of demands are often incompatible with each other. The latter, e.g., demands for restrictions on racist or sexist speech or practices, requires restricting precisely those practices that demand immunity under the first type of demand.

In this article, I explore the merits of these conflicting demands. I argue that both demands are based on genuine interests of individuals and hence are prima facie justifiable. Once the prima facie value of the conflicting demands is illustrated, I set up criteria for properly balancing these demands in cases of conflict, as well as briefly explore the proper institutional means to guarantee the satisfaction of these demands.

2. Social Preconditions of Well-Being: A Liberal Perspective

An exploration of the proper boundaries of tolerance in modern society should be based on its impact on the well-being of individuals.[1] The specification of what well-being consists of and the methods of measuring and comparing the well-being of different individuals in instances of conflict differ under different political theories.

Under a liberal conception, the ability of individuals to promote their own life projects, to pursue their own conception of the good, and to live in accordance with self-chosen goals and relationships are important components of one's well-being.[2] Liberals do not deny that there are other aspects of one's well-being that might sometimes conflict with these interests. However, they argue that in the case of such conflicts the interest of individuals in leading their own life is an important (although not always an overriding) consideration.[3]

The interest individuals have in living in accordance with their freely made choices imposes a duty on the state to promote and reinforce this interest. It is traditional within liberal theory to point out two central duties derived from this interest:

    1. The state has a duty to avoid interfering in freely chosen pursuits of individuals unless it has powerful reasons to do so.

    2. The state has a duty to safeguard individual choice against (undue) interference by others, including individuals and collective bodies, such as religious or cultural institutions.

Both of these are established duties of a liberal state. However, as has recently been made clear, they are not sufficient to enable individuals to live according to their choices.[4] Individual choice is always made within a particular social context. A social context can be more or less conducive to such choice. Various explanations have been provided by political philosophers as to the importance of social context in facilitating individual choice. These include the claim that the capacity for choice can be nurtured only within the boundaries of a community;[5] that meaningful choice requires social confirmation of one's values;[6] and that a rich social context is a prerequisite for providing meaningful and socially defined and determined pursuits and activities.[7] All these claims share the view that individuals can engage in meaningful choice only in a social context that encourages and supports such activity.[8]

There are two ways of understanding the claims about the social prerequisites for meaningful choice. Under a weak interpretation, claims affirming the importance of a social context for choice are conceptual but do not entail any duties beyond those that are already contained in the ones mentioned above, namely, the duty of the state to avoid interference in freely chosen ways of life and its duty to protect such ways of life from interference by others. The strong interpretation requires adding an additional duty:

    3. The state has a duty to sustain and reinforce a social context conducive to individual choice.

The liberal conception of well-being as presented here is sympathetic to the role of the state in reinforcing individual choice. It is clear, however, that under the liberal conception the state can contribute only indirectly to the provision of a fertile context for individual choice. This duty of the state cannot be fulfilled by directly *creating* or *producing* a social context that is conducive to choice. It can be fulfilled only indirectly, by promoting and reinforcing existing social structures in a way conducive to individual choice.[9]

So far, some duties of the state, namely, those that are derived from the liberal conception of well-being, have been discussed on a general and abstract level. Providing a more specific description of the social prerequisites for meaningful choice, as well as the duties of the state in sustaining and promoting those social prerequisites, requires an exploration of the particular types of interests individuals share. These interests cannot be analyzed independently of the social context in which the individuals operate. More specifically, they differ according to the social group to which the individuals belong, because these are interests individuals share not *qua individuals* but rather *qua members of particular communities*. Such interests are conceptually tied to membership in a community or a social group and hence *cannot logically be shared* by outsiders.[10]

This article will identify three interests individuals can share qua members of particular communities, each of which has important social and legal implications. The first is the interest individuals might have in participating in intolerant practices and sharing intolerant beliefs, when those practices and beliefs form part of a comprehensive way of life. The second is the interest they might have in the existence and flourishing of minimally supportive communities. The third is the interest they might have in "egalitarian intolerance," namely, in the exclusivity of egalitarian values. Let me elaborate on each one.

A. *The Indivisibility of Ways of Life*

Orthodox Jews might genuinely believe that their religion entails certain views of the role of women in society or certain positions about the moral standing of homosexuality. Admittedly, it is not logically impossible to be an Orthodox Jew and at the same time a feminist or a gay liberationist. But for many religious Jews, the antifeminist position or the condemnation of so-called "unnatural" sexual practices form part of a comprehensive worldview and are routinely manifested in the practices related to such a worldview.[11]

This example illustrates that intolerant views, opinions, or values can be an aspect of a wider net of opinions and sensibilities that, taken together, form a distinctive style or way of life. Expressing disagreement, condemnation, hostility, and intolerance can be valuable as a means of affirming one's own values or as an integral component of one's way of life.[12] The complex cluster of values and practices that comprise a particular way of life cannot be interfered with by the state without undermining the integrity of that way of life.

In order for practices that form integral parts of comprehensive ways of life to command our respect, such practices must satisfy two conditions. First, it is necessary to show that the intolerant practice is indeed an integral part of a way of life. Second, it must be shown that the way of life as a whole is a valuable one. It is certainly possible that some intolerant practices are integral parts of ways of life that are not valuable and hence need not be protected. The difference between one's attitude toward such practices as those of fundamentalist religious groups, on the one hand, and those of the KKK, on the other, can be explained by the claim that whereas the former are valuable (although they might contain repugnant values and practices), the latter lack any value.

The requirement that we respect values and practices that constitute integral parts of comprehensive ways of life can be explained in terms of the holistic, indivisible nature of ways of life. They are often conceived by their participants as indivisible clusters of values and practices. Respect shown to a way of life as a whole entails taking seriously the internal perspective of its participants, including their perception that it consists of an indivisible cluster of values and practices. A selective attempt to regulate some of those practices or restrict the promulgation of certain values can therefore be interpreted as an expression of disrespect toward the way of life as a whole.[13]

It might seem as if this argument is applicable only to fanatical communities, because intolerance supposedly can only be a component of a fanatical worldview. This assumption is misleading. Individuals who hold egalitarian sentiments can sometimes demonstrate intense intolerance toward racist or sexist ideas or practices. The fact that egalitarian intolerance of racism or sexism might be morally justified does not detract from the fact that this intolerance can be a means of affirming one's own egalitarian worldview.

A genuine interest in sharing intolerant ideas or participating in intolerant practices as a means of affirming one's own values does not necessarily entail a *moral obligation* on the part of others to respect or tolerate those ideas and practices, but it might provide *good reasons* for tolerating them. This interest might justify more than merely *legal* protection of intolerant practices that are essential to one's way of living. It could also imply that we have reasons to respect, rather than merely tolerate, intolerant values and practices when they constitute an integral part of a comprehensive worldview. The respect shown to the intolerant values and practices that form part of a valuable way of life is a byproduct of the respect shown to that way of life as such.[14]

Understanding the role of ideas and practices that form part of comprehensive ways of life can have important policy implications. It is common to argue that practices that are permissible if performed by secular individuals for secular purposes should also be permissible if performed by individuals for religious purposes, and, conversely, those that are justifiably prohibited if performed by individuals for secular purposes should also be prohibited if performed by individuals for religious purposes.[15]

The analysis presented above illustrates the falsity of this position. Religious practices are part of comprehensive ways of life. Under the above description, the protection granted to ideas and practices is based on the role they play within such ways of life. Hence, it is not inconsistent to grant immunity to practices when they are conducted as part of comprehensive ways of life, for example, when they are conducted as part of religious life, while at the same time to prohibit those very same practices when they do not reflect components of such a way of life.[16]

Our argument so far is a limited justification for tolerating intolerance. Though it might lead us to grant legal protection to intolerance as well as to sympathize, understand, and tolerate it, this argument cannot provide us with reasons for *being intolerant*.[17] Are we ever justified in being intolerant rather than merely in tolerating or respecting manifestations of intolerance? In the next two subsections, I explore this possibility.

B. Minimally Supportive Communities

I argued earlier that individuals need a fertile social context in which to exercise individual choice. Social context consists mainly of a supportive community that shares one's values and practices. The emergence of competing ways of life can be detrimental to the existence of a supportive community, and thus can be detrimental to one's interest in living one's chosen way of life. Members of cultural minorities have often found themselves in conditions that have endangered the fulfillment of their interest in living within a supportive community. History has shown that individual rights and liberties granted to the majority resulted in the erosion of the traditional values of cultural minorities. Some cultural minorities have reacted by initiating campaigns favoring some restrictions on individual rights for the sake of reinforcing the values of such cultures.[18] We cannot ignore the possibility that the interest of individuals in the existence of a supportive community might override the interests other individuals have in participating in practices or advocating views that threaten the survival of that supportive community.

This might seem to be a very radical suggestion. If left unqualified, its oppressive potential is almost unlimited. One central qualification can already be formulated.

One's interest in the existence of a supportive community rarely requires or justifies intolerance. I can express an interest in the viability of a secular community that can typically be fully satisfied without imposing any restrictions on the religious practices of religious communities. Of course, the larger the secular community, the more it can support and enhance secular lifestyles. But if a sufficiently large secular community exists, the marginal benefit the secular person derives from a further enlargement of that community is nil or close to nil. Consequently, the secular person's interest in the survival of a secular community can usually be satisfied without imposing any restrictions on religious practices. The need to impose restrictions in order to protect secular communities from the threat of extinction will arise, therefore, only when the secular community is too small or weak to provide meaningful life for its members without the aid of such regulation.

One's interest in a supportive community can therefore be more accurately described as an interest in a *minimally* supportive community, that is, the smallest community capable of providing adequate support for one's chosen way of life. The crucial element here is not necessarily the size of the community but its ability to provide adequate support. Once this interest is guaranteed, any further interest in enlarging and strengthening the supportive community is too weak to justify intolerance. Consequently, with the exception of minority cultures that cannot provide adequate support for their members, one's interest in the existence of a supportive community cannot justify the endorsement of legal or social intolerance.

It is important to draw out the implications of this argument. Unlike the duties derived from the interest concerning the indivisibility of ways of life, those relating to the interest in sustaining minimally supportive communities are not necessarily derived from the internal perspective of the members. The latter interest could sometimes require tolerance toward practices of the community that are essential to its viability, but it could also include policies unrelated to community practices, such as subsidies, immigration policies designed to protect the community, inheritance laws, and so on.[19]

So far I have described two types of interests individuals share qua members of communities: respect granted to their intolerant values and practices when those constitute an integral part of their way of life, and sustaining a minimally supportive community. Both interests can be classified as exclusionary, that is, interests of members of the community in reinforcing their separateness from a larger social body. Yet members of communities also share inclusionary interests, that is, the interests they have in becoming an integral part of a broader society. Inclusionary interests, as we shall see, present a much greater challenge to a liberal society.

C. Egalitarian Intolerance

The feminist movement is fighting to suppress pornography. Human-rights organizations are struggling to suppress racist propaganda. The aim of these struggles is to facilitate integrating women and Blacks into a broader social body. Both campaigns are motivated by the interests members of the relevant groups have in becoming full participants in the broader community in which they live. They are therefore paradigmatic instances of policies designed to promote the inclusionary interests shared by members of the these groups.

Claims of this type present a difficult challenge to a liberal society. Exploring the content of the demand to suppress racist or sexist forms of speech can explain the source of the difficulty in meeting these demands. The interest that would justify suppressing pornography is not merely women's interest in the survival of a nonsexist supportive community but their interest in totally eliminating sexist attitudes and practices. Similarly, the interest Blacks supposedly share is not merely the existence of a nonracist supportive community but eliminating racist sentiments altogether. The alleged threat to the welfare of women in a sexist society, and of Blacks in a racist society, is not that a community that shares egalitarian values is not a minimally supportive one but the very existence and prevalence of sexist or racist sentiments. Consequently, only the elimination of sexist and racist sentiments can satisfy the demands of these groups.[20]

These demands differ fundamentally from those based on the indivisibility of ways of life or the need to protect the survival of a minimally supportive community. Unlike the former (analyzed in sections A and B), this latter demand insists on granting exclusivity to a specific set of values; more particularly, it is a demand to grant exclusivity to egalitarian values. Its unique character stems from the exclusive role to be played by a particular set of values if those demands are to be met.[21]

What is the justification for demanding the exclusivity of egalitarian values? Can this demand be justified on the basis of the genuine interests of members of marginalized groups? It is beyond the aims of this article to provide a full defense of this demand. However, it is useful to point out an important interest of members of marginalized groups that gives special force to their demand.

Membership is considered an important good and is often a prerequisite for various entitlements. Individuals can be full members of traditional societies without being conceived as possessing the same status as other members. For instance, some major religions recognize women as members of religious communities while assigning them different and, some would argue, inferior roles.[22] Modern societies, on the other hand, regard equality of some sort as a prerequisite for membership. Hence racial minorities cannot be considered both inferior and at the same time full members of the community. Denying equality is therefore interpreted in modern societies as a denial of membership itself. Its particular importance is a byproduct of its relations to the concept of membership in modern society.

This observation suggests that being a member of a modern society is tantamount to being an equal member. Denying equality is therefore denying membership as such. Hence, eliminating discriminatory attitudes and practices is a prerequisite for membership.

One can easily detect a potential conflict between the interests of members of some communities in enjoying immunity for their values and practices and the interest of others in the exclusivity of egalitarian values. For example, a conflict might emerge between the interest of women in eliminating sexism and the interest of Orthodox Jews in living their lives in accordance with their sexist values. The former interest provides us with reasons for manifesting legal or social intolerance toward sexism with the intention of eliminating it, whereas the latter interest, as I argued above, can provide us with reasons for tolerating and even respecting this form of intolerance. The multiplicity of considerations described above—in particular, the coexistence of exclusionary interests of members of traditional communities (namely, their interest in enhancing the separateness of their practices from those of the rest of the society) and inclusionary interests of members of marginalized groups (namely, their interest in becoming part of a broader social body)—can explain the persistence of the conflicting demands at the focus of this article. In the last section, I explore the means of reconciling these conflicting interests.

3. Toward a Reconciliation of Inclusionary and Exclusionary Interests

I have so far pointed out some considerations suggesting that the exclusionary interests of individuals *qua members of communities* provide, under certain circumstances, reasons to tolerate and respect intolerant practices when these are indivisible components of a valuable way of life or when tolerating them is necessary for the survival of minimally supportive communities. On the other hand, it has been shown that the inclusionary interests of individuals *qua members of communities* can provide reasons to grant exclusivity to egalitarian values. These two interests, it has been claimed, often lead to conflict.

Inegalitarian practices and sentiments are particularly harmful to the inclusionary interests of marginalized groups when adopted by individuals or communities with a significant impact on the lives of members of marginalized communities, that is, when the lives of members of different communities are intertwined. The more individuals and communities are integrated into a broader society that does not share their values, the more harmful their inegalitarian sentiments can be. Thus, an important factor in determining the degree of immunity to be granted to cultural practices is the degree to which those practices have spillover effects. The more isolated the communities that participate in these practices, the less serious their impact on the inclusionary interests of marginalized groups. The strength of the demands made by Native Americans in the United States and Canadian Aboriginals to immunize their practices from interference is based on these groups' isolation, and hence on the limited impact their values and practices have on the society at large.

Spillover effects can be partially manipulated by institutional methods of granting immunity to cultural communities. The sovereignty of Native American reservations is often perceived as a device intended to protect the interests of Native Americans. It can, however, also be described as a means of realizing the inclusionary interests of marginalized groups in the society at large. Sovereignty is a device used by the society at large to respect, but at the same time distance itself from, the practices of Native Americans, which are incompatible with its own egalitarian values.

This last observation provides us with an important lesson often ignored in the current literature. The institutional means of protecting the interests of individuals *qua members of communities* are as important as the scope of the protection itself. Protecting practices of Native Americans from interference can be carried out by different means. Granting sovereignty to those communities is particularly useful because it is a powerful symbolic recognition of the exclusionary interests of Native Americans as well as a powerful statement by means of which society at large can dissociate itself from these practices and consequently enhance the inclusionary interests of members of other marginalized groups.

Tolerance is a liberal value, but liberalism also points out the limitations of tolerance. These limitations might require us to respect intolerant practices in contexts in which they are conducive to the exclusionary interests of individuals or to suppress intolerant practices when they are detrimental to the inclusionary interests of minorities. There is no guarantee that these conflicting interests can always, or even often, be reconciled. However, legal and other institutional mechanisms can sometimes alleviate the tension between them.

Notes

1. This claim can be derived from a more general claim, which Raz calls "the humanistic principle": "[t]he explanation and justification of the goodness or badness of anything derives ultimately from its contribution, actual or possible, to human life and its quality." See J. Raz, *The Morality of Freedom* (Oxford: Clarendon, 1986), 194.

2. For a formulation of the liberal conception of well-being, see Raz, 369.

In this context, I prefer to use Raz's formulation, emphasizing the successful pursuits of self-chosen goals and relationships. See Raz, 370. This construction, if broadly interpreted, encompasses one's ability to pursue freely chosen life projects as well as one's interest in living according to one's conception of the good. It also includes one's interests in pursuing one's judgments in matters that cannot be described as either life projects or conceptions of the good.

3. The liberal conception of well-being as presented here regards the ability to choose as *one* component of well-being. It is therefore weak enough to be acceptable to communitarians. It is labeled the "liberal conception of well-being," however, because liberals will tend to attribute more importance to this aspect of well-being than adherents of most other philosophical persuasions.

4. See W. Kymlicka, *Liberalism, Community and Culture* (Oxford: Clarendon, 1991).

5. C. Taylor, "Atomism," in C. Taylor, *Philosophical Papers*, vol 2: *Philosophy and the Human Sciences* (Cambridge: Cambridge University Press, 1985), 207. For a critique of this view, see Kymlicka, 74ff.

6. R. Smith, *Liberalism and American Constitutional Law* (Cambridge, Mass.: Harvard University Press, 1985) 170. For a critique, see Kymlicka, 61ff.

7. See Raz, 308–13; Kymlicka, 164–78.

8. There is, however, an important difference between various attempts to characterize the role of social context in facilitating or enhancing individual choice. Some attempts are based on claims of the dependence of the agent's or the agency's capacities on proper social context. Other attempts locate the role of social context in shaping the circumstances of choice rather than in facilitating agency itself.

9. There are various reasons for the liberal insistence on the indirect role of the state in facilitating and enhancing a social context conducive to choice. First, there are institutional factors concerning the limits of the role of the liberal state and the risks of manipulating social context in a way that is not conducive to individual choice. Second, there are conceptual problems, in particular, the logical incoherence of free individual choice with decisions determined not by the agent but by circumstances shaped and manipulated by external forces.

10. This does not imply that outsiders could not have interests that coincide with interests held by members of the community qua members of a particular community. I might, for example, have an interest in the future existence of the Islamic religion because I am sympathetic to that religion or because, after reflection, I might one day discover its merits and convert to Islam. The future existence of Islam provides me with opportunities I would otherwise not have had, for example, to join it in case I find its doctrines compelling.

But this interest is different from that of a person who is already practicing Islam. The interest one has in the future existence of the particular community one belongs to is an interest in sustaining the way of life one has already chosen. This interest coincides with that of an outsider who has an interest in having the opportunity to make the same choice, but it is nevertheless a different interest.

11. See Joseph Raz, "Free Expression and Personal Identification," *Oxford Journal of Legal Studies* 11 (1991):303, 321.

12. I use the term "way of life" to denote what Raz labels "form of life" or "style of life." See ibid., 309–10.

13. It should be noted that intolerant practices and values can be indivisible components of a way of life even if a proper interpretation of the more fundamental values underlying these ways of life would in fact require one to abandon these intolerant practices and values. Some Orthodox Jews criticize the sexist practices of Orthodox Judaism, claiming that they are based on an incorrect interpretation of the Scripture. This criticism might be valid with respect to the Scripture, but it is irrelevant to the issue at hand. It is not the correctness of the sexist interpretation of the Scripture by Orthodox Judaism that provides reasons for respecting these practices, but rather the role these practices play within the lives of Orthodox Jews.

14. I do not deny that there are often powerful reasons to interfere in intolerant practices. In particular, interference can often promote the interests of members of the intolerant community who are the victims of its intolerance. The argument is only intended to illustrate a powerful prima facie reason to respect intolerant views and practices. I believe that the victims of intolerant attitudes of cultural or religious communities sometimes have to choose either to exit their community altogether or attempt to demonstrate to other members that the intolerant practices and ideas are based on a false understanding of their own cultural tradition.

15. This position is adopted by Locke:

> By this we see what difference there is between the church and the commonwealth. Whatsoever is lawful in the commonwealth cannot be prohibited by the magistrate in the church. Whatsoever is permitted unto any of his subjects for their ordinary use, neither can nor ought to be forbidden by him to any sect of people for their religious uses. If any man may lawfully take bread or wine, either sitting or kneeling in his own house, the law ought not to abridge him of the same liberty in his religious worship; though in the church the use of bread and wine be very different, and be there applied to the mysteries of faith and rites of divine worship. But those things that are prejudicial to the commonweal of a people in their ordinary use, and are therefore forbidden by laws, those things ought not to be permitted to churches in their sacred rites. (John Locke, *A Letter Concerning Toleration*, ed. Mario Nontuori [The Hague: Martinus Nijhoff, 1963], 67)

This view is derived from Locke's claim that it is not coercion as such that is evil but coercion undertaken for certain reasons or certain ends. Hence, only a restriction on religious practices motivated by religious reasons is unjustified. See J. Waldron, "Locke, Toleration and the Rationality of Persecution," in J. Waldron, *Liberal Rights: Collected Papers* (Cambridge: Cambridge University Press, 1993), 88, 104–7.

16. Several qualifications should be made. First, the protection that should be granted to religions should not be absolute. Second, it is not claimed that only religions form comprehensive ways of life. Secular lifestyles also deserve protection to the extent that they are valuable. Third, there could be institutional reasons to be reluctant to give the executive or the judiciary the right to make the distinction between those practices that form part of comprehensive ways of life and those that do not. If indeed there are institutional reasons of this sort, it might be inadvisable to adopt the policy of granting broader immunities to practices when they form part of comprehensive ways of life because of the inability of the courts to make the relevant judgments.

In practice, the legal system provides ample instances in which religious practices enjoy special immunity. The "free exercise" clause of the United States Constitution singles out religion for special treatment, as do some of the decisions of the United States Supreme Court. In *Wisconsin v. Yoder* (1972), 406 U.S. 205, the court reasoned in terms very similar to those analyzed above, exempting Amish parents from the duty to provide their children with a secondary education. The court relied on two factors. First, it concluded that compulsory secondary education is incompatible with the attitudes, goals, and values of Amish life. In the terms used above, the court reasoned that the absence of secondary education is indeed an integral part of the Amish way of life. Second, it relied heavily on the fact that the Amish community has been a law-abiding and productive community. The court therefore concluded that the Amish way of life is a valuable one and hence deserves special immunity from duties that would otherwise be imposed on it.

There is, however, one feature in *Yoder* that differentiates the arguments in *Yoder* from my analysis. Forcing the Amish children to go to secondary schools is not *in itself* incompatible with the Amish way of life. It is only the consequences of such education, in particular, the alien influence inculcated through this education, which are detrimental to the Amish way of life. My analysis, on the other hand, focuses on the importance of tolerating intolerant practices that are *in themselves* constitutive to valuable ways of life.

17. Unless, of course, we are members of a community that adopts intolerance as part of its worldview.

18. See Kymlicka.

19. See Kymlicka.

20. The legal system sometimes (justifiably) recognizes (in a limited manner) the interest of women or minorities in the exclusivity of antisexist or antiracist practices. For example, human-rights laws prohibit discrimination on the basis of gender or ethnicity even in private businesses. Other laws, in particular in Europe, prohibit speech that reinforces sexist or racist values.

I have argued in favor of granting exclusivity to egalitarian values in the context of the debate on the boundaries of freedom of expression. See A. Harel, "Bigotry, Pornography and the First Amendment: A Theory of Unprotected Speech," *Southern California Law Review* 65 (1992):1887; A. Harel, "Review Essay: Free Speech Revisionism: Doctrinal and Philosophical Challenges," *Boston U. L. Rev.* 74 (1994):687.

21. The difficulty in meeting the demand to grant exclusivity to egalitarian values is aggravated once the broad meaning attributed to the notion of equality is fully understood. Two factors related to this meaning make satisfying this demand particularly difficult.

First, minority groups have often exposed the subtle discriminatory nature of established institutions and practices. Equality of women or gays could, under the broad meaning attributed to this term, require us to suppress pornography, change our abortion laws, expand the legal and social definitions of family to include single mothers and gays, etc. Granting exclusivity to egalitarian values might therefore require us to grant exclusivity to a very broad and demanding conception of equality.

Second, the interpretation given to the term "equality" is often deliberately intended to fit the perspective of members of minority or otherwise marginalized groups, and hence might be alien to the perspective of privileged groups. Meeting the demand to grant exclusivity to egalitarian values could mean granting exclusivity to a conception of equality as conceived from the perspective of marginalized communities. This claim is often made by feminists. See, e.g., C. MacKinnon, *Towards a Feminist Theory of the State* (Cambridge, Mass.: Harvard University Press, 1989), 83–154.

22. Dworkin has argued that equality interpreted abstractly as "equal concern and respect" is the starting point of any acceptable tradition. See Dworkin, *Law's Empire* (Cambridge, Mass.: Belknap Press, 1986). On Dworkin's view, if a traditional society wants its sexist practices to be respected, it must show that those practices do not infringe on women's rights to equal concern and respect, but rather represent a different conception of equality.

I believe that this is an artificial attempt to attribute a central value of our culture to traditional communities that do not share those values. The very act of comparing the concern and respect granted to different individuals is alien to traditional societies. Therefore, attempts to interpret the practices either as an expression of inequality or as an expression of a different conception of equality are bound to be arbitrary.

On my view, the acceptability of practices of inequality in traditional societies is not based on the ability to interpret them as reflecting a different conception of equality but rather on the fact that equality is not a prerequisite for membership in these societies.

8

Toleration and the Struggle against Prejudice

DAVID A. J. RICHARDS

THE ARGUMENT for toleration was of pivotal importance not only in the development of the civil liberties of religion, free speech, and privacy,[1] but in the abolitionist criticisms of slavery and racism in America, Britain, and elsewhere and their correlative expressions in law (for example, American constitutional principles of equal protection).[2] My theme here is the pivotal role that the argument for toleration played in the first sustained criticism in human history of slavery as an institution and the associated criticism of racial prejudice. The analysis of racial prejudice, as a political and constitutional evil, was, I argue, very much a generalization of the rights-based analysis of religious intolerance as an evil. The analysis of anti-Semitism, which has taken the form of both religious intolerance (Christian anti-Semitism) and modernist racism (anti-Christian anti-Semitism), will be a central case study for this argument as an explanatory model for the correlative political evil of American-style racism against Blacks. Both the development of these political evils and their criticism as political evils share a history that is, in ways I hope to make clear, structurally interdependent.

My argument uses American political and constitutional experience as a useful starting point in the analysis of phenomena that are, I believe, universal in the long and still incomplete struggle of free people everywhere for rights-based constitutional government under the rule of law. Hopefully, the account will, by its end, suggest important continuities and even points of mutual influence in the experience of many peoples (including the impact of American understanding of the evil of European anti-Semitism on American criticism of its own racism). The argument, if plausible, also suggests why contemporary forms of rights-based constitutional democracies have distinctively developed doctrines and institutions to identify and condemn the force of racism and similar prejudices in democratic politics. The interest of the argument is the fruitful use to which it puts the argument for toleration as a powerful explanatory and normative tool in the struggle for a deeper and more complete understanding of what the struggle for universal human rights means and should be taken to mean.

1. Abolitionist Ethical Criticism of Slavery: The Analogy of Anti-Semitism

Theodore Weld, one of the most important and influential of the early American abolitionists, presented in his widely circulated *American Slavery as It Is*, not only a factual picture (gathered largely from southern newspapers) of life in the South under slavery, but a normative argument in light of which those facts should be interpreted. The normative argument took it to be fundamental that persons have "inalienable rights."[3] The abridgment of such inalienable rights (including "free speech and rights of conscience, their right to acquire knowledge"[4]) required a heavy burden of justification.

Weld identified an important analogy between the inadequacies of the justifications in fact offered by southerners and the comparably inadequate arguments offered in support of religious persecution, whether Puritan persecutions of the Quakers,[5] Roman persecution of Christians, or Christian persecutions of pagans and heretics.[6] The key to understanding the political evil of both religious persecution and slavery was the intrinsic corruptibility of human nature by political power over certain kinds of questions. The worst corruption was of conscience itself—a fact that was, he argued, well reflected in the cumulative blinding of Southern public morality to the evils of slavery.[7]

In the most important studies of the morality of slavery by an American philosopher in the antebellum period, William Ellery Channing had temperately stated the ethical dimensions of the abolitionist case for both the evil of slavery and the need for abolition in a similar way.[8] In order to understand the subversion of conscience that slavery required, Channing, like Weld, drew an analogy to the history of religious persecution, whose injustice often rested on the corruption of conscience.[9] Making pointed reference to anti-Semitism,[10] Channing drew instruction from the history of religious persecution, because it exemplified both an abridgment of inalienable human rights and a familiarly inadequate way in which such abridgments have been justified. Pro-slavery views exemplified the same structure of argument and should be condemned for the same reason.

We need now to explore what this abolitionist argument was and what role the example of the wrongness of anti-Semitism played in it.

2. The Argument for Toleration

The argument for toleration assumed by both Weld and Channing was an American elaboration of the argument for universal toleration that had been stated, in variant forms, by Pierre Bayle and John Locke.[11] The context and motivations of the argument were those of radical Protestant intellectual and moral conscience reflecting on the political principles requisite to protect its enterprise against the oppressions of established churches, both Catholic and Protestant.

That enterprise arose both from a moral ideal of the person and the need to protect that ideal from a political threat that had historically crushed it. The ideal was of respect for persons in virtue of their personal moral powers both rationally to assess and pursue ends and reasonably to adjust and constrain pursuit of ends in light of the equal moral status of persons as bearers of equal rights. The political threat to this ideal was the political idea and practice that the moral status of persons was not determined by the responsible expression of their own moral powers, but specified in advance of such reflection, or the possibility of such reflection, by a hierarchical structure of society and nature in which they were embedded. That structure, classically associated with orders of being,[12] defined roles and statuses in which people were born, lived, and died, and exhaustively specified the responsibilities of living in light of those roles.

The political power of the hierarchical conception was shown not only in the ways in which people behaved but in the ways in which it penetrated into the human heart and mind, framing a personal, moral, and social identity founded on roles specified by the hierarchical structure. The structure—religious, economic, political—did not need to achieve its ends by massive coercion precisely because its crushing force on human personality had been rendered personally and socially invisible by a heart that felt, and a mind that imaginatively entertained, nothing that could render the structure an object of critical reflection. There could be nothing that might motivate such reflection (life being perceived, felt, and lived as richly natural).

In light of the moral pluralism made possible by the Reformation, liberal Protestant thinkers like Bayle and Locke subjected the political power of the hierarchical conception to radical ethical criticism in terms of a moral ideal of the person having moral powers of rationality and reasonableness; the hierarchical conception had subverted the ideal and, for this reason, distorted the standards of rationality and reasonableness to which it appealed.

Both Bayle and Locke argued as religious Christians. Their argument naturally arose as an intramural debate among interpreters of the Christian tradition about freedom and ethics. An authoritative Pauline strand of that tradition had given central weight to the value of Christian freedom.[13] That tradition, like the Jewish tradition from which it developed, had a powerful ethical core of concern for the development of moral personality; Augustine of Hippo thus offered a model of God in terms of the elements of moral personality.[14] Indeed, the argument for toleration arose from an internal criticism by Bayle of Augustine's argument for the persecution of the heretical Donatists; to wit, Augustine had misinterpreted central Christian values of freedom and ethics.[15] The concern was that religious persecution had corrupted ethics and, for this reason, the essence of Christianity's elevated and simple ethical core of a universal brotherhood of free people.

The argument for toleration was a judgment of, and response to, perceived abuses of political epistemology. The legitimation of religious persecution by both Catholics and Protestants (drawing authority from Augustine, among others) had rendered a politically entrenched view of religious and moral truth the measure of permissible ethics and religion, including the epistemic standards of inquiry and debate about religious and moral truth. By the late–seventeenth century (when Locke and Bayle wrote), there was good reason to believe that politically entrenched views of religious and moral truth (resting on the authority of the Bible and associated interpretive practices) assumed essentially contestable interpretations of a complex historical interaction between pagan, Jewish, and Christian cultures in the early Christian era.[16]

The Renaissance rediscovery of pagan culture and learning reopened the question of how the Christian synthesis of pagan philosophical culture and Jewish ethical and religious culture was to be understood. Among other things, the development of critical historiography and techniques of textual interpretation had undeniable implications for reasonable Bible interpretation.[17] The Protestant Reformation both assumed and further encouraged these new modes of inquiry, and encouraged as well the appeal to experiment and experience that were a matrix for the methodologies associated with the rise of modern science.[18] These new approaches to thought and inquiry had made possible the recognition that there was a gap between the politically entrenched conceptions of religious and moral truth and inquiry and the kinds of reasonable inquiries that the new approaches made available. The argument for toleration arose from the recognition of this disjunction between the reigning political epistemology and the new epistemic methodologies.

The crux of the problem was this. Politically entrenched conceptions of truth had, on the basis of the Augustinian legitimation of religious persecution, made themselves the measure both of the standards of reasonable inquiry and of who could count as a reasonable inquirer after truth. But, in light of the new modes of inquiry now available, such political entrenchment of religious truth was reasonably seen often to rest not only on the degradation of reasonable standards of inquiry but on the self-fulfilling degradation of the capacity of persons reasonably to conduct such inquiries. In order to rectify these evils, the argument for toleration forbade, as a matter of principle, the enforcement by the state of any such conception of religious truth. The scope of legitimate political concern must, rather, rest on the pursuit of general ends like life, basic rights, and liberties (for example, the right to conscience). The pursuit of such goods was consistent with the full range of ends free people might rationally and reasonably pursue.[19]

A prominent feature of the argument for toleration was its claim that religious persecution corrupted conscience itself, a critique we have already noted in the American abolitionist thinkers who assume the argument. Such corruption, a kind of self-induced blindness to the evils one inflicts, is a consequence of the political enforcement at large of a conception of religious truth that immunizes itself from independent criticism in terms of reasonable standards of thought and deliberation. In effect, the conception of religious truth, though perhaps having once been importantly shaped by more ultimate considerations of reason, ceases to be held or to be understood and elaborated *on the basis of reason.*

A tradition that thus loses its sense of its reasonable foundations stagnates and depends increasingly for allegiance on question-begging appeals to orthodox conceptions of truth and the violent repression of any dissent from such conceptions as a kind of disloyal moral treason. The politics of loyalty rapidly degenerates, as it did in the antebellum South's repression of any criticism of slavery, into a politics that takes pride in widely held community values solely because they are community values. Standards of discussion and inquiry become increasingly parochial and insular; they serve only a polemical role in the defense of the existing community values and are indeed increasingly hostile to any more impartial reasonable assessment in light of independent standards.[20]

Such politics tends to forms of irrationalism in order to protect its now essentially polemical project. Opposing views relevant to reasonable public argument are suppressed, facts distorted or misstated, values disconnected from ethical reasoning; indeed, deliberation in politics is denigrated in favor of violence against dissent and the aesthetic glorification of violence. Paradoxically, the more the tradition becomes seriously vulnerable to independent reasonable criticism (indeed, increasingly in reasonable need of such criticism), the more it is likely to generate forms of political irrationalism (including scapegoating of outcast dissenters) in order to secure allegiance.

I call this phenomenon the paradox of intolerance. The paradox is to be understood by reference to the epistemic motivations of Augustinian intolerance. A certain conception of religious truth was originally affirmed as true and was politically enforced in the society at large because it was supposed to be the epistemic measure of reasonable inquiry (i.e., more likely to lead to epistemically reliable beliefs). But the consequence of legitimizing such intolerance over time was that forms of reasonable inquiry, outside the orthodox measure of such inquiry, were repressed. In effect, the orthodox conception of truth was no longer defended on the basis of reason but was increasingly hostile to reasonable assessment in terms of impartial standards not hostage to the orthodox conception. Indeed, orthodoxy was defended as an end in itself, increasingly by non-rational and even irrational means of appeal to community identity and the like. The paradox appears in the subversion of the original epistemic motivations of the Augustinian argument. Rather than securing reasonable inquiry, the argument now has cut off the tradition from such inquiry. Indeed, the legitimacy of the tradition feeds on irrationalism precisely when it is most vulnerable to reasonable criticism, contradicting and frustrating its original epistemic ambitions.

The history of religious persecution amply illustrates these truths and, as the abolitionists clearly saw, no aspect of that history more clearly so than Christian anti-Semitism. The relationship of Christianity to its Jewish origins has always been a tense and ambivalent one.[21] The fact that many Jews did not accept Christianity was a kind of standing challenge to the reasonableness of Christianity, especially in its early period (prior to its establishment as the church of the late Roman Empire) when Christianity was a proselytizing religion that competed for believers with the wide range of religious and philosophical alternative belief systems available in the late pagan world.

In his recent important studies of anti-Semitism,[22] the medievalist Gavin Langmuir characterizes as anti-Judaism Christianity's long-standing worries about the Jews because of the way the Jewish rejection of Christianity discredited the reasonableness of the Christian belief system in the pagan world. Langmuir argues that the Christian conception of the obduracy of the Jews and the divine punishment of them for such obduracy were natural forms of anti-Judaic self-defense, resulting in the forms of expulsion and segregation from Christian society that naturally expressed and legitimated such judgments on the Jews.[23] In contrast, Langmuir calls anti-Semitism proper the totally baseless and irrational beliefs about ritual crucifixions and cannibalism of Christians by Jews that were "widespread in northern Europe by 1350";[24] such beliefs led to populist murders of Jews usually (though not always) condemned by both church and secular authorities.

Langmuir suggests, as does R. I. Moore,[25] that the development of anti-Semitism proper was associated with growing internal doubts posed by dissenters in the period 950–1250 about the reasonableness of certain Catholic religious beliefs and practices (for example, transubstantiation) and the resolution of such doubts by the forms of irrationalist politics associated with anti-Semitism proper (often centering on fantasies of ritual eating of human flesh that expressed the underlying worries about transubstantiation). The worst ravages of anti-Semitism illustrate the paradox of intolerance, which explains the force of the example for abolitionists. Precisely when the dominant religious tradition gave rise to the most reasonable internal doubts, these doubts were displaced from reasonable discussion and debate into blatant political irrationalism against one of the more conspicuous, vulnerable, and innocent groups of dissenters.

Langmuir's distinction between anti-Judaism and anti-Semitism proper is an unstable one. Both attitudes rest on conceptions of religious truth that are unreasonably enforced in the community at large; certainly, both the alleged obduracy of the Jews and their just punishment for such obduracy were sectarian interpretations of the facts and not reasonably enforced at large. Beliefs in obduracy are certainly not as unreasonable as beliefs in cannibalism, and segregation is not as evil as populist murder or genocide. But both forms of politics are, on grounds of the argument for toleration, unreasonable in principle. More fundamentally, anti-Judaism laid the corrupt political foundation for anti-Semitism. Once it became politically legitimate to enforce at large a sectarian conception of religious truth, reasonable doubts about such truth were displaced from the reasonable discussion and debate they deserved to the irrationalist politics of religious persecution. In the Christian West, the Jews have been the most continuously blatant victims of that politics, making anti-Semitism "the oldest prejudice in Western civilization."[26]

The radical criticism of political irrationalism implicit in the argument for toleration, once unleashed, could not be limited to religion proper but was naturally extended by John Locke to embrace politics as such.[27] Reflection on the injustice of religious persecution by established churches was generalized into a larger reflection on how political orthodoxies of hierarchical orders of authority and submission (for example, patriarchal political theories of absolute monarchy like Filmer's[28]) had been unreasonably enforced at large. The generalization of the argument for toleration naturally suggested the political legitimacy of some form of constitutional democracy (in which the principle of toleration would play a foundationally central role) as a political decision procedure more likely to secure a reasonable politics that respected human rights and pursued the common interests of all persons alike.[29]

The argument for toleration was motivated by a general political skepticism about enforceable political epistemologies. Such politics enforced at large sectarian conceptions of religious, moral, and political truth at the expense of denying the moral powers of persons to assess these matters in light of reasonable standards and as reasonable persons.

The leading philosophers of toleration thus tried to articulate some criteria or thought experiment in terms of which such sectarian views might be assessed and debunked from a more impartial perspective. Bayle thus put the criterion in terms of a contractualist question: "Is such a practice just in itself? If it were a question of introducing it in a country where it would not be in use and where he would be free to take it up or not, would one see, upon examining it impartially that it is reasonable enough to merit being adopted?"[30]

Bayle's use of a contractualist test was generalized by Locke into a comprehensive contractualist political theory.[31] Though Locke is not clear on the point, contractualism has nothing to do with history; nothing in the argument turns on the actual existence of a state of nature. Rather, as Jeffrey Reiman has strikingly put it, in contractualism "[t]he state of nature is the moral equivalent of the Cartesian doubt."[32] Descartes was not, of course, an ultimate epistemological skeptic but rather a philosopher of knowledge worried by the unreliable ways in which beliefs were conventionally formed; he was, for this reason, concerned heuristically to discover what could count as a reasonable basis on which reliable beliefs could be formed, and the Cartesian doubt was a way of articulating what he took that basis to be.

In the same way, neither Bayle nor Locke were moral, political, or religious skeptics; they were concerned, rather, by the unreliable appeals to politically enforceable conceptions of sectarian truths (i.e., politically enforceable epistemologies) and articulated a thought experiment of abstract contractualist reasonableness to assess what might legitimately be enforced through law. Bayle's use of a contractualist test made this point exactly: abstracting from your own aims and the particular customs of your society, what principles of legitimate politics would all persons reasonably accept? The test is, of course, very like Rawls's abstract contractualist test in the absence of knowledge of specific identity, and serves exactly the same political function.[33]

Such a contractualist test assumes that persons have the twin moral powers of rationality and reasonableness in light of which they can assess human ends, their own and others'.[34] The principles of prudence enable us to reflect on the coherence and complementarity among our ends and the more effective ways to pursue them subject to principles of epistemic rationality; the principles of moral reasonableness enable us to regulate the pursuit of our ends in light of the common claims of all persons to the forms of action and forebearance consistent with equal respect for our status in the moral community. These self-originating powers of reason enable us to think for ourselves not only from our own viewpoint but also from the moral point of view that gives weight, or should give weight, to the viewpoints of everyone else.

Reason—epistemic and practical—can have the power that it does in our lives because it enables us to stand back from our ends, to assess critically how they cohere with one another and with the ends of others, and to reexamine and sometimes revise such judgments in light of new insights and experience and to act accordingly. Reason can reliably perform this role only when it is itself subject to revision and correction in light of public standards that are open, accessible, and available to all. Public reason—a resource that enables all persons better to cultivate their moral powers—requires a public culture that sustains high standards of independent, critically tested and testable, revisable argument accessible to all. In order to perform the role that it should play in the exercise of our internal moral powers, public reason cannot be merely or even mainly polemical. It must afford sufficient public space within which we can comfortably express what doubts we might have or should have about our ends, lives, and communities, and deliberatively discuss and resolve such doubts.[35]

Respect for our capacity for reason, thus understood, requires a politics that respects the principle of toleration. Forms of traditional wisdom that have a basis in public reason will not be subject to the principle. But the principle does deny that convictions of sectarian truth *can be enforced through law solely on that basis* (the role of such convictions in private life is, of course, another matter). The principle thus limits the force in *political* life of convictions that draw their strength solely from the certainties of group loyalty and identification that tend, consistent with the paradox of intolerance, most to insulate themselves from reason when they are most reasonably subject to internal doubts.

3. Slavery as a Political Evil

It was no accident, but fundamental to their vindication of the right to conscience against majoritarian American complacency, that the abolitionists—the most principled nineteenth-century advocates of the argument for toleration in the United States—should have come to see the abolition of slavery as the central critical test for American contractualism.

The theory of toleration not only supplied the internal ideals of the supremacy of critical conscience that motored the abolitionist project, but supplied a diagnosis of the underlying political and constitutional problem. American constitutionalism, ostensibly based on the argument for toleration, had betrayed its own central ideals by allowing a politically entrenched sectarian conception of the religious and political legitimacy of slavery to be the measure of legitimate political debate about this issue. The consequence was what the argument for toleration would lead one to expect: the debasement of public reason about the political morality of slavery and about issues of constitutional interpretation relating to slavery. In the South, the paradox of intolerance ran amok; reasonable doubts about slavery were brutally suppressed, and the politics of group loyalty displaced these doubts into increasingly irrationalist pride and violence that culminated in an unjust and illegitimate civil war.[36]

Political abolitionists, like Theodore Parker and the founders of the Republican Party, developed a unified theory to explain the force of this debasement, namely, a slave power conspiracy that permeated the fabric of American political life.[37] Abolitionists brilliantly analyzed the political pathology of southern pride and violence and northern indifference and cowardice, because they saw so clearly their common roots in an irrationalist intolerance that American constitutional institutions and traditions had proven unable to contain. In so doing, they articulated an argument of principle that rendered their defense of human rights not hostage to the abolition issue alone.

4. The Political Evil of Racism

In addition to the criticism of slavery, one group of abolitionist Americans had also long urged the full inclusion of Blacks into the political community on terms of equal citizenship with white Americans. Their thought was understandably to be pivotally important once the nation embraced such inclusion. The argument for toleration was central to this claim and to its underlying political analysis of the evil of racism.[38]

The abolitionist theory of racism offered a cultural analysis of both the construction of irrationalist prejudice and how it was sustained. American racism arose reactively as a way of justifying cultural boundaries of moral and political community—ostensibly universalistic in their terms—that had already excluded a class of persons from the community. Slavery was such an excluding institution, and it was historically based on a folk bias against Africans that centered on their unfamiliar culture and for which color became a kind of proxy. A public culture, based on the principle of toleration, is and should be open to all persons on fair terms of freedom of conscience and moral and cultural pluralism. American slavery violently disrupted and intolerantly degraded the culture of African slaves. The peculiarly onerous conditions of American slavery (prohibitions on reading and writing, on religious self-organization, and on marriage, and limitations and eventual prohibitions on manumission)[39] deprived Black slaves of any of the rights and opportunities that the public culture made available to others; in particular, Black Americans were deprived of the respect for their creative moral powers of rational and reasonable freedom in public and private life. The nature of American slavery and the associated forms of racial discrimination against free Blacks both in the South and in the North had socially produced the image of Black incapacity that ostensibly justified their permanent heathen status (outside the community capable of Christian moral freedom).

For these abolitionists, consistent with the argument for toleration, slavery and discrimination were forms of religious, social, economic, and political persecution motivated by a politically entrenched conception of Black incapacity. That conception enforced its own vision of truth against both the standards of reasonable inquiry and the reasonable capacities of both Blacks and whites that might challenge the conception. A conception of political unity, subject to reasonable doubt as to its basis and merits, had unreasonably resolved its doubts, consistent with the paradox of intolerance, in the irrationalist, racist certitudes of group solidarity on the basis of unjust group subjugation.

Black Americans were the scapegoats of southern self-doubt in the same way European Jews had been the victims of Christian doubt. Frederick Douglass, the leading Black abolitionist, stated the abolitionist analysis with a classical clarity:

> Ignorance and depravity, and the inability to rise from degradation to civilization and respectability, are the most usual allegations against the oppressed. The evils most fostered by slavery and oppression are precisely those which slaveholders and oppressors would transfer from their system to the inherent character of their victims. Thus the very crimes of slavery become slavery's best defence. By making the enslaved a character fit only for slavery, they excuse themselves for refusing to make the slave a freeman.[40]

Abolitionist analysis of the evil of racism focused on the corruption of public reason that its defense required. Its defense had, by the nature of the evil to be defended, required depriving the basic rights of whites as well as Blacks, for example, to free debate about the evils of slavery and racism. The abolitionists—the only consistent advocates of the argument for toleration in antebellum America—were for this reason pathbreaking moral and constitutional dissenters of conscience from, and critics of, the stifling tyranny of the majority of Jacksonian America. The ethical impulse that motivated abolitionists was the corruption of conscience that slavery and racism, like religious persecution, had worked on the spiritual lives of Americans. To sustain these practices and institutions, pro-slavery theorists had, consistent with the paradox of intolerance, repressed criticism precisely when it was most needed. Instead, they fostered decadent standards of argument in the use of history, constitutional analysis, Bible interpretation, and even in science, whose effect had been to corrupt the public sense of what ethics was. From the abolitionist perspective, such attitudes could, consistent with respect for human rights, no more legitimately be allowed political expression than could religious intolerance with its analogous corruption of public reason. Religion, the first suspect classification under American constitutional law, should, as a matter of principle, be generalized to include cognate forms of classification highly likely to be actuated by comparable forms of irrationalist prejudice that are inconsistent with respect for human rights.

As we have seen, abolitionists often made their point by analogy to anti-Semitism. It confirms the power of their analysis to show how it clarifies the related development of European anti-Semitism into racism.

5. Anti-Semitism as Racism

If American politics in the nineteenth century was preoccupied by the issue of the terms and scope of political community (including the status of Blacks), the comparable political issue in Europe was posed by the emancipation of the Jews against the background of the principles of Enlightenment thought embodied in the French Revolution[41] and the ancient anti-Judaism and anti-Semitism we earlier discussed. In the medieval period, both the expulsions of the Jews and their segregation were justified on the ground that they were legitimately the serfs or slaves of Christian princes, because of their culpable failure to adopt Christian belief.[42] Segregating Jewish communities from the life, occupations, and responsibilities of Christian communities—intended, as it was, to stigmatize their culpability—created a Christian image of Jewish culture as inferior, the kind of cultural degradation that was, as we have seen in the case of American Blacks, the context of American racism. It was, as we shall now see, also part of the historical background of the modern European form of racism we call anti-Semitism.

Modern European anti-Semitism, sometimes marked by its students as anti-Christian anti-Semitism,[43] arose in the context of the tense relationship between emerging European principles of universal human rights, sponsored by the French Revolution, and nineteenth-century struggles for a sense of national identity and self-determination. When the French Revolution took the form of Napoleonic world revolution, these forces became fatally contradictory. The emancipation of the Jews fatally occurred in this tense environment and became over time its most terrible victim. The Jews, whose emancipation was sponsored by the appeal to universal human rights, were identified with a culture hostile to the emergence of national self-determination. Their very attempts at assimilation into that culture were, on this view, marks of their degraded inability for true national culture.

The struggles for national identity in nineteenth-century Europe—against the background of balkanized German principalities, Italian kingdoms, and imperialistic domination by non-Germans and non-Italians—were not obviously religious struggles.[44] Indeed, many of them were self-consciously secular and some of them deeply antireligious (thus, German anti-Christian anti-Semitism). Religion was not usually the rallying call of national identity, but culture was—culture often understood in terms of linguistic unity as the basis of a larger cultural and ultimate national unity (thus, Pan-Germanism). National unity, particularly in Germany, was increasingly identified with forging a cultural orthodoxy centering on the purity of the German language, its ancient "Aryan" myths,[45] its high culture. This search for cultural unity arose in part in reaction to the French imperialistic and assimilationist interpretation of universal human rights. That history invited the search for an alternative, linguistically and culturally centered concept of national unity.

But cultural unity—when hostile to universal human rights—is, as under southern slavery, an unstable, highly unprincipled, and sometimes ethically regressive basis for national unity. It can unreasonably enforce at large highly sectarian values by deadly polemical reaction to its imagined spiritual enemies; and it is all too historically comfortable to identify those enemies with a group already historically degraded as culturally inferior. Blacks were this group in America; in Europe, Jews performed this role, a highly vulnerable, historically stigmatized cultural minority—the paradigm case of cultural heresy, as it were. In the German case, where there was little solid humane historical background of moral pluralism on which to build, romantic aesthetic values increasingly dominated over ethical ones; Italy's Mussolini, in contrast, had the history of Roman pluralistic toleration of Jews to appeal to in rebuking Hitler's very German anti-Semitism.[46] Richard Wagner, a major influence on the development of German anti-Semitism, thus preposterously regarded his artistic genius as sufficient to entitle him to articulate, as a prophetic moral leader like Lincoln, an ethical vision for the German people in the Aryan myth embodied in his opera Parsifal. Such a confusion of the categories of aesthetic and ethical leadership reflects the underlying crisis in ethical and political culture.[47]

These deadly confusions are brilliantly displayed in Houston Chamberlain's immensely influential book The Foundations of the Nineteenth Century,[48] a work much admired and indeed used by Hitler.[49] Chamberlain, Wagner's son-in-law, offered a cultural history of the world in which Aryan culture was the repository and vehicle of all value and Jews, as rationalists lacking creative imagination, the embodiment of negative value. In effect, Chamberlain called for a politically enforceable cultural orthodoxy centering on Aryan culture against corrupting non-Aryan (Jewish) culture.

Chamberlain's argument clearly exemplified the paradox of intolerance; he admitted that there were reasonable scientific doubts about the equation of language and race (which underlay his thesis), but he resolved these doubts by appeal to a certitude expressive of the political irrationalism of the will: "Though it were proved that there never was an Aryan race in the past, yet we desire that in the future there may be one. That is the decisive standpoint for men for action."[50] Jesus of Nazareth, whom Chamberlain claimed to much admire, must, of course, be a non-Jew, an Aryan in fact. We are in the never-never land where wishes become, magically, facts.

As in the evolution of American racism, religious intolerance became racist subjugation under the impact of decadent standards of public reason. Chamberlain thus gave an essentially cultural argument a racial interpretation (transmogrifying religious or cultural intolerance into racism) at a time precisely when such scientific racism, as he (like Hitler[51]) clearly recognized, was under examination and attack among students of language and of culture more generally.

Franz Boas, a German Jew and anthropologist who emigrated to the United States and became a central architect of the modern human sciences of culture, had begun seriously to debunk the racial assumptions of European and American anthropology as early as the 1890s.[52] In a way that had not been the case earlier, racial theory was now under sharp attack as scientifically unsound. Yet it was in this context that the increasingly well understood irrationalism of racial thinking was accorded its fullest and most dangerous political expression in the legitimation of a new conception of the basis of political unity and identity.

The malignant consequences of the dynamic of such irrationalism, when it is actually seriously harnessed to political power that is aggressively hostile to human rights, was played out in the history of modern political anti-Semitism and the racial genocide of some six million European Jews to which it ruthlessly led.[53] Political leaders obtained or retained populist political support for governments that violated human rights (and whose legitimacy was therefore in doubt) by appealing to racist fears as the basis of national unity. This strategy included the blatant falsification and distortion of facts that, self-consciously consistent with the aims of Chamberlain and Hitler, inspired the national will with an unreasonable certitude (for example, the Dreyfus affair in France and the Protocols of the Elders of Zion in imperial Russia).[54]

In the German world, political anti-Semitism became, under Hitler's leadership, the very core of the success of Nazi politics in a nation humiliated by the triumphant democracies in World War I.[55] Reasonable standards of discussion and debate on issues of race and human rights were brutally suppressed by a government-sponsored pseudoscience of race enforced by totalitarian terror.[56] Nazism was self-consciously at war with the idea and practice of human rights, including the institutions of constitutional government motivated by the construction of a politics of public reason that respects human rights.[57] Its politics of an artificially constructed group solidarity of myth, ritual, and pseudoscience, having no basis whatsoever in public reason, was motivated by the internal dynamic of the paradox of intolerance to manufacture a basis of unity in an irrationalist will to believe in the fantasized, degraded evils of the Jews. The social construction of racism was carried in Nazi politics to its most irrationalist and immoral extremes because the basis of unity of Nazi politics was essentially a social solidarity of political unreason.

6. Concluding Comparisons

Events in America after the Civil War reveal a not dissimilar dynamic of increasingly powerful political racism; a comparison of these developments to those in Europe would clarify one of the most important interpretive developments in our time, the constitutional acceptance and later repudiation of state-sponsored racial segregation in the United States. As I argue at length elsewhere,[58] American critical understanding and repudiation of its racism was crucially advanced by its confrontation with, and victory over, a racist state (Nazi Germany) genocidally at war with the theory and practice of universal human rights.

On my analysis, identifying and criticizing both slavery and racism as evils (and properly interpreting constitutional principles and doctrines that reflect this mode of criticism) arise within the context of a rights-based contractualist interpretation of political legitimacy as such. In this paper, I have tried to show how and why this is so. The argument for toleration plays the central role that it does in this enterprise because it condemns not only the unreasonable abridgment of the human rights of one person, but, a fortiori, the unreasonable abridgment of the human rights of whole classes of persons. It is for this reason that constitutional democracies, concerned as they are to protect basic equal liberties of religion, speech, and privacy, are increasingly concerned as well to protect persons against the unjust subjugation from their status as bearers of human rights expressed in the irrationalist populist politics of race and gender and sexual preference.[59]

My argument tries to show not only the important role the argument for toleration plays in properly understanding and justifying these developments, but how easily the force of the argument can be abusively circumscribed by forms of putative emancipation that darkly betray the promise of universal toleration. I have, of course, largely focused on American experience as a kind of important constitutional experiment of the uses and abuses of the argument for toleration from which all peoples can learn. But even that focus has necessarily had to be enlarged to include the larger human experience that American culture often importantly reflects. The moral tragedy of American racism is one with the tragedy of European anti-Semitism. I hope to have shown how both the promises and the betrayals of universal toleration are universal to all peoples. The struggle for universal human rights, in which the argument for toleration has played a pivotal role, is the struggle of all people and peoples against their myopia and insularity. Constitutional government, if I am right, must play a central role in that battle by constructing forms of governance that adequately express a principled articulation of the reasonable demands of the argument for toleration. A constitutional culture, actuated by the demand to justify political power in terms of respect for universal human rights, must, as a matter of principle, condemn equally the populist politics of both religious persecution and its ugly modernist expressions in the group solidarity of irrationalist prejudice.

Notes

1. I develop and explore this theme in David A. J. Richards, *Toleration and the Constitution* (New York: Oxford University Press, 1986); for an elaboration of the argument exploring the foundations of the American idea of an enduring written constitution, see David A. J. Richards, *Foundations of American Constitutionalism* (New York: Oxford University Press, 1989).

2. For a much fuller expression of this argument, on which I draw here, see David A. J. Richards, *Conscience and the Constitution: History, Theory, and Law of the Reconstruction Amendments* (Princeton, N.J.: Princeton University Press, 1993).

3. See Theodore Dwight Weld, *American Slavery as It Is* (New York: Arno Press and The New York Times, 1968) (originally published 1839), p. 123; see also pp. 7–8, 143–44, 151.

4. Ibid., 7–8.

5. See ibid., pp. 112–13.

6. See ibid., pp. 118–20.

7. See ibid., pp. 113–17, 120–21, 123–25, 146, 184–86.

8. See *Slavery*, pp. 688–743; *Remarks on the Slavery Question*, pp. 782–820; and *Emancipation*, pp. 820–53, in William E. Channing, *The Works of William E. Channing* (New York: Burt Franklin, 1970). For commentary on Channing and his background, see Andrew Delbanco, *William Ellery Channing: An Essay on the Liberal Spirit in America* (Cambridge, Mass.: Harvard University Press, 1981); Daniel Walker Howe, *The Unitarian Conscience: Harvard Moral Philoso-*

phy, 1805–1861 (Middletown, Conn.: Wesleyan University Press, 1988). See also D. H. Meyer, *The Instructed Conscience: The Shaping of the American National Ethic* (Philadelphia: University of Pennsylvania Press, 1972).

9. See Channing, *Slavery*, pp. 704–5, 714, 715, 722; Channing, *Emancipation*, pp. 839–43.

10. See Channing, *Emancipation*, p. 840.

11. For fuller examination of the argument in Locke and Bayle and its American elaboration notably by Jefferson and Madison, see Richards, *Toleration*, pp. 89–128.

12. See, in general, Arthur O. Lovejoy, *The Great Chain of Being* (Cambridge, Mass.: Harvard University Press, 1964).

13. See Richards, *Toleration*, pp. 86–87.

14. See ibid., pp. 85–88.

15. See ibid., pp. 89–95.

16. See ibid., pp. 25–27, 84–98, 105, 125. For an important recent study of the use and abuse of the interpretation of Judaism in this general context, see Frank E. Manuel, *The Broken Staff: Judaism through Christian Eyes* (Cambridge, Mass.: Harvard University Press, 1992).

17. See Richards, *Toleration*, pp. 125–126.

18. For a recent review of the question, see I. Bernard Cohen, ed., *Puritanism and the Rise of Modern Science: The Merton Thesis* (New Brunswick, N.J.: Rutgers University Press, 1990).

19. See Richards, *Toleration*, pp. 119–20.

20. See, in general, John Hope Franklin, *The Militant South 1800–1861* (Cambridge, Mass.: Belknap Press of Harvard University Press, 1956); cf. W. J. Cash, *The Mind of the South* (New York: Vintage Books, 1941).

21. For a useful study of the early Christian period, see John A. Gager, *The Origins of Anti-Semitism: Attitudes toward Judaism in Pagan and Christian Antiquity* (New York: Oxford University Press, 1983). The classic general study is Leon Poliakov, *The History of Anti-Semitism*, vol. 1, trans. Richard Howard (New York: Vanguard Press, 1965); vol. 2, trans. Natalie Gerardi (New York: Vanguard Press, 1973); vol. 3, trans. Miriam Kochan (New York: Vanguard Press, 1975); vol. 4, trans. George Klin (Oxford: Oxford University Press, 1985).

22. See Gavin I. Langmuir, *Toward a Definition of Antisemitism* (Berkeley: University of California Press, 1990); Langmuir, *History, Religion, and Antisemitism* (Berkeley: University of California Press, 1990).

23. See Langmuir, *Toward a Definition of Antisemitism*, pp. 57–62.

24. Ibid., p. 302.

25. See R. I. Moore, *The Formation of a Persecuting Society: Power and Deviance in Western Europe, 950–1250* (Oxford: Basil Blackwell, 1987).

26. Langmuir, *Toward a Definition of Antisemitism*, p. 45.

27. See Richards, *Toleration*, pp. 98–102; Richards, *Foundations*, pp. 82–90.

28. See Robert Filmer, *Patriarcha* (originally published, 1680), reprinted in Johann P. Sommerville, ed., *Patriarcha and Other Writings* (Cambridge: Cambridge University Press, 1991), pp. 1–68.

29. See Richards, *Foundations*, pp. 78–97.

30. Pierre Bayle, *Philosophical Commentary*, trans. Amie Godman Tannenbaum (New York: Peter Lang, 1987), p. 30.

31. See Richards, *Foundations*, pp. 82–90; Richards, *Toleration*, pp. 98–102.

32. Jeffrey Reiman, *Justice and Modern Moral Philosophy* (New Haven: Yale University Press, 1990), p. 69.

33. See John Rawls, *A Theory of Justice* (Cambridge, Mass.: Harvard University Press, 1971).

34. For a fuller account of these powers, see David A. J. Richards, *A Theory of Reasons for Action* (Oxford: Clarendon Press, 1971).

35. For a useful discussion of all these points, see Onora O'Neill, *Constructions of Reason* (Cambridge: Cambridge University Press, 1989). For Kant on public reason, see "An Answer to the Question: 'What Is Enlightenment?'", in Hans Reiss, ed., *Kant's Political Writings* (Cambridge: Cambridge University Press, 1970), p. 55: "The *public* use of man's reason must always be free."

36. For fuller discussion, see Richards, *Conscience and the Constitution*, pp. 73–80.

37. See, in general, Theodore Parker, *The Slave Power*, ed. James K. Hosmer (Boston: American Unitarian Association, n.d.); David Brion Davis, *The Slave Power Conspiracy and the Paranoid Style* (Baton Rouge: Louisiana State University Press, 1969); William E. Geinapp, *The Origins of the Republican Party 1852–1956* (New York: Oxford University Press, 1987), pp. 353–65.

38. For fuller discussion, see Richards, *Conscience and the Constitution*, pp. 80–89.

39. On the special features of American slavery, in contrast to slavery elsewhere, see Stanley M. Elkins, *Slavery*, 3d ed., revised (Chicago: University of Chicago Press, 1976); Kenneth M. Stampp, *The Peculiar Institution* (New York: Vintage, 1956); Eugene D. Genovese, *The World the Slaveholders Made* (Middletown, Conn.: Wesleyan University Press, 1988); John W. Blassingame, *The Slave Community*, 2d ed. (New York: Oxford University Press, 1979); Carl N. Degler, *Neither Black Nor White* (Madison: University of Wisconsin Press, 1986); Peter Kolchin, *Unfree Labor: American Slavery and Russian Serfdom* (Cambridge, Mass.: Harvard University Press, 1987).

40. Frederick Douglass, "The Claims of the Negro Ethnologically Considered," in Philip S. Foner, ed., *The Life and Writings of Frederick Douglass*, vol. 2 (New York: International Publishers, 1975), p. 295.

41. See Arthur Hertzberg, *The French Enlightenment and the Jews* (New York: Columbia University Press, 1990).

42. See Langmuir, *Toward a Definition of Antisemitism*, pp. 156–7.

43. See, in general, Uriel Tal, *Christians and Jews in Germany*, trans. Noah Jonathan Jacobs (Ithaca, N.Y.: Cornell University Press, 1975).

44. See, in general, E. J. Hobsbawm, *Nations and Nationalism since 1780: Programme, Myth, Reality* (Cambridge: Cambridge University Press, 1990); Ernest Gellner, *Nations and Nationalism* (Ithaca, N.Y.: Cornell University Press, 1983). Such struggles, of course, strikingly continue today in not dissimilar forms. For an important recent study of Pan-Africanism along these lines as a kind of reaction to Western racism, see Kwame Anthony Appiah, *In My Father's House:*

Africa in the Philosophy of Culture (New York: Oxford University Press, 1992). For an important general study of the construction of national identity in a post-colonial world, see also Benedict Anderson, *Imagined Communities: Reflections on the Origin and Spread of Nationalism* (London: Verso, 1983).

45. For a superb treatment, see Leon Poliakov, *The Aryan Myth: A History of Racist and Nationalist Ideas in Europe*, trans. Edmund Howard (London: Sussex University Press, 1971). For an important recent treatment of longstanding anti-Semitic features of German culture as such, see Paul Lawrence Rose, *Revolutionary Antisemitism in Germany: From Kant to Wagner* (Princeton, N.J.: Princeton University Press, 1990).

46. See Poliakov, *The Aryan Myth*, p. 70.

47. See Poliakov, *The Aryan Myth*; Poliakov, *The History of Anti-Semitism*, vol. 3, chap. 11. On Wagner's actual confused state of belief, see Jacob Katz, *The Darker Side of Genius* (Hanover, N.H.: University Press of New England, 1986). For good general studies of Wagner and Wagnerism (including their political uses by Hitler), see L. J. Rather, *Reading Wagner: A Study in the History of Ideas* (Baton Rouge: Louisiana State University Press, 1990); David C. Large and William Weber, eds., *Wagnerism in European Culture and Politics* (Ithaca, N.Y.: Cornell University Press, 1984).

48. Houston Stewart Chamberlain, *The Foundations of the Nineteenth Century*, trans. John Lees (London: John Lane, 1911), 2 vols.

49. See Adolf Hitler, *Mein Kampf* (New York: Reynal and Hitchcock, 1940), pp. 116, 307, 325, 359, 369, 395, 413, 605. On Chamberlain's admiration and support for Hitler, see David C. Large and William Weber, eds., *Wagnerism in European Culture and Politics*, pp. 124–25.

50. Chamberlain, *The Foundations of the Nineteenth Century*, vol. 1, p. 266n.

51. For Hitler's clear recognition "that in the scientific sense there is no such thing as race," see Rather, *Reading Wagner*, p. 286 (quoting conversation with Hitler reported by Rauschning).

52. See Franz Boas, "Human Faculty as Determined by Race," in George W. Stocking, Jr., ed., *A Franz Boas Reader* (Chicago: University of Chicago Press, 1974) pp. 221–42, originally published in American Association for the Advancement of Science *Proceedings* 43 (1894): 301–27. For Boas's fullest statement of his views, see Franz Boas, *The Mind of Primitive Man* (Westport, Conn.: Greenwood Press, 1963) (first edition published, 1911). On Boas's critical influence on modern social theory, see George W. Stocking, *Race, Culture, and Evolution* (New York: Free Press, 1968); Carl J. Degler, *In Search of Human Nature* (New York: Oxford University Press, 1991). For a useful comparison of American and British antiracist thought and argument, see Elazar Barkan, *The Retreat of Scientific Racism: Changing Concepts of Race in Britain and the United States between the World Wars* (Cambridge: Cambridge University Press, 1992).

53. See Raul Hilberg, *The Destruction of the European Jews*, vol. 3 (New York: Holmes and Meier, 1985), pp. 1201–20. On anti-Semitism, see, in general, Poliakov's magisterial *The History of Anti-Semitism*, 4 vols.

54. See Poliakov, *The History of Anti-Semitism*, vol. 4.

55. See Peter Pulzer, *The Rise of Political Anti-Semitism in Germany and Austria*,

rev. ed. (Cambridge, Mass.: Harvard University Press, 1988); Jacob Katz, *From Prejudice to Destruction* (Cambridge, Mass.: Harvard University Press, 1980).

56. See, in general, Hannah Arendt, *The Origins of Totalitarianism* (New York: Harcourt Brace Jovanovich, 1973).

57. See ibid.

58. See Richards, *Conscience and the Constitution*, pp. 160–70.

59. I explore this argument further in Richards, *Conscience and the Constitution*, chap. 5, and, with respect to sexual preference in particular, in Richards, "Sexual Preference as a Suspect (Religious) Classification: An Alternative Perspective on the Unconstitutionality of Anti-Lesbian/Gay Initiatives," *Ohio State Law Journal*, 55 (1994): 491.

9

The Ring: On Religious Pluralism

AVISHAI MARGALIT

CAN JUDAISM, Christianity, and Islam be pluralistic? The question is not whether they can tolerate one another, but whether they can accept the idea that the other religions have intrinsic religious value. Christians, said Goethe, want to be accepted, not tolerated. This is presumably true of Jews and Muslims as well. The question is whether each of these groups is willing to accept the others, that is, to ascribe value to the others' life-style, so that, if they have the power, they will not only refrain from perse-cuting the others but will also encourage the flourishing of their way of life.

Put differently, do the three religions allow their adherents to ascribe intrinsic value to competing religious ways of life? In competing ways of life, beliefs and values essential to one of them contradict beliefs and val-ues essential to the other. The life of a nun and that of a prostitute are an extreme example of a contradiction that is more than mere incompatibil-ity. To contradict, however, is not necessarily to reject. The tension of attraction and rejection between the prostitute and the saint, between Salome and John, is a familiar theme.

My question is about the possibility of interreligious rather than in-trareligious pluralism, where the latter includes the acceptance of Protes-tants by Catholics, of Sunnis by Shiites, and of Reform Judaism by the Orthodox. If a religion can adopt a pluralistic stance with respect to other religions, this does not necessarily imply that it can also adopt such a stance toward heterodox streams within itself. Religious expectations from people perceived as belonging to one's own religion are liable to be much more demanding than those relating to people on the outside.

The Parable of the Rings

The lore of discussions about religious pluralism is accompanied by the folklore of the parable of the three rings, a story made famous by Lessing in his play *Nathan the Wise*. This story has many different medi-eval ancestors, but I will jump through the rings regardless of historical precedence.

A king leaves a legacy of three rings to his three sons. Only one of the rings is real, and its owner is the king's legitimate heir. But the father has mercy on his other children and gives them imitation rings that look like the real one. The analogy is clear. The king is the Heavenly Father, who is the king of the universe, and the three sons are Moses, Jesus, and Muhammad. The real ring is the true revelation.

The story of the one real ring is an antipluralist story. There is one true religion, and the others are false. An imitation ring—for example, one with glass instead of a diamond—not only is valueless but can even have negative value if it pretends to be a real ring.

In the above version, the father did indeed leave two imitation rings and one real one, but no one else knows for certain which ring is the real one. This doubt should lead to an attitude of "respect and suspect," because it is possible that the truth is in another religion.

Another, more radical reading of the parable claims that none of the rings is real. The genuine ring is actually somewhere else. The three rings are only a means for discovering the genuine one. This version of the parable, in which the real ring is not one of the three, has two different interpretations. One is a mystic interpretation, which can be found, for example, in the writings of the thirteenth-century Jewish mystic Abulafia. This interpretation claims that the degree of religious perfection represented by the genuine ring cannot be attained by any of the three traditional religions. Religious perfection can be achieved only by the mystic, who is the sole possible owner of the real ring. The second interpretation of this version claims that the real ring is philosophy. Only philosophy permits the supreme religious knowledge that constitutes religious perfection. (Spinoza is probably the most radical advocate of the philosophical ring.) None of the three rings is real, but this does not mean that they are not effective, that is, able to promote the creation of a social order that enables the real ring to be found—in other words, a social and political order that permits doing philosophy.

Yet another version of the parable, that of Lessing in his play, is that none of the rings has intrinsic value in the sense that a gold ring has such a value, which is the worth of the gold it is made of. Rather, the worth of a ring is in the attitude of its owner. A religion is genuine in the sense that a wedding ring is. It is the person's belief in its significance that makes it effective, for example, by leading to love or good deeds. For someone who does not believe in it, the ring is worthless. All three rings can be valuable or valueless; their worth is in the eye of the beholder.

This last version of the parable raises the question of what it means for a ring to be genuine. Here there are three possibilities that need to be distinguished. One is that the ring is made out of the material it is supposed to be made of. A gold ring is genuine if it is made of eighteen-karat gold. The analogy to this is that the belief is true. The second possibility is that the ring is real if it is effective, if faith in it leads to desirable actions. The analogy here is to religious practice; a religion is genuine if it leads to the proper worship of God. The third possibility is that the ring is real if it truly determines who the father's legitimate heir or representative is. Here the analogy is to the question of who truly constitutes the source of religious authority—more precisely, who the true prophet is, from among the three claimants for legislative revelation.

Of course, there is yet another important version of the parable. A ring made of impure gold, which was the best available in its time, is replaced by a ring of purer, "more real" gold. This is a possible Christian or Muslim interpretation of the story, and the analogy is clear. The ring that was once "real" represents Judaism; now its time has passed, and the father has provided a "more real" ring, in all the senses of "real" I have discussed.

My ring stories do not have Boccaccio's mocking Renaissance charm or Lessing's moral sublimity, but their dry schematism has the advantage of suggesting, if only in parable form, the approaches *to* religion and *within* religion that bear on religious pluralism.

I intend to approach the discussion of religious pluralism indirectly. I will present an antipluralist argument, the argument of the one genuine ring. Possible rebuttals of the premises of this argument, if any, would then constitute a basis for the claim that religious pluralism is possible. Thus this possibility requires the rebuttal of at least one of the premises, and the stance of religious pluralism will be only as convincing as this rebuttal.

The One-Ring Argument

Premise 1: Revelation is propositional.

Premise 2: Revealed truths are constitutive of religion and of redemption through religion.

Premise 3: Religions acquire their intrinsic value by providing a framework for redemption (that is, for achieving religious perfection).

Premise 4: There are contradictions between the constitutive revealed truths of each pair of the three traditional religions.

Premise 5: The fact that the source of religious truths is revelation implies that false religious propositions are valueless (as opposed to scientific errors, for example, which could have value).

Premise 6: Premises 1–5 fit the historical reality of the three religions.

Conclusion: A religion based on constitutive, redemptive, revealed
               truths cannot ascribe value to a religion that contradicts
               these truths. Thus each religion sees itself as the only true
               religion and ascribes no value to the others. In other
               words, there is no room for religious pluralism.

I will now examine this argument.

Propositional Revelation

Propositional revelation is the transmission of truths from the Divinity to
humankind by means that transcend the ordinary course of nature. This
does not necessarily imply that the revelation must actually occur in a
linguistic form, but only that what is transmitted in the revelation can be
formulated in language. When the revelation is transmitted in book form
(the Koran, for example), the transmission itself is propositional.

A proposition is generally an indicative sentence that makes a statement that can be either true or false. However, I see the concept of propositional revelation as including commandments as well, such as "Remember the Sabbath day to keep it holy." Moses Mendelssohn thought
that the Jewish concept of revelation refers to laws rather than to a creed.
Thus, on Mendelssohn's account, a revelation formulated in imperative
sentences should be considered propositional. The reason for not distinguishing between indicative and imperative sentences in the presentation
of a revelation as propositional is that every imperative sentence can be
formulated as an indicative sentence stating that the command is an expression of God's will.

Premise (1) of the one-ring argument is that revelations are propositional. This contradicts a view that has become very widespread, especially in the twentieth century and particularly in Protestant thought. This
view claims that revelation is not propositional but rather has to do with
the divine presence in historical events. But even if one claims that revelations have an experiential nature, as encounters of divine significance,
this does not necessarily, as I see it, prevent the revelation from having
propositional content. Saying that Protestants oppose the idea that revelation is propositional does not necessarily mean claiming that they play
their religion on the organ. Opposing the idea of propositional revelation
is a way of expressing opposition to the notion of Church dogma rather
than to the linguistic nature of revelation. According to the view of revelation as "nonpropositional," it is a living dialogue rather than a list of
commands and articles of faith. Revelation is meant to be an encounter
with "the living God," not with an institution issuing metaphysical truths

or authoritarian commands. Revelation for the believer is a "belief in," which cannot be reduced to a "belief that." It is in this sense that it is non-propositional, not in the sense that the revelatory encounter cannot be formulated in propositional language.

Constitutive Truths

The one-ring argument rests on the premise that the truths received in revelation are those that are constitutive of the religion, whether in the form of dogmas to be held or commands to be obeyed. In either case, they are the truths that define the religion. The definition of the religion is thus essentially dependent on revelation. Revelations can come in various sizes and shapes. The "shapes" can vary from the direct presence of God to the appearance of an angel; they can occur in a vision or a dream. The various "sizes" are the number of people receiving the revelation—an individual or a group, a large group or a small one.

What is crucial for the present discussion is not the form of the revelation but its significance. I distinguish between constitutive revelations, which reveal the religious path, and secondary (instructive) revelations, which bring strayers back to the known straight path. In Judaism the constitutive revelation is to Moses, whereas in Islam it is to Muhammad. The case of Jesus in Christianity is more complicated. In one sense Jesus *is* the revelation, but in another sense the revelation is to Jesus. In either sense, however, this revelation is constitutive of Christianity. In Judaism the distinction between constitutive and secondary revelations is a sharp one. "One must not obey a divine voice, because the Torah was already given at Mount Sinai." That is, any revelation that contradicts the constitutive one at Mount Sinai must be ignored. Moreover, anyone who claims to have received such a revelation is by definition a false prophet.

Premise (2) of the one-ring argument claims that there is a constitutive element in the religion that is given through revelation. A stronger traditional claim is that every constitutive element in the religion is given through revelation. This stronger claim, however, is not necessary for the present argument. On the other hand, the weaker notion put forward by Bultmann and Tillich, which suggests that the purpose of revelation is to release religious life from the pettiness of the everyday, is not sufficient for the present argument.[1] The importance of revelation lies not in the fact that it is dramatic rather than banal, but in the fact that it is essential for the religion.

One well-known argument against giving a constitutive status to the truths of revelation is the argument from God's benevolence: it is impossible that God should give revelatory truths to one person or group and keep these truths from other people. God's truths must be available to everyone. In a radical (deistic) formulation, this is an argument against revelation in general. In a more moderate formulation, it is an argument against truths that cannot be attained through reason and yet are constitutive of a religion. The idea is that constitutive truths should be subject to human understanding, whereas revelatory truths should serve only to delineate the conditions and the method of applying constitutive principles. Thus, for example, the necessity of giving thanks to God is a matter of reason and a basic principle. The particular way of giving thanks—that is, the method and timing of the prayers—is given by revelation.

In other words, what can be given through revelation is the religious lifestyle, not the principles. According to this view, the truths of revelation in the various religions do not stand in contradiction to one another.

Intrinsic Value

The one-ring argument demonstrates that each religion denies the others intrinsic religious value, the sort of value that is the basis of pluralism, as opposed to mere tolerance. As premise (3) says, intrinsic religious value is attributed to a system that presents a framework for attaining religious perfection, in other words, for redemption. Calling the religiously perfect state "redemption"—whether in the personal or the public realm—is not acceptable to the same extent, or in the same sense, in all three religions. This term fits the Christian sense, and to a lesser extent the Jewish formulation, but it hardly fits the Muslim use. Nevertheless, I intend my use of the term "redemption," as referring to whatever has intrinsic religious value, to be neutral between the three religions. Thus, for example, the state of religious perfection that I am calling "redemption" can include a state in which the right God is worshiped in the right way. I have deliberately left open the description of the state of redemption. My claim is merely that only this state can confer intrinsic value on a religion, as opposed to instrumental value, such as being a tool for preserving the public order.

The advantage of using the concept of redemption only for what grants religion its intrinsic value is that redemption is thereby perceived as a ticket to the world to come, a passport to the City of God. The equivalent of the presumptive Jewish promise "All Israelites have a share in the world to come" exists in the other two religions as well. One place to examine the possibility of religious pluralism is in the willingness of each religion to grant members of the other religions citizenship in the world to come. It makes no difference for the present discussion whether "the world to come" is meant literally or metaphorically. Thus the test of whether a given religion allows for pluralism is whether that religion is willing to recognize the citizenship of members of other religions in the world to come. This test can be refined: is the ticket to the world to come offered *in spite* of, or *because* of, the candidate's being a member of another religion? This is obviously a distinction that makes a difference.

There is no salvation outside the Church, says an ancient Church doctrine. The Koran, for its part, says (sura 3, verse 18): "The only true faith in Allah is Islam." These statements seem to be judgments that other religions have no intrinsic value. But, as mentioned, the way to test the stringency of these pronouncements is to find out whether the members of other religions have a share in the world to come. Maimonides incorporated in his code the view that "the pious of the nations of the world have a share in the world-to-come" (*Mishneh Torah, Hilkhot Teshuvah* 3:5). This inclusion in the Heavenly Club is not enough to establish religious pluralism. The righteous among the gentiles can be included in spite of the fact that they belong to another religion, rather than because of it.

Contradictory Truths

Premise (4) in the one-ring argument is that there are contradictions between the revealed truths of the different religions. This premise refers not to just any revealed truth but to important truths that are constitutive of the religion, especially those vital for redemption. If the Christian outlook is defined by the belief that Jesus is the Redeemer, and redemption requires this belief as a necessary component, then it is clear that Judaism denies it. Christianity, for its part, of course claims not only that there is nothing in the Jewish revelation that contradicts the belief in Jesus' redemptive role, but that the Bible as a source of revelation for the Jewish people attests to that very belief. This example demonstrates that the issue of contradiction here is not a matter for the logician but for the believer. Jewish believers might see a contradiction just where Christian believers see evidence supporting their belief. In order to say whether there is a contradiction between religions, it is necessary to specify for whom it is supposed to be a contradiction.

Another note might be in order here. It is not difficult to recognize the possibility of religious pluralism, even with respect to the religions based on historical revelation, if one believes that these revelations are addressed to different groups of people. The Jewish Midrash (*Exodus Rabbah* 5) says that the pronouncements made on Mount Sinai were conveyed to all the nations in seventy languages. If this is taken figuratively to mean that every nation received a different revelation, then there is no contradiction between them.

At any rate, the problem of religious pluralism arises when a contradiction is found between revelations, a contradiction in matters essential to the religion and particularly to the issue of redemption. If the area in which the contradiction is found is an issue that prevents redemption, then the competing religion must be considered lacking in intrinsic value. Not every element that is constitutive of a religion is necessarily vital for redemption. One might consider such a commandment as circumcision vital to Judaism without seeing it as a necessary condition for redemption. (It is interesting to note that the question of whether circumcision is vital for redemption is actually debated in the New Testament. On the one hand, the Jewish Christian from Judea warns: "Except ye be circumcised after the manner of Moses ye cannot be saved" (Acts 15:1). On the other hand, according to Paul: "If ye be circumcised Christ shall profit you nothing" (Galatians 5:3).)

The issue of contradictions between the three revelatory religions is a complicated one. As mentioned, there is a lack of symmetry among the religions with respect to such contradictions. Christianity and Islam affirm the revelations of Judaism, but not vice versa. It sometimes seems as if the controversy between Judaism and Islam is not about the truths of revelation but about principles of the kind governing the firing of employees. Judaism holds the principle of "Last in, first out," Muhammad being the last one in this case. The Islamic principle, on the other hand, is "First in, first out," in this case, Moses. According to the latter principle, the revelation to Muhammad has priority because it came later than those to Moses and Jesus. Islam recognizes that the Torah and the New Testament were taken from the same heavenly tablets as the Koran, but because the Koran came last, it has the power to cancel what was said before.

What does it mean to abrogate what was given in previous revelations? In Islam it is common to use a path metaphor: Islam is seen as the guide to the straight path. Thus we can present our question in terms of this metaphor. There is a difference between two of its usages. One is the idea that a short, straight path leading to the City of God was revealed to Muhammad, but the old paths, even though they are winding and full of pitfalls, still lead to the same place. The other idea is that the old paths were closed off after the new, straight one was revealed, and so they can no longer bring the traveler to the City of God. In the second case, unlike the first, using the old paths contradicts the only set of directions that can lead to redemption. The one-ring argument is based on the idea that all the other paths to redemption are closed off. In this sense, one can speak of a contradiction between the religions.

A move that is familiar to us from Wittgenstein questions the whole idea that religious discourse can be presented in terms of contradictions. If I say the deposed interior minister will be put on trial during the coming year and you say he will not, then our assertions are contradictory. In contrast, if you claim that on the Day of Judgment I will be put on trial before the heavenly throne and I, as a nonbeliever, deny this, our disagreement cannot be described in terms of contradictions. A sentence about the Day of Judgment is a framework sentence, and framework sentences cannot be contradicted, because it is only within a framework that the idea of contradiction makes any sense. A person who rejects such a proposition is living within a different framework but does not hold a contradictory proposition.

As I see it, however, it is precisely between the religions of historical revelation that there is sufficient agreement, including agreement about many framework sentences, that sentences affirmed by one religion and negated by another can be seen as disagreements rather than misunderstandings. The idea is that in general not everything that seems formally to be a contradiction (one sentence negating another) actually is one. In most cases, it is a manifestation of misunderstanding rather than disagreement. In order for the disagreement between two views to be focused enough to constitute a contradiction, there must be a broad basis of agreement in their judgments. The broader and more varied the basis of agreement between two views, the more focused are the contradictions generated by the disagreements between them. Because this is indeed the situation with the religions of historical revelation, it is appropriate to speak of contradictions between them.

Another claim is that the unit of religious communication is not the proposition but the symbol, and that the opposition between religions is an opposition of symbols. The same symbol, for instance, the cross, is seen as attractive in one religion and as loathsome in another. What is difficult in religious pluralism is overcoming the feelings of loathing aroused by the symbols of the other religion, rather than trying to reconcile propositions. There is some truth in this claim, but it is entirely parasitic on the fact that symbols gain their currency from propositions. Propositions are not everything in the psychological acceptance of others, but they are a central element to a normative acceptance of them.

Revelation and Error

Pluralism has a far-reaching requirement: ascribing value to forms of life based on error, precisely what is denied in premise (5). One way of justifying this requirement is to say that the possibility of choosing a mistaken path is necessary for the individual's autonomy and the community's self-definition. Respecting the autonomy of individuals means respecting their choices even if these are mistaken.

Must we accept this claim? It seems that the same argument about error could be raised with respect to evil in general. After all, a necessary component of free choice is the possibility of doing what is bad. Then must we respect evil just because we respect free choice? No. For one thing, what is predominantly bad about evil is that it harms others. One reason for not tolerating evil, even if it is an expression of free choice—which is a good thing in itself—is because of the harm to others.

One antipluralist stance in the religious realm is based on the idea that error and evil should not be distinguished. Religious error constitutes sin if the person committing the error ought to have known better. Toleration of error is like toleration of evil, it is a manifestation of sloth, the worst of the seven deadly sins. In Judaism, Islam, and Catholicism, there is a conception of a religious collective that does not permit them to adopt the distinction between harm to oneself and harm to others. Locke's view, which is based on the idea that religion is a voluntary organization for the purpose of attaining private redemption, is not acceptable to those religions, or at least not to important divisions of them.

The one-ring argument relies on the assumption that, because the revelatory religions claim the authority of revelation for their basic truths, this renders whatever is done on the basis of error devoid of intrinsic value, whether it is the error of people whose revelation was false to begin with (i.e., not really a revelation) or of people whose revelation has become outdated. There is a specific reason for not ascribing value to religions based on error: it is because the truths constitutive of religion—those concerning the worship of the right God in the right way—are given by revelation, not reason.

We might call the specific argument about the connection between revelation and the worthlessness of a life based on error the crystal-ball argument. Suppose we have a crystal ball that tells us medical truths and suggests treatment methods. If the goal is curing people, an error in treatment resulting from not relying on the crystal ball would be a foolish act that should not be respected from any point of view. If, on the other hand, it is scientific medicine that is in question, then errors in theory or treatment could still be considered rational. What gives the errors value is the fact that they are the result of the rational act of hypothesis testing. In other words, the possibility of error has a constitutive function in scientific activity, and a society that relies on scientific rationality must be an open society that encourages competition among hypotheses, including those that bear a high risk of being false. When truth is given by revelation, or when medicine is a crystal-ball practice, errors are not a constitutive element in attaining truth. Errors have no value, and when they occur in a way of life, or in medical treatment, they become sins.

Historical Faithfulness

Premise (6) of the one-ring argument is that the previous antipluralistic premises are faithful to the historical reality of the relations among the three religions. Although my question relates to the possibility of interreligious pluralism rather than to the reality of the relations among the religions, the claim of historical faithfulness, if correct, is relevant to the discussion. The question about the possibility of interreligious pluralism is, after all, being asked with respect to religions that are historical givens. It is not a question about every possible revelatory religion but about serious possibilities. The given state of the religions must provide us with a sense of the various possible relationships among them. The history of these religions is half as old as time. It may be presumed that in such a long history it will always be possible to find some quotation to support any position we want to ascribe to any of the three religions. It is therefore important to ascertain whether the quotation is an authentic one, and thus indicates a serious possibility, or whether it is merely an eccentric curiosity. In the realm of historical possibilities, it would seem that the modal rule, "what exists must be possible," does not always hold. If we ask, for example, whether there can be three popes at the same time, we will obviously get a negative answer. Even if there once were three popes, this is irrelevant to the present judgment. This is the sense of possibility that is not empirical but normative. A church headed by three popes is liable to be considered by believers to be so corrupt that the three popes will not be recognized as legitimate, even if there was nominally a time when three persons were called "pope." In order to ascertain what is possible in a long cultural tradition, judgment is sometimes more important than logic. For acquiring discerning judgment, the protagonist's point of view has an advantage over the spectator's.

As a spectator, I accept that there is a great deal of descriptive truth in the premises of the one-ring argument. I am therefore convinced that the burden of proof is on those who believe in the possibility of religious pluralism. Be that as it may, one thing is clear: the pagan Ovid got it right when he said, "A ring is worn thin by use."

Note

1. Rudolf Bultmann, *Kerygma and Myth I*, ed. Hans Werner Bartsch, trans. R. H. Fuller (S.P.C.K., 1953). Paul Tillich, *Systematic Theology*, vol. 1, p. 1, *Reason and Revelation* (James Nisbett, Digswell Place, n.d.).

10

The Instability of Tolerance

GEORGE P. FLETCHER

TOLERANCE is an unstable virtue. The reason, I will argue, is that tolerance presupposes a complexity of two sentiments: the first, an impulse to intervene and regulate the lives of others, and the second, an imperative—either logical or moral—to restrain that impulse. This complexity readily gives way to a range of simple and straightforward sentiments. At the one extreme, is intolerance toward activities deemed harmful to others. Since John Stuart Mill's proposal in *On Liberty*, the conventional justification for the state's casting intolerance into coercive laws is the protection of secular interests, such as life, health, privacy, reputation, and property. Of course, there are many activities that could generate a risk of harm to these interests, and it is a matter of debate whether a slight risk can justify the state's prohibition. Tolerance can come into play in deciding when the threshold of risk is crossed. The more tolerant we are of risks, the less likely we are to intervene.

At the opposite extreme from intolerance lies a posture of indifference toward what other people do. There is no issue of tolerance, properly understood, in my contemplating my neighbor's choice of television shows or the hours she keeps or the way she spends her money. These things are none of my business. Even if I disapprove of her taste and style of life, I am not in a position to be either tolerant or intolerant of the way she lives. Calling my hands-off attitude a matter of tolerance cheapens the virtue and arrogates too much power to myself.

Tolerance comes into play, therefore, between a ceiling of harm that rules out forbearance and a threshold of concern that makes someone else's behavior my business. The classification of a matter as one for tolerance easily veers off to these extremes. If pornography is harmful to women the way assault is harmful, there is no case for tolerance. If practicing a religion is a matter of private entertainment, something like playing cards or watching television, there is no serious debate about tolerance.

On a tangential axis, we find the attitude of acceptance or respect toward my neighbor's living habits or the religion she practices. Respect differs radically from tolerance. It is a single-stage attitude. When T. S. Eliot said, "The Christian does not wish to be tolerated," presumably he meant that the Christian desires acceptance and respect. I suppose we would all prefer to have our religion, our political views, or our sexual orienattion respected rather than merely tolerated. Yet, as I shall argue, there is merit in maintaining in some situations a posture of tolerance as opposed to both indifference and respect.

Indifference and respect are both simple, first-order attitudes. Tolerance suffers from the complexity of its being a virtue attitude about a first-order attitude of disapproval and rejection. At the second level, the tolerant decide—for reasons yet to be explored—not to follow their first-order instincts. In this respect, tolerance resembles mercy, a second-order virtue that does not come into play unless one has good reason to condemn and punish another.

The core of tolerance lies in the internal conflict of the tolerant. If they could, tolerant people would wish the tolerated behavior out of existence, but they nonetheless recognize that the intervention required to realize that wish is either impossible or unadvisable. They must suffer what they would rather not confront. This element of suffering in tolerance is more evident in other languages, in which there seems always to be a strong connection between "patience" and "tolerance." The connection is patent in Hebrew (*savlanut* and *sovlanut*), in German (*Geduld* and *Geduld-samkeit*), in Russian (*terpenie* and *terpimoct'*) and presumably in numerous other languages. To be tolerant, therefore, is to suffer what we cannot stand because we ought not, for a variety of reasons, intervene.

This element of suffering, I contend, generates the instability of tolerance. Those who suffer understandably prefer an easier way. Their natural inclination is to figure out an effective way of intervening to change the behavior they disapprove of, or the tolerated behavior will become a matter of indifference. As a third option, the tolerated will press and gain acceptance and even respect. The new advocates against hate speech and obscenity think they can safely intervene and excise some speech that they dislike. Following the example of T. S. Eliot, gays and lesbians now seek, in many countries, to go beyond tolerance and demand full acceptance (Eliot himself would probably not appreciate the analogy). Tolerance is unstable, because no one wishes either to tolerate when intervention is possible or to be tolerated when there is an option for something better. Let us examine how these forces play themselves out in the classic arenas of religion, speech, and sex.

1. Religion

In order to take the problem of religious tolerance seriously, we have to make several assumptions that were common when John Locke wrote in the late–seventeenth century but which can only seem peculiar to most educated people in the industrialized world today. We have to believe first that there is something called "salvation" of individuals (Christians) or of the people (Jews); that this salvation, or eternal life with God, depends on whether one lives correctly, according to the true faith; and that this loving God requires that we bear at least some responsibility for the salvation of our neighbors. If any one of these three premises fails to obtain, the problem of tolerance disappears or at least should disappear. Let us see why.

If there is no salvation, or if salvation bears no relation to correct beliefs and practices, I do not see why I should give a hoot whether my neighbor believes in one god or ten, whether she thinks that wine is transformed in church into the blood of her savior, or accepts any of a hundred other random religious doctrines. Without salvation or some or other ultimate concern at stake, these beliefs become personal idiosyncracies, something like believing in astrology or reading coffee grounds. At this level of casualness, the religious beliefs of my neighbor are no more my business than other matters of taste and style.

But let us suppose that having the correct religious beliefs and practices bears on the human condition at least as much as we now think that health is central to the good life. Suppose my neighbor is overweight, eats red meat, and smokes two packs a day. I find this behavior horrendous, and as a friend I try to persuade her to change her ways. She refuses. Even though I am convinced that she is eating and smoking her way into her grave, it seems to me that I have no basis for interfering further in her life. My carrying on a campaign against her smoking—say, by slipping notes under her door and leaving messages on her answering machine—would be a violation of her privacy and arguably subject to legal sanctions. My abstaining from further intervention is required not only by the principle of tolerance but by the basic assumption of nonaggression in an orderly society.

If this were the way seventeenth-century Christians thought about the salvation of their neighbors, there would never have been need for a principle of tolerance. Just as we now let others smoke themselves into their graves, Christians would have allowed their neighbors to go to hell with their incorrect vision of God. It is only when saving the souls of others becomes our mission and duty that we encounter a problem of tolerance. For passionate Jews today, the problem of tolerance is particularly acute, for the religion holds that all Jews are responsible for each other and further that the Messiah will come (the Jewish version of salvation) only when all Jews observe all the mitzvoth, or commandments. When an observant Jew encounters one who refuses to perform the commandments, he or she can feel only pain and the yearning to find a way to induce a fellow Jew to comply with what he or she takes to be God's law.

The closest a modern secularist can come to Locke's context in arguing for toleration is to imagine that we are all deeply concerned about each other's physical health and that we are convinced that certain practices are harmful and others are conducive to good health. What do we do with dissenters who insist on smoking, eating red meat, and lying down whenever they get the urge to exercise? Must we tolerate their bad practices when we care so much about them? It would be painful to do so; we would feel trapped in contradiction. Yet the only way to intervene might be the extreme of imposing penalties for self-destructive behavior like smoking and eating too much fat. Admittedly, health is only one value to be balanced against others, such as privacy and pleasure. No one would want to live in a society that so devalued these competing elements of the good life that smokers had to sneak their puffs in the closet and meat eaters had to go beyond the three-mile limit to have a good steak.

Yet imagine an issue like health that takes precedence over all matters of personal pleasure and privacy. This is the only way to think about salvation in a culture that takes religion seriously. No other value comes close to eternal life with God. Now the question becomes: why not force others to save themselves by adhering to the true religion? Paradoxically, John Locke had a relatively easy time with this issue, because he devised a knockdown argument to show that intervention against those following the false religion would be counterproductive. Salvation, he reasoned, requires a personal quest, a self-actuated identification with the beliefs and practices that bring about the state of grace. State coercion, intervention "by the magistrate," as he quaintly put it, prevents this personal quest from taking place. Tolerance is required of other Protestant sects, because there is no choice.

The argument works insofar as Protestant salvation by faith alone is our concern. The argument works less well for Catholics among themselves (salvation by works rather than faith) and seemingly not at all for Jews relative to other Jews (non-Jews not being their concern). The internal Jewish position appears, at first blush, to be the opposite of Locke's. A long tradition supports the view that it is not intention but external compliance with the mitzvoth that counts. So long as matzo passes over the lips during Passover, a Jew fulfills the commandment of eating matzo. Whether one intends to eat unleavened bread is supposedly irrelevant.

Yet a version of Locke's argument applies as well in the Jewish context. According to the late, revered theologian Yeshayahu Leibowitz, the proper posture of the Jew in fulling the commandments is submission to God's authority.[1] Doing the same act without being commanded to do so is less worthy, for it does not testify to God's sovereignty as lawgiver. Now if a Jew observes the commandments solely because the magistrate has commanded it, the action fails to testify to God's supremacy over all other lawgivers. Acting out of fear of secular sanction rather than out of respect for God's command is to do the right deed for the wrong reason.[2] It would be good to fulfill the commandment but less holy than if the state had not coerced it. Not surprisingly, Leibowitz regarded the state as the primary enemy of the religious life.

There is a general argument, then, of this form: neither the state nor other coercive bodies can intervene to bring about desired behavior, because, in the nature of things, individuals must do it on their own, and coercive threats—from the state or anybody—prevent (or tend to prevent) individuals from acting with internal motivation. Call this the logical argument against intervention. Locke uses the argument. Kant uses it. Leibowitz uses it. It is probably the most ingenious argument ever devised to curtail the power of the state. The argument forces us to stand back and recognize the limits of our power over other individuals. We cannot intervene and force them to do the right thing. Nor can we get the magistrate to do it for us.

Of course, the logical argument for nonintervention works only if we take seriously ultimate values, such as salvation (Locke), transcendent reason (Kant), and the kingship of God (Leibowitz). These are the ideas that generate our need to defer to the individuals' acting on their own internal springs of action. Without these ultimate values, the reasons for nonintervention and the basis for tolerance collapse.

A second way to generate a case for tolerance, it seems, is to weaken the bonds of reciprocal concern for living right according to the true religion. Locke goes surprisingly far in this direction when he argues, "If any man err from the right way, it is his own misfortune, not injury to thee: nor therefore art thou to punish him in the things of this life, because thou supposest he will be miserable in that which is to come."[3] Locke writes later in the same *Letter* that "the greatest duty of a Christian" is to "employ as many exhortations and arguments as possible as he pleases, toward another man's salvation."[4] Exhortations are all right, but coercion is not. It is not clear whether Locke should be read as indifferent to the fate of others when he writes that their going to hell is "no injury to thee." What he means, it seems, is that it is not the kind of injury that can either justify or be remedied by the magistrate's intervention. There are hints of skepticism in the remark that "thou supposest" knowledge of the true religion. If this were merely a supposition, it is not clear why there should be any duty at all "toward another man's salvation."

However Locke should be read, the attitudes presaged in his writing— a high degree of indifference and at least some skepticism—are the hallmarks of the modern approach to religious liberty. A century after Locke's *Letter*, at a time when many states had established churches, the principle of "free exercise of religion" came to be entrenched in the First

Amendment to the United States Constitution. John Rawls incorporates the same attitude toward religious liberty in a more general concept of liberty to which each person is entitled to a maximum amount compatible with a like liberty enjoyed by others.

The First Amendment and the Rawlsian conception of religious liberty reflect a structure of thinking suggested in Locke's distinction between activities that are within the domain of traditional (Judeo-Christian) religious practice and those that impinge on the domain of civil society. The magistrate, Locke concedes, can intervene to execute equal laws designed to protect civil interests, such as life, liberty, health, and property.[5] Rawls agrees that liberty of conscience is limited by the "common interest in public order and security."[6]

These terms are, of course, vague, and they provide little guidance in resolving difficult cases, such as animal sacrifice in Santeria rites, recently resolved by the Supreme Court.[7] The Santeria religion coalesced in Cuba as a fusion of native East African beliefs and Catholicism; its adherents sacrifice small animals, such as chickens and turtles, in order to nourish the "orishas" that guide personal destinies. When the residents of Hialeah, Florida, learned that practitioners of the Santeria rites had immigrated from Cuba, they enacted a special ordinance to suppress the "ritual sacrifice" of animals. The problem under Mill's principle is whether the unnecessary killing of animals (i.e., not for food consumption) represents a harm to other individuals in Hialeah or elsewhere.

It is obviously not enough that the local residents were offended by the practice of killing chickens and turtles in church. If being offended by thinking about others' engaging in the practice were sufficient, anything might qualify as harm to others. The best argument for the city was that the unnecessary killing of animals created a danger to public health. Creating a risk of disease would be sufficient to justify official intolerance and intervention against animal sacrifice. This argument persuaded the two lower courts that the city had a sufficiently strong interest to justify the apparent restriction on official freedom. But the same argument failed at the level of the Supreme Court, because the justices were impressed by the apparent failure of the City of Hialeah to address other equally urgent risks to public health, such as the restaurants' disposing of organic waste and hunters' bringing home dead carcasses. The selective nature of the local ordinance convinced the court that the motive for legislative intervention was not the public good but discriminatory intolerance. That the ordinance was aimed specially at one religious group and its practices made it constitutionally unacceptable.

If we leave the issue of discrimination, we encounter problems in applying the conventional criteria for deciding when the "magistrate" may intervene to prevent harm. On the one hand, Locke holds that things that are "not lawful in the ordinary course of life . . . neither are they so in the worship of God."[8] In the same passage, however, he opines that there should be no law against sacrificing a calf "for no injury is thereby done to anyone."[9] There is no way to predict whether Rawls would conclude that animal sacrifice encroaches on "the common interest in public order and security." The Supreme Court seems all too often to have come to that conclusion—in cases ranging from Mormons' engaging in polygamy[10] to Native Americans' smoking peyote as part of their ritual.[11]

The focus on injury to the common interest illustrates how easy it is to move from the threshold of making someone's practice the business of others to the ceiling, where harm to the public good requires prohibition under the criminal law. It is almost as though the window of tolerance between these two extremes has disappeared. As soon as religious practices become a matter of community interest, they appear to be harmful to some common interest, such as public health. The realm of tolerance is squeezed out. If religion remains in the private sphere, limited to prayers and other traditional rites, these acts of personal liberty are nobody's business. As soon as religious life encounters the slightest resistance of others, as soon as it properly becomes of concern to others, the argument is easily made that the practice is injurious to the common interest and therefore properly enjoined.

It seems that in the United States, we want to ensure that religious practices are never upsetting to anyone. As soon as they become upsetting, as when people have multiple wives or smoke peyote or slaughter animals, we think up neutral laws (or apply old ones) that cover the case and prohibit the activity. Significantly, the Supreme Court has explicitly upheld religious liberty primarily in cases in which the complainant desires to abstain from an objectionable practice, such as saluting the flag, working on the Sabbath, or taking a blood transfusion.[12] It is relatively easy to be tolerant of these abstentions and more difficult to accommodate assertions of the religious spirit that encroach affirmatively on existing laws.

Before turning to the problem of free speech, consider one practical example in which tolerance is in fact operative in the field of religion. The uneasy truce between the religious and secular forces in Israel reflects not indifference, not acceptance, but at most tolerance. The struggle in Israel is for the shape of the public culture, for the style of life that is visible on the street and in the mall. It makes an enormous difference to the religious forces whether public buses operate on the Sabbath, whether the state airline serves only kosher food, and whether Jewish stores sell leavened bread during Passover. The secular regard all of these religiously motivated restrictions, none of which would be thinkable in the United States, as violations of their civil liberties. Significantly, Israel is one of the few countries in the world where the religious and the secular do not clash on the issue of abortion. Their energies are spent fighting about the state's enforcement of Jewish practices.

Both the religious and the secular in Isreal would like to be accepted and respected by the other side, but by and large they have only contempt for each other. Yet neither side can do much to make the lives of the other more uncomfortable without violating the criminal law. This is a case in which intervention is not logically, but only practically infeasible. There are few options available. The compromise that has evolved in Israeli society allows each side some symbolic victories. El-Al serves only kosher food, but other airlines are available to and from Ben-Gurion Airport. By and large, buses do not run on the Sabbath, but privately owned cars do, except in neighborhoods reserved for the ultrareligious. You will not find pork on the menu, but "white steak" (the same thing) is readily available. This is a species of toleration that is likely to remain stable. It is not likely to flip over as acceptance and respect; nor is it likely to diminish to the level of indifference. It stands in contrast to the interwoven pattern of indifference and of mutual respect that has developed among Protestant sects, between Catholics and Protestants (save in Northern Ireland), and between Christians and Jews.

2. Free Speech

As compared with words and rites directed toward God, words and gestures directed toward others offer more than ample opportunities for tolerance. These words that come at us are often offensive. They contain expletives that we would rather not hear, political opinions that attack our beliefs, and often racist, anti-Semitic, sexist, and homophobic slurs. These are words that wound. Pictures, particularly of sex acts, can be even more disturbing, and moving pictures are the most effective means of propagating lies and hate that the world has ever devised. All these words and pictures seem easily to pass the threshold of indifference and enter the realm where tolerance is required.

It is not hard to grasp why personally directed verbal attacks and insults are the business of the person addressed. It is harder to explain why discursive speech, not directed toward anyone in particular, becomes the business of particular groups or even of everyone. Why should it be my business if some revisionist historian denies that the Holocaust ever happened? Why should it matter to me as an American if someone burns an American flag in a demonstration and thereby communicates contempt for the United States? Both of these speech forms are constitutionally protected in the United States but, mutatis mutandis, prohibited in most other advanced industrial societies. If they are not prohibited, then they are a fit object for tolerance. (Indifference seems unlikely, and respect is out of the question.) Yet we need some account of why these verbal acts count as invasive, as my proper concern, when the recitation of prayers in a religion I regard as false can be accepted and ignored.

Holocaust denial and flag burning are examples of political speech. Both could easily be treated as political nonsense. No educated person believes the revisionist Holocaust historians, and flag burning does not visibly hurt the nation whose flag is torched. Yet regardless of the likelihood of tangible harm, it seems right for each of us to be concerned about the dissemination of political nonsense that, if believed, could be harmful. The reason for this proper concern, I submit, is not the risk of realization but rather a function of speech that, with some risk of misunderstanding, I describe as mystical.

Uttering falsehoods is the closest we can come to creating falsehoods. It is almost as though by claiming that the Holocaust never happened, one is creating a world—the world that comes to be between speaker and listener—in which it never did happen. As literature becomes its own reality, systematic political misrepresentation becomes a detached, sealed world in which one lie validates another. Flag burning has mystical overtones in another sense. Displaying the flag is itself a form of speech but a more profound mode of speech than, as the Supreme Court dismissively puts it, a form of symbolic representation of the nation.[13] The flag is not the symbol of the nation in the way a Christmas tree is the symbol of Christmas. For those who believe in it, the flag invokes the nation state's presence. Burning it symbolically negates its presence and its power. This accounts for the use of the religious term "desecration" to name the offense of flag burning.[14]

Tolerance toward speech is important, for self-expression is so easily suppressed. It might be hard to prevent someone from screaming insults on the street corner, but it is easy to prevent distribution of pictures and of the written word. The police can simply seize newspapers and film prints before they reach their intended audience. They can prevent the "wrong" people from appearing on radio and television. Censorship is an ever-ready remedy for speech that we do not like. There is not much an individual can do against a neighbor who is distributing hate propaganda or pornography, but the state can readily intervene and prevent the vicious stuff from spreading.

In many cases, speech does directly cause harm. When it does, states have no qualms about intervening to punish, or provide civil sanctions against, for example, criminal solicitation, blackmail, extortion, copyright infringement, and defamation. Where speech falls short of causing harm but nonetheless offends some people, why should the state not intervene when it can do so easily? The Lockean logical argument does not strictly apply; the state can suppress speech without contradiction. Yet precisely because intervention is so easy and tempting, an extended version of the Lockean argument comes into play.

One argument is that being forced to tolerate opinions we detest exercises the virtue of tolerance.[15] Yet the same argument could be made about harmful activities that we suppress. Tolerating noxious speech must make sense on its own terms not simply because it enables us to tolerate more of the same.

Another argument is that censors initiate a process that easily goes to extremes. If it is a crime to use a conventional racial epithet, then soon it will be a crime to call a woman a "bitch" or a politician a "crook." If it is a crime to deny the Holocaust, then perhaps it should be a crime to question the reigning view of historians about other troubling historical events. What if someone could show that Lincoln did not care about emancipating the slaves, that he was interested only in the economic value of the Union? Should this view be suppressed? This is the slope that becomes too slippery to stop the slide toward ever more censorship. The only way to check the danger is to prohibit censorship altogether.

A related argument holds that intervention against irresponsible revisionist historians gives them more attention than they deserve. This seems to be the observation of many who witnessed the Alberta prosecution of James Keegstra, the high school teacher who taught his students that the Holocaust was a Jewish fabrication. Bringing Keegstra to trial, calling witnesses, putting the factual issue in doubt, allowing him to defend himself—this official recognition only gave his lies greater respectability. Even though he was convicted, more people probably had doubts after the trial about whether the murder of the six million ever occurred.[16]

Locke himself used a version of the "slippery slope" argument when he argued that it was dangerous even to suppress religions that were patently false and sinful, such as those that practiced idolatry. Locke could imagine that the officials evaluating religion might not be Christians, but Muslims or pagans: "And what if . . . to them, the Christian religion seems false and offense to God?"[17] He concluded that punishing idolaters would establish a precedent that, if generalized, could easily lead to the punishment of Christians. The "slippery slope" argument acknowledges that the evaluation of offensive ideas as well as sin is far from objective and scientific. The practice of suppressing religion and censoring offensive speech always begins in clear and appealing cases. It is the later cases, the ones yet to be heard before less wise decision makers, that become the object of concern.

A strong position in favor of free speech reflects an attitude toward the distasteful ideas that is tolerance in its purest form. The attitude toward racist and sexist speech is neither indifference nor acceptance. We suffer speech that we find offensive because we sense that it is too dangerous to intervene and excise just that arena of freedom and nothing more. Our fear of overkill is undoubtedly heightened by our appreciation for speech as a privileged form of freedom, an essential medium of democratic politics, artistic creation, and an unrestrainedly expressive life.

The instability of this tolerance derives from the relentless drive to find some harm in offensive speech and thus push it into the category of suppressible behavior. The latest version of the argument is that racist speech and obscenity violate the constitutional guarantee of equal protection of the laws. The repeated use of racist, ethnic, homophobic, and misogynist slurs reinforces the subordinate positions of the affected groups in society. Put in its most attractive light, the argument is not that a single speech act implying the inferiority of others effects their subordination, but that ongoing patterns of "surpremacist" speech reinforce attitudes of subordination already existing in American society. The argument undoubtedly has a point, and it increasingly finds an audience. The way obscenity affects subordination and generates a violation of equal protection is less clear, but the view has its advocates, notably the relentless Catharine MacKinnon. Many countries agree with the arguments against hate speech but balk at the necessity of controlling obscenity. In the United States, at least, it is not clear whether the advocates of tolerance will be able to hold the line against those who think they can excise some "harmful" forms of speech without heading down the slippery slope of ever-more-vigilant demands for censorship.

3. Sex

People seem to care passionately about what other people do in the bedroom. Twenty-two American states (the figure usually given) still prohibit acts of sodomy between consenting adults. Less than a generation ago, oral sex between consenting adults (a form of foreplay now recommended by pulp sex manuals) was thought to be so disgusting, so deeply "unnatural" and wrong, that it was treated as a crime in most states. Not even married couples were exempt. The principle of intolerance toward so-called deviant sexuality rests on a long tradition of obsessive interest in the way other people receive their sexual pleasure. Even the great liberal Immanuel Kant writes offhandedly that people engaging in sex with animals should be exiled, for they are obviously unfit to live with human beings.[18]

At first blush, this seems most curious. Why should we think it our business what strangers do with their genitals? The Bible is not to blame, for the legal regime generated by the Bible comprehensively regulates the use of bodily orifices. If what you put in your mouth is a fit object for divine guidance, if the Talmud devotes chapters and chapters to the proper response to bodily excretions, then it is not surprising that Jewish law would pay attention to sex. Yet the Western legal tradition ignored issues of diet and excretion and concentrated exclusively on channeling sexual activity into perceived patterns of normalcy.

English law, obviously influenced by Christian sexual repression, turned out to be more intolerant of sexual diversity than was the Bible. True, some biblical prohibitions escaped the lawmakers' vigilant eye. It was never a crime, so far as I know, to have sex with both a mother and a daughter (remember *The Graduate?*) or to engage in any number of the imaginative variations prohibited in Leviticus. Yet the English legal tradition extended the prohibition against homosexual sodomy to stigmatize "unnatural" lovemaking between heterosexuals and lesbians. The English also expanded the range of impermissible liaisons branded as incest; for example, marrying your niece is all right for the Jews but not for the English. These perpetuators of sexual intolerance obviously had a vision of a normal sexual world, and they believed that they could use the repressive power of the state to realize that vision in English, and later in American, society.

As curious as this traditional form of sexual intolerance is, there has been an extraordinary and very recent shift in American and Western European attitudes toward sexual acts that not long ago were branded as "unnatural." It is hard to find anyone who regards oral sex as anybody's business except the consenting adults who are enjoying it. The attitudinal shift here has been from intolerance, backed by criminal sanctions, to benign indifference. Attitudes toward homosexuality are in a much greater state of flux. Americans are deeply divided between those fearful of gays and lesbians in the military and trendsetters in the media and the universities who routinely denounce homophobia along with racism and sexism.

Among those more tolerant of homosexuality, the problem is distinguishing among the sentiments of indifference, acceptance, and tolerance in the narrow sense. The problem is complicated by the ascendancy in this century of privacy as a moral and constitutional value. We no longer feel it appropriate to think about what consenting adults do with each other in bed. In the doctrine-breaking *Griswold* decision, Justice Douglas invoked the horror of police searching "the sacred precincts of marital bedroom for telltale signs of the use of contraceptives" to argue that purchasing and using birth control was within a constitutionally protected domain of privacy.[19] In *Roe v. Wade*, the Supreme Court extended the principle of privacy to encompass abortion prior to the viability of the fetus.[20] The notion of privacy has spawned the rhetoric of the "pro-choice" movement, which demands acceptance not of abortion but of the principle that, in certain matters, the state should not intervene in the mother's decision whether to bear her child or not. True, in a widely criticized decision, the court refused to extend the principle of privacy and tolerance for personal choices to include sodomy in private, whether between heterosexual or homosexual consenting adults.[21] Nonetheless, among those now more tolerant of homosexuality, the dominant idea seems to be that what goes on in private between the sheets is not the business of the public or of the legal system.

It is not clear whether this privacy-conditioned attitude should be described as tolerance. Respecting the privacy of others inclines us toward indifference to what they do in private. Yet a version of the Lockean argument suggests that perhaps tolerance is the proper description. Recall that the Lockean argument is based on the logical impossibility of intervention. In the context of free speech, the argument appears in warnings against embarking on the slippery slope of censorship. As to homosexual behavior, the argument for tolerance would be that one would prefer to prohibit and punish certain sexual acts but that the invasion of privacy required to enforce the law is worse than the behavior in question. A version of the same argument enters the abortion debate: trying to control the decision about reproduction will only drive women to the more dangerous alternative of illegal, back-alley abortions. The justification for tolerance in all these cases is that, although one would like to intervene, one cannot do so safely and effectively. Toleration is always the second-best solution.

Understandably, activist gays and lesbians do not like to be treated as second best. Paraphrasing T. S. Eliot, they do not wish merely to be tolerated. They wish to be accepted and respected for their own normal mode of coupling. This acceptance would be expressed by legally recognizing same-sex marriages and by presenting these marriages in our educational system (e.g., in reading primers) as a normal and respectable way of life. Within religious orders, the issue of acceptance, as opposed to tolerance, is captured in the question of whether gays and lesbians should be recognized in leadership roles as rabbis, ministers, and priests.

I confess to a certain amount of sympathy for this push toward acceptance rather than tolerance or indifference toward homosexuality. The core cases of tolerance—religion and speech—express a refined reciprocity. The tolerated are also tolerant; they return what they receive. If you do not interfere with my religion, I will not interfere with yours. If you do not suppress my outrageous political views, I will not suppress yours. In the case of homosexuality, this subtle balance crashes on one side. Homosexuals have no trouble accepting and respecting the way men and women do it together. Yet the favor is not returned. If they did not insist on acceptance, gays and lesbians would be in a position of submitting to tolerance. They would surrender to a status less favorable than that which they accord straight society.

The instability of tolerance is evident in cases of religion, speech, and sex. In the first case, tolerance tends toward indifference; in the second, arguments of harm seek to push tolerance over the threshold and justify the state's intervention against hate speech and obscenity; in the third case, sexual orientation, tolerance is constantly subject to the demand for respect and acceptance. The two-step thinking required for tolerance—I do not like it, but intervening is impossible or unadvisable—is constantly replaced by the one-step logic implicit in indifference, justified intervention, or acceptance. The complexity of tolerance gives way to simpler responses, and the social struggle in any particular area of dispute defines itself by the option most likely to replace tolerance.

Notes

1. See Yeshayahu Leibowitz, *Judaism, Human Values and the Jewish State*, ed. and trans. E. Goldman (Cambridge, Mass.: Harvard University Press, 1992).

2. On this point, see Meir Dan-Cohen, "In Defense of Defiance," *Philosophy and Public Affairs* 23 (1994).

3. J. Locke, *A Letter Concerning Toleration*, ed. J. Horton and S. Mendus (London: Routledge, 1991).

4. Ibid., 42.

5. Ibid., 17.

6. John Rawls, *A Theory of Justice* (Cambridge, Mass.: Harvard University Press, 1971), 212.

7. See *Church of Lukumi Babalu Aye v. Hialeah*, 113 S. Ct. 2217 (1993).

8. Locke, *Letter*, 36.

9. Ibid.

10. *Reynolds v. United States*, 98 U.S. 145 (1879).

11. See *Department of Human Resources of Oregon v. Smith*, 494 U.S. 872 (1990).

12. For a survey and interpreation of these cases, see my treatment in George P. Fletcher, *Loyalty: An Essay on the Morality of Relationships* (New York: Oxford University Press, 1993), 89–99.

13. See *United States v. Eichman*, 110 S.Ct. 2404 (1991).

14. For an analysis of these religious overtones, see Fletcher, *Loyalty*, 129–34.

15. See, generally, Lee Bollinger, *The Tolerant Society: Freedom of Speech and Extremist Speech in America* (New York: Oxford University Press, 1986).

16. This is the informal report of Irwin Cotler, who surveyed the reactions of his students at McGill University to the Keegstra trial.

17. Locke, *Letter* 39.

18. Immanuel Kant, *The Metaphysics of Morals*, trans. Mary Gregor (Cambridge: Cambridge University Press, 1991), 168.

19. *Griswold v. Connecticut*, 381 U.S. 479, 485 (1965).

20. *Roe v. Wade*, 410 U.S. 113 (1973).

21. *Bowers v. Hardwick*, 478 U.S. 186 (1986).

11

Freedom of Expression

JOSHUA COHEN

IN APRIL 1989, students at the University of Michigan walked into a class and were faced with a blackboard that read, "A mind is a terrible thing to waste—especially on a nigger." This message followed closely on the appearance of a flier at the university declaring "open season on Blacks." A month later, an African student at Smith College found a message slipped under her door that read, "African nigger do you want some bananas? Go back to the jungle."[1]

Responding to a pattern of such incidents and the long-standing American traditions of racial hatred and violence reflected in them, a substantial number of colleges and universities have adopted codes regulating racist and other forms of hate speech. These regulations have been the object of intense controversy. Denounced by some as the work of "tenured radicals,"[2] they have also been the target of more serious criticism. The University of Michigan's own speech code was found constitutionally infirm by Judge Avern Cohn.[3] Considering the university's record in implementing that code, Cohn's objections were well taken.[4]

Still, critics commonly sweep too widely. The United States is, after all, unique internationally in its legal toleration of hate speech.[5] And the Michigan rule is not the only model. Consider, for example, Stanford's regulation on discriminatory harassment (overturned in February 1995; see first note to this chapter). The Stanford code regulates "speech or other expression" that is

1. *intended* to insult or stigmatize individuals on the basis of their sex, race, color, handicap, religion, sexual orientation, or national and ethnic origin;

2. addressed *directly* to the individual or individuals whom it insults or stigmatizes; and

3. makes use of insulting or "*fighting words*" or nonverbal symbols that are "commonly understood to convey direct and visceral hatred or contempt for human beings on the basis of their sex, race, etc."

Expression is only regulable if it meets all three conditions. So here we have a not very restrictive regulation that can be endorsed consistently with a strong commitment to freedom of expression and to the toleration associated with that commitment.[6] It does restrict some expression. But it is not very restrictive.[7] There is no violation if a student in a course or at a political rally says, "the Holocaust is a Zionist fraud" or "slavery was a great civilizing influence." Indeed, the regulation does not prohibit very much at all—for example, probably not the Michigan or Smith cases I mentioned at the outset.

Putting the extent of prohibition to the side, what is the rationale for it and similar regulations? The aim is not to encourage civility, shelter people from offensive comments, or punish malign ignorance. They are motivated instead by various costs associated with discriminatory harassment: direct psychological injury to targets, indirect injuries from encouraging assaults on targeted groups; and, in particular, damage to prospects of equality that comes from undermining equality of educational opportunity within the university and from contributing to an environment in which unacceptable forms of discrimination seem reasonable. Judge Cohn's opinion in *Doe v. University of Michigan* gives special notice to concerns about equality. He begins by noting that it is an "unfortunate fact of our constitutional system that the ideals of freedom and equality are often in conflict." Responding to this unfortunate fact, he indicates in the concluding section of his opinion that the court is "*sympathetic* to the University's obligation to ensure equal educational opportunities for all of its students," but emphasizes that "such efforts must not be at the *expense* of free speech."[8]

Why not? What is the "expense" of regulating free speech? Why is this expense of such magnitude that in the face of it concerns about such substantial values as equality rise only to the level of "sympathetic" concern?

My aim here is to address these and related questions. To that end, I leave aside for now the immediate controversies about speech codes, though I return to the Stanford code at the end, indicating why a pallid endorsement of it is consistent with affirming stringent protections of expressive liberties. Principally, however, I argue for the pallor of the endorsement by discussing some reasons for the protections. The discussion will show that support for such regulations need not reveal a disdain for the values of freedom of expression, and that lack of enthusiasm for them need not reveal indifference to the destructive potential of hate speech. To claim otherwise—to draw a line of principle around regulations of this kind—is to provoke a divisive and unnecessary conflict between liberal and egalitarian commitment.

I start (section 1) by describing what I mean by "stringent protections of expressive liberties." Then (in section 2) I sketch and criticize two strategies for defending such stringency. The first, which I call "minimalist," holds that expression deserves stringent protection not because it is so valuable but because it is costless ("just speech"), because the costs it imposes cannot permissibly be taken into consideration by the state, or because government is especially untrustworthy when it comes to regulating expression: the common thread running through the several variants of minimalism is that the defense is to proceed without recourse to the thesis that expression has substantial value. "Maximalist" views, by contrast, concede the costs of stringent protections but argue that the transcendent value of expression guarantees that it trumps the costs (except when they are of equally transcendent value).

Maximalism and minimalism are not formal theories about freedom of expression. Still, each represents an important tendency of thought in this area.[9] Moreover, their attractive simplicity encourages the assumption that they exhaust the field of justifications. Because neither is compelling, nihilism about freedom of expression lives parasitically off their defects— the nihilism urged, for example, in Stanley Fish's claim that "there's no such thing as free speech and it's a good thing, too."[10] Put less colorfully, the nihilist claims that all there really is—all there could be—when it comes to decisions about restricting or permitting speech is an *ad hoc* weighing of costs and benefits in particular cases using the scales provided by "some particular partisan vision."[11] No general presumption in favor of protection can withstand inspection.

But maximalism and minimalism do not exhaust the strategies of argument for stringent protections.[12] The central burden of my argument (in sections 3 and 4) is to present an alternative to maximalism and minimalism and thereby to defuse some of the temptations to nihilism. Less simple than the alternatives, this view proposes that stringent protections emerge as the product of three distinct considerations:

1. Certain fundamental interests—expressive, deliberative, and informational—are secured by stringent protections of expressive liberty.
2. The costs of expression can, in an important range of cases, be addressed through, as Justice Brandeis put it, "more speech."
3. Certain features of human motivation render expression vulnerable to underprotection, and so recommend rigid protections for it.[13]

Stringent protections, then, help to advance a set of fundamental interests and are recommended principally by the importance of those interests, by the prospects of using expression as a preferred strategy for combating the costs of expression, and secondarily—but only secondarily—by concerns about our tendency to underprotect expression or fears of government regulations of it.[14] I see no rationale that is at once simpler and as compelling. To be sure, the complexity may prompt charges of manipulability: providing a set of relatively unstructured elements that, with suitable adjustments, can be made to deliver any result. I do not think the view has that defect. In any case, I think things are just this complex and see no gain in substituting an arbitrary truncation of relevant considerations for a complex but hard-to-manage structure.[15]

One feature of the account that I want especially to emphasize is that it does not depend on a freestanding preference for liberty over all competing values, in particular, not on a freestanding preference for liberty over equality and an associated condemnation of any restrictions of expression that (like hate-speech regulations) are undertaken in the name of the value of equality.[16] The idea that a commitment to freedom of expression depends on a freestanding preference for liberty over equality is, I believe, a serious mistake. It fosters an unnecessary and destructive hostility to freedom of expression among friends of equality and an unnecessary and destructive hostility to equality among friends of expressive liberty. Where reconciliation is possible, it promotes division; where disagreement is possible on common ground, it insists on drawing false lines of principle.

This point bears special notice because of the current state of debate about freedom of expression. For much of the twentieth century, egalitarians of the political Left have been among the most insistent defenders of stringent protections of expressive liberty, arguing that freedom of expression is both an intrinsic aspect of human liberation and a precondition of popular democratic politics. Over the past fifteen years, this conjunction of egalitarian and libertarian commitment has been subjected to increasingly severe strain. Regulations of political spending aimed at enhancing the voice of less-wealthy citizens have been condemned as unacceptable abridgments of expressive liberty. And free-speech values have been advanced as an obstacle to regulating pornography and hate speech. Because these regulations, too, are in part about promoting equality, the suggestion has emerged that egalitarian and libertarian commitments have come to a parting of the ways. I disagree and aim to state a case for stringent protections of expressive liberty in the tradition of free-speech egalitarianism.

Finally, I explore some of the implications of the view. In particular, the basic framework of argument for stringent protections suggests a different treatment of hate-speech regulations than that advanced in Justice Scalia's opinion in the 1992 case of *R. A. V. v. St. Paul.* So in section 5, I discuss some reasons for rejecting Scalia's reasoning and explore the consistency of a certain style of pornography regulation with the view advanced here. Finally, I return to the Stanford regulation (section 6), indicating how an endorsement of it is consistent with my case for stringent protections of freedom of expression.

One last introductory point: throughout, I help myself freely to examples, terms, and ideas drawn from First Amendment law.[17] My aim, however, is not to interpret the U.S. Constitution but to provide a rationale for stringent protections.

1. Stringent Protections

I begin by explaining what I mean by "stringent protections of expressive liberties." My explanation proceeds by setting out four familiar themes suggested by the free-speech tradition. Nothing I say about these themes is original, or even unfamiliar; each could be expressed in different ways; and not much turns on the particular formulations. But I do need some statement of themes at hand to fix the idea of stringent protections sufficiently to be able to consider the bases for it.

Presumption against Content Regulation

It is common to distinguish regulations of expression that focus on content—including viewpoint and subject matter—from those that are content-neutral. A prohibition on advocating adultery restricts viewpoint; a prohibition on discussing adultery restricts subject matter; a prohibition on debating the merits of adultery (or anything else) on my street at 3:00 A.M. is content-neutral. The first theme, then, is that there is an especially strong (if rebuttable) presumption against regulating expression by virtue of subject matter and, still more particularly, viewpoint: a presumption against regulations animated by a concern for what a person says or otherwise communicates, or consequences flowing from what he or she says.[18]

Categorization

Despite this general presumption, some kinds of content regulation seem intuitively less troubling: for example, regulations of express, direct incitement; truth in advertising; private libel; fighting words; bribery; espionage; and nonobscene child pornography.[19] Because content-regulation is in general objectionable, these exceptions need to be confined. So a second main theme recommends a special approach to handling content regulations. Sometimes called "categorization,"[20] the approach singles out of a small set of categories of expression—in First Amendment law, for example, child pornography, commercial speech, obscenity, fighting words, and express incitement—for lesser protection, specifying conditions for permissible regulation of expression in each category.[21] For content-neutral regulations, by contrast, the second theme recommends a more-or-less-explicit balancing, with a thumb on the scale for speech and an especially heavy thumb when the burden of a content-neutral regulation is especially great for groups with restricted means for conveying their views.[22] (I revisit this last point about "weighted balancing" below, in "Fair Access").

Costly Protections

Expression sometimes has unambiguous costs: a price.[23] It is sometimes offensive, disgusting, or outrageous; it produces reputational injury and emotional distress; it requires protection from hecklers; when it is delivered through leaflets, someone has to clean up the mess; and, concentrated in sufficient numbers on billboards, telephone poles, and buses, it can add to the general ugliness of an urban environment. But—here is the third theme—the presence of such costs does not generally suffice to remove protection from expression. Neither offense, nor cleanup costs for taxpayers, nor reputational injury, nor emotional distress, for example, suffice by themselves to deprive expression of protection.[24]

I am not suggesting that all libel law is inconsistent with stringent protections of expression, that the intentional infliction of emotional distress always deserves protection, or that fines for littering always offend the ideal of freedom of expression.[25] I mean only that even uncontested facts of reputational injury, emotional distress, or mess are not always sufficient to deprive expression of protection, as when the target of expression is a public figure or when the expression focuses on a subject of general interest. When, for example, *New York Times v. Sullivan* required a showing of "actual malice" in order for a public figure to win a libel judgment,[26] or when *Hustler v. Falwell* required actual malice in cases of the intentional infliction of emotional distress,[27] there was no suggestion that actual malice is necessary for reputational injury or emotional distress. Instead, it was held, in effect, that the values associated with a system of free expression outweigh those injuries.

Fair Access

A system of stringent protections of expressive liberties must assure fair opportunities for expression, that is, the value of expressive liberties must not be determined by a citizen's economic or social position.[28] Taking the unequal command of resources as a fact, a system of stringent protections must include measures aimed expressly at ensuring fair access to expressive opportunities. Such measures might include keeping traditional public forums (parks and streets) open and easily accessible; expanding the conception of a public forum to include airports, train stations, privately owned shopping centers, and other places of dense public interaction; affirming the importance of diverse broadcast messages and the role of fair access in contributing to such diversity; financing political campaigns through public resources; and regulating private political contributions and expenditures. The requirement of fair access supports a strong, general presumption against content-neutral regulations with substantially disparate distributive implications—for example, regulations on distributing handbills or using parks and sidewalks that impose disproportionate burdens on people who otherwise lack the resources to get their message out.

Several preliminary comments on this inclusion of fair access in the account of stringent protections are in order. First, the measures I listed for ensuring fair access are all content-neutral, and all are addressed to remedying problems of unfair access that reflect inequalities of material resources. But it is an open question whether and to what extent fair access can be assured through content-neutral remedies. A lack of fair access—social and political exclusion—is sometimes said to result precisely from what others say and not from the distribution of resources.[29] This tension between the demands of content-neutrality and fair access lies at the heart of Catharine MacKinnon's argument for regulating pornography on grounds that—because of its content—it silences women and so prevents fair access.[30] Here I want simply to call attention to this concern. Later, I will suggest some ways to address it and so to broaden the range of cases in which values of fair access and content-neutrality can be reconciled (pp. 200–204).

Second, it might be objected that including requirements of fair access abuses the phrase "stringent protection," that ensuring fair access is really a matter of "positively" expanding expressive opportunities rather than "negatively" protecting expressive liberty. I have a more formal and a more substantive response to this objection.

The formal response is that my four points define "stringent protection" for the purposes of the paper. So the terminological issue does not interest me very much. More substantively, I disagree that this inclusion abuses or stretches the term "protection." When owners of shopping malls wish to prevent people from leafletting on the premises and the state bars them from doing so, the state *is* protecting at least some expression from efforts (by the owners) to silence it. It is tendentious to describe this as an effort by the state to expand opportunities for the leafletters rather than as an effort to protect their liberty from intrusion: tendentious, because that description imports a presumptive right of owners to exclude into the distinction between protection and expansion.[31] The real issue is whether fair access to expressive arenas ought to be ensured as a matter of right to citizens, including those who otherwise lack the resources for participating in such arenas. In grouping these four themes together as "protections," I do not mean to have answered, or even to have addressed, that question.

So here we have four components of a system of stringent protections of expressive liberty: a strong presumption against content regulation; categorization as a method for handling such regulation; a willingness to protect expression despite its costs; and assurances of a fair distribution of expressive opportunities. I now consider some reasons for endorsing a scheme of stringent protections, thus understood.

2. Two False Starts

Earlier I briefly sketched minimalist and maximalist styles of argument for stringent protections. Taking "stringent protections" now to be defined by the four features I presented in the last section, I want to discuss these strategies in more detail.

Minimalism

Generically described, minimalism aims to defend stringent protections without attaching any elevated importance to expression: to make the case for stringent protections by concentrating, so to speak, on the magnitude of the evil those protections prevent rather than the magnitude of the good they protect. One familiar minimalist strategy—I call it "no-cost minimalism"—rests on an expression/action distinction. Relying on that distinction, the minimalist argues that expression, as distinct from action, is not *in itself* costly or harmful and that the harms that might flow from it *in conjunction with* its surrounding conditions can always be addressed without abridging expression. The no-cost case does not rest on attaching an especially significant value to expression itself: the harm principle suffices to generate the protections.

Other minimalists emphasize as well the remedial side of stringent protections, arguing that they are required by the pervasive tendency of people generally (or, in some versions, of political officials) to silence expression for insubstantial or impermissible reasons: for example, to protect officials from criticism, or enforce social morality. Ronald Dworkin, for example, has argued that a right to consume pornography is one implication of a general ban on enforcing preferences about the proper way for other people to conduct their lives; the right serves as a protective device against the legal imposition of moralistic preferences and is required, because such imposition would constitute a demeaning denial of the abstract right of citizens to be treated as equals.[32] This defense of the right to consume pornography is minimalist, beause it does not turn on any special value of expression generally, or of sexual expression in particular, or on the claim that restrictions of expression are especially burdensome, but—only on the abstract right to be treated as an equal, the claim that that right is violated by the legislative imposition of external preferences, and the factual assumption that regulations of expression that emerge from the democratic process commonly are rooted in such preferences.

Minimalism makes two important points: it registers a concern about tendencies to excessive abridgment; and it emphasizes the importance of avoiding the injuries of expression by means other than the restriction of expression, where that is possible. Both points will figure in my own account. But minimalism generally, and no-cost minimalism in particular, is pretty much hopeless as a foundation for stringent protections.

Consider, for example, the third element in the scheme of stringent protection: using "expression" in its ordinary English sense, expression is sometimes harmful, and so protecting it has a price.[33] Denying the cost is simply insulting to those who pay it. Moreover, protecting people with unpopular messages and assuring outlets for expression is costly: sometimes you have to pay for police protection or to sweep the streets to clean up leaflets. It is not clear how no-cost minimalism proposes to capture these components of a scheme of stringent protections. The minimalist might of course be understood as introducing a new technical sense of expression: call something "expression" only if it carries no costs. But then minimalism will offer no help in understanding the rationale for stringent protections of expression as characterized here, because they protect expressive liberty in a much wider sense than the technical one just noted, that is, even when expression has costs.[34]

Or consider the style of minimalism that supplements the case for stringent protections by emphasizing a concern for tendencies to restrict expression for demeaning reasons. This still seems insufficient as a rationale for a system of free expression. It is difficult, for example, to see the justification for a "thumb on the scale" for expression in the case of content-neutral regulations or in the face of a wide range of costs of expression, unless we premise an *affirmative value* for expression and not simply a requirement to abjure demeaning justifications for restrictions of liberty. Consider some content-neutral reasons for restricting expression: to keep *not trusting gov't?*

streets clean, clutter under control, noise levels down, and traffic flow-ing smoothly. Nothing here seems to involve a troubling (because de-meaning) failure to treat people as moral equals. The problem with, for example, sharp restrictions on political demonstrations enacted for these reasons is that they give insufficient weight to the value of expressive lib-erty.[35] It is true, as I indicated earlier, that content-neutral regulations are sometimes troubling because of their disparate impact, that is, because they are especially burdensome for citizens who lack the means to get their message out. And it might be thought such unequal burdensomeness signals the presence of a demeaning rationale for the regulations. But without an antecedent reason for treating expressive liberties as funda-mental, I doubt that the conclusion can be supported, unless all forms of disparate impact are demeaning.[36]

Finally, none of the forms of minimalism seems to provide a good rationale for the fourth feature of stringent protections: assurances of fair access to expressive opportunity.

Maximalism

Maximalism inverts the minimalist strategy. Generically described, the maximalist proposes that expression merits stringent protection, because its great value guarantees that the benefits of protection trump the costs.[37] The maximalist might, for example, argue that the dignity of human be-ings as autonomous and responsible agents is so immediately at stake in any act of expression or so immediately threatened by any regulation of expression—or at least any regulation of expression on grounds of its communicative impact—that abridgments of it represent intolerable vio-lations of human dignity.[38]

The maximalist view has something right, and I will say what it is when I discuss in section 3 fundamental expressive and deliberative inter-ests. Still, maximalism is too simple to capture the contours of freedom of expression. In its simplicity, it either exaggerates the stakes in particular cases of regulating expression or else manipulates the notion of auton-omy to make it fit the complexity of the terrain.[39]

For example, maximalism does not help us to understand why there are cases in which costs do seem relevant to justifying regulations: why regulations of group libel might be more problematical than restrictions on individual libel; why it might make sense to distinguish the treatment of reputational injury to public and nonpublic figures; or why autonomy does not simply trump reputational injury altogether. Similarly, maxi-malism does not seem to be a promising route to understanding why false or misleading advertising seems less worthy of protection than false or misleading claims offered in the course of political or religious argument.[40] In each of these cases, maximalism has troubles with an intuitive idea or distinction. Perhaps there is, in the end, nothing more to these "intuitions" than second nature masquerading as first. But they do have some presumptive weight, and so raise troubles for maximalism.

Furthermore, if considerations about the transcendent value of expression are understood only to provide grounds for rejecting regulations on grounds of communicative impact, then they will provide no limit at all on content-neutral regulations—no weighted balancing—and no basis for a concern with fair access. On the other hand, if considerations of autonomy are understood to ground a uniform presumption against all regulation of expression because of the uniform connection between expression and autonomy, then either the uniform presumption will be very low and protections will be weak or the uniform presumption will be very high and we will all have lots of listening to do.

More fundamentally, the main idea behind the variant of maximalism I focus on here is that expression always trumps other values because of its connection with autonomy. This suggests that a commitment to freedom of expression turns on embracing the supreme value of autonomy as a human good. But this threatens to turn freedom of expression into a sectarian political position. Is a strong commitment to expressive liberties really available only to those who endorse the idea that autonomy is the fundamental human good, an idea about which there is much reasonable controversy? I do not doubt that such a strong commitment *is* available to those whose ethical views are of this kind, but I wonder whether such views are necessary. The force of this concern about sectarianism will become clearer as I describe an alternative to minimalism and maximalism. Suffice it to say for now that it would be desirable to frame an account of the values at stake that is capable of receiving wider support: an account that would free the doctrine both from the insulting idea that expression is costless and from the sectarian idea that it is priceless.

3. An Alternative Strategy: Foundations

The difficulties with maximalist and minimalist strategies recommend a different angle of approach, one which gives stringent protections as a conclusion but does not assume that expression is costless or priceless. More precisely, I will present a view that gives more weight to the value of expression than minimalism, while retaining its emphasis on the desirability of nonrestrictive remedies for harms and its concern with tendencies to overregulate, and that has greater discriminating power than maximalism, while preserving its emphasis on the importance of expression. I propose that three kinds of considerations work together to generate upward pressures for protection and so to provide the basis for the scheme of stringent protections:

1. an idea of the fundamental *interests* that are protected by a system of freedom of expression;

2. an account of the *cost* structure of these protections; and

3. a set of more-or-less commonsense factual claims that I refer to as *fundamental background facts*.

I consider each of these in turn and then in the next section discuss the case for protection produced by their joint operation.

Interests

Freedom of expression is commonly associated with such values as the discovery of the truth, individual self-expression, a well-functioning democracy, and a balance of social stability and social change.[41] I do not wish to dispute these associations but rather to connect more transparently the importance of expression with certain fundamental interests.

In particular, I distinguish three interests protected by stringent assurances of expressive liberty whose importance makes the demand for substantial protection reasonable. I call them the *expressive, deliberative, and informational* interests. Before describing those interests, however, I want to highlight the background to my account of them.

Earlier I accused maximalism of sectarianism. Because I want to steer clear of sectarianism, my presentation of these interests and of their importance is framed to accommodate the idea of reasonable pluralism.[42] In brief, the idea of reasonable pluralism is that there are a plurality of distinct, conflicting, fully reasonable understandings of value. An understanding of value is fully reasonable—which is not the same as *true*[43]—just in case its adherents are stably disposed to affirm it as they acquire new information and test it through critical reasoning and reflection.[44] I emphasize that "test through critical reasoning and reflection" is itself a normative notion: a view is not reasonable simply because of the dogged persistence of its adherents, who preserve their disposition to affirm it after hearing (though not listening to) all the arguments. The contention that there are a plurality of such understandings is suggested by the absence of convergence in reflection on issues of value—the persistence of disagreements, for example, about the values of autonomy, welfare, and self-actualization; about the value of devotions to friends and lovers as distinct from more diffuse concerns about abstract others; and about the values of poetic expression and political engagement.

Acknowledging the pluralism of reasonable evaluative conceptions has important implications for political justification. It suggests that we ought to conduct such justification in terms of considerations that provide compelling reasons within other views as well. When we restrict ourselves in political argument to the subset of moral considerations that others who have reasonable views also accept, we are acknowledging that their views are not unreasonable, even if they do believe what we take to be false.

Assuming reasonable pluralism, then, I look to characterize interests whose importance provides a basis for stringent protections and that are located on common ground shared by different reasonable conceptions. Because different views disagree in their substantive characterization of what is valuable, the basic interests will inevitably be presented in abstract terms. But this abstractness is no metaphysical or philosophical predilection; instead it is the natural consequence of taking seriously the diversity that issues from the free exercise of practical reason.

First, then, there is the *expressive* interest: a direct interest in articulating thoughts, attitudes, and feelings on matters of personal or broader human concern, and perhaps through that articulation influencing the thought and conduct of others.[45] When we think of expression quite generally as a matter of outwardly indicating one's thoughts, attitudes, feelings (or at least what one wants others to believe those inner states are), then the importance of the expressive interest might seem elusive. Drawing some distinctions within the general category of expression, however, will clarify the asserted importance of the interest and one source of the burdensome quality of regulations of expression.

A feature shared by different evaluative conceptions is that the conceptions themselves single out certain forms of expression as especially important or urgent; the conception implies that the agent has weighty reasons for expression in certain cases or about certain issues.[46] The failure to acknowledge the weight of those reasons for the agent, even if one does not accept them, reflects a failure to appreciate the fact of reasonable pluralism. Consider in particular three central cases in which agents hold views that state or imply that they have very strong, perhaps compelling, reasons for expression, and so three central cases illustrating the importance of the expressive interest:

First, in a range of cases, the limiting instance of which is a concern to "bear witness," a person endorses a view that imposes an *obligation* to speak out, to articulate that view and perhaps to urge on others a different course of thought, feeling, or conduct. Restricting expression in such cases would prevent the person from fulfilling the obligation assigned by the view; it would impose conditions that the person reasonably takes to be unacceptable. Here, expressive liberty is on a footing with liberty of conscience, and regulations are similarly burdensome.[47]

In a second class of cases, expression addresses a matter of political justice. Here the importance of the issue, indicated by its being a matter of justice, provides a substantial reason for addressing it. The precise content and weight of the reason is a matter of controversy. Brandeis, for example, urged that "public discussion is a political duty."[48] Perhaps so. But even if expression on such issues is not a matter of duty, still, it is a requisite for being a good citizen—in some cases, for sheer decency—and as such is characteristically supported by substantial reasons within different moral-political conceptions, even though those conceptions might disagree about the precise importance of civic engagement and the occasions that require it.

In a third class of cases, expression is not a matter of personal obligation, nor does it address issues of justice. It is moved by concerns about human welfare and the quality of human life; the evident importance of those concerns provides substantial reasons for the expression. A paradigm here is expression about sexuality, say, artistic expression (whether with propositional content or not[49]) that displays an antipathy to existing sexual conventions, to the limited sensibilities revealed in those conventions, and the harms they are perceived as imposing. In a culture that is, as novelist Kathy Acker says, "horrendously moralistic," it is understandable that such writers as Acker challenge understandings of sexuality "under the aegis of art, [where] you're allowed to actually deal with matters of sexuality."[50]

Another paradigm is social satire (or analogously, caricature). Lenny Bruce's biographer described him as a "man with an almost infantile attachment to everything that was sacred to the lower-middle class. He believed in romantic love and marriage and fidelity and absolute honesty and incorruptibility—all the preposterous absolutes of the unqualified conscience. . . . Lenny doted on human imperfection: sought it out, gloated over it—but only so he could use it as a *memento mori* for his ruthless moral conscience. . . . The attempt to make . . . him a hippie saint or a morally transcendent *artiste*, was tantamount to missing the whole point of his sermons, which were ferociously ethical in their thrust."[51]

There are further important cases here, including an interest in creating things of beauty. But the three I have mentioned are central cases of the expressive interest and suffice to underscore the basis of its importance. They work outward from the case of fully conscientious expression, the paradigm of expression supported by substantial reasons from the agent's point of view. To be sure, diverse evaluative conceptions carry different implications about what is reasonable to say and do. But they all assign to those who hold them substantial reasons for expression, quite apart from the value of the expression to an audience, and even if there is no audience at all.

One alternative line of argument about freedom of expression focuses entirely on public discussion and locates the contribution of expression to public debate at the core of the ideal of freedom of expression. Such views miss the parallels between expressive liberty and liberty of conscience. As a result, they are insufficiently inattentive to the weight of the expressive interest and are likely to be too narrow in the scope of their protections.

Cass Sunstein, for example, has recently defended a two-tier conception of freedom of expression, with political speech occupying the upper, stringently protected tier.[52] Although Sunstein's immediate focus is the proper interpretation of the First Amendment, his case rests in part on general political values and so intersects with my concerns here.[53] Sunstein defines speech as political when "it is both intended and received as a contribution to public deliberation about some issue."[54] This conception of political speech is very broad and is understood to encompass "much art and literature," because much "has the characteristics of social commentary."[55] It is not boundless, however, in that it excludes from highest level protection commercial speech, bribery, private libel, and obscenity.

Because of the breadth of Sunstein's conception of political speech, the practical differences between his approach and mine might turn out to be rather subtle. Still, it strikes me as a mistake to make core protection contingent on the role of expression in contributing to public discussion, in particular on how it is received. Should the level of protection of, for example, Kathy Acker's literary exploration of sexuality be made to depend on whether people find her *Hannibal Lecter, My Father* or *Blood and Guts in High School* challenging or instructive rather than offensive, disgusting, or, simply, out-of-control, post-modernist, identity-deconstructive raving?[56] Should the level of protection of a doctor's conscientious efforts to advise a pregnant patient on the alternatives available to her depend on that advice being intended or received "as a contribution to public deliberation" about reproductive choice.[57] Expression of these kinds is often supported by very substantial reasons, quite apart from how it is *received*. As my discussion of the expressive interest indicates, an account of freedom of expression ought not to disparage those reasons.

In response, it might be urged that the justification for establishing an upper tier occupied by political speech does not depend on assessing the relative *value* of different sorts of speech but on assessing their relative *vulnerabilities*: because the government has such strong incentives to regulate political speech, it is especially vulnerable; because it is so vulnerable, it requires especially strong protections.[58]

This response is not convincing. The evidence of special vulnerability is at best uncertain.[59] In any case, the reasons for special protection extend beyond vulnerability. As I have indicated in my discussion of the expressive interest, very substantial interests *are* at stake. I see no compelling reasons—of political theory, general constitutional theory, or American constitutional tradition—to deemphasize the weight of those interests and shift focus to assessments of vulnerability.[60]

We proceed, then, to the second basic interest: the deliberative interest. This interest has two principal aspects. The first is rooted in the abstract idea, shared by different evaluative conceptions, that it is important to do what is best (or at least what is genuinely worthwhile) not simply what one now believes best (or what one now believes worthwhile). For this reason, we have an interest in circumstances favorable to finding what is best, or at least what is worthwhile, that is, to finding out which ways of life are supported by the strongest reasons.

The second aspect of the deliberative interest is rooted in the idea that it is important that one's evaluative views not be affirmed out of ignorance or out of a lack of awareness of alternatives. So alongside the interest in doing what is in fact supported by the strongest reasons, we also have an interest in understanding what those reasons are and the nature of the support they give. This, too, leads to an interest in circumstances favorable to such understanding.

The connection between these two aspects of the deliberative interest and expression lies in the familiar fact that reflection on matters of human concern typically cannot be pursued in isolation. As Mill emphasized, it characteristically proceeds against the background of an articulation of alternative views by other people.[61] So here, again, there is an interest in circumstances suited to understanding what is worth doing and what the reasons are that support it, for example, circumstances featuring diverse messages, forcefully articulated.[62]

Finally, and most straightforwardly, I assume a fundamental interest in securing reliable information about the conditions required for pursuing one's aims and aspirations.

Having described these three interests, I return to the complaint I registered earlier about the sectarianism of autonomy-based, maximalist views of freedom of expression. It might now seem that my own view is not, after all, so sharply distinct from them. I respond briefly by noting three sorts of differences.

First, autonomy has a capaciousness that strikes me as a vice in an account of expressive liberty. Each of the basic interests I have mentioned is sometimes included within the value of autonomy, but they are importantly different interests. Bringing out these differences helps both to clarify the importance of those interests within different evaluative conceptions and to provide the basis for a theory of expressive liberty that is able to capture intuitive distinctions among different sorts of expression. Second, I am not supposing, with the maximalist, that the three interests always trump other values. Nor, third, do I assume that the interests are uniformly implicated in different sorts of expression; for example, I do not think they are equally at stake in commercial, political, and artistic expression. (I return to this point in my discussion of categorization in section 4).

There are, then, at least these three basic interests rooted in diverse, determinate, evaluative conceptions and in the second-order concerns collected under the deliberative rubric.[63] A first component of the case for stringent protection, then, lies in the ways that such protection secures favorable conditions for advancing these fundamental interests. In the case of the expressive interest, the grounds for protecting expression lie in the importance of the expressive activity itself, as specified by the agent's reasons; in the case of the deliberative and informational interests, the grounds for protecting expression lie in the importance of the interests to which expression contributes. In short, the reasons for protection are partly intrinsic, partly instrumental. I see no basis for deciding (nor any reason to decide) which is more fundamental.

I return later to a more detailed discussion of connections, but first the costs and background facts.

Costs

What then of the costs of expression? Commentators since Justice Holmes have noted that protection for expression cannot be premised on faith in its impotence.[64] As Harry Kalven put it, "Speech has *a price*. It is a liberal weakness to discount so heavily the price. [It] is not always correct to win [the protection of speech] by showing [that the] danger [it threatens] has been exaggerated."[65] Underscoring Kalven's point about the price of speech and the weakness of characteristic arguments for protection, recent "outsider" jurisprudence has portrayed the injuries that hate speech imposes on its targets, by narratively recounting those injuries.[66] If we abjure both the minimalist denial of the price and the sectarian route of maximalism, then the idea of stringent protections could seem simply indefensible, and the skeptical response—"there is no such thing"—could seem a natural alternative.

What kinds of costs does expression impose? In answering this question, I want to organize them along just one axis, distinguishing three types of costs by the pattern of their etiology.

First, there are direct costs. Here I have in mind cases in which, intuitively, nothing intervenes between the expression and its price, where "the very utterance inflicts injury":[67] I shriek at a neurasthenic with a weak heart; disrupt the peace and quiet with loud shouting; falsely tell an elderly mother that her child has just died; spread defamatory falsehoods about a colleague; use offensive language in a public setting; offer a raise or a higher grade in return for sex. When I have said my piece, the damage is done, and it is done by what I said—and in the latter four cases, by its content.

A second category of costs are "environmental." Thus expression could help to constitute a degraded, sickening, embarrassing, humiliating, obtrusively moralistic, hypercommercialized, hostile, or demeaning environment. It might, for example, combine with other expressive actions to contribute to an environment of racial or national antagonism, or to one in which dominance and submission are erotized. Here the harm is not the expression by itself, because in the absence of other similar sayings the environment would not be degraded, hypercommercialized, or hostile; we might be unable to trace particular injurious consequences to particular acts of expression that help to constitute the unfavorable environment.[68] Instead, the price of the expression lies in its contribution to making an environment hostile to, for example, achieving such fundamental values as racial or sexual equality.

Finally, there are straightforwardly indirect costs. Here the injury results from the expression's causing (by persuasion, suggestion, or providing information) someone to do something harmful, as when someone persuades others to purchase too much of a scarce resource or to join the Ku Klux Klan or to support a war that results in massive death and destruction.

Background Facts

To complete the picture of the bases of stringent protections, I now come to the background facts.[69] These facts are sociological and anthropological claims that play a central role in arguments about freedom of expression, though often only as an implicit, half-articulated, thus easily manipulable background.[70] Whatever their common treatment, their importance will eventually become clear. My aim here is simply to make them explicit.

I group the facts into three broad categories, which I label the "facts of reasonableness," the "bare facts of life," and the "unhappy facts of life." Intuitively, the difference among the three categories is that the facts of reasonableness are considerations that would favor protecting speech even under fully ideal conditions; the bare facts favor protection and are unalterable; the unhappy facts of life are considerations that now favor protection but that we might hope are alterable features of our circumstances.

Among the facts of reasonableness, are

1. The fact of reasonable pluralism: under conditions of expressive liberty, people will arrive at conflicting, reasonable evaluative convictions.

2. The fact of reasonable persuasion: people have the capacity to change their minds when they hear reasons presented, and sometimes they exercise that capacity. This assumption lies behind Brandeis's remark that "if there be time to expose through discussion the falsehood and fallacies, to avert the evil by the process of education, *the remedy to be applied is more speech*, not enforced silence."[71] But for the fact of reasonable persuasion, more speech would be a diversion rather than a remedy.

As bare facts of life, we have

1. The fact of resource dependence: expression depends on resources, and access to those resources is commonly unequally distributed.

2. The fact of innocent abuse: if expression is relatively uninhibited, people will sometimes, even without malign intent, say things that are false, offensive, insulting, psychically injurious, emotionally distressing, and reputationally damaging. As James Madison put it, "Some degree of abuse is inseparable from the proper use of everything."[72]

3. The cold (chilling) facts: if sanctions are attached to expression for being false, offensive, insulting, psychically injurious, and so on, then people will be reticent to express themselves (chilled), even if they think their expression is true, inoffensive, not insulting, and so on. Moreover, if the regulation of expression proceeds in ways that are highly uncertain—because standards are vague (e.g., if sanctions attach to remarks that are offensive, deeply disturbing, "outrageous" insults[73]) or because their application depends on weighing competing considerations in each case—then many people will be reticent to express themselves, even if their views deserve protection.

Finally, I count among the unhappy facts of life

1. The fact of power: most people, particularly those with power, do not like to be criticized or disagreed with and are tempted to use the means at their disposal to avoid criticism or disagreement.[74]

2. The fact of bias: we tend to confuse what we would prefer other people to do with what would be best for them to do or with what they must do on pain of immorality.[75]

3. The fact of disadvantage: in a society with relatively poor and powerless groups, members of those groups are especially likely to do badly when the regulation of expression proceeds on the basis of vague standards whose implementation depends on the discretion of powerful actors.

4. The fact of easy offense: putting sociopaths to the side, everyone is offended by something.[76]

5. The fact of abuse: against a background of sharp disagreement, efforts at persuasion sometimes proceed through exaggeration, vilification, and distortion.[77]

IV. An Alternative Strategy: Implications

I want now to bring the different pieces together into a case for a scheme of stringent protections. I will proceed through the four themes discussed in section 1, showing how each can be explained by reference to the elements I have just sketched. In my explanation, I place principal emphasis on the expressive and deliberative interests and the facts of reasonableness. The aim is to show that stringent protections are driven principally by the substantive value of expression and the possibilities of using speech to combat the harms of speech; such protections are only secondarily remedial, only secondarily driven by fear and mistrust underwritten by our tendency, or the tendency of government, to undervalue or suppress expression.

Content Regulation

Take first the presumption against content regulation. This presumption is driven in part by the fundamental expressive and deliberative interests. Content regulation presents the possibility that regulation could effectively exclude certain views from the marketplace, that is, not only drive them into another market niche but drive them out altogether. Content-neutral regulation also presents that possibility, but the threat from content-discriminatory regulations is greater because the targeting is more precise. Because of this threat, content regulations pose a more substantial danger that people will be prevented from expressing views despite, as they see it, the existence of substantial reasons for such expression. In short, they represent a direct threat to the expressive interest.

Moreover, the limits imposed by content regulations on the range of messages threaten the deliberative interest. By directly reducing the diversity of expression, they distort, as Meikeljohn said, the "thinking process of the community."[78] More immediately, by restricting the range of views and establishing official dogma, they limit reflection on alternative views and, therefore, on the reasons for holding one's own views. The problem is *not* that content regulation keeps people from being persuaded to change their minds; rather, it prevents us from figuring out just what our minds are on some subject and what the reasons are for not changing them.

The fact of power points in the same direction. Those with power often wish to insulate themselves from criticism, and the power to regulate content is an especially refined instrument of such insulation. This is particularly true of viewpoint regulation. By contrast, content-neutral regulations are blunter and so less desirable instruments of insulation. To be sure, blunt instruments are still instruments. And if someone expects the distribution of messages to be unfavorable, that someone will want to reduce the level of expression. Moreover, content-neutral regulations can have more or less transparently discriminating effects with respect to classes of speakers. So content-neutral regulations, too, raise serious concerns. But the point suggested by the fact of power remains: there is typically no motivation to reduce the quantity of expression of the same kind and intensity as the motivation to target certain topics, or more particularly certain views. So content-neutral regulations are often less troublesome.

These considerations about the interests and the fact of power indicate why content regulation is especially troubling. Given those troubles, the fact of reasonable persuasion helps to secure the case for a presumption against such regulations. It suggests that the damaging consequences of expression with objectionable content can, apart from the case of direct costs, be addressed with more expression. Because such address is preferable to imposing sanctions, we ought to establish a general presumption in favor of relying on it.

In the case of political speech, for example, these pressures for protection exercised by the basic interests and the facts of power and reasonable persuasion are very strong. So some rule of the sort advanced in *Brandenburg v. Ohio* is naturally suggested: advocacy of violent political change can legitimately be restricted only when "such advocacy is directed to inciting or producing imminent lawless action and is likely to incite or produce such action."[79] Advocacy of the kind addressed by this rule is not the only kind that threatens harm, nor is the expected value of the harm necessarily the greatest. But it is the only case in which circumstances preclude the preferred remedy.

Categorization

We come next to categorization as an approach to handling content regulations. Recall that the idea of categorization is to confine exceptions to a general presumption against content regulation by singling out a small set of categories of expression—for example, child pornography, commercial speech, obscenity, fighting words, and express incitement—for lesser protection, specifying conditions for permissible regulation of expression in each category. The rationale for this strategy divides naturally into two parts.

We need first to account for the distinctions between more and less important kinds of expression. Judgments of importance proceed principally by considering the connection of the expression to the fundamental interests, and secondarily by considering the prospects of addressing the harms through more expression and the fragility of expression given the bare and the unhappy facts of life.

So, for example, political expression is especially important, because it is so closely connected to each of the basic interests and because of its fragility in light of the fact of power. Because it is commonly a form of political speech, group libel is more strongly connected to expressive and deliberative interests than expression that threatens individual libel, and the injuries are more easily remedied with group libel than individual. For these reasons, it is important to confine reduced protection to a category of individual libel, even though people can be harmed by libeling groups to which they belong or with which they identify. The idea that group libel ought to be more strongly protected than individual libel is not contingent on a liberal individualist failure to acknowledge the possibility of harm through group libel, any more than the protection of the libel of public figures requires a denial of its harm.[80]

Commercial speech is, or can be, a source of information. But it is less important than political expression, because it is not so closely connected to the expressive or deliberative interests.[81] Moreover, the cold facts and the fact of innocent abuse have much less force in the case of commercial speech.[82] The economic interests fueling commercial speech ensure that it is less susceptible to regulatory chill, and the fact that commercial advertisers are best situated to know the accuracy of their claims reduces concern about the chilling effects of requiring accuracy in commercial speech.

Even if—and here we come to the second part of the case—we can provide an account of relative importance, why filter judgments of relative importance by categorization rather than working case by case?[83] Here the main burden is carried by the chilling facts and the unhappy facts of power, bias, and disadvantage. Together they suggest that ad hoc regulation will err on the side of excessive interference, on the side of underprotecting what should be protected. Moreover, ad hoc judgments are likely to raise greater concerns about chilling expression. Categories, then, serve as a protective device, a device of self-binding, against excessive interference in a context in which a very substantial value is at stake.

To elaborate, unless expression falls into a less-protected category, we impose very high barriers to regulating it. And before we can consider more substantial regulation of some act of expression, we need to find a general category into which it falls such that we are prepared to reduce the protection for all expression in that general category. The result might be greater protection for some expression than we are inclined to think suitable.[84] If the facts are right, however, then the alternative would be insufficient protection to some expression. Of course, the claim that categorization plays this role assumes that the categories are—whether for semantical or psychological reasons—not so utterly manipulable and indeterminate that they serve no channeling function at all. If they are not thus manipulable, if the facts are as stipulated, and if the choice of regulatory form does have the proposed consequences, then it is reasonable to pursue the strategy of protection through categorization.

Digression: Nihilism Redux

Earlier I mentioned free-speech nihilism, the idea that "there is no such thing as free speech." The pieces are now in place for a response to it.

What does the nihilist denial of free speech come to? Echoing Holmes's remark that "every idea is an incitement" and Kalven's "speech has a price," Fish explains it this way: "There is no such thing as 'speech alone' or speech separable from harmful conduct, no such thing as 'mere speech' or the simple nonconsequential expression of ideas."[85] Beginning from these familiar observations, Fish concludes that decisions about the permissibility of speech always require a balancing of benefits and costs in particular cases by reference to "some particular partisan vision."

I have two disagreements with this conclusion: first, with the idea that decisions about cases must be a matter of ad hoc balancing and, second, with the idea that such balancing must proceed by reference to a particular partisan vision.

As to the first, Fish himself acknowledges the importance of general categories and principles in deciding how to handle particular cases, and for roughly the reasons I just sketched in my remarks on categorization. He says that "free speech principles function to protect society against over-hasty outcomes; they serve as channels through which an argument must pass on its way to ratification."[86] This acknowledgment of the role of "free speech principles" in protecting against "over-hasty outcomes" shows that Fish is not really, as it might have seemed, offering balancing as the mandatory way to resolve particular cases. Neither metaphysics nor politics condemns the resolution of cases by reference to general, free-speech principles that serve (as we see it) to tie our hands against over-hasty outcomes. So the mere fact that speech is consequential carries no implications at all about the proper, much less the necessary, forms for regulating expression.

If free-speech nihilism is not nihilism about principles and a corresponding embrace of ad hoc balancing as the proper form of regulation, then perhaps it registers a point about justifying the principles used to decide cases: because speech is "never free of consequences,"[87] any justification of principles for resolving cases must take into account the values that a scheme of restrictions and permissions promotes and the costs it imposes.

This thesis is indisputable, but also uncontested. Justice Black, for example, urged free-speech absolutism as a doctrine about *decision making under* the First Amendment—"no law" means "no law"—not as a theory about the *justification of* that amendment. He did not deny the importance of a "balancing of conflicting interests" in justifying the First Amendment prohibition on laws restricting freedom of speech; he thought instead that the authors of the First Amendment did all the balancing necessary when they settled on the phrase "shall make no law."[88]

Perhaps, then, free-speech nihilism consists neither in the rejection of principles as guides to decision making nor simply in the claim that a justification of such principles must take the consequences of speech into account. Perhaps it is the claim that justification must always proceed in terms of the aims, interests, and aspirations of particular groups, in terms of "some particular partisan vision";[89] that is, there are no common or shared interests that can serve as a basis for justification. Thus understood, nihilism suggests a pair of practical precepts: if you are weak, argue as forcefully as you can for an encompassing protection of speech in the hope of gaining some political space for your vision; if you are strong, "refashion" principles "in line with your purposes" and then "urge them with a vengeance."[90]

But—here I come to my second disagreement—expressive, deliberative, and informational interests do, I claim, provide common ground among a range of genuinely different views and "particular partisan vision[s]." Of course neither those interests nor any other general scheme of values resolves all controversy about specific cases. But if nihilism amounts only to the thesis that judgments in this area are controversial and contestable, then it wins a quick and uninteresting victory.

Some views, to be sure, do deny the importance of expressive and deliberative interests, so it might be said that endorsing those interests is itself partisan. But partisanship in this sense—not being accepted by all—is consistent with holding that these interests provide common ground for a wide range of *distinct* moral-political views, that they are not the exclusive possession of one particular partisan vision. As to the views that deny these interests, we need to consider actual cases in order to see whether the positions have any serious claim to be reasonable and whether the partisanship they embrace is not still more narrow and particular. In short, we need to consider cases to decide whether the partisanship is really troubling.

Take, for example, a "rationalist fundamentalist."[91] This person denies the idea of reasonable pluralism, affirming instead that it lies within the competence of reason to know that salvation is the supreme value, that there is a single path to salvation, that there is no salvation among the damned, that there are no expressive and deliberative interests, and that free expression is to be condemned along with liberty of conscience. This is not a common view, if only because it claims for reason territory more commonly reserved for faith.[92] But if people advance it, then one ought to say that they are simply mistaken about the powers of reason.[93] Even if the views of the rationalist fundamentalist are all rationally permissible, reason surely does not mandate them, and in insisting that it does the fundamentalist is not acknowledging the facts. So the fact that expressive and deliberative interests are not recognized by the rationalist fundamentalist does not seem very troubling.[94] To be sure, other cases might present greater difficulties. But that needs to be shown. It is not enough to point to the fact of disagreement and conclude that there are only particular partisan visions.

We now return to the case for stringent protections.

Costly Protections

What about protecting expression despite its costs? Why is the fact that expression imposes conditions that are reasonable to want to avoid not sufficient to remove the presumption of protection from it?

To address this question, I start with the special case of offensive expression, in particular, expression that disturbs our sensibilities. We cannot ensure fair opportunities for expression while protecting people generally from offensive expression. Given the fact of easy offense and the associated ubiquity of offense, such protection would have to take the form of substantially restricting expression. But the weight of the expressive and deliberative interests is much greater than the weight of the interest in not being offended, so those restrictions would be intolerable. Moreover, it will not help to confine regulatory efforts to "grossly offensive" expression, because the likely vagueness in regulations of the "grossly offensive" threatens to chill acceptable expression.[95]

I do not deny that offensive expression imposes costs; indeed, its costs are direct. Instead, I claim that the costs of avoiding offense are to be borne by those subject to it, they must, for example, "avert their eyes."[96]

Offensive expression is, as I said, a special case. Moving beyond it, then, the general strategy in deciding whether to protect expression despite its price is to consider the importance of the expression (with attention to the role of categories), how direct and serious the harm is, and the vulnerability of the expression to underprotection, given the background facts. Let me illustrate with three kinds of cases.

In cases of the first type, expression belongs to an important category, is vulnerable, and imposes environmental or indirect costs. Then the reasons against restriction are especially strong, even if the cost is substantial.

Consider, for example, the pornography ordinances adopted in Minneapolis and Indianapolis in the 1980s. According to the Indianapolis ordinance, pornography is the "graphic, sexually explicit subordination of women, whether in pictures or in words," that also meets one of the following conditions:

> (i) women are presented as sexual objects who enjoy pain or humiliation; or (ii) women are presented as sexual objects who experience sexual pleasure in being raped; or (iii) women are presented as sexual objects tied up or cut up or mutilated or bruised or physically hurt; or (iv) women are presented being penetrated by objects or animals; or (v) women are presented in scenarios of degradation, injury, torture, shown as filthy or inferior, bleeding, bruised, or hurt in a context that makes these conditions sexual; or (vi) women are presented as sexual objects for domination, conquest, violation, exploitation, possession, or use, or through postures or positions of servility or submission or display.[97]

As this language indicates, those ordinances, by contrast with obscenity regulations, included no provision for the artistic, literary, scientific, or political value of the expression they sought to regulate. So they were inattentive of the importance of the expressive, deliberative, and informational interests associated with sexually explicit expression. But expressive interests are important in this area, because advancing views about human sexuality is supported by substantial reasons from the point of view of the expresser. I noted this in my earlier discussion of expressive interests. Moreover, deliberative and informational interests are at stake:

> [The existence of pornography] serves some social functions which benefit women. Pornographic speech has many, often anomalous, characteristics. One is certainly that it magnifies the misogyny present in the culture and exaggerates

the fantasy of male power. Another, however, is that the existence of pornography has served to flout conventional sexual mores, to ridicule sexual hypocrisy and to underscore the importance of sexual needs. Pornography carries
many messages other than woman-hating: it advocates sexual adventure, sex
outside of marriage, sex for no other reason than pleasure, casual sex, anonymous sex, group sex, voyeuristic sex, illegal sex, public sex.[98]

Apart from their inattention to basic interests, the ordinances were
vaguely drawn, suggesting inattention to the historical vulnerability of
sexual expression to moralistic overregulation.[99] And they did not consider alternative ways to address the injuries they associated with pornography. For example, if the problem with pornography is that it sexualizes,
and thereby legitimates, abuse, then one natural step would be to target
sexual abuse—the abuse of women as women—directly and seriously.
Such targeting might, for example, include a tort of domestic sexual harassment modeled on workplace sexual harassment, including elements
of quid pro quo and hostile-environment harassment.[100] If the injury of
pornography is that it silences women, then, taking seriously Brandeis's
idea of combating the harms of speech with more speech, there could be
regular public hearings on sexual abuse, perhaps subsidies for women's
organizations to hold such hearings,[101] or easier access for women to
broadcast licenses.

To be sure, the regulations of pornography did claim to address its
harms. But their breadth of coverage makes the arguments about costs
look suspect: given the importance of the regulated target, the claims
about costs seems too speculative to sustain the case for regulation.

These criticisms of the speculative character of the connections between the availablity of pornography and its alleged costs derive their
force in part from the broad sweep of the regulations and so from the
importance of the expression they sought to regulate. The case does not
rest entirely on freestanding doubts about the speculative quality of the
connections between the expression and the costs. Less sweeping regulations, drafted with more attention to the value of sexual expression,
ought to trigger correspondingly less concern about the need for a conclu-
sive showing of injury and so demand less-exacting scrutiny.

Consider, for example, a regulation targeted on the "pornographically
obscene": the subset of the constitutionally obscene (prurient, offensive,
and minimally valuable expression) that erotizes violence. The case
against this regulation would be weaker, because of the weak relation of
obscenity to the fundamental interests. Given that weak relation, it is less
important that the costs are not direct and that the arguments in support
of the costs are speculative.[102] (I provide a more detailed case for this
conclusion later on).

I come now to a second type of case, in which expression belongs to an important category and is vulnerable, but the costs are direct and unavoidable. In such a case, expression is still to be protected. Paradigms here are expression that causes emotional distress or reputational injury to public figures.

Consider, for example, the case of *Hustler v. Falwell*. In a *Hustler* parody of a Campari ad, the Reverend Jerry Falwell was represented as having had his first sexual encounter while drunk, in an outhouse, and with his mother. Falwell won a substantial settlement for the intentional infliction of emotional distress. The Supreme Court overturned the settlement, rejecting the idea that tort law protections should define the scope of expressive liberty. Without denying the reality of Falwell's distress, dismissing it as merely "mental" or emotional, or disputing *Hustler's* responsibility for it,[103] the Court nevertheless argued that the parody was protected, absent a showing of actual malice. The decision did not simply protect offensive expression; emotional distress is not a matter of being offended. Nor did it reflect the view that the liberty to inflict emotional distress is, *in general*, of greater weight than the injury of such distress. The decision turned instead on Falwell's standing as a public figure and the importance of freewheeling, sharp criticism of public figures. In a world in which carefully crafted personal images play a central role in politics, and in which fundamental interests depend on the operation of the political arena, equally well targeted efforts at deflation deserve strong protection. By requiring actual malice, the Court in effect licensed increased emotional distress in order to protect the values associated with expressive liberty.

In a third type of case, importance and vulnerability diminish, and there are direct costs. Here, restriction is permitted. Take, for example, the case of libel of private figures. The vulnerability of reputations, the difficulty of repairing them through more speech, and the fact that such libel is typically not supported by weighty expressive or deliberative interests combine to reduce the appropriate level of protection.

Fair Access

Finally, we come to the requirement of ensuring fair access to expressive opportunities. Three main lines of argument converge on this conclusion.

The first begins by underscoring the central role played in the account of stringent protections by the fact of reasonable persuasion and Brandeis's associated counsel that we remedy the harms of speech with more speech. By holding out the hopeful prospect of reconciling stringent protection of expressive liberties with other substantial political values (including the value of equality), Brandeis's point helps to remove the sectarian edge from freedom of expression. Instead of winning arguments by always insisting that the "danger has been exaggerated," we take the costs seriously and embrace expression as the preferred strategy for addressing them.

But if we help ourselves to Brandeis's thesis, then we must also take its implications on board. When Brandeis urged more speech, in the case of *Whitney v. California*, the context was subversive advocacy.[104] But his remarks were not addressed to the advocates: Anna Whitney was using speech; the state was shutting her up. Brandeis was reminding political elites of the vast means at their disposal for addressing arguments for revolutionary change: they might, for example, try to cure the social ills that prompt such arguments or to present the case against a revolutionary solution.

Addressed to less powerful groups, with restricted access to means of expression, the easy injunction "More speech!" loses its edge. If we insist that "more speech" is the preferred remedy for combating the harms of speech and appeal to the Brandeisian injunction in criticizing content regulation, then we also have an obligation to ensure fair access to facilities of expression where the additional speech might plausibly help the "deliberative forces" to "prevail over the arbitrary."[105] Put otherwise, any argument in which Brandeis's thesis figures as a premise must count assurance of fair access among its conclusions. It is simply unacceptable to impose a high burden on justifying restrictions on expression, to justify that burden partly in terms of the possibilities of combating the harms of speech with more speech, and not to endorse the requirement of ensuring such facilities.

A second line of argument for fair access is rooted in the expressive interest. The argument follows a generic egalitarian strategy of argument for substantively egalitarian norms. Described abstractly, the strategy begins with a more formal and less controversial political norm—for example, the norm of formal equality of opportunity—and then argues that the best justification for that norm provides a rationale for a more egalitarian norm, for example, substantive equality of opportunity.[106]

To put the point less abstractly and apply it to the issue at hand, the rationale for the more formal requirement of an equal right to expressive liberties rests centrally on a conception of the human interests served by that guarantee. More specifically, the reason for protecting expressive liberties against content regulation or other forms of undue restriction lies partly in the importance of assuring favorable conditions for pursuing the expressive interest. But once we acknowledge the need for favorable conditions for realizing this basic interest, we are naturally led from a more formal to a more substantively egalitarian requirement, because the latter more fully elaborates the range of favorable conditions. In particular, given the fact of resource dependence, favorable conditions for realizing the expressive interest will include some assurance of the resources required for expression and some guarantee that efforts to express views on matters of common concern will not be drowned out by the speech of better-endowed citizens.

The deliberative interest provides the foundation for a third, more instrumental rationale for fair access. The cornerstone of this deliberative case is provided by the Millian thesis that favorable deliberative conditions require a diversity of messages. Such diversity might be encouraged in a variety of ways. But one natural means to diversity is to ensure that all citizens have fair opportunities for expression, the expectation being that the breadth of subject matters and viewpoints will increase if the extent of expressive opportunity is not determined by economic or social position.[107]

I have already indicated some ways to achieve fair access in a world of unequal resources (pp. 178–80). One requirement is to endorse a more "functional" conception of a public forum,[108] rejecting the conception of such forums as places that are by tradition or explicit designation open to communicative activity, and instead accepting a presumption that any location with dense public interaction ought to be treated as a public forum that must be kept open to the public.[109] Another condition of fair access is a heightened presumption against content-neutral regulations that have substantially disparate distributive implications, when, as with regulations on distributing handbills or using parks and sidewalks, they work to impose disproportionate burdens on those who otherwise lack the resources to get their message out.

Furthermore, fair access recommends financing political campaigns through public resources, at least to ensure reasonable floors, and regulating private political contributions and expenditures.[110] In *Buckley v. Valeo*, the Supreme Court drew a sharp distinction between regulations of contributions, which are acceptable because they help to prevent the appearance and reality of corruption, and regulations of expenditures, which are an unacceptable burden of expressive liberty.[111] In arguing against expenditure limits, the Court appealed in part to the greater burdens imposed by such regulations. More fundamentally, however, the majority condemned restrictions (even if content-neutral) on expressive liberty imposed in the name of "enhanc[ing] the relative voice of others"[112] and thereby "equaliz[ing] access to the political arena."[113] The Court did not deny that expenditure limits would work to "equalize access" but instead held that regulations of expression aimed at such equalization were "wholly foreign to the first amendment."[114]

Whatever their connection to the First Amendment, it is difficult to understand how any plausible account of expressive liberty would regard content-neutral regulations enacted in the name of fair access as foreign to its concerns. In any case, I have suggested that requirements of fair access share a common justification with other stringent protections of expressive liberty; rather than being "wholly foreign," they are on a par.

Thus far I have focused on measures for ensuring fair access that are content-neutral and concerned to remedy the effects of inequalities of material resources on access to expressive opportunities. But, as I indicated in the discussion of fair access in section 1, it is not clear that content-neutral regulations suffice when it comes to addressing problems of fair access that do not reflect the distribution of material resources. In the case of pornography, for example, the mechanisms of exclusion have been tied directly to what is said. Consider the argument that pornography works by silencing women. Responding to the Brandeisian "more speech" argument, MacKinnon explains the problem of silencing and the consequent tension between content neutrality and fair access this way:

> The situation in which women presently find ourselves with respect to the pornography is one in which more *pornography* is inconsistent with rectifying or even counterbalancing its damage through speech, because so long as the pornography exists in the way it does there *will not be more speech by women*. Pornography strips and devastates women of credibility, from our accounts of sexual assault to our everyday reality of sexual subordination. We are stripped of authority and devalidated and silenced. Silenced here means that the purposes of the First Amendment, premised upon conditions presumed and promoted by protecting free speech, do not pertain to women because they are not our conditions. . . . Any system of freedom of expression that does not address a problem where the free speech of men silences the free speech of women, a real conflict between speech interests as well as between people, is not serious about securing freedom of expression in this country.[115]

I agree with the last claim about the implications of a serious commitment to freedom of expression, and later I present a style of pornography regulation that is less encompassing than MacKinnon's proposals but consistent with the perspective I have advanced in this article. I do wish, however, to resist jumping too quickly to the conclusion that content regulation is the only way to ensure fair access. Other measures of empowerment that are more affirmative than regulations of expression could show real promise in addressing silencing and exclusion, at least as much promise as restricting pornography. In particular, alongside efforts to address the general unjust inequalities of men and women—to overcome the division of household labor and the labor-market segregation of women[116]—alternative ways to meet the problems of silencing directly should be explored. Earlier, for example, I mentioned a tort of domestic sexual harassment, regular public hearings on sexual abuse, perhaps subsidies for women's organizations to hold such hearings, and easier access of women to broadcast licenses.

Indeed, it is not clear that MacKinnon would disagree about the plausibility of these remedies. Responding to the Brandeisian idea of addressing the harms of speech with more speech, she asks, "would more speech remedy the harm [of pornography]?" Her response is instructive: "In the end, the answer may be yes, but not under the *abstract system* of free speech, which only enhances the power of pornographers while doing nothing to guarantee the free speech of women, for which we need civil equality."[117] MacKinnon is right in saying that a serious commitment to freedom of expression cannot be sharply distinguished from a program of civil equality. For that reason, the proposals I have mentioned are not exclusively about "the abstract system of free speech"; they aim directly to enhance the speech of women and are part of a program of "civil equality." So it is unclear why they should be expected to do less well than a restrictive strategy for addressing the harms at issue.

5. Hate Speech, Pornography, and Subcategorization

At several points in the discussion—for example, in my remarks on regulating the pornographically obscene—I have suggested that a commitment to stringent protections of expressive liberty is consistent with a certain style of restriction on expression. Other examples of the style, apart from regulations of pornographic obscenity, are regulations of racist fighting words or "sexually derogatory fighting words."[118] The idea of such regulations is to restrict expression within a less important class (obscenity, fighting words) by targeting a particular subcategory (pornographic, racist, sexually derogatory) of the broader class on grounds of the special harmfulness of that subclass. For example, rather than targeting fighting words generally, regulations focus on racially insulting fighting words; rather than targeting obscenity generally, they focus on obscenity that erotizes violence. Subcategorization is a distinctive and controversial style of regulation because, to put the point abstractly, the defining features of the subcategory would not provide a permissible basis for regulation outside the less protected category. To be a little less abstract, the strategy raises the following question: why is it permissible to regulate hateful fighting words or pornographic obscenity while acknowledging that a general regulation of hate speech or pornography would not be acceptable?

The acceptability of subcategorization will be important to my concluding comments on the Stanford regulation. But it was the target of sharp criticism by Justice Scalia, writing for the Court in the 1992 case of *R. A. V. v. St. Paul*. Although I am not concerned here with the constitutional issue as such, Scalia's objection raises important issues about regulating expression that are not narrowly constitutional.

Background

The facts in *R. A. V. v. St. Paul* are straightforward and uncontested. Robert A. Viktora (a juvenile at the time of prosecution) and his friends burned a cross in the yard of a Black family; he was arrested and charged under a St. Paul bias-motivated crime ordinance. The ordinance provides that "Whoever places on public or private property a symbol, object, appellation, characterization or graffiti, including, but not limited to, a burning cross or Nazi swastika, which one knows or has reasonable grounds to know arouses anger, alarm or resentment in others on the basis of race, color, creed, religion or gender commits disorderly conduct and shall be guilty of a misdemeanor."[119] Viktora challenged the ordinance, arguing that it was overbroad and impermissibly content-based. The Minnesota Supreme Court rejected the challenge. Central to the court's holding was its construction of the phrase "arouses anger, alarm or resentment in others" as restricted to "fighting words." As defined in *Chaplinksy v. New Hampshire*, fighting words are directed to individuals, they form "no essential part of any exposition of ideas," and their "very utterance inflicts injury" or "tends to incite an immediate breach of the peace."[120] Assuming that the First Amendment does not protect fighting words,[121] the Minnesota court held that the ordinance was neither overbroad nor an impermissible form of content regulation.

The U.S. Supreme Court rejected the conclusions of the Minnesota court and agreed unanimously on the infirmity of the St. Paul ordinance. This consensus, however, emerged from a convergence of two distinct lines of argument about the sources of that infirmity. Writing for the Court, Justice Scalia maintained that the regulation, understood to be restricted to fighting words, was an impermissible form of content discrimination; rejecting this contention, the separate concurrences by Justices White and Stevens held that it was not really restricted to fighting words and so was objectionably overbroad.[122] I am concerned here with the majority's claim: *even as restricted to fighting words*, the regulation is impermissibly content-discriminatory. To state the problem more exactly, assuming, as the majority does, that fighting words are a proscribable category of expression, is it permissible to focus a regulation on the particular subcategory of fighting words mentioned in the ordinance? Let us call the subcategory "hateful fighting words." We have two competing proposals, then: (1) regulating hateful fighting words represents an impermissible regulation of subject matter (and perhaps viewpoint); and (2) regulating hateful fighting words represents a permissible targeting of a subcategory of concededly low value and regulable expression on grounds of the special injuriousness of that subcategory.

Three Points of Agreement

To situate the disagreement between these two proposals more precisely, we need first to clarify three points of common ground.

First, proscribable expression is not without protection. From the fact that the government could proscribe a whole category of expression, say, child pornography, it does not follow that every less-inclusive regulation proscribing a subclass and permitting the rest is also acceptable: think of a child pornography statute restricted to that in which at least one actor wears an "I like Dan Quayle" button; or a regulation of obscenity produced after supper. Regulations targeted on those subcategories are unacceptable. So the argument for restricting hateful fighting words cannot count among its premises the claim that every subcategory of a proscribable category can permissibly be targeted.

Second, subcategories can sometimes be restricted on the basis of their content. Agreeing that fighting words (along with obscenity and defamation) are proscribable because of their content, the majority accepts further that regulations can target certain subcategories of proscribable expression in virtue of the distinctive content of those subcategories. The federal government, for example, can "criminalize only those threats of violence that are directed against the President."[123] So the argument against regulating hateful fighting words cannot count among its premises the claim that *all* content-based regulations of subcategories of fighting words are impermissible.

Taking these first two points together, the disagreement is about the specific subcategory singled out by the St. Paul ordinance. That disagreement, in turn, is sharpened by a third point of agreement between the two positions: It is impermissible to proscribe all speech that arouses anger, alarm, or resentment on the basis of race, color, creed, religion, or gender.[124] Such a regulation would aim at, and almost certainly produce, an unacceptable "suppression of ideas." The issue, then, is whether a regulation targeted specifically at *fighting words* that "arouse anger, alarm, or resentment" is acceptable.

Regulating Hateful Fighting Words

With these three points in place, we can fix the precise disagreement and assess the alternative positions.

The first view is that a regulation of hateful fighting words triggers exactly the same suspicion about the suppression of ideas as would be triggered by a *general* hate-speech regulation, directed to all speech that arouses anger, alarm, or resentment in others on the basis of race, color, creed, religion, or gender. The underlying principle that bars a general regulation of hate speech (the third point of agreement) is that hateful messages are not proscribable because of their content. They do not forfeit that immunity because they travel in a vehicle that is, for reasons other than the hate message, dangerous. Thus, immediate provocative speech can be regulated. But the fact that a hateful message is conveyed, for example, in an immediately provocative way does not make it permissible to target it as distinct from other messages conveyed in an equally (or more) provocative way.

Content regulation threatens us with the official suppression of ideas; so the question is always whether the "official suppression of ideas is afoot."[125] That question, according to the first view, loses none of its force when a regulation is targeted on a proscribable category of speech; the fact that expression falls into a less-protected category does not make it permissible to use a regulation of such expression as a device to restrict concededly protected messages.[126]

The alternative view is that there is indeed less concern about content discrimination, less concern about the suppression of ideas, when regulated speech falls into a proscribable category. Why? The neatest answer would be this: "How could there be any concern about the suppression of ideas? Expression in proscribable categories conveys no ideas." But that will not do; different obscene movies, for example, can convey competing ideas about the pleasures of different sorts of sex.[127] More to the point, if hateful fighting words did not communicate anything, there would be no point in targeting them. Nor would it be right simply to insist that if a category is proscribable then we are less concerned about protecting it. That is of course true in some way. But it does not indicate any reason for reduced concern about content discrimination, and it threatens to fly in the face of the first point of agreement noted earlier, that proscribable expression has some protection. The explanation for the reduced concern about content regulation cannot lie in the bare fact that expression belongs to a proscribable category but must instead be provided by the reason for treating it as proscribable in the first place.

Consider, then, the category of fighting words. Such words are provocations directed to individuals and comprise "no essential part of the exposition of ideas." For that reason, concerns about the official suppression of ideas are naturally reduced when regulations are targeted on them; it is, intuitively, difficult to see how a regulation targeted on expression that is no essential part of the exposition of ideas could seriously threaten to drive certain ideas, topics, or viewpoints from the marketplace of ideas or the forum of political debate.[128]

More specifically, recall the reasons for being especially troubled about regulations targeted on content (pp. 192ff.): they represent especially serious threats to the deliberative and expressive interests; the relative precision of their targeting raises the specter of the abuse of power in an especially acute way; and, even if such regulations are targeted on real evils, the fact of reasonable persuasion should lead us to trust more speech to address those evils.

Fighting words, however, are insults or provocations directed to individuals. So they do not make a significant contribution to discussion. The threat to deliberative interests seems, then, relatively small. Moreover, insofar as they serve as vehicles for expression, for advancing the expressive interest, proscribing them leaves a wide range of alternative vehicles. And the reasons for expression in the form of fighting words do not seem especially substantial. Taking these points together, it seems much less plausible that a regulation targeted on hateful fighting words would severely suppress ideas or would be motivated by a desire to suppress them than that a regulation targeted on hate speech generally would have that unacceptable effect or illegitimate motivation. So there does appear to be a substantial difference in the fears about suppression that would reasonably be triggered by a general regulation of hate speech and a regulation targeted specifically on the hateful subset of fighting words.

Of course, given the facts of power, easy offense, and abuse, concerns about suppression could be revived if a regulation were focused on a relatively insignificant harm. But racial subordination, for example,[129] is a serious evil, and it is at least plausible that racist fighting words play some role, perhaps a significant role, in maintaining racial inequality. They contribute to an environment of fear, suspicion, hostility, and mistrust that makes racial division so resistant to remedy. So the regulation does not pick out an arbitrary class of fighting words but a class that is especially damaging to fundamental political values, for example, the value of racial equality. Finally, it seems especially implausible that the injuries produced by hateful fighting words can be remedied with more speech. The anger, fear, and suspicion that they produce is not easily addressed by verbal reassurances.

The regulation, then, is targeted on a category with only a minimal connection with the fundamental deliberative and expressive interests, and within that category it focuses on a subcategory that is plausibly more injurious than other elements of the category and whose effects are plausibly more recalcitrant to expressive cure. There are three responses to this argument, each of which aims to reinstate suspicions about the suppression of ideas in a regulation of hateful fighting words.

The first is that there is a straightforward basis for the suspicion: it is agreed, as I indicated earlier, that a *general* hate-speech regulation would threaten us with the suppression of ideas. But if it is unacceptable to single out hateful words for special regulation, why is it not also unacceptable to restrict the hateful subset of fighting words? Contrast that restriction with one that singles out the fighting words that are especially likely to incite breach of the peace. Fighting words are low value in part because they tend to incite breach, so there could be no objection to singling out those fighting words that threaten, in more extreme form, the very evil that prompts the reduced protection in the first place.[130] But a regulation of hateful fighting words (arguably) does not pick out the especially provocative. So it is objectionable.

The problem with this objection is that it fails to take into consideration the bases for reduced protection for fighting words and the reasons for special concerns about content regulation. The category of fighting words is such that restricting expression within the category does not present a substantial threat of the suppression of ideas. But the suppression of ideas is the main threat posed by content regulation. So the explanation of the reduced protection for fighting words also explains why regulating hateful fighting words does not threaten the suppression of ideas and so accounts for the legitimacy of a form of content discrimination that would be unacceptable outside the limited context of fighting words.

A second reason for the concern might be a familiar "camel's nose" concern: once we allow the suppression of some subcategory of hate speech, we will be tempted to regulate hate speech generally. But that regulation is not legitimate.

The problem here is that the argument proves too much: it provides a case for an absolute ban on content regulation, a position that no one in the debate occupies (see the second of the three points of agreement noted above). Moreover, although the concern about excessive regulation is real, the point of carving out such less-protected categories as fighting words, obscenity, and commercial speech is precisely to address that concern. To endorse the strategy of categorization as a device against temptations to overregulate and then to revisit concerns about those temptations in the context of regulating subcategories strikes me as an exaggerated form of distrust, and one that runs up against the premise, accepted by the Court majority, that fighting words themselves are low value.

The third reason is that, although hateful fighting words are certainly offensive and insulting, even gross offensiveness and insult cannot provide a basis for regulation.[131] But to say that the "price" is offensiveness represents a tendentious misstatement of the harms. The harms of hateful fighting words are several and include the role of such words in sustaining racial division and preserving racial inequality.[132] This is a very great harm. Of course, not every restriction of expression that contributes to avoiding it is, for that reason, acceptable. But a regulation that might contribute, and do so without threatening to suppress ideas (for example, a regulation of hateful fighting words), is acceptable.

Pornographic Obscenity

In introducing this discussion of regulations of hateful fighting words, I presented such regulations as one example of the more general strategy of regulation by subcategorization. I have now indicated why the strategy is, as a general matter, unobjectionable. To clarify the basis of this view, I want now to say more about an example I discussed earlier, the case of pornographic obscenity.

I will assume the *Miller* test for obscenity.[133] According to that test, a work is obscene just in case it meets three conditions: the average person, applying community standards, finds that the work taken as a whole appeals to the prurient interest; the work presents an offensive depiction of sexual conduct; and it lacks serious literary, artistic, political, or scientific value. The intuition is that sexually preoccupied, offensive junk does not merit stringent constitutional protection. It is an interesting question, which I will not pursue here, why the sexual preoccupation makes a difference.[134] It does not appear to diminish the value of the expression, which by stipulation is not very great; furthermore, because the costs lie in offensiveness and expression can be offensive without being sexually preoccupied, the sexual content is not required for the costs. So why is it not permissible to regulate violence-preoccupied, offensive junk? Or offensive junk preoccupied with frightening people? Or with moneymaking? Or with cruelty? Leaving these questions for another occasion, I assume for the sake of argument that obscenity merits reduced protection. I want to ask about the implications of that assumption for regulating subcategories of the obscene.

Consider, then, three obscenity regulations. The first targets all obscene forms of expression. The second targets obscene expression in which
women are subjected to violence, what I referred to earlier as the "pornographically obscene." I stipulate a regulation covering all obscenity in
which women are subjected to violence, rather than obscenity in which
that violence is applauded, because I want the regulation to be content-
based but viewpoint-neutral.[135] The third regulation targets "grossly" obscene expression, by which I mean expression that is obscene and *grossly*
offensive by the lights of the community: perhaps golden-shower movies
and movies featuring oral sex with animals fall into this class.

Paralleling the earlier discussion of hateful fighting words, I distinguish
two natural responses to these regulations. The first is constructed on
analogy with a view that accepts a regulation targeted on extremely provocative fighting words but not one targeted on hateful fighting words. So
it would accept regulations of all the obscene or of only the grossly
obscene, but not of only the pornographically obscene.

Why would a regulation focused on the grossly offensive subcategory
be acceptable? Although the determination of gross offensiveness is a
matter of content (prohibitions on golden-shower movies and movies displaying oral sex with animals are subject-matter restrictions), and content
regulations are generally objectionable, offensiveness is precisely the reason for reducing the protection of the obscene in the first place. So if it is
permissible to target all offensive, prurient junk without engendering concern about suppressing ideas, then surely it is permissible to target the
grossly offensive, prurient junk without engendering such suspicion.

A regulation of the pornographically obscene is, like a regulation of the
grossly obscene, not subject-matter-neutral. But, this first line of response
emphasizes, it singles out for regulation a subcategory of the obscene on
the basis of considerations other than those that render it obscene in the
first place; the subclass of the violent might not correspond to the subcategory that is either *especially* prurient or *grossly* offensive in its prurience.
Moreover, a general regulation of pornography seems unacceptable, for
the reasons I indicated earlier. Because the feature that defines the subcategory is unrelated to obscenity, and because that feature *would* trigger
concern about the suppression of ideas if applied outside the context of
obscenity, it might be thought to trigger that concern here. Defenders of
the regulation will, to be sure, argue that the regulation is justified by
reference to the distinctive harms of the pornographically obscene. But if
those alleged harms cannot justify regulating pornography generally,
then why should they provide an acceptable rationale for regulating the
pornographically obscene?

Here again we meet the central concern: the fact that a whole category of expression is proscribable does not imply a reduced concern about the evil of a kind of content discrimination that would be unacceptable if applied to a wider category of expression.

Once more, however, an alternative view—constructed on analogy with the position that approves regulating hateful fighting words—seems more plausible. This alternative would accept the regulation of the pornographically obscene.[136] The contention fueling this second line of argument is that *if* obscenity is low value in the first place, then it is permissible to restrict pornographically obscene representations on grounds that such representations are injurious,[137] *even though* the alleged injuries would be insufficient to sustain the regulation of pornography generally. The reason is that regulating pornography generally does, for reasons I discussed earlier, present a substantial threat to fundamental expressive and deliberative interests. (This might be conceded even by those who argue that the threat is overpowered by injuries reasonably attributed to pornography.) But the basis for treating obscenity as low value is that it contributes little to the fundamental interests, thus, regulating it would not present a substantial threat to those interests. Because it would not, the concerns that provide the basis for opposing content discrimination are diminished. Because they are diminished, the injuries associated with the fusing of sex and violence by the pornographically obscene provide sufficient basis for regulation. Indeed, there is a better case for this regulation, which is focused on genuine harms, than for regulating either obscenity generally or grossly offensive obscenity. Those regulations aim to prevent the uncertain evil of offensiveness rather than the genuine evil of injuries to women.

6. Reflections on the Stanford Case

Finally, I come back to the Stanford regulation. At the beginning of this article, I promised to fit a pallid endorsement of it into the conception of freedom of expression I have outlined here. Everything I have said should suffice to explain the lack of enthusiasm (though I will add a few more considerations later on). What are the bases for the endorsement?

Recall that the regulation restricts "speech or other expression" that is (1) *intended* to insult or stigmatize individuals on the basis of their sex, race, color, handicap, religion, sexual orientation, or national and ethnic origin; (2) addressed *directly* to the individual or individuals whom it insults or stigmatizes; and (3) makes use of insulting or "fighting words" or nonverbal symbols that are "commonly understood to convey direct and visceral hatred or contempt for human beings on the basis of their sex, race, etc."

My endorsement reflects three features of the regulation, each of which indicates sensitivity to the case for stringent protection that I have presented here:

1. The regulation is directed to remarks that are *intended* to insult, and the insult must be directed to an individual or small group. So the regulated expression bears at most a loose connection to the fundamental expressive and deliberative interests.

2. The insult must be conveyed through fighting words, particularly words that insult or stigmatize on the basis of sex, race, color, and so on. Because of the requirement of immediate provocation and injury associated with fighting words, some of the costs are direct and there is no deflecting them with "more speech."

3. The rule singles out an exceptional category and does not represent an open-ended invitation to balancing the benefits and costs of expression. So it is attentive to concerns about vulnerability.

Given the minimal interests, direct costs, and attention to potential abuse, the supports for protection are substantially reduced, and it seems appropriate (or at least permissible) to shift the burden of restraint to the speaker.

To be sure, the regulation is not without its troubles, principally because (as interpreted) it would be viewpoint-discriminatory; for example, racist remarks addressed to Black students could (depending on conditions) count as a form of discriminatory harassment; racist remarks to white students do not.[138] Is the general presumption against such discrimination rebuttable in this case?

In assessing the troublesomeness of the viewpoint discrimination, we need to keep in focus the requirements of intent and fighting words and the stipulation that the words be directed to an individual or group with the intent to insult or stigmatize. Expression meeting these conditions has only a marginal claim to protection in the first place. So, as I indicated in the discussion of hateful fighting words, it seems *permissible* to deny protection to a subcategory of it in order to promote the substantial value of ensuring equality of educational opportunity for the groups singled out in the regulation.

Of course "permissible" does not imply "recommended." Other considerations are relevant to deciding that issue. How much injurious expression would actually be avoided? Would the regulation be at all effective in combating the underlying problems reflected in hate speech? Furthermore, apart from addressing these questions about the regulation itself, we need to consider the wisdom of focusing energy and attention on regulating hate speech (or pornography) rather than on taking more affirmative measures to combat the harms that the regulation aims to avoid.

The focus on regulating expression has at least three defects: it can distract energy from other measures; it divides people who are allied in their commitment to equality; and it suggests a depressingly profound loss of constructive, egalitarian, political and social imagination.

Together, these considerations strike me as good grounds for skepticism. To be sure, such skepticism is not costly for those of us who are not now targets of hate speech.[139] This point has some force, and so I do not treat my skepticism about effectiveness as a basis for rejecting the regulations as inconsistent with a commitment to stringent protections of expressive liberty.

But ineffectiveness could in turn lead to pressure for more stringent regulations in the name of equality. And this could represent a serious challenge to the conception of freedom of expression I have sketched here. If the harms of subordination cannot be fought with more speech and other nonrestrictive remedies, then, the world being as it is, a commitment to substantive equality simply cannot be reconciled with a strong affirmation of expressive liberties. If my account of the basis of freedom of expression is correct, then that conclusion would not show that we ought to give up on the value of equality, because, as I indicated early on, nothing in the defense turns on a freestanding preference for liberty over all competing values, particularly a freestanding preference for liberty over equality. Nor would it show that we ought to give up on the value of liberty. Instead, we would face a grim standoff between concerns about expressive liberty and concerns about equality.

So those of us who celebrate the values of equality, toleration, and expressive liberty—and the remedial powers of speech in reconciling these values—ought to conduct our celebration by getting to work.

Notes

* An earlier version of this paper appeared in *Philosophy and Public Affairs* 22, 3 (summer 1993): 207–63. I have made exclusively editorial and stylistic changes in preparing this version and wish to thank Carol Roberts for her many helpful suggestions. In particular, I have not modified the paper to take account of the February 1995 decision of Santa Clara County Superior Court in *Corry v. Stanford* to overturn the Stanford speech code, which I discuss below at pp. 173–74 and 212–14. The court's decision relied on Justice Scalia's opinion in *R. A. V. v. St. Paul*, 112 S. Ct. 2538 (1992). I criticize that opinion in section 5. I have presented talks based on earlier drafts of this paper at Haverford College, the University of California (Davis), the John F. Kennedy School of Government, Wellesley College, the University of Illinois (Chicago), Northwestern University, Amherst College, New York University, the Inter-Africa Group Symposium "On the Making of the New Ethiopian Constitution," and the Society for Ethical and Legal

Philosophy. I am grateful to my audiences for their criticisms and suggestions. I also thank C. Edwin Baker, Randall Forsberg, John Rawls, John Simmons, and Cass Sunstein for comments on previous versions, and Archon Fung for his research assistance. More generally, I am very much indebted to Thomas Scanlon's papers on freedom of expression, in particular his "Freedom of Expression and Categories of Expression," *University of Pittsburgh Law Review* (1979): 519–50.

1. See Charles Lawrence, "If He Hollers Let Him Go: Regulating Racist Speech on Campus," *Duke Law Journal* (1990): 431–83; Mari Matsuda, "Public Response to Racist Speech: Considering the Victim's Story," *Michigan Law Review* 87 (1989): 2320–81; Richard Delgado, "Campus Antiracism Rules: Constitutional Narratives in Collision," *Northwestern University Law Review* 85 (1991): 343–87.

2. See, for example, George Will, "Curdled Politics on Campus," *Newsweek*, May 6, 1991, 72; Chester E. Finn, "The Campus: 'An Island of Repression in a Sea of Freedom,'" *Commentary* (September 1989): 17–23.

3. *Doe v. University of Michigan*, 721 F. Supp. 852 (E.D. Michigan, 1989).

4. See ibid. at 865–66 for discussion of cases of enforcement against comments made in the course of classroom discussion.

5. See David Kretzmer, "Freedom of Speech and Racism," *Cardozo Law Review* 8 (1987): 445–513; Eric Stein, "History against Free Speech: The New German Law against the 'Auschwitz'-and Other 'Lies,'" *Michigan Law Review* 85 (1986): 275–324; Kenneth Lasson, "Racism in Great Britain: Drawing the Line of Free Speech," *Boston College Third World Law Journal* 6 (1987): 161–81; Robert Sedler, "The Constitutional Protection of Religion, Expression, and Association in Canada and the United States: A Comparative Analysis," *Case Western Reserve Journal of International Law* 20 (1988): 577–621; Matsuda, "Public Response to Racist Speech"; Delgado, "Campus Antiracism Rules."

6. But it does appear to be inconsistent with the current view of the Supreme Court on permissible forms of state regulation of speech. See *R. A. V. v. St. Paul*, 122 S. Ct. 2538 (1992). I discuss this view in section 5.

7. In saying that it is not very restrictive, I do not mean to say that it is, therefore, an acceptable restriction. "No one whose first name includes the letters *z* and *y* may criticize impressionist painting" is not very restrictive but is also not acceptable.

8. *Doe v. University of Michigan* at 853, 868, emphases added. Cohn did not indicate the sorts of measures that might be consistent with the First Amendment.

9. As much in informal conversations about these issues as in the legal and philosophical literature.

10. See Stanley Fish, "There's No Such Thing as Free Speech," *Boston Review* 17 (January–February 1992): 3–4, 23–26. I do not mean "nihilistic" as tendentious labeling or as a term of criticism, but only as a way to capture the "there is no such thing" point in the quotation in the text. The view could be called "pragmatism" about expression, but this misses its critical edge.

11. Ibid., p. 26.

12. For a response to nihilism, see below, pp. 195–97.

13. See, for example, Vincent Blasi, "The Pathological Perspective and the First Amendment," *Columbia Law Review* 85 (1985): 449–514.

14. For an argument based more fundamentally on mistrust, see Richard Epstein, "Property, Speech, and the Politics of Distrust," *University of Chicago Law Review* 59 (1992): 41–90. For criticisms, see Frank Michelman, "Liberties, Fair Values, and Constitutional Method," *University of Chicago Law Review* 59 (1992): 91–114.

15. Cass Sunstein criticizes my view along these lines. He suggests that legal principles emerging from it might be "too complex, ad hoc, and unruly." See Sunstein, *Democracy*, p. 146. I address this concern in my discussion of specific issues in sections 4 and 5.

16. For the suggestion that it does so depend, see Ronald Dworkin, "Two Concepts of Liberty," in *Isaiah Berlin: A Celebration*, ed. Edna Ullmann-Margalit and Avishai Margalit (London: Hogarth Press, 1991), pp. 100–109.

17. In this connection, I thank Ed Baker for pointing out a number of blunders that marred the penultimate draft of the paper.

18. The classic statement of the general concern is Justice Marshall's in *Police Department of Chicago v. Mosley*, 408 U.S. 92, 95–96 (1972): "[A]bove all else, the First Amendment means that government has no power to restrict expression because of its message, its ideas, its subject matter, or its content." On viewpoint discrimination, see *Texas v. Johnson*, 491 U.S. 397, 414 (1989). For discussion, see John Hart Ely, "Flag Desecration: A Case Study in the Roles of Categorization and Balancing in First Amendment Decisions," *Harvard Law Review* (1975): 1482–1508; Geoffrey Stone, "Restrictions of Speech Because of its Content: The Peculiar Case of Subject-Matter Restrictions," *University of Chicago Law Review* 46 (1978): 81–115, and "Content-Neutral Restrictions," *University of Chicago Law Review* 54 (1987): 46–120; and T. M. Scanlon, Jr., "Content-Regulation Reconsidered," in *Democracy and the Mass Media*, ed. Judith Lichtenberg (Cambridge: Cambridge University Press, 1990), pp. 331–54.

19. For example, on incitement, see *Brandenburg v. Ohio*, 395 U.S. 444 (1968); on commercial speech, *Virginia State Board of Pharmacy v. Virginia Citizens Consumer Council*, 425 U.S. 748 (1976), *Central Hudson Gas and Electric v. Public Service Commission of New York*, 447 U.S. 557 (1980), *Posadas de Puerto Rico Associates v. Tourism Company of Puerto Rico*, 106 S. Ct. 2968 (1986); on fighting words, *Chaplinsky v. New Hampshire*, 315 U.S. 568 (1942); on child pornography, *Ferber v. New York*, 458 U.S. 747 (1982).

20. I emphasize that I am using this protean term exclusively as a label for the approach to content regulation described here.

21. For doubts about the virtues of categorization and corresponding skepticism about categorically formulated prohibitions on content regulation, see John Paul Stevens, "The Freedom of Speech," *Yale Law Journal* 102 (1993): 1293–1313.

22. For a subtle discussion of the structure of argument about content-neutral regulations and of the extent to which the thumb gets put on the balance for different sorts of regulations, see Stone, "Content-Neutral Restrictions."

23. By "costs" or a "price," I mean, quite generically, conditions that it is reasonable to want to avoid.

24. See *Schneider v. State*, 308 U.S. 147 (1939) (on cleanup costs); *New York Times v. Sullivan*, 376 U.S. 254 (1964) (on reputational injury); *Cohen v. Califor-*

nia, 403 U.S. 15 (1971) (on offense); *Hustler v. Falwell*, 485 U.S. 46 (1988) (on intentional infliction of emotional distress).

25. Say, a fine for leaving a pile of leaflets sitting on a bench for people to pick up.

26. *New York Times v. Sullivan*, 376 U.S. 254, 279–80 (1964).

27. *Hustler v. Falwell*, 485 U.S. 46, 50 (1988).

28. On the idea of the value of a liberty, see John Rawls, *A Theory of Justice* (Cambridge, Mass.: Harvard University Press, 1971), pp. 204–5. On the rationale for requiring a fair value for political liberty in particular and the permissibility of (content-neutral) regulations of political speech in order to ensure that fair value, see John Rawls, "The Basic Liberties and Their Priority," *Political Liberalism* (New York: Columbia University Press, 1993), lecture 8, secs. 7, 12.

29. See Frank Michelman, "Universities, Racist Speech, and Democracy in America," *Harvard Civil Rights–Civil Liberties Law Review* 27 (1992): 352.

30. See, for example, Catharine MacKinnon, "Francis Biddle's Sister," in *Feminism Unmodified* (Cambridge, Mass.: Harvard University Press, 1987), pp. 163–97; for discussion of the silencing argument, see Frank Michelman, "Conceptions of Democracy in American Constitutional Argument: The Case of Pornography," *Tennessee Law Review* 56 (1989): 291–319; and the critical appraisal in Ronald Dworkin, "Two Concepts of Liberty."

31. For an extended elaboration of the importance of this point for free speech doctrine, see Cass Sunstein's discussion of a New Deal for speech in "Free Speech Now," *The University of Chicago Law Review* 59 (1992): 255–316, esp. 263–77, 316.

32. Ronald Dworkin, "Do We Have a Right to Pornography," in *A Matter of Principle* (Cambridge, Mass.: Harvard University Press, 1985), pp. 335–72. For an excellent discussion of the limits of this argument, see Rae Langton, "Whose Right? Ronald Dworkin, Women, and Pornographers," *Philosophy and Public Affairs* 19 (1990): 311–59. Dworkin's recent discussions of expressive liberty seem less minimalist. In "What Is Equality? Part 3: The Place of Liberty," he ties the value of expressive liberties to the formation of "authentic preferences" (*Iowa Law Review* 72 [1987]: 34–36). In "The Coming Battles over Free Speech," he notes the importance of an active side to personal responsibility (*New York Review of Books*, June 11, 1992, 57).

33. For criticism of the project of founding an account of freedom of expression on a prior expression action distinction, see T. M. Scanlon, "A Theory of Freedom of Expression," *Philosophy and Public Affairs* 1 (1972): 205–8.

34. Indeed, as Scanlon emphasizes, the central task for a theory of freedom of expression is to explain why this should be so. See ibid., p. 204.

35. See *Schneider v. State*, 308 U.S. 147, 161 (1939).

36. To put the point in a constitutional slogan: you cannot derive the First Amendment from the equal-protection clause of the Fourteenth Amendment.

37. The maximalist need not hold that the value is intrinsic, nor that there is just a single value associated with expression. I am indebted to Connie Rosati for urging this clarification.

38. See, for example, Scanlon's listener-autonomy theory in "A Theory of Freedom of Expression," pp. 204–26, and his criticisms of that theory in "Free-

dom of Expression and Categories of Expression," pp. 534–35. In "Persuasion, Autonomy, and Expression," *Columbia Law Review* 91 (1991): 334–71, David Strauss aims to rescue a version of Scanlon's theory from these criticisms. Strauss condemns restrictions of speech justified by reference to the harmful results of the speech's persuasive power as inconsistent with listener autonomy.

39. This complaint is registered in Scanlon, "Freedom of Expression and Categories of Expression"; Steven H. Schiffrin, *The First Amendment, Democracy, and Romance* (Cambridge, Mass.: Harvard University Press, 1990), chap. 4. On the contrast between the complexity of the terrain and the simplicity of familiar theories, see Harry Kalven, *A Worthy Tradition: Freedom of Speech in America*, ed. Jamie Kalven (New York: Harper and Row, 1988), p. 23.

40. In "Persuasion, Autonomy, and Expression," Strauss argues that persuasion is "a process of appealing, in some sense, to reason" (p. 335) and that we ought not to regulate expression when its harmful effects come from its power to persuade. Thus false advertising gets reduced protection because it does not work by persuasion, as though we were in no danger of being persuaded by liars; nonobscene pornography is protected because it does work by persuasion, as though the scenes of the Washington Monument and American flag featured at the start of some triple-X-rated movies were representative. Here I lose my hold on his conception of persuasion, and so of his argument about commercial speech.

41. See, in general, Thomas Emerson, *The System of Freedom of Expression* (New York: Random House, Vintage, 1971). Lee C. Bollinger emphasizes as well the importance of encouraging tolerance in *The Tolerant Society* (Oxford: Oxford University Press, 1986); and Vincent Blasi examines the role of freedom of expression as a check on official misconduct in "The Checking Value in First Amendment Theory," *American Bar Foundation Research Journal* 3 (1977): 521–649.

42. For fuller discussion, see my "Moral Pluralism and Political Consensus," in *The Idea of Democracy*, ed. David Copp, Jean Hampton, and John Roemer (Cambridge: Cambridge University Press, 1993), pp. 281–87; also see Rawls, *Political Liberalism*, pp. 35–38.

43. There is, for example, this logical distinction: two inconsistent views can both be fully reasonable, though they cannot both be true.

44. I take this formulation from Mark Johnston.

45. I say "perhaps" because expression often has nothing to do with communication. See C. Edwin Baker, *Human Liberty and Freedom of Speech* (Oxford: Oxford University Press, 1989), pp. 51–54. I am grateful to Randall Forsberg for her helpful comments on an earlier draft in which I characterized the expressive interest much too narrowly.

46. My emphasis on reasons in the description of the expressive interest distinguishes my treatment from conventional discussion of the value of self-expression and self-fulfillment. When someone fulfils what they take to be an obligation (as specified by their moral views, for example), it is wrong to treat this as a matter of self-expression or self-fulfillment.

47. Here I follow a suggestion advanced in Rawls's discussion of liberty of conscience: the rationale for liberty of conscience lies in obligations that religious

and moral views assign to those who hold them, and this rationale can in some measure be extended to other liberties. See *Theory of Justice*, p. 206.

48. *Whitney v. California*, 274 U.S. 357, 375 (1927) (Brandeis, J., concurring).

49. See, for example, *Barnes v. Glen Theatre, Inc.*, 111 S. Ct. 2456 (1991) (White, J., dissenting).

50. See Kathy Acker, "Devoured by Myths: An Interview with Sylvère Lotringer," in *Hannibal Lecter, My Father* (New York: Semiotext(e), 1991), and the interview of Acker in *Angry Women*, ed. Andrea Juno and V. Vale (San Francisco: Re/Search, 1991), pp. 184–85.

51. Cited in Edward de Grazia, *Girls Lean Back Everywhere: The Law of Obscenity and the Assault on Genius* (New York: Random House, 1992), pp. 459–60.

52. See his "Free Speech Now" and *Democracy and the Problem of Free Speech* (New York: Free Press, 1993).

53. See, in particular, his four reasons for special protection for political speech, only the first of which is concerned specifically with constitutional interpretation, in *Democracy*, pp. 132–37. Of course, his view is also controversial as constitutional interpretation.

54. Ibid., p. 134.

55. Sunstein, "Free Speech Now," p. 308.

56. Just for the record, I think it is neither instructive nor raving.

57. Expression that falls outside the upper tier is not for that reason without protection. Thus the formulation in terms of "level of protection."

58. See Sunstein, *Democracy*, pp. 134–35.

59. Absent a precise delineation of the category of political speech, the empirical issue is hard to adjudicate. But some reasons for doubting the case for special vulnerability are suggested in de Grazia, *Girls Lean Back Everywhere*, and William Noble, *Bookbanning in America* (Middlebury, Conn.: Erikson, 1990).

60. On the issue of American constitutional tradition, Sunstein associates his own conception of freedom of expression with Brandeis's focus on deliberation rather than Holmes's marketplace of ideas. See Sunstein, *Democracy*, pp. 23–28. But Brandeis's concurrence in *Whitney v. California* is perhaps the classic statement of the very great constitutional weight of the interests protected by the right to freedom of expression; it is not about the special vulnerability of political speech to government restriction. 274 U.S. 357, 373–78 (1927).

61. This is the force of Mill's contention that censorship robs the human race and that for this reason is does not matter whether all censor one or one censors all. Mill does not focus on the harm or robbery to the person who is censored. See the first paragraph of *On Liberty*, chap. 2, par. 1.

62. Robert Post has suggested a tension among various conditions required for satisfying the deliberative interest in a diverse community. In particular, deliberation depends on civility, but requiring civility puts the community in danger of making one particular understanding of civility authoritative for the community. I am not sure how deep this tension goes. To be sure, civility has its place in public deliberation. But so do anger, disgust, bitter criticism, and open expressions of

hostility. Post's immediate concern is with a parody of Reverend Jerry Falwell in Larry Flynt's *Hustler* magazine. Suffice it to say here that the parody of Falwell was, in my view, a contribution to public debate, even if it was not civil and not an invitation to Falwell to have a conversation with Flynt. See Robert Post, "The Constitutional Concept of Public Discourse: Outrageous Opinion, Democratic Deliberation, and *Hustler Magazine v. Falwell*," *Harvard Law Review* 103 (1990): 601–86.

63. Joseph Raz proposes that part of the case for a right to freedom of expression turns on the "fundamental need for public validation of one's way of life" together with the fact that acts of expression serve the purpose of "validation" in three ways: they inform the public about "ways of life common in certain segments of the public"; they reassure "those whose ways of life are being portrayed that they are not alone"; and they provide a "stamp of public acceptability" for those ways of life. See Raz, "Free Expression and Personal Identification," *Oxford Journal of Legal Studies* 11 (1991): 311, 324. I agree with Raz about the importance of the interest in validation, but believe that it can be accounted for in terms of the expressive, deliberative, and informational interests.

64. *Abrams v. U.S.*, 250 U.S. 616, 629 (1918) (Holmes, J., dissenting).

65. Cited from Kalven's notes in the editor's introduction to *A Worthy Tradition*, p. xxii.

66. See, in particular, Matsuda, "Public Response to Racist Speech"; Lawrence, "If He Hollers Let Him Go"; Delgado, "Campus Antiracism Rules."

67. *Chaplinsky v. New Hampshire*, 315 U.S. 568, 571–72 (1942). Or, where the "evil" is "created by the medium of expression itself," as in the case of signs posted on utility poles, as distinct from leaflets handed to individuals. See *City Council v. Taxpayers for Vincent*, 466 U.S. 789, 810 (1984).

68. A work environment, for example, can be actionably hostile under Title VII of the Civil Rights Act either because of the severity or the pervasiveness of conduct. See *Meritor Savings Bank v. Vinson*, 477 U.S. 57, 67 (1986). For discussion of severity and pervasiveness, see *Ellison v. Brady*, 924 F.2d 872 (9th Circuit, 1991).

69. Scanlon discusses the importance of "linking empirical beliefs" in arguments about right to expressive liberty. His discussion overstates, I believe, the importance of beliefs specifically about the role of government in suppressing expression. See "Freedom of Expression and Categories of Expression," p. 534.

70. For a general discussion of the tendency of legal-doctrinal argument to suppress reference to background factual assumptions, see Roberto Unger, *The Critical Legal Studies Movement* (Cambridge, Mass.: Harvard University Press, 1982). In the case of freedom of expression, Bollinger claims that the "fortress model" of speech protection presumes a set of irrational tendencies to suppress speech that conflicts with the assumption of rational competence that drives the ideal of an open market of ideas. So the conjunction of these two doctrines in a justification of free expression is untenable because it requires inconsistent background beliefs. See *The Tolerant Society*, pp. 92–93.

71. *Whitney v. California*, 274 U.S. 357, 375–76, 377 (1927) (concurring).

72. Cited in *New York Times v. Sullivan*, 376 U.S. 254, 271 (1964).

73. On the problems of regulating outrageous insults, see *Hustler v. Falwell*, 485 U.S. 46 (1988).

74. This is of course true of public officials but hardly unique to them. It is commonly said that they are especially untrustworthy, but I know of no evidence for the claim that political power breeds arrogance more surely than economic power.

75. As Mill put it, "No one acknowledges to himself that his standard of judgement is his own liking." See *On Liberty*, chap. 1, par. 6. The point is not that standards of judgment are, in general, simply matters of liking and disliking but rather that, even when they are, we do not see them that way.

76. Bollinger in effect argues that there is a fundamental conflict between appealing to the facts of reasonableness and to the unhappy facts of life. See *The Tolerant Society*, pp. 92–93. I do not see the conflict.

77. Paraphrasing Justice Roberts in *Cantwell v. Connecticut*, 310 U.S. 296, 310 (1940).

78. Alexander Meikeljohn, *Political Freedom* (New York: Harper and Brothers, 1960), p. 27.

79. *Brandenburg v. Ohio*, 395 U.S. 444, 447 (1968).

80. Here I disagree with the defense of group libel laws in "A Communitarian Defense of Group Libel Laws," *Harvard Law Review* 101 (1988): 682–701. The main reason for rejecting regulations of group libel is not that such libel is harmless. See, for example, Justice Black's dissent in *Beauharnais v. Illinois*, 343 U.S. 250 (1952). Black does not deny the costs but emphasizes the extensive "inroads" on expression that would result from accepting regulations of group libel.

81. Edwin Baker proposes that commercial speech ought to have no First Amendment protection in part because such speech reflects the coercive logic of profit maximization rather than the choice of the speaker. This explanation strikes me as a strained defense of the idea that regulations of commercial speech are less burdensome, not least because it suggests that advertising by price-setting monopolists, which is less subject to the coercive demands of profit maximization, ought to be more protected. See *Human Liberty and Freedom of Speech*, chap. 9.

82. See *Virginia State Board of Pharmacy v. Virginia Citizens Consumer Council*, 425 U.S. 748, 771 (note 24) (1976), and 777–81 (Stewart, J., concurring).

83. My discussion here is influenced by Ely, "Flag Desecration," pp. 1496–1502.

84. This concern is expressed in *Hustler v. Falwell*, 485 U.S. 46 (1988).

85. Fish, "There's No Such Thing," p. 23.

86. See ibid., p. 26. I am indebted to Duncan Kennedy for discussion of this point.

87. Ibid.

88. Black, "The Bill of Rights," *New York University Law Review* 35 (1960): 879.

89. Fish, "There's No Such Thing," p. 26.

90. Ibid.

91. I take this example from my "Moral Pluralism and Political Consensus," p. 286.

92. It is an analog to "creation science," operating in the domain of salvation. The proper response is the same in both cases.

93. Most fundamentalists are not rationalist fundamentalists and would, I think, agree with this response.

94. I offer the rationalist fundamentalist simply as one illustration. The case of the nonrationalist fundamentalist, who affirms that the basis of religious conviction lies in faith, is more complicated. The latter might wish to distinguish truths delivered by faith from the bases of political justification, and so might be prepared to acknowledge expressive and deliberative interests, at least in the context of political argument.

95. See *Hustler v. Falwell*, 485 U.S. 46 (1988).

96. See *Cohen v. California*, 403 U.S. 15 (1971).

97. Indianapolis, Ind., City-Council General Ordinance No. 35 (June 11, 1984), cited in MacKinnon, *Feminism Unmodified*, p. 274, n. 1. I present a more detailed account of pornography regulation in "Liberty, Equality, Pornography," in *Justice and Injustice in Law and Legal Theory*, ed. Austin Sarat and Thomas Kearns (Ann Arbor: University of Michigan Press, 1996, forthcoming).

98. Lisa Duggan, Nan Hunter, and Carole Vance, "False Promises: Feminist Antipornography Legislation," in *Caught Looking: Feminism, Pornography and Censorship* (East Haven, Conn.: Long River Books, 1992), p. 82. The authors were members of the Feminist Anti-Pornography Task Force.

99. Though the rationale for the regulations was emphatically not moral. See Catharine MacKinnon, "Not a Moral Issue," in *Feminism Unmodified*.

100. I take the proposal from Duncan Kennedy, "Sexual Abuse, Sexy Dressing and the Eroticization of Domination," *New England Law Review* 26 (1992): 1318.

101. For a more general discussion of associative approaches to reconciling egalitarian and liberal commitment, see Joshua Cohen and Joel Rogers, "Secondary Associations and Democratic Governance," *Politics and Society* 20 (1992): 393–472.

102. See, for example, Cass Sunstein's proposal in "Pornography and the First Amendment," *Duke Law Journal* 4 (1986): 589–627. He sharply narrows the class of pornographic expression, defining the class in a way that aims to make it low value. It amounts, more or less (and implicitly), to substituting "erotizes violence and subordination" for "offensive" in the definition of obscenity.

103. There was, for example, no suggestion that Falwell was really responsible for the distress because of a hypersensitivity to accusations of sin.

104. *Whitney v. California*, 274 U.S. 357 (1927) (Brandeis, J., concurring).

105. Ibid., 375.

106. As, for example, in Rawls's argument that reflection on the ideal of natural liberty leads to the ideal of democratic equality. See *Theory of Justice*, pp. 65–74; and my discussion of the bootstrapping strategy in "Moral Pluralism and Political Consensus," pp. 278–79.

107. Reasoning of broadly this kind can be found in *Metro Broadcasting, Inc. v. FCC*, 100 S. Ct. 2997 (1990), where the Court upholds an FCC program aimed

at increasing broadcast diversity by increasing the number of minorities holding broadcast licenses. For criticisms, see Charles Fried, "*Metro Broadcasting, Inc. v. FCC*: Two Concepts of Equality," *Harvard Law Review* 104 (1990): 107–27.

108. See Owen Fiss, "Silence on the Street Corner," *Suffolk University Law Review* 26 (1992): 13–14.

109. Current tendencies in doctrine are, more or less, opposite to the suggestion here. See *U.S. v. Kokinda*, 110 S. Ct. 3115 (1990); and the discussion in Fiss, "Silence on the Street Corner."

110. For an argument—close to the perspective in this article—that the current private scheme of campaign financing violates requirements of equal protection, and a sketch of alternative directions of reform, see Jamin Raskin and John Bonifaz, "Equal Protection and the Wealth Primary," *Yale Law and Policy Review* 11 (1993): 273–335. For an instructive discussion of campaign finance that focuses more or less exclusively on the deliberative interest, see Charles Beitz, *Political Equality* (Princeton, N.J.: Princeton University Press, 1989), chap. 9.

111. *Buckley v. Valeo*, 424 U.S. 1 (1976). It is consistent with *Buckley* to move to a system of voluntary public financing, with matching funds for candidates whose opponents opt for private contributions, or to spend their own money. For a sketch of such a system, see Ellen S. Miller, "Money, Politics, and Democracy," *Boston Review* 18 (March/April 1993): 5–8.

112. *Buckley v. Vale*, 424 U.S. 1, 48–49 (1976).

113. Ibid.

114. Ibid.

115. MacKinnon, "Francis Biddle's Sister," p. 193.

116. For discussion, see Susan Moller Okin, *Justice, Gender, and the Family* (New York: Basic Books, 1989).

117. MacKinnon, "Francis Biddle's Sister," p. 193 (my emphasis).

118. I take the term from *R. A. V. v. St. Paul*, 112 S. Ct. 2538, 2546 (1992).

119. Minnesota Legislative Code §292.02 (1990), cited in ibid., 2541.

120. *Chaplinsky v. New Hampshire*, 315 U.S. 568, 571–72 (1942). For a recent statement of doubts about the fighting-words doctrine, see "The Demise of the *Chaplinsky* Fighting Words Doctrine: An Argument for Its Interment," *Harvard Law Review* 106 (1993): 1129–46.

121. This is the basis of the reasoning by the Minnesota court. Scalia's opinion emphatically rejects this claim. See *R. A. V. v. St. Paul*, 112 S. Ct. 2543.

122. The Minnesota court said it was restricted to fighting words. But the concurrences rejected that court's construal of the fighting-words test. Ibid., 2558–60.

123. Ibid., 2546.

124. See ibid., 2558–60 (White, J., dissenting). This point is not very controversial, even among defenders of hate-speech regulations. See, for example, Lawrence, "If He Hollers Let Him Go."

125. *R. A. V. v. St. Paul*, 112 S. Ct. 2547.

126. Even this misses the full subtlety of the majority view. They suggest that the Title VII ban on hostile work environment sex discrimination "may" permissibly regulate "sexually derogatory 'fighting words', among other words" (ibid., 2546). But it is permissible to regulate sexually derogatory fighting words in the

workplace only as an "incidental" effect of a general protection against hostile work environments. The fact that the regulation of speech was an incidental part of a general code of conduct would immediately answer the concern that the speech itself was being regulated because of its message rather than because of its harmful effects.

127. Thus Scalia's firm distinction between "no part" of the exposition of ideas and "no essential part." Ibid., 2544. Implicit in these remarks is that the suggestion that the concurrences endorse the tempting but implausible view I note in the text.

128. There is certainly no "prohibition of public discussion of an entire topic." *Boos v. Barry*, 485 U.S. 312, 319 (1988).

129. I say "for example," because the St. Paul ordinance was not simply addressed to racial hate speech nor, more particularly, to racial hate speech targeted on African Americans or other groups subordinated on the basis of race. For the suggestion that such a narrower and "openly asymmetric regulation" might have been less constitutionally suspect, in light of the Thirteenth Amendment ban on badges of servitude, see Akhil Reed Amar, "Comment: The Case of the Missing Amendments: *R. A. V. v. City of St. Paul*," *Harvard Law Review* 106 (1992): 155–61. See also my discussion of the asymmetry in the Stanford regulation, below pp. 212ff.

130. See *R. A. V. v. St. Paul*, 112 S. Ct. 2545: "When the basis for the content discrimination consists entirely of the very reason the entire class of speech is proscribable, no significant danger of idea or viewpoint discrimination exists."

131. This appears to be the force of Scalia's remark that "What makes the anger, fear, sense of dishonor, etc. produced by violation of this ordinance distinct from the honor fear, sense of dishonor, etc. produced by other fighting words is nothing other than the fact that it is conveyed by a distinctive idea, conveyed by a distinctive message." Ibid., 2548.

132. Here I agree with Amar that a cleaner focus on the nature of the harms and a more discriminating discussion of the differences among the categories mentioned in the ordinance—"race, color, creed, religion, or gender"—would have sharpened both the regulation and the Court's assessment of it. See Amar, "The Case of the Missing Amendments," pp. 155–60.

133. *Miller v. California*, 413 U.S. 15 (1973).

134. See *Roth v. United States*, 354 U.S. 476, 512 (Douglas, J., dissenting); and Harry Kalven, "The Metaphysics of the Law of Obscenity," *The Supreme Court Review: 1960*, ed. Philip B. Kurland (Chicago: Univeristy of Chicago Press, 1960), 18–19.

135. I am not sure that an obscene movie could present violence against, or humiliation of, women in an unfavorable light, because by so doing, it would plausibly have serious political value, thus defeating the categorization as obscene.

136. Indeed, I suspect that many who hold this second view would be more inclined to regulate the pornographically obscene than the grossly obscene. But I will put this matter to the side.

137. But not on grounds of viewpoint.

138. According to clarification offered in a debate in the Faculty Senate. See the discussion in Nadine Strossen, "Regulating Racist Speech," *Duke Law Journal* (1990): 494 n. 110, and accompanying text; and the less measured discussion in Charles Fried, "The New First Amendment Jurisprudence: A Threat to Liberty," *University of Chicago Law Review* 59 (1992): 22ff.

139. I say "not now," because I was not infrequently called "kike," "bagel bender," etc., when I was growing up.

12

The Difficulty of Tolerance

T. M. SCANLON

1. What Is Tolerance?

Tolerance requires us to accept people and permit their practices even when we strongly disapprove of them. Tolerance thus involves an attitude that is intermediate between wholehearted acceptance and unrestrained opposition.[1] This intermediate status makes tolerance a puzzling attitude. There are certain things, such as murder, that ought not be tolerated. There are limits to what we are able to do to prevent these things from happening, but we need not restrain ourselves out of tolerance for these actions as expressions of the perpetrators' values. In other cases, where our feelings of opposition or disapproval should properly be reined in, it would be better if we were to get rid of these feelings altogether. If we are moved by racial or ethnic prejudice, for example, the preferred remedy is not merely to tolerate those whom we abhor but to stop abhorring people just because they look different or come from a different background.

Perhaps everything would, ideally, fall into one or the other of these two classes. Except where wholehearted disapproval and opposition are appropriate, as in the case of murder, it would be best if the feelings that generate conflict and disagreement could be eliminated altogether. Tolerance, as an attitude that requires us to hold in check certain feelings of opposition and disapproval, would then be just a second best—a way of dealing with attitudes that we would be better off without but that are, unfortunately, ineliminable. To say this would not be to condemn tolerance. Even if it is, in this sense, a second best, the widespread adoption of tolerant attitudes would be a vast improvement over the sectarian bloodshed that we hear of every day, in many parts of the globe. Stemming this violence would be no mean feat.

Still, it seems to me that there are pure cases of tolerance, in which it is not merely an expedient for dealing with the imperfections of human nature. These would be cases in which persisting conflict and disagreement are to be expected and are, unlike racial prejudice, quite compatible with full respect for those with whom we disagree. But while respect for each other does not require us to abandon our disagreement, it does place limits on how this conflict can be pursued. In this article, I want to investigate the possibility of pure tolerance of this kind, with the aim of better understanding our idea of tolerance and the difficulty of achieving it. Because I particularly want to see more clearly why it is a difficult attitude and practice to sustain, I will try to concentrate on cases in which I myself find tolerance difficult. I begin with the familiar example of religious toleration, which provides the model for most of our thinking about toleration of other kinds.

Widespread acceptance of the idea of religious toleration is, at least in North America and Europe, a historical legacy of the European Wars of Religion. Today, religious toleration is widely acknowledged as an ideal, even though there are many places in the world where, even as we speak, blood is being spilled over what are at least partly religious divisions.

As a person for whom religion is a matter of no personal importance whatever, it seems easy for me, at least at the outset, to endorse religious toleration. At least this is so when toleration is understood in terms of the twin principles of the First Amendment to the Constitution of the United States: "Congress shall make no law respecting an establishment of religion, or prohibiting the free exercise thereof." Accepting these principles seems to be all benefit and no cost from my point of view. Why should I want to interfere with other people's religious practice, provided that they are not able to impose that practice on me? If religious toleration has costs, I am inclined to say, they are borne by others, not by me.

So it seems at first (although I will later argue that this is a mistake) that for me religious toleration lacks the tension I just described: I do not feel the opposition it tells me to hold in check. Why should I want to tell others what religion to practice, or to have one established as our official creed? On the other hand, for those who do want these things, religious toleration seems to demand a great deal: if I thought it terribly important that everyone worship in the correct way, how could I accept toleration except as an uneasy truce, acceptable as an alternative to perpetual bloodshed, but even so a necessity that is to be regretted? Pure toleration seems to have escaped us.

I want to argue that this view of things is mistaken. Tolerance involves costs and dangers for all of us, but it is nonetheless an attitude that we all have reason to value.

2. What Does Toleration Require?

This is a difficult question to answer, in part because there is more than one equally good answer, in part because any good answer will be vague in important respects. Part of any answer is legal and political. Tolerance requires that people who fall on the "wrong" side of the differences I have mentioned should not, for that reason, be denied legal and political rights: the right to vote, to hold office, to benefit from the central public goods that are otherwise open to all, such as education, public safety, the protections of the legal system, health care, and access to "public accommodations." In addition, it requires that the state not give preference to one group over another in the distribution of privileges and benefits.

It is this part of the answer that seems to me to admit of more than one version. For example, in the United States, the requirement that each religious group is equally entitled to the protections and benefits conferred by the state is interpreted to mean that the state may not support, financially or otherwise, any religious organization. The main exception, not an insignificant one, is that any religious organization can qualify for tax-exempt status. So even our idea of "nonestablishment" represents a mixed strategy: some forms of support are prohibited for *any* religion, others are allowed provided they are available for *all* religions. This mixture strikes me more as a particular political compromise than as a solution uniquely required by the idea of religious toleration. A society in which there was a religious qualification for holding public office could not be accounted tolerant or just. But I would not say the same about just any form of state support for religious practice. In Great Britain, for example, there is an established church, and the state supports denominational as well as nondenominational schools. In my view, the range of these schools is too narrow to reflect the religious diversity of contemporary Britain, but I do not see that just any system of this kind is to be faulted as lacking in toleration. Even if it would be intolerant to give one religion certain special forms of support, there are many different acceptable mixtures of what is denied to every religion and what is available to all. The particular mixture that is now accepted in the United States is not the only just solution.

This indeterminacy extends even to the area of freedom of expression, which will be particularly important in what follows. Any just and tolerant society must protect freedom of expression. This does not mean merely that censorship is ruled out, but requires as well that individuals and groups have some effective means for bringing their views before the public. There are, however, many ways of doing this.[2] There are, for example, many ways of defining and regulating a "public forum," and no one of these is specifically required. Permitted and protected modes of expression need not be the same everywhere.

Let me now move from the most clearly institutional aspects of toleration to the less institutional and more attitudinal, thereby moving from the indeterminate to the vague. I have said that toleration involves "accepting as equals" those who differ from us. In what I have said so far, this equality has meant equal possession of fundamental legal and political rights, but the ideal of equality that toleration involves goes beyond these particular rights. It might be stated as follows: all members of society are equally entitled to be taken into account in defining what our society is and equally entitled to participate in determining what it will become in the future. This idea is unavoidably vague and difficult to accept. It is difficult to accept insofar as it applies to those who differ from us or disagree with us, and who would make our society something other than what we want it to be. It is vague because of the difficulty of saying exactly what this "equal entitlement" involves. One mode of participation is, of course, through the formal politics of voting, running for office, and trying to enlist votes for the laws and policies that one favors. But what I now want to stress is the way in which the requirements of toleration go beyond this realm of formal politics into what might be called the informal politics of social life.

The competition among religious groups is a clear example of this informal politics, but it is only one example. Other groups and individuals engage in the same political struggle all the time: we set and follow examples, seek to be recognized or have our standard-bearers recognized in every aspect of cultural and popular life. A tolerant society, I want to say, is one that is democratic in its informal politics. This democracy is a matter of law and institutions (a matter, for example, of the regulation of expression.) But it is also, importantly and irreducibly, a matter of attitude. Toleration of this kind is not easy to accept—it is risky and frightening—and it is not easy to achieve, even in one's own attitudes, let alone in society as a whole.

To explain what I have in mind, it is easiest to begin with some familiar controversies over freedom of expression and over "the enforcement of morals." The desire to prevent those with whom one disagrees from influencing the evolution of one's society has been a main motive for restricting expression—for example, for restricting religious proselytizing and for restricting the sale of publications dealing with sex, even when these are not sold or used in a way that forces others to see them. This motive supports not only censorship but also the kind of regulation of private conduct that raises the issue of "the enforcement of morals." Sexual relations between consenting adults in the privacy of their bedrooms are not "expression," but it is no mistake to see attempts to regulate such conduct and attempts to regulate expression as closely related. In both cases, what the enforcers want is to prevent the spread of certain forms of behavior and attitude both by deterring it and, at least as important, by using the criminal law to make an authoritative statement of social disapproval.

One form of liberal response has been to deny the legitimacy of any interest in "protecting society" from certain forms of change. (The analog of declaring religion to be purely a private matter.) This response seems to me to be mistaken.[3] We all have a profound interest in how prevailing customs and practices evolve. Certainly, I myself have such an interest, and I do not regard it as illegitimate. I do not care whether other people, individually, go swimming in the nude or not, but I do not want my society to become one in which nude bathing becomes so much the norm that I cannot wear a suit without attracting stares and feeling embarrassed. I have no desire to dictate what others, individually, in couples or in groups, do in their bedrooms, but I would much prefer to live in a society in which sexuality and sexual attractiveness, of whatever kind, was given less importance than it is in our society today. I do not care what others read and listen to, but I would like my society to be one in which there are at least a significant number of people who know and admire the same literature and music that I do, so that that music will be generally available, and so that there will be others to share my sense of its value.

Considered in this light, religious toleration has much greater risks for me than I suggested at the beginning of this article: I am content to leave others to the religious practices of their choice provided that they leave me free to enjoy none. But I will be very unhappy if this leads in time to my society becoming one in which almost everyone is, in one way or another, deeply religious, and in which religion plays a central part in all public discourse. Moreover, I would feel this way even if I would continue to enjoy the firm protection of the First Amendment. What I fear is not merely the legal enforcement of religion but its social predominance.

So I see nothing mistaken or illegitimate about at least some of the *concerns* that have moved those who advocate the legal enforcement of morals or who seek to restrict expression in order to prevent what they see as the deterioration of their society. I might disagree with them in substance, but I would not say that concerns of this kind are ones that anyone should or could avoid having. What is objectionable about the "legal enforcement of morals" is the attempt to restrict individuals' personal lives as a way of controlling the evolution of mores. Legal moralism is an example of intolerance, for example, when it uses the criminal law to deny that homosexuals are legitimate participants in the informal politics of society.

I have not tried to say how this informal politics might be regulated. My aims have been, rather, to illustrate what I mean by informal politics, to point out what I take to be its great importance to all of us, and to suggest that for this reason toleration is, for all of us, a risky matter, a practice with high stakes.

3. The Value of Tolerance

Why, then, value tolerance? The answer lies, I believe, in the relation with one's fellow citizens that tolerance makes possible. It is easy to see that a tolerant person and an intolerant one have different attitudes toward those in society with whom they disagree. The tolerant person's attitude is this: "Even though we disagree, they are as fully members of society as I am. They are as entitled as I am to the protections of the law, as entitled as I am to live as they choose to live. In addition (and this is the hard part) neither their way of living nor mine is uniquely *the* way of our society. These are merely two among the potentially many different outlooks that our society can include, each of which is equally entitled to be expressed in living as one mode of life that others can adopt. If one view is at any moment numerically or culturally predominant, this should be determined by, and dependent on, the accumulated choices of individual members of the society at large."

Intolerant individuals deny this. They claim a special place for their own values and way of life. Those who live in a different way—Turks in Germany, for example, Muslims in India, and homosexuals in some parts of the United States—are, in their view, not full members of their society, and the intolerant claim the right to suppress these other ways of living in the name of protecting their society and "its" values. They seek to do this either by the force of criminal law or by denying forms of public support that other groups enjoy, such as public subsidies for the arts.

What I have just provided is description, not argument. But the first way of making the case for tolerance is simply to point out, on the basis of this description, that tolerance involves a more attractive and appealing relation between opposing groups within a society. Any society, no matter how homogeneous, will include people who disagree about how to live and about what they want their society to be like. (And the disagreements within a relatively homogeneous culture can be more intense than those within a society founded on diversity, like the United States.) Given that there must be disagreements, and that those who disagree must somehow live together, is it not better, if possible, to have these disagreements contained within a framework of mutual respect? The alternative, it seems, is to be always in conflict, even at the deepest level, with a large number of one's fellow citizens. The qualification "even at the deepest level" is crucial here. I am assuming that in any society there will over time be conflicts, serious ones, about the nature and direction of the society. What tolerance expresses is a recognition of common membership that is deeper than these conflicts, a recognition of others as just as entitled as we are to contribute to the definition of our society. Without this, we are just rival groups contending over the same territory. The fact that each of us, for good historical and personal reasons, regards it as *our* territory and *our* tradition just makes the conflict all the deeper.

Whether or not one accepts it as sufficient justification for tolerance, the difference that tolerance makes in one's relation to those who are "different" is easy to see. What is less obvious, but at least as important, is the difference tolerance makes in one's relation with those to whom one is closest. One's children provide the clearest case. As my children, they are as fully members of our society as I am. It is their society just as much as it is mine. What one learns as a parent, however, is that there is no guarantee that the society they will want is the same one that I want. Intolerance implies that their right to live as they choose and to influence others to do so is conditional on their agreement with me about what the right way to live is. If I believe that others, insofar as they disagree with me, are not as entitled as I am to shape the mores of our common society, then I must think this of my children as well, should they join this opposition. Perhaps I hold that simply being *my children* gives them special political standing. But this seems to me unlikely. More likely, I think, is that this example brings out the fact that intolerance involves a denial of the full membership of "the others." What is special about one's children is, in this case, just that their membership is impossible to deny. But intolerance forces one to deny it, by making it conditional on substantive agreement with one's own values.

My argument so far is that the case for tolerance lies in the fact that rejecting it involves a form of alienation from one's fellow citizens. It is important to recognize, however, that the strength of this argument depends on the fact that we are talking about membership in "society" as a political unit. This can be brought out by considering how the argument for tolerance would apply within a private association, such as a church or political movement.[4] Disagreements are bound to arise within any such group about how their shared values are to be understood. Is it then intolerant to want to exclude from the group those with divergent views, to deny them the right to participate in meetings and run for office under the party label, to deny them the sacraments, or stop inviting them to meetings? It might be said that this also involves the kind of alienation I have described, by making others' standing as members conditional on agreement with our values. But surely groups of this kind have good reason to exclude those who disagree. Religious groups and political movements would lose their point if they had to include just anyone.

In at least one sense, the ideas of tolerance and intolerance that I have been describing do apply to private associations. As I have said, disagreements are bound to arise within such groups, and when they do it is intolerant to attempt to deny those with whom one disagrees the opportunity to persuade others to adopt their interpretation of the group's values and mission. Tolerance of this kind is required by the very idea of an association founded on a commitment to "shared values." In what sense would these values be "shared" unless there were some process—like the formal and informal politics to which I have referred—through which they evolve and agreement on them is sustained?[5] But there are limits. The very meaning of the goods in question—the sacraments, the party label—requires that they be conditional on certain beliefs. So it is not intolerant for the group as a whole, after due deliberation, to deny these goods to those who clearly lack these beliefs.

Tolerance at the level of political society is a different matter. The goods at stake here, such as the right to vote, to hold office, and to participate in the public forum, do not lose their meaning if they are extended to people with whom we disagree about the kind of society we would like to have, or even to those who reject its most basic tenets. One can become a member of society, hence entitled to these goods, just by being born into it (as well as in other ways), and one is required to obey its laws and institutions as long as one remains within its territory. The argument for tolerance that I have been describing is based on this idea of society and on the idea that the relation of "fellow citizen" that it involves is one we have reason to value. The form of alienation I have mentioned occurs when the terms of this relation are violated: when we deny others, who are just as much members of our society as we are, the right to their part in defining and shaping it.[6]

As I have said, something similar can occur when we deny fellow members of a private association their rightful share in shaping it. But the relation of "fellow member" that is violated is different from the relation of "fellow citizen," and it is to be valued for different reasons. In particular, the reasons for valuing such a relation often entail limits on the range of its application. It would be absurd, for example, for Presbyterians to consider everyone born within the fifty United States a member of their church, and it would therefore not be intolerant to deny some of them the right to participate in the evolution of this institution. But the relation of "fellow citizen" is supposed to link at least everyone born into a society and remaining within its borders. So it does not entail, and is in fact incompatible with, any narrower limits.

4. The Difficulty of Tolerance

Examples of intolerance are all around us. To cite a few recent examples from the United States, there are the referenda against gay rights in Oregon and Colorado, attempts by Senator Jesse Helms and others to prevent the National Endowment for the Arts and the National Endowment for the Humanities from supporting projects of which they (Helms et al.) disapprove, recent statements by the governor of Mississippi that "America is a Christian nation," and similar statements in the speeches at the 1992 Republican National Convention by representatives of the Christian right.

But it is easy to see intolerance in one's opponents and harder to avoid it oneself. I am thinking here, for example, of my reactions to recurrent controversies in the United States over the teaching of evolution and "creation science" in public schools and to the proposal to amend the Constitution if necessary in order to allow organized prayer in public schools. I firmly believe that "creation science" is bogus and that science classes should not present scientific theory and religious doctrine as alternatives with similar and equal claim to the same kind of assent. I therefore do not think that it is intolerant per se to oppose the creationists. But I confess to feeling a certain sense of partisan zeal in such cases, a sense of superiority over the people who propose such things and a desire not to let them win a point even if it did not cost anyone very much. In the case of science teaching, there is a cost, as there is in the case of school prayer. But I am also inclined to support removing "In God We Trust" from our coinage and to favor discontinuing the practice of prayer at public events.

These changes appeal to me because they would make the official symbolism of our country more thoroughly secular, hence more in line with my own outlook, and I can also claim that they represent a more consistent adherence to the constitutional principle of "nonestablishment" of religion. Others see these two reasons as inconsistent. In their view, I am not simply removing a partisan statement from our official symbolism, but at the same time replacing it with another; I am not making our public practice neutral as between secularism and religiosity but asking for an official step that would further enthrone secularism (which is already "officially endorsed" in many other ways, they would say) as our national outlook. I have to admit that, whatever the right answer to the constitutional question might be (and it might be indeterminate), this response has more than a little truth to it when taken as an account of my motives, which are strongly partisan.

But why should they not be partisan? It might seem that here I am going too far, bending over backwards in the characteristically liberal way. After all, the argument that in asking to have this slogan removed from our money I am asking for the official endorsement of *ir*religiosity is at best indirect and not really very persuasive. Whereas the slogan itself does have that aggressively inclusive, hence potentially exclusive "we": "In God *We* Trust." (Who do you mean "we"?)

Does this mean that in a truly tolerant society there could be no public declarations of this kind, no advocacy or enforcement by the state of any particular doctrine? Not even tolerance itself? This seems absurd. Let me consider the matter in stages.

First, is it intolerant to enforce tolerance in behavior and prevent the intolerant from acting on their beliefs? Surely not. The rights of the persecuted demand this protection, and the demand to be tolerated cannot amount to a demand to do whatever one believes one must.

Second, is it intolerant to espouse tolerance as an official doctrine? We could put it on our coins: "In Tolerance We Trust." (Not a bad slogan, I think, although it would have to be pronounced carefully.) Is it intolerant to have tolerance taught in state schools and supported in state-sponsored advertising campaigns? Surely not, and again for the same reasons. The advocacy of tolerance denies no one their rightful place in society. It grants to each person and group as much standing as they can claim while granting the same to others.

Finally, is it contrary to tolerance to deny the intolerant the opportunities that others have to state their views? This would seem to deny them a standing that others have. Yet to demand that we tolerate the intolerant in even this way seems to demand an attitude that is almost unattainable. If a group maintains that I and people like me simply have no place in our society, that we must leave or be eliminated, how can I regard this as a point of view among others that is equally entitled to be heard and considered in our informal (or even formal) politics? To demand this attitude seems to be to demand too much.

If toleration is to make sense, then, we must distinguish between one's attitude toward what is advocated by one's opponents and one's attitude toward those opponents themselves: it is not that their *point of view* is entitled to be represented but that *they* (as fellow citizens, not as holders of that point of view) are entitled to be heard. So I have fought my way to the ringing statement attributed to Voltaire,[7] that is, to a platitude. But in the context of our discussion, I believe that this is not only a platitude but also the location of a difficulty, or several difficulties.

What Voltaire's statement reminds us is that the attitude toward others that tolerance requires must be understood in terms of specific rights and protections. He mentions the right to speak, but this is only one example. The vague recognition of others as equally entitled to contribute to informal politics, as well as to the more formal kind, can be made more definite by listing specific rights to speak, to set an example through one's conduct, to have one's way of life recognized through specific forms of official support. To this we need to add the specification of kinds of support that *no* way of life can demand, such as prohibiting conduct by others simply because one disapproves of it. These specifications give the attitude of tolerance more definite content and make it more tenable. One *can* be asked (or so I believe) to recognize that others have these specific rights no matter how strongly one takes exception to what they say. This move reduces what I earlier called the vagueness of the attitude of tolerance, but leaves us with what I called the indeterminacy of more formal rights. This residual indeterminacy involves two problems.

The first is conceptual. Although some specification of rights and limits of exemplification and advocacy is required in order to give content to the idea of tolerance and make it tenable, the idea of tolerance can never be fully identified with any particular system of such rights and limits, such as the system of rights of free speech and association, rights of privacy, and rights to free exercise (but nonestablishment) of religion that are currently accepted in the United States. Many different systems of rights are acceptable; none is ideal. Each is therefore constantly open to challenge and revision. What I will call the spirit of tolerance is part of what leads us to accept such a system and guides us in revising it. It is difficult to say more exactly what this spirit is, but I would describe it in part as a spirit of accommodation, a desire to find a system of rights that others (all those within the broad reach of the relation "fellow citizen") could also be asked to accept. It is this spirit that I suspected might be lacking in my own attitudes regarding public prayer and the imprint on our coins. I need to ask myself the question of accommodation: is strict avoidance of any reference to religion indeed the only policy I could find acceptable, or is there some other compromise between secularism and the many varieties of religious conviction that I should be willing to consider?

The second, closely related problem is political. There is little incentive to ask this question of accommodation in actual politics, and there are usually much stronger reasons, both good and bad, not to do so. Because the boundaries of tolerance are indeterminate, and accepted ways of drawing them can be portrayed as conferring legitimacy on one's opponents, the charge of intolerance is a powerful political coin.

When anyone makes a claim that I see as a threat to the standing of my group, I am likely to feel a strong desire, perhaps even an obligation, not to let it go unanswered. As I have said, I feel such a desire even in relatively trivial cases. But often, especially in nontrivial cases, one particularly effective form of response (of "counterspeech") is to challenge the limits of the system of informal politics by claiming that one cannot be asked to accept a system that permits what others have done, and therefore demanding that the system be changed, in the name of toleration itself, so that it forbids such actions.

The pattern is a familiar one. For example, in the early 1970s, universities in the United States were disrupted by protesters demanding that speeches by IQ researchers, such as Richard Herrnstein and William Schockley, be canceled. The reason given was that allowing them to speak aided the spread of their ideas and thereby promoted the adoption of educational policies harmful to minority children. Taken at face value, this seemed irrational, because the protests themselves brought the speakers a much wider audience than they otherwise could have hoped for. But the controversy generated by these protests also gained a wider hearing for the opponents. Because "freedom of speech" was being challenged, civil libertarians, some of them otherwise friendly to the protesters' cause, others not so friendly, rushed into the fray. The result, played out on many campuses, was a dramatic and emotional event, provoking media coverage and anguished or indignant editorials in many newspapers. Whether the challenge to the prevailing rules of tolerance made any theoretical sense or not, it made a great deal of sense as a political strategy.

Much the same analysis seems to me to apply to more recent controversies, such as those generated by campus "hate-speech" rules and by the Indianapolis and Minneapolis antipornography statutes. I find it difficult to believe that adopting these regulations would do much to protect the groups in question. But *proposing them*, just because it challenges accepted and valued principles of free expression, has been a very effective way to bring issues of racism and sexism before the minds of the larger community (even if it has also had its costs, by giving its opponents a weapon in the form of complaints about "political correctness").

Challenging the accepted rules of tolerance is also an effective way of mobilizing support within the affected groups. As I have already said, victims of racist or anti-Semitic attacks cannot be expected to regard these as expressing "just another point of view" that deserves to be considered in the court of public opinion. Even in more trivial cases, in which one is in no way threatened, one often fails (as I have said of myself) to distinguish between opposition to a message and the belief that allowing it to be uttered is a form of partisanship on the part of the state. It is therefore natural for the victims of hate speech to take a willingness to ban such speech as a litmus test for the respect that they are due.[8] Even if this is an unreasonable demand, as I believe it often is, the indeterminacy and political sensitivity of standards of tolerance make it politically irresistible.

Because of the indeterminacy of such standards—because it is always to some degree an open question just what our system of toleration should be—it will not seem out of the question, even to many supporters of toleration, to demand that one specific form of conduct be prohibited in order to protect a victimized group. This can be so even when the proposed modification is in fact unfeasible because a workable system of toleration cannot offer this form of support to every group. On the other hand, because of this same indeterminacy, a system of toleration will not work unless it is highly valued and carefully protected against erosion. This means that any proposed modification will be politically sensitive and will elicit strong opposition, hence valuable publicity for the group in question.

Moreover, once this protection has been demanded by those speaking for the group—once it has been made a litmus test of respect—it is very difficult for individual members of the group not to support that demand.[9] The result is a form of political gridlock in which the idea of tolerance is a powerful motivating force on both sides: on one side, in the form of a desire to protect potentially excluded groups; on the other, in the form of a desire to protect a workable system of tolerance. I do not have a solution to such problems. Indeed, part of my point is that the nature of tolerance makes them unavoidable. The strategy suggested by what I have said is to try, as far as possible, to prevent measures inimical to the system of tolerance from becoming "litmus tests" of respect. Civil libertarians like me, who rush to the defense of that system, should not merely shout "You can't do that!" but should also ask the question of accommodation: "Are there other ways, not damaging to the system of tolerance, in which respect for the threatened group could be demonstrated?"[10]

5. Conclusion

I began by considering the paradigm case of religious toleration, a doctrine that seemed at first to have little cost or risk when viewed from the perspective of a secular liberal with secure constitutional protection against the "establishment" of a religion. I went on to explain why toleration in general, and religious toleration in particular, is a risky policy with high stakes, even within the framework of a stable constitutional democracy. The risks involved lie not so much in the formal politics of laws and constitutions (though there may be risks there as well) but rather in the informal politics through which the nature of a society is constantly redefined. I believe in tolerance despite its risks, because it seems to me that any alternative would put me in an antagonistic and alienated relation to my fellow citizens, friends as well as foes. The attitude of tolerance is nonetheless difficult to sustain. It can be given content only through some specification of the rights of citizens as participants in formal and informal politics. But any such system of rights will be conventional and indeterminate and is bound to be under frequent attack. To sustain and interpret such a system, we need a larger attitude of tolerance and accommodation, an attitude that is itself difficult to maintain.

Notes

I am grateful to Joshua Cohen and Will Kymlicka for their helpful comments on earlier drafts of this paper.
    1. As John Horton points out in his contribution to this volume.
    2. More exactly, there are many ways of trying to do it. I believe that our ideas of freedom of expression must be understood in terms of a commitment both to certain goals and to the idea of certain institutional arrangements as crucial means to those goals. But the means are never fully adequate to the goals, which drive

their constant evolution. I discuss this "creative instability" in "Content Regulation Reconsidered," in *Democracy and the Mass Media*, ed. J. Lichtenberg (New York: Cambridge University Press, 1991).

3. Here I draw on points made in section 5 of my article, "Freedom of Expression and Categories of Expression," *University of Pittsburgh Law Review* 40 (1979): 479–520.

4. Here I am indebted to very helpful questions raised by Will Kymlicka. I do not know whether he would agree with my way of answering them.

5. As Michael Walzer has written, addressing a similar question, "When people disagree about the meaning of social goods, when understandings are controversial, then justice requires that the society be faithful to the disagreements, providing institutional channels for their expression, adjudicative mechanisms, and alternative distributions." *Spheres of Justice*. (New York: Basic Books, 1984), p. 313.

6. Intolerance can also be manifested when we deny others the opportunity to *become* members on racial or cultural grounds. But it would take me too far afield to discuss here the limits on just immigration and naturalization policies.

7. He is said to have said, "I disapprove of what you say, but I will defend to the death your right to say it."

8. See, for example, Mari Matsuda, "Public Response to Racist Speech: Considering the Victim's Story," *Michigan Law Review* 87 (1989). Matsuda emphasizes that legal prohibition is sought because it represents public denunciation of the racists' position.

9. I am thinking here particularly of the Salman Rushdie case. The Ayatollah Khomeini's demand that *The Satanic Verses* be banned was unreasonable. On the other hand, many Muslims living in Britian felt they were treated with a lack of respect by their fellow citizens. Even if they could see that the Ayatollah's demand was unreasonable, it was difficult for them not to support it once it had been issued. Here the situation was further complicated (and the appeal to "unfeasibility" clouded) by the existence of a British blasphemy law that protected Christianity but not Islam. The result was gridlock of the kind described in the text.

10. I do not mean to suggest that this is always called for. It depends on the case, and the group. But the difficult cases will be those in which tolerance speaks in favor of protecting the group as well as against the measure they have demanded.

Index of Names and Cases

BRITAIN'S COLONIAL WARS 1688–1783

MODERN WARS IN PERSPECTIVE

General Editors: *H.M. Scott and B.W. Collins*

This ambitious new series offers wide-ranging studies of specific wars, and distinct phases of warfare, from the close of the Middle Ages to the present day. It aims to advance the current integration of military history into the academic mainstream. To that end, the books are not merely traditional campaign narratives, but examine the causes, course and consequences of major conflicts, in their full international political, social and ideological contexts.

ALREADY PUBLISHED

BRITAIN'S COLONIAL
WARS 1688–1783

BRUCE P. LENMAN

An imprint of **Pearson Education**

Harlow, England · London · New York · Reading, Massachusetts · San Francisco
Toronto · Don Mills, Ontario · Sydney · Tokyo · Singapore · Hong Kong · Seoul
Taipei · Cape Town · Madrid · Mexico City · Amsterdam · Munich · Paris · Milan

Pearson Education Limited
Edinburgh Gate
Harlow
Essex CM20 2JE
England

and Associated Companies throughout the world

Visit us on the World Wide Web at:
http://www.pearsoneduc.com

First published 2001

ISBN 0 582 42401 1 (ppr)   0 582 42402 X (csd)

British Library Cataloguing-in-Publication Data
A catalogue record for this book is available from the British Library

Library of Congress Cataloging-in-Publication Data
A catalog record for this book is available from the Library of Congress

Transferred to digital printing 2004

Printed and bound by Antony Rowe Ltd, Eastbourne

Typeset by 35 in 11/13pt Baskerville MT
Produced by Pearson Education Asia Pte Ltd

CONTENTS

CONTENTS

LIST OF MAPS

ACKNOWLEDGEMENTS

This book, like the larger project of which it is the second part, has taken many more years to complete than I had originally envisaged. Over a dozen years have passed since the original contract was signed and there had been a great deal of thinking, reading and researching invested in what are now key parts of it in the previous decade. I am therefore more than usually indebted to others for the fact that it has reached publication, albeit in a much-changed format. First and foremost I owe thanks to Pearson Education for their patient and constructive encouragement in recent years; for their willingness to re-contract; and for their admirably professional editorial procedures from which I have derived much benefit.

I cannot say, as did one eminent English historian recently, that every word of his major work was written abroad. I stand heavily indebted to bodies such as the National Library of Scotland and the British Library. Within the latter my obligation to what used to be the India Office Library and Records and is now the Oriental and India Office Collections is such that I simply cannot express it in words. From my first worthwhile experience in historical research there in the early 1960s to the ongoing encouragement and companionship of its scholarly guardians now, I have derived immense benefit. When purely local library resources ceased to be of any utility, as they did as early as 1996, it was bodies like these, and their American cousins which enabled me to continue this project. Amongst the latter I must record assistance with relevant material going back to 1982. Among my major benefactors have been the Newberry Library of Chicago; the John Carter Brown Library of Providence, Rhode Island; the Folger Library in Washington DC; the Virginia Historical Society; and the Huntington Library of San Marino, CA. To list individuals would be invidious and interminable, but the courtesy, and respect for scholars and scholarship which characterises all the libraries I have mentioned, alone makes the historian's always self-isolating, and often sullen craft tolerable.

In the Department of Modern History in St Andrews I have learned much from the students who have endured my honours classes in North American colonial warfare; and on His Late Sacred Majesty King James VI & I and his kingdoms, as well as my special subject on the East India

Company and India. They have made me defend my positions, and indeed beat one or two hasty retreats, to all our benefit. The department has underlined for me the mutual dependence of teaching and research, while the School of History has been both understanding and generous in supporting my research. From colleagues at the College of William and Mary and from a colleague in Emory University I learned much that compensated for my ignorance in areas important to this book. Of all my colleagues, it is not invidious to single out my long-suffering series editor Professor Hamish Scott for support above and beyond the call of duty, including bibliographical knowledge of matters imperial truly impressive even from a scholar in the apostolic succession of Edinburgh diplomatic historians deriving from Sir Richard Lodge.

Though I was able to incorporate the most important relevant works appearing in 1999, I regret that Fred Anderson's distinguished *Crucible of War* (Alfred Knopf, New York, 2000), came out after my own book was in galley proof. I am relieved to find that though our approaches and frames of reference could not be more different, I am in complete agreement with its main conclusions. The wonderful narrative style which makes it the twenty-first century replacement for Francis Parkman's classic nineteenth-century narratives is quite beyond my range. I end by dedicating this volume not to an individual but to a national tradition to which I am a very minor adherent. The Scots historians of empire trace their ancestry to the Scottish Enlightenment and to the man who was much its greatest all-round figure – the Very Reverend Principal William Robertson, Moderate divine and historian of Scotland, America and India. In recent decades scholars like my old teacher Archie Thornton, and my own contemporaries like Gordon Stewart and John Mackenzie, have maintained that tradition. Their gritty integrity and scholarly bite has not always endeared their work to others swayed by contemporary fashions in thought. May this work add rather than detract from a tradition of which my own small nation, indeed any nation, should be proud.

Bruce Lenman
St Andrews
July 2000

Colonies, identities, Marx and Mars

The United Kingdom of Great Britain, which was formed by an incorporating union of the kingdoms of England and Scotland in 1707, only modified in 1999, was controversial for much of the first half of the eighteenth century. That does not mean that it was difficult to get the union through the Scots parliament in 1707. A combination of principled unionism on the part of a section of the Scots parliament which saw some sort of union as the key to securing the Protestant succession and to economic development, government office-holders, and the great host of the venal ensured that English ministers could probably have obtained a measure of union in 1702, when it was under discussion, or even earlier. In 1702 the main problem seems to have been lack of interest on the part of English ministers when they grasped the fact that there was no guarantee that Scots MPs incorporated into Westminster would accept ministerial direction. *A fortiori* similar considerations seem to have ruled out a legislative union with Ireland, where a coalition among the exclusively Protestant landed ascendancy comparable to the Scottish unionist coalition might have been formed. There was some concern in elite circles in Ireland as Anglo–Scottish union proposals were discussed that Ireland might be losing out on possible benefits.

Again, the unlikelihood that Irish politicians could easily be subsumed into the predominant Westminster party system seems to have been the key to official lack of interest in an Anglo–Irish union. Modern continental European historiography, with its obsession with 'State Formation', might well see the union of 1707 and the Declaratory Act of 1720 – in which the British parliament at Westminster relegated the Irish parliament to a subordinate role – as having created in effect an archipelagic 'imperial state', but in practice matters did not work out that way because Westminster governments were more interested in 'managing' Scottish and Irish interests than they were in actually ruling Scotland or Ireland. The governments of William III, Queen Anne, and the early Hanoverians were usually heavily European oriented, even if, like the long administration of Sir Robert Walpole, the main government interest was in trying to avoid being sucked into major European wars. What they wanted from peripheral parts of the monarchy was absolute stability, preferably prosperity, at all times willingness to pay taxes. By the 1720s fairly stable systems had emerged whereby the management of both Scotland and Ireland was being run by delegation of power to local power-brokers. In Scotland they were aristocratic magnate-managers, who at their greatest became unofficial viceroys like Lord Islay or Henry Dundas. They had, however, no legislature of their own, though much patronage. In Ireland, with a parliament of its own which was far from powerless, and even the originally 'Anglo-Irish' new nobility beginning to acquire a stronger Irish identity, there were few magnates. The most powerful 'managers' like William Connolly were quite different from a duke of Argyll. Managers had to share power and patronage with an English viceroy, but could exploit a potent Irish lobby in Westminster. 'Britishness' was not much of a force anywhere until quite late in the century, broadly after 1760 when, mainly because of external factors, London governments began to think, more or less for the first time, of Ireland in an 'imperial' context.[1]

The role of overseas plantations and trading companies in this monarchy around 1700 was not negligible, but they can only be described as 'even more marginal' appendages to it, and there is no way the evidence can be twisted to suggest they were central to its interests and identity – which has not stopped ideologically driven historians from trying. The most complicated, if not necessarily the most sophisticated, attempt is probably that of Immanuel Wallerstein, which involved two volumes and much talk of 'cores', 'peripheries', and even 'semi peripheries' within a 'world system'. None of these terms, useful though 'core' and 'periphery' can be descriptively, is notably precise, and the 'world system' as Wallerstein seems to define it is frankly unconvincing.[2] Too often he falls back on the crude, lachrymose Marxism of Christopher Hill which sees negroes, and Ireland, as victims of 'the navigation system which gave England her world hegemony'.[3] The Acts of Navigation were significant, but they never did that. Wallerstein's final conclusion is keyed to the Peace of Paris of 1763, which saw quite spectacular colonial gains for Great Britain at the expense of both Spain and France. It is that:

> The British thus won a century-long struggle for the eventual succession
> to the Dutch hegemony of the mid seventeenth century. This victory of

certain segments of the world bourgeoisie, who were rooted in England, with the aid of the British state, can be adequately accounted for only by an analysis of how the state of Britain was politically able to help create and enlarge the socio-economic margin British entrepreneurs had over competitive forces rooted in France.[4]

This extraordinary mixture of jargon and dogmatism is all the more remarkable for its complete omission of military or naval considerations in the assessment of a peace treaty which, as peace treaties are wont to do, ended a war. The attempt to reconcile this particular peace with conviction that somehow, somewhere, there has to be a 'Bourgeois Revolution' – however complex and veiled in form – and that this is part of a predetermined pattern of global social evolution, no longer even serves to over-simplify world history conveniently (as the convoluted nature of Wallerstein's material shows), and is much better dumped in historiography's rubbish bin. Apart from anything else, the Peace of Paris was not the irreversible conclusion of a century of predictable evolution. It was a new balance of power between the Crowns of France and Great Britain, much of it based on remarkable successes for British arms in the previous five or six years. The balance was extremely fragile, indeed arguably self-destructive, and it was to be shattered within twenty years.

The whole game of trying to find an over-arching explanation for 'British Imperialism' before 1783 or so rather presupposes that the phenomenon is a coherent one and that there is consistency in it over time from the sixteenth to the eighteenth centuries. Neither presupposition is in fact correct, so even the most sophisticated mega-explanations run into trouble in the period 1550–1783. There is, for example, much to be said for the 'Gentlemanly Capitalism' hypothesis of P.J. Cain and A.G. Hopkins, from the nineteenth century onwards.[5] They point out the unwisdom of trying to tie British overseas expansion too tightly to what economic historians used to be happy to call the Industrial Revolution in Britain. Insofar as a truly significant spurt in manufacturing activity and in 'Britain's' margin of comparative advantage in manufactured goods can be identified, it came embarrassingly late in the eighteenth century. Not all of the British Isles left European norms behind. Belfast may have, County Kerry certainly did not. Glasgow, like nearby and very similar Belfast, did; but in the north of Scotland Sutherland did not. The Cain and Hopkins emphasis on the City, that London-based complex of financial interests which – partly due to its proximity to Westminster, but more because of its inherent and enduring weight – had more influence over the formulation of government policy than any manufacturing interest, is shrewd. City magnates' loans were propping up English government as early as the reign of James VI and I. City magnates dominated the leadership of the original East India Company (EIC). Certain regimes in Westminster, like the Rump Parliament in the early 1650s, were exceptionally open to mercantile pressures. Some aristocratic politicians, like the Elder Pitt, gloried in City connections and support.

However, it is no accident that Cain and Hopkins' first volume, which covers the period 1688–1914, is notably thin on everything before the 1790s. It does make the valid point that long before that date there had been widespread recognition of the often close interlocking of the landed and financial interests. Wealthy aristocrats held extensive investments in forms other than land and it was possible, over two or three generations, for a wealthy financier to buy land and eventually engineer the recognition of his grandchildren as landed gentry. There was also intermarriage between City wealth and the aristocracy, though much less than was once thought. Nevertheless, it is very difficult to find capitalists, gentlemanly or otherwise, determining state policy, let alone programmes of imperial expansion geared to war.

Even an apparent exception like Sir Josiah Child, who led the EIC into armed confrontation with the Moghul Empire in 1688–89, turns out to be much less of a fundamental decision-taker than he appears on the surface. All his life, he was dependent on large customers. The first was the Protectorate navy, for he started out a supplier of naval stores. His political colouring, appropriate to the years between the execution of Charles I in 1649 and the Restoration of the Stuarts in 1660, had been republican. After 1660 he eventually became reconciled to Charles II. Though he owned a lot of EIC stock he was primarily a leader of the shipping interest in the company – interested in freighting ships for the company monopoly trade. To defend that monopoly, and himself, he committed the company to a Tory and royalist position. When that led to military defeat in India followed by political disaster at home, he adjusted yet again to become a Williamite under William and Mary, obliging the new king with the presents he had persuaded the EIC to make to the old one.

Child's concept of 'Dominion' in an increasingly unstable and dangerous Indian sub-continent in the end came down to having fortified bases which would guarantee the security of their employees and goods. Madras the EIC had long ago fortified by agreement with a local ruler. Bombay was a Crown possession which they leased and by 1700 understood they had to pay to fortify adequately. In Bengal, where they had lost a war through making outrageous demands on one Moghul governor, was a province in which they eventually fortified their new settlement of Calcutta by agreement with another Moghul governor, who was alarmed by a rising against his Muslim regime by a local Hindu rajah. Child was much less of a mover and shaker than he looked. His voluminous writings, and especially his

Discourse of Trade (1696), which was often republished, revealed a mind which supported the protectionism of the Acts of Navigation because they defended the shipping interest, especially in the colonial trades. He had reservations about colonies like the New England ones, preferring staple-producing colonies which created need for shipping. Shipping, he argued, was a key to defence. Child was a dependant, all his life, of large institutions and especially the state, on which he leaned in the belief that it was a prime duty of government to make trade 'easy and necessary'.[6]

If merchants were very seldom, if ever, instigators of war, mercantile considerations entered largely into the calculations of governments, especially after 1650 when, for the first time, some sort of 'imperial' policy began to emerge. It has been argued that the protectionist Acts of Navigation were primarily designed to build up naval power by fostering a powerful mercantile marine, and that by 1675 the English had consciously created an Atlantic empire, primarily of commerce and shipping. It was based on an implicit but fundamental social compact in which the metropolitan government was permitted by colonists and merchants to regulate trade flows created almost entirely by private enterprise, and to draw revenues from them, in exchange for protection in the dangerous contemporary world and the ability to move freely about in a very large trading area. British diplomacy was active in trying to uphold this protected Atlantic system whilst pushing at the envelope to improve access to other powers' colonies (especially Spanish ones), even at the cost of extensive licit or illicit trade with foreigners.

Self-sufficiency was not truly an exclusive objective, at least before 1750, provided there was enough self-sufficiency to guarantee control of adequate maritime power. As we shall see, the social compact of adequate protection in exchange for acknowledgement of the London government's authority was one more honoured in the breach than in the observance by that government before about 1715. Thereafter, the 'system' was distinguished by more or less effective mutuality until after 1763 changes in the attitudes of both the London government and colonial elites placed it under intolerable, shearing pressure leading to a break-up formalised in 1783.[7]

The tendency to see the Anglo–Dutch wars of the period 1652–74 and the Navigation Acts of 1651, 1660, and 1662 as but 'the *mise en scène* in an unfolding drama of commercial competition and imperial expansion', which is seen as the prelude to a 'second Hundred Years' War' with France (finishing in 1783 or 1815, depending on taste) can in recent years be traced back, more often than not, to John Brewer's brilliant synthesis *The Sinews of Power*.[8] That influential book, published in 1989, was very much in the tradition of comparative analysis of European state formation. It traced the story of the weak early Stuart state evolving into the later Stuart naval

5

imperialist machine whose weaknesses were eventually tackled successfully under the stress of the great land and sea wars of William III. The transformation associated with the so-called Financial Revolution of the 1690s left eighteenth-century British government based on a parliamentary monarchy with formidable tax-raising powers buttressed by a central bank, the Bank of England, founded in 1694. The latter was the creation of a powerful group of City merchants and financiers working closely with the treasury. The contribution of the aristocracy was negligible. By way of contrast, the Bank of Scotland, established a year later by legislation of the Scots parliament, could lean on no such massive financial interest. On the contrary, 'the support of the aristocracy and landed gentry was crucial for the establishment of the Bank'.[9]

Brewer depicted the eighteenth-century British state, with its massive, well-sourced, permanent (and largely war-related) national debt, as just much more efficient at the game of competitive pursuit of wealth and power than rivals like the United Netherlands, France, or Prussia. Very significantly, Brewer cites another brilliant synthesiser, Adam Smith: 'According to Smith and others, this performance was orchestrated by a number of powerful commercial and mercantile interests, most notably chartered and regulated companies of merchants and investors, which manoevered government policy into serving their own ends.' He added his own opinion that 'This view has much to recommend it.'[10] Unfortunately, Adam Smith's paranoia, which was useful for him because it was self-serving, is no basis for a realistic analysis of the patterns of English and British imperial expansion and contraction before 1776, the date of the publication of Smith's *An Inquiry into the Nature and Causes of the Wealth of Nations*.

In much the same mode, an admirable collection of essays, based on a Princeton seminar series partly stimulated by Brewer's *Sinews of Power*, takes up his theme and then deftly pushes it rather further than he did. He stopped in 1783, and these essays annex a further stretch of historical territory for the argument by moving it forward to 1815, but within a general framework which assumes that his views have much to recommend them not just as an explanation of the emergence of the 'English' state (Brewer draws no distinction at 1707) as a great power, but also as a particularly useful tool to explain its imperial dimension. One contributor does warn that applying generalisations derived from the period after 1763 to earlier decades is particularly dangerous and adds, absolutely correctly if not very acceptably to some of the most prominent schools of contemporary historical discourse, that 'the Atlantic empire was a "back-yard" in which sinews of war were generated for use in the "front yard", that is to say in Europe and European seas'.[11] The rulers of the late seventeenth- and eighteenth-century British monarchy, a multi-national, geographically dispersed polity with a significant Atlantic dimension, made the inhabitants of the United Kingdom of Great Britain after 1707 the most heavily taxed, albeit also one of the most prosperous, peoples in Western Europe, primarily in order to play what they saw as an essential role in the wars and threats of war which regulated the European balances of power. Certainly in the first half of the eighteenth century, the result was often that colonial warfare broke out in the wake of European conflicts, and its impact on British colonies could be extremely erratic since even in valuable and vulnerable colonies, such as those in the Leeward Islands, the London government's policy was to keep defence expenditure in peacetime to a minimum.

The Leeward Islands was not the only overseas colony with very limited capacity for self-defence. In January 1755, after a shooting war had already broken out in America between British and French forces in the Ohio valley, Governor Arthur Dobbs of North Carolina drew the attention of the Board of Trade to the completely defenceless state of the province; to the lack of forts, arms, and ammunition; and to its long, undefended coastline.[12] Geographical remoteness had hitherto been its main security, and this was ceasing to be a sure shield from the enmity of other Europeans. The news that formal war was on the verge of being declared in Europe in 1756 filled colonial governors with gloom, for they knew that that development might make it even more difficult for them to secure money, troops, and munitions from the London government. In practice, in the latter part of the war, colonial governments received more metropolitan aid than they can have expected at the start of the war.

The thesis has recently been advanced that by 1760 Britain's interest in the politics of continental Europe was in decline, and that a major reason for this was a radical French revision of strategic priorities, which had concluded that Britain rather than the Austrian Habsburgs was the most dangerous enemy of France. The strain of massive land and maritime war efforts had deeply damaged the fiscal viability of the Bourbon monarchy. By 1764 French state debt had risen to about 2350 million livres, an increase of nearly 1000 million livres on the figure ten years before. By the end of the 1760s some 60 per cent of the French monarchy's annual revenues was going on debt servicing, and it was known that for the next generation at least half of all revenue would have to be so dedicated. France was in military and diplomatic decline in Europe from 1758. The duc de Choiseul, who became the first minister of France in late 1758, had taken a conscious decision to give the colonial wars more priority than the continental European campaigns. France was perceived as having lost much of its ability to dominate Europe.[13]

On the other hand, there was genuine fear that the British, with their ability to use naval superiority to close other powers off from access to the

7

high seas, might achieve a virtual monopoly of the ready wealth derived from maritime commerce which was such a valuable sinew of war and especially a source of wartime credit-worthiness. One result was that France came to value the alliance of the Spanish Bourbons much more highly. In 1765 Choiseul described Spain as 'an indispensable power'. Her colonial interests more or less guaranteed endless friction with a Britain anxious to penetrate these markets. For much of the period 1749–83 (and beyond) British strategists toyed with, and occasionally tried to implement, plans for destabilising the Spanish Americas by triggering or cooperating with a revolt of disaffected Creole elites. As Sir John Dalrymple remarked in May 1780: 'England might very well put up with the loss of America, for she would then exchange an empire of dominion which is very difficult to be kept for an empire of trade which keeps itself.'[14] It was therefore not difficult for France in the 1760s to encourage Spain's naval building programme, with a view to a Franco–Spanish naval combination in the next war which would have some chance of matching British naval power.

Nevertheless, this line of argument can be pushed too far. Both Britain and France retained an intense interest in European politics and diplomacy after 1763. They were just not very successful in that arena, where the rise of the Eastern powers – Russia and Prussia – made the situation much less easy to manipulate. The British search for a European ally failed partly because the British had little to offer, but more because nobody was interested in building coalitions against a less menacing France. The French were extremely anxious to try to block the westward thrust of Russian power by fighting Russia through various proxies. They did not succeed, that was all. Their failure was highlighted by the 1772 partition of France's traditional client, Poland-Lithuania. Only in 1787 did Britain successfully intervene again in a major European crisis, in the Netherlands, and only after 1792 did France resume its career as an incipient European hegemon.[15]

The two decades between 1763 and 1783 were therefore most unusual. The French were anxious to weaken their British rivals by depriving them of at least some of the financial benefits they thought flowed from their Atlantic Empire. France valued its remaining West Indies colonies, especially St Domingue (now Haiti), the 'pearl of the Antilles' – as well it might, for by the 1780s the 7000 slave-powered plantations in this sugar and coffee colony accounted for 40 per cent of French overseas trade. There was, however, no desire on the part of the French Crown to re-create the larger Atlantic Empire lost in 1763, though 'few doubted that a French invasion of Canada would receive massive local support'.[16] The very different British Crown, whose government machine was based on Westminster, had turned late in the day to regard the coherence and identity of its war-inflated Atlantic Empire as an issue of high priority in the decade 1765–75, and as a result found itself plunged into another cycle of war which reshaped British, but more especially English, identities as no wars had since the alienation of the Old English in Ireland in the late sixteenth and early seventeenth centuries. Whilst wars have to be seen in their social and economic – as well as their political – contexts, war and its contingencies remain a force in their own right in the story of the making and breaking of empires and identities in the fluid, and often marginal, world of European trans-oceanic expansion between 1688 and 1783.

Notes and references

1. David Hayton, 'Constitutional Experiments and Political Expediency', in Steven G. Ellis and Sarah Barber (eds.), *Conquest and Union: Fashioning a British state 1485–1725* (Longman, London, pbk edn, 1995), pp. 276–305.

2. Immanuel Wallerstein, *The Modern World System: Capitalist agriculture and the origins of the European world-economy in the sixteenth century* (Academic Press, New York, pbk edn, 1974), laid down the basic model.

3. *Idem, The Modern World System II: Mercantilism and the consolidation of the European world economy* (Academic Press, New York, pbk edn, 1980), p. 266.

4. *Ibid.*, pp. 257–58.

5. P.J. Cain and A.G. Hopkins, *British Imperialism: Innovation and expansion 1688–1914* (Longman, London, pbk edn, 1993), and *British Imperialism: Crisis and deconstruction 1914–1990* (Longman, London, pbk edn, 1993). The latest volume devoted to discussing the 'Gentlemanly Capitalism' thesis, Raymond E. Dumett (ed.), *Gentlemanly Capitalism and British Imperialism: The new debate on empire* (Longman, London, 1999), hardly mentions anything before 1800 and devotes very little space to anything before 1880.

6. I am very grateful to the kindness of my colleague Dr Julian Crowe in allowing me to read his father's thesis: A.L. Crowe, 'Sir Josiah Child and the East India Company' (unpublished University of London PhD thesis, 1956).

7. Daniel Baugh, 'Maritime Strength and Atlantic Commerce: The uses of "a grand maritime empire"', in Lawrence Stone (ed.), *An Imperial State at War: Britain from 1689 to 1815* (Routledge, London, 1994), pp. 185–223.

8. John Brewer, *The Sinews of Power: War, money and the English state 1688–1783* (Alfred A. Knopf, New York, 1989).

9. Richard V. Saville, *Bank of Scotland: A history 1695–1995* (Edinburgh University Press, Edinburgh, 1996), pp. 3–4.

10. Brewer, *op. cit.*, p. 168.

11. Daniel Baugh, *op. cit.*, in *An Imperial State at War*, p. 203.

12. Desmond Clarke, *Arthur Dobbs Esquire 1689–1765* (The Bodley Head, London, 1958), p. 115.

13. Daniel A. Baugh, 'Withdrawing from Europe: Anglo-French maritime geopolitics, 1750–1800', *International History Review*, 20 (1998), pp. 1–32, pushes a good argument a little far.

14. Alan Frost, 'The Spanish Yoke: British schemes to revolutionise Spanish America, 1739–1807', in Alan Frost and Jane Samson (eds.), *Pacific Empires: Essays in honour of Glyndwr Williams* (Melbourne University Press, Melbourne, 1999).

15. For an expansion and modification of Baugh's views *vide* Hamish Scott, 'The Decline of France and the Transformation of the European State System, 1756–1792', which Dr Scott kindly made available to me before its publication in Paul W. Schroeder and Peter Krüger (eds.), *The Transformation of the European States System, 1648–1945* (Cambridge University Press, New York, in press).

16. David P. Geggus, *Slavery, War and Revolution* (Clarendon Press, Oxford, 1982), pp. 6 and 17.

PART ONE

The English Nation and the Rise of Imperial Britain to 1760

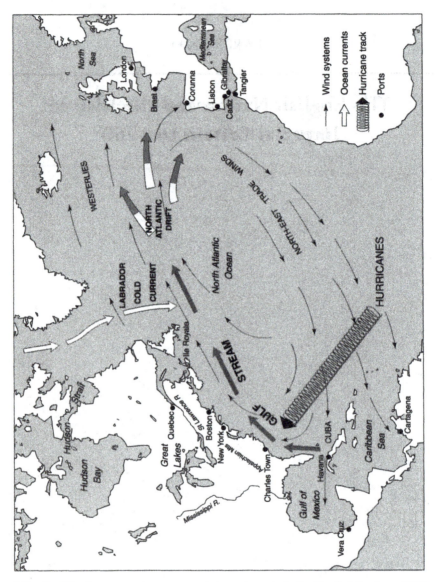

Map 1 Weather systems, currents and strategic ports in the North Atlantic, *c.* 1700

CHAPTER ONE

Atlantic monarchy, English America and two wars, 1689–1713

Prelude

In the English-speaking American world the two great wars which followed the overthrow of James VII and II and his replacement by the joint monarchy of his son-in-law William of Orange and his daughter Mary are usually referred to as King William's War and Queen Anne's War – after William of Orange and his successor after 1702, Mary's sister Anne (Mary died in 1693). The implication is that English monarchs in some way imposed conflict on their American subjects. Nothing could be further from the truth. The War of the English Succession, better known to historians of continental Europe as the Nine Years' War or the War of the League of Augsburg (after the name of the coalition which fought the aspirations of Louis XIV's France to a standstill between 1689 and 1697), came at a point at which conflict between the French and their allies, and the English and their allies, in North America had proven irrepressible, despite the increasing willingness of King James to appease King Louis. Insofar as the Glorious Revolution of 1688–89 can be seen as the event which raised the stakes by leading Protestant England into all-out conflict with the might of Louis XIV's Roman Catholic absolutism, it has to be said that the English colonies were, as the use of the term 'provincial' as an alternative to 'colonial' to describe them or their troops reminds us, provinces of England. New England was more rabidly supportive of the Glorious Revolution than was Old England, where many conservative Anglicans were very distressed about the whole business. New France was also essentially a French province, and insofar as any European monarch imposed his or her will in bellicose fashion on North America, it was Louis XIV who did that when he laid down a particular strategy for the French war effort there in the second spasm of conflict, the War of the Spanish Succession, which was fought out between 1702 and 1713. America was bound to be involved in that war since the fate of the Spanish dominions in the western hemisphere was one of the main points at issue, and a matter of obsessive interest to English Americans, then and later. Tremendous tensions there were between provincial Englishmen in America and the metropolitan authorities of what by 1713 had become a British monarchy but, though affected by local circumstances, they were not different in kind from the tensions between those authorities and other English provinces, and they were in some ways less acute than the tensions between the metropolitan core and the non-English parts of the monarchy's periphery.

Anglo–French hostility had boiled over into near war in the Duke of York's province of New York after 1685. The reigning governor of that province was then Colonel Thomas Dongan, an Irish Catholic soldier originally patronised by the duke's friend the Earl of Tyrconnell. After a spell in the Tangier garrison, Dongan went out in 1683 to govern New York, where he had a particular responsibility for the relationship between the Crown of England and the League of the Iroquois. In 1677 representatives of the English colonies and the Iroquois had met at Albany and concluded an alliance known as the Covenant Chain. Technically, it included all the English colonies from Virginia to Massachusetts, but in practice New York was the key English participant. Quite what the Covenant Chain meant depended on to whom you were talking and where. The English liked to claim to other Europeans that it made the Iroquois their subjects. Some New York expansionist propagandists of the eighteenth century like Cadwallader Colden went on to claim that the Iroquois were dependants of the province of New York. This was nonsense and the meaning of the Covenant Chain is clear enough from the way it functioned. It was a cross-cultural alliance in which the participants retained their sovereignty, but it was a vital alliance for both the Iroquois and New York since both needed the other as a guard or guarantee against a French bid to obliterate them. Competition for control of the western fur trade between the French and Iroquois had been becoming ferocious, especially in the Illinois country west of Lake Michigan. After Governor La Barre of Quebec had been compelled to back off from an attempt to intimidate the Iroquois in 1684, his successor, the marquis de Denonville, launched in 1687 a massive invasion of the territory of the Senecas, the most westerly Iroquois people, at the head of 1600 regulars, 400 Indian allies, and 400 Canadian militia. Villages were burned, vast corn stocks destroyed, livestock slaughtered, and graves pilfered. Dongan, who had been upgrading the New York militia in preparation for a confrontation with the French and who had warned the

French that he regarded the Iroquois as English subjects, took a force of militia reinforced by regulars from his garrison up to Albany later in that year to deter further French aggression, but he lost the confidence of his Iroquois allies because his expedition was too little, too late to matter, and he incurred heavy financial charges, of nearly £6500. The Dutch-speaking Scotsman Robert Livingstone, who was Dongan's close ally and the provincial Indian agent, presented a bill for over £20,000 for his share of supplying the troops.[1]

Sir Edmund Andros, first and last governor of the Dominion of New England, who assumed power over both New York and New Jersey in the autumn of 1688, almost immediately thereafter fell out with the French on the eastern frontier of the dominion. He tried to stabilise its boundary on the St Croix River, which is indeed the modern eastern limit of Maine, but in 1688 there were a few French settlements as far west as the Penobscot River, a mere eighty miles from Boston. Making a bad situation worse, Andros started to enforce the Acts of Navigation by seizing ships and goods which represented defiance of that legislation. Boston merchants trading with French Acadia suffered and moaned. Castine, a French trader married to the daughter of an Abenaki chief, suffered loss of goods and replied by organising Indian war parties against the English. Disputes over fisheries further poisoned the atmosphere. Equipped with ammunition by the French authorities in Quebec, the Abenaki soon had the outlying English settlements calling for assistance. Andros was not prepared to resort to the network of fortified townships which had helped win King Philip's War, because such a strategy necessarily strengthened the all-too-autonomous townships. Instead he chose to set off in the winter of 1688 to blunder around in the Maine woods with a significant force but with little result, and then to leave 700 men in small forts beyond the Merrimack, forts past which the enemy easily slipped. He was denounced for trying to 'Hedge in the Cuckow' and for failing to kill a single hostile Indian.[2] The Dominion of New England had been justified in some measure as necessary for defence against the French and their Indians. Its record in that respect was not calculated to secure for it the local constituency it desperately needed to create a strong regime.

There was a note of desperation in the reports penned by the three commissioners James II had appointed to talk with French commissioners about implementing the 'Instrument for the Quieting of all Disputes between the English and French in America', which is what the Treaty of Neutrality of 1686 purported to be. The Earl of Middleton, Lord Godolphin, and even the notoriously complaisant Earl of Sunderland – normally anxious to sing only tunes James wished to hear – were clearly shaken by the sudden attack on three Hudson Bay Company forts in James Bay successfully led by Pierre Le Moyne d'Iberville, and by the intransigence of their French counterparts. The English commissioners suggested that to secure any redress for an attack against unprepared, sleeping garrisons in a time of peace, 'it may be fitt for your majesty to support the Company of Hudson's Bay in the recovery and maintenance of their Right'. Otherwise there would be no end to French violence. Equally, the commissioners were taken aback by the rhetoric of the French negotiating team on the subject of the recent massive French strike against the Iroquois, whom the English claimed as subjects, on territory to the south of the Great Lakes claimed by New York on the same sort of bogus prescriptive rights which underpinned French pretensions in North America. The French had already tried 'Christian solidarity' as a means of asking the English not to arm their Indian allies whilst the French made access to firearms a major incentive to conversion for theirs. The Jesuit mission to the Hurons in the mid-seventeenth century had prefigured virtually every aspect of the pressures which the Jesuits were now placing on the Iroquois, especially the Mohawks. Then guns had been made available only to Christian chiefs, and deep factionalism had been built into Huron society to the point of fatally weakening its coherence in the face of external attack. The fact that a fair number of traditionalist Hurons had voluntarily joined the Iroquois in the early 1650s as the Huron nation disintegrated under the pressures of famine, plague, defeat, and cultural fragmentation, had led the Jesuits to try to insert themselves into, and divide, Iroquois society by accompanying Huron refugees.[3] The French commissioners now demanded that the English desist from arming the Iroquois and inciting them to attack the French. In fact the Senecas' main crime in French eyes had been to compete too efficiently in the western fur trade. The English commissioners, one of whom (Middleton) was a Scot, were clear that their king had to support the Iroquois and tell his officials to 'give them all necessary aid and assistance and to oppose the French in case of another Invasion', for the sake of the security of his own dominions, which was sufficiently threatened for them to recommend that Dongan be encouraged to construct forts at appropriate sites. What was at issue was whether the French truly sought peace or regarded the talks, for they were hardly negotiations, as war pursued by other means. The English Crown could only try to stop Iroquois attacks on the French and secure compensation for damage done if the French ceased to reach out aggressively for military and ideological mastery over the Iroquois confederation, but that was the name of the French game.[4] It is a platitude of the self-flagellant school of the history of European expansion that Europeans approached other races sheathed in an impenetrable armour of sanctimonious self-justification, but they did that so well because that was the way they usually approached each other.[5]

The commissioners were vexed by the clash of jurisdictional claims in Maine, and suggested that the matter be referred to James' governor in New England for clarification. Once the Glorious Revolution had seen off both monarch and governor in a decisive repudiation throughout the English world of any drift towards a Catholic absolutism as the future, and war had broken out between the English and French Crowns, the conflict on New England's eastern frontier became as much a sectarian as a racial one. It was bound to be so. Religion was a very powerful tool for all Counter-Reformation Catholic monarchies, and only the use of religion for politico-military ends seemed to offer the 11,000 or so inhabitants of New France any chance of holding at bay the enormously bigger English communities on the seaboard of North America. The 13,000 militia of New England alone outnumbered the entire French Canadian population, but religion enabled the rulers of New France to penetrate, control up to a point, and deploy militarily the all-important Indian allies without whom it was impossible to wage effective inter-colonial war. When the marquis de Denonville returned to France from governing Canada in 1689, he assured the authorities there that it was in the interest of the civil government and of French commerce to keep missionaries in the Indian villages because missionaries 'alone are able to maintain them in our interests and to prevent them from revolting against us'. By 1699 at least six Jesuits were living with Abenaki groups within territory claimed by Massachusetts. When in 1700 Governor the Earl of Bellomont had the New York and Massachusetts legislatures pass laws banning Jesuits, priests, and popish missionaries from 'His Majesty's territories' under pain of death under certain circumstances, he was being realistic. They would be French agents and quite likely war hawks. Bellomont was not an unreasonable man. He shared the views of Judge Samuel Sewall that the fundamental obstacle to better Anglo–Abenaki relations was the shameless way English settlers robbed the Indians of their ancestral lands.[6]

It was the Jesuits who had succeeded in splitting the Mohawks, the most easterly of the Iroquois nations, by converting a significant part of it and persuading the converts to move to New France, to the mission settlement of Caughnawaga. Bitterness and division on this scale profoundly weakened a proud people. Equally, it was the Jesuits with their unprecedented mastery of very difficult Indian languages who could persuade some Abenaki to go a 15- to 20-day journey to distant Quebec to trade rather than make a 2-day trip to better, cheaper trade goods in English posts. Intolerance of rival Christian denominations tended to be total in seventeenth-century Europe, and this world view could be transmitted, albeit with difficulty, to native American peoples. Perhaps the most remarkable achievement of the Jesuit missionaries in transferring social patterns was their radical redefinition of the role of women in such Indian peoples as the surviving Huron and Montagnais, all of whom they proudly described as meek and humble Christians by the latter part of the seventeenth century. Jesuit humanism regarded the Indians as 'savages' in thrall to Satan. In this view they differed not at all from their Spanish or English contemporaries. However, they were equally clear that the Indians could be 'civilised' by accepting not only Christian doctrine but also the strict social discipline and hierarchy which they regarded as an essential part of the Christian life. The fact that Indian women were traditionally far freer than European women, sexually and socially, and enjoyed a relationship of complementarity with men explains why they often opposed a religious conversion which had as an integral part of its method the subjugation of women to the point where they would normally be dominated and disciplined by men. Demoralising catastrophe or radical separation from tribal traditionalists was often the key to incorporating Indian groups within the baroque absolutism of the Counter-Reformation world.[7] Where the relationship with Christian proselytisers was more a matter of negotiation, Indian women could adapt to and even subvert the social and economic changes forced on them by Europeans.[8] There were always Indians the French could not manipulate successfully, as they were reminded in July 1689.

Round One: 1689–1701

Aware of the outbreak of war in Europe, and locked in continuing conflict with the French, who highly resented the Iroquois determination to secure what were to them vitally important supplies of furs from the lands of other Indian peoples north of Lakes Ontario and Erie, the Iroquois struck in late July 1689, with a force of 1500 men, against the French farming community of Lachine, some ten miles upstream from Montreal. As massacres go, it was not much of one. Immediate casualties numbered about 200, and the final death toll was no more than 106, including some 40 soldiers and Indian auxiliaries, for whom this sort of death was a professional hazard. The Iroquois then withdrew and the French reoccupied Lachine. Smaller Iroquois raids were less effective. Behind the league's willingness to fight lay the assumption on the part of its sachems or council leaders that the English would soon be in the field. To their horror, the sachems found that English effort and morale were so poor that they had to be told by the sachems, after a few opening setbacks, that these were only preliminary rounds and that they should cheer up and get on with the hard pounding of war.[9] Governor the comte de Frontenac, who had come out to rule New

France for the second time in September 1689, had a preferred strategy to redeem the situation, and one which appealed to his monarch. It would have been to strike hard at New York by land through Albany from Canada at the same time as a strong French naval force launched an amphibious onslaught from the Atlantic approaches. Obdurate and heretical inhabitants were of course to be driven out after the conquest. Mentally, this was total war between rival civilisations. Fortunately, practicalities intervened. With no hope of diversion of major naval units from European waters and only 1500 troops and 2000 militia, Frontenac had to settle for less than the ideal. He still had hopes, because New York was in political chaos after the seizure of power at the time of the revolution by Jacob Leisler, one of the militia captains. His regime was high handed and alienated many conservatives. In Albany it was simply repudiated from the start. What Frontenac eventually did, very successfully, was to launch three long-range spoiling raids against New England's frontiers with mixed French–Indian forces. In the winter Schenectady and Salmon Falls were devastated, and in May Fort Loyal near present-day Portland in Maine was captured by a large raiding party whose Indians, to whom European conventions about surrender were absurd, massacred what was left of the garrison after it yielded on terms. The same sort of panic spread through New England as Lachine had created in New France, though in absolute terms the casualties were not serious. The intendant, the second most important official in Canada, had argued that a single heavy strike should go in against Albany, demonised as the power behind the Iroquois, but certainly vital to them as a market and supply source. Instead, Frontenac had divided his forces against settlements with no history of zeal to fight New France and had done about the only thing that would unite the selfish, short-sighted, and feuding English colonists.[10]

Their first attempt to hit back was led by Sir William Phips, than whom a more appropriate leader for a counter-attack on the French settlements nearest to Maine could hardly be found. He had been born on the Kennebec River in Maine, son of an immigrant English gunsmith. Starting as an apprentice ship's carpenter in Boston, Phips had climbed up socially, at first by the wholly orthodox means of marriage to a wealthy widow, and then by a spectacular coup in which he recovered a quarter of a million pounds sterling in silver from the wreck of the *Nuestra Senora de la Concepción*, the almiranta or vice admiral ship of a Mexican treasure fleet. The *Concepción* had struck on a coral reef north of Hispaniola and sunk in 1641. Phips had gone to the court of Charles II, the central political institution of the monarchy into which he had been born, to secure not only authorisation from the king, but also financial backing from a group of City of London businessmen and prominent courtiers like Christopher Monck, second Duke of

Albemarle – a financially embarrassed chancer who was a friend and backer of Henry Morgan and briefly governor of Jamaica. His physician, that remarkable Ulsterman Sir Hans Sloane, future father of the British Museum, went to Jamaica with him and cannot have been greatly surprised by his patron's premature death, for he has left us a description of how unfit the alcoholic duke was before the idea of restoring his fortunes by going to the West Indies penetrated a mind which was often 'somewhat out of order'.[11]

In London Phips had forged an alliance with Increase Mather, who was part of the formidable father-and-son clerical team of Cotton and Increase Mather and who was lobbying relentlessly for the restoration of the charter privileges of Massachusetts. On the back of this and his fabled luck, Phips was in one day in March 1690 rocketed into the Boston elite by being baptised and admitted to full membership of Boston North Church, as well as being made a freeman, major general, and commander in chief of a forthcoming expedition against the main French settlement in Acadia, Port Royal on the Bay of Fundy. Boston merchants were anxious to curb Acadian privateering against their shipping, so Phips headed a strong force of 700 sailors and militiamen when in May he easily forced Port Royal to surrender on terms which seem predictably to have been violated by the systematic looting which followed. Although he made no effort to garrison and therefore hold Port Royal, Phips returned in triumph, despite creditable anger among Boston councillors at allegations that Phips had stolen the personal possessions, ostensibly protected by the surrender document, of the French governor. Logically enough, New England opinion was of the view that the way to stop more destructive frontier raids was to take out the base from which they were mounted by attacking Canada. The decision to do so by land and sea had been taken at an inter-colonial conference independently sponsored by both Massachusetts and the Leisler regime in New York, and held in the city of New York on 1 May 1690. The conference boded ill for effective cooperation. No colony south of the Hudson sent delegates, who came only from Massachusetts, from a New Plymouth destined soon to disappear into Massachusetts, and from Connecticut. Virginia insisted it could not afford to offer support. Maryland offered only a hundred men. Still, after the successful assault on Port Royal, morale was high enough to launch two offensives. The diversionary land attack by 1500 Indians and 500 whites from New York and Connecticut was crucial to hopes of success, for it alone could prevent Frontenac from concentrating all his forces against a never very overwhelming amphibious attack down the St Lawrence. Under Colonel Winthrop – and plagued by smallpox, supply shortages, and internal quarrels – the land offensive collapsed at the foot of Lake Champlain in mid-August. That 150 men did move down that water corridor to raid villages near Montreal was better than nothing, but not much better. The naval expedition was fatally delayed by shortages of arms and ammunition and inability to raise men, who had to be pressed despite irresponsible assurances of loot after a walkover victory. Due to adverse weather at sea, Quebec was not reached until early October, when it was much too near to winter for an original force of 2300 reduced effectively to half by smallpox, facing well-entrenched and resolute forces of comparable if not greater strength, and absurdly short of gunpowder for both muskets and land and sea ordnance – to the point where they could scarce have fought a well-conducted engagement (not that they were capable of that). Storms and ship losses sent them home. Leisler's goose was cooked by the failure. He was arrested after ill-advisedly resisting the installation of a new royal governor and judicially murdered by his local enemies in 1691. William III had him exonerated in 1695, a shade late. Massachusetts added £40,000–50,000 to its debt and paid off mutinous troops with depreciated paper money. Had King William been interested enough to intervene in 1690 to sort out the governance of the demoralised northern colonies, from which petitions were being forwarded for the restoration of the desirable aspects of unity under the dominion of New England, appalling future problems might have been moderated, but he was not interested.[12]

Outside Albany the Dutch community had been disproportionately supportive of Leisler. His fall 'set the fate of the Dutch'. Since the conquest they had defended the rights granted them by the articles of surrender, and many in 1689 must have hoped that with a Dutch prince on the throne it might be possible to strengthen their identity in the province. Instead, they 'could not escape their fate of being the first Europeans to confront the pressures of English culture and society in North America'. They were the first of many such groups and by 1800 their cultural patterns remained strong only in a few areas, especially in the upper Hudson valley.[13] The general effect of a traumatic and protracted war was to re-emphasise the indivisibility of the fate of the Atlantic-linked English world.

The central strategic issue of the war was not dissimilar to the one which was to dominate strategic argument in the United Kingdom during the First World War. Ultimately, those with the power of decision believed that it was essential to concentrate the maximum naval force in European waters and the maximum weight of land forces available to the coalition fighting Louis XIV in Flanders, where alone a decision could be reached in the face of the main fighting force of the French army, if only in the form of checking any French threat to William's beloved United Netherlands. After a naval defeat for the Anglo–Dutch fleet off Beachy Head in 1690, there was a very real threat of a successful Franco–Jacobite invasion of England. In the spring of 1692 the exiled James II was poised to return with French troops and a disposition, to judge by his proclamations at the time, to make those who had overthrown him or who would dare to resist him pay heavily for their conduct. God knows how the Saints of New England would have fared under a new restoration, but it would certainly have been the end of their long career of prevarication and covert republicanism. As it happened, a decisive allied naval victory at the Battles of Barfleur and the Hogue in 1692 crushed all hopes for James Stuart's armada.[14] Louis XIV was more willing to send regular troops to America than William III, but neither monarch was prepared to detach significant parts of his naval or military forces for service in the western hemisphere. Nevertheless, the whole North Atlantic was ultimately a single war zone with informed observers acutely conscious of the linkages between what was happening in the metropolitan archipelago off Western Europe and the seas around it and the cockpit of Flanders, and events in North America and the West Indies.

The English provincials were nervously aware that Frontenac had played with the idea of an all-out assault on Boston or New York. In practice, action was confined to their northern sea and land frontiers, but it was frightening enough. Several Royal Navy frigates had to be placed on convoy duty off the New England coast to ensure that French privateers did not totally disrupt English trade. Even when they were successful, the actions could be bloody. One account which reached London in 1690 described 'an obstinate fight at half muskett-shot distance near two hours' between a 30-gun French man-o'-war and a Royal Navy escort frigate with similar armament but without the enlarged crew of its antagonist. A merchant ship of the convoy which joined in saw grenade throwers and musketeers fall from the Frenchman's fighting tops 'like pidgeons'. On fire and badly holed, the Frenchman eventually sheered off, but leaving the captain of the escort frigate dead, as well as many other dead and wounded.[15] By the end of the war Royal Navy frigates were being supplemented by a provincial Massachusetts naval force of sloops, ketches, and galleys (sailing ships usually with a flush deck and the ability to be propelled by large oars or sweeps when in shallow waters or rivers). The unity of the North Atlantic as a field of operations was demonstrated even in failure. A naval squadron was sent from England under Sir Francis Wheler to campaign in the West Indies in the winter of 1692–93. The plan was that it would then move up to New England in the early summer of 1693. Waiting there would be forces under the command of Sir Thomas Phips, who had become the first royally nominated governor of Massachusetts under the colony's revised 1691 charter. Together they would rerun the 1690 assault on Quebec. Phips had at least learned from failure. The fleet arrived too late in July in his view to set out for the St Lawrence without undue risk of being caught in unacceptable weather. Phips had been unable to assemble adequate provincial forces. The fleet was riddled with disease. Only half the ships' complements survived and of two regiments aboard only 650 soldiers. Phips vetoed the enterprise, and Wheler headed north to try to strike a blow in the Anglo–French war of attrition in Newfoundland, where he pillaged St Pierre but achieved little else before storms scattered his ships. Massachusetts was spared fresh waste of funds, which – given its heavily taxed state, its debts, and its inability to secure cooperation from other colonial governments – was just as well. It was also just as well that after 1694 the authorities of New France could not obtain sufficient naval support from France seriously to attack the heart of English America.

In the West Indies, though the French started with the big advantage of having in Martinique an outstanding naval base and headquarters, success or failure largely hinged on the amount of support that got through from Europe to reinforce the local forces, and before 1697 there was never enough to make a decisive difference. In 1689 the French seized control of St Kitts. The only significant Jacobites left in English America were Irish Roman Catholic servants and settlers in Montserrat and Antigua, and they were thought to be a potentially dangerous fifth column; but naval support and some troops from home, supplemented by a regiment from Barbados plus the emergence of a dynamic new leader, Christopher Codrington, commander in chief of the Leeward Islands 1689–98, enabled the English to mount a counter-offensive. Codrington was such a wealthy planter that he could supplement the funding of his operations from his own pocket. The year 1690 saw him recapture St Kitts. In 1691 he would have over-run Guadeloupe after a successful landing but was let down by his naval support withdrawing. In 1693 his invasion of Martinique was similarly frustrated. Many of his fellow planters did not really want to bring French competition in the sugar market within the English protectionist system by conquest.[16] Stalemate ruled. Though in 1683 French and Dutch buccaneering captains had combined in a sensational sack of Vera Cruz, which had been infinitely more profitable than Morgan's sack of Panama, it turned out that in the Nine Years' War the French could not even seriously interrupt Spanish commerce with the Caribbean. *Flotas* sailed successfully for Vera Cruz in 1688, 1689, 1692, 1695, 1696, and 1698. The *Galeones* reached Cartagena safely in 1690 and 1695.[17] William III was aware of the importance of the Caribbean plantations to the revenues of the Crown of England. His servants could effectively make the point that if there was intelligence of the fitting out of a squadron in France with troops aboard and aimed at the West Indies, the threat to the English colonies, which could not defend themselves against a large metropolitan French expedition, simply had to be met by a similar English effort to preserve plantations 'wherein your Majesty's Revenue and the Navigation of the Kingdome are so highly concerned'. Any French squadron could try to cap success in the Caribbean with a potentially devastating sweep up to the Chesapeake, New York, and New England on its way home. William also had to prop up his Spanish allies, 'the preservation of whose Colonies in those parts and their Flota and Gallions [is] so important to Your Majesty'.[18]

William III and the various sections of the English nation were united only in their opposition to France. Otherwise they fought the same war with significantly different agendas. With the establishment of the Bank of England, a national debt, and deficit funding as a normal government expedient, the king has been seen as one of the founders of the 'British version of the fiscal-military state',[19] albeit one who left problems of political management and taxation patterns to be sorted out in subsequent reigns. Clearly he did leave a heritage to the state rooted in England which in the next two centuries under various names was able to incorporate a fluctuating proportion of the British Isles and to form equally fluctuating patterns of overseas dominion, but William was not consciously any kind of state builder. He was Dutch, a member of an early-modern community which had become a nation to avoid the need to build a central state. He was a Dutch patriot who was also an aristocratic military adventurer and spectacular risk taker. Above all, he was determined to fight Louis XIV to a standstill, using any resources he could lay his hands on. He very nearly wrecked the economy of Old England by the vast deficits, econocidal naval policies, and ruinous monetary policies he ruthlessly imposed in the name of military necessity. But for a massive recoinage in 1695–97, the pound would have collapsed. As it was, 'survival to the peace, signed at Ryswick in September 1697, was a very close-run thing indeed'.[20] The enormous discontent which the Dutch monarch's rule provoked among those who had to pay for his policies is entirely understandable. So was the apparent shortsightedness of the English political establishment. Edward Randolph – who was appointed surveyor general of customs in America again in 1698, with as close a relationship with the new Board of Trade set up in 1697 as he had had with their predecessors the Lords of Trade and Plantations – had been agitating since 1676 for stronger royal control in the American colonies. In 1695 he had returned to London with detailed material on the general evasion of law in the colonies, and with a detailed plan for rationalising the mosaic of colonial jurisdictions as a prelude to building some degree of coherence and reasonable cooperation between the colonies and the Crown, as well as between the colonies themselves. His case was overwhelming. Failure to act constructively was to breed dismal consequences, yet the House of Lords chose in 1696 to initiate important legislation not to grasp a political nettle, but to tighten up the administration of the revenue-yielding Acts of Navigation. Like King William, their lordships were for minimising potential political trouble while maximising existing revenue yields needed to fund the war: they knew the monarchy and the English nation were on the verge of bankruptcy.[21]

For much of the war raid and counter-raid therefore swayed back and forth on the periphery of English spheres of influence in America without decisively tipping the balance. From western Massachusetts to eastern Maine the French and their Indian allies repeatedly pounced on settlements too small to defend themselves, inflicting loss even when significant numbers of the inhabitants did manage to reach defended houses with thick, bullet-proof walls which offered a measure of protection against what were essentially hit-and-run raids. English seasonal counter-raids led by experienced fighters like James Converse and Benjamin Church could not win decisive victories, but did usefully destroy Indian villages and food supplies, and hindered the Abenaki from concentrating in numbers adequate for serious action. In western New York a different war of attrition was going on, while in Newfoundland and on Hudson's Bay, despite the outstanding abilities of French commanders like d'Iberville, success went usually to the side which had had the most recent dose of reinforcement. At the very end of the war there was no doubt that the French were in the ascendant. They had destroyed nearly all the English fishing settlements in Newfoundland, and the sending in the summer of 1697 by Louis XIV of 'the most formid-able fleet ever sent to Hudson's Bay'[22] enabled the French to capture York Factory, the main Hudson's Bay Company settlement on the strategic Nelson River, which they were to hold until the Peace of Utrecht of 1713. It was the same story on the Maine frontier. There a period of stalemate was broken when stone-built Fort William Henry – which Phips had had con-structed at great expense, with assurances of reimbursement by the Crown, to secure the Pemaquid settlement – fell after a disgracefully token resist-ance from its provincial garrison to a powerful expedition from Quebec led by d'Iberville in August 1696. The persistent, essentially pacific traders of the Hudson's Bay Company still held on in James Bay, the area nearest to their arch-enemies in Montreal, and an English fleet did redress the bal-ance in Newfoundland at the last minute, but the French were undoubtedly marginal victors in these northern combats.

On the western marches of New York, the French scored a victory which was far from marginal. It finally eliminated the Iroquois threat to New France, and thereby massively weakened the English position. In the open-ing years of the war the Iroquois had struck heavy blows against the French, but the failure of the English colonists' invasion of Quebec in 1690 had shaken Iroquois confidence, and then they had found that increasingly they were not receiving any effective support from their allies in the Covenant

Chain. An Oneida chief, Cheda, demanded to know of the governor of New York in 1692 why his people were fighting alone in what was supposed to be a general war of the Anglo–Iroquois alliance. He went on, 'how come Maryland, Delaware River, and New England to be disengaged from this War? – How can they and we be Subjects of the same great King, and not be engaged in the same War?'[23] There was an answer, of course, but that was that the incoherence of the English polity did indeed make it a hopeless ally. Connecticut was perhaps the extreme case. Its geographical position allowed its leaders to wrangle about inter-colonial parity and local control, and to prevaricate endlessly over costs. The colony was not directly threatened. It wanted the Iroquois and Albany to defend it while it shirked serious contributions. It could not or would not see that the Iroquois were not fools and that sending 150 dragoons to Albany, long after a massive French punitive strike had hit the Mohawks in February 1693 and withdrawn, was merely to add insult to injury.[24] The year that the French attacked the Mohawks with six hundred troops was also the year Phips wisely aborted another plan to invade Canada. The Iroquois began to reach out for negotiation with the French, nor were they misled when in 1694 Governor Benjamin Fletcher of New York tried to talk them out of the idea, with assurances of support they knew he could not deliver. In 1696, two thousand French troops and Indian allies devastated the villages of two more Iroquois nations – the Onondagas and Oneidas. The western tribes hostile to the Iroquois gathered for the attack in the 1690s, actually settling in territories long claimed by the Iroquois, who were not included in the peace in 1697. Eventually, the Iroquois sachems negotiated a treaty with New France in 1701. They could not stop the establishment of French forts at Detroit and by 1720 at the vital Niagara portage, but their hands had been strengthened by an understanding with the once seriously hostile Ottawa people to the north. Mutual recognition and free passage to Albany through the Iroquois heartland was irresistible to a trading people like the Ottawa, who were weary of war. The French settled for Iroquois neutrality. Despite the anger of New York, the Iroquois also allowed Jesuits to reside in their lands. The mental takeover and control which the French hoped for never occurred, but the epidemic- and war-decimated Iroquois gained a respite to rebuild population and prosperity. They were only a few thousand strong and no more powerful than they had been in 1640. New York effectively followed their example in the next war by pursuing tacit neutrality, apart from a couple of half-hearted flirtations with military activity in 1709 and 1711.[25] As an Atlantic imperial people the English nation had failed irreversibly by 1700. Self-government by colonial charter and even modest functional unity proved incompatible, and imperial appeasement of colonial protests and intransigence merely encouraged more intransigence.

Yet ducking the problem by shouldering more and more of a war effort mainly needed to protect the colonists from the consequences of their meanness and folly was in the end London's preferred option.

The authorities there were not short of advice stressing the strategic facts of American life, such as the imperative necessity of keeping an active alliance with the Iroquois, if possible, because, though they were few in number, the combination of their forest warfare and scouting skills with the military potential of the English colonies and the power of the Royal Navy was in theory more than enough to overwhelm New France. The problem was the collapse of all coherence with the disintegration of the Dominion of New England.[26] William III was probably the last monarch who could have secured some degree of rationalisation in the northern colonies, but he was primarily interested in financial contributions from the parliament of Old England for his war, and in the Americas the even distribution of eight regular infantry companies in the mid-1690s between the West Indies and New York showed that there he was primarily anxious to defend the web of maritime links which guaranteed payment of his plantation duties.[27] Nor did the new prominence of the Westminster parliament due to war finance help the imperial problem. By the mid-1690s critics of the American situation were suggesting that legislation by that parliament should be used to over-ride local obstruction. Precedents such as the Acts of Navigation and the status of the English in Ireland could be cited, but misleadingly so. Poyning's Law was a reasonable assertion of sovereignty, but of the king's sovereignty, which was ultimately the only formal sovereignty. A monarch might utilise any one of the parliaments or assemblies which were expressions of his or her majesty for more general ends, purely for practical convenience, but once one of those bodies tried to use the royal sovereignty for its own purposes against other such bodies, the game had changed and ceased to carry the same moral weight.[28] By 1697 the Board of Trade could articulate to the king the central problem: no sane observer doubted the need for more unity in the northern colonies, but there was nothing but backbiting and mutual antagonism when means were discussed. The appointment of the needy Irish nobleman the Earl of Bellomont as governor of Massachusetts, New Hampshire, and New York after 1695, with even wider military responsibilities, was designed to build more cohesion, but foundered on the bloody-mindedness of the individual assemblies – one of which, Rhode Island, this Irish Whig described as 'the most Irregular and Illegal that ever any English Government was'.[29]

Virtually every part of the composite monarchy over which William III reigned was showing signs of acute political stress by the time of his death in 1702. His Scottish reign had started with a civil war. The great achievement of the Scottish aristocracy had been to contain it, preventing any

27

repetition of the devastating events of 1644–45, when the royalist Marquis of Montrose had inflicted untold damage and suffering on the country for very little practical result. A highly pragmatic approach to cooperation across ideological lines had also enabled the Scottish political nation to foil William's attempt to preserve most of the fundamentally irresponsible system through which the favourites of James VII had misgoverned his ancient kingdom.[30] Thereafter the pressures of war, famine, disease, economic depression, and the frequently ruthlessly high-handed actions of the Williamite executive in Scotland – notably in connection with the massacre of a minor Jacobite clan in Glencoe and the subsequent cover-up – ensured that Jacobitism (i.e. support for the exiled main branch of the Stuart dynasty which had taken up residence in the palace of St Germain in France) was far more pervasive in the Scotland of 1702 than it had been in 1688, when very few had turned out to fight for King James.[31]

Ireland was, by the turn of the century, also showing signs of giving trouble, even though it was firmly under the control of an overwhelmingly Protestant aristocracy. The minority of Roman Catholic landowners who had clung to their estates in the restoration era and who for a brief period when James II was a resident king in Ireland looked as if they might recover a great deal more, had been broken by the outcome of the Williamite wars in Ireland. Ironically, William himself had not wanted to divert his energy and forces into an Irish campaign and would have preferred some sort of negotiated settlement with James' lord deputy, Richard Talbot, Earl of Tyrconnell. However, the chances of any compromise between the aspirations of the Old English nobility, which were essentially embodied in Tyrconnell, and the substantial confirmation of the restoration Irish land settlement, which is what Protestant opinion would have pressured William for, made an agreed outcome unlikely. Though at various points in the campaigns groups in the Jacobite camp argued for negotiation based less on any specific division of land ownership and more on religious toleration and a free market in land, they never gained the upper hand. The new regime was therefore based on an Anglican nobility and gentry, an almost homogeneous political nation which represented the final, exclusive triumph of the New English interest, which had been wrestling with others in Ireland since the sixteenth century. Precisely because there was no surviving serious challenge to their ascendancy, this political nation could then describe itself as Irish with genuine enthusiasm and adopt traditional Old English constitutional arguments to defend the Dublin parliament and administration against English attempts to subordinate or control them. And they had good reason to oppose such control, since they correctly believed that King William was much more interested in appeasing his Roman Catholic allies like the emperor or the king of Spain than he was in endorsing the draconian measures which would have been required to root out the Roman Catholic Church in Ireland. Most of the Penal Laws against Catholics were passed under Queen Anne, and were by then too little, too late seriously to eradicate the central achievements of the Counter-Reformation in Ireland. On top of these considerations, the Anglican rulers of Ireland were suspicious that the London government was exploiting divisions within Irish Protestantism by patronising the Presbyterians of Ulster, where that community received additional reinforcement and showed new assertiveness as a result of a big influx of Scottish refugees from the dreadful Scottish famines of the 1690s. These people were more alarming in some ways to the rulers of Ireland than the Roman Catholic peasantry. From the Tory Dean Swift to the radical Whig Wolfe Tone, patriotic and articulate Irish Protestants were liable to expound the lamentably unrealistic view that Counter-Reformation Catholicism would simply wither away in the face of social, intellectual, and economic progress. Swift and William Molyneux could therefore defend the autonomy of Ireland on strictly constitutional grounds.[32] Molyneux and two fellow graduates of Trinity College, Dublin – Robert, Viscount Molesworth, and John Trenchard – were to expound a principled hostility to the domination of the composite monarchy by London.[33] It was a view which the Westminster parliament could defy by asserting its authority over Ireland by the Declaratory Act of 1720, but it was a view which was biding its time, and war brought that time, though not in the reign of Anne. Even so, when the Irish elite watched breathlessly the great Western European battles of her day, they did so in a spirit essentially anti-French rather than pro-British.

Round Two: fighting France and making Britain 1702–1713

The composite Atlantic monarchy to which Queen Anne succeeded after William's death in 1702 was therefore a deeply divided structure with acute tensions, not just between the different political nations of which it was composed, but also within the communities over which those nations presided. These internal tensions did not find institutional expression in Scotland or Ireland, but the core national group, the English nation, was a different story. Its Atlantic-wide political structure was a contradictory shambles in many ways. War with a Catholic France which was perceived as absolutist united the English, but had also demonstrated in the 1690s their chronic inability to cooperate at even minimally sensible levels in North

America, and war was coming again, over the issue of the Spanish succession. It was so clear that there would be a crisis due to the failure of direct heirs to the sickly and impotent Charles II, the last male Spanish Habsburg, that Louis XIV and William III had negotiated not one but two highly controversial partition treaties. These were designed to solve the problem that there were two serious claimants to the succession, the Austrian Habsburgs and the French Bourbons, and a third, weaker one from the Bavarian Wittelsbachs, and that neither of the first two would willingly accept a massive strengthening of the other. The maritime powers, England and the United Netherlands, were naturally averse to the idea that the French Bourbons gain control over the Spanish overseas dominions. The first Partition Treaty of 1698 gave the bulk of the inheritance to the weakest dynasty in the form of the electoral prince of Bavaria, with compensation to France and Austria in Italy. When that prince died, a second treaty in 1700 gave Spain, its overseas dominions, and the southern Netherlands to a younger son of the House of Austria, while France was more heavily compensated in Italy. An enraged Spanish court, which had not been consulted, backed the strategy embedded in the will of Charles II, which coopted French power to defend the unity of the Spanish Empire by willing everything to the second grandson of Louis XIV, Philip of Anjou – with the unacceptable rider that rejection of the offer would mean it would be transferred in its entirety to the younger son of France's arch-rival, the Austrian Habsburg Emperor Leopold I. Military men were toasting the prospect of war as early as 1699, and though the Dutch and English acknowledged the accession of the Bourbon Philip V to the Spanish thrones in 1701, there was no way they could stay out of the fighting between Louis XIV and Leopold I which began that year. Louis occupied barrier forts vital to Dutch security in the Spanish Netherlands; acknowledged the heir of James VII and II as legitimate ruler of the Stuart dominions; and on top of this endorsement of Jacobitism, behaved in such a fashion with respect to the Spanish overseas empire as to suggest that he meant to use French power to colonise it from within. The unavoidable Anglo–French war was formally declared in May 1702.[34] Neither side had wanted it, but the dead William III had prepared for it.

The war was bound to involve the overseas dominions of France, England, and Spain. Indeed, the destiny of the resources represented by the Spanish American Empire was one of the main issues of the war, though the allied opponents of Louis XIV clearly meant to settle that issue on European battlefields. In 1701, with war with England impending, Louis XIV therefore took the fundamental decision to use the French presence in North America as a means of tying up hostile resources in a strategic side-show. Previously, the French had fought for the Canadian objective of controlling the western fur trade despite their inability to compete on purely commercial terms. Now Louis ordered a systematic attempt to corral the English settlements east of the Appalachian Mountains. He urged, against strong Canadian commercial opposition which saw them as wasteful and dangerous, two important developments. One was a fort and colony at the narrows between Lakes Erie and Huron. This was Detroit, and it was meant to keep the English out of the north-west completely. Much more dramatic was the founding of a new colony, Louisiana, at the mouth of the Mississippi to forestall possible English settlement from the Carolinas, and to establish an interior line of control along that river, the Great Lakes, and the St Lawrence. East of it the native allies of France were to be welded into an exclusive block sealed off from cultural, economic, and political contact with the English. The fur trade was subordinated to politics, and indeed to the regular officers of the colonial line commanding at the interior forts. The problem was that commitments south of the Great Lakes made little commercial sense in an era of glutted fur markets, and were politically provocative. The furs there were inferior to those of the north-west where the high quality of their trade goods, the excellence of the river transportation, and the universal Cree trading language would have made it easy for the French to maintain an indefinite ascendancy.[35] Above all, as Louis XIV's great minister Jean-Baptiste Colbert had warned in the late seventeenth century, any policy based on an aggressive dog-in-the-manger challenge to the future of the English settlements was bound eventually to provoke a backlash which would threaten the very survival of New France. He was right.[36] In many ways the new imperial strategy was surreal, since it involved continental pretensions on the back of pathetically inadequate realities, such as the colony of Louisiana which Pierre Le Moyne d'Iberville started to establish on the shore of Biloxi Bay in February 1699. D'Iberville moved his colonial headquarters to Mobile Bay in 1702 for better access to nearby Indian tribes.

The tone of the colony was well expressed by its leader's speech, translated by his younger brother, Jean-Baptiste Le Moyne de Bienville, for the benefit of Chickasaw and Choctaw Indian delegates at a meeting in March 1702. D'Iberville berated the Chickasaws for having 'foolishly followed the advice of the English', and threatened that the French would assail them in alliance with the Choctaws, Mobilians, and Tahomes, unless they instantly expelled all the English from their territory. The southern region between the Mississippi and the most southerly of the English colonies, South Carolina, was already unstable and violent, partly due to the search by traders from the Carolinas for Indian slaves as well as the deer skins which the French soon worked out were the most valuable available export from Louisiana, but which could not be had except from the Indians, and then only if large amounts of gunpowder were traded in exchange. In 1708 the colonial population of Louisiana was composed of 122 soldiers and sailors, 80 Indian slaves, and 77 settlers. The slaves were an early fruit of conflict with small coastal tribes, some of which were among the first Indian peoples to be wiped out by the two main gifts the new colony bestowed on the region: epidemic disease and higher levels of violence. Plantation agriculture to produce tropical staples like indigo required black slaves and Louisiana acquired its first handful of them from the sack of Nevis by d'Iberville in 1706, after which that remarkable Canadian naval officer died of yellow fever in Havana. Despite a phase of mass immigration arranged by the Scotsman John Law's Company of the Indies in 1717–21, death rates were such that there were still only 2000 colonists in 1731, but 4000 black slaves. Louisiana had fought its first large-scale genocidal war when it put down a 1729 rising of the Natchez Indians, and by paying the Choctaws for Chickasaw scalps and slaves had launched what the French hoped would be an endless struggle between the two tribes. The Chickasaw proved tough opponents. Their fortified villages were so engineered that they could absorb pounding by heavy French cannon. It remains extraordinary how much mayhem so small a French colony could cause.[37]

The War of the Spanish Succession, misnamed Queen Anne's War in English America, involved conflict there on both Anglo–French and Anglo–Spanish borders. The unfortunate Spaniards in northern Florida had to face French pressure from the west as well as a northern threat, from the Carolina colony which had been established by 1670. North Carolina acquired a separate governor in 1710. The Spanish fort at Pensacola, established just before Louisiana became a reality, held the western marches and the war saw an uneasy Franco–Spanish alliance, for the Spanish overseas empire opted for the French candidate for the throne. The Carolina slave dealers and their Creek Indian allies were a different proposition. They had successfully raided Apalache and the Franciscan mission to the Timicuans. A Spanish punitive column had been routed at the Flint River in the summer of 1702 by the Carolinians and Creeks. Governor James Moore of South Carolina was well aware of d'Iberville's hopes not just for Franco–Spanish cooperation, but also for an offensive which would start with the destruction of Carolina and then systematically roll up the other southern English colonies until it conquered the Chesapeake region. Predictably ultra-aggressive, utterly unrealistic, and deeply counter-productive when its outline became common knowledge, d'Iberville's master plan was a great help to Moore.

In 1702 Moore invaded Florida, doing vast damage and capturing San Augustin but failing due to lack of heavy cannon and mortars to capture its central fortress, the Castillo de San Marcos. He was forced to retreat with the loss of his ships when a relief force arrived from Havana. By 1704 the debts of the Carolina colony were such that Moore had to fund from the wealth he had accumulated as planter, trader, and slaver a colonial and Indian army which devastated the Apalache missions. Thereafter the Carolinian alliance with the Creeks, renewed formally in 1705, and subversion of French and Spanish Indian allies enabled partisan warfare to destroy irreversibly the mission-controlled Indians who were the thin northern bulwark of a Florida whose interior Indians had always defied and detested the Spaniards. By 1707 Pensacola had been burned and there were plans for an assault on Mobile which foundered due to funding problems, factional disputes among provincial leaders, and Bienville's outstanding Indian diplomacy. An attack on Charles Town, seat of the Indian trade, by French ships and Spanish troops in 1706 was decisively defeated.[38] By 1710 the war was a stand-off, but with the Carolinian position much enhanced, so much so that it was possible for South Carolina to send decisive aid to North Carolina against the rising of the Tuscarora Indians of the inner coastal plain, a section of whom had finally been driven to despair by pressure from whites following the arrival of a wave of Swiss and Palatine German settlers in 1710. Virginia sent some provisions, but Governor Spotswood dropped a plan to send two hundred militia after a row with the North Carolinians over money. South Carolina sent a typical mixed provincial and Indian force under veteran partisan commander John Barnwell. Fascinatingly, the Tuscaroras twice defied their opponents from state-of-the-art forts, artillery-resistant and defended by trenches, ditches, outworks, and the sharpened stakes which were the eighteenth-century equivalent of barbed wire. They were far from crushed decisively. Barnwell left after treacherously seizing Indians as slaves after inviting them to a peace celebration, but that was essentially unscrupulous business practice – there was no other way of making his war pay, and the North Carolinians were angry at his lack of interest in obliterating the enemy. James Moore led the second South Carolinian intervention. Many Tuscaroras fled to be incorporated in the Iroquois confederacy, or to Virginia. Others accepted settlement on a reservation under a 1713 agreement. Guerrilla warfare sputtered on for years, but these coastal Indians did not have the demographic weight to hold up the post-1713 immigrant tide.[39]

Decision in the War of the Spanish Succession was sought by concentrating on Europe. It was the strategy of William III more effectively executed. That monarch's administration in London had been warned, in the interlude of peace, of the potentially exposed nature of the American colonies. Edward Randolph had argued that Bermuda could be surprised and taken by five hundred men.[40] Robert Livingstone had conveyed to William Blathwayt his sense in 1701 that the impending French settlement with the

Iroquois was a potential disaster for the English, and his despair at the fact that no response to this crisis was possible.[41] It was true that when it became clear that the French had concentrated 42 warships with 1200 troops aboard in Martinique on the eve of war, and that they and their Spanish allies were proposing to open informal hostilities at once, instructions went out to governors of West Indian islands that they must be ready for action; but they were also assured that the Royal Navy squadron sent to the Caribbean under Vice Admiral John Benbow was ready to protect trade and colonies and to react aggressively to any provocation.[42] The eventual fleet action was indecisive. Two of Benbow's captains were later condemned to be shot for cowardice, while the admiral himself died of wounds. However, by then battle, disease, and Franco–Spanish distrust had destroyed the French squadron's potential for mischief. The main controller of high strategy under Queen Anne, John Churchill, Duke of Marlborough, was understandably hostile to side-shows. In 1710 he wrote that 'I dare not speak against the project of sending troops to the West Indies, but I will own very freely that I think it can end in nothing but a great expense and the ruining of those regiments.'[43] Marlborough's view of the disease environment in the West Indies was not unduly pessimistic, for though the range of human diseases there was wide in the seventeenth century, there was a marked increase in lethality from the 1690s into the eighteenth century. The two dominant diseases were malaria and yellow fever, both conveyed to humans by the domesticated mosquito *Aedes aegypti*. Malaria over the long run probably killed slightly more soldiers than yellow fever, but the latter was more lethal and was to dominate the era of expeditionary warfare in the Caribbean. Originally a West African disease, it became endemic in the Caribbean only after a severe epidemic in Martinique in 1690. All the virus then needed to break loose was an influx of a large body of non-immune hosts like an expeditionary force. Though it made forays as far as Boston in the summer, yellow fever really needed the sustained high temperatures of the tropics, for its host mosquito only flourished at above 80° Fahrenheit.[44]

Combat in the West Indies in the War of the Spanish Succession therefore soon settled down to mutual attrition, extremely expensive in lives and property, but with no decisive edge being established by either side after the early conquest of the French part of St Kitts by Christopher Codrington the younger, who achieved an easy victory – partly by offering the French planters generous terms with guarantees for their church and clergy and for their property in negro slaves. Thereafter it was significant that when he invaded Guadeloupe, he was out to destroy, not conquer. Planters on both sides were averse to acquiring new rivals within their respective economic systems by conquest. They were also increasingly reluctant to fight. When the French sacked Nevis in 1706 the negro men did not accept the planters' abject capitulation, which among other things allowed d'Iberville to start collecting negro slaves for shipment as loot. Instead the negroes retreated into the interior and went on fighting in a way which shamed their masters and drove d'Iberville into a very ugly humour indeed.[45] Planters could not see profit in pointless resistance. Governor Daniel Parke, a Virginian planter and Marlborough aide who came out as governor general of the Leeward Islands after the devastation of Nevis, expressed the cynical despair of many when he asked London, tongue firmly in cheek, to 'Send me over 10,000 Scotch, with oatmeal enough to keep them for three or four months.' With these self-sustaining minions he promised either to destroy Martinique, the core of French regional power, or kill off the Scots. Either way this splendid English chauvinist implied that the world would be a better place. He was rebuked by London on the grounds that after the recent union with Scotland all British subjects must be accorded equal respect.[46] Parke himself was a paranoid and greedy bully, to the point where, as planter confidence returned towards the later part of the war, his subjects were prepared to fight him. He was brutally murdered in 1710 in Antigua. It was indeed the wild west.

If the Caribbean colonies ended with a stalemate of balanced devastation, the mainland North American colonies contrived to stalemate all French attempts to strike at the heart of their economic and demographic strength. They had learned some lessons from former, partially self-inflicted disasters. There had always been considerable military and even more naval potential in New England to meet the challenge of a much smaller French Canada. In the previous war there had been wailing about losses to French privateers, but it is clear from the squabbles about non-payment of the Crown's fifth of the value of enemy prizes taken into New England ports that these include more than just the odd ship described as a 'rich prize'.[47] When Governor de Vaudreuil launched spoiling attacks on the Maine frontier with the usual mixture of Canadian militia, regular officers (themselves increasingly Canadian), and Abenaki allies, he hit a much better prepared enemy. Massachusetts militia had already moved in to strengthen the northern frontier. A screen of designated fortified settlements, with permanent garrisons of about fifty volunteers who were capable of concentrating against a specific enemy force once it had declared itself, proved on the whole adequate to contain what were essentially terrorist attacks by the enemy. The system was not foolproof. In early 1704 the town of Deerfield was surprised, with the usual small-scale massacre and over a hundred captives abducted, but the overall effect of this act of calculated terrorism was to enrage rather than to intimidate New England. Drawing on experience of the last war, Massachusetts deployed flying columns of rangers under experienced Indian fighters like Benjamin Church. They used Indian methods and tactics, from snowshoes to ambush and surprise raids on settlements, both Indian and French. In response to Deerfield, Church devastated fields and outlying settlements of the French Acadian population on the Bay of Fundy. Calls for stronger measures led to the raising of two volunteer regiments in 1707, and a thousand men with cannon attacked the main Acadian settlement, Port Royal, twice – in the spring and then the summer of 1707. Both attacks failed miserably, so aid was solicited from London and from other colonies.

It was hardly surprising that someone should suggest a rerun of the Phips attack on the heart of French Canada by way of the St Lawrence. Every raid, every loss to privateers, suggested that the simplest answer was to crush the heart of the beast, but it was significant that the mind behind the latest proposal was that of a Scot, Samuel Vetch, who had become a New England merchant involved in illegal trade with French Canada after participating in the unsuccessful bid to establish a Scottish colony at Darien on the Isthmus of Panama. That venture had been the subject of sarcasm from Governor Daniel Parke of the Leewards. Certainly the Company of Scotland Trading to Africa and the Indies would have been far wiser to concentrate on smuggling to willing Spanish settlers rather than listening to the charismatic London Scot, William Paterson, with his plans for an emporium in a rainforest where the Indians were anti-Spanish but hardly a viable consumer market.[48] If the Scots vision had been emporial rather than imperial in Panama, there is no doubt that their failure there was an important part of the background to their acceptance of the Treaty of Union of 1707, which like Darien was to them an attempt to gain more clout within the Anglo–Scottish relationship. Afraid that English talk of empire was a mere mask for domination over Scotland, the Scots wanted an ideological recasting of the English into a new British Empire after 1707, so that it became an extension of a new identity.[49] They never sold the idea to the elites of Old England, let alone of New England or the Chesapeake, but they tended to hyperactivism to set a seal on their commitment. Vetch, who had married a daughter of the New York grandee Robert Livingstone, had been a British negotiator in both Acadia and Quebec. He was for attacking both. Unfortunately, a proposed expedition in 1709 aborted when the Crown's contribution of ships and troops had to be diverted to shoring up the faltering military effort of Portugal. That kingdom had joined the Grand Alliance against Louis XIV in 1703, after witnessing an Anglo–Dutch fleet destroy a returning Spanish bullion fleet and its French escort at Vigo Bay, but was not truly capable of sustaining a war effort against Bourbon Spain. From the start allied naval forces had had to be used to protect Portugal's vital Brazil trade, but both in 1709 and in 1710 colonial hopes of support from the London government for an attack on Quebec were frustrated by diversion of resources to Portugal.[50] The year 1709 was particularly galling because large colonial forces had been concentrated at Boston and at the southern end of Lake Champlain. The capture of Port Royal by a combined force of such Crown troops as had reached America and provincial units in 1710 was viewed as a second best, though it was very desirable to contain the privateer menace, and it represented a realistic expression of the regional balance between New England and New France.

When the new Tory government, anxious for overseas victory, reversed the Europe-first priorities of its Whig predecessors in 1711 by sending out a significant force on forty-six transports escorted by fifteen warships with Admiral Sir Hovenden Walker and the politically well-connected Brigadier John Hill in joint command, the upshot showed the wisdom of the Whig priorities. The whole idea of the expedition, designed to mount the usual thrust at Quebec by sea, with a diversionary land attack, had been hyped relentlessly in London by the visit of four Iroquois sachems, referred to as 'kings', in the spring of 1710. The idea seems to have come, through Vetch, from serving provincial officers anxious for Crown backing for a knock-out blow against New France. They were shrewd.[51] A few hundred Iroquois warriors did participate in the offensive. However, the presence of 6000 regulars, 5000 seamen, and 1500 provincial troops posed terrible supply problems in a Boston with 9000 inhabitants. The amphibious operation started too late and without adequate local pilots for the St Lawrence. In the era of the so-called expansion of Europe printed maps of other continents tended to be very general and navigation extremely unreliable until the late eighteenth century.[52] The exiled Stuarts had collected maps of Scotland at St Germain and much of their collection survives, but it did not prevent the aborting of the 1708 rising by a directionally-challenged French admiral.[53] In bad weather in late August, Walker lost eight transports and a sloop and eight hundred men on the breakers on the north shore of the St Lawrence, when he thought he was approaching the south shore. Vetch, commanding the provincial troops, wanted to go on. Walker and a council of war, probably rightly, decided to go home. Reliable power-projection on a tight schedule over several thousand miles was beyond the capacities of the era's technology.

The year 1710 had been marked by the decisive defeat of the reigning Whig party in a British general election, the first British election as such, but one decided in the English constituencies. Whig policy had been identified with the crippling taxation and huge casualties of an increasingly unpopular war. Marlborough's run of battlefield victories had concluded with Malplaquet in 1709, a limited victory bought with a fearsome butcher's bill which was a gift to his Tory critics. The continental Europe-first strategy of Marlborough and his great political ally Sidney Godolphin had always had a risk factor built into it. Despite all the talk about a military revolution expanding vastly the size of standing armies – which has helped to keep historians employed as they either try to push it back from its original late-sixteenth/early-seventeenth-century time frame, or insist it did not really happen until much later, or ascribe it to tactical and technological innovations, or deny it had any such roots[54] – the fact is that the wars of King William had seen a peak in the trend towards relentless expansion in military and naval establishments in the handful of European monarchies capable of competing in the top league. The 'military–fiscal state' was usually a monarchy with a bureaucracy resting on an aristocracy which was not keen on taxes and which could obstruct their collection. This modified the ratchet effect of competition, which was probably the basic mechanism behind expansion, and imposed limits and therefore selectivity. Louis XIV had plenty of warships after 1695 but chose not to pour money into battle fleet operations, because he needed it for his armies. It was still true that the seas around the British Isles were a facility for invaders, not a moat, and the Franco–Jacobite enterprise of 1708 showed this. The incorporating Union Treaty of 1707, which Queen Anne's English ministry had pushed through the Scots parliament by persuading and bribing the dominant aristocracy, was meant to guard England's northern frontier against the Jacobite menace in the middle of a great European war, but as the treaty was deeply unpopular in Scotland, it in practice greatly helped the Jacobite cause. The extraordinarily devious Highland chief, Simon Fraser of Lovat – who was in France as a refugee from a rape charge but who was a sort of a Jacobite and deep down under many layers of self-serving equivocation a Scottish patriot – suggested that if the young James Francis Edward Stuart, whom Louis had recognised as rightful heir to his father James VII and II, could be conveyed to Scotland with a small French force, he could easily take over the Stuarts' ancient kingdom. Simon then suggested, quite brilliantly, that the Scots rerun their successful strategy of the bishops' wars against Charles I and occupy the north-east of England sources of London's fuel supply, forcing England not to defeat but to negotiate with a Franco–Scots alliance. There were simply no forces to oppose the invasion, which failed not because of the presence of the Royal Navy, but because the French admiral sent to execute it failed to take advantage of his window of opportunity by atrocious navigation which left him beating back slowly against the wind, having overshot his mark, and giving the Royal Navy the time it should never have had.[55] The American colonies outwith the Caribbean were always liable to suffer from privateers and the odd French squadron of warships, but they were safe from massive French intervention by the very nature of Louis' American strategy, and they were not divided in the way the Scots were, which might have allowed a small French force to be the catalyst of rebellion. They also benefited massively from the new Tory government in London, even though its America initiative culminated in a fiasco.

William Blathwayt's old friend and client Joseph Dudley – who had succeeded as governor of Massachusetts and New Hampshire in 1701, and who clung to the post despite serious attempts to have him removed in 1707 on charges of bribe taking and covert connection with merchants trading illegally with Quebec – was an unlikely candidate for survival, let alone achievement. Yet despite the failure of offensive operations under his aegis, his thirteen years of office showed very substantial defensive achievements. Frontier defence was so effective that only two major settlements came to grief – Deerfield and Haverhill. The Board of Trade had at various points been in despair about its inability to organise any inter-colonial cooperation, but Dudley contrived to recruit for the Crown two companies of volunteers who were sent to serve in the royal garrison of Jamaica, another American colony and one with which Massachusetts had closer commercial links than it had with many mainland ones.[56] He had also taken stern action against pirates, recovering 800 ounces of gold for the London treasury in the process, and this was another area in which there had been positive achievement since 1697. Around 1695 there were complaints that pirates based on ports in the English colonies in America were responding to increasing official hostility to their activities by moving into Asian waters, where they could cause infinite trouble for the English EIC by indiscriminate attacks on local shipping, rendered all the more damaging by their loud assurances that they would not attack English ships – assurances which convinced Asian rulers that the EIC was in league with the pirates. It was not. Its trade was suffering from a variety of problems, from government leasing of its biggest ships to serve as 60–70 gun warships, to heavy losses to French privateers in the South Atlantic, to the chartering of a rival company in 1697 with which they only managed to amalgamate finally as late as 1709. Add in a ceaseless cold war with the United Dutch East India Company (known as the VOC), their Dutch equivalent and rival, and the murder of their president in China in a mutiny of Buginese mercenaries which destroyed an agency he was trying to establish on an island off the mouth of the Mekong in 1702;[57] and they just did not need the plundering in the Red Sea of Gujerati and, worse, imperial Moghul ships by an Englishman calling himself 'Henry Avery', assisted by pirate ships from Rhode Island and Philadelphia. 'Avery' and his crew divided their loot in the Bahamas on their return before infiltrating themselves back into Ireland and England. The Scot William Kidd had set out, with backing from Whig politicians and a commission to take action against such pirates, but once in Asian waters plundered European and Moghul shipping, and even chased EIC vessels. The wrath of the company ensured his sub-sequent arrest and hanging at Execution Dock in 1701.[58]

He had reneged on his contract rather than outlived his time, for the War of the Spanish Succession was a great age of licensed privateering in Europe which turned into a great age also of piracy in Anglo-America, not in the mainland colonies where governors and elites were less inclined to connive at it, but in the Bahamas. There, exactly what London had been told would happen did happen. In 1703 a Franco–Spanish expedition from Havana devastated Nassau, the main settlement, and carried off the acting governor. Spanish raids of 1704 and 1706 completed the destruction of ordered life, turning the archipelago into a paradise for pirates, uncon-trolled by a London government which jibbed at the expense of ships and troops, let alone by the increasingly notional lords proprietors. There were at least a thousand active pirates in the Bahamas by 1713, on the whole stealing from Spaniards because that was easiest, but not under the letters of marque which a Henry Morgan had carried on every voyage. These persons (a few were female) were honest thieves. They probably damaged imperial Spain more than any formal British regime in the islands after 1707 could have done.[59] They were part of an extremely loose coalition of interests which fought the war against the Bourbon regimes in France and Spain in the wider Atlantic world. It was a conservative coalition of vested interests not unlike the one with which Queen Elizabeth had fought the Spain of Philip II and Philip III in the late sixteenth century. The contribu-tion of the Crown was real but severely limited, and the coalition, like the Elizabethan one, was full of tensions and clashes of interest.[60] On balance it proved sensible for the Crown to leave most of the colonies north of Jamaica to help themselves, even if it meant some had to bear a heavy burden of self-help, while a few helped very little, and some helped them-selves to rather too much, too indiscriminately. Greatly enhanced Crown commitment was impractical and would only have encouraged in the planta-tions the culture of obstruction, dependency, and ingratitude which had flowered so noxiously in the previous war.

Rather a different coalition of interests in Old England had agreed to fund the vast armies and navies needed to fight Louis XIV in Western Europe and the Mediterranean. Had the English political leadership been willing to accept earlier that the Anglo–Portuguese crusade to drive the Bourbon king out of Spain was essentially impractical, the final terms would have been even better from a British point of view. As it was, Louis' last commander, Marshal Villars, was able to fight through to the point where the Tory government after 1710 was as desperate for peace as was France, and prepared to betray allies to get it. Of the two leading figures in the new government, Harley and St John, Harley (later earl of Oxford) had a plan simultaneously to expand and secure British overseas trade and to stabilise war-torn state finances. By 1710 he was discussing with the Dutch how best to check the growing French domination of Spanish overseas trade and in 1711 a new South Sea Company was founded with himself at its head. In exchange for a nine-and-a-half-million-pound loan to help fund public debt, it gained a chartered monopoly of all South American trade on either coast, with the exceptions of Portuguese Brazil and Dutch Surinam, where a freedom to trade already existed. An armistice in 1711 gave English ships interim access to Spanish ports, though the first two South Sea Company ships were only ready to sail in 1715.

The Treaty of Utrecht signed in April 1713 saw Louis XIV make concessions overseas in order to avoid concessions in Europe. His grandson retained the throne of Spain and its overseas empire, though the emperor was confirmed in compensatory conquests in Italy and was awarded the dubious prize of the southern Netherlands. The thrones of France and Spain were never to be united and France forswore any special privileges in trade with the Spanish Empire. This was a retreat from a major French war aim, for Louis had said as late as 1709 that the principal object of the current war was the wealth-generating commerce of the Indies.[61] The British were confirmed in the sole possession of St Kitts and Newfoundland. France held Canada, Cape Breton Island, and Prince Edward Island, but surrendered Nova Scotia and Acadia to the British, the latter under extremely vague terms which were a recipe for future trouble. The local Micmac Indians, notably independent-minded people who had made no secret of their contempt for many aspects of French culture, fought off attempts by British settlers to move into their territory. They were encouraged, on a somewhat different agenda, by the Jesuit mission at Bay Verte on the peninsula connecting Nova Scotia to the mainland. The Micmacs kept the British to their main settlement in Port Royal until 1750 or so. As ever in the colonial period, a balance of force was salutary.[62] New England was rid of a privateer nest, but the Micmac nation did not experience the expropriation which the treaty invited the only-too-eager New Englanders to practise against the Abenakis.[63] The Hudson's Bay Company had managed to fight off an assault on its Fort Albany in 1709. Utrecht gave it back Fort York and, apart from a French raid in 1782, marked the end of the involvement of these canny traders with European wars.

All of this was rather more than the situation on the ground justified, and though the provincials of English America griped, they had done very well out of a European emphasis which generated gains and thirty years of peace with New France for them. Some American historians still see their dissatisfaction as 'another step on the road to eventual revolution', but this is pure retrospective state-myth construction and the reverse of the contemporary truth, which was that the provincials were frustrated imperialists who knew that they still very much operated within parameters set by the potentially vastly superior forces of European monarchies, and that the two versions of Bourbon monarchy still established in North America were antipathetic to the politics, culture, and dominant religion of English America. Apart from the acquisition of the two key Mediterranean naval bases, Gibraltar and Minorca, Old England secured few concrete gains at Utrecht. Like New England, it derived satisfaction from being able to insist on the expulsion of the Jacobite pretender from France (though he only moved to nearby Lorraine), and it set high hopes on developing trade with Spanish America. As an earnest of these hopes, the South Sea Company was given in the treaty a 30-year grant of the *asiento* or contract to furnish Spanish America with negro slaves from Africa, as well as a wedge in the door of general trade in the shape of a right to send one ship a year. The new British government was left after 1713 with the unresolved old structural problems of the English Atlantic monarchy, plus some of its own. Coalitions which win wars tend to fall apart in peace, and the British monarchy was a fragile coalition. What is remarkable is not that there were crises but that they were kept more or less under control for another sixty years, during which the subjects of that monarchy not only expanded their North American territorial bases, but also acquired extensive, if politically ambiguous, territorial ascendancies in the Indian sub-continent.

Notes and references

1. Robert C. Ritchie, *The Duke's Province* (University of North Carolina Press, Chapel Hill, NC, 1977), pp. 189–90.

2. Richard R. Johnson, *Adjustment to Empire: The New England colonies 1675–1715* (Leicester University Press, Leicester, 1981), pp. 85–86.

3. Bruce C. Trigger, *Natives and Newcomers: Canada's 'Heroic Age' reconsidered* (Manchester University Press, Manchester, pbk edn, 1985), pp. 262–80.

4. Papers and memorandum submitted in December 1697 by Sunderland, Middleton, and Godolphin, in Blathwayt Papers, Huntington Library, San Marino, CA (hereafter BPHL), Box III, BL 34 (A, B, C, D, E).

5. An example of a book written round this theme is Mark Cocker, *Rivers of Blood, Rivers of Gold: Europe's conflict with tribal peoples* (Jonathan Cape, London, 1998).

6. James Axtell, *The Invasion Within: The contest of cultures in colonial North America* (Oxford University Press, Oxford, 1985), pp. 247–49.

7. Karen Anderson, *Chain Her by One Foot* (Routledge and Kegan Paul, London, pbk edn, 1993), p. 228.

8. *Vide, Negotiators of Change: Historical perspectives on native American women*, ed. Nancy Shoemaker (Routledge and Kegan Paul, London, 1995).

9. Francis Jennings, *The Ambiguous Iroquois Empire* (Norton, New York, 1984), pp. 195–96.

10. W.J. Eccles, *The Canadian Frontier 1534–1760* (University of New Mexico Press, Albuquerque, NM, rev. edn, 1983), pp. 120–21.

11. Peter Earle, *The Wreck of the Almiranta* (Macmillan, London, 1979), p. 162.

12. Philip S. Haffenden, *New England in the English Nation 1689–1713* (Clarendon Press, Oxford, 1974), pp. 84–93.

13. Ritchie, *Duke's Province*, p. 238.

14. Philip Aubrey, *The Defeat of James Stuart's Armada 1692* (Leicester University Press, Leicester, 1979).

15. 'Abstract of a letter from Falmouth the 10th July 1690', BPHL, Box III, BL 291.

16. Richard Dunn, *Sugar and Slave: The rise of the planter class in the English West Indies 1624–1713* (Jonathan Cape, London, 1973), pp. 134–35.

17. *The New Cambridge Modern History Vol. VI*, ed. J.S. Bromley (Cambridge University Press, Cambridge, 1970), p. 354, fn. 1.

18. Board of Trade to William III, 3 December 1696, BPHL, Box IV, BL 420.

19. John Brewer, *The Sinews of Power: War, money and the English state 1688–1783* (Alfred A. Knopf, New York, 1989), p. 250.

20. D.W. Jones, 'The Economic Consequences of William III', in Jeremy Black (ed.), *Knights Errant and True Englishmen: British foreign policy, 1660–1800* (John Donald, Edinburgh, 1989), p. 38.

21. Michael G. Hall, *Edward Randolph and the American Colonies 1676–1703* (University of North Carolina Press, Chapel Hill, NC, 1960), Chap. 7.

22. Peter C. Newman, *Company of Adventurers* (Penguin, London, pbk edn, 1985), p. 160.

23. Jennings, *Ambiguous Iroquois Empire*, p. 205.

24. Harold E. Selesky, *War and Society in Colonial Connecticut* (Yale University Press, New Haven, CT, 1990), p. 42.

25. Thomas Elliot Norton, *The Fur Trade in Colonial New York 1686–1776* (University of Wisconsin Press, Madison, WI, 1974), Chaps. 2, 3, and 8.

26. Lavinus van Schaik, 'Report on Indian Affairs in North America delivered to Mr Blathwayt May 16, 1696 – at the Hague, by Charles Pilsworth', BPHL, Box IV, BL 192.

27. Board of Trade *c.* 1696, 'List of the Forces in the West Indies, and the Independent Companies', BPHL, Box IV, BL 422.

28. *Vide* van Schaik 'Report', *supra.*

29. Johnson, *Adjustment to Empire*, p. 300.

30. Bruce P. Lenman, 'The Scottish Nobility and the Revolution of 1688–1690', in Robert Beddard (ed.), *The Revolutions of 1688* (Clarendon Press, Oxford, 1991), pp. 137–62, and *idem*, 'The Poverty of Political Theory in the Scottish Revolution of 1688–90', in Lois G. Schwoerer (ed.), *The Revolution of 1688–89: Changing perspectives* (Cambridge University Press, Cambridge, 1992), pp. 244–59.

31. Bruce P. Lenman, *The Jacobite Clans of the Great Glen 1650–1784* (Scottish Cultural Press, pbk edn, 1995), Chap. 4, 'The Nadir of Government'.

32. Nicholas Canny, 'Identity Formation in Ireland: The emergence of the Anglo-Irish', in Nicholas Canny and Anthony Pagden (eds.), *Colonial Identity in the Atlantic World, 1500–1800* (Princeton University Press, Princeton, NJ, pbk edn, 1987), pp. 159–212.

33. Caroline Robbins, *The Eighteenth-Century Commonwealthman* (Harvard University Press, Cambridge, MA, 1961), p. 10.

34. William Roosen, 'The Origins of the War of the Spanish Succession', in Jeremy Black (ed.), *The Origins of War in Early Modern Europe* (John Donald, Edinburgh, 1987), pp. 151–75.

35. W.J. Eccles, 'The Fur Trade and Eighteenth-Century Imperialism', in *idem*, *Essay on New France* (Oxford University Press, Toronto, 1987), pp. 79–95.

36. W.J. Eccles, *Canada under Louis XIV, 1663–1701* (Oxford University Press, London, 1964), pp. 247–49.

37. Daniel H. Usner, *Indians Settlers and Slaves in a Frontier Exchange Economy: The lower Mississippi valley before 1783* (University of North Carolina, Chapel Hill, NC, 1992), Chaps. 1–3.

38. Verner W. Crane, *The Southern Frontier 1670–1732* (Norton, New York, pbk edn, 1981), Chap. 4.

39. There is an outstandingly good entry on the Tuscarora War by T.C. Parramore in Alan Gallay (ed.), *Colonial Wars of North America 1512–1763: An encyclopedia* (Garland, New York, 1996).

40. Edward Randolph, 'To the Lords Commissioners for Trade —', 15 November 1700, BPHL, Box V, BL 305.

41. Robert Livingstone to William Blathwayt, 23 May 1701, *ibid.*, BL 149.

42. Lords Justices to Governor William Selwyn of Jamaica and *mutatis mutandis* to the governors of Barbados and the Leeward Islands, 23 October 1707, *ibid.*, BL 343.

43. Cited in *The Cambridge History of the British Empire. Vol. I: The Old Empire*, eds. J. Holland Rose, A.P. Newton, and E.A. Benians (Cambridge University Press, Cambridge, 1929), p. 326.

44. John R. McNeill, 'The Ecological Basis of Warfare in the Caribbean, 1700–1804', in Maarten Ultee (ed.), *Adapting to Conditions: War and society in the eighteenth century* (University of Alabama Press, Tuscaloosa, AL, 1986), pp. 26–42.

45. Richard Pares, *A West India Fortune* (Longman, London, 1950), pp. 46–49.

46. *Cambridge History of the British Empire*, Vol. I, p. 520.

47. Edward Randolph to Board of Trade, April 1696, 'A Computation of the 5th parts of Prizes not accounted for in North America', BPHL, Box IV, BL 144.

48. Bruce P. Lenman, *An Economic History of Modern Scotland 1660–1976* (Batsford, London, 1977), pp. 49–51.

49. David Armitage, 'Making the Empire British: Scotland in the Atlantic World 1542–1717', *Past and Present*, No. 155, May 1997, pp. 34–63; and *idem*, 'The Scottish Version of Empire: Intellectual origins of the Darien venture', in *A Union for Empire* (Cambridge University Press, Cambridge, 1995), pp. 97–118.

50. A.D. Francis, *The Methuens and Portugal* (Cambridge University Press, Cambridge, 1966).

51. Richmond P. Bond, *Queen Anne's Indian Kings* (Clarendon Press, Oxford, 1952), pp. 32–33.

52. R.A. Skelton, *Explorers' Maps* (Spring, London, 1958).

53. Margaret Wilkes, *The Scot and His Maps* (Motherwell, Scottish Library Association, 1991), p. 9.

54. The best discussion of this is probably Clifford J. Rogers, 'The Military Revolution in History and Historiography', in *The Military Revolution Debate* (Westview Press, Boulder, CO, 1995), pp. 1–10.

55. John S. Gibson, *Playing the Scottish Card: The Franco–Jacobite invasion of 1708* (Edinburgh University Press, Edinburgh, 1988).

56. Johnson, *Adjustment to Empire*, p. 349.

57. Charles Boxer, 'William and Mary and the World of Maritime Asia', *History Today*, 38 (1988), pp. 52–58.

58. Robert C. Ritchie, *Captain Kidd and the War Against the Pirates* (Harvard University Press, Cambridge, MA, 1986).

59. Michael Craton, *A History of the Bahamas* (Collins, London, 2nd edn, 1968), Chap. 9.

60. Nicholas A.M. Rodger, *The Safeguard of the Sea: A naval history of Britain. Vol. I: 660–1649* (HarperCollins, London, pbk edn, 1997), pp. 432–34.

61. Ragnhild Hatton, *Europe in the Age of Louis XIV* (Thames and Hudson, London, 1969), pp. 99–100, and fn. 8, p. 215.

62. Alan Gallay (ed.), *Colonial Wars of North America*, p. 756.

63. Richard Middleton, *Colonial America* (Blackwell, Oxford, 2nd edn, 1996), pp. 343–47.

CHAPTER TWO

The House of Hanover, internal stresses and external delusions 1713–1748

Stabilising core and periphery 1713–1731

The Peace of Utrecht was acutely controversial in Great Britain. It was a Tory peace pushed through in the face of bitter Whig opposition which did succeed in watering down the massive commercial rapprochement with France that was an integral part of Tory plans. Crucially, the elector prince of Hanover, Georg Ludwig, who in 1714 by the Act of Settlement became Anglicised as Queen Anne's successor, George I, blamed the Tories for abandoning Hanover and other German allies of the emperor by making a separate peace in 1713. Since Emperor Charles VI had been the unsuccessful allied candidate for the Spanish throne when a mere archduke not expected to succeed to the imperial dignity, there was real bitterness when he and his allies had to sign, after a year's further futile war with France, the Peace of Rastadt in March 1714. It did not seriously modify the provisions of Utrecht. George I therefore distrusted Tories to the point where he was sure to allow Whigs to dominate his early governments. Some Tory participation in a subordinate capacity was as far as he was prepared to go towards mixed-party administration, but here Tory delusions of grandeur proved suicidal. Two leading Tories who were asked to join the government shortly after the arrival of King George in September 1714 refused. They wanted equal representation, not what they saw as tokenism.[1]

Thereafter, the Tory slide to disaster was fast. The principal civil and military architects of the peace, Harley and Ormonde, were threatened with indictment for high treason. Harley went to the Tower of London. His colleague Bolingbroke's nerve broke. Henry St John, 1st Viscount Bolingbroke, was a man who had reached the peerage in 1712 after a meteoric

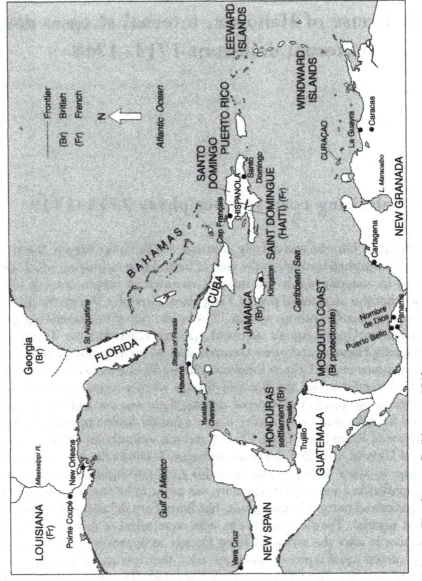

Map 2 The Greater Caribbean, *c.* 1740

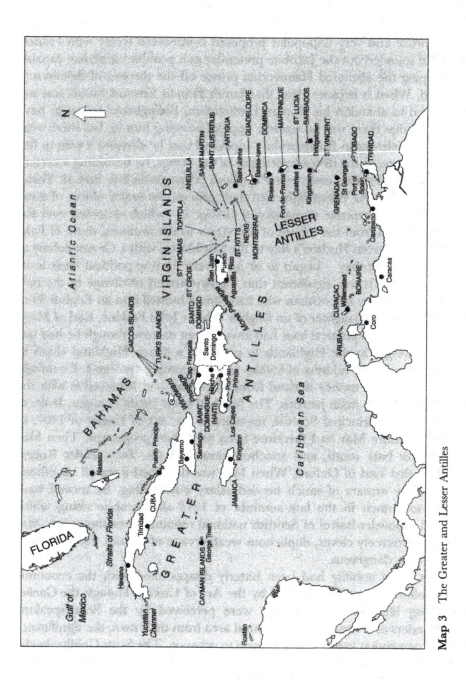

Map 3 The Greater and Lesser Antilles

49

rise through the Secretaryship at War to be Secretary of State. A passionate advocate of closer relations with France, he had favoured abandoning Britain's continental allies for the sake of a quick peace and was identified with an abortive and very unpopular proposed commercial treaty with France. He had sounded out the Jacobite pretender as a possible candidate capable of keeping the alienated Hanoverian prince off the thrones of Britain and Ireland. When it became clear that James Francis Edward Stuart was not prepared to abandon his Roman Catholicism, Bolingbroke seems to have accepted that there was no realistic hope of bringing him in, but there were so many skeletons in Bolingbroke's cupboard that he deemed it wise to flee abroad where, to the ill-concealed glee of the Whigs, by becoming secretary to the pretender he assisted their specious propaganda line that all Tories were Jacobites. As Whigs tightened their grip on the major offices of state, the complex composite monarchy of George I – which sprawled over the Atlantic world from the mouth of the Weser to the southern shore of Lake Ontario, and from Hudson's Bay to the Caribbean, with a Crown colony as far away as Bombay – began to sit on a very narrow political basis in its core territory. It was significant that the first armed challenge to the new regime was led by a Scotsman who had turned himself into an English Tory and married the daughter of an English Whig – John Erskine, Earl of Mar.[2]

Mar's Scottish political base had always been narrow, though he had just enough weight in the Highlands to persuade a dozen Highland chiefs to sign a sycophantic address of loyalty to the incoming George I. Essentially Mar needed the money derived from office and had achieved it with the assistance of two main patrons. The first had been James Douglas, Duke of Queensberry, principal Scottish manager of the Act of Union of 1707, of which measure Mar had therefore been an ardent proponent. Then Mar shifted his base south, and attached himself to the Tory leader Robert Harley, first Earl of Oxford. When Mar was dismissed from all his offices, with heavy arrears of much needed salary outstanding, he moved back north to launch in the late summer of 1715 the Jacobite rising which ignited a powder-barrel of Scottish national resentment at the union. Mar was an extremely clever, duplicitous weathervane of politics. He had never been more dangerous.

The Scots nobility had been bitterly disappointed with the economic and political pay-offs generated by the Act of Union. Though the Gaelic-speaking Highlands and Islands were perceived by the Scots-speaking Lowlanders as a very different cultural area from their own, the significance of this perception varied from occasion to occasion. The Scots Gaidhealtachd had achieved an identity distinct from the Irish one due to social, religious, and literary developments; albeit the distinction remained ragged at the margins of contact, especially around the margins of the Dalriadic Sea between Ulster and Argyll.[3] However, in the course of the seventeenth century the Highland aristocracy, who had long ago learned to combine feudal and tribal structures to generate and sustain clanned power, had become fully integrated into the politics of the Scottish community of the realm. The results of this, as the destructive campaigns of the Marquis of Montrose showed in the 1640s, could be far from happy.

Nevertheless, 1715 was clearly an occasion when it was the Scottishness of the Highlanders which was important, rather than their cultural difference. They were the shock troops of a national rising, because they had to be. Only in the Highlands could large numbers of armed men be quickly and safely assembled. After visiting his Lowland estates Mar moved to his Highland properties to confer with Jacobite chiefs, and to raise the standard on the Braes of Mar in September 1715. There was widespread Lowland support for the rising, not by any means confined to the admittedly strongly Jacobite north-eastern counties of Aberdeenshire and Banff. The rebels had no difficulty in taking over most of the east coast trading burghs, from Aberdeen to Dundee and Perth, nor did they hesitate to hold open elections in them in the correct belief that such elections would yield stoutly Jacobite town councils. After the failure of the rising, the massive obstruction of attempts to enforce effective forfeiture of condemned Jacobites' estates, an obstruction led by the judges of the supreme courts in Scotland, merely underlined the depth of Scottish sympathy for the rebellion.[4]

The Scottish aristocracy had remained very Scottish. Neither the regal union of 1603 nor the Act of Union of 1707 had led to any significant Anglicisation of the Scots elites. They had a British dimension, but it was just that, not a new identity. Common Anglo–Scottish Protestantism had promoted a degree of cultural integration, but this was deceptive, both for contemporaries and for some modern historians, in that it encompassed profound ecclesiastical and political differences; and even as a cultural bond it worked primarily against a perceived Roman Catholic 'other'. It could not generate any monolithic cultural entity, let alone an identity shared by English and Scots.[5] New Englanders were English, of their kind. Scots were not, and forty years after her departure to England to marry, under scandalous circumstances, the Duke of Monmouth, the Duchess of Buccleuch could insist in 1720 that 'The Scotts hart is the same I brought to England, and will never chang, as I find by long experience.'[6] The role of the exiled Stuarts was to act as the symbol of unity for a coalition of disgruntled elements, led by the Scots, which had a fair chance of shaking the uncertain grip of the House of Hanover on the British thrones.

The groups which could conceivably have coalesced into a truly dangerous uprising were otherwise divided by both nationality and sectarianism. Scottish Roman Catholics were, understandably, usually Jacobites, but

Roman Catholics were a small minority, even in the Highlands. The core of committed Scottish Jacobitism was the Protestant episcopal community, and their clergy, often ousted from charges they had once held in the Kirk by Law Established, were the arch-ideologues of the movement. To them the Glorious Revolution was sin against the Lord's Anointed, sin whose punishment by God in the shape of plague, famine, and war was inevitable and would only cease when repentant peoples bowed before God's plan for mankind – indefeasible hereditary right – and restored the exiled dynasty.[7] It was, however, crucial for the Scots Jacobites to link up with the small simultaneous rising in the north-east of England, where Roman Catholic and high church Anglican nobles and gentry of a Tory persuasion were caught between the anvil of falling revenues, due to low agricultural prices and technical problems in their coal mines, and the hammer of the new Whig political ascendancy. Had Mar been able to march triumphantly across the Anglo–Scottish Borders to link up with the English rebels before sweeping into Lancashire with a view to rousing its large Roman Catholic population, a hotbed of active plotting for a rising in support of a French invasion since 1689, George I would have been reduced to fighting for life and thrones probably just north of London.

The 1715 failed so miserably for purely military reasons. Mar totally lacked the flair and drive necessary for the leader of a rising. When his passage south was blocked by the Whig general and principal chief of the Clan Campbell, Argyll, who occupied the strategic lynchpin of Scotland at Stirling, Mar needed to act fast. He had a superiority of numbers so great that he could have destroyed Argyll's army in a couple of days' indecisive attritional fighting. Instead Mar procrastinated. He sent his best general, Macintosh of Borlum, on an abortive flanking movement with inadequate force. Eventually Borlum wandered through the Borders, linked up too late with the English rebels, and was caught and forced to surrender by government troops at Preston in Lancashire. Mar did realise he was no soldier, but the professional military man he brought with him to Scotland at the start of the rising to compensate for his own lack of expertise was, in the opinion of a young Jacobite participant who was later to die in battle as a Prussian field marshal, totally unsuited to the job:

> Lord Mar brought along with him Lieutenant General Hamilton, who tho' an old officer, was not the least equal to the affair he was to undertake, for tho' he had served long . . . in the Dutch troops, yet being a man whom only experience, not natural genious, had made an officer, he did not know how to make use of his new troops, who are of a disposition as hot and quick as the Dutch are slow and flegmatick; and this certainly was the occasion of his misfortune at the affair of Dumblain . . .[8]

A successful Jacobite restoration would not only have meant the repeal of the Act of Union, but also traumatic and possibly terminal chaos in the English Atlantic community. Much would have hinged on where the loyalty of the Royal Navy ultimately settled. With naval power, a Stuart monarch could no doubt have cowed the West Indian islands, but most of the North American colonies had gone too far to knuckle under a restored Roman Catholic dynasty closely associated with Bourbon absolutism. God knows what the upshot of the resulting struggle might have been, and what price France and Spain might have tried to exact for assistance in bringing the heretical provincials to heel. In the event, an unsuccessful rising greatly strengthened the hand of the new Whig Hanoverian regime as the Jacobite cause withered in the aftermath of the indecisive Battle of Sheriffmuir, near Dunblane, in November 1715. By December the Dutch had shown their commitment to the Protestant succession in Britain by despatching six thousand troops to uphold it. The despatch of £15,000 of Spanish gold from Calais in a small ship which wrecked in St Andrews Bay merely provided the advancing Hanoverian soldiery with an unusually lucrative species of fishing.[9]

Spanish covert support for the 1715 was the product of a network of circumstances. Both Louis XIV and his successor as ruler of France, the Regent Orleans, suggested to the Spanish government, at different times, that it secretly take up the sponsorship of Jacobitism, as France was by public treaty committed to accepting the Protestant succession in Britain. So was Spain, but that was less important in deterring its new Bourbon monarch Philip V from offering such sponsorship than two other factors. One was that the Bourbon government of Spain had inherited an empty treasury. The other was that the prime Spanish policy objective was the reversal of the part of the peace settlement which had stripped Spain of its old imperial status and territories in Italy, to the benefit mainly of the Emperor Charles VI. Philip V of Spain, almost as great a genetic disaster as his Habsburg predecessor Charles II, was dominated by his strong-willed Italian second wife, Elizabeth Farnese, a niece of the Duke of Parma. Since she expected Philip V to die first, her objective – to the benefit of one of several sons of his first marriage – was to secure the reconquest of Parma, Piacenza, and Tuscany to which she and her children could then retire as rulers in her widowhood. The British position on Italy was marginally ambiguous. Spain vacillated between backing a compliant Jacobite candidate and buying Hanoverian acquiescence with commercial concessions. The signature by Spain of a commercial treaty with George I in December 1715 showed that even during the rebellion the policy of accommodation with Britain advocated by the rising Italian priest-politician Cardinal Julio Alberoni was winning out.[10] However, by 1717, when Spain had invaded and over-run Sardinia, and even more by 1718 when a large Spanish expedition invaded Sicily, it had become clear that Anglo–Spanish cooperation was impossible because the British really wanted more trade concessions in Spanish America, which Spain was no more prepared to grant than Britain was to allow a fundamental destabilisation of the Utrecht settlement and the alienation of her traditional Austrian ally by condoning a wave of Spanish conquests in Italy.

Admiral Sir George Byng was sent to the Mediterranean with orders to secure a secession of arms if possible but, if this did not prove feasible, he was 'with all your power, to hinder and obstruct' Spanish operations. Byng found the court of Madrid and the Spanish commander who had over-run Sicily obdurate, so on 11 August he completely destroyed the Spanish fleet under Don Antonio de Castaneta, off Cape Passaro, effectively marooning the Spanish army in Sicily. A desperate Cardinal Alberoni, caught between his own wilful sovereigns and an unyielding Britain, played his last card: a Jacobite would-be trump. It failed, as the Jacobite army commander, the exiled Irish Tory Duke of Ormonde, warned Alberoni it was almost bound to do unless the Hanoverians could be caught completely by surprise.[11] In practice British intelligence completely penetrated Jacobite schemes. The British ambassador in Paris, the Scots Whig soldier John Dalrymple, second Earl of Stair, had detailed knowledge of Jacobite preparations to invade England with five thousand men, and deemed the scheme a military absurdity. As it happened, storms destroyed the main Jacobite fleet. A minor, purely diversionary force, led by Jacobite Highland chiefs, landed in the west Highlands to be promptly crushed by the Royal Navy and Major General Wightman, who marched adequate forces down from Inverness to disperse the Jacobites in a battle in Glenshiel.[12]

An Anglo–French–Austrian alliance had emerged in 1718, with a definite settlement plan for southern Europe. Apart from very minor concessions in Tuscany, Spain was asked to renounce Italian territorial ambitions. The Emperor Charles VI was to do what he had hitherto avoided doing: renounce his claims to Spain. He was allowed to exchange Sardinia for Sicily. There were further public guarantees of the English and French successions as recognised at the Peace of Utrecht, thus securing the House of Hanover and keeping open to the Regent Orleans the chance of succession to France if the young Louis XV died. A combination of British naval power and a French invasion of Catalonia compelled the Spanish royal pair to sack Alberoni in December 1719 and accede to the allies' settlement in January 1720 by joining them in what had become known as the Quadruple Alliance. So little had the war been about imperial issues that Earl Stanhope, George I's English general and leading minister, who had been the main architect from 1716 of Anglo–French entente, had offered to return Gibraltar to Spain – a sweetener for Spain's accession to Anglo–French terms. That, however, had been before Byng's naval victory. The Spaniards remembered the proposed concession, forgot its context, and added Gibraltar for themselves to Italian ambitions they still retained, for Elizabeth Farnese's sons.

The Hanoverian dynasty's grip on the British Isles, and its prestige in Europe, was vastly more impressive in 1720 than it had been in 1715. Unsuccessful rebellion strengthens a challenged regime, and the debacle of the 1718 further discredited the exiled Stuarts, seen as Spanish catspaws. Debate within the Scottish elites between Jacobite nationalists and unionists had moved decisively in favour of the latter by 1720, purely on grounds of practicality. Their vision was attainable.

In North America there was another zone of conflict between Spain and England on the southernmost frontier of the English settlements. With the establishment of English settlements in the Carolinas from the early 1660s, and especially after an enlarged grant by Charles II in 1665 had laid down nominal English claims as far south as latitude 29 north, which was well within the Spanish northern mission and settlement area, endless bickering was guaranteed. The Spaniards originally regarded the main English settlement at Charles Town in what was to be South Carolina as an intolerable threat to Spanish bullion fleets using the Bahama Channel as they sailed north picking up the Gulf Stream, but they lacked the capacity to do anything about it. The Anglo–Spanish Treaty of Madrid in 1670 was out of date on the ground when signed. In any case, Carolina settlers, many of whom came from the Caribbean, treated it as important mainly because of its abandonment of Spanish claims to exclusive rights in the Americas.[13] A settlement organised by Lord Cardross at Stuart's Town, mainly as a refuge for Scottish religious dissenters, was wiped out by Governor Juan Cabrera of Florida. Even if he accepted the Treaty of Madrid of 1670 (which he did only grudgingly), the Marquis Cabrera deemed any foreign settlements south of the Ashley River as violating its terms. Then the Scots followed an extremely risky and aggressive Indian trade policy which armed and encouraged the Timicuan Indians to attack the Spanish establishments in the Timicua mission province, one of the three frontier mission provinces which were the cutting edge and defensive shield of Spanish imperialism on the east coast of North America. Though alarmed and amazed by the Spanish amphibious strike of 1686 which burned and destroyed Stuart's Town, already weakened by disease, the English in Charles Town were probably not truly sorry to see the end of an intrusive alien group who had tried to muscle in on the vital Indian trade.

Carolina was swift to emerge as the dominant force in trade with the south-western Indian tribes. It was slow to develop viable agricultural staple crops. Even rice-growing, its first great agricultural success story, may have begun to assume commercial proportions only after 1695, but Carolina was close to the hunting territories of the Catawbas and the Cherokee. There were no serious mountain barriers to westward penetration, as there were for more northerly colonies, and after the resistance of the Westo Indians had been broken in the early 1680s, trade expansion along the Savannah River corridor was easy.[14] This uniquely rapid – amongst English colonies – commercial penetration of Amerindian societies involved extensive physical contact with indigenous peoples as the Charles Town traders and their pack horses plodded westwards. It also guaranteed eventual confrontation with a dynamic French frontier moving west from the Mississippi delta, and immediate confrontation with an undynamic but sulky and resentful Spanish Florida. Once the original Carolina proprietors had, by the 1690s, ceased to be capable of attempts to monopolise the trade, it boomed. Originally, Indian slaves loomed large in the business. The Westo wars ensured an early supply of slaves, and this pattern continued through the Tuscarora and Yamassee wars of the early eighteenth century, though by then the internal market for Indian slaves was drying up. By 1708, when the total colonial population in South Carolina was 9580 (including 2900 negroes) there were only 1400 Indian slaves. Victims of the defeat of the Yamassees and Tuscaroras tended to be shipped as slaves to the West Indies. Furs and hides dominated exports from Charles Town, the only English-American port south of the Chesapeake. From 1699 to 1715 England's annual import of Carolina deerskins was 54,000.

As the *South Carolina Gazette* stressed in 1736, this trade was 'the Means by which we keep and maintain the several Nations of the Indians surrounding this Province in Amity and Friendship with us, and thereby prevent their falling into the Interests of France or Spain'.[15] Superior English trade goods were vital. They enabled the Carolinians easily to be the predominant influence with the Lower Creek Indians until 1715. The Creeks were the objectives of Spanish garrisons and friars in the frontier region of Guale, but showed so little enthusiasm for these unsolicited disciplines that the Spaniards denounced them as disobedient subjects. By 1690 Indians had migrated in large numbers away from the north-west frontier of Spanish Florida to the upper reaches of the Altamaha River, much closer to the English settlements in Carolina. Effectively, Carolina had a Creek shield between itself and Spanish power.

The Yamassee War profoundly weakened Carolina's Indian bulwarks. Temporarily, it totally paralysed the Indian trade. That could be rebuilt after the traumas of 1715–17, but only with difficulty, for the war had been a revolt against the whole Carolina trading system, as well as a less important reaction to the ravages that expanding European cattle farming was inflicting on Indians who lived near the eastern coast. In the end, the Carolinians repaired their alliance with the Cherokee, thereby securing military aid and a path through to the loyal Catawba. By 1717 they had patched up a sort of peace with the Creeks still within their sphere, but the Yamassee, themselves an important Creek tribe, had chosen to migrate back to their old haunts on the Chattahoochee, near the Spaniards, rather than accept defeat. Spain became a serious contender for a Creek alliance rather than a non-starter.

The crisis was primarily local. Metropolitan Englishmen's withers were unwrung, even if they knew about the misfortunes of their Carolina brethren, and most did not. What did excite active interest in metropolitan circles was the prospect of penetrating the markets of Spanish America through the mechanism of the South Sea Company, with its *asiento* or contract to supply slaves to the Spanish colonists, guaranteed in the Peace of Utrecht, and its right to send an 'annual' ship to the great fairs of Central America. Its first ship, the *Royal Prince*, was launched in 1715 but departed on her maiden voyage only in 1717, to be driven off by the Spaniards, who by 1718 were fighting a war with Great Britain in Europe. The company's second ship, the *Royal George*, was launched in 1718, in the middle of the war. By then, the Spanish government had violated the *asiento* agreement, but the company had loaned large sums to the British government and coopted George I as its governor. The year 1719 saw a wild speculative boom in France, engineered by the Scots economist-gambler John Law, whose Bank and Company of the Indies had absorbed the tobacco monopoly; the right to coin money; and the stock and privileges of the East India, China, Senegal, and African companies; as well as the collection of royal revenues. By early 1720 Law had been made comptroller general of finance, qualifying for office by adopting Roman Catholicism. The South Sea Company was simultaneously offering to take over £7,567,000 of the British national debt, in exchange for a 5 per cent interest payment annually until 1727 and 4 per cent afterwards. A South Sea bubble of speculation, matching the lunacies of speculation in Paris, took hold in London. It was rumoured that Earl Stanhope had been approached by the Spanish Crown with an offer of four ports in Peru in exchange for Gibraltar and Minorca.[16] By the end of 1720 both Law and the bubble were bust, but the illusion about Spanish America lingered.

The implication that free trade in Spanish America was buyable was mad. Any British trade or activity there was bitterly resented by Spain, and relations in the Caribbean were deteriorating. Spain had acknowledged English occupation of Jamaica in 1670, but the Spanish Crown and its principal lieutenants in Central America did not understand until much later that this would involve an English, later British, presence on the

Mosquito shore of Nicaragua, where English traders from the brief colony on Providence Island had contacted Indians at Cape Gracias a Dios as early as 1633. French and English buccaneers used the Rio Coco as a way into the settled core of Nicaragua, plundering the town of Nueva Segovia in 1654 and reaching and attacking the principal Spanish settlement at Grenada on Lake Nicaragua by 1665. By 1700 buccaneering of this kind was in decline, but by the second decade of the eighteenth century British planters, traders, and log-cutters were settling on the shore and a local Sambo–Mosquito monarchy was emerging as effectively a Jamaican protectorate. In 1720 the British governor in Jamaica negotiated a treaty with the Mosquito Indians which involved supplying them with arms, nominally to enable them to recapture and return runaway Jamaican slaves, but really for use against the Spaniards.[17]

There was nothing odd about this arrangement. The Spanish conquest of Central America had been brutal, even by the standards of the original Mexican conquest. It had been driven through over a long period by a group of endlessly squabbling *conquistadores*, whose quarrels were perpetuated in the complex jurisdictional frontiers of the colonial era and, above all, it had been very incomplete. Spaniards predictably preyed on the richer soils and denser human populations which existed south and west of the mountain ranges that formed a 1000-mile-long spine of the region from Chiapas to Costa Rica. The much less attractive soils which ran down from the crest of the mountains to the Caribbean coast, with landscapes ranging from pine barrens to dense tropical forest lashed by torrential rain, and with fiercely independent Indian peoples who repulsed Spain's occasional bids to establish supremacy through soldiers or priests, were beyond Spanish capacities. The loose collection of Spanish colonial provinces looked to the Pacific rather than the Caribbean. At the northern and southern ends of the region Anglo-Saxon penetration did provoke major Spanish countermeasures. By 1700 the governors of Panama and Porto Bello had forced the surrender of the Scots trying to establish an emporium at Darien, and the governor of Yucatán had hounded English logwood cutters into the forests of Belize, where he could not reach them. Elsewhere, the Spaniards abandoned their pretensions on the Honduran coast, apart from one defended port of call; stood on their mountain frontier inland; and often blundered into disaster because of sheer ignorance, as when they would pit a coastguard schooner against a large fleet of Sambo dugout canoes. Logwood yielded dyes in demand in British textile mills, and there was enough profit in pine timber and other naval stores, tortoiseshell, sarsaparilla (a medicinal root), sugar, and rum to ensure that British entrepreneurs increasingly put economic muscle behind Indian autonomy.[18]

Though infuriating to Spanish colonial governors, developments such as this were just not worth a war from the point of view of Elizabeth Farnese.

After 1720 she still sought principalities in her native Italy for her sons, next time round in alliance with Emperor Charles VI – who played her like a fish, hoping for subsidies and commercial concessions, but did not stand by her when George II and Philip V went to war. It was a brief war from January 1727 to March 1728, in which Spain broke its teeth on the rock of Gibraltar in an unsuccessful siege, and British shipping in the Caribbean suffered from sustained assault and seizure by Spanish naval forces. Inevitably, the British government mounted a blockade of Spanish home ports by the Royal Navy. The new United Kingdom of Great Britain was a more dangerous animal than England because its armed forces were an attractive career opportunity, not only for a numerous Scots aristocracy with a martial tradition, but also for some of Scotland's numerous graduates. A lord of the admiralty warned an influential Scots politician seeking a berth as a surgeon's mate for a young man in 1726, 'There are more surgeons come from Scotland to gett into the service of the Navy, than would fill the whole places, tho' none other apply'd.'[19] A naval build-up prior to war was to such men a potential career opportunity.

Patiño, the Spanish naval minister since 1717 and secretary of the Office of the Indies after 1726 – on his way to secretary of state and effective first minister to Philip V 1733–36 – would probably have preferred an accommodation with Britain until he had rebuilt Spanish naval power for a decisive confrontation in the Americas, but to keep his job he had to sell to the Spanish Crown the idea of using harassment of British ships in the Caribbean as a means of pressuring the British into cooperation with limited Spanish objectives in Italy. Patiño did ditch the pointless Austrian alliance, and formal Anglo–Spanish war ended with a convention in 1728 lifting the British naval blockade in return for a promise of the return of seized British ships and assets, but in practice Patiño unleashed war on legal as well as illicit British trade in the seas off Spanish America. He used the ships of the *guarda costas*, licensed warships theoretically on customs and law-enforcement work, as instruments of undeclared naval war. Any foreign ship searched and found to have Spanish coins aboard was deemed to be a smuggler. Given the global use of the silver *real de a ocho*, the piece of eight, this was naked aggression.

Patiño also harassed French trade by systematic obstruction in the great monopolistic peninsular centre of Seville, whence most French goods were despatched to the Americas. The idea was to persuade France and Britain to help Spain to introduce garrisons into Parma and Tuscany, in exchange for easing of pressure on their Atlantic trade. This pressure France and Britain bowed to by the Treaty of Seville of 1729, only to find the Spanish naval harassment redoubled to make sure they delivered on their European promises. By 1730 the Spanish war on British trade had reached a point where only countervailing state force would sober it, and Rear-Admiral Stewart on the West Indies station was authorised to take reprisals from Spanish merchant shipping if illegal seizures were not returned. The South Sea Company, worried about its legal trade, persuaded him to concentrate on checking the *guarda costas*. Meanwhile Spain had signed the first Family Compact with France in 1733, an originally secret deal in which, in exchange for most favoured nation trading status, France acquiesced in Spanish conquest, completed by 1734, of Naples and Sicily for Don Carlos, Elizabeth Farnese's elder son. In theory, France was also committed to supporting Spain if Britain attacked her, and to persisting until Gibraltar was reconquered and British pretensions in the American trade curbed.[20] France proved less keen to deliver than to promise, but it was clear that the Anglo–French entente which had enabled Sir Robert Walpole's regime to coexist with those of the duc d'Orléans and later Cardinal Fleury, with continual tension but with some assurance that the Jacobite menace would not receive serious French sponsorship, was over by 1731.

Aggressive confrontation with the Bourbon powers 1732–1748

By 1732 a royal charter of George II had laid the foundations of a new British colony, Georgia, which was bitterly resented by Spain and feared by France. It was on land which the British government regarded as well within the extensive boundaries granted to the Carolina proprietors in 1663, but to the French it looked like British expansion round the southern end of the Appalachians, menacing the French line of forts between Louisiana and Canada, a line openly designed as a threat to the future of British North America. To the Spaniards, Georgia was aggression on Florida's bounds, aggression all the more objectionable as it made future Spanish raids on South Carolina impractical. French and Spanish reactions alone indicated that Georgia was a good strategic option for British North America, yet the original motivation behind the project was genuinely philanthropic. Its roots lay in the problem of insolvent debtors released from debtors' prison by legislation of 1729, but unable to secure employment. The Anglican divine Dr Thomas Bray, active in missionary work in the colonies, especially among negroes, became interested. On his death in 1730, the torch passed to the High Anglican Tory soldier James Edward Oglethorpe. Indigents, debtors, slaves, and foreign Protestant refugees were amongst those for whom Oglethorpe envisaged a colonial haven. Slavery was to be banned. Nevertheless, the promoters had to broaden the basis of the colony, stressing commercial opportunity and land grants, to bring aboard the venture leading London merchants whose additional political clout was essential to securing the charter.[21]

In an age of embittered sectarian rivalries, the English and later the British Crown had always considered that foreign Protestant refugees from a triumphalist Counter-Reformation in continental Europe were more politically reliable than groups of Roman Catholic subjects from any of the three kingdoms as settlers in the new southern colonies established after 1660. Refugees were also, if the French Huguenots were typical, likely to assimilate to an English host culture, as the large and influential Huguenot element in London showed. Charles II had sent Huguenots to Carolina as early as 1679. By the early eighteenth century, German refugees were supplementing a continued flow of Huguenots in the Carolinas, and in 1710 the British government assisted persecuted German Protestants from the Palatinate to settle in New York and North Carolina. Georgia was always meant to offer a refuge to Germans, initially from the archbishopric of Salzburg, where the incumbent archbishop was anxious to eliminate heretics from his ecclesiastical principality. The First Transport of Salzburg refugees was conducted to Georgia in 1733–34 by Philipp von Reck. Two years later he brought over the Third Transport and wrote a report which makes it clear that early Georgia lay between two war zones. In 1736 the friendly Chickasaw Indians had come to treat with the Georgia authorities after defeating a recent French punitive column, and the Georgia settlers had already started to skirmish with the Spaniards to the point where Oglethorpe was preparing an expedition against Florida. Von Reck recorded that 'People talked about nothing but the expedition against the Spaniards . . . and they were happy to be able to show the Spaniards their old English courage.'[22]

Spain was aware of a split between doves and hawks in the English ministry, but miscalculated that a truculent note demanding evacuation of Georgia under threat of war would strengthen the hand of the pacifically inclined Sir Robert Walpole. It had the opposite effect, making it politically impossible for Walpole to surrender on the Georgia issue. Oglethorpe had angrily accused Walpole to his face of being instinctively inclined to sell the new colony down the river to appease Spain. However, when it became clear that the Georgia colonists were not only pugnacious, but could also mobilise enough politically effective support to compel the British government to stand by them (the trustees of the colony could sway key votes at Westminster), Spanish truculence waned. By 1736 the issue was the negotiable one of Georgia's frontiers, not its existence. War was not inevitable because of frontier clashes in peripheral areas, especially if the British response to failed negotiations was to build up crushing naval superiority.

From early 1734 such a build-up had been in full swing, gathering its own constituency of hawkish naval officers or would-be officers whose zeal for conflict must have been known to the Spanish ambassador in London, who devoted much of his time to guessing whether the British really were prepared to fight, if all else failed.

One such excited hopeful, defining line-of-battle ships as being of 40 guns and upwards, reported that 'There is in Commission just now 33 Ships of the line of battell and there is to be put in Commission in a week or two 28 more which in all makes 61 besides 25 twenty Gun Ships that are in Commission at present.' He grasped the importance of the Westminster parliament's willingness to fund 'a great Armament at Sea', and of the wild scramble for patronage which inevitably ensued as men chased officers' commissions within the 20,000 expansion in naval manpower authorised by parliament.[23] As the first lieutenant of HMS *Kinsale* remarked in 1734, he needed an English patron to help him break out of the right circle of fellow Scots on 'a perfect scots ship' since without 'a good back to my interest, there is now such vast interest making for ships that I dare not ask one'. His ship was under orders for Jamaica and was to have its hull copper sheathed, which augured a long stay in tropical waters.[24]

Loss of a patron was like the loss of 'my sheatanchor', and there was general expectation by April 1734 that the great fleet riding at anchor off the Downs was bound soon to smell powder 'in the ensuing war'. When the fleet was stripped to send an admittedly superbly furnished squadron of 25 ships of the line towards the Spanish coast, it became clear that outright war might be avoided.[25] Patiño never had a navy comparable with his Atlantic ambitions before he died in 1736. His successor, Sebastian de la Quadra, was a much more realistic man, well aware that Spain still had aspirations in Italy where her policies, though successful, had been hideously expensive. An active Spanish foreign policy was dependent on the uninterrupted flow of bullion from the Americas into the Iberian peninsula. War disrupted that flow. Even as events drifted out of hand in 1738-39, British naval moves were as much deterrent as threatening.

They were also shrewd. For example, Royal Navy units on station off West Africa, where there was no Spanish presence, were ordered, with one exception which was recalled home, to proceed to the West Indies. It was possible to concentrate a formidable battle squadron at Jamaica whilst also reinforcing the Leeward Islands squadron with a heavy ship. On the contentious Georgia frontier far to the north, Colonel James Oglethorpe had permission to deploy a regiment he was raising in England. A first detachment of 680 men had sailed in December 1737, in three transports escorted by HMS *Phoenix*. A reinforcement was despatched in June 1738, escorted by HMS *Hector* and HMS *Blandford*. The three warships were to stay to strengthen the North American squadron; HMS *Hector* off Virginia, HMS *Phoenix* off South Carolina, and HMS *Blandford* off Georgia. Nor was the British government unaware of the fact that the Spaniards might open hostilities with a sudden attack on one or both of the Mediterranean bases they had lost to the British by the Treaty of Utrecht. That is what they had done in 1726 when they failed before Gibraltar. Minorca, vulnerable to a descent from the Catalan ports, seemed a more likely target in 1738, but Admiral Haddock was sent with reinforcements to the Mediterranean to cruise between the two main Spanish bases of Cartagena and Barcelona.[26]

Technically, it was difficult to fault these dispositions, which did not fail to impress a Spanish government that was hardly ready for war and that was increasingly whistling in the wind by trying to place frantic emotional pressure on France to join in, offering in return 'a mere appeal to the sentimental cant of kinship which the rulers of the House of Bourbon employed when they wanted each other's help for nothing'.[27] Cardinal Fleury knew that France ultimately could not abandon its horrendous investment in blood and treasure in the Bourbon succession in Spain, and that he could not allow massive British aggrandisement at the cost of imperial Spain, but that did not mean he would offer help without in exchange extracting one of the king of Spain's eye-teeth with an advantageous commercial treaty for France signed the same day. Also, he knew Elizabeth Farnese's ambitions would ultimately generate a general European war if encouraged, so he moved with glacial speed. Despite Admiral Vernon's subsequent early success with the British Jamaica squadron against Porto Bello in 1739, there was reason to expect that Spanish America would prove a tougher nut to crack than British chauvinists expected. Vernon himself was sceptical about the military feasibility of taking and holding large islands like Cuba, and indeed believed that even a coup against a port had to be executed quickly at the start of a war with forces on station before the Spaniards could mobilise properly and before disease struck. He did just this, but his second target, Cartagena, was by his own definition more difficult and had been heavily fortified since it had been captured by the French in 1697.[28]

Spain would never swallow formal defiance of its huge claims in the Indies. Its council of the Indies reacted with fury on 8 July 1739 when 'King' Edward of the Mosquitos' proposal for a treaty of peace and commerce with Spain reached it. The Spanish line still was that papal bulls had given them Edward's land and people, long ago. In alliance with Jamaica from late 1739, the Mosquitos conducted the only meaningful dialogue possible with Spain by disrupting, with continuous raids, trade from Granada to Cartagena and Porto Bello, and making the Veragua gold mines unworkable. Until they were deserted and betrayed by the British government after

1786 for diplomatic reasons (and in the face of considerable public revulsion by British opinion at the sell-out), the Indians of the Mosquito Coast demonstrated that it was perfectly possible to live with 'impossible' Spanish legal claims. The trick was to ignore them and counter-punch hard enough to make the Spaniards back off from an excess of zeal in trying to turn legal fantasy into physical reality.[29]

Effectively, Spain had been waging a naval conflict against the British in American waters, on and off, since 1718, sometimes declaring war (usually for purely European motives), but often without benefit of declaration. Attempts to negotiate redress, as in the 1730s, tended to encourage Spanish escalation of the war. Counter-violence was desirable, indeed essential. A spasm of tough British action followed by effective menace was the ideal scenario, all in that twilight zone of non-declared war Spain had made her own, but there were British ministers spoiling for war in the Walpole government. These were led by Thomas Pelham Holles, Duke of Newcastle, the principal secretary of state – a much younger politician than Walpole – who as early as 1737 had veered towards a much stronger official response to Spanish depredations against British shipping. By 1739 he was in open conflict with a Walpole anxious to avoid if at all possible a rupture between the two Crowns. The formed opposition in the Westminster legislature, which had been driven to despair by Walpole's political longevity, and especially by his survival of the high-water mark of their combination of parliamentary obstruction and outdoor agitation in the Excise Bill crisis of 1733–34, clearly welcomed war as a destabilising factor in which either success or failure would serve their purpose. Then there was the mercantile interest, especially in London, which was divided; there was a large vested interest in uninterrupted trade with Old Spain, but vocal exponents of the need for a tough response to alleged Spanish excesses – such as Sir John Barnard (lord mayor in 1737–38) and Micajah Perry (lord mayor 1738–39). Both men had been leaders of City of London opposition to the Excise Bill.[30]

Nevertheless, the formal war, absurdly misnamed the War of Jenkins' Ear after a legitimate merchant who appears to have had his ear sliced off by *guarda costas* in 1731 despite or because of their inability to find even a piece of eight on his ship to justify their depredations, was not inevitable. Patiño had died in 1736. His successor, La Quadra, was far more reasonable and realised Spanish naval power could not take on the British. Spain's aggressive harassment of British shipping had always been playing with fire. Walpole's stubborn determination to negotiate a pragmatic compromise came within an ace of success in the shape of the Convention of the Prado signed at that Spanish royal residence in January 1739. Walpole's diplomatic support was outstanding. His brother Horace, former ambassador to France and then to the United Netherlands, may have been unpopular because of his manner, but he was well informed and acted as the government's consultant for European treaties. Benjamin Keene, ambassador to Spain, was perhaps the finest technical diplomat to serve Britain at that unspeakably dreary court. The trouble was that he doubled up as the official representative of the South Sea Company, which proceeded to undermine the convention by insisting that it would only pay an acknowledged debt to the Spanish Crown at its own crooked undervaluation of the currency involved. As a major creditor of the British government, with votes at its disposal at Westminster and ability to tap into opposition rhetoric and out-of-doors agitation, the company proved impossible to move. War came between two states because the company wrecked nearly successful negotiations between two governments anxious for peace.

On the other hand, there had been cold and hot war with Spain for over twenty years. Much of the 'cold' war had been very violent. The most famous *guarda costa* of the period 1720–32 was a mulatto ex-slave called Henriquez sailing out of Puerto Rico. Essentially a corsair, he was abetted by a governor who in 1728 issued privateering patents allowing seizure of British shipping purely on grounds of nationality.[31] Between 1732 and 1737 Spanish pressure on British shipping in the Americas had been much more restrained, but smuggling by foreigners to willing Spanish colonists assumed such proportions that in 1737 desperate governors of Spanish islands persuaded local entrepreneurs to fit out privateers to check this trade. It was the capture of a dozen British ships by these privateers which launched the crisis that led to Anglo–Spanish war in 1739. On the way the Westminster parliament in 1738 resolved to recruit 10,000 sailors and allocate £500,000 for their pay.[32] It was a familiar scenario which had been repeated over and over again. The usual scramble for commissions reached the point of frenzy when war broke out.

Whilst drafts from line regiments sent to serve as marines in the amphibious attack planned against the Spanish Caribbean were hopelessly drunk on the king's bounty money, their officers were trying to spot future admirals whose ascent in war would make them valuable patrons,[33] or cursing the expedition commander, Lord Cathcart, for not doling out to them one of the limited number of commissions at his disposal.[34] One disappointed officer who shifted his hopes to patronage from the Duke of Argyll was in despair when Argyll resigned all his offices in the course of a political quarrel with Walpole.[35] The same man went out eventually in a supernumerary capacity under Cathcart, hoping against all the odds that something would turn up.[36]

These men were far from stupid in their driving ambition to get in on the act. A lucky officer, especially in the navy, could make a lot of money. Admiral Sir Peter Warren, scion of a County Meath Roman Catholic gentry family, is a classic case. Brought up Protestant, like another of his brothers, to qualify for a naval career, he joined the Royal Navy in Dublin in 1716. His mother's Protestant relatives included Admiral Matthew Aylmer, who rose to an Irish peerage in 1718 as Baron Aylmer of Balrath in County Meath. Peter Warren sailed in Irish and West Indian waters before patronage from Admiral Norris secured him a 70-gun ship in the Baltic squadron. The years 1727–28 saw him serve in Gibraltar and sail to the West Indies. In 1731 he married into the De Lancey family, wealthy Huguenot fur-traders of New York related to the Dutch Van Cortlandt dynasty. The war after 1739 rocketed Warren to wealth and high eminence, mainly as a successful capturer of rich prizes in American waters in 1739–43 and then as second-in-command to Admiral George Anson in the Western squadron in the Atlantic between 1745 and 1748. Operations on the London money market, expanding estates run for him by his Roman Catholic brothers in Ireland, property on Long Island, and vast estates in the Mohawk valley in upper New York marked his success.[37]

Warren's rapid rise to fortune during the war owed much to the amended British prize law of 1708 under which the Crown and the treasurer of the navy surrendered their claims to a share of prizes, which were to be shared between the crew of their captor, with a distribution so skewed by rank that the captain secured three-eighths of the value. Documents from the Vice Admiralty Court in Gibraltar, a well-organised base for British privateers, especially in the years 1745–48,[38] underline how more egalitarian the share-out was among their crews. One example shows the skipper taking four shares. Two men received two, half a dozen pocketed one and a half shares, forty-three received one share, and one poor soul – who if he were not the cabin boy should have been – collected three-quarters of a share.[39] Still, the general pattern is clear: whatever the outcome of the clash between the Spanish and British states, its occurrence enabled many seafaring men on both sides to make money by ship capture. The British offered more targets than the Spaniards, so they too suffered.

Neither government could control the activities of their more aggressive subjects on their mutual sea and land frontiers. These men had agendas of their own, often wildly imperialistic. The south-western corner of the North American contact zone between, uniquely, three European imperialisms – French, Spanish, and British – was a classic case. The white settlers of South Carolina had always had plans to seize lands and expand west and south to the Gulf of Mexico and the Mississippi.[40] Injured innocents caught in the fires of metropolitan rivalries they were not. Nor were their Indian allies, whom they never reduced to mere pawns, though they did relent-lessly try to impose on their loose groupings of autonomous townships the concept of 'nations', to make them more coherent and manipulable blocks.

The Yamassee 'nation' was largely the product of cooperation with South Carolina in war, slave-raiding, and trade. The Muskogean peoples were much more resistant to such redefinition. Despite terrible demographic losses due to disease, slaving, and war, the Indians of the southern back country, like the Choctaws and Chickasaws, were strongly placed in the skin and fur market, and could afford to play off French and British buyers.[41] Big Euro–American war parties leaving Georgia to attack the underfunded and indefensible Spanish Indian missions of Florida would contain several, different, aggressive agendas, often mutually contradictory.[42]

What proved a total fiasco was the attempt to knit all these zones of conflict into a coherent, successful war effort directed from London. Newcastle was reading, at the start of the war, Jonathan Swift's classic pamphlet *The Conduct of the Allies* (1711), which had advocated attacks on the Spanish Caribbean and a primarily naval war. The fruits of reliance on the writings of a deranged Church of Ireland dean, penned nearly thirty years before when Swift was a political priest using his formidable literary talents to puff the chances of the Tory party, were as disappointing as might be expected.[43] Talk of capturing Spanish bullion fleets, usually accompanied by rhetoric about Drake and Cromwell, had always been unrealistic in the sense that neither Drake nor Cromwell had ever come near to capturing the main *flota* from Cuba, that well-escorted fusion of the Mexican galleons from Vera Cruz and the galleons from the fairs at Cartagena and Porto Bello, Peru's Atlantic ports. The *azogues*, fast ships which in the frequent years when the galleons did not sail took out the mercury essential for economic silver-smelting and returned with bullion, were a target which Admiral Haddock was told to aim at four months before war was declared, but they were elusive and, forewarned, slipped safely into Santander in Galicia rather than the usual destination, Cadiz. Thereafter all the precedents suggested bullion flows could be delayed during the war, but hardly captured.

The one exception proves the rule. It was the capture of the Manila galleon which plied regularly between Manila in the Philippines and Acapulco in Mexico by Commodore Anson in 1743. It was not an unprecedented feat in any respect. Anson circumnavigated the globe on his voyage, but so had Captain Woodes Rogers in 1708–11. He, too, had captured the Manila galleon and his pilot, William Dampier, had been on his third circumnavigation. George Shelvelock had circumnavigated the world in 1719–22 in the course of a less successful plundering raid on the west coast of Spanish America during another Anglo–Spanish war, and in 1726 had published an account of his voyage, the track of which was not dissimilar to Anson's. The latter's voyage started with shockingly bad manning. Amphibious operations were envisaged, but instead of troops 259 Chelsea Pensioners were sent aboard. They died, as did virtually everyone who set out in the original 7-ship squadron which sailed from Plymouth. There were the usual rich pickings of plate and jewels from Spanish settlements and coastal shipping in the Pacific, but Anson was down to HMS *Centurion* and 201 men (only 45 of them able seamen) when he left Canton, where he had recuperated and secured supplies, to cruise for the galleon.[44]

The papers of his second-in-command Philip Saumurez, a Channel Islander, make it clear that the crew of the *Centurion* thought themselves amazingly lucky in that the galleon commander, misinformed of the state of Anson's ship and crew, was foolishly willing to risk an engagement with a specialist 60-gun warship with a lean and hungry crew.[45] Accounts of the voyage, including a virtually official one, became best-sellers, and the 32-wagon procession to the Tower of London which conveyed the £400,000 of captured bullion was a stage performance. Governments always hype military success and play down failure. Strategically, the voyage was an irrelevance, though Anson was promoted to flag rank and went on to be an outstanding first lord of the Admiralty from 1751, with one short break, until his death in 1762.

The whole Anglo–Spanish War was dominated by a pattern of humiliating British failure to achieve absurdly unrealistic objectives. Because the war had been used by a frustrated opposition as a means of undermining Sir Robert Walpole, the early successes of Vice Admiral Edward Vernon were hyped to the skies. He had been an opposition MP in 1729 when another British sailor, Admiral Hosier, had failed miserably in an attack on Porto Bello, a major base for Spanish naval power in the Caribbean, and more especially for the outfitting of *guarda costas*. Vernon had then said that the operation had been botched and that he could take Porto Bello with six ships, which is precisely what he did ten years later. By early 1740 this opposition Whig admiral had captured the important fort of San Lorenzo, as well as the town of Chagre. He failed in 1741 in an attack on the great city of Cartagena, though his capture of the outlying fort of San Luis in May briefly deluded domestic opinion in England into thinking the city itself had fallen. Disease compounded the inevitable loss of military impetus, as Vernon himself had privately expected. The hysterical adulation of Vernon back in England by every means from street parties with bonfires to books, pamphlets, plays, and prints – all designed to show him as a hero of British and Protestant liberty – is a measure of the widespread degree of popular alienation from the ministry, but otherwise about as closely connected with reality as the hype surrounding the South Sea Bubble or the similar Mississippi Scheme bubble in France.[46]

Historians have been taken to task because in studying the expansion of Georgian Britain 'the best-known accounts have tended to eschew ideological and cultural forces in favour of the "great events": battles won and lost, military and naval strategies' and the techniques used to consolidate conquest. It has been pointed out that such an approach, valid in its own terms, 'is of limited usefulness to those who wish to know the meaning and significance of empire at home'.[47] The trouble with changing the emphasis of scholarship from naval and military reality to mushroom personality cults in Old England, like that formed round Vernon, is that they were invariably rooted in widespread alienation from the ruling ministry and in an often cynical exploitation, by opposition politicians, of the unreasonable expectations of the contemporary media and populace – whose frustration was ascribed to the treachery, corruption, and inefficiency of a ministry which was usually accused of deliberately starving the opposition naval celebrity of the resources he needed for decisive victory. In the highly factionalised and divided Britain of the era of the War of the American Revolution, once opposition began to build up to the ministerial policy of continuing to use force against the American colonists after France entered the war, a similar wave of opposition hysteria built up round Admiral Augustus Keppell in 1778–79 – after that opposition Whig had failed decisively to crush the French fleet off Ushant in the summer of 1778.[48]

Reality had a way of breaking in and bursting these bubbles. The Jenkins' Ear one would have been punctured far earlier and far more decisively but for two fortuitous developments. One was the way in which a pretty predictable early French intervention in the naval struggle came to naught. Cardinal Fleury had made it clear in the summer of 1739 that France would not tolerate a serious change in the balance of power in America. Despite the quick early victories scored by Vernon, the main British expedition to the Caribbean was slow to get off its mark, not because of particular incompetence by the government, but because of an unavoidable set of circumstances ranging from the need to assemble an adequate land force to tackle potential targets like Havana or Cartagena; to the need to replace substandard victuals; to the provision of a powerful escort in the face of French as well as Spanish squadrons in the Atlantic; to adverse winds. By the time the expeditionary force was more or less available in the Caribbean – after losing many men, including its commander, Lord Cathcart, to disease – the French colonies in the region were giving Spain all aid short of war. Fleury had despatched the Brest and Toulon squadrons of the French fleet to the Caribbean with orders which virtually guaranteed a clash and Anglo–French war. Faced with the potential hostility of joint Franco–Spanish fleets, Vernon was frightened for the security of Jamaica and so anxious to preserve his own fleet that he refused to accept the attrition rates needed to push the attack on Cartagena through to success.[49]

It was sheer luck that hurricanes and disease destroyed the French squadrons' capacity to operate effectively. Even more unpredictable was the invasion of Silesia late in 1740 by the army of the young King Frederick of Prussia. By 1741 that crisis had broadened into the War of the Austrian Succession, with France allied to Prussia. Despite Fleury's reservations, a war party led by Marshal Belleisle could not resist the opportunity to exploit the occasion of the disputed succession of a woman, Maria Theresa, to the Austrian Habsburg dominions to try to deal a deathblow to the old enemy. Elizabeth Farnese's Spain managed to land troops in Italy late in 1741 and early in 1742 to pursue claims to Habsburg duchies. The British Mediterranean fleet under Admiral Haddock was too weak to prevent this development. France's resources were drawn into war in Germany and Italy, which put off war with Britain but also guaranteed it would come, given that Britain had a Hanoverian king and could not afford to let France demolish Austria. By 1743 France and Britain were fighting a European war only formally declared in the spring of 1744.

For both, the naval and colonial struggle assumed less importance than the European land campaigns. The wild delusions about extensive conquests in Spanish America which had been rampant in British minds early on had never been realistic, if only because heavy Spanish investment in fortification of key colonial positions paid off, and the Spanish colonial army not only performed adequately but vastly outnumbered British land forces in the Americas.[50] But for the raising of an enlarged four-battalion regiment – Gooch's American Foot – from the British-American colonies from New England to North Carolina, it would have been impossible to assemble the minimum land force deemed essential for operations in the Caribbean. This unit had its troubles and a fairly predictable attempt has been made to weave its story, and the details of friction between North American colonists and the few regular units of the Crown with which they ever came into contact, into a pre-history of the national identity created after the Declaration of Independence of the United States in 1776.[51] The attempt is inherently unconvincing. There were marginal frictions between all early-modern armies and all early-modern populations. What the War of Jenkins' Ear showed was that settlers from Maine to South Carolina were not 'Colonial Americans' so much as provincial Englishmen with all the chauvinism, imperial delusions, and aggressive greed which flourished in Great Britain between 1739 and 1744. Former Governor Alexander Spotswood of Virginia died whilst training provincial troops for Caribbean service in Annapolis, Maryland. George Washington's beloved elder half-brother called the family home Mount Vernon after his old commander at Cartagena.

What riled the British North Americans was failure to get what they wanted from the war. On the southern frontier the Georgians had been understandably nervous before 1739 in the light of stories that the French and Spanish had signed a secret agreement for a joint offensive against Georgia and the Carolinas in the event of war. As Oglethorpe pointed out, the chances of serious support from other British North American governments was minimal, so he had to be given considerable Royal Navy cover and a regular regiment of 600 men for the defence of Georgia, created by assigning to it all the effective enlisted men of the 25th Regiment of Foot. The next step was clearly to try to destroy St Augustine, the only Spanish base capable of threatening Georgia. Oglethorpe's second invasion of Florida after the outbreak of war tried to do just that and failed, as so many other British attacks had failed, because of resolute Spanish defence of up-to-date fortifications. The Westminster government had spent nearly £92,000 on Georgia between 1738 and 1743.[52] It was reasonable to say the colony had to be capable of looking after itself by 1743, which it was.

A combination of bastion-defended artillery-proof low ramparts, swamps, and naval defences which kept Oglethorpe's gunners frustrated and at a distance had saved St Augustine. Roughly similar techniques saw off the Spanish counter-attack on Oglethorpe's capital of Frederica in June–July 1742, despite the nearly 2000 men and over 50 vessels from Cuba and Florida which launched it. The Spaniards did eventually take the main British artillery defences on St Simon's Island, but were defeated in an ambush when they tried to move inland. They withdrew for fear of being caught between superior British naval power and an undefeated colonial force: if they could not win quickly, they could not linger. It was a measure of the growing Britishness of the metropolitan elites that Oglethorpe and the Georgia trustees had from 1736 imported Scottish Highlanders, caught between rising rents and falling cattle prices, to establish a fortified boundary settlement at the significantly named site of Darien, on a branch of the Altamaha River. Deliberately chosen as soldier-settlers and disproportionately from Speyside – where the Macintosh, chief of Clan Chattan, had become interested in the project (his brother was with Oglethorpe in Georgia) – they were prominent, with Indian allies, in raids on Florida and in the final defensive victory. Their swampy settlement area barely sustained agriculture, and though Oglethorpe and the trustees opposed slavery, it was the opening of Georgia to black slaves and rice culture which gave the area economic vitality.[53]

As the loose coalitions of quasi-autonomous interests which the British monarchy brought into global wars repeatedly fell apart during or just after the conflict, it was local demographic, military, and economic vitality which determined the viability of each interest group. In 1742 Georgia could survive. New England, with much more demographic and economic weight, could do better than that, but only with assistance from the Crown. The New Englanders, as the more perceptive French Canadians grasped, would probably have been happy to accept the idea of tacit neutrality with nearby French settlements, but were provoked and enraged by a raid mounted from the island fortress of Louisbourg against the New Englanders' fishing base at Canso in Nova Scotia. Compounded by an unsuccessful French attack on Annapolis Royal (formerly Port Royal) in the Bay of Fundy, these raids stimulated Governor William Shirley of Massachusetts to organise an attack on Louisbourg, widely feared in New England as a privateer base. Four thousand New Englanders eventually disembarked on Isle Royale to besiege Louisbourg, with financial help from New York and Pennsylvania and a vital escort from the Leeward Islands squadron of the Royal Navy under Peter Warren. He blockaded French warships inside the harbour whilst making a fortune capturing French ships outside it.

In fact, Louisbourg was more legend than stern reality. The French spent so much on its fortifications that Louis XV said its streets must be paved with gold. Yet its defences were overlooked, badly built, and succumbed to each of its two sieges within seven weeks. The French Ministry of Marine, remote from colonial realities, was insistent in the 1730s that Louisbourg was impregnable, the vital guardian of Canada, and a good base for offensives against the British. It was none of these things. At best it was a base for a frigate guard for the security of French cod fishermen on the nearby Grand Banks.[54] Shirley had hopes of a New England takeover in that fishery, but the whole operation was blown up by propaganda to national and heroic proportions. Shirley was made a colonel after the fall of Louisbourg. William Pepperrell, the New Englander who commanded the militia, was knighted. French Canada could survive very well without Louisbourg, which in no way controlled the sea approach to Quebec. Plans to develop an attack on Quebec after the fall of Louisbourg in June 1745 simply withered away. It would have been a popular move in all parts of the British monarchy to keep Isle Royale, but the French had won the war, mostly in Flanders. Total restitution of all conquests in the East and West Indies was a basic provision of a peace treaty primarily concerned with European adjustments.

French armies enjoyed both a substantial advantage in numbers over their allied opponents in Flanders, and the leadership of one of the truly great commanders of the century: the marshal de Saxe. In 1743, George II in person had fought at the head of a so-called 'Pragmatic Army' to defeat a French force at Dettingen on the Main. However, the victory had few consequences and in May 1745 de Saxe opened his roll of victories by heavily defeating George's son, the Duke of Cumberland, at Fontenoy. Though the vulnerability of Hanover rather suited the French, and they had originally found the Hanoverian succession in Britain not inconvenient, they were by 1743 sick of British meddling and muddling in Europe to the point of preparing to execute a standard contemporary gambit: an invasion of another realm without benefit of declaration of war. They dredged up Charles Edward Stuart, the Jacobite Prince of Wales, to act as figurehead for a sudden invasion of the south of England led by de Saxe. The trouble was that de Saxe proved unenthusiastic.[55] That sensible man could see little point in opening a risky second front when he knew he could win indefinitely on the Flanders one. The launching of a Jacobite rebellion in the western Highlands of Scotland in the late summer of 1745 by Prince Charles, largely on his own initiative, was therefore primarily a ploy to force the French Crown to reactivate the project for an invasion of England which it had dropped in 1744. The fact that Charles originally set out with two ships, one a leased French battleship with uniformed French cadets and arms from French royal arsenals aboard, makes it difficult to absolve French ministers from holding their own covert agenda for a spoiling attack designed not to succeed but to divert British resources from the continent. As such, the rising proved an unqualified success, the principal beneficiaries being de Saxe and the slaver-privateer entrepreneurs of Nantes, who put Charles into Scotland and eventually rescued him in 1746. The latter benefited when Royal Navy ships were diverted from convoy work to Scottish waters.[56]

What made the rising so profitable to French interests was its unexpected temporary success. It tapped a vein of dynastic loyalism, discontent, and anti-union Scottish nationalism which proved a potent combination. The clanned societies of the Gaelic-speaking Highlands were changing fast under the impact of commercialisation but had just enough coherence left to provide the bulk of the Jacobite army. The endless debate on the size of the Lowland contribution is profitless and pointless in the sense that though we know there was a significant Lowland minority in the Jacobite army, the main Lowland contribution was economic. It was by seizing control of the Lowlands virtually without fighting, and then confirming that grip by fifteen minutes of successful attack at Prestonpans, that the Jacobites gained control of the fiscal and material resources which enabled them to raise and equip a second army at home whilst launching a controversial reconnaissance in force into England. By the time it reached Derby virtually everyone except Charles was clear he had no serious support in England. There was no point in imposing an unpopular, and therefore chronically unstable, ruler so retreat began, ending in the relatively infertile area around Inverness which, like the west where the rising started, could not fund an army. Scottish Roman Catholic leaders had worked out that association with the Stuarts, though popular with their small flock, was an embarrassment. It was Protestant episcopalians who mainly clung to the cause, not just as the unpaid, starving army which went to defeat at Culloden[57] but even after, as their *beau idéal* the Gentle Lochiel demonstrated. He spurned very reasonable terms from Cumberland because he wanted to fight on after Culloden, and thereby called down the terrible devastation of Lochaber by Hanoverian troops. In exile in France before his death in 1748 he argued for another rising.[58]

The 1745 showed how fragile 'British' identity remained. There was shock and anger in Whig circles. Whigs were astonished that after the fall of Edinburgh to a horde of Highland 'Robbers and Banditti' there had been willingness on the part of 'so many Noblemen and Gentlemen, who had the character of Men of Honour and good Sense, and Men of good Fortunes too, to raise a great Army in the Low Country, and join the wild and desperate Highlanders'.[59] Fear lay behind the anti-Papist Hanoverian propaganda denouncing the (notably well-behaved) Highland army as 'savages' which was churned out during the rising, but the most eminent churner, the novelist Henry Fielding, knew perfectly well that only a minority even of Highlanders were active Jacobites. Defeat was inevitable for the Jacobites, themselves devoid of effective cavalry and artillery, once they met steady regular troops who could check Jacobite shock tactics with musket volleys, canister shot from well-served field guns, and serried bayonets. Though at Falkirk excellent Jacobite musketry killed a hostile cavalry charge, routed Jacobites were very vulnerable to a strong cavalry after Culloden. By 1749 only Prince Charles believed another rising was feasible. Ex-Jacobite Scots were beginning to work their passage back to a Hanoverian port.

By then the Peace of Aix-la-Chapelle had put a tombstone on the grave of Jacobitism. As Lord Chancellor Hardwicke's son, Colonel the Honorable Joseph Yorke, who was serving with Cumberland in the summer of 1746, told his brother, the key to daunting the clans was a demonstration that royal troops would devastate the lands of any recalcitrant group, and a realisation that Cumberland had the rank and will to 'stand the clamour that a just severity must raise against him'.[60] Irresponsibly conceived and increasingly erratically executed, the 1745 destroyed Highland autonomy by dragging a reluctant and uninterested Hanoverian Crown into the mountains. It ultimately strengthened George II's throne, though it also contributed to his defeat in the general war. There was no serious hope of arresting the advance of de Saxe, who had over-run much of Dutch Flanders and stormed Bergen-op-Zoom. British hopes that the Dutch would be revitalised by an Orangist coup in 1747 which made William IV stadtholder and captain general proved illusory. Britain's Austrian ally was negotiating for a separate peace with France.

Even at sea, the British record was mixed. The amphibious war with Spain had been a failure. Once France entered the war both the French and British devoted most of their naval energy to commerce protection and raiding. Marginally, the British may have done better than the French and Spaniards in ships captured, but both sides captured over three thousand enemy ships, and it was little comfort to the traders of Bristol to know that Peter Warren was making a fortune off Louisbourg when their slave ships from Africa were being picked off regularly east of the Leeward Islands and they had lost half their ships engaged in the South Carolina trade.[61] The situation of the EIC was equally galling. Both they and their French equivalent, the Compagnie des Indes, had hoped that the normal rule of neutrality in Asian waters would obtain. Indeed, the directors of the French company had written late in 1743 to François Dupleix, intendant of Pondicherry – their main trading station on the Coromandel or south-east coast of India – saying that with the approach of war with Britain, with its dampening effect on trade, expenses in India must be halved, partly by suspending expensive work on the fortifications of Pondicherry.

Dupleix ignored not the general order to cut costs, but the ban on completing the fortifications, paying the costs out of the large fortune he had made in inter-Asian trade. As his directors were unable to fund cargoes for company ships trading with China, Dupleix furnished these himself, effectively privatising the company, to his own vast potential profit. Both he and his directors were desperate for a neutrality pact with the nearby British EIC government in Madras. However, the latter were aware that a Royal Navy squadron under Commodore Barnett was in Asian seas specifically to capture French ships trading with China, and that they would soon be off Madras with their prizes, prizes which involved massive financial loss for Dupleix.[62] Despite the fact that the EIC directorate was as keen on neutrality as their French counterparts, Barnett triggered a cycle of violence and retaliation which, between 1744 and 1748, cost a fortune and saw the French capture Madras in 1746 and Admiral Boscawen fail to recapture it in 1747.

Though it has been argued that the conflicts of 1739–48 'had some role, though an unspectacular one, in the process by which British trade and imperial profits outstripped those of its competitors',[63] even this very cautious conclusion may be doubted. All wars were setbacks to trade, though the wars of 1689–1713 only weakened further an already weakening English overseas trading performance. The wars of 1739–48 had a much higher opportunity cost, for they held back a trade expansion which was very strong and which boomed after 1748. For a generation, no more, the fastest British trade growth derived from the export of manufactures to British North America, Ireland, and Asia, and this was reinforced by the revitalisation of the torpid re-export trade by mid-century by new products such as Carolina rice, China tea, and West Indian coffee. After 1776 the simple fact that there were 150,000,000 people in Europe and only 3,000,000 in the new United States helped return British manufactured exports to more traditional European markets.[64]

Even the privateering entrepreneurs who were probably the greatest gainers by the most successful aspect of these wars from the British point of view were finding life tougher by the end. Commodore George Walker, who made spectacular captures off the Spanish coast at little cost for his employers, ended up slugging it out with a 74-gun Spanish man-o'-war, one of the battleships the Spaniards had taken to using for bullion movements. That Spanish 74 had already fought off two Royal Navy attacks and sent her bullion ashore at the Groyne near Ferrol before she succumbed to Walker's privateer squadron known as 'The Royal Family' and two Royal Navy ships, one of which was blown out of the water. The privateers' heroic performance may in the end have been worth only £4000 to them by the time that prize was sold.[65]

The British Crown was lucky in that bad harvests and soaring state indebtedness made the French monarchy anxious for peace and not concerned to extract full advantage from its victories. Eighteenth-century war was often as much about prestige and honour as about concrete gain, and the French army had its mantle of glory by 1748, and rightly so. The French navy had endured diminishment, becoming 'the object of a very select group of contending interests rather than an effective instrument of state power'. In the spring of 1746 11,000 men in 25,000 tons of shipping, warships, and transports had been despatched from France to redeem the loss of Louisbourg. Illness, inadequate logistics, storms, and the general problems of long-range power projection at sea led to complete disaster, including the death of the commander, the duc d'Enville. Mounted mainly to advance the career of Minister of Marine Maurepas, the expedition achieved nothing except a viral massacre of a third to a half of the Micmac Indians.[66] The latter had been urged into lethal contact with the disease-ridden expedition by French missionaries who wanted the Indians to collect weapons and instructions at Chibouctou (the future Halifax), where the expedition made landfall, with a view to cooperating in a preliminary attack on Annapolis Royal, which never happened.

Colonial British-American ports – especially Boston, Newport, New York, Philadelphia, and, to a lesser extent, Charles Town – did very well out of privateering. Charles Town was handicapped by shortage of ships and white seamen. Blacks did serve on colonial ships, but the Stono rebellion of slaves in 1739 had led to draconian slave surveillance legislation which discouraged arming of slaves as privateersmen. The more than three hundred privateers sailing from British-American ports drove up seamen's wages due to their need for big crews, but their successes, even late in the war, could be spectacular. The Spaniards were so annoyed by the unlucky loss of a register ship carrying bullion and worth £48,000 to a Boston vessel with letters of marque that they held up the Aix-la-Chapelle peace negotiations.[67] Nevertheless, there was no question that, as a matter of prestige, the French Crown had to recover Louisbourg at the end of a victorious war, and New England had no capacity whatever to stop the return. The British were lucky that an Anglo–French *uti possedetis* settlement gave them back Madras, by definition.

The whole concept of an evolving triumphalist British identity based on imperial trade, imperial swagger, and Protestantism growing and evolving between 1739 and 1748 is sheer *post facto* constructionism by historians. Defeated by Spain, thrashed by France, and humiliated by very Protestant Scottish episcopalian Jacobites, the British monarchy staggered out of wars which had highlighted the violent clashes of interest within the devolved, multi-national, Atlantic, and global web of interests it ruled or half-ruled or hardly ruled at all. As Sir Lewis Namier long ago pointed out, imperial trading interests, even the well-entrenched West Indian one, were never the most potent economic interests in the Westminster legislature where home agriculture was 'the massive mountain range against which any single interest stood out as a minor peak', and 'cloth, coal and iron, shipping, brewing and banking' and even cider could all flex formidable lobbying muscles when threatened.[68] Great Britain was in 1746 an unstable European kingdom, with an Atlantic periphery, which after the puncturing of the Jenkins' Ear imperial bubble had been shown to be truly peripheral.

Indeed, the main problem posed by the British Atlantic and Asian periphery was that it might, given the unsatisfactory and untidy nature of the 1748 settlement, generate dangerous conflicts between British and French regional interests, themselves barely controllable by their respective monarchies, but capable because of the prestige factor of precipitating general war. The interests of the Duke of Newcastle were almost entirely in Europe and not outside it,[69] and he ran British foreign policy. There were endless disputes over Anglo–French colonial boundaries, especially in Nova Scotia, where the British in 1749 created the town of Halifax as a counter to Louisbourg, and in the West Indies. There, ownership of four islands – St Lucia, St Vincent, Dominica, and Tobago – was disputed. Attempts to secure French cooperation in demilitarising and, at one point, in evacuating the islands pending what British colonial as well as metropolitan authorities hoped would be 'a speedy and amicable conclusion' to 'this great affair' proved difficult to the point of driving the British governor of the Leeward Islands to despair, and helping to undermine his health.[70] War in India between the servants of rival East India companies could not be stopped even by their directorates, but it was to be in the Ohio valley that an attempt to put a term to a chronic tendency to shuffle into war for causes neither Crown deemed worth a major war ironically precipitated just that. Both in India and in North America, military developments ran out of hand.

Notes and references

1. Wilfred Prest, *Albion Ascendant: English history 1660–1815* (Oxford University Press, Oxford, 1988), p. 121.

2. Edward Gregg, 'The Jacobite Career of John Earl of Mar', in Eveline Cruickshanks (ed.), *Ideology and Conspiracy: Aspects of Jacobitism 1689–1759* (John Donald, Edinburgh, 1982), pp. 179–200.

3. Jane Dawson, 'The Gaidhealtacht and the Emergence of the Scottish Highlands', in Brendan Bradshaw and Peter Roberts (eds.), *British Consciousness and Identity: The making of Britain, 1533–1707* (Cambridge University Press, Cambridge, 1998), pp. 259–300.

4. Bruce P. Lenman, *The Jacobite Risings in Britain 1689–1746* (Scottish Cultural Press, Aberdeen, 2nd edn, 1995), Chaps. 5–6.

5. Jane Dawson, 'Anglo-Scottish Protestant Culture and Integration in Sixteenth-Century Britain', in Steven G. Ellis and Sarah Barber (eds.), *Conquest and Union: Fashioning a British state 1485–1725* (Longman, London, pbk edn, 1995), pp. 87–114.

6. Cited in Keith M. Brown, 'The Origins of a British Aristocracy: Integration and its limitations before the Treaty of Union', in Ellis and Barber (eds.), *Conquest and Union*, p. 249.

7. Bruce P. Lenman, 'The Scottish Episcopal Clergy and the Ideology of Jacobitism', in Cruickshanks (ed.), *Ideology and Conspiracy*, pp. 36–48.

8. From *A Fragment of a Memoir of Field Marshal James Keith Written by Himself 1714–1734*, partially excerpted in Bruce P. Lenman and John S. Gibson (eds.), *The Jacobite Threat* (Scottish Academic Press, Edinburgh, 1990), p. 118.

9. Bruce P. Lenman, *The Jacobite Cause* (Richard Drew and National Trust for Scotland, Chambers, Edinburgh, 2nd edn, 1992), pp. 57–58.

10. L.B. Smith, 'Spain and the Jacobites, 1715–16', in Cruickshanks (ed.), *Ideology and Conspiracy*, pp. 159–78.

11. Ormonde to Alberoni, Corunna, 22 March 1719, printed in William Kirk Dickson (ed.), *The Jacobite Attempt of 1719* (Scottish History Society, lst series, Vol. 19, Edinburgh, 1895), pp. 90–93.

12. Stair to Secretary Craggs, 11 March 1719, in *ibid.*, pp. 229–30.

13. Wesley Frank Craven, *The Southern Frontier 1670–1732* (Norton, New York, pbk edn, 1981), pp. 9–11.

14. Wesley Frank Craven, *The Southern Colonies in the Seventeenth Century* (Louisiana State University Press, Baton Rouge, LA, pbk edn, 1970), pp. 356 and 405–7.

15. Cited in Craven, *Southern Frontier*, p. 115.

16. Viscount Erleigh, *The South Sea Bubble* (Peter Davies, London, 1933), pp. 65–66.

17. Craig L. Dozier, *Nicaragua's Mosquito Shore: The years of British and American presence* (University of Alabama Press, Tuscaloosa, AL, 1985), pp. 7–16.

18. Troy S. Floyd, *The Anglo–Spanish Struggle for Mosquitia* (University of New Mexico Press, Albuquerque, NM, 1967), pp. 1–188.

19. John Cockburne, Lord of Admiralty to Sir John Clerk of Penicuik, 2 June 1726, Clerk of Penicuik Papers, Scottish Record Office (hereafter CPP, SRO), GD18/4153.

20. John Lynch, *Bourbon Spain 1700–1808* (Basil Blackwell, Oxford, 1989), pp. 133–39.

21. Geraldine Meroney, 'The London Entrepôt: Merchants and the Georgia colony', *William and Mary Quarterly*, 3rd series, xxv (1968), pp. 230–44.

22. From George Fenwick Jones, 'Von Reck's Second Report from Georgia', *William and Mary Quarterly*, 3rd series, xxii (1965), p. 327.

23. John Christie to Sir John Clerk of Penicuik, 2 February 1734, CPP, SRO, GD18/4162.

24. Francis Holborne to Sir John Clerk of Penicuik, 10 October 1733 and 23 March 1734, CPP, SRO, GD18/4163.

25. Same to same, 5 June 1735, CPP, SRO, GD18/4163.

26. Herbert W. Richmond, *The Navy in the War of 1739–48* (2 vols., Cambridge University Press, Cambridge, 1920), Vol. I, pp. 6–8.

27. Richard Pares, *War and Trade in the West Indies, 1739–1763* (Clarendon Press, Oxford, 1936), pp. 136–37.

28. *Ibid.*, p. 91.

29. Jean Preston, *The Mosquito Indians and Anglo–Spanish Rivalry in Central America, 1630–1821* (University of Glasgow, Latin American Studies, Occasional Paper No. 48, 1987), pp. 15 and 24–26.

30. The best survey of the coming of the war is Philip Woodfine, *Britannia's Glories: The Walpole ministry and the 1739 war with Spain* (Royal Historical Society, Boydell Press, Woodbridge, 1998).

31. Jean O. McLachlan, *Trade and Peace with Old Spain* (Cambridge University Press, Cambridge, 1940), pp. 88–89.

32. *Ibid.*, p. 110.

33. Patrick Clerk to Sir John Clerk of Penicuik, 24 February 1740, CPP, SRO, GD18/4175.

34. Same to same, 20 March 1740, CPP, SRO, GD18/4175.

35. Same to same, 18 July 1740, CPP, SRO, GD18/4175.

36. Same to same, 19 July 1740, CPP, SRO, GD18/4175.

37. Julian Gwyn, *The Enterprising Admiral* (McGill–Queen's University Press, Montreal, 1974).

38. See a settlement of 22 October 1745 between a Dr Haskell, civilian lawyer and agent, and the crew of the privateer *Enterprize*: Grant of Monymusk Papers, Scottish Record Office (hereafter GMP, SRO), GD1/32/37, ff. 4v–5r.

39. 'Scheme of a Division of the prize *San Joseph* . . . among the crew of the privateer sloop *Enterprize*', 1745: GMP, SRO, GD1/32/37, ff. 1v–2r.

40. Verner W. Crane, 'Projects for Colonization in the South, 1684–1732', *Mississippi Valley Historical Review*, 12 (1925), pp. 23–27.

41. Michael Pate Morris, 'The Bringing of Wonders: The effect of European trade on the Indians of the southern backcountry' (unpublished Auburn University PhD thesis, 1993).

42. David J. Weber, *The Spanish Frontier in North America* (Yale University Press, New Haven, CT, 1992), pp. 141–46; and Verne Chatelain, *The Defences of Spanish Florida* (Carnegie Institute, Washington DC, 1941).

43. Woodfine, *Britannia's Glories*, p. 224.

44. J.C. Beaglehole, *The Exploration of the Pacific* (A. and C. Black, London, 3rd edn, 1966), pp. 165–78; Richard Walter and Benjamin Robins, *A Voyage Round the World in the Years 1740–44 by George Anson*, ed. Glyndwr Williams (Oxford University Press, London, 1974); George Shelvelock, *A Voyage Round the World*, ed. W.G. Perrin (Cassell, London, 1928).

45. Leo Heaps, *Log of the Centurion* (Hart Davis, MacGibbon, London, 1973), pp. 215–27.

46. Kathleen Wilson, 'Empire, Trade and Popular Politics in Mid-Hanoverian Britain: The case of Admiral Vernon', *Past and Present*, 121 (1988), pp. 74–109.

47. Kathleen Wilson, *The Sense of the People: Politics, culture and imperialism in England, 1715–1785* (Cambridge University Press, Cambridge, 1995), pp. 135–36.

48. *Ibid.*, Chaps. 3 and 5.

49. Richard Harding, *Amphibious Warfare in the Eighteenth Century: The British expedition to the West Indies, 1740–1742* (Royal Historical Society Studies in History 62, Boydell and Brewer, Woodbridge, 1991).

50. Woodfine, *Britannia's Glories*, p. 179, n. 177, quote from J.M. Fernandez, *Officiales y soldados en el ejécito de America* (Seville, 1983), p. 167.

51. Douglas Edward Leach, *Roots of Conflict: British armed forces and colonial Americans, 1677–1763* (University of North Carolina Press, Chapel Hill, NC, pbk edn, 1986). For a fairly comprehensive and convincing demolition of his central thesis *vide* R.H. Harding, 'The Growth of Anglo-American Alienation: The case of the American regiment, 1740–42', *Journal of Imperial and Commonwealth History*, 17 (1989), pp. 161–84.

52. Trevor R. Reese, *Colonial Georgia* (University of Georgia Press, Athens, GA, 1963), p. 83.

53. Anthony W. Parker, *Scottish Highlanders in Colonial Georgia: The recruitment, emigration and settlement at Darien, 1735–1748* (University of Georgia Press, Athens, GA, 1997).

54. John R. McNeill, *Atlantic Empires of France and Spain: Louisbourg and Havana, 1700–1763* (University of North Carolina Press, Chapel Hill, NC, 1985), Chap. 4.

55. F.J. McLynn, *France and the Jacobite Rising of 1745* (Edinburgh University Press, Edinburgh, 1981), Chap. 1.

56. John S. Gibson, *Ships of the '45* (Hutchinson, London, 1967).

57. Jean E. McCann, 'The Organization of the Jacobite Army, 1745–46' (unpublished Edinburgh University PhD thesis, 1963).

58. John S. Gibson, *Lochiel of the '45: The Jacobite chief and the Prince* (Edinburgh University Press, Edinburgh, 1994).

59. *A Few Passages Shewing the Sentiments of the Prince of Hesse and General Hawley with Relation to the Conduct, Measures and Behaviour of several Persons, both Civil and Ecclesiastick in the City of Edinburgh since the Commencement of the present Civil War and Rebellion* (London, 1746, and sold at the pamphlet shops), pp. 4–5.

60. Col. the Hon. Joseph Yorke to the Hon. Philip Yorke, 3 June 1746, printed in Philip C. Yorke, *The Life and Correspondence of Philip Yorke Earl of Hardwicke* (3 vols., Octagon Books reprint, New York, 1977), Vol. I, pp. 542–43.

61. Merchant Venturers of Bristol to Lords of the Admiralty, 28 November 1747, and covering letter to Bristol MPs of same date, printed in *Politics and the Port of Bristol in the Eighteenth Century* (Bristol Record Society's Publications, Vol. 23, 1963), p. 65.

62. G.B. Malleson, *History of the French in India from the Founding of Pondicherry in 1674 to the Capture of that Place in 1761* (Allen and Unwin, London, 1893), pp. 98–102.

63. M.S. Anderson, *The War of the Austrian Succession* (Longman, London, 1995), p. 192.

64. Ralph Davis, 'English Foreign Trade, 1700–1774', reprinted in W.E. Minchinton (ed.), *The Growth of English Overseas Trade* (Methuen, London, 1969), pp. 99–120.

65. See H.S. Vaughan (ed.), *The Voyages and Cruises of Commodore Walker* (Cassell, The Seafarers Library, London, 1928).

66. James Pritchard, *Anatomy of a Naval Disaster: The 1746 French naval expedition to North America* (McGill–Queen's University Press, Montreal, 1995).

67. Carl E. Swanson, *Predators and Prizes. American privateering and imperial warfare, 1739–1748* (University of South Carolina Press, Charleston, SC, 1991), p. 53.

68. Sir Lewis Namier, 'The Treasure Islands', in *idem, Crossroads of Power: Essays on eighteenth-century England* (Hamish Hamilton, London, 1962), pp. 173–83.

69. Derek McKay and H.M. Scott, *The Rise of the Great Powers* (Longman, London, pbk edn, 1983), p. 183.

70. See Henry to George Grenville, 8 February 1749, and enclosed petition in French from 'The Governor, Council and Legislative Assembly of Your Majesty's Island of Barbados'; same to same, 28 February 1749; Henry Grenville to the Duke of Bedford, 13 March 1750 (copy). This last piece contains the words cited. Henry to George Grenville, 28 April 1750; 22–23 June 1750; and Lords Justices of Great Britain Leave of Absence to Henry Grenville, then Governor of the Caribee Islands (on grounds of ill health), 31 August 1752; all in Stowe Collection, Huntington Library (hereinafter STG), Box 24 (14), (17), (18) and (25); and Box 25 (1), (12), (20) and (48) respectively.

CHAPTER THREE

Under whose flag?: The erratic emergence of the East India Company as a military power 1688–1757

The brief spasm of EIC imperialism in India in 1688–90 under Sir Josiah Child was an aberration. Sir Josiah clung to power within the EIC, but that body entered an unstable era after 1689, culminating in the chartering of a rival New East India Company in 1698. The struggle between the two organisations benefited nobody, though the older one turned out to hold the whip hand in terms of competitive trading in Asia. Eventually, though with great difficulty, the two bodies came together to form the United Company in 1709. In practice the spirit of the EIC dominated the United Company, but not in the style of Sir Josiah, who had died in 1699. Military conquest was anathema to the leadership of the United Company after 1709. Yet the EIC always had contacts with the military world and, after 1668, an ironic heritage from Charles II committed it to maintaining indefinitely a small standing force of regular soldiers.

The EIC was, oddly enough, a major supplier of a vital component of gunpowder in the shape of saltpetre or potassium nitrate. Small amounts could be produced in England, but it occurred in bulk in Orissa in eastern India. The sulphur needed along with charcoal and saltpetre to make up gunpowder came from the Mediterranean. Gunpowder was a royal monopoly, but the EIC was allowed to make gunpowder for its own use. Charles I alleged angrily at one point that the EIC was making a surplus which it was marketing, to the detriment of the value of the leases of his monopoly, which of course he sold for all he could get.[1]

At a time when Courteen's associates were blithely talking about seizing and fortifying the large island of Hainan off the south China coast as a base for their trade with China,[2] the EIC had been perfectly willing to supply firearms and munitions of war to friendly Asian rulers, especially if the ruler in question was being bullied by the Dutch. A case in point was the king of

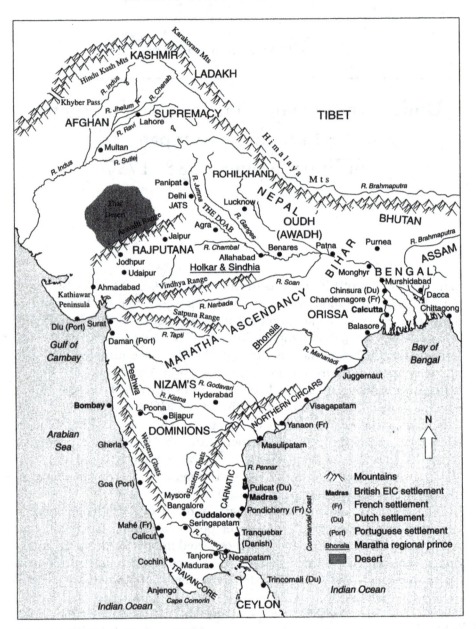

Map 4 Sub-Moghul India, *c.* 1750

Bantam in Java who asked the EIC in 1639 for 300 muskets, 300 barrels of powder, and 1000 round iron shot. The company did not have the shipping to send immediately more than 50 muskets and 200 iron shot, but this it did. To avoid an open quarrel with the Dutch, it told its local representative to give the king such powder as was to hand, under pretence of sale, and promised to send more.[3] Willingness to supply up-to-date weaponry to Asian rulers was a sure sign of absence of any design for conquest. In this, the gut instincts of the EIC were quite different from those of Charles I or, indeed, of Charles II after 1660.

The restoration regime was primarily navalist, but there was a military side to its imperialism. As well as Bombay Island, Charles II had received Tangiers as part of Catherine of Braganza's dowry. It was spoken of as 'the foundation of a new empire'. It was seen as giving the English monarchy a 'Nursery of its own for soldiers', instead of its previous expedient of sending chosen officers for periods of service with the French army. Tangiers was a bastion of crusading Christendom in the midst of the Moors, but also a position from which the Crown of England aspired to dominate the Straits of Gibraltar, 'the great passage to the wealth of Africa and America'. Its military government and hard-boiled professional garrison were harbingers of a future firm smack of authority which the royal Stuarts had always believed Englishmen needed badly.[4]

When the Earl of Sandwich led in 1662 the expedition which installed English control and a garrison of two thousand or so troops, he saw at once that it was essential to give Tangiers an all-weather harbour, and that the only way this could be done was by the construction of a massive mole. It proved by far the biggest and most expensive civil engineering project embraced by the English state in the late seventeenth century. The mole eventually achieved a length of more than 450 yards at a staggering total cost of £340,000. Sir Jonas Moore, the outstanding restoration applied mathematician, was taken out to Tangiers and subsequently produced a 'Mapp of the Citty of Tanger' which in its printed version consisted of three sheets, together making up a map more than 4 feet by 2.[5] It is more of a prospect than a plan and was probably designed primarily as visual propaganda for the whole Tangiers affair. The return of the mole, which would have created the harbour, was never built. The cost of supplying the garrison was huge. It was involved from the start in what have been called 'skirmishes' with the locals, as if actions in which a senior English commander and four hundred men were killed are skirmishes. Outright war with the Empire of Morocco, with which Elizabethan Englishmen had sensibly maintained a cordial commercial relationship,[6] came by 1678. Though a long siege in 1680 was broken by the sending out of heavy reinforcements, the whole enterprise had by then become an unfundable fiasco.

People like Samuel Pepys, the diarist and naval administrator, who had been up to his neck in the project of establishing Tangiers as a major outpost of Stuart imperial power, started to backtrack and write down the whole business retrospectively when it became clear that Tangiers would have to be abandoned, a decision which had been taken by 1683 and which was implemented in 1684. It was a huge waste of resources and a humiliating defeat. Added to the shameful end of the second Dutch war, and the spectacular failure of the outrageously ambitious strategic and political objectives with which Charles II had started the third in 1672, Tangiers was a grim reminder that the restoration military were no better than their naval colleagues when it came to trying to secure decisive victory over a determined opponent. The Duke of York had always been the leading imperial hawk in the councils of his brother, so it was entirely consistent that his short reign as James II and VII was marked by the ill-advised and calamitously unsuccessful amphibious assault on the Moghul Empire.

The restoration monarchy did resist the temptation to throw good money after bad in the pursuit of imperial stature in Bombay, but in general it is clear that the Glorious Revolution of 1688–89 which overthrew James II was hardly the turn towards empire which some historians have said it was. Of course, writers started trying to impose their interpretation on the Glorious Revolution as it occurred. John Dryden, who had been at the heart of the two great Tory propaganda offensives which helped secure public compliance in the drastic measures that secured the power of Charles II after 1683, and whose pen was kept busy supporting the policies of James II,[7] had his own particular line to plug. In his later works there is a consistent insinuation that the sacrilegious deposition of the Stuarts had been followed by a terrible collapse in English moral standards – as if the collection of fanatics, cynically opportunistic rogues, pimps, whores, French spies (like Charles II's mistress, the Duchess of Portsmouth), and bravos who made up the restoration courts were not, even in the mephitic world of baroque courts, in a league by themselves. It is almost equally absurd to see 1688–89 as an era when Englishmen turned to a combination of Protestantism and empire for the shaping of their identity. With James II's fall, a series of attempts to create a particular kind of imperial identity finally ground to a halt, and in places like India sensible Englishmen turned their back with relief on the crusading militarism of their late sovereign.

Yet the EIC was left in Bombay with a military commitment originally shouldered by Charles II. Local Portuguese officials insisted that Bombay harbour was one 'with which that of Lisbon cannot be compared'. They resisted the hand-over, as did their compatriots in Tangiers. However, Portugal had reasserted its independence from Spain only in 1640 and secured it only in 1668. As well as the resources of the 'King's plantation' of Brazil, it needed England as an ally to hold off Spanish reconquest. The island of Bombay had been sacked by an Anglo–Dutch fleet in 1626. The Cromwellian protectorate had shown a passing interest in acquiring it. There was therefore a pre-history of English interest in the island when Sir Abraham Shipman arrived with a force of some 450 men in September 1662 to claim Bombay. He was transported by a fleet commanded by James Ley, third Earl of Marlborough, a sailor with an impeccable royalist record in the civil wars and a strong hereditary interest in the West Indies. He was indeed to die governor-elect of Jamaica when he was killed in action against the Dutch fleet in the summer of 1665.[8] His 1662 voyage was rendered unhappy by the deliberate obstruction of local Portuguese officials from the viceroy of Goa downwards. They were convinced that 'India will be lost on the same day in which the English nation is settled in Bombay'. If by this was meant Portuguese India, the forecast proved untrue, but by sustained obstruction the Portuguese eventually forced Shipman to land his force on a barren island south of Bombay, where he and all but one of his officers, and most of his men, died. When Shipman's secretary was eventually allowed, as the result of diplomatic pressure, to land on a narrowly defined Bombay Island in February 1665, he had with him only 1 ensign, 111 other ranks, a surgeon and surgeon's mate, and 2 gunners and 2 gunners' mates. He could not control the islands in the harbour or the neighbouring island of Salsette. In the face of a Dutch threat he had to hire forty 'Portugals of Europe' to reinforce his troops. In 1666, Sir Gervase Lucas arrived as governor with sixty reinforcements, but died in 1667.[9]

Despite the pathetic nature of the early history of the Bombay garrison, it was a crucial precedent, for Charles II was committed by the treaty with Portugal to a garrison of 500 in Bombay, to protect local Roman Catholics (presumably from the Dutch). Maintaining such a garrison, in the face of a climate unhealthy for Europeans, and with Portuguese 'allies' whose behaviour killed many more English soldiers than ever fell to the hostile Dutch, was not easy. Lucas' successor recruited Frenchmen and locals to reinforce the ranks. The latter were known as topasses, and though the early historian of the British military in India, Robert Orme, thought that this term derived from their headwear, an early form of what became the solar topi, it almost certainly comes from the Persian *top-chi*, meaning a musketeer. That is what they were: local firelock musketeers. They were Indian Christians with Portuguese names but no Portuguese blood, defined by their religion, and adequate security guards rather than warriors. When the Dutch threatened to attack in 1667 the garrison was a motley crew, 285 only in number, and of those only 93 English; the rest were French, European Portuguese, topasses, or Hindu Marathas from the nearby mainland. By 1668 Charles II had contrived to shed the expensive burden of Bombay by transferring it to the EIC, at an annual rent of £10 in gold, but with the same obligation as to a garrison.

Sir George Oxenden, who had been knighted by Charles II in 1661 and appointed in 1662 president of the EIC council in Surat, had in 1663 experienced the trauma of a plundering attack on that principal trading centre in Gujerat. Surat was a gem in the diadem of the Moghul Empire, but that empire had raised, among other problems, the resurgence in power of the Marathas, whose native land lay due east of Bombay. Their great warrior-king, Sivaji, struck at Surat with a force of 4000 horse. The Moghul governor retired within this fort, allowing Sivaji to lift a huge booty, but not the contents of the EIC factory or fortified warehouse – where £80,000 worth of goods was stoutly defended by Oxenden and his staff, to the point where they were commended by the Emperor Aurangzeb and granted a year's exemption from customs. In September 1667, Oxenden took over Bombay from its royal administration. Unsurprisingly, he successfully offered the officers and men of the garrison inducements to transfer to what became the first EIC military establishment in India. Oxenden died in Surat in 1669, but the EIC now had an alternative on the west or Malabar Coast of India to the increasingly unstable conditions in that city.[10] Its settlement of Bombay, which had perhaps 10,000 inhabitants when the EIC assumed control, had over 60,000 by 1674. It offered shelter to local peoples from the twin banes of their lives: the inability of Moghul government to ensure security, and the relentless cultural aggression of Portugal's Counter-Reformation regime in Goa.

Oxenden's successor at Surat, Gerald Aungier, presided over Bombay's fortunes between 1669 and 1677. He fortified the island. There had always been an artillery element in the garrison. As early as 1668, the court of the EIC sent out an 'able gunner' to Bombay. Yet the cosmopolitan element remained a feature of the regime there. In 1671, Aungier appointed as chief engineer a German, Colonel Herman Blake, who had reached India via Persia. More significantly, Aungier organised in the 1670s a militia of all the freemen or landholders. The officers were mainly English, but the ranks were filled by Indians assimilated to Portuguese culture. As late as 1803, when war had stripped out regular troops, 600 'Portuguese' militia garrisoned Bombay.

Bombay, as well as its excellent harbour, also boasted by the early 1670s a substantial fort at the south-east corner of the island. A contemporary account said that it mounted no fewer than 120 cannon and also held 60 field guns, mounted on carriages designed for movement beyond the fort walls. There were good reasons for this accumulation of ordnance. A Dutch naval attack had to be discouraged. Then there were the endemic local feuds between Indian powers which continually threatened to involve Bombay.

The Moghul admiral on the west coast, the Siddi, habitually brought his fleet into sheltered anchorage at Bombay between June and September, when the south-west monsoon made the idea of beating out into the Indian Ocean unattractive. His sailors were a rowdy menace. His idea of a ploy to keep them busy was to launch plundering, slaving attacks on adjacent Maratha territory. Maratha retaliation was inevitable. Eventually their admiral, the Angria, was to command a fleet of fast, light inshore vessels, very like the Siddi's fleet, in the sense that its activities were indistinguishable from those of the numerous active local pirates. The EIC garrison was therefore a necessity, though not one the company was very willing to fund – even after a clash with the nearby, poisonously hostile Portuguese led to the creation of a rapid-reaction force of 40 cavalry, under a veteran of the Dutch wars of 1665–67 and 1672–74, Captain Richard Keigwin. His main achievement in Bombay was to lead a largely justifiable mutiny against the mean-minded company.

So it is not very convincing to argue that the EIC was always an incipient imperial hegemon. The cosmopolitan riff-raff it employed to guard its valuable stocks of goods could occasionally perform well behind defences, but normally their record was remarkable for pusillanimity and a tendency to mutiny. This is not to deny that there had always been an element of force in English trade with India. There had to be. When the EIC was founded in 1600 England was at war with a Spanish Habsburg monarchy which included Portugal. The Portuguese were absolutely determined to exclude other Europeans from Moghul ports by brute force, and they went on trying to batter the EIC into accepting Portuguese hegemony in Indian waters until the Convention of Goa of 1635 finally signalled an Anglo–Portuguese truce. By then it had become clear that the Dutch were just as violent and monopolistic as the Portuguese had been in their heyday. Moghul central authority was always remotely benign towards foreign merchants, but Moghul local officers regarded them as milch cows, until the merchants proved otherwise. Sir Thomas Roe, in the early seventeenth century, had expressed the sincere conviction of the EIC leadership that conquest and expensive fortification were ineffective, delusive solutions to an acknowledged security problem, but that was because he was confident that EIC naval power alone could compel respect – not just from rival Europeans but also, by threat of blockade, from the Moghul governor of Surat. He also believed that English attacks on Moghul shipping between Surat and the Red Sea could 'stir these people to know us and fear us'. Fear was better than feigned love. Fear was the root of respect.

All of this was platitudinous, and true. In the late seventeenth century, as relations between centre and periphery in the Moghul Empire began to become fluid, capacity for a measure of self-defence was essential for mercantile survival. Even the moderate Gerald Aungier warned the EIC directorate in 1676 that 'the times now require you to manage your general commerce with your sword in your hand'. Indian merchants flocked to the fortified EIC settlements of Bombay and Madras for security.[11] The company began to regard security of the modest kind which its major settlements could offer as not just an essential, but also as a marketable commodity.

There was always also an undercurrent of violence in relations between Europeans in India. After British and Dutch pressure had forced the Habsburg emperor of the Holy Roman Empire to suspend the Asian trade of the Ostend Company in his Netherlands early in 1727, one of the emperor's subjects in his Austrian lands, a merchant in Linz, had the bright idea of securing authorisation from the king of Poland to trade in Asia. His two ships sailed from Spain, but one came from Ostend; they carried a cargo of silver bullion (the key to Asian trade) belonging to the Ostend Company, and its agents in Asia were urged to give the voyage every assistance. It looked like a not very subtle attempt to get round the ban on the Ostend Company and when the small flotilla reached the Ganges and anchored there, it found its exit blocked by an Anglo–Dutch fleet of 'four large ships, two galleys, and severall sloops'. This fleet fired on the first of the two nominally Polish ships that tried to run the gauntlet and seized her, forcing the remaining ship to pay off its crew and over-winter for fear of sharing its companion's fate. The resulting diplomatic row guttered like a candle in the wind, for nobody treated Count Watzdorff, the Polish king's representative in London, as a serious player in the Asian game. When Lord Harrington wrote to the count on 22 April 1731 about the incident, he acidly reminded him that 'if one prince grants his flag and passports to the subjects of another prince to Trade, in violation of a treaty concluded with their Sovereign and lawful master, it would render all treaties and conventions for the regulation of commerce entirely vain and fruitless'.[12]

Relations between the EIC and the French East India Company, on the contrary, were distinctly cordial in the early eighteenth century. Disputes there were – as when in April 1731 the EIC Court of Directors formally appealed to their French counterparts about the seizure in the Ile de France (Mauritius) of the brigantine *Amity*, sent out from Madras on a voyage to the coast of Africa and the Malabar Coast, under the authority of the EIC council at Madras. It was represented to the French that:

> After so many years of perfect harmony and agreement between our
> Governors and others at our several Settlements in the East Indies, and
> the reciprocal freedom of trade allowed in the several ports belonging to
> both nations, we were very much surprized with the account we have
> received that the President and Superior Council of the Isle of Bourbon

had declared that they had orders from Europe to prohibit that freedom of trade.

The EIC hoped that this action lacked any foundation, and stressed that it had not so far given reciprocal orders of this kind to its own settlements. The French response was conciliatory, not defiant.[13] The English and French companies truly did cooperate. It was to their mutual advantage so to do. That same summer a representative of the French company wrote to London enclosing a list of tea prices alleged to have been paid in Canton by their recently returned China ships. In return, he asked the EIC to send a note of its own purchase prices at Canton, when available, as a cross-check on the buyers.[14]

The disintegration of Anglo–French relations at local level in India was always a possibility. In 1722–25 there was considerable trouble on the Malabar Coast of India, where the EIC had a long-standing settlement at Tellicherry by permission of the local ruler, the Zamorin of Callicut. Close to it, the French established their own fortified settlement, using a grant from 'one Byanore, a rebel prince'. In this situation of endemic civil war, the EIC was soon complaining that the French were seizing and pillaging their small vessels whilst 'They have protected the said Boyanore's vessels and supplied him with ammunition and men in order to oppose and root out the English.' The English response was to build another fort nearby at Moylan, with the Zamorin's permission, and to appeal to the directors of the EIC to approach the French. What was at stake locally was the Callicut pepper trade, into which the French were determined to insert themselves. Significantly, the Callicut representatives of the EIC deplored the way their French rivals were refusing to respect the stable Anglo–French peace in Europe after 1714, not least because of the heavy cost of all this local fighting.[15]

In the last analysis, the rising levels of violence between competitors for the succession to a dying Moghul Empire made some fortification, with guards and mounted ordnance, essential. On the east coast of India, the EIC's servants had constructed from 1640 Fort St George, the nucleus of the future city of Madras, on land granted by a local rajah and under the mistaken assumption that the rajah would pay for it. By the time the London directors' veto of the idea reached India, the fort existed. By 1690–91 a company of European artillerymen and a troop of horse supplemented the usual racially mixed infantry garrison there. At this time, the English started to build Fort St David south of Madras at Cuddalore. Nearby, the French had had a settlement at Pondicherry since 1672. They lost it to the Dutch in 1693–94 but recovered it by the Peace of Ryswick which concluded the War of the League of Augsburg in 1697. Urgent requests from Fort St George for reinforcement in 1705–07 produced no response before

1732 when a large reinforcement was sent out by EIC directors clearly becoming nervous about French attitudes, to which their attention had been drawn by the *Amity* episode. They were, however, so ignorant as to have to ask Fort St George what the French were up to on the south-east (or Coromandel) coast of India. The reply cannot have been wholly reassuring, for in 1737 the parsimonious directors sent out more reinforcements and a large amount of military stores. This was just as well, for in 1741–42 Maratha armies swarmed into the Carnatic hinterland of Madras, plundering that sub-Moghul Muslim-ruled principality and demanding tribute from Fort St George. Faced with defiance, they besieged it unsuccessfully in June and again in December 1741, drawing off eventually to attack the French at Trichinopoly, which they captured in March 1742. The Marathas were eventually driven out by the Moghul viceroy of the Deccan, the virtually independent Nizam ul Mulk of Hyderabad, in 1744, but guards were a necessity, not an option, for traders; and when war broke out between Britain and France in 1745, the combined garrisons of Fort St George and Fort St David contained only 150 European soldiers as compared with a French garrison of 436 at Pondicherry.

None of this would have mattered had the usual conventions obtained between the French and English East India companies: that war between their respective Crowns in Europe did not extend to Asia, where the men of commerce maintained neutrality during European hostilities. With the rise of British naval supremacy, this arrangement clearly worked to French advantage, so in 1745 the Westminster government vetoed a proposed neutrality pact. A Royal Navy squadron commanded by Commodore Barnett made a profitable cruise in waters east of Cape Comorin, capturing valuable French shipping on the trade routes between the Coromandel Coast and the great emporium of Manila in the Philippines. Most unfortunately, this involved heavy personal loss for Joseph Dupleix, the senior French official on the coast. After a vain attempt to secure redress by approaching Fort St George, Dupleix embarked on a process of redress by force. Barnett died in April 1746. By 3 September, Madras faced a French fleet with 1100 European troops and 800 coloured soldiers, 400 of them Indians known to history as sepoys. Dupleix's predecessor, Dumas, had begun the practice of hiring Indians to turn them by European drill into sepoys. They were cheap. Indian labour was a bargain by European standards. For the same cost, an employer could have four or five good sepoy companies, or one European company. Adding in the 2000 seamen aboard the fleet, the odds against the motley EIC garrison of 200 were hopeless. After being battered by two mortar batteries, Madras surrendered on 10 September. The Royal Navy had left the scene earlier, after an indecisive action against the large but undergunned French flotilla.[16]

The French state was much more willing to commit military resources to India than the British, so it was creditable that the British in Cuddalore, one of their Coromandel settlements south of Madras, fought off a French attempt to seize the town. Early in 1748, Major Stringer Lawrence, a retired regular soldier and a veteran of Culloden, had reached Cuddalore with authority to command all company troops on a salary of £840 a year plus the king's brevet making him 'major in the East Indies only'. He imposed real discipline on the motley band of Europeans and topasses garrisoning Fort St David, the EIC's stronghold near Cuddalore. Meantime, the French threat had grown much more serious because of developments following the seizure of Madras. A quarrel over the loot between Dupleix and the equally greedy naval commander de la Bourdonnais was predictable. Dupleix simply could not have taken Madras without the squadron de la Bourdonnais had brought from the Isle of France (Mauritius) and the French sailors had been active in the siege. After his squadron had been damaged by a storm which warned him of the serious danger posed by the impending north-west monsoon on the harbourless Coromandel Coast, de la Bourdonnais extracted a large ransom from the English and vanished over the horizon. He never returned and with him went a crucial local naval superiority.

More significant still proved a quarrel between Dupleix and the ruler of the Carnatic, Nawab Anwar-ud-din, technically a vassal of the Moghul Empire and a subordinate of its viceroy in the Deccan, the nizam of Hyderabad. He objected to European wars on his soil, and had been led to believe that Dupleix would turn Madras over to him, something Dupleix never intended to do. The nawab sent his eldest son, Mafuz Khan, with 10,000 horse to take over the city. On the estuary of the Adiyar River, south of Madras, on 24 October 1746 Mafuz Khan's army tried to block French reinforcements of 1000 men – commanded by a Swiss mercenary engineer officer called Paradis – which were heading for Madras. The 700 Indian troops in Paradis' force were sepoys, not the peons which were the French equivalent of the EIC's topasses. Certainly, on that day on the Adiyar, the sepoys proved their worth. They formed up on either flank of the French European infantry and then advanced in a three-deep line in the face of a battery of heavy slow-firing Indian cannon, which belched out a round before becoming irrelevant. The sustained musketry of the advancing line was too much for the massed horse awaiting them. Under the eye of its elephant-mounted general, the nawabi army broke. The action was south of the old Portuguese settlement of St Thomé, just occupied by French troops coming out from Madras to escort Paradis in. When these troops poured volley fire into the rear of Mafuz Khan's already reeling army, it disintegrated and fled. Already the French in Madras had won skirmishes with Mafuz Khan's encircling cavalry, by smashing their charges with rapid discharge of case shot, whereby a fan of musket balls was projected from a canister, probably by short four-pounder guns.[17] The effect was equivalent to machine-gun fire.

None of this meant cavalry was obsolete if properly handled. The nawabi cavalry had maintained their blockade of Madras until Paradis appeared, by withdrawing out of canister-shot range, and the same troopers routed a French force marching to attack Fort St David in December 1746 by a surprise dawn attack which swept over the French camp.[18] Nevertheless, in set-piece battle, it was now clear that sepoys armed with flintlock muskets and bayonets, supported if possible by fast-firing light field guns, could see off most cavalry attacks, and could themselves only be stopped by a similar force. Sepoys were quite essential if European military entrepreneurs were to be able to exploit the relative edge which European methods of organising and waging war had probably given them over their Asian contemporaries, both on sea and land, since possibly the sixteenth and certainly the seventeenth century.

Sustained competition in a multi-polar European political system had created conditions under which states had continually to update their war-making capacities if they wanted to survive. In Europe, war was pervasive. Between 1618 and 1660 there was no year without serious war between states somewhere in Europe, and many years when several wars went on simultaneously. A cosmopolitan mercenary officer class moved between armies, facilitating transfer of techniques and technology.[19] It has been argued that advances in Europe's art of war between 1600 and 1750, based partly on the ability of armies to protect the core economies of the warrior states, had created a 'self-sustaining feedback loop . . . that raised Europe's power and wealth above levels other civilizations had attained'.[20] Here lay a root of global imperialism, but in Asia before 1800 distance effectively neutralised the superiority of the professional forces forged in the military–industrial complexes of Europe's predominantly church-state monarchies.[21] Logistics ruled out a French invasion of India. Only Indians could conquer India.

The French system of raising sepoy forces was the first sign that Europeans might act as military managers within an otherwise essentially Indian military scene, but of course naval factors remained vital when two European trading companies clashed. Dupleix's first bid to crown the seizure of Madras and defeat of the nawab by the capture of the last English stronghold on the Coromandel Coast, Fort St David, was foiled when a Royal Navy squadron under Commodore Thomas Griffin re-established local British naval superiority and landed reinforcements. The second French bid to take out Fort St David was decisively defeated in June 1748. Major

Stringer Lawrence had had six months to instil some discipline into the garrison. By an ostentatious abandonment of Cuddalore, which persuaded the French he meant to make a serious defence only of Fort St David itself, he lured a French force of 800 Europeans and 1000 sepoys into an almost casual occupation of the town, which Lawrence had regarrisoned after dark. A lethal discharge of musket balls from muskets and cannon shattered the French advance.

It was really still a war of position, and the positions were the European fortified coastal enclaves. Dupleix had spent freely on the latest bastion defences for Pondicherry, defying orders from home in 1743 to suspend such work as an economy measure.[22] As a result, he was able in August–September 1748 to hold off a massive amphibious assault on the place led by Admiral Edward Boscawen, who had a fleet of 30 ships and 7500 troops, including 4000 Europeans. Because of the impending north-west monsoon, which his ships could not ride out on a harbourless coast, Boscawen's available time was short. He wasted too much of it on besieging an outlying fort which should have been neutralised by a masking force, and by beginning his trenches too far from the outer defences of Pondicherry. Disease ravaged his men, while it proved impossible to warp his warships close enough in to bring their main armament effectively to bear on the seaward artillery defences of the town. In September the siege had to be raised. The garrison was a formidable 1800 Europeans and 3000 sepoys, so any assault might have proved bloody within the 50-day operational period available. Robert Orme, the contemporary military historian of the British in India, who drew on a printed account by one of Boscawen's officers, concluded that 'the reputation of superior skill in the defence of fortified places, which the French nation had at this time established in all parts of the world, was exaggerated in the opinion of the troops before Pondicherry by a sense of the errors committed by themselves'.[23] Certainly, the France of Louis XIV and XV, the France which had produced in Sébastien Le Prestre de Vauban the first military engineer to gain a marshal's baton, was out ahead of its British rivals in the art of fortification before 1750. In 1725, it was said that under Vauban's example, 'the French nobility embraced the art of engineering'.[24] The EIC did not have engineers on a proper military basis before 1759, making do with foreign adventurers or army and navy officers on secondment before that date.[25]

The Peace of Aix-la-Chapelle, which involved the mutual return of overseas conquests, was greeted with predictable joy by the directors of the EIC. They sent off a message via the Middle East to inform their servants in Fort St David, telling them that in accordance with the general peace signed on 19 April at Aix-la-Chapelle 'all hostilities either by sea or land against the French are to cease in the East Indies six months after the said 19th April, which must be complied with accordingly'. They also told their servants to appoint commissioners (one of whom was to be Major Stringer Lawrence) to receive the return of Madras from the French. Until further notice, Madras was to be 'a subordinate settlement'.[26] By 1749, Madras was British again, but did not become the seat of an EIC presidency again before 1753.

By then it had long become clear that the servants of the French East India Company simply did not intend to desist from the use of force in India after 1748. They had made the fatal twin discovery of the cheapness of sepoy troops and their lethal effectiveness against the cavalry armies of the Moghul tradition. They had also discovered how easy it was to attain their objectives by backing a compliant Indian prince militarily in the endless succession and sovereignty disputes of the sub-Moghul states. The Carnatic was the best-publicised cock-pit, but the situation in the EIC's Bombay presidency was no different. By early 1752, the chief and council of the EIC at Tellicherry in south India were advising their superiors in Bombay that their fort at Madacarra was under siege, being bombarded by batteries mounting twelve and eighteen pounders. In theory the assault was the product of a local civil war. In practice, as the Tellicherry council insisted, 'this war is no other than a French war'. French troops and French guns were the core of the besieging force. To protests, the French council in the nearby French settlement of Mahé replied that they were merely supporting a princely ally, and of course defending such grants of land and trade as he had given them or might choose to give them. Troops sent from Bombay to raise the siege did not distinguish themselves. They panicked and fled when their young lieutenant was shot dead in an assault on the main hostile battery. There was fear that a French 60-gun ship might intervene in the road off Tellicherry under guise of escorting a convoy of rice ships from Mangalore whose cargo was vital for France's local ally's military and political survival.[27]

This sort of speculative intervention in an Indian succession dispute was much more likely to be profitable to the servants of the Compagnie des Indes than trade. Since its formation in 1664, the French company had only been very intermittently profitable. It was horribly vulnerable in Asia or at sea during a European war. The War of the League of Augsburg from 1689 to 1697 cut its Asian establishments off from Europe, as did the War of the Spanish Succession in the period 1703–14. Privatisation of its monopoly after 1714 was replaced by tight state control from 1719. When in 1722 its servants were allowed private trade, they concentrated on intra-Asian trade. The years between 1731 and 1741 proved prosperous, but a financial crisis in 1741, turmoil in India, and Anglo–French war from 1744 effectively destroyed the Compagnie des Indes as a trading structure. Even in the halcyon era between 1731 and 1741, the state-sponsored company had relied very heavily on a partnership with private traders. By 1744 the company claimed to be on the verge of bankruptcy. It probably had overall been profitable in the period to 1741, but at low rates of profit, below what could be obtained by fairly safe investment in France itself. Troubles in India led to concentration on the China trade, but then the British navy captured its homecoming China convoy in 1745. The servants of the French company, who had always lived very high on the hog in India when given the opportunity, were virtually unemployed by 1744. Trade was impossible, but India was unstable. The crushing defeat of the Moghul emperor and fall of Delhi in 1739 to the arms of the invading Persian warlord Nadir Shah had convinced Dupleix that instability was going to be the pattern of the future. Between 1744 and 1748 he had become a successful military entrepreneur. After 1748, when trade was again feasible, he preferred to rent out his security system. His troops were for sale. It was not the course which his directorate wished to see, and since they were overseen by a state commissioner responsible to a government committee, the Conseil des Indes, it was clearly not preferred state policy, but Dupleix was out of hand.[28]

His decision to back a claimant by the name of Chanda Sahib to the title of nawab of the Carnatic was a calculated gamble. Chanda Sahib was an able general and administrator who had been captured by the Marathas. His release from a lengthy, though not very rigorous imprisonment was the result of obscure financial transactions which certainly did not amount to his being ransomed by the impecunious French.[29] He did have some Maratha troops at his disposal, and he soon allied with Muzaffar Jang, grandson of the deceased nizam of Hyderabad, who claimed his grandfather had willed the Moghul viceregality of the Deccan to him. Early in 1749, a triple alliance was formed between these two Muslim military adventurers and the French. It was essentially a speculative partnership which hoped to defeat the reigning nawab of the Carnatic, Anwar-ud-din (whose troops had been routed at the Adiyar River), and seize his country for Chanda Sahib, whom Muzaffar Khan could then legitimise in his capacity as nizam. This, and the death of Anwar-ud-din, was duly achieved in a battle at a mountain pass near Ambur, where the reigning nawab of the Carnatic chose to try to fight off the triple alliance. The French contingent bore the brunt of the action. Arcot, the nawabi capital, fell to the invaders.

There ensued a complex series of events which culminated in the defeat and killing of the reigning nizam, Nazir Jang, late in 1750 by a mixture of intrigue with discontented Pathan chiefs in his army and a direct assault on the divided nizami camp by the French under Louis d'Auteuil. Absolutely predictably, as well as splitting a great deal of loot from the vanquished Nazir Jang's coffers, the allies sealed their league with further deals. Muzaffar Khan wanted to occupy the viceregal capital of Aurangabad formally to confirm his authority over the Deccan, but needed a French contingent with his army to ensure victory. He appointed Dupleix his deputy south of the River Kistna and granted the French the right to the revenues from territories from which Dupleix naively hoped to extract an annual income of 3.5 lakhs (350,000) of rupees. That done, Muzaffar Khan marched into the interior accompanied by French troops commanded by the very able Charles de Bussy. The latter's 500 Europeans and 2000 sepoys were the heart of the army. When Muzaffar Khan was killed in a skirmish on the way, de Bussy did not flinch. He decided to sponsor the deceased man's uncle, Salabat Jang, whom he duly installed at Aurangabad as nazim. The French were the power behind yet another throne, though propping this one up against threats from the Marathas and local rebellions proved a full-time job which removed de Bussy's troops indefinitely from the Carnatic theatre.

There the British were left clutching an alliance with Mohammed Ali, son and surviving heir of the defeated Anwar-ud-din. Stringer Lawrence had departed for England after disputes over his pay and authority, but a new governor of the EIC Madras presidency, Thomas Saunders, grasped the fact that Dupleix would use his influence over the rulers at Arcot and Aurangabad to squeeze the EIC out of the Deccan. Mohammed Ali had taken refuge in the southern city of Trichinopoly, where he had once been the governor. He knew that he had no hope against Chanda Sahib and his French allies without British support. There had been a clear perception among Indian elites since the early eighteenth century that European discipline, battle tactics, and artillery skills were in some respects superior to anything available within India's military cultures. Clement Downing, an English sailor who sailed in Indian waters between 1715 and 1723, at one point with a force which tried unsuccessfully to strike hard enough at the ports and shipping of the Angria to discourage him from molesting EIC shipping, has left an interesting record of this. He met the commander of a Moghul army operating against the Marathas and dissident Muslim vassals of the empire in and around Gujerat. After being carefully quizzed about European battle technique, which he explained involved much stricter discipline and closer-order formations than were conceivable in a Moghul army, he was asked about his skills as an artillerist and hired as a gunnery officer. His account of the several actions and sieges in which he participated shows the importance of artillery. It was crucial in sieges, but also on several occasions vital in battles, where it fired the equivalent of canister (Downing talks of 'Partridge shot') against cavalry charges. However, it is clear that the guns were relatively immobile and that, to be effective battle weapons, they required two preconditions. One was a set battlefield such as an opposed crossing of the only tactically relevant ford of a river. The other was that after the establishment of a 'Platform of Cannon', usually in a linear deployment, they ideally needed to be concealed so that they opened up without warning on the advancing enemy. Camouflage was standard practice.[30]

Ideally, Indian rulers could simply incorporate European infantry training and manoeuvrable field-artillery into their armies. In the longer run, they were to do so to a great extent, but a ruler like Mohammed Ali, who controlled only a fraction of the territory he claimed, could not control subordinate officials as long as they suspected Chanda Sahib would destroy him quite soon. He had to assign parts of his revenue-yielding territories to the EIC at the behest of Governor Saunders to pay for the cost of EIC troops attached to his army. The Madras presidency of the EIC alone had the power to create a modern infantry-based field force capable of checking the French. Once they started to expand their sepoy forces, and scored some sort of success to engender confidence, they had a far superior economic base on which to build. Unlike the French, the British were rooted in a viable, profitable trading company with a large cash-flow and networks of credit. The key decision came in August 1751 when a junior captain in the EIC service called Robert Clive led out 200 Europeans and 300 sepoys from Madras to launch a diversionary attack on the nawabi capital of Arcot, in order to lift pressure from Mohammed Ali and a small British force besieged in Trichinopoly by the French and Chanda Sahib. The venture succeeded beyond all reasonable expectation.

The French had made plenty of enemies by their high-handed actions and soon were facing an inherently superior coalition in the inevitable confrontation around Trichinopoly in 1752. The British had a better command team. Stringer Lawrence returned to command the army, but he was one of the few men to whom Robert Clive could defer. They worked well together, whereas the French commander, Jacques Law, though brave and intelligent, proved indecisive. Outmanoeuvred, he surrendered in his entrenched camp on Sriringham Island in June, and when the news of this reached Paris the French directorate resolved that Dupleix's wars must stop. Their company was being bankrupted to no good purpose. In fact, the fighting around Trichinopoly continued, with the fortunes of war fluctuating almost as much as the alliance patterns between the French, the British, and nearby Indian powers like the states of Mysore and Tanjore – not to mention that supremely mobile menace, the Marathas. Lawrence gradually forged a formidable Madras presidency army with a sepoy force second to none. Its commander, Yusuf Khan, was deeply respected by both Lawrence and Clive, and rightly so. Yet he too gained from the turmoil of the period, for he was originally a low-caste Hindu who escaped caste by embracing Islam, and then rose by working for the EIC at its new trade of war.

When he did not have a cooperative local ally, Lawrence did suffer from want of cavalry, especially for reconnaissance. On the battlefield both the

French and the British made unprecedented use of light, quick-firing field guns to hold off hostile horse.[31] In the final battle before Trichinopoly in May 1754, three British brass six-pounders spewed out a murderous slew of musket balls which stopped the advancing French infantry line at a crucial point in the engagement.[32] The loss of impetus proved fatal when Captain Caillaud launched the EIC infantry line forward. One volley finished off the work of the six-pounders, breaking the French line. As the French had already failed in a daring attempt at a night escalade of the defences of Trichinopoly, ending up trapped in a 'killing zone' between two of its rampart-systems and taking heavy casualties before the assault force had to surrender, there were no more cards left in the French hand. The arrival of Commissioner Charles Godeheu in 1754 in India marked the end of Dupleix's career. Superseded, he returned to France, where he was to die bankrupt, with the bailiffs in residence. It was not as unfitting a fate as Victorian British imperialists thought. He had not founded an empire, nor had he tried. He had gambled and lost on the military market in south India. It was known that the British government had been provoked into sending regular troops to India, though they had not yet arrived. Godeheu sought cessation of arms and negotiated peace.

The greatest monument Dupleix left behind was the new military capability of his arch-rivals. The EIC acquired the independent military muscle which was to enable them to expand not commercially but territorially only because they had perceived a naked French threat to their own traditional 'open door' policy in India and had had to create a sepoy army to match the French one.[33] It always operated as part of a kaleidoscopic regional alliance system, but it turned out to have certain outstanding advantages over other local forces, including even the French. By the end, Dupleix was simply running out of money whereas, despite the stresses and dreadful costs of war, the EIC troops – European and Indian – on the whole had steady pay and therefore better discipline. Then there was the question of battlefield edge. Beyond any doubt, the new EIC sepoy army had an edge. Its close-order drill and capacity to maintain a steady rolling fire with its flintlock muskets, with their bayonets for close impact situations, made it formidable both in attack and defence. In hollow square formation, well-led EIC sepoys were difficult to destroy. Indian states rapidly set out to imitate it.

By 1770 Mysore had 20 battalions of sepoy infantry, as well as 20,000 horse. There were always European mercenaries available as drill masters. In north India, the nawab-vizier of Oudh (or Awadh) soon had eighteen battalions 'as well disciplined as any belonging to the Company'. In 1780 the ruler of Mysore, Hyder Ali, wiped out a significant British force near Madras. It was still true that the European way of war was a profitable ploy in India. Timing was vital. There was a lag. The sub-Moghul states of India needed time to catch up. Some, like the Carnatic, could not even start the race because of European parasitism on their fiscal systems. Others adapted faster in some areas than others. Field artillery is a case in point. It was not just the European quick-firing guns which were superior. So were their wheels, carriage mounts, and ammunition limbers. Mysore had field artillery in the 1770s but not until the Maratha wars of the early nineteenth century did the British face Indian field artillery so good that they could incorporate captured pieces.[34]

Yet up to the formal outbreak of a new Anglo–French conflict in 1756, the London and Paris directorates hoped to avoid further expensive wars. In a letter from Paris dated 21 March 1753, the Secret Committee of the French company approached the Secret Committee of its British counterpart saying that they had delegated Director Duvelaer to confer with the British committee, with an eye to restoring tranquillity by means of a formal accommodation between the two bodies. To this proposal for a treaty, the EIC was positively warm. It said that:

> The Committee of the United Company, as the most certain means for restoring and preserving Tranquillity between the two companies, and with the Indian Powers, did propose that each Company should renounce every possession and acquisition obtained since the breaking out of the late war between the two nations and to retire within their ancient limits, resting their motives thereto on three Arguments:
> The sufficiency of such limits for commercial views;
> The charge of maintaining the new Acquisitions against the country governments desirous of repossessing them.
> The disputes which may arise from the proximity of these possessions by the imprudence of the officers of either Company.[35]

That said it all: the EIC did not want more territory in India; it did not want to fight the French company; and its directors simply assumed, correctly, that the belligerence of French and British company representatives in India was a major problem for both.

An immense amount of energy was invested in trying to reach an understanding. The French opening gambit envisaged firstly steps to restore peace and tranquillity; secondly, 'liberty of trade without exclusion'; thirdly, a 'settlement of the affairs of the government of Arcot and Coast of Coromandel', and fourthly, and most contentiously, a perpetual neutrality. To the first and second items, the EIC heartily agreed. The territorial settlement on the coast was clearly going to require difficult negotiations, and the EIC was well aware that the British government, and particularly Secretary of State Lord Holderness, was likely to jib at a cast-iron perpetual neutrality, unless the likely course of Anglo–French relations were to suggest that an indefinite period of peaceful coexistence lay ahead. Nevertheless, the EIC itself made it clear to its French counterpart that it was willing, as part of a real settlement, to press the case for a neutrality pact in India on its own government.

The underlying problem was lack of trust. Though Dupleix's wilder schemes had been defeated in the Carnatic wars after 1751, the French company and French troops were still strongly posted both on the coast of Coromandel and in the nizam's capital of Hyderabad. Experts consulted by the EIC Secret Committee were liable to express admiration for the French, as having 'chosen their Ground judiciously and to have never lost sight of war and commerce'. They were also admired for their shrewd placement of a line of forts deemed to display 'The traces of an Engineer'. Yet there was a basic fear that behind all of this lurked the demon of reversal to rapid self-funding conquest when circumstances allowed it. Only a return to the pre-war (i.e. pre-1745) situation could exorcise it, at least from British minds.[36]

By June 1754, agreement appeared close. There was a meeting between the Earl of Holderness, the French ambassador, a Captain Mabbot, and no less a French grandee than the duc de Mirepoix in the Arlington Street residence of Holderness, on the eleventh day of that month. Holderness was reluctant to commit himself finally to anything in the absence of EIC representatives, but he seems to have concurred in the French statement that agreement between the two companies was feasible. He then summarised the British position on the two outstanding issues. One was that both companies must recognise Mohammed Ali as nawab of the Carnatic, and in the event of his death or legal deposition not intervene in any succession dispute or 'enter into the discussion of what prince, has, or has not, the right of nomination to the nabobship; but both companies agree to acknowledge the person who shall be confirmed by the Great Mogul'. Even more interesting was his lordship's second point to the effect that there was no British objection to French trading posts on the northern parts of the coast of Coromandel 'provided such settlements are not accompanied with territory or revenue'. If, of course, a settlement grew commercially important, 'each company may fortify; but if either were to begin with a fortification, before it can be certain, whether trade can be drawn to such parts, it must appear to the other Company, to be done with intent to govern the country, by means of garrisons; and that cannot be admitted'.[37] What the EIC wanted was assurance that trade, not empire, would be the field in which French and English merchants would compete.

Thereafter, the EIC became increasingly sceptical of the chances of a positive outcome to the negotiations. They wanted an end to what they diplomatically called 'The Troubles' in India but in early October 1754 the Secret Committee told Holderness that they were 'sorry to say, we find the state of the negociation relative to the troubles in India subsisting between our East India Company and that of France, remains in the same state it was in when we had the honour to attend the cabinet council on the 23rd day of May last'.[38]

By 8 November 1754 the Court of Directors was imploring the government to assist the company 'with such a force by sea and land as may protect the Company's trade and settlements in the East Indies and give weight to such measures as His Majesty may think proper for the Company to agree to'. The directors were depressed by the endless disputes with the Crown of France and not unreasonably worried by the way the Westminster government was depriving them of control over their own fate whilst not backing them with naval and military power in the way the French Crown supported its commercial interest in India.

The EIC was disturbed by the growth of French power in India and shocked when, at a conference at Sadrass to try to reach an accommodation, the French representatives had insisted that Dupleix be recognised as governor of the Deccan from Cape Comorin to the River Kistna. The EIC had sent out to its settlements 'very large supplies of men and military stores',[39] from time to time, and would send more, but it was a commercial business which Dupleix would be able to throttle if all his claims were acknowledged. Fortunately, by this time Dupleix was heading home to die in obscurity a decade later.

Godeheu, who, as commander and director general of the Compagnie des Indes, wielded extensive authority, agreed a provisional truce with Thomas Saunders, governor of Fort St George and president for the EIC on the coasts of Coromandel and Orissa. Done at Fort St George on 31 December 1754, the text of the provisional treaty was available in London by June 1755. It was a notably sensible standstill agreement. The French and English companies kept their existing settlements, agreed that access to navigation on major rivers be free, balanced their military guards in outlying areas where they had adjacent factories, and agreed to cooperate militarily against any third party who tried to establish themselves within the existing bounds of the English and French. The extreme pretensions to overlordship of a vast stretch of the Deccan, on the strength of some very dubious grants, Godeheu conspicuously abandoned. Inconspicuously, he did not abandon French supremacy at Hyderabad where Charles de Bussy continued to display a rare mixture of diplomatic and military talent in sustaining Nizam Salabat Jang against challenges as diverse as the Marathas and his elder brother, Ghazi-ud-din.

De Bussy himself thought that by 1753 the nizam's throne was secure enough for the French to withdraw with honour from Hyderabad, but fear that English influence would replace French made Dupleix persuade him to return. Pressure on the nizam from rebellion in Berar enabled the French to obtain grants of land revenues worth 30 lakhs of rupees, from which they maintained at a cost of 25.5 lakhs an army of 900 Europeans and 4000 sepoys. With its assistance, the financially embarrassed nizami government was able to launch a profitable plundering raid into Mysore to refill its coffers with 'tribute'. However, the fact was that Hyderabad was now dominated by a self-funding foreign-controlled army and the nobility of the nizami state, led by its first minister Shah Nawaz Khan, were anxious to expel it. Dupleix, before his fall, thought the prospects so good that he had arranged for de Bussy to be betrothed to one of Madame Dupleix's daughters by a previous marriage. Though it came to naught, the engagement underlined plans for a permanent Dupleix family business controlling much of the Deccan. Godeheu was anxious to sustain French power in Hyderabad after the fall of Dupleix, for fear of English influence. In real terms, Godeheu had only agreed to withdraw from a couple of French positions on the Orissa coast, and that conditionally. Elsewhere, the French dug in, in de Bussy's case literally, in the nizam's capital in the summer of 1756 when Shah Nawaz Khan tried to dismiss him. A stout defence and the way Jacques Law fought his way through with reinforcements of 160 Europeans and 700 sepoys with five guns confirmed the permanency of the French cuckoo in the nest.[40]

Anglo–French relations in North America had been characterised by much the same use of force to back endless jockeying for advantage, but with the defeat of Braddock on the Monongohela in 1754 the upshot, as the next chapter will show, had been a major land war between the two Crowns, a war which was likely to engulf the Indian representatives of France and England, and which duly did so. However, India was different because of the Godeheu–Saunders truce and the genuine anxiety of the EIC directors for a dismantling of the structures of European entrepreneurial violence in Indian politics. Godeheu's position over the French presence at Hyderabad raises the question whether the French company was ever prepared to accept the logic of mutual withdrawal and, of course, the servants of the EIC were deeply and corruptly involved in the chaotic finances of the nawab of Arcot.

Where the Indian and North American situations were close was in the remarkable ignorance of rival Europeans as to the nature of the continental mass within which they sought one another out and grappled. Robert Clive, in a letter he wrote to the EIC from Queen's Square in London in December 1754, said flatly that:

The Kingdom of Mysore, before the late Troubles was known to the Europeans only by name, we had no Idea of the power, riches and

grandeur of that empire, before the inhabitants thereof came to the
relief of Trichinopoly, it is a country equal in extent to the nabob's
[Nawab of the Carnatic] dominions, lies upon the back of them . . .

Clive said he did not know Mysore's revenues, but a minister of Mysore
had told him they were over £3,000,000 per annum. In the seat of Anglo–
French war on the Coromandel Coast, Clive reckoned the three territorial
unit revenues, in peace, as 100 lakhs of rupees for the province of Arcot,
and 50 lakhs of rupees each for the kingdoms of Trichinopoly and Tanjore.
Arcot's 100 lakhs was equivalent to £1,250,000 and the total of 200 lakhs
for the region had a sterling equivalent of £2,500,000. This, Clive said,
was mainly derived from the grain crops of the region, and was not truly
impressive if compared with the yield of a two shillings in the pound land
tax in Great Britain. Yet these revenues in the Carnatic, Tanjore, and
Trichinopoly were 'that we were contending for', to pay for the sepoy
armies which were the prime instruments of power, and to underwrite
private fortunes based on trapping Indian princes into unrepayable debt at
high interest.[41]

As late as January 1755, the president and council at Fort St George
were arguing to the Court of Directors that the truce was essential, because
French power was basically superior and French interest with the country
powers much greater. The burden of war, with only a bankrupt nawab of
the Carnatic as an ally, was 'too heavy for a trading Society' and if war
should come 'from a superiority of country force especially horse they would
be able to protect their own, and destroy our Districts', thereby choking off
EIC revenue.[42] In practice, the business of settling precise claims to specific
villages, which was part of the truce, proved bad tempered. In March 1755,
the Fort St George council reported 'Numberless Complaints having been
made both by the Nabob and the French of the infringements of the suspension of arms, by the seizure of several villages' and added that in these
disputes with the nawab, French officers were playing for time.[43] Well they
might, for not only was war between the two Crowns raging in America,
but it was also about to explode in Europe and India.

Even if it had limited confidence in its warmaking capacity, the EIC
Madras presidency was by 1755–56 profoundly militarised. It had been
fighting for its life, off and on, since 1746. It had copied and developed the
French technique of raising sepoy battalions, and it had built up a corps of
battle-hardened officers from Stringer Lawrence to Robert Clive. It was
also about to receive heavy reinforcements from the royal forces, naval and
military. Compared with Madras, the Calcutta presidency of the EIC, for
all its commercial importance, was living in a time-warp and was less capable of holding off an attack than Oxenden and his men had been when the

Marathas invaded Surat in 1663. One reason why Governor Saunders had been unable to assist, as was his hope, Shah Mawaz Khan's coup designed to expel de Bussy from Hyderabad was that the attentions and resources of the Madras officials were focused on the dramatic fall of the EIC's settlement at Calcutta to the nawab of Bengal, Siraj-ud-daula, in June 1756.

The account of the fall of the settlement written by John Zephaniah Holwell, though that of an eyewitness penned in July 1756, is predictably self-serving, but it makes some key points. The nawab first fell on the EIC post at Kasimbazar, which surrendered. Either the money and goods he seized there had to be returned at a settlement or he had to drive the EIC from Bengal, which with the aid of 'the cannons ammunition and military stores he became possessed of' at Kasimbazar, he went on to do at Calcutta. There the EIC defences were masked by speculative building and the garrison a motley crew of '45 of the train [i.e. gunners] and 145 infantry and in both only 60 Europeans'. There was, as in Bombay, a militia, but it was not impressive. In Holwell's words:

> in the Militia were about 100 Armenians who were entirely useless, and
> then that number amongst the black militia boys and slaves, who were
> not capable of holding a musket, so that in fact when the seafaring people,
> who most of them appeared only on the first muster were draughted off
> on board the vessels, of which we had in port about 30 sail of every craft,
> our garrison did not consist of 250 fighting men, officers included.

Deserted by the bulk of the militia, whose officers fled to the ships and whose other ranks just fled, this minuscule force could not hold off the nawab's army, especially after the bulk of the EIC top brass decided, disgracefully, to run away on the ships.[44] It was a predictable debacle by a motley, cosmopolitan mercantile rabble which had outlived its welcome and, more seriously perhaps, failed to upkeep its fortifications.

Siraj-ud-daula was much vilified by Victorian British writers of the imperialist school. The fall of Calcutta was followed by the deaths of a large proportion of his British captives by suffocation in the notorious Black Hole of Calcutta. It was John Zephaniah Holwell who publicised the episode in a contemporary pamphlet as part of a campaign to have himself seen as the 'hero' of the siege. He depicted the nawab as a cruel tyrant whose minions threatened his captives with such fates as being blown from a cannon's mouth.[45] In fact, the young nawab of Bengal was a fairly typical Muslim Indian ruler. His grasp of reality had been weakened by the unavoidable sycophancy of a court upbringing, and his understanding of European realities was very limited, but he knew he needed revenues and he was well aware of the depth of faction-fighting within his entourage. He put down a

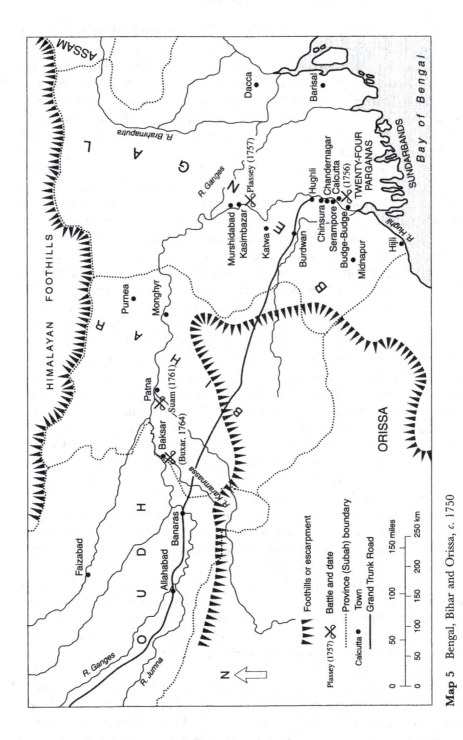

Map 5 Bengal, Bihar and Orissa, *c.* 1750

rebellion by his cousin, Shaukat Jang, after he had humbled the British and extracted large payments from the French and Dutch settlements on the river. This campaign revealed to all the world that Siraj-ud-daula was on very bad terms with his bankers, the Hindu Seth family. It also showed that he distrusted his own generals to the point of fearing that they might try to assassinate him. In this, he showed insight. What he could have no insight into was the power of the military and naval forces available in Madras for the EIC counterstrike.

It was not just the new sepoy army in Madras which made the British dangerous. Clive had returned in November 1755 from a spell in England with three companies of the Royal Artillery. At Bombay he should have found a superior regular officer, Captain Caroline Scott, a competent and brutal Scotsman who had won the favour of Captain General the Duke of Cumberland by his role in the defeat of the 1745 Jacobite rising. He had stoutly defended Fort William, at the southern end of the Great Glen, from a Jacobite siege. After Culloden, he had mounted notably vicious 'pacification' operations. He came to India to inspect EIC fortifications. There he died. Clive, with a lieutenant-colonel's commission 'in the East Indies only', had expected to fight as an 'auxiliary' to a Maratha attack on the Nizam of Hyderabad which the EIC hoped would compel the nizam to dismiss de Bussy. When the Bombay presidency got cold feet about the idea, a frustrated Clive teamed up with Vice Admiral Charles Watson, a senior officer of the powerful Royal Navy squadron in Bombay harbour. Amphibious operations and prize money were at the heart of their plans. Watson and Clive opened their partnership with a successful assault on the Angria's long impregnable fortress port of Gheria, which saw its defences blasted into submission by short-range fire from the main gun batteries of Watson's squadron, with their powerful thirty-pounder guns.

What was different was the ability of Watson's squadron to navigate safely into such short range. European maps of the wider world were surprisingly unreliable to a late stage in the history of the great age of European overseas expansion. European mapping of Asian waters was distinctly uneven. The London Scot, John Ogilby, who invented the road strip map and in the late 1660s started to publish his multi-volume *English Atlas*, had published 'A New Map of Asia' dedicated to the governors of the EIC in 1673, but its functions were informative and decorative rather than navigational. Another Scot, Alexander Hamilton, published *A New Account of the East Indies* in Edinburgh in 1727, in which he simply denied the possibility of truly accurate map-making on any useful scale in Asia and reverted, very sensibly, to the older tradition of the rutter or pilot's guide based on landmarks and experience.[46] Watson had not solved the big problems of global mapping like longitude, but he had with him outstanding naval surveyors who made the operational charts which allowed their commander to bring his guns to bear. No Indian state had ships which could match a European man-o'-war. Now such men-o'-war were much more effective as weapons of amphibious warfare.

The point can hardly be overstressed, for the operations which set the EIC on the path to empire in India were essentially amphibious.[47] Colonel Adlercron, commanding the regular 39th Foot, which was on loan to the EIC, refused to allow his regulars to serve under Clive when the latter reached Madras and was designated commander of land forces in the expedition which the EIC was sending to succour its Bengal establishments. Vice Admiral Watson, who was to transport Clive's force, nevertheless had the seniority to force Adlercron to disgorge three companies of the 39th to act as marines on his ships. So it was a combination of EIC troops (European and sepoy), regular infantry, and Royal Navy ships that approached the River Hugli in December 1756. They first fought their way by river and land, past the fort at Budge Budge fifteen miles up the river. Watson's ships had to pound that fort, but Fort William at Calcutta surrendered after a few rounds. Clive's forces occupied Calcutta. They then participated in a raid on the port of Hugli just up the river before falling back to fight off the nawabi army led by Siraj-ud-daula in a fierce action outside Calcutta.

The nawab would have been happy to cut a deal at this point, but news had arrived of the declaration of Anglo–French war and Admiral Watson's ships, after a protracted and bloody action, pounded the powerful French defences at their settlement of Chandernagore, up river from Hugli, into submission in the stiffest fighting of the campaign. The subsequent action by Clive's small army on 23 June 1757 at Plassey required nerve and boldness in the face of vastly superior numbers. Bloody it was not. Nor were arms alone the key to the outcome. Siraj-ud-daula's forces were riddled with disaffection. His senior general, Mir Jafar, was conspiring with Clive to replace him as nawab of Bengal. Above all, the giant banking house of Jagat Seth, which was deeply entrenched throughout Bengal and its sister province of Bihar, where the Gangetic port city of Patna had emerged as a great national entrepôt, was deeply disaffected. The Seths were unusual in the complex world of *shroffs* and *kothiwals*, to use the Indian terms closest to 'banker', for their profound involvement with politics. Handling government finances and remitting the tribute still paid to the imperial court at Delhi was lucrative work, but risky. It was probably to decrease the risk of conspiracy against a violent Muslim ruler who had verbally and physically abused the Hindu Seths that the latter insisted the British be brought into the conspiracy.[48] The result was no 'Anglo–Banian raj', for the British were basically always suspicious of the *shroffs'* power, but nawabi government was distinctly undermined on 23 June 1757, and that was what counted. Watson's account of Plassey did not mention Clive. Yet Watson died soon after, and Plassey made Clive master of Bengal in the sense that the new ruler, Mir Jafar, was dependent on him and on the large sepoy force which Clive at once started to build with revenues which, by hook or by crook, he had transferred to the EIC's control.

The servants of the EIC Madras presidency had followed the example of their French predecessors. At a time when it had become difficult to make money by normal commercial means, they had turned to a frontier of war and plunder where it was possible for them to pile up enormous personal fortunes, if they were very lucky. Most of them did no such thing. The majority were traditionally thought to die within two monsoons of arrival in India. Those who, like Clive, did not just survive but flourished, found themselves with a window of opportunity in 1757 when circumstances placed at their disposal a uniquely powerful combination of EIC and government naval and military power. At the same time, occasion arose to deploy it in the wealthiest sub-Moghul state in the sub-continent: Bengal and Bihar.[49] Apart from decisive combat leadership, Clive displayed a real genius for identifying and exploiting the political fissures within a deeply divided Bengali ruling establishment. He had always, perhaps, had unusual access to the currents of local Indian politics through his mastery of Portuguese and contacts with the thin veneer of priests and people left by former Portuguese expansion scattered along the Indian coasts. Of course, the company itself in the long run did not benefit from this swing towards violence. It began to go the way of its French rival. Nor were the territories in the Carnatic, Bengal, and Bihar dominated by EIC sepoy armies legally British. They had Moghul-sanctioned nawabi administrations. What mattered to the greedy servants of the EIC was that Mohammed Ali in the Carnatic was financially complaisant and, as Holwell said to a Westminster select committee in 1767, 'The Natives are a quiet timid people not addicted to war . . . the Revenue may be collected from them with very great facility.'[50] There were fortunes to make.

Notes and references

1. 'Order of the Privy Council, June 16, 1632', *Calendar of the State Papers, Colonial Series, East Indies and Persia 1630–34*, ed. W. Noel Sainsbury (London, HMSO, 1892), 266, No. 276.

2. 'Notes Concerning the Trade in China, etc.', March 1638. *Calendar of the Court Minutes . . . of the East India Company 1635–1639* (Clarendon Press, Oxford, 1907), p. 294.

3. 'A Court of Committees, September 18, 1639', *ibid.*, p. 326.

4. Stephen Saunders Webb, *Lord Churchill's Coup: The Anglo-American Empire and the Glorous Revolution reconsidered* (Alfred A. Knopf, New York, 1995), pp. 19–25.

5. Frances Willmoth, *Sir Jonas Moore: Practical Mathematics and Restoration Science* (Boydell Press, Woodbridge, 1993), pp. 130–36.

6. T.S. Willan, *Studies in Elizabethan Foreign Trade* (Manchester University Press, Manchester, 1959), Chap. 4.

7. Phillip Harth, *Pen for a Party: Dryden's Tory propaganda in its contexts* (Princeton University Press, Princeton, NJ, 1993).

8. *Dictionary of National Biography* (hereafter *DNB*), Vol. XI, p. 1086.

9. Sir Patrick Cadell, *History of the Bombay Army* (Longman, Green and Co., London, 1938), Chap. 3.

10. *DNB*, Vol. XV, pp. 9–10.

11. I. Bruce Watson, 'Fortifications and the "Idea" of Force in Early English East India Company Relations with India', *Past and Present*, 88 (1980), pp. 70–87.

12. The EIC's office file of transcripts of documents relevant to this episode are preserved in I/1/1 Part 1, ff. 28–48, Oriental and India Office Collections (hereafter OIOC).

13. *Ibid.*, ff. 49–56.

14. A translation of Fromaget to Cavalier, 28 July 1731, can be found in *ibid.*, f. 63.

15. *Ibid.*, transcripts, extracts from letter from Callicut dated 28 October 1728, and draft protest, ff. 84–86.

16. P.J. Begbie, *History of the Services of the Madras Artillery* (Madras, 1852), Chap. 1.

17. Henry Dodwell, *Dupleix and Clive. The beginning of Empire* (Archon Book reprint, Shoe String Press, Hamden, CT, 1968), p. 19.

18. James P. Lawford, *Britain's Army in India from its Origins to the Conquest of Bengal* (George Allen and Unwin, London, 1978), p. 79.

19. M.S. Anderson, *War and Society in the Europe of the Old Regime 1618–1789* (Fontana, London, pbk edn, 1988).

20. William H. McNeill, *The Pursuit of Power: Technology, armed force and society since AD 1000* (University of Chicago Press, Chicago, IL, 1982), p. 117.

21. P.J. Marshall, 'Western Arms in Maritime Asia in the Early Phases of Expansion' in *idem*, *Trade and Conquest: Studies in the rise of British dominance in India* (Variorum, Aldershot, 1993), Chap. 10.

22. G.B. Malleson, *History of the French in India from the Founding of Pondicherry in 1674 to the Capture of that Place in 1761* (W.H. Allen, London, 1893), pp. 97–99.

23. Robert Orme, *A History of the Military Transactions of the British Nation in Indostan from the Year 1745* (John Nourse, London, 1773), Vol. 1, p. 109.

24. The Chevalier de Guignard in his *L'Ecole de Mars* (1725), cited in Christopher Duffy, *The Fortress in the Age of Vauban and Frederick the Great 1660–1789. Vol. II: Siege Warfare* (Routledge and Kegan Paul, London, 1985), p. 96.

25. *Ibid.*, p. 254.

26. I/1/1 Pt 1, f. 90, OIOC.

27. Excerpts from the Tellicherry Council's letter of 22 March 1752 to Governor and Council in Bombay; the Tellicherry Council's protest to Mahé, and the reply of the French Council in Mahé are in 'Extracts from the East India Company's Advices regarding the Conduct of the French on the Coast of Mallabar and the Country Government there', in *ibid.*, ff. 92–103.

28. Catherine Manning, *Fortunes à Faire. The French in Asian trade, 1719–48* (Variorum, Aldershot, 1996).

29. Dodwell, *Dupleix and Clive*, pp. 32–38.

30. Clement Downing, *A History of the Indian Wars*, ed. William Foster (Oxford University Press, Oxford, 1924), pp. 140–87.

31. Orme, *Military Transactions*, Vol. 1, p. 159.

32. *Ibid.*, p. 358.

33. Peter J. Marshall, 'British Expansion in India in the Eighteenth Century: A historical revision', in Marshall (ed.), *Trade and Conquest*, pp. 28–43.

34. Bruce P. Lenman, 'The Weapons of War in Eighteenth-Century India', *Journal of the Society for Army Historical Research*, 46 (1968), pp. 33–43.

35. There is an account of the beginnings in 'A narrative of what formerly passed towards offering an Accommodation between the English and French Companies in the East Indies', in I/1/1 Pt 1, ff. 162–69, OIOC.

36. Joseph Frowke to the Gentlemen of the Committee of Secrecy of the East India Company, 29 May 1753, I/1/1 Pt 2, ff. 170–73, OIOC.

37. 'Arlington Street June 11th 1754: Minute received from the Earl of Holderness, 12 June 1754', *ibid.*, ff. 223–25.

38. Secret Committee to Lord Holderness, 4 October 1754, copy I/1/3, ff. 20–21, OIOC.

39. Directors of EIC to Sir Thomas Robinson, Secretary of State, 8 November 1754, *ibid.*, ff. 21–24.

40. H.H. Dodwell (ed.), *The Cambridge History of India. Vol. 5: British India 1497–1858* (3rd Indian reprint, S. Chand and Co., New Delhi, 1968), pp. 134–39.

41. 'Letter from Captain Clive relating to the revenues of Arcot Tanjour etc.', 4 December 1754, I/1/3, ff. 62–64, OIOC.

42. General Letter of President and Council at Fort St George to Court of Directors, 12 January 1755 (recd 25 June 1756), *ibid.*, f. 147.

43. Same to same, 8 March 1755 (recd 11 September 1756), *ibid.*, f. 152.

44. 'Copy of a letter by John Zephaniah Holwell Esq., dated at Muxadavad the 17th July 1756 to the Governor and Council of Bombay', in I/1/2, ff. 206–08, OIOC.

45. The text of J.Z. Holwell, *A Genuine Narrative of the Deplorable Deaths of the English Gentlemen and Others, etc.* (A. Miller, London, 1758), is conveniently reprinted in Irish Macfarlane, *The Black Hole or the Making of a Legend* (Allen and Unwin, London, 1975), pp. 283–311.

46. Bruce P. Lenman, 'The Scottish Linschoten: Alexander Hamilton and the development of Scottish knowledge of Eastern waters to 1727', *South Asia Library Group*, 42 (January 1995), pp. 4–18.

47. Bruce P. Lenman, 'The Transition to European Military Ascendancy in India 1600–1800', in John A. Lynn (ed.), *Tools of War: Instruments, ideas and institutions of warfare, 1445–1871* (University of Illinois Press, Urbana, and Chicago, IL, 1990), pp. 100–30.

48. Kumkum Chatterjee, 'Collaboration and Conflict: Bankers and early colonial rule in India, 1757–1813', *The Indian Economic and Social History Review*, 30 (1993), pp. 283–310.

49. J.D. Nichol, 'The British in India 1740–1763: A study in imperial expansion into Bengal' (unpublished PhD thesis, University of Cambridge, 1976).

50. Cited in Macfarlane, *Black Hole*, p. 275, footnote.

CHAPTER FOUR

From Armageddon to millennium: English America and the destruction of New France 1748–1760

The unstable nature of the Peace of Aix-la-Chapelle can hardly be exaggerated. It reflected a fiscal rather than a military stand-off between the Crowns of France and Britain. The French public in particular found it difficult to comprehend why their considerable military achievements in the Low Countries gave them so little positive reward. This was even more puzzling in the light of the generally miserable British military performance in a war which had seen the Hanoverian dynasty humiliated by a Jacobite invasion of England that reached Derby, the main British field army under Cumberland clearly outmatched by the marshal de Saxe in Flanders, and significant reverses for British interests on the Coromandel Coast of India. In North America the capture of Louisbourg had been a surprise, but it in no way shook the military confidence of French officers. They were clear that the disciplined, militarised society of New France might be outnumbered by the Anglo-Saxons, but remained more than a match for them in combat where its cult of authority in church and state enabled it to act decisively, seizing the all-important initiative.

The Ohio valley proved to be the source of a clash of interests so violent as to make coexistence, even competitive coexistence, difficult if not impossible. Here was a vast stretch of territory into which all sorts of groups of native peoples had been driven to join groups already there. It was both a refuge and a bastion of native American identity, balanced between rival European empires but jealous of its own autonomy, and valuable to Europeans immediately as a source of trade, especially in furs. In the longer run, of course, the rich lands of the Ohio were a magnet for European settlers' greed. There were Indian groups whose power stretched into this area who had, at least in European eyes, ties to a European monarchy – notably the Iroquois, recognised as British subjects by the 1713 Treaty of Utrecht.

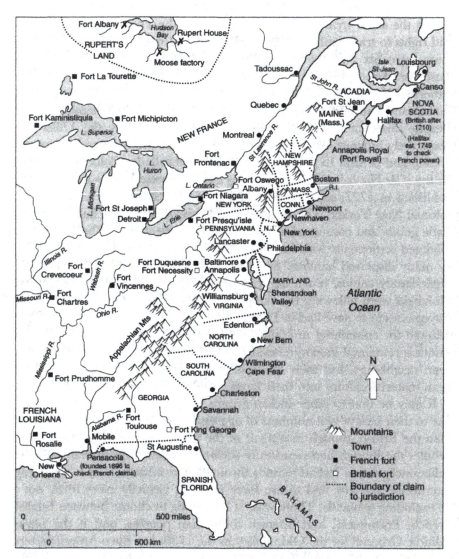

Map 6 European rivalries on the Eastern seaboard of North America, 1690–1754

Yet the same treaty guaranteed that both the French and the English had rights to trade with the Five Nations of the Iroquois. By the early 1720s there were Six Nations in the League of the Iroquois. Survivors of the Tuscarora tribe defeated a decade earlier in a war with the aggressive settlers of North Carolina had resettled further north under Iroquois protection and had been recognised as the league's youngest member nation. Despite this demographic reinforcement the Iroquois by the 1730s were desperately anxious for peace based on a diplomatic balance between the French and British. In practice the title of Cadwallader Colden's book, *The History of the Five Indian Nations Depending upon the Province of New-York in America*, published in 1727, expressed a truth as well as the wishful prejudice of a colonial New Yorker. The Iroquois were dependent. Their culture needed trade goods and consumed alcohol to its own great hurt. Their once consolidated settlements with large, handsome longhouses had been replaced by many dispersed hamlets. By 1750 most Senecas seem to have lived in single-family cabins, much like Euro-American settlers. The Oneidas and Mohawks were following the same trend, and only the more conservative Cayugas seem to have had in 1750 at least one town with several longhouses adapted for communal multi-family occupancy. The mental world of the Iroquois remained incomprehensibly different from that of all their European neighbours, but their life-style underlined the penetration of European material culture into their lands.[1]

It may be that to other Indian groups in the Ohio valley, the French – due to their lack of vast numbers of aggressive settlers – were less of a threat than the British, though in pursuit of the power of command over Indian peoples the French had repeatedly shown themselves more than happy to deliberately divide Indian nations through their missionaries; to encourage internecine warfare; and to use force freely at virtually every level, not at all excluding genocide. There was, at base, little to choose between English, French, Portuguese, and Spanish for Indian peoples, and if the phrase 'Middle Ground' for the Ohio valley in the 1750s is a Euro-American term of art, it nevertheless encapsulates an understandable desire on the part of its native American inhabitants to keep meaningful autonomy for themselves.[2] In 1713 an ambiguous compromise with free trade for both neighbouring European empires was clearly envisaged, but by the late 1740s the French had grasped the fatal snag in this arrangement for them. British trade goods were cheaper and better. The French reply was predictable – to use force to assert sovereignty and thereby establish monopoly access. It was an extraordinarily dangerous option to embrace, for it ran the risk of destroying the aversion of British officials, colonial and imperial alike, towards the prospect of another general war in America. William Shirley, for example, was both a colonial American and an imperial place-hunter, but he resided in Paris after 1749 as a member of the Anglo–French commission which vainly sought a peaceful resolution to the problems of western frontiers, and by the time he returned to Massachusetts in 1753 he had married a young Frenchwoman as his second wife. To depict the British elites of the mid-eighteenth century as rabid francophobes is nonsense. Their involvement with French culture was often intimate.

Long after war had broken out, Shirley emphasised that he saw the central object of the conflict as being the laying, with the help of Divine Providence, of a solid foundation 'for a general Tranquillity in North-America' and 'securing all the English Colonies there against the Future Depredations of the French and reclaiming the Indians to their Interest'. Admittedly, by the time he said this Shirley wanted a decisive rolling back of what he saw as aggressive French frontier expansion, and a breaking of what he rightly regarded as an inherently provocative French concept of continuous French sovereignty from Louisiana along the Mississippi to New France, but he most emphatically did not envisage the destruction of either New France or Louisiana. It is fashionable in some historical circles, especially those whose expertise lies primarily in polemical pamphlet literature, to argue that since all events are reflected through ideology, ideological splits more or less make conflict inevitable and contingent events which precipitate a conflict are almost incidental.[3] If this were generally so, the activities of theologians alone would have doomed mankind to mutual extermination centuries ago. The relationship between event and ideology is complex, but ideologically incompatible societies, and incompatible ideologies within a society, can and do coexist all the time, not least because most people are less ideological than ideologues would like them to be. It is contingent events and conscious choices that more often than not turn ideology into mobilised political polarisation. Just as the rising in Ulster in 1641 precipitated a crisis in the English ruling elite over control of the army needed to contain it and so forced civil war on a reluctant nation, so French choices in the Ohio valley in the 1750s threatened to precipitate an Anglo–French war few Britons wanted.

The success of General Pepperrell's New England infantry and Admiral Warren's English fleet in capturing Louisbourg in the previous war may have been hailed by the colonial poet Samuel Niles as part of 'God's wonder-working Providence for New England', but there was widespread appreciation in the British colonies in the early 1750s of just what a hard, dangerous struggle a war with New France was likely to prove. Partly this was a tribute to the way in which French and British nationals spied compulsively on one another during the long era of Anglo–French confrontation in North America. One result was a very realistic understanding of French fighting potential. The experience of combat between 1744 and

1748 had left an indelible impression on the minds of many British colonists, and it was by no means uniformly an impression of easy victory; quite the reverse. Alexander Hamilton, a Scots physician who had emigrated to Maryland, where he practised in Annapolis, has left an account of the declaration of war against France in 1744 in Philadelphia, where Hamilton just happened to be in the course of an extensive summer tour. There were privateers fitting out in the river, for the declaration had been long foreseen. When Governor Thomas processed to the Court House stairs to make his official announcement, he was accompanied by 'about 200 gentlemen', but the procession was 'led by about 30 flags and ensigns taken from privateer vessels and others in the harbour which were carried by a parcell of roaring sailors'.[4] There was a great deal less cockiness around in these maritime circles after the war had been fought.

Peter Kalm, a young Swedish botanist and pupil of the great Linnaeus, was sent by the Swedish Academy to North America in 1747 in search of plants capable of thriving on Swedish soil. In November 1749 he was in New Jersey, where he spoke with 'an Englishman who had been a privateer for several years during the last war'. The conversation moved to the prowess of the French in sea battles. Whereas Kalm's informant considered Spanish shipping relatively easy meat, he was clear that if

> The French had a vessel with sixteen guns and a hundred men and the English likewise one with just as many men when they started to fight, the result would ordinarily be that they would have to leave one another, each having received equal injury. They cannot conquer one another, since the French are said to be merciless fighters on the seas.[5]

Kalm's *Travels* (originally published in Swedish in 1753–61) appeared in an English version in 1770. It showed that he was well aware of the extent to which the strength of French Canada was a reflection of the will and commitment of the French Crown. The inhabitants paid little or no taxes, though in 1748 a 3 per cent duty had been laid on imported goods. The fortresses of Quebec, Fort Chambly, Fort St Jean, Fort St Frédéric (or Crown Point), Montreal, Frontenac, and Niagara were all made formidable by royal funding, just as the economy of New France was sustained by a very high level of state inputs of men, money, and goods. Other fortified trading places were private, but the Indian trade was, Kalm noted, only available to those who bought licences from the governor general of New France. He stood at the apex of a society deliberately designed as the sword of the monarchy in North America. Buttressed by a totally intolerant Gallican Catholic Church, New France was a potentially lethal opponent, and Kalm was clearly not the only contemporary observer to understand this.[6]

It is interesting, in the light of the 16-gun ship example used by the ex-privateer in conversation with Kalm in New Jersey, to note that in a report smuggled out from a Quebec prison in 1757, Colonel Peter Schuyler of the New Jersey Blues (captured at Oswego) reported that of the forty-three French vessels that had reached Quebec in that summer 'some of the Merchantmen were very large, carrying from sixteen to twenty-six guns'. They had been accompanied by two 64-gun men-o'-war and a 36-gun frigate. New France was armed to the teeth, with a resident force of 'Regulars, Canadeans, and Indians' which Schuyler guesstimated at 24,000. It is true that some of the better informed British North American colonial soldiers had worked out after several years of war that New France was basically weaker in defensive than in offensive mode. Schuyler was acutely aware that his own prisoner's diet was meagre because of a general shortage of supplies in New France.[7] Other prisoners such as Major John Smith, 'Commander of a Company of Rangers on the frontiers of Virginia', reached similar conclusions. Smith was arguing in a journal dated 1756–57, a copy of which was forwarded to the British government in 1757, that it would not be inherently difficult, provided some key Indian groups could be won over, to seize control of 'the whole hunting Country, the best in America, from the Ohio to the river Illonoise'. One reason Smith was confident of over-running French positions west of Fort Niagara was the situation of the French forts:

> There not being one Great Gun, in any of French forts in all that Country,
> to oppose us in any incursion to be made amongst them, which Major
> Smith thinks very practicable, more especially in Winter, and early in the
> Spring . . . for that Enterprise he thinks 1000 Woods men are sufficient,
> with some Cherokees or Catabas Indians, . . .

Smith was a chronic optimist. He had been captured by a French and Indian raiding party 'towards the Head of James River on the 25th of June 1756', and his information as to the relatively slight nature of French western defended posts seems to have been gleaned during eleven months as a prisoner of war.[8] He was, in fact, a very good example of the vulnerability of British North American colonial frontiers to the sort of Franco–Indian onslaught which any informed person in the early 1750s realised was likely to be the first consequence of a formal outbreak of Anglo–French war.

British America had contributed substantially to the rhetorical war against the French from the late seventeenth century. A circle of Whig literary refugees – who had fled England during the period of the 'Stuart revenge' from the failure of the Ryehouse Plot to assassinate Charles II in 1683 to the reign of James II – settled in New England. There they continued to write in a stridently anti-French, anti-Catholic, and anti-Stuart vein fuelled ultimately by their fear of French-backed, Stuart Roman Catholic absolutism in metropolitan England. It was the distinctive achievement of colonial American-English literature to link the concept of French perfidy to 'Indian Barbarism'.[9] By the mid-eighteenth century the threat of French power in North America was very real. The French and their Indian allies seemed poised to deprive Anglo-America of the trans-Appalachian territory which that arch-exponent of English American interests, Benjamin Franklin, described as 'well known both to the English and French, to be one of the finest in North America, for the extreme richness and fertility of the land'. Yet this threat did not diminish the usual reluctance of Rhode Island and the Quakers of Pennsylvania and New Jersey to fund any military effort. New York, which had suffered greatly from Indian raids, still found it difficult to raise funds for military purposes. When in 1754 Franklin placed a plan for a federation designed to ensure 'Security and defense' before the Albany Congress of colonial governments, it was opposed by both colonies and Crown. In any case, the British West Indies, Georgia, and Nova Scotia had not been invited to attend, and Virginia and New Jersey chose to abstain. The Scots literary gadfly, Dr Adam Thomson, might support Franklin's attempts to organise effective colonial force by invoking 'all ye Powers That guard *Britannia's* lofty Towers', but colonial elites were parochial, mean, provincial, and English. They demonised the Indian allies of France, but out of fear rather than as a cant prelude to conquest, and their fear was all the more pervasive because they sensed their own visceral inability to use that fear to forge effective military cooperation between the British colonies.[10]

There were, of course, groups and individuals in those colonies which were strongly expansionist. Using official grants to gain control of vast amounts of American land for risible sums of money, with a view to either developing them or, more frequently, speculating on a rising land market, had been a standard means of self-enrichment for the well connected for decades. The greatest of Virginia's colonial governors, Alexander Spotswood, contrived by various means, some of debatable legality, to accumulate 85,000 acres during his spell in office between 1710 and 1722. He had gone to London to secure his land titles by appropriate lobbying after he demitted, and had then returned to set up a remarkable slave-run charcoal-fuelled iron industry on his princely estates. It is no accident that it was he who had led the famous symbolic trip in September 1723 on which he was accompanied by sixty-three Virginians, many prominent politicians, when they all moved across the Blue Ridge of Virginia to claim not just the Shenandoah valley but all North America to the Mississippi for George I. It was the beginning of Manifest Destiny, and an outrageous pre-emptive land grab.[11]

In Pennsylvania, Franklin was a militant expansionist, as were the tough 'Scotch–Irish' immigrant communities which started to emigrate in large numbers into Pennsylvania after 1717. These were Protestant Ulstermen and their migration steadily gathered momentum throughout the 1720s, 1730s, and 1740s. The Cumberland valley became their central settlement area, where down to the revolution 90 per cent of the settlers were of Ulster stock. From the start, colonial authorities deliberately used this militant community as a shield against the Indians. James Logan, secretary of the province, wrote to a friend in November 1729 saying:

> a considerable Number of good Sober People came in from Ireland, who wanted to be settled, at the Same time it happen'd that we were under some apprehensions from northern Indians of whose claims to the Lands on Sasquehannah I was not then sensible . . . I therefore thought it might be prudent to plant a Settlement of fresh men as those who formerly had so bravely defended Derry and Inniskillen as a frontier in case of any Disturbance.

Since Logan was himself an Ulsterman, the pride in the martial achievements of his people was perhaps overdone, but in practice they proved self-reliant frontiersmen continually spreading out as fresh migrations reinforced them, and at odds with the Quaker proprietary government of the province – which was not averse to cheating Indians out of land by such outrageous measures as the 'Walking Purchase of 1737' and the Albany Purchase of 1754, but which jibbed at military measures to contain the smouldering Indian wrath which exploded after 1755.[12]

Nevertheless, the Pennsylvania authorities did drag their feet about mounting an effective military riposte to the Franco–Indian threat until as late as 1756, when the Quakers finally lost control of the provincial assembly, never to regain it wholly. It was Virginia which triggered, on the British side, what contemporaries originally called 'the Ohio war'.[13] The key to this was the way Governor Robert Dinwiddie (technically a lieutenant governor, like most rulers of the eighteenth-century colony) became heavily involved in the Ohio Company. Dinwiddie ruled Virginia from 1751 to 1757. He was a Glasgow businessman turned colonial bureaucrat and not young, but this paunchy Scot forged a political alliance with some of the most aggressive expansionists, including some from the quasi-autonomous Northern Neck of Virginia, an area between the Potomac and Rappahannock rivers which was held as a proprietary grant by the Lords Fairfax, originally by grant of Charles I. In 1740, the leading families of the Northern Neck had helped the then Lord Fairfax not only to defeat a challenge to his grant from the Virginia legislature, but also to extend its boundaries beyond the

Blue Ridge. His Lordship moved his residence to the Shenandoah valley.[14] The young George Washington was an active frontier surveyor and Fairfax protégé. As early as 1747, a group of influential Virginians, nearly all from the Northern Neck, had, with the help of some Marylanders and a few influential London merchants, established the Ohio Company. By 1749, they had a royal grant of some 200,000 acres near the Forks of the Ohio, where the Monongahela and Allegheny rivers joined. Washington worked for the Ohio Company. Dinwiddie had expressed his willingness to aid it in every way in 1751. In 1752 he became a shareholder in it. That was the year the company built a trading fort on the Monongahela. Governor Dinwiddie had the Ohio Company's 'success and prosperity . . . much at heart'. By 1753 it had built a stockade at the Forks of the Ohio.

It was the seizure of this stockade by the French in 1754 which proved the detonator for Anglo–French conflict in North America. Some 1500 French troops, with Indian allies, had landed on the southern shore of Lake Erie in the spring of 1753 and had started building forts and roads. It was a detachment of 800 men from this force that had seized control of the Forks. To George Washington, despatched by Dinwiddie to remonstrate with the French late in 1753, French officers in their cups boasted that they knew the English could raise two men to their one, but 'that it was their absolute Design to take possession of the Ohio, and by God they would do it' because they were confident that the English response would be 'too slow and dilatory to prevent any Undertaking of theirs'. Dinwiddie rushed Washington's official report to him, which recorded these remarks, into print. William Hunter, the colony's official printer, published it in Williamsburg, Virginia's capital, in 1754.[15] Dinwiddie needed all the help he could get to mobilise colonial opinion. Washington himself admitted later that many Virginians saw the looming conflict as a conspiracy by a wealthy and greedy minority to involve Virginia in a war, purely to protect their speculative land claims. There were other opportunities for speculative land investment in a southward direction which did not involve a clash with the French. The colonial legislators of Virginia were not falling over themselves to fund an Ohio war. At least one of them said he understood that the Ohio country was indeed French. Dinwiddie believed that in 1756 Virginia had 293,742 inhabitants, of whom 173,316 were white. He had, with difficulty, extracted a grant of £10,000 from the legislature which represented the latter for defence of the colony in the face of the crisis which came to a head in 1754. It was not a lot.[16]

There were doubts about Dinwiddie's authority to send troops into the Ohio country, parts of which were claimed by Pennsylvania as well as France, but he nevertheless despatched several hundred volunteers embodied as the Virginia Regiment to support the Ohio Company. Joshua Fry, a former professor of mathematics at the College of William and Mary, commanded it as colonel, and when he died he was succeeded by his lieutenant colonel, George Washington. It was the swift juxtaposition of victory and defeat for the latter which brought a shooting war to the Ohio. In May 1754, Washington gave the French a taste of their own standard medicine and ambushed a French force, with crucial help from Indian allies, killing its commander, the Sieur de Jumonville. Even more significant was his capture of an important French Indian agent, Commissary La Force. By 19 July, the Williamsburg *Virginia Gazette* was running the story but, before it appeared, Washington had had to surrender to the inevitable French counter-attack on 3 July. His attempt to sit it out in a stockaded position christened Fort Necessity failed because of his faulty judgement in entrenching a site overlooked by good firing positions.

There was widespread awareness of the level of stakes for which the two sides were playing. John Carlyle, a wealthy Chesapeake merchant whose great stone house still stands in the port of Alexandria, was related to Washington, whom he described as 'A Brother of My Late Brother in Laws'.[17] He was active in the Ohio Company, and was prompt to send the printed version of Washington's report of his mission to challenge the French over their initial incursion in strength to his brother, George Carlyle, who still lived in the north of England.[18] Previously, in soliciting a loan, John had pointed out that 'our land Increases Near double in Seven Years in Vallue'.[19] John Carlyle was anxious to spread knowledge of the American conflict in England proper, not just by correspondence but also by sending over copies of provincial American newspapers. He was acutely aware of the way the French attempt to link Canada with Louisiana along the Mississippi, corralling English settlements east of the Appalachians and turning the Indians against them, would blight the long-term future of English America, but even at his most optimistic, after he had seen several colonial governors confer in his Alexandria house with the commander of a substantial regular British army striking force, his objectives were limited to repelling the French invasion of the Ohio valley. He hoped Governor Shirley of Massachusetts could mount an effective thrust against the French at Fort Niagara because 'to us Virginians Nothing less than Shirley's Takeing Niagaria, can do Us any good, which would stop the French's Communication from Canida to Fort Duquesne, which is At preasant Open'.[20]

Fort Duquesne was the stronghold built by the French to confirm their grip on the Forks of the Ohio. Governor Shirley of Massachusetts was a hard-line imperial administrator who had been alerted to the new and hyper-aggressive note in French policy when he had to take vigorous counter-measures against a French attempt to occupy territory at the top of the Kennebec River, with a view to building a string of forts down it threatening

Massachusetts' northern fiefdom of Maine. He warned his legislature that this presaged a continent-wide French bid to close down the English trade with the Indians by force (which indeed it did), and to erect an impenetrable barrier against any further English settlement. As he said, the French 'seem to have advanced further towards making themselves Masters of this continent within these last 5 or 6 years, than they have done ever since the first Beginning of their Settlements upon it'.[21] The situation was all the more frightening because the mixed populations of Iroquois, Shawnee, Delaware, and other Indians of the Ohio valley had no illusions about the underlying land-grabbing policies of the major English colonies. The more perceptive of Indians could see, as one said in 1753, that both French and English presumptuously claimed 'ownership' of Indian hunting grounds to the point where if an Indian found a bear in a tree a European 'owner' would appear, claim the land the tree grew on, and forbid hunting. Nevertheless, it was a parcel of rogues from Pennsylvania, Connecticut, New York, and Virginia who had of late been cheating Indians out of Ohio land.

The French were out to establish physical and ideological sovereignty. They tried to conceal their claims to territorial sovereignty from the Indians they needed as allies and meant to make subjects, by devices as ludicrous as secretly burying plaques inscribed with statements of the sovereign rights of Louis XV on appropriate pieces of territory. To fellow Europeans, of course, they trumpeted the claims they tried to hide from Indians. Since religion was a system of power, their missionary offensive matched their troops' movements in importance. The Canadian missionaries so active among the Seneca were consciously aiming at using that tribe as a lever to swing the entire Iroquois confederacy into the French camp. It did not require great insight to grasp the potentially limitless nature of French ambitions in the Americas.

The response of the Westminster government to this threatening situation was to seek a negotiated settlement, based on enlightened appeasement of the French. There was absolutely no desire for war in the Westminster government dominated by the Pelham brothers after 1746. Premier Henry Pelham tended to isolationism, not because he was imperially oriented, but because he was a treasury man who saw peace as the key to reduce debt-service charges and taxes. His brother was the Duke of Newcastle, secretary of state for the Northern Department after 1748 and eventually the happy possessor of a compliant colleague, Lord Holderness, in the Southern Department after 1751. Newcastle dominated foreign policy, and was passionately European in his views. Britain, he argued flatly, needed continental alliances to contain the incipient hegemony of France, and had to regard the subsidies needed to sustain them as a cheap insurance policy against cripplingly costly war. That he could not retain the Austrian alliance he favoured and ended up after a 'Diplomatic Revolution' allied to Prussia was hardly his fault. America was not a priority. In accordance with the terms of the 1748 peace congress, Anglo–French commissioners had begun to meet in 1749 to try to settle outstanding issues. Prisoners and prizes proved perfectly negotiable. Land boundaries and the ownership of West Indian islands proved intractable. France was determined to keep St Lucia, and to bottle up the British in Nova Scotia and east of the Appalachians. A new president of the Board of Control after 1748, the vigorous Lord Halifax, could read the military implications of the French position and stiffened Newcastle's occasionally incipiently supine spine.

Not that Newcastle ever contemplated a conscious sell-out in America. On the contrary, he would have regarded that as a threat to the European balance. He said, 'If we lose our American possessions or the influence and weight of them, in time of peace, France will, with great ease, make war with us whenever they please hereafter.' A very low-level war had developed in Nova Scotia by 1750. From 1752 Newcastle personally directed an accelerated drive for settlement in Paris at ambassadorial level. The developments in the Ohio country were ominous. In June 1754 the British cabinet officially recorded its view that French aggression threatened both British trade and the long-term viability of the American colonies. When news of Washington's defeat reached Newcastle, he was clear that unless a check was given to French power, 'All North America will be lost.' With a surplus of £100,000 on his current budget, Newcastle envisaged, very reluctantly, funding American colonial forces to fight back. They would be cheaper than British regulars, and both Lord Chancellor Hardwicke and Lieutenant General Sir John Ligonier told him they would also be more effective than regulars in forest warfare.

Unfortunately the divisions among the colonies and their lack of stomach for fighting the French meant that, short of forcing them into a union, which any fool could see might well become a potentially independent state, there was no way of matching French military potential purely from colonial sources. Even more reluctantly, and under heavy pressure from Captain General the Duke of Cumberland, Newcastle agreed to send Major General Edward Braddock with two regiments from the Irish establishment which, when augmented in the colonies, would give a force of 1500 men. With a wilful suspension of disbelief, Newcastle still deluded himself that the total cost to the treasury would be close to the budget surplus, saying 'we must do it as cheap and inoffensively as we can'. By early 1755 a French ambassador, the duc de Mirepoix, who believed in mutual withdrawal in America, was negotiating with Newcastle, who wanted the same, in London. The trouble was that Mirepoix's Crown refused formal talks without an armistice for fear of the effects of the coming British military backlash. The campaign was meant to include attacks on all major French posts in disputed areas, though success was to be followed by slighting and withdrawal.[22]

It was in fact an eminently sound policy. It compares very well with Neville Chamberlain's appeasement of Hitler in the 1930s or Westminster's protracted twentieth-century appeasement of the Irish Republican Army. Newcastle grasped that appeasement was only viable if the other party was treated with the utmost toughness on the run-up to meaningful negotiation. Mirepoix was not really offering more than continued intransigence in a flawed and protracted peace process, poisoned by definition by the position held by his Crown. The French decision to send reinforcements to Louisbourg compelled Newcastle to concentrate a fleet in the Channel and detach a section of it under Vice Admiral Edward Boscawen to try to cut off the reinforcements for Canada by cruising off the mouth of the St Lawrence. Newcastle firmly rejected suggestions that he try to intercept the reinforcements in European waters, on the grounds that this would certainly be treated as a *casus belli* by the French. Boscawen's failure to capture more than a couple of ships from the French convoy made a bad situation worse.

It was still the case that neither Newcastle nor the Duke of Cumberland wanted all-out war. They hoped to keep the colonial clash of arms distinct from any hint of a general European war. Whilst there was widespread perception of the inherent superiority of British power in North America, could it but be adequately mobilised, Newcastle did not want even a general war in North America. The French colonies were administered by the Department of Marine Affairs, so the regular garrison troops in French-American possessions were known rather misleadingly as the Independent Companies of Marines (in French *Les Compagnies Franches de la Marine*). They were, in fact, regular French infantry, though their officers were usually locals. A cadet corps for the sons of the elites of Canada, Louisbourg, and Louisiana had been set up in 1730. By 1755 there were 40 marine companies in Canada, 36 in Louisiana, 24 in Louisbourg, 20 in the Windward Islands, 10 in Guyana, and 32 at Saint-Dominique. To these must be added the Canadian militia, theoretically 15,000 strong (though it was impractical to mobilise more than a fraction of that number). There were also the Indian allies of France, the so-called 'Christian Indians', mainly drawn from the Hurons of Lorette, the Abenaki of St Francis and Batiscan, the Iroquois of Caughnawaga and La Présentation, and the Algonquins of the Two Mountains on the Ottawa. They were noted for theological ambiguity (despite the best efforts of their Jesuit mentors); chronic alcoholism, which underlined the role of Bacchus as the European deity most successful in winning their devotion; and, as the marquis de Montcalm was to write to his wife, for making war 'with astounding cruelty, sparing neither men, women nor children'.[23] War against such a military establishment was likely to be protracted and costly. Even the vaunted British naval superiority was a slow and costly weapon to bring to bear. In the event, British naval superiority in Canadian waters was scarcely established before 1758.[24] Newcastle, in particular, was appalled by the thought of the cost of protracted campaigning.

His aim was to save money in the long run by giving the French the only experience at all likely to make them rethink the basic thrust of their policy in America – a series of sharp military rebuffs. Only in Nova Scotia did the policy basically work. Only there did events not run ahead of Newcastle's ability to control them. Colonel Monckton turned the French out of Fort Beauséjour in June 1755 and renamed it for Cumberland (despite the fact there already was a Fort Cumberland in North America). The fall of the heavily fortified and well-garrisoned French stronghold was partly due to collapse of morale. There was no relief column from Louisbourg. The Acadians who had been summoned to assist the fort (many of them British subjects in terms of international law) largely vanished when it became clear that the British meant business. Highly effective mortar fire also helped. Surrender became inevitable when a British mortar bomb destroyed a casemate or secure chamber within the thickness of the rampart, killing the section of the garrison sheltering there. There was no reason at all why Fort Duquesne at the Forks of the Ohio should prove more of a problem than Fort Beauséjour on the Missaquash River frontier of Nova Scotia, provided Braddock could bring his command to it. In Nova Scotia the British were already close to their target: their Fort St Lawrence stood on the opposite river bank from Beauséjour.[25]

Braddock's problems were in the first instance logistical. His orders, though based on the best information available to the Duke of Cumberland, were simply unrealistic, showing no real grasp of geographical and political difficulties. Braddock was soon reporting a dire shortage of carriages, a lack of dry forage, the reluctance of Maryland men to cross the Potomac, and the need to carry all his food supply with him. In Alexandria, he conferred with colonial governors and William Johnson, the Indian expert from western New York, though concrete help came mainly from Commodore Augustus Keppel of the Royal Navy, who produced stores, manpower, and timber.[26] The construction of boats from the last named facilitated water carriage. The problem of land carriage remained acute. John Carlyle, the Alexandrian merchant in whose house Braddock had conferred with the governors, was appointed by Braddock – in the capacity of C-in-C North America – 'Storekeeper of all the Provisions, Arms, Ammunition, Bagage of all other kinds whatever belonging to the forces under my Command which are now in Alexandria or shall at any time hereafter be brought thither'.[27] From a petition which Carlyle submitted to the Virginia House of Burgesses in 1762 seeking reimbursement for an expense incurred it is clear that Carlyle then acquired much more extensive responsibilities, for the petition set forth that:

> Robert Dunwiddie, Esq, late Governour of this Colony by Commission under the Seal of the Colony, bearing the Date the 27th Day of January 1754 appointed the Petitioner Commissary of Provisions and Stores for an Expedition then intended to the River Ohio, with full Power and Authority to appoint such and so many Deputies to be aiding and assisting, for the more expeditious transporting the said Provisions and Stores to the aforesaid Fort, as should be found expedient for the Service: . . .[28]

Carlyle appointed deputy commissaries, and it is clear that Braddock's offensive was built on the development of the seaports and merchant networks of the Chesapeake, with landward penetration exploiting such technologies as the wagons that had been developed to supplement the deep navigable rivers which ran into the heart of the middle colonies. Of these most famous was the Conestoga wagon which was becoming pervasive just behind the frontier of settlement in the era of the mid-century Anglo–French confrontation. The future Revolutionary War patriot general, Daniel Morgan, left his home in the Shenandoah valley to serve as a wagoner with Braddock's expedition, in the course of which he received five hundred lashes for assaulting an officer.[29]

Progress of the expedition still remained funereal. At one point Braddock was prepared to give up because of a hopeless shortage of wagons, but Benjamin Franklin, who happened to be at his headquarters as a special envoy for the Pennsylvania Assembly, pointed out that virtually every farmer in that colony had a serviceable wagon and, for a price, arranged for an appropriate number of them to be made available to the general. Braddock did not regard Fort Duquesne as his prime target, telling Franklin that 'Duquesne can hardly detain me above three or four days; and then I can see nothing that will obstruct my march to Niagara'.[30] From there he was to move on Fort Frontenac, if the season allowed. The first two parts of the plan were reasonable. The estimate for the siege of Duquesne was generous. Beyond the original Fort Cumberland, Braddock was, of course, hacking a 12-foot wide road through forest over rough country in order to move his men, wagons, and artillery, but it was not the logistics of the campaign that led to disaster, but the fact that Mars is as fickle a deity as Venus.

On 9 July 1755 the Anglo-American army successfully completed its crossing of the fords of the Monongahela, in good order and heart, for it was now very close to its objective, Fort Duquesne. French opposition to the river-crossing had been feared, and could have been effective owing to the steep nature of the far bank. Until the very beginning of the month, French forces in the fort had been so weak that no serious opposition could have been offered. A few days lost by Braddock, mainly due to the dishonesty of colonial contractors, which created a supply problem for him, were in the event crucial, for there were by 9 July some 1600 Frenchmen and Indians concentrated round the fort: quite enough for at least an ambush designed to delay and maul the enemy. Braddock had accepted advice during his march. He had valued his Indians, of whom he would have liked more. He had flattered the young George Washington into joining his military 'family' of aides. He had kept flank guards out and beaten off previous surprise attacks. His force still had a small wagon train despite having left the bulk of it behind in a base camp. The army had to close in its formation as it moved up a wooded slope along a narrow newly cut track. Then the French struck. What followed has been a matter of bitter controversy ever since.[31]

What is fact is that after three hours of confused fighting the British force was totally routed with the loss of a third of its men, including the commander and his senior subordinate commanders such as Sir Peter Halkett. The battle has taken on a life of its own, particularly with those of a teleological bent, who see in Braddock everything the American Revolution was rightly against. He did despise colonial troops originally, though before he died he seems to have recognised that they had fought better than the regulars. His flanking parties were driven in by the first stages of the attack. Militarily the position was then grave but not insuperable. A bayonet charge would probably have driven reinforced flanks out again, at least enough, given the colonial troops' acknowledged ability to fight in the forest. Captain Robert Cholmley's batman's narrative (whose survival is quite astonishing) relates that 'there might be two hundred of the American Soldiers that fought behind Trees and I believe they did the moast Execution of Any'.[32] Even so, the rational response once the position was held was probably withdrawal, a difficult feat in the face of an enemy far from heavily outnumbered, and with the advantage of surprise and position.

On balance, it looks very much as if there were no valid options for Braddock, a man of 60 whose orthodox responses may well have been as good as any going. The initial tactical failure was that of Thomas Gage, commander of the van.[33] It was he who failed to occupy heights on the right of the line of march, when this standard procedure would have revealed the ambush. The central fact about the battle is that the regulars disintegrated as coherent units at the first shots, with cries that the dreaded, demonised Indians were on them. It was these disorganised troops who staggered about showing the standard, suicidal tendency of panicking infantry to huddle together for comfort when the narrow track made the eventual run for safety and jettisoning of equipment difficult to achieve at once. As one anonymous backbiting anti-Braddock account which appears to have been written by one of his officers admits, after the vanguard panicked under French fire they were then hit by British cross-fire as well as French sniping. That the troops milled around under these two fires for over two hours made the situation worse, for:

> both together Contributed not a little to a general disorder; after which, The General would have Changed his disposition (or more properly made one) but the Men were then turn'd stupid and insensible and would not obey their officers in makeing the intended movements which were unhappily too late attempted. The officers behaved extremely well . . . which fact is strengthened by the number of kill'ed . . .[34]

It was a repeat of the panic and confusion of regular units of dubious quality before Jacobite charges at Prestonpans and Falkirk, without the option of instant flight.

Apart from this decisive failure, there was much to admire in the British performance in mounting an offensive whose logistics were so complex. By definition naval cooperation was indispensable, not only to transport the force across the Atlantic, but also to make it possible to concentrate dispersed Crown forces in America. Braddock was given the power to summon to a council of war not just the Royal Navy commander-in-chief North American station but also, if he wanted, 'such other officers of His Majesty's Fleet who are of Equal Rank with Field Officers in the King's army'.[35] There was extensive discussion of pay scales and deductions therefrom for specific contingencies, precisely in order to have a clear basis for adjusting 'the difference of the Pay and Allowances in the most reasonable and equal manner' in the event that 'the Troops now at Nova Scotia should at any time Act in Conjunction with the other Troops under the General's Command'.[36] Because of its conclusion, there had been a tendency to underestimate grossly the remarkable administrative sophistication of the Braddock episode. Thus, the actual payment of the troops was an immensely intricate international operation. They were to be paid in Spanish dollars in gold or silver, this being reckoned both the stablest and the most acceptable of American currencies. What is impressive is the capacity of the British state to set up such an arrangement.

Since all the British American colonies had their own currencies, nominally sterling but in practice discounted at different levels to reflect the state of each provincial economy, dollars were far more sensible. On 29 November

1754 the treasury settled articles of agreement with John Thomlinson and John Hanbury of London, merchants. The latter were described as:

> willing and desirous to contract and agree to take and receive all such Sum and Sums of Money as shall from time to time be issued or wanted for the purposes aforesaid, and to invest the same in the purchasing Spanish milled dollars and other Spanish coined Silver and Spanish and Portugal coined Gold either in England or in the Colonies as they shall find such Silver and Gold may be purchased on the most advantageous Terms for the Service of the publick, and to pay over such Monies at Williamsburgh in Virginia or Boston in New England as they shall be wanted for the Service of the said Troops ...[37]

Surveys of the ordnance available to the Crown in North America late in 1754 in Annapolis Royal, Halifax, St John's, and Placentia provided a disturbing overview of inadequate, mixed provision, much of it French or Spanish in origin.[38] It also led the British government to take stock of the situation at the southern end of its chain of colonies on the North American mainland. John Reynolds, governor of Georgia, reported to Sir Thomas Robinson, 'One of His Majesty's Principal Secretaries of State', that his province was 'a Frontier Country to all His Majesty's Dominions in North America', surrounded everywhere except on the north-west by Indian nations 'whose Allegiance to His Majesty is very precarious'. Reynolds had reports from 'Reputable Traders in the Indian Country' that the French governor at Mobile was going to great lengths to seduce the Indians and persuade them 'to attack the English'. This was at a time when Reynolds could say 'there is neither Cannon, small Arms, Ammunition nor Fortifications in the Province that are fit for Service, nor soldiers (except a small Detachment from the three Independent Companies at South Carolina)'. He appealed for a regular company of at least 150 men to reinforce his militia in the event of an attack. He also begged for any ordnance which could be spared.[39]

Braddock, by virtue of a clause inserted in the annual Mutiny Bill at Westminster, was to have the right to subject all provincial troops under his command to the same military law and discipline as his own regulars.[40] There was an unmistakable determination on the part of the metropolitan authorities both to assess the North American situation as a whole and to establish a firm centralised grip on their military response to it. Both characteristics boded ill, in the long run, for the French. They had never truly faced up to a British Crown in North America which combined overall vision with determination to keep them in their place. James II's American vision had been primarily about making his authority over his own subjects real, and his frontier agreement with Louis XIV in North America had been regarded as a sell-out by his own military intimates. Yet it must be stressed that just as the whole Braddock expedition was designed by Newcastle as a firm rebuff which would push the French back from positions and policies that would otherwise inevitably breed war, so the objectives of the British authorities in North America in 1754, even at their most ambitious, remained tied to specific frontier issues. Jockeying not so much for position as positions which promised long-term security and stability was what the game was all about.

This is very clearly illustrated by a memorandum available in high British military circles, which examined the rival claims of the English and French to Fort Frontenac, which 'is built upon the North East Edge of the Lake Ontario at the distance of about 100 miles from Montreal, and Situated near the head of a River, which takes its rise from the said Lake, and discharges itself in the River St. Lawrence at the Island of Montreal'. That opening statement alone should have warned any British observer that the French would go to the utmost lengths to defend Fort Frontenac as a position blocking a key invasion route into the lower St Lawrence valley. In fact, the memorandum went on ingeniously to turn the cartography of France against itself. Englishmen, in both North America and India, in the eighteenth century often showed an easy familiarity with the very distinguished contemporary French schools of map-making. It was therefore possible for the memorialist to point out that 'upon the French Charts of the best Authority' the country between Montreal and Fort Frontenac was habitually marked '*pais des Inroquois du Nord*, or *les Iroquois du Nord* in Contradistinction to the *Iroquois* (under which General appellation the French Comprehend the Several Cantons of Indians call'd by the English the five Nations)'.[41]

From this point the old arguments came out: that the French had inserted the fort under guise of setting up a trading post in 1672, that in the Peace of Utrecht of 1713 'the five Nations are declared to be subject *to the Dominions of Great Britain*', that by the Treaty of Aix-la-Chapelle of 1748 it was agreed that the American dominions of the French and British should be in a state '*as they ought of right to have been in*' before the recent war, and so on. French 'encroachments' in Nova Scotia and at Niagara and Crown Point were denounced for the same reasons.[42] In fact, these latter incursions and fortifications were menacing rather than defensive, seriously threatening the security of Nova Scotia and upstate New York. A memorandum for operations in North America in 1755 which may be from William Shirley, the governor of Massachusetts who had been the brains behind the successful assault on Louisbourg in 1745, underlines the quest for security which lay behind British thinking. One of Shirley's sons was Braddock's secretary, and died with him at the Monongahela. Shirley himself held major general rank and was temporary commander-in-chief North America after Braddock's death. If the memo was not by him, it certainly reflected his views. It urged the need to pierce the French net round the British colonies by cutting communications between the northern and southern French settlements. Reinforcement of the Oswego and Albany garrisons, plus naval supremacy on Lake Ontario, was then to be followed by a diversionary thrust from Nova Scotia, coinciding with an assault by New England and New York forces plus British regulars, especially artillery, against the French forts at Niagara and Crown Point, 'which if we succeed in, all His majesty's Settlements on this side the Lakes Ontario and Erie, will then be secured'.[43]

That was the height of British military ambition in 1755. To achieve it, they knew they had to fight their own inherent disunity. They knew that a royal proclamation in America banning trade which would send supplies to Quebec would be ineffective without a Royal Navy blockading squadron off Cape Breton, a squadron whose job would be more to capture British-American blockade runners than French. Shirley, whose military rank had been granted in February 1755, had been one of the five governors who conferred with Braddock in Alexandria, Virginia, in April of that year, when it was agreed to move against the Forks of the Ohio, Crown Point, and Niagara. Shirley was to fail completely in his advance on Niagara, turning back in the face of a superior French force. Braddock's own total defeat at the Forks in July 1755 seemed to show that even limited objectives were beyond the reach of the British in North America.

It is true that their paper plans had been over-simple and tended to run into difficulties when confronted with reality. Their reliance on specie for funding the war, for example, created serious problems of security and flexibility in rapidly changing theatres of combat. Bills of exchange rapidly resurfaced as a necessary expedient.[44] Nevertheless, the inherent weight and incipient coherence of the British military effort, masked by a fearsome tactical debacle, meant that failure with limited objectives was always likely to be followed by the embracing of much more radical ones. In January 1755 the British high command's strategy was already being criticised by local insiders with access to the ears of the colonial and military leadership, on the grounds that it would be less troublesome in the long run to go for the jugular or, as the well-informed clergyman Michael Houdin was reported as saying in January 1755, 'He is for striking at the Root of all our Evils at once, by attempting Quebec, and Montreal at the same time, without attempting Crown Point or any other of their Forts.' The tough outer defences of French Canada ultimately drew all their resources from these two centres which were vulnerable to a converging attack from up the St Lawrence and down the Richelieu River from Fort Frontenac.[45] The

British knew perfectly well that the defences of Louisbourg, which they had already taken once, were radically defective and could not easily be rectified or repaired,[46] so the outer defences of the entry into the St Lawrence were less impressive than they looked at first sight.

The far-flung nature of French claims in North America made their positions elsewhere look even more fragile, but Edmond Atkin, a Charleston Indian trader and member of the governor's council in South Carolina, pointed out that the French had a river-based strategy:

Since the French open'd and establish'd some years ago a shorter
Communication between Canada and Louisiana by way of the River
Wabash, instead of the Illinois River, into the Mississippi, they have bent
all their Measures to the making themselves Masters of the River Ohio,
the Hogohege or Great Cherokee River, and other rivers that run from
the Eastward into the Same; and to the advancing upon, and confining
our Possessions within the Heads of the Rivers that run into the Atlantic
Ocean –[47]

Atkin thought that a diplomatic offensive by the French among the Six Nations of the Iroquois in the north from 1745 had marked the beginning of a new aggressiveness in the French implementation of their policy of corralling English America in order to check its relentless, if disorganised, expansion. He was clear that French power on the south-west frontiers he knew best did not rest on their small and widely scattered forts, most of which could probably be overwhelmed by the Indian nations surrounding them. It rested on the assiduous cultivation of Indian alliances, cemented by French willingness to sell Indians arms and ammunition and to keep in their forts gunsmiths willing to repair Indian weapons.

Atkin knew that the British had access to more and better trade goods than the French. In his view, what was needed was a radical reorganisation of British–Indian relations under Crown aegis, with a northern and southern Indian Department, each headed by a superintendent. Not only might such a system discipline the unruly and irresponsible British North American Indian trader community and limit their abuse of Indians, especially with liquor, but it might also lead to commitment of Crown troops. Forts and blockhouses should be built, and each fort should have a gunsmith willing to oblige Indians. It was a splendid plan. Up to a point it was implemented.

From 1756 until his death in 1761, Atkin was superintendent of the Southern Indian Department, but the extra resources of men, munitions, and money which were integral to his plans proved elusive. Atkin had rather to make bricks without straw. In the aftermath of Braddock's defeat he earned the ire of the young George Washington because of his inability to supply reliable Indian allies or scouts to Washington and his Virginia Regiment as it desperately tried to hold back French-sponsored Indian raids on Virginia's devastated frontier settlements. Atkin embarked on interminable conferences with the Cherokee, the Catawba, and other Indians to some effect in the end, for in August 1757 Governor Dinwiddie described the Indians as behaving 'pretty well'.[48]

The British leadership was obsessed with the northern theatre of war. General Braddock, it is true, reported from Fort Cumberland on 5 June 1755 that of his 2000 effective men, 1100 were 'Americans of the Southern Provinces', but he promptly added that their 'Slothful and languid Disposition renders them very unfit for Military Service'. This was, however, Braddock's style, for he castigated 'a General Want of Spirit in the People to forward the Expedition'. He complained bitterly that only Benjamin Franklin, 'Postmaster of Pennsylvania, and a man of great Influence in that Province', had been able to produce a reasonable number of horses and wagons for the army. Contractors had been awkward, colonial agents crooked. He had been at this point seriously short of Indian allies, for which he blamed the misconduct towards Indians of the government of Virginia. One had to recall that much of this was standard civilian behaviour, reflected through a peppery military mind. Braddock was counting on New England forces mounting a diversion from Nova Scotia, and the province of New York sustaining offensives towards Niagara and Crown Point.[49] No doubt he was over-optimistic about the effectiveness of the supporting thrusts and he was certainly a victim of outrageous dishonesty by contractors, but he arrived near his objective with plenty of force. His regular troops quite simply let him down.

There was a fair amount of demoralisation and fear around after the defeat. Again, the regulars led the way, notably Colonel Thomas Dunbar who, having been left in command of Braddock's base camp with a force available of 1500 men, could easily have stood his ground, but chose instead to burn his wagons and baggage and race back to Fort Cumberland with proposals for withdrawal into winter quarters at Philadelphia, in high summer.[50] The merchants, traders, and planters of South Carolina and Georgia anxiously reminded the British government that 'these Provinces are by their Situation more exposed to the Incursions of the French and Spaniards, and of the Indians depending on them and in their Interest, than any other of His Majesty's Dominions in North America'. They went on to point out that with recent developments in plantation agriculture, several good harbours, and a risible resident defence force of two independent companies scattered in frontier garrisons, they were a tempting target for the French.[51]

General Shirley, the new commander-in-chief, was much less faint hearted. He could only push Dunbar as far as Albany (he would have liked him to mount another attack on Fort Frontenac). His own march on Fort Niagara had bogged down and finished as a reinforcement to Fort Oswego. William Johnson, the Irishman appointed Superintendent of the Northern Indian district, had been supposed to march against Crown Point. He never reached it. On 8 September, a detached unit of his force was ambushed just like Braddock, though more inexcusably for it had thrown out no flank guards. Thereafter, the scenario was different. The ambushed men fell back on Johnson's camp, where the French rush was met and stopped with loss. Finally, a counter-attack caught the French off-balance. For a messy victory which owed little to him, Johnson was made a baronet, but his immediate achievement was limited to completing Fort William Henry, designed to check and mask Crown Point. It was not even to stop the French from building Fort Ticonderoga ten miles south of Crown Point, where Lake George connects with Lake Champlain.

Still, Oswego had been reinforced and effective action had been taken in Nova Scotia. There the French had challenged British control of the peninsula with Forts Beauséjour and Gaspereau. They could count on the active or passive sympathy of the Acadian inhabitants of the territories transferred to Britain in 1713, most of whom had refused the oath of allegiance to a Hanoverian monarch, and their fighting priest, the abbé Le Loutre, could head several hundred Abenaki and Micmac Indians to war to supplement French regulars from the great offshore fortress of Louisbourg. Shirley had seen early that this ulcer needed to be excised. He persuaded Massachusetts to raise two thousand militia who were transported to Nova Scotia where, with the British regular garrison, they destroyed the forts and routed French forces. An unrestricted oath of allegiance was still refused by the Acadians under the influence of their clergy. After forty years' prevarication the British removed the potential fifth column by deporting some six thousand Acadians, scattering them in British colonies rather than reinforcing Quebec with them. Later, another six thousand were treated in the same way at the capture of Cape Breton and Prince Edward Island. It was ruthless but dictated by military logic as well as the sectarian logic of the French priests, and it worked. Many Acadians eventually returned, but not as active participants in total cultural war. Even after the Monongahela, Shirley remained aggressive and confident, with some reason. He wanted to see the reduction of French forts on the Great Lakes from Niagara to Fort Detroit between Lakes Erie and Huron, as well as Michilmackinac between Lakes Huron and Superior. This, he was convinced, would:

not only secure the back parts of his Majesty's Western Colonies from future Incroachments but reduce the whole Southern Country behind the Apalachian or Alleghenny Mountains to the Crown of Great Britain, and have a further Effect, to render Canada itself of little or no value to the French . . .

He believed the costs of administering 'a Country so barren' would greatly exceed its yield, with the loss of the Indian trade and the rupture of links with Louisiana.[52] Canada was, in fact, a fiscal burden even without such losses.

Though strategically shrewd and indomitable, Shirley was a slapdash administrator, abused by rascally associates. In March 1756 he was recalled to London and replaced as commander-in-chief by the middle-aged Scottish Whig soldier John Campbell, Earl of Loudoun. Technically Britain and France had been at peace throughout 1755, but on 18 May 1756 the British government finally declared war. As the French and Indian War, it had already been raging in America. In Europe, as it ended in 1763, it became known as the Seven Years' War. As such, it did not start well, and the early loss of Minorca, the main British naval base in the western Mediterranean, was a disaster to set beside the defeat of Braddock. Lieutenant General the Earl of Loudoun and his two major-generals, James Abercromby and Daniel Webb, faced a new French military leadership, for the marquis de Montcalm had been appointed to command in Canada, where he had arrived in April 1756. Assisted by two excellent subordinates in the chevaliers de Lévis and Bourlamaque, he rapidly displayed great vigour on the forward positions of Canada.

After an inspection of Fort Carillon, which was under construction at Ticonderoga, where he left Lévis to command, Montcalm went to Fort Frontenac, whence he easily overwhelmed the disease-weakened Anglo-American garrison at Oswego, giving the French complete control over Lake Ontario. Loudoun was clear that repeated tactical disasters fighting in difficult, remote country could best be overcome by mounting a direct assault down the St Lawrence on Quebec with a powerful army of 5500. Given naval supremacy, it was quite possible to bypass Louisbourg in much the same way as US forces were to bypass and doom to futility Japanese garrisons on strategically irrelevant Pacific islands in the Second World War. The driving force behind Loudoun's highly concentrated strategy appears to have been primarily technical. If French victory on the Monongahela had made war inevitable, every French tactical victory on the colonial frontiers made a direct British strike against Quebec a more attractive option. There is no reason to think that the originally limited British war aims had seriously changed. The ministers with whom Loudoun worked, like the Duke of Newcastle and Lord Hardwicke, saw gains in North America as pieces which should and largely would be traded against the return of Minorca and other French territorial gains in Europe at a peace settlement. Loudoun had not found it easy to create any kind of coordinated military union among the British colonies, so he envisaged a predominantly colonial but purely defensive stance by 7700 or so men on the Virginian, New York, and northern frontiers. One result of his arrival in the St Lawrence valley would be to force Montcalm to abandon any aggressive strategy in order to concentrate his forces for defence. The Duke of Cumberland, captain general and overlord of the war effort, heartily approved Loudoun's strategy, and he was a man of sense, if no tactical genius.[53]

It was William Pitt who superseded this simple vision with a much less tidy one of his own. If it did not absolutely compel Loudoun to attack Louisbourg first, it certainly placed him in a cruel dilemma because of strong emotional pressure, from George II as much as Pitt, to do just that. Also, Pitt intervened unilaterally over such basic issues as allocation of troops to specific colonies. Lateness, atrocious weather, and strategic confusion generating division in the British council of war led to Loudoun and his army being stranded in Halifax until it was too near the period of unacceptably bad weather to do anything in 1757. Nevertheless, a strategy of total overthrow had been adopted largely for pragmatic reasons, and in Pitt, who was briefly driven from office only to return soon with enhanced authority, Westminster had produced a most unusual minister, one who believed that it was positively desirable to drive France completely out of North America.[54]

Sir William Johnson, despite his own close links with the Iroquois confederacy, and particularly intimate links with the Mohawk tribe, was as much a long-term exploiter of Indians as anyone. Perhaps that gave him the insight to see that the French held the upper hand in terms of Indian alliances, and would continue to do so unless the British swallowed 'a Treaty of Limitation of Country with the Indians' whereby the British would persuade the Indians to expel the French presence in the Ohio, in exchange for a pull-back of British frontier claims. Johnson was clear that epidemic colonial greed for Indian land probably ruled out any such proposal.[55] He then went on to point out that the dilemma was insoluble (and he should have known),[56] unless the British made 'such considerable Conquests, as will force the Indians to side with us, as Conquerors upon this Continent'.

But contemporaries were aware that as well as solving dilemmas, a knock-out blow against French Canada which was not at least partially cancelled at the final peace might carry with it a heavy price. It might clear the way for a radical change of identities in the British North American colonies. Johnson was an Irishman from County Meath of mixed Roman Catholic and Protestant background, though probably of Celtic stock which had Anglicised McShane into Johnson. He was very conscious of his Irish nationality, as his bacchanals on St Patrick's Day and importation of an Irish harper into the Mohawk valley testified. But he was also British, as well as American, and sort of Mohawk. His descendants became Canadian. Governor Shirley, a loyal British-American whose commitment to the Crown was real, admitted in 1755 that if the French threat were lifted there were 'Apprehensions . . . that they will in time unite to throw off their Dependency upon their Mother Country, and set up one General Government among themselves.' He deprecated the idea, saying colonial divisions, Indian allies of the Crown, a 7000-man garrison, and independently funded colonial Crown executives would make this impossible.[57] That might have been true had not most of the pillars of Crown authority on which he rested his case been either fantasies (like the independently funded executives) or unsustainable like the garrison and Indian threat, or fond hopes like the inability of such different colonies to cooperate against the Crown.

Provinces whose populations, as Shirley admitted, were doubling every twenty years and which were already substantially self-governing were unlikely to accept the tilting away from them of the metropolitan–provincial balance. Even Shirley's vision implied that British identity was extremely fragile, and tested to the limit by war. The Hanoverian dynasty did not possess the sort of hegemonic culture which enabled its Bourbon opponents to exploit the power of the Gallican Church as a cement capable of holding its American subjects and allies together. In every substantial French force which thrust towards British frontier positions the regulars and Canadian militia were accompanied by a significant number of Indian allies, always shepherded, in so far as wolves could be, by a gaggle of priests. Those recruiting for regiments in the Hanoverian service in the 1750s in North America were formally warned against recruiting Roman Catholics, whether of Irish or any other nationality.[58] The assumption behind the warning (regularly breached by officers desperate for recruits) was that the religious divisions within the British world ran deeper than the loyalties and institutions uniting it. It was a sensible assumption. Protestants could scarcely desert to Catholic France easily, but in large parts of British North America few Protestants belonged to their King's church.

The failure of Loudoun to achieve anything, denounced by Benjamin Franklin as a disgrace 'to our Nation', owed more to Pitt than to Loudoun, though Pitt bitterly denounced Loudoun in the House of Commons in December 1757 when he 'loaded him with all the asperity peculiar to his style'. Contemporaries applied the term 'bombast' to Pitt's lucubrations, but bombast deflected blame and Pitt was determined to exercise more control.[59] Franklin had not defined 'our Nation' (though he probably meant English). There were plenty of people in British North America who thought of themselves as neither English nor British, like the German Palatines who had settled just north of the Mohawk at a place christened German Flats, and had made a secret neutrality agreement with the French. Great was their indignation in November 1757 when a French and Indian force descended to sack their village, seize their cattle, scalp fifty or so of them, and kidnap three times as many. War was a great shatterer of illusions. To a French commander one set of heretics was much as another. The Palatines learned the hard way that they were at least honorary Brits.

Though leading French officers like the future explorer Louis Antoine de Bougainville regarded their own Indian allies as 'barbarians' and 'monsters',[60] they could see that they needed them for that brisk war of raids and thrusts which the long frontiers of the British colonies made so attractive to a professional French soldier anxious for distinction and conscious of the near impossibility of effective defence at an acceptable price for the British against a mobile foe. The most effective and economical British defence was to take out Montreal and Quebec. Shirley had at one point complained about 'a map entitled "a map of the Middle British Colonies in America etc" haveing been lately Published here by one Lewis Evans', in which, to Shirley's horror, 'Fort Frontenac, and the whole north side of Lake Ontario, are marked as part of New France, and the River Iroquois Called St Lawrences River, and in the Introductory notes to it are asserted to belong to the French by Virtue of the Treaty of Ryswick'. Worse still, in Shirley's view, was the fact that British subjects were beginning to accept this. So they were, and their cartographic admission showed they did not share the old colonial governor's zeal to push the French back beyond the point where the security of the core of New France might be permanently in danger.[61] By 1757 the French were doing Shirley's work for him with every victory and every atrocity by French Indian allies.

The long absence of the main British forces in Nova Scotia enabled Montcalm to move south from Ticonderoga with six thousand troops and a couple of thousand Indians to assault a key British defence of the invasion corridor to Albany: Fort William Henry at the top of Lake George. It had already repulsed a French attack in March but its garrison was in terrible shape, wracked by illnesses such as smallpox, and its Scottish commander, Lieutenant Colonel George Munroe, had been disappointed of adequate reinforcement from his superior, the literally palsied Major General Daniel Webb. After a short siege in early August, Munroe surrendered. He had only suffered lightish casualties, but he was outgunned. All his own artillery pieces had burst, and the Massachusetts militia in his garrison complained of betrayal and threatened to desert. There was no point in trying to stand a storm. The correct decision was to accept Montcalm's offer of honourable terms.

What followed was to provide the pivotal episode in James Fenimore Cooper's frontier romance *The Last of the Mohicans*, published in 1826. Its treatment there is something historians have tended until recently to regard as exaggerated but recent excavations on the site have confirmed most of the gorier details, as well as the lamentable health of the garrison. As the two thousand men of the garrison started to move off with baggage, arms, and horses, the French Indian allies, nominally 'controlled' by four priests, started first to rob, then to maul, then to massacre the column. The Indians had already massacred the sick left behind in a makeshift hospital in the casern or temporary barracks in the fort. By the time the French grudgingly intervened, two hundred men had been killed and another two hundred kidnapped. The New England prejudice which regarded the Indian allies of France as fiends incarnate received a boost which has, over the imaginative bridge provided by Fenimore Cooper, survived in images which became icons of late twentieth-century Anglo–American cinema. The Indians at Fort William Henry were being, in their view, cheated out of plunder and scalps by their French allies, and the 'massacre' was their counterstrike.[62] Other than for the science of semiotics (or symbols), the massacre was unimportant in the long run, a minor feature of a serious military defeat. It most certainly did not invincibly prejudice the British high command against French Canadians, or weaken their strong desire for military alliance with as many Indians as possible. In the royal instructions issued to Lord Loudoun's successor, Major General James Abercromby, there is heavy emphasis on the need to cooperate with Johnson and Atkin, the northern and southern Indian superintendents, and to keep an eagle eye on the 'Value of the Presents that shall be voted or ordered by the Assemblies of Our different Colonies and Provinces', to ensure that they really reached the Indians they were meant to conciliate, and proved an effective instrument in the general drive 'to engage the said Indians to take Part, and act with Our Forces, in all Operations'.[63]

What did change, to some extent, was the degree of strategic autonomy the commander-in-chief North America was allowed. An assault on Louisbourg was taken for granted in plans for troop provision for 1758, with an assurance that this time 'There will be a proper Train of Artillery for this Service also'.[64] William Pitt, happily in control of that part of the royal prerogative relating to operational command, made no bones about talking to Abercromby in 1758 about the troops, battering train, and stores 'which you have been directed to send to Halifax, to be employed in the Siege of Louisbourg'.[65] There has been almost endless historiographical debate over the role of the Elder Pitt in securing the overwhelming triumph of British arms in the French and Indian or Seven Years' War. Since Pitt was a theatrical megalomaniac who suffered from acute manic depression, his own claims for his achievements were never cast in modest vein, for they all emanated from the manic side of his personality.

There is much to be said for the sceptics who point out that over distances of several thousand miles and with the communication systems of the period, never mind the fog of war and vagaries of nature, Pitt could not possibly have exercised detailed control over the American war fronts. Continuity was a marked feature of British military policy as soon as the dramatic impact of Braddock's defeat had been wholly absorbed. When appointed commander-in-chief, Abercromby was told that he would duly receive 'the proper Commissions, and Instructions for this Purpose, which have been prepared, in every Respect the same, as were done for Lord Loudon'.[66] Nor, as has been seen, were some of Pitt's interventions entirely happy. What is clear enough is that by 1758 he was dictating strategic options. The taking of Louisbourg before any expedition thrust down the St Lawrence was not open to discussion. It was part of the commander-in-chief's remit. Pitt covered all the bases. His North American strategy contained nothing new. Nevertheless, it was in two respects original. It combined Shirley's original limited but ambitious programme of offensives against French positions south of and on the Great Lakes, with all the other options such as the taking of Louisbourg and convergent thrusts along the Richelieu River corridor and into the mouth of the St Lawrence. Refusal to choose amongst options to secure economy of force could have been fatal but for the second aspect of originality. Pitt poured unprecedented quantities of men, munitions, and money into the North American theatre. In terms of ordnance alone, vast amounts of artillery – including heavy 24-pounder and 12-pounder siege cannon, and 8-inch howitzers, complete with round shot, 'tin case shot' for anti-personnel fire, and shells for the howitzers – started to flow to North America. They were accompanied by thousands of muskets, with all necessary accoutrements, from entrenching tools down to sandbags.[67]

Some of Pitt's obsessions, like embargoing trade between British colonies and provinces and New France, were hoary.[68] The repetition of metropolitan demands for the imposition by colonial governors of an effective, coordinated embargo was a sign of the impracticability of any water-tight ban on illicit trade. Pitt could order imperiously, but not produce results. Where he could exercise control, he did. He searched for experienced, competent generals in the school of warfare in central Europe. Abercromby was simply informed that the Louisbourg expedition, within his theatre of command, would be undertaken by Colonel Jeffrey Amherst, who would be given the rank of major general and who was daily expected in England from Germany. He was also urged in the same letter to raise in America 'as considerable a Number of Rangers as may be practicable' for scouting and other forward operations, at least six hundred of whom were to accompany the Louisbourg expedition, as long as the requirement did not lead to delay.[69]

None of this meant that Pitt's orders were obeyed in every detail. A company was a hundred men and it appears that in the end Robert Rogers sent only four Ranger companies to Cape Breton Island for the siege of Louisbourg.[70] That was not at all a bad record when dealing with Rogers, who had signed up to serve under William Shirley to evade prosecution for counterfeiting New Hampshire currency. In 1746, Shirley had made him captain of an independent Ranger company, paid from British government funds. Amherst promoted him major of nine Ranger companies in 1758. In 1760, he was to be sent to Detroit to receive the surrender of the French western posts. From start to finish he was a dishonest, unreliable, administratively incompetent financial desperado. After negotiating with both sides at the start of the American Revolution, he died a poverty-stricken Loyalist refugee in London in 1795.[71] That Pitt grasped the crucial importance of effective scouting is clear. It was no great insight. What was different was his willingness to pay for it. There were companies of Rangers on most British war fronts by the end of 1758. There were, for example, a couple in Nova Scotia. The annual cost of one to the British government seems to have been roughly £1750–£2000.[72]

The British war effort was now being coordinated by a very strange, often very ill man. His subordinates had to explain that his signature looked odd on important communications because 'the inclosed is signed by Mr Pitt in an extremely violent fit of the Gout, which is the reason that his signature is different from what it usually is, when he has the free use of his hand'.[73] As the success of British arms was the condition of Pitt's political survival, his fiscal liberality was more or less mandatory, because it was the only way to activate the overwhelming concentrations of force which guaranteed victory. By the spring of 1758 the Iroquois could sense the change in the balance of power and were assuring Sir William Johnson that they were resolved 'never more to listen to the French' but to honour their Covenant Chain with the English.[74] All of these developments reflected a justifiably upbeat view of the military prospects for the British in North America. Thomas Pownall, governor of Massachusetts, wrote triumphantly to Abercromby in March 1758 that the General Court of the province had voted 'for raising a sufficient number of men in conjunction with his Majesty's Regular Troops under your command'. This vote envisaged several thousand provincial troops, with accompanying Ranger units. Pownall hoped other provinces would follow the Massachusetts example, pointing out that if they did, even on a conservative basis, over 20,000 troops could be mobilised. Pownall, like other colonial governors, was hungry for military command, and proposed to raise and lead a significant proportion of the colonial troops himself, promising Abercromby that if this were permitted 'you wou'd see again such people as took Cape Breton'.[75]

It was an optimistic view. Even after the early setbacks, colonial legislatures could be only grudgingly cooperative. New Hampshire would only raise eight hundred men for nine months and blatantly violated the royal prerogative by wanting a voice in the choice of officers. The slowness with which Abercromby eventually moved his over six thousand regulars and nearly six thousand provincial troops from Schenectady and Albany for a thrust against Ticonderoga owed something to the graceless behaviour of provincial legislatures, but the disaster which followed was all of his own making. Moving out in June, he was near Ticonderoga and Fort Carillon, at the foot of Lake Champlain, in early July. Montcalm seems to have thought that a delaying action, followed by a withdrawal of his eight battalions of irreplaceable regulars to Crown Point, was the best he could do. His men had built an *abatis* of felled trees, with a bristling line of sharp points pointing out and a sandbagged firestep behind, across the peninsula which held the fort. It was outflankable at either end – especially on the north-east, where low ground rose up towards it. Abercromby was reluctant to wait for his full artillery train, for fear of the arrival of French reinforcements, but instead of encircling the *abatis* he launched a frontal assault. Losses were appalling, only about 350 provincials but over 1600 regulars including most of the best combat officers. The 42nd Regiment, the premier Highland regiment known as the Black Watch, was massacred on the *abatis*. Abercromby still had the men and guns to stop, rest, bring up the siege train, and try again after artillery preparation, but one hot afternoon on 8 July had broken his nerve. He retreated, never having personally reconnoitred the defences which had foiled him. He deserved his eventual recall.

Amherst's offensive against Louisbourg showed the professional command capacity so lacking in Abercromby, who was more politician than soldier (he had been an MP since the 1730s). Amherst cooperated well with Admiral Edward Boscawen and had among his senior officers James Wolfe, future conqueror of Quebec. The successful landing on a defended beach owed as much to luck as to skill, but the tactical opportunism which spotted the one weak point in the elaborate French defences was the product of leadership from the front by Wolfe. Thereafter the vastly superior British siege train and weight of naval broadsides simply battered Louisbourg and the hopelessly outmatched naval squadron within its harbour into honourable surrender by 27 July. All French forces in Cape Breton Island and Prince Edward Island surrendered as prisoners of war. Civilians were deported, those from the town of Louisbourg to France. By the time this victory had been won, news of Ticonderoga really ruled out any attempt on Quebec before the winter, though the defeated Abercromby had detached a force of 3600 men under Colonel John Bradstreet which not only reinforced the new Fort Stanwix on the Oneida Lake at the head of the Mohawk River but also moved on Fort Frontenac. The final approach to the fort was by boat, and once Bradstreet was ashore his vast superiority in numbers and cannon forced a French surrender, after which the fort was destroyed. Montcalm thought his position now extremely critical, but had not been able to reinforce Fort Frontenac for fear of a renewed assault on Ticonderoga. Abercromby had contemplated this. Amherst talked him out of it at the end of the year, when he also replaced him as commander-in-chief.

New France was facing an almost impossible situation. The ailing General John Forbes, who died in Philadelphia in March 1759, had late in 1758 effectively re-run the Braddock campaign, though he insisted on a more direct route to the Forks of the Ohio and a new and easier road through Pennsylvania rather than the Virginian forests. George Washington commanded one of his three brigades. On 13 September 1758 the French and their Indian allies successfully repulsed a rash and weak challenge from eight hundred or so Virginians and regulars from Montgomery's Highlanders under the over-ambitious Major James Grant, but on 14 November Forbes, when still a few miles short of his main objective, heard that the French had evacuated and burned the fort, and vanished.[76] They had taken the only sane decision. A siege would have lost them the garrison as well as the fort. The inexorable advance of Forbes was the product of a steady knitting together of strands of policy which enabled the British to deploy something like their full potential in war in North America for the first time.

Colonial efforts, though disproportionately funded by Westminster, were assuming very serious dimensions. Stephen Hopkins, governor of Rhode Island, told Abercromby in March 1758 that his General Assembly had noted to raise 1000 men, as a 10-company provincial regiment for the forthcoming campaign. He reminded Abercromby that there were probably no more than six thousand men fit to bear arms in his small colony and 'one Thousand of that Number are now absent from the Colony in private Vessels of War'. Finally, he added that he had embargoed trade with the enemy.[77] If this sort of effort massively reinforced British military and naval efforts, changing patterns of Indian allegiance materially assisted British campaigns. Edmund Atkin, the southern Indian superintendent, was rather successful in persuading Cherokee and Catawba Indians to offer their services to General Forbes.[78] The latter regarded them as a very mixed blessing. The Iroquois were appalled by the prospect of these southern warriors crossing their land, but it was essential to have them as long as the western Ohio Indians, like the eastern Delaware and Shawnee, were pro-French. In the end, the Cherokee largely went home,[79] and an elaborate negotiation was set in motion. The British distinguished between southern Indian nations, deemed 'friendly', and northern ones, either hostile like the Delaware or ambiguous like the Iroquois. They were unhappy about bilateral negotiation, as when 'King Teedeyuscung' and other Delaware chiefs made a unilateral peace offer to the Cherokees.[80] The British ideal was that they should call the shots in the game of negotiation between Indian groups important to them. It was a naive hope.

If Indians were the supreme individualists on the North American stage, they were not the only ones. White settlers ran them a close second. Virginia had started the war. Even in the period 1756–57 when the Virginia Regiment was well under strength, it cost the colony about £1500 a month. Scalp bounties, pensions to disabled soldiers, payments to widows, wages for mobilised militia, and costly 'presents' needed to cement the Cherokee alliance ran taxes higher. By the beginning of 1757, the Virginia legislature had invested £125,000 in the war. By its end that figure had more than quadrupled. Yet the gentry leadership of the colony baulked at the idea of effectively mobilising, let alone conscripting, the white 'lower orders' whom everyone assumed should bear the main burden of conflict. From 1758 a bounty-based volunteer system was the basis of the colony's war effort.[81] It was simply taken for granted that even white trash, often from a very violent background, would insist on using violence on its own terms. Virginia had to pay for what can only be described as a semi-professional provincial army.

This was the norm among the British North American colonies active in the latter stages of the war. Though at periods of acute danger whole militia units could take the field as regiments – as several did in 1757 – the main function of the provincial militia had become to supply volunteers for annually recruited provincial armies. Amongst the New England colonies, there had been a detailed study of the forces raised by Massachusetts. It argues that the relatively egalitarian society maintained by the quarter of a million or so inhabitants of the colony in the 1750s was profoundly alien in culture to the hierarchical, authoritarian society of Hanoverian Britain. From this point of view, the contractual, libertarian bias of nearly all procedures in New England was a measure of the extent to which its culture had diverged fundamentally from that of Old England, and the horror which provincial soldiers incorporated with British forces showed when faced with the frequent floggings and regular military executions inflicted on British regulars was a precursor of the spirit which sustained the American Revolution. Equally, when Lord Loudoun, exasperated by the reluctance of Massachusetts to feed its own troops for fear certain procedures might undermine the Crown's assurance that it would give the province reimbursement for provisioning its units, complained that America was a lawless country where every man did as he pleased, this is seen as a measure of a vast incomprehension rooted in incompatibility.[82] There is clearly something in this, but it is also an example of the plundering of the past to find 'roots' for the present. Most eighteenth-century civilians were liable to regard men under regular military or naval discipline as in a sense 'slaves'. Colonel, later General, George Washington had little sympathy with this gut reaction. He thought discipline the soul of an army, was not averse to military execution in extreme cases, and thought the use of the lash salutary in the face of dereliction of duty in the ranks. Meanness and irresponsible selfishness had at least as much to do with the foot-dragging of colonial legislatures as assertions of libertarian principles.

The West Indian legislatures, representative of white oligarchies presiding over a slave-driven sugar economy, were very much like their fellow British-American mainland counterparts when it came to cooperation with the war effort. They consulted first their own interests. This meant that, although they were reluctant to say so, they traditionally did not want to see French sugar islands conquered and annexed, for that would mean an increased supply of sugar from within the British dominions, and therefore reduced prices in the domestic market. The re-export trade to Europe had been destroyed by the fact that the British islands simply could not compete with the cheaper product of the French and Dutch. What the British planters wanted to see was the mounting of purely destructive attacks on French islands, with a view to knocking them out as producers for a period. The French planters were no keener on conquest, for similar reasons. Because they were chronically short of labour, they preferred raids on British islands to hijack large numbers of slaves.

Both the French and British islands had white militias, but the relentless engrossing of smaller plantations by large ones had so reduced the potential pool of militiamen that most island colonies were notoriously reluctant to send reinforcements to help compatriots under attack in other islands, for fear of leaving themselves incapable of holding off foreign attack or of suppressing a slave rebellion. Barbados was infamous for sending only good wishes to other beleaguered British islands. French militiamen could be just as selfish. When in 1759 a British force attacked Martinique and was quite unexpectedly defeated by the embodied French militia, it moved off to attack Guadeloupe, but the victorious militia were conspicuously reluctant to leave Martinique in order to help their sister island. In any case, the military quality of the militias on the British islands was lamentable. In Nevis there was a widespread conviction that 'discipline is the first step to tyranny'. Antigua in 1756 passed a supplementary militia law, one of whose clauses forbade any private to turn out with a negro to carry his weapons for him. In 1760 Lieutenant Governor Moore complained bitterly to the Jamaica Assembly that the fines for non-attendance at compulsory militia training were so nugatory as to encourage most planters to shirk and pay them. In any case, it was alleged that in the late 1750s the Jamaican authorities either failed to build emplacements at likely invasion points or neglected to mount guns and guards at sites with emplacements.

Nearly every island had a coastal fortress where shipping could lie secure under its guns. Some of the French islands had mountain redoubts, but by and large militiamen were well aware that a landing party could kidnap slaves, burn cane fields, and burn houses and works without bothering to assault fortified positions. So there was less and less zeal for mounting any active defence. In all the many wars between France and England in the West Indies, only one small territory had ever changed hands formally – the formerly French half of St Kitts, retained at the Peace of Utrecht, apparently mainly to stop illicit trading. St Kitts therefore became British as a minor piece of bureaucratic tidying up. Given this sort of track record and the massive vested interests whose selfish ends usually dictated opposition to serious effort, let alone conquest, the amazing fact is that the Seven Years' War did see the British conquer all the Windward Islands and annex the neutral islands: St Vincent, Dominica, St Lucia, and Tobago. These four were small islands whose debatable international status had never been deemed worth a war. Since the Seven Years' War was primarily about North America, this burst of activity in the Caribbean looks all the odder, until it is placed in context. It was all the work of the Westminster government, and no decisive step was taken until after the fall of Louisbourg.[83]

The news of the fall of Niagara, Ticonderoga, and Crown Point to British forces had reached London almost simultaneously in September 1759. The European war, which was quite crucial in its ability to tie up a large proportion of French fiscal and military resources, had taken a sharp turn for the better in early August, when Ferdinand, Prince of Brunswick, commander of the Anglo–Hanoverian army guarding Hanover from French attack (and Frederick of Prussia's flank), decisively defeated the marquis de Contades' French army at Minden. Nevertheless, peace was being very seriously discussed by Britain and her allies between June and October 1759. Frederick of Prussia was being worn down by the sheer weight of Austrian and Russian attacks. The British treasury and more and more of the political class were extremely worried about the mounting debt and endless funding crises generated by the war. The French administration was weary of an expensive and unsuccessful conflict. At this period Pitt was not as intransigent as might be supposed. Even after the outlying French stronghold in North American waters, Louisbourg, had fallen, virtually depriving France of any chance of recapturing the initiative in North America, he was flexible. Louisbourg had to cease to be a threat, but that could mean permanent demilitarisation rather than annexation by Britain. The future of Quebec was fluid in his mind. In North America the only non-negotiable points were the original British war aims: a frontier on the Great Lakes and Mississippi and the blocking of the corridor into New England via Crown Point. Pitt accepted that conquests would have to be returned to secure peace.[84]

The end game in America was to some extent about picking up bargaining counters to be traded for European pieces, like Minorca, the important British naval base in the western Mediterranean lost early in the war. As early as the late summer of 1757 Pitt had initiated the accumulation of a siege train of 30 heavy brass guns, 6 light pieces of ordnance, and 38 brass mortars, with over 3300 barrels of powder, all designed to take Martinique, specifically as an exchange for Minorca. The attack was not launched until 1759 and was successful only when repeated in 1762. By the latter occasion tactical lessons had been learned. A series of feints against coastal positions led to dispersal of the French planter militia, and its demoralisation at the threat of the destruction of its assets by British landing parties. Since the British had granted generous terms to Guadeloupe, guaranteeing the island's French cultural identity whilst giving its highly competitive sugar access to British markets big enough to lift it from recession to prosperity, the Martinique militia were probably ambiguous at the prospect of conquest. They certainly had no stomach to stand protracted bombardment in their far from impregnable main fortress, Fort Royal. Yet the assaults on Louisbourg and later Quebec required even greater trains of ordnance than were deployed by the British in the West Indies, and it was a measure of William Pitt's willingness to buy victory with massive commitment that – despite the virtually insuperable problems faced by the Board of Ordnance in its attempts to increase British gunpowder production – he was prepared in North America to supply colonial as well as regular British forces generously with gunpowder and ordnance.[85]

What turned British war objectives from limited to potentially unlimited in North America was naval victory in European waters. It is clear that the naval side of the war was run principally by the prestigious first lord of the Admiralty, Admiral Anson. Pitt believed in departmental government, so Anson's grip was never even threatened by his flamboyant colleague. The Anson regime, though impressively professional and marked by exceptional attention to the victualling and health of seamen, was essentially traditional in nature. Anson's ability to control the Board of Admiralty was very limited.[86] Pitt, during his brief first ministry of 1756–57, did contrive to place at the head of the Board of Admiralty his arrogant brother-in-law Lord

Temple, but that arrangement was not repeated in the coalition ministry he formed with the Duke of Newcastle later in 1757. Naval strategy had been hammered out in previous wars. It was mostly obvious, involving an attempt to contain the French fleet by blockade, to protect British shipping, and to interdict French Atlantic trade and the despatch of reinforcements to colonies.[87]

Facing defeat, France had been forced to concentrate her resources on a massive planned invasion of England. This was the last time the French proposed to use the exiled Stuart dynasty as a political pawn; it was also a gamble which failed. In November 1759 in Quiberon Bay, in a gale, Admiral Hawke destroyed the French fleet. David Garrick's musical tribute 'Heart of Oak' was deserved, but froth compared with the fact, long acknowledged by historians, that the action, by freeing British troops for Germany and ruling out reinforcements for French America, marked the point at which defeat became disaster for France.[88] In an age of sail, when weather was an all-important factor, this did not mean that the French could not mount hard-hitting naval sallies. For example, in the summer of 1760 the British squadron at Louisbourg had to seek out and destroy a small French squadron which had penetrated the southern part of the Gulf of St Lawrence and was trying to hide in the mouth of the River Restigouche. Even after their ships were destroyed, the matelots escaped to rally two thousand local Acadians for a spell of guerrilla warfare which lasted for four months before surrender. A much more sensational example came after Spain had joined the war in 1762. A French expeditionary force seized St John's in Newfoundland in June of that year. It slighted Fort William, captured or destroyed 460 fishing boats, and devastated British settlements before being chased off by British forces from Cape Breton and Nova Scotia. It was a horribly expensive footnote to the war, but everyone knew that only small French squadrons could now operate in these waters.[89]

Naval supremacy was a necessary, but not a sufficient condition for total British victory in North America. It allowed a large force of 30 men-o'-war to escort no fewer than 140 vessels, originally assembled at Louisbourg, into the St Lawrence in June 1759, carrying the predictable expeditionary force against Quebec under the command of Major General James Wolfe. Admiral Saunders, the naval commander, had access to inaccurate French charts and one English chart of the St Lawrence, but these were corrected by surveys conducted by, amongst others, the future great explorer Captain James Cook. Captured French seamen and careful sounding also helped.[90] Yet even when the entire fleet reached the basin below Quebec safely, there could be no guarantee that the expedition would succeed against a city upon a hill which defied Wolfe's best efforts to within a week of the period where inclement weather, the sufferings of his men, and the looming threat of ice closing the St Lawrence would have compelled the British to sail away. Though the French commander, the marquis de Montcalm, was a chronic pessimist who looked for ways of transferring blame for defeat at the start of every campaign, his troops were in far better heart than he was. When on 31 July an increasingly baffled Wolfe tried to force the pace by a direct assault on the left of the French line before Quebec, his troops were beaten back with heavy loss by the Montreal militia whom he despised as 'peasants'.[91] They shot his regulars down from behind the defences as efficiently as Anglo-American militiamen firing from behind a redoubt were to shoot down British troops at the Battle of Bunker Hill in 1775.

There was a widespread feeling in the French camp in September 1759 that the siege of Quebec was virtually over, and was ending in glory for the defenders. General Jeffrey Amherst, the British commander-in-chief North America, spent most of that summer taking and rebuilding French forts and heavily entrenching the area of Crown Point – hardly an offensive measure or one envisaging the elimination of New France. The landing upstream from Quebec which enabled Wolfe to fight and win the Battle of the Heights of Abraham on 13 September was extremely risky; it was too close to Quebec by far and would have had to have been abandoned in the face of any serious opposition.[92] Montcalm's decision to rush pell-mell at his enemy verges on the inexplicable. Wolfe's position was not even in sight of Quebec's walls. Ten miles to his rear there was a crack French force of 3000 regulars, militia, and light artillery under Louis Antoine de Bougainville, more than capable of cutting off Wolfe's retreat to the Anse au Foulon, where he had landed. Wolfe had no reserves. His own confidence in his army was total, but rooted in a misplaced contempt for the Canadian militia and a conviction of the low quality of the French regulars which was just wrong. Montcalm needed to wait for a few hours before he overwhelmed Wolfe with superior forces. His successor François-Gaston de Lévis was to defeat Wolfe's army under Wolfe's successor under the walls of Quebec in April 1760. As it was, Montcalm's premature assault enabled Wolfe, at the cost of his own life, to smash the French with perhaps the two most disciplined volleys ever fired on an eighteenth-century battlefield. Bayonets and Highland broadswords then cleared the field, though the bulk of the French army escaped. It is difficult not to agree with W.J. Eccles, the eminent Canadian historian, that the action on the Heights of Abraham 'gives one to think that perhaps the most overlooked determining factor in history has been stupidity'.[93]

Thereafter, British naval superiority was decisive. De Lévis could whip Brigadier Murray before Quebec but his spring offensive to recover Quebec entirely depended on the arrival of a French fleet capable of seeing off the Royal Navy. It was not to be. Short of food, ammunition and troops (the militia had deserted *en masse*), the French had to surrender Montreal in September 1760, in the face of a triple offensive by Murray from Quebec, Lieutenant Colonel William Havilland from Lake Ontario, and General Jeffrey Amherst whose glacial progress down the Richelieu River from Lake Champlain had compelled Murray to endure a siege in Quebec. Fortunately, de Lévis simply did not have the siege guns to batter Murray into surrender, while the latter had quite enough guns to rule out an attempt by an unreinforced de Lévis to storm.

Had Wolfe failed, as he should have, the chances of another massive British effort would have been remote. The Seven Years' War was already posing lethal fiscal problems for the French and British Crowns. For the French, a war which cost twice as much annually as the previous one meant an accumulation of debt which their social structure prevented them from handling by the conversion or reduction schemes employed by the British or Dutch. Treated as sacrosanct, this huge debt was the root cause of the fiscal crisis which between 1787 and 1793 destroyed the Bourbon regime.[94] In Britain, soaring debt had generated an incipient political crisis. Large sections of the conservative ruling class, including from 1760 the new king and his minister, Lord Bute, were desperate for peace. Once New France had fallen, however, there was a consensus that, despite the case for retaining a potentially profitable Guadeloupe rather than a loss-making Canada, Canada should be retained. As Lord Chesterfield wrote to Newcastle on 30 November 1760: 'I think we should keep Quebec and Canada as preventatives of future war'.[95]

Perceptive commentators like the Duke of Bedford, who had long been aware of the underlying futility of Anglo–French conflict and who could see that the destruction of New France would remove one of the few real constraints on the virtual independence of most British North American colonies, were not wanting. Men on the spot – like the Scots ex-regular officer Walter Rutherford, who had married and settled in New York – insisted that a Great Lakes frontier and Louisbourg gave Britain the ascendancy in furs and fish which alone was worth having, and that a surviving French presence would justify a British military establishment capable of securing the loyalty of the colonies.[96] The French had long grasped the reality of the virtual independence of the British colonies and the incipient incoherence of the British Atlantic empire. As early as 1710, when the comte de Ponchartrain, the minister of marine, hoped to foment rebellion in New England and New York, he stressed that 'these provinces [have] always maintained themselves in a sort of republic, governed by their Councils'.[97] The decision to keep all Canada in the final peace settlement not only created grave problems of governance for the British monarchy in North America, but also drove another nail into the coffin of the cohesion of the English Atlantic community.

A process of mythologising the conduct and implications of the war was well advanced long before it was over. William Pitt, by maintaining an ostentatiously 'independent' and 'Patriot' stance, enabled a loose coalition of country Whigs, Tories, and 'middling sorts' from the City of London to project on to him their fantasies about the virtuous 'Patriot' minister, and to give this image resonance in newspapers, magazines, prints, and pamphlets. In fact, it was in the closet with George II that Pitt could exercise most influence. The king still had an effective veto on military and diplomatic policy, and the German war, which was a *sine qua non* of Pitt's survival as a minister of the Crown, and indeed an integral part of his overall strategy, was always unpopular with his vociferous coalition of extra-parliamentary supporters. Latterly that coalition was disintegrating, not least because of inattention from Pitt.[98]

As a pinchbeck messiah, Pitt did not wear too well in the eighteenth century. What did resound after his resignation in 1761 was simply the unique string of British victories, commemorated by the historian and painter Francis Hayman in four giant 12-foot high and 15-foot long canvases erected in Vauxhall Pleasure Gardens. Painted between 1761 and 1764, these remarkable history paintings celebrated the surrender of Montreal to Amherst, Hawke's triumph at Quiberon Bay, Robert Clive's seizure of control in Bengal after the Battle of Plassey, and the glories of the British generals, including the deceased Wolfe.[99] The deification of Wolfe gathered pace with the appearance in 1771 of an influential prime icon in the shape of Benjamin West's painting *The Death of Wolfe*. Its relationship to reality was less than appeared at first sight, including as it did an Indian close to a general who despised and detested Indians.[100] West was an American who was to be somewhat ambiguous in the face of an American Revolution which occurred after he had irreversibly transferred his professional career to London. He is an example of the contradictory, fractured nature of eighteenth-century British identity. Informed contemporaries could be less gullible in the face of 'Patriot' mythology rooted in neo-classical ideals than some modern historians have been.

The war in America saw a massive Scottish presence in the regular ranks, with ex-Jacobites like Simon Fraser of Lovat bringing his own Highland regiment over to fight in a theatre where the government's Black Watch Highland Regiment campaigned, at times under notably incompetent Lowland Scots generalship. British conquests were a mechanism for advancement and in certain cases political reintegration for ambitious Scots,[101] but these men did not necessarily buy the retrospective hype. In 1774, two of Wolfe's former brigadiers, George Townshend and James Murray (a Scot from a Jacobite-tainted family) corresponded about the conquest of Quebec. Townshend admitted to being bored by the whole overdone business and more interested in contemporary campaigns in Tanjore in south India, but he advised Murray not to attack in print a Wolfe the public had been taught to revere. Murray, always a jealous but often a shrewd critic of Wolfe, replied: 'God forbid My Lord I should interrupt your Amusements: Tanjour you may quietly Enjoy, while I am knocking my obstinate Scotch head against the Admiration, and Reverence of the English Mob for Mr Wolfe's memory.'[102]

The nineteenth and twentieth centuries were to see more and more determined attempts to insert providential significance into the military events of 1759-60. The great New England historian Francis Parkman saw the defeat of New France, like the sweeping aside of the American Indian peoples against whom he held profound prejudices,[103] as pre-ordained event. Absolutism and Romish superstition had been defeated by Anglo-Saxon liberty and reason. In his eyes, the Peace of Paris, which confirmed the loss of Canada to France, 'ended the chequered story of New France; a story which would have been a history if faults of constitution and the bigotry and folly of rulers had not dwarfed it to an episode'.[104] For Parkman the fall of New France was but a stage in the providential plan for the emergence of a mighty, independent United States of America whose historic destiny had been confirmed in his own lifetime by the triumph of the union in the American Civil War.

In the United Kingdom in the early twentieth century, ardent imperialists, conscious of the inevitable decline in the relative power of their country and fearful of the palpable political incoherence of what was called then the British Empire, resurrected a messianic Elder Pitt as a beacon for their flickering faith in a future of greatness. In the light of modern research, their icon simply does not hold up to scrutiny. He worked in a government of departments. He could not possibly control in detail over thousands of miles. Though a good administrator in handling specific projects like the attacks on Martinique and Guadeloupe, he was a fiscal desperado, dependent on the Duke of Newcastle's flair for raising the vast sums required by a policy of endlessly upping the ante in the face of failure.[105] Newcastle, before, during and after the war, has been unreasonably denigrated. It was his reputation's misfortune that in the 1930s his personality was held up to scorn by influential historians like Sir Lewis Namier, and even by the vastly better balanced and erudite Richard Pares.

In the last analysis, though the layer upon layer of iconography, rhetoric, and sustained self-deception is a fascinating study in its own right, it is not of prime importance in understanding the significance of the military outcome of the Seven Years' War in America. That outcome, later selectively incorporated into versions of US and UK identity, was rightly seen at the time by many thinking observers as creating two major and inter-connected crises. One was a political crisis over the funding of a huge war debt. The other was a crisis in the coherence and identity of the ramshackle structure of an over-extended British Atlantic monarchy. Few victories have turned sour so fast, or so predictably.

Notes and references

1. Daniel K. Richter, *The Ordeal of the Long House: The peoples of the Iroquois League in the era of European colonization* (University of North Carolina Press, Chapel Hill, NC, 1992), Chap. 11.

2. Richard White, *The Middle Ground: Indians, empires and republics in the Great Lakes region, 1650–1815* (Cambridge University Press, Cambridge, 1991).

3. Ethan Howard Shagan, 'Constructing Discord: Ideology, propaganda, and English responses to the Irish rebellion of 1641', *Journal of British Studies*, 36 (1997), pp. 4–34, is an extreme example.

4. Entry for Monday, 11 June 1744, in Hamilton's 'Itinerarium', printed in Wendy Martin (ed.), *Colonial American Travel Narratives* (Penguin Classics, New York, 1994), pp. 194–95.

5. Entry for 15 November 1749 in Adolph B. Benson (ed.), *Peter Kalm's Travels in North America: The English version of 1770* (Dover Publications, New York, 1 vol. pbk edn, 1987), pp. 632–33.

6. *Ibid.*, entry for 5 October 1749, pp. 540–41. This is the last part of the *Travels* that achieved contemporary publication, but the set of notes known as the 'Supplementary Diary' which was discovered in modern times can be used as a source for contemporary conversations, as in the text above.

7. 'Intelligence from Colonel Peter Schuyler', printed in Isabel M. Calder (ed.), *Colonial Captivities, Marches and Journeys* (Macmillan Company, New York, 1935), pp. 140–42.

8. 'Extract from the Journal of Major John Smith, 1756–57', *ibid.*, pp. 137–39.

9. David S. Shields, *Oracles of Empire: Poetry, politics, and commerce in British America 1690–1750* (University of Chicago Press, Chicago, IL, 1990), pp. 196–97.

10. *Ibid.*, pp. 221–23.

11. Bruce P. Lenman, 'Alexander Spotswood and the Business of Empire', *Colonial Williamsburg. The journal of the Colonial Williamsburg Foundation*, Autumn 1990, pp. 44–55.

12. Wayland F. Dunaway, *The Scotch–Irish of Colonial Pennsylvania* (Geneological Publishing Co. reprint, Boston, MA, 1979), pp. 144–48.

13. 'Journal of Major John Smith', *loc. cit.*, p. 139.

14. Bruce P. Lenman, 'The Old Imperialist and the Young Soldier', *Colonial Williamsburg*, Spring 1994, pp. 32–41.

15. *The Journal of Major George Washington*, Williamsburg, Printed by William Hunter, 1754 (Facsimile, Colonial Williamsburg Foundation, Williamsburg, VA, 1959), p. 13.

16. Alf J. Mapp Jr, *The Virginia Experiment: The old dominion's role in the making of America (1607–1781)* (Dietz Press, Richmond, VA, 1957), pp. 229 and 242.

17. John Carlyle to George Carlyle, 18 April 1754, transcript in 'Carlyle Correspondence Indexing Project' by the staff of Carlyle House, Alexandria, VA. I am most grateful to the staff for making this material available to me.

18. *Ibid.*

19. Same to same, 11 August 1753, *loc. cit.*

20. Same to same, 3 July 1754, *loc. cit.* There is a useful biography of John Carlyle: James D. Munson, *Col. John Carlyle, Gent., 1720–1780* (Northern Virginia Regional Parks Authority, 1987).

21. Douglas E. Leach, *The Northern Colonial Frontier 1607–1763* (Holt, Rinehart and Winston, New York, 1966), pp. 196–99.

22. By far the best detailed study of Newcastle's American policy, in its British and European context, is in Reed Browning, *The Duke of Newcastle* (Yale University Press, New Haven, CT, 1975), Chaps. 5 and 6.

23. Philip Katcher, *Armies of the American Wars 1753–1815* (Osprey Publishing, Reading, PA, 1975), pp. 2–4.

24. Julian Gwynn, 'The Royal Navy in North America, 1712–1776', in Jeremy Black and Philip Woodfine (eds.), *The British Navy and the Use of Naval Power in the Eighteenth Century* (Leicester University Press, Leicester, 1988), pp. 138–40.

25. Alan Gallay (ed.), *Colonial Wars of North America*, pp. 63–65.

26. Rex Whitworth, *William Augustus Duke of Cumberland: A life* (Leo Cooper, London, 1992), pp. 165–66.

27. Copy, letter of appointment issued by Braddock, 10 April 1755, in Alexandria, in 'Carlyle Correspondence', original in Huntington Library, California.

28. Petition of John Carlyle, 8 November 1762, in *ibid.*, original in Journals of the House of Burgesses of Virginia.

29. Oscar and Lilian Handlin, *A Restless People* (Anchor Press/Doubleday, New York, 1982), pp. 16 and 110.

30. Lee McCardell, *Ill-Starred General: Braddock of the Coldstream Guards* (University of Pittsburgh Press, Pittsburgh, OH, 1958), p. 174.

31. Paul E. Kopperman, *Braddock at the Monongahela* (University of Pittsburgh Press, Pittsburgh, OH, 1977), is the latest and in many ways the best summary of evidence and literature.

32. Charles Hamilton (ed.), *Braddock's Defeat: The journal of Captain Robert Cholmley's batman; The journal of a British officer; Halkett's orderly book* (University of Oklahoma Press, Norman, OK, 1959), p. 29.

33. Robert L. Yaple, 'Braddock's Defeat: The theories and a reconsideration', *Journal of the Society for Army Historical Research*, 56 (1968), pp. 191–201.

34. 'Anonymous Letter of Braddock's Campaign', printed in Stanley M. Pargellis (ed.), *Military Affairs in North America 1748–1765* (American Historical Association, New York, 1936), p. 116.

35. Thomas Robinson [1st Baron Grantham] to Major General Braddock, Whitehall, 26 November 1754, contemporary copy, Loudon Papers, Huntington Library, San Marino, California, CA (hereafter LO), 516.

36. 'Memorandum relating to troops in North America', 27 November 1754, contemporary copy, Treasury Chambers, Whitehall, LO518 A.

37. Articles of agreement between HM Treasury and Messrs Thomlinson and Hanbury, 29 November 1754, contemporary copy and enclosure in Thomlinson and Hanbury to London, 8 May 1756, LO520 A and B.

38. Board of Ordnance, 'State of Ordnance . . . in North America', November 1754, LO32.

39. John Reynolds to Sir Thomas Robinson, 5 December 1754, contemporary copy, LO524 A.

40. Sir Thomas Robinson to Major-General Braddock, 31 December 1754, draft LO525.

41. 'Claim of the English and French to the possession of Fort Frontenac, Stated and Examined', [1754], LO6196. This is probably by William Shirley. It certainly reflects his views.

42. *Ibid.*

43. 'Memorandum, For Operations in North America Anno 1755' [William Shirley?], LO723.

44. Minutes relating to the contract between the Commissioners of the Treasury and Thomlinson and Hanbury, 28 November 1754–26 November 1755, LO519.

45. Houdin, 'Advice in relation to an attack on Quebec and Montreal', January 1755, copy, LO548. Houdin was a missionary 'at Trenton in the Jerseys and lived several years at Quebeck', so in a paradoxical way his recommendation came from an insider's view of New France. *Vide* 'List of Commissions

Granted by His Excellency the Right Honorable the Earl of Loudon', printed in Pargellis, *Military Affairs*, p. 363.

46. 'State of the Town and Port of Louisbourg in the year 1754', LO529.

47. Edmond Atkin, 'To ... the Lords Commissioners for Trade and Plantations', copy (partly in Atkin's hand), LO578. This MS has been edited and published by Wilbur R. Jacobs.

48. Cited in Wilbur R. Jacobs, *Indians of the Southern Colonial Frontier. The Edmond Atkin report and plan of 1755* (University of South Carolina Press, Columbia, SC, 1954), XXV.

49. Edward Braddock to Sir Thomas Robinson, 5 June 1755, from Fort Cumberland at Will's Creek, LO581.

50. Howard H. Peckham, *The Colonial Wars, 1689–1762* (University of Chicago Press, Chicago, IL, 1964), p. 147.

51. South Carolina and Georgia merchants, traders, and planters memorial to the Lords Regents of Great Britain, [July 1755?], LO5931.

52. William Shirley to Henry Fox, 12 August 1755, 'Camp on the Great Carrying place of Oneida near the Head of the Mohawk River', LO624.

53. Stanley M. Pargellis, *Lord Loudon in North America* (Yale University Press, New Haven, CT, 1933), pp. 211–30.

54. *Ibid.*, pp. 237–52.

55. Sir William Johnson to Thomas Pownall, Albany, 8 September 1757, in James Sullivan (ed.), *The Papers of Sir William Johnson Vol. II* (State University of New York, Albany, NY, 1922), p. 737.

56. The distinctly flattering view of Johnson in Milton W. Hamilton, *Sir William Johnson Colonial American 1715–1763* (Kennikat Press, Port Washington, NY, 1976), is corrected with some acerbity in Julian Gwynn's piece in *Dictionary of Canadian Biography. Vol. 4: 1771 to 1800* (University of Toronto Press, Toronto, 1979), pp. 394–97.

57. Sir William Shirley to Henry Fox, 15 August 1755, Camp at Oneida Lake, LO632.

58. 'Recruiting Instructions for the Officers of His Majesty's 45 Regiment of Foot Commanded by Major General Warburton', Item 2, Halifax, 3 September 1755, LO642.

59. Commons debate, 14 December 1757, report in R.C. Simmons and P.D.G. Thomas (eds.), *Proceedings and Debates of the British Parliaments Respecting North America 1754–83 Vol. I: 1754–1764* (Kraus, New York, 1982), p. 241.

60. Edward P. Hamilton (ed.), *Adventure in the Wilderness: The American journals of Louis Antoine de Bougainville 1756–1760* (University of Oklahoma Press,

Norman, OK, 1964), entries for 19 September 1756 and 24 July 1757, pp. 41 and 142–43.

61. William Shirley to Henry Fox, 19 December 1755, LO700.

62. Ian K. Steele, *Betrayals: Fort William Henry and the 'Massacre'* (Oxford University Press, New York, 1990).

63. George II, 'Instructions for Our Trusty and Wellbeloved James Abercromby Esquire', St James, 30 December 1757, Abercromby Papers, Huntington Library, San Marino, CA (hereafter AB), 7.

64. 'Troops destined for the Siege of Louisbourg', 30 December 1757, Whitehall, AB851.

65. William Pitt to General Abercromby, 9 January 1758, AB12.

66. Same to same, Whitehall, 30 December 1757, AB9.

67. *Vide* List of ordnance 'for Pensilvania', Whitehall, 9 January 1758, and 'for Halifax', and 'for New York', same date, all enclosed in William Pitt to James Abercromby, 9 January 1758, AB858–60.

68. William Pitt to James Abercromby, 11 January 1758, AB13.

69. William Pitt to James Abercromby, 27 January 1758, AB18.

70. 'Major Robert Rogers Account against the four Ranger Companies gone to Cape Breton. Enclosed to Lieut. Gov. Monkton, 30 June 1758', AB16.

71. *Dictionary of American Biography*, pp. 108–09.

72. 'An Account of several Military Services the charge of which is stated in the Estimate for Nova Scotia for 1758 transmitted by Governor Lawrence to the Board of Trade', AB850.

73. Robert Wood to James Abercromby, Whitehall, 11 February 1758, AB22.

74. Sir William Johnson, Minutes of an Indian conference, 11 March 1758 at Fort Johnson, enclosed in Sir William Johnson to James Abercromby, 24 March 1758, AB36.

75. Thomas Pownall to James Abercromby, 12 March 1758, AB37.

76. Douglas E. Leach, *Arms for Empire. A military history of the British colonies in North America, 1607–1763* (Macmillan, New York, 1973), pp. 423–44.

77. Stephen Hopkins to General Abercromby, 20 March 1758, AB57.

78. Edmond Atkin to William Byrd, Charleston, 24 March 1758, plus enclosed copy of letter to Cherokees, AB70.

79. Francis Jennings, *Empire of Fortune: Crowns, colonies and tribes in the Seven Years' War in America* (Norton, New York, 1988), pp. 375–77.

80. Proceedings of a Council of Officers at Fort Loudon Virginia concerning a peace offer by the Cherokees to the Delaware, 30 March 1758, AB93.

81. James Titus, *The Old Dominion at War. Society, politics and warfare in late colonial Virginia* (University of South Carolina Press, Columbia, SC, 1991), pp. 113 and 143–48.

82. Fred Anderson, *A People's Army. Massachusetts soldiers and society in the Seven Years' War* (W.W. Norton, New York, pbk edn, 1984).

83. For the Anglo–French confrontation in the Caribbean in the Seven Years' War, Richard Pares, *War and Trade in the West Indies, 1739–1763* (Clarendon Press, Oxford, 1936), remains the classic work.

84. Richard Middleton, *The Bells of Victory. The Pitt–Newcastle ministry and the conduct of the Seven Years' War* (Cambridge University Press, Cambridge, 1985), pp. 130–35.

85. Jenny West, *Gunpowder, Government and War in the Mid-Eighteenth Century* (Royal Historical Society, Boydell Press, 1991), Chap. 6 and Conclusion.

86. Stephen F. Gradish, *The Manning of the British Navy during the Seven Years' War* (Royal Historical Society, London, 1980), pp. 209–11.

87. Richard Middleton, 'Pitt, Anson and the Admiralty, 1756–1761', *History*, 55 (1970), pp. 189–97.

88. Geoffrey Marcus, *Quiberon Bay* (Hollis and Carter, London, 1960), pp. 177–80.

89. Julian Gwynn, 'The Royal Navy in North America, 1712–1776', in Black and Woodfine (eds.), *The British Navy*, p. 140.

90. Richard Hough, *Captain James Cook: a biography* (Hodder and Stoughton, London, 1994), pp. 18–20.

91. George F.G. Stanley, *New France. The last phase 1744–1760* (Oxford University Press, London, 1968), p. 227.

92. C.P. Stacey, *Quebec, 1759: The siege and the battle* (Macmillan of Canada, Toronto, 1959), pp. 131–32 and 172–73.

93. W.J. Eccles, 'The Battle of Quebec: A reappraisal', in *idem, Essays on New France* (Oxford University Press, Toronto, pbk edn, 1987), p. 133.

94. James C. Riley, *The Seven Years' War and the Old Regime in France. The economic and financial toll* (Princeton University Press, Princeton, NJ, 1986), p. 236.

95. Cited in Sir Lewis Namier, *England in the Age of the American Revolution* (Macmillan, London, 2nd pbk edn, 1961), p. 276.

96. *Ibid.*, p. 281.

97. Cited in Eccles, 'New France and the French Impact on North America', *Essays on New France*, p. 138.

98. Marie Peters, *Pitt and Popularity. The Patriot minister and London opinion during the Seven Years' War* (Clarendon Press, Oxford, 1980).

99. Brian Allen, 'Rule Britannia? History painting in eighteenth-century Britain', *History Today*, 45 (1995), pp. 12–18.

100. Ann Uhry Adams, *The Valiant Hero: Benjamin West and grand-style history painting* (Smithsonian Institution Press, Washington DC, 1985).

101. Bruce P. Lenman, *The Jacobite Clans of the Great Glen 1650–1784* (Scottish Cultural Press, Aberdeen, pbk edn, 1995), pp. 179–93.

102. Murray to Townshend, 5 November 1774, cited in Stacey, *Quebec*, pp. 175–76.

103. Wonderfully demonstrated in Francis P. Jennings, 'A Vanishing Indian: Francis Parkman versus his sources', *Pennsylvania Magazine of History and Biography*, 87 (1963), pp. 306–23.

104. Francis Parkman's original seven volumes on the Anglo–French confrontation are conveniently condensed into two in *France and England in North America* (The Library of America, New York, 1983). The quote is in Vol. 2, p. 1477.

105. Apart from Middleton, *Bells of Victory*; Marie Peters, 'The Myth of William Pitt, Earl of Chatham, Great Imperialist. Part I: Pitt and imperial expansion 1738–1763', *Journal of Imperial and Commonwealth History*, 21 (1993), pp. 31–74, is a realistic assessment.

PART TWO

The Struggle for Control of Imperial Futures and the Final Fissuring of the Englishry 1760–1783

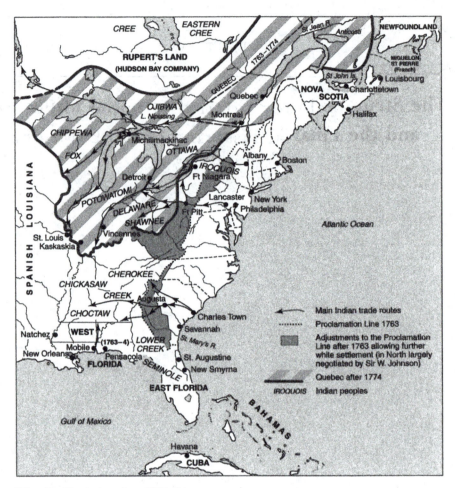

Map 7 North America, 1763–74

CHAPTER FIVE

'To the victor the spoils' – but which victors after 1760?

The question of ending the war which had begun on the Monongahela in 1754 had been prominent in informed circles as early as 1759–60, when the first serious bout of tentative negotiation had taken place between French and British representatives. In the course of these unsuccessful discussions, William Pitt had at least sketched the parameters of what he thought desirable. It was, by later standards, restrained. He had already resisted pressure to commit himself necessarily to the retention of Louisbourg. In the negotiations, he did not insist on the retention of either Louisbourg or Quebec and the core of New France. Rather did he insist on a defensible northern boundary for the British colonies, one which by including the forts at Niagara and Crown Point would close the sally ports of Canada, establish the Anglo–French frontier on the Great Lakes, and thereby put an end to any French pretensions in the Ohio valley. That would still have left a viable French Canada with a huge fur-bearing hinterland out west and between the northern settlements on the St Lawrence and the trading territories of the Hudson's Bay Company in the regions draining into Hudson's Bay. Pitt was probably still more interested in trade than in territory for its own sake. Beyond North America, he accepted that it would be politically necessary to insist on the return of the western Mediterranean naval base of Minorca, if only because its loss had been one of the events which had generated the sense of crisis that had enabled him to achieve major office and control of the war effort. Though he was interested in some Caribbean island conquests, he was not particularly concerned about Guadeloupe, which was eventually to loom large in the debates on the final peace terms. Interestingly, he was much more concerned at this stage to retain the West African forts and trading posts of Senegal and Goree, to which his attention had first been drawn by the Quaker London merchant Thomas Cumming, late of New York. Pitt had taken a personal interest in the two expeditions in 1758 that had captured these trading complexes, which were so situated as to give control of the trade in gum senega, used in large quantities in the manufacture of some silk and linen fabrics, and which also sustained a less important but lucrative trade in slaves.[1] About India, Pitt was at this stage silent. His view that there must be substantial returns of conquests as well as big gains seems to have commanded the support of most of his cabinet colleagues.

It was a different story after the successful campaigns of 1760 had confirmed sweeping victories. Bilateral negotiations in the spring of 1761 saw Pitt demand both the secession of all Canada and the exclusion of the French from the Newfoundland cod fisheries. His intransigence was almost certainly partly motivated and exaggerated by a sense of insecurity following the accession to the throne of the young George III, and the rise to office and influence of the young monarch's personal friend and mentor, the Scots Earl of Bute. In any case, the position of a war minister usually deteriorated when peace negotiations became a central part of the political agenda. By the summer of 1761 not only was a second bout of Anglo–French negotiation in progress, but also the British government was split over how hard it should press its undoubtedly strong hand. The new king and Bute, who as groom of the stole held only a court appointment but wielded great influence, were known to be anxious to end the war. Colleagues of Pitt, like the Duke of Bedford, were developing a far-reaching critique of what they saw as the dangerous implications of Pitt's hard line. Bedford believed that the terms offered by the French in 1761 were almost too good to be true. He did not grasp they were designed to ditch strategic liabilities in a war of revenge. Bedford also warned Pitt that if he were to be seen reaching out to destroy France as a naval power, leaving Britain totally ascendant at sea, he would trigger a violent reaction on the part of all the other European powers.[2]

In many ways, the French position in 1761 was far more devious than it seemed on the surface. That the duc de Choiseul, the principal French minister, was ready in 1761 to surrender all of New France should have given British ministers occasion for thought, the more so as Choiseul was as inflexible about refusing to accept French exclusion from the Newfoundland fisheries as he was flexible on New France. The fisheries were nurseries of seamen, and did make a vital marginal difference to the naval potential of France. Combined with the not very secret renewal of the Bourbon Family Compact with a Spain which had her own quarrel with Britain over the Newfoundland fisheries, and a new French insistence that the peace settlement had to include a settlement of Anglo–Spanish differences (an idea unanimously repudiated by British ministers), the outlines of a scheme for a French empire of trade rather than territory in the Americas – coupled to a naval war of revenge, free of the strategic handicap of New France – was emerging. Spain was an early example of the European backlash Bedford feared, for its real motive for moving closer to France was alarm at the threat to its American empire posed by the overwhelming nature of the British triumph in North America. Choiseul, who raised cynicism to an art form, intended to suck Spain into the war partly for the sake of Spanish assistance in the new round of campaigns which would follow the breakdown of the current round of negotiations, and partly in the hope that if the war was still lost, he could pay for French failures with Spanish assets.

The French navy was simply outclassed by its British counterpart. There had always been tremendous problems for the French Crown in raising the funds necessary seriously to challenge the Royal Navy. It had been a platitude for years in French naval circles that the flourishing maritime commerce of Britain generated revenues which enabled that state to support its naval preponderance. The comte de Maurepas, who had been dismissed as secretary of state for the navy in 1749, had been the recipient of numerous memoranda to the effect that a more powerful navy was a precondition for the flourishing of French overseas commerce, all the more so as the commerce of the Spanish dominions was of vast significance to France. This meant that the French navy needed to be able also to defend access to it[3] but, given the competition for limited royal funds from the French army, with its European commitment, one of Maurepas' correspondents argued that naval expansion could only be funded by the broadening of the tax base to include new taxes aimed not at the already burdened poor, but at the more prosperous classes in French society – many of whom (and not just the nobility) had exemptions from direct taxes.[4] Politically, this was not practical. After the naval battles of 1759 had destroyed the best part of half of the French navy and exposed French overseas commerce to serious interruption, it became clear that shortage of funds precluded swift repair or replacement of warships. The already old suggestion that maritime commerce should fund naval expansion through a system of levies was also impractical.[5] There had always been an underlying pessimism among even resolute defenders of French overseas interests, like one of Maurepas' successors, the able Jean-Baptiste de Machault. He expected the British to dismantle the French overseas possessions, so he deemed provocative French moves in India undesirable, and just hoped that European conquests could be used as bargaining counters by France to restore the colonial position in any peace negotiation.[6] Choiseul's hopes of successful Franco–Spanish cooperation did not survive the failure of an attempt to relieve a beleaguered Martinique in 1762 and, despite fiscal reforms which re-established its credit, the French navy had proved incapable of much more than pinpricks by the time Choiseul was driven to the negotiating table in November 1762. By then Pitt's paranoid anti-Bourbonism and demands for a pre-emptive strike on Spain before she formally entered the war had proved too much for colleagues bent on peace, and he had been forced out of office in October 1761.

It hardly mattered. For structural reasons the two Bourbon monarchies were in poor shape to try to turn the tide of fortune in the naval and colonial war. Without Pitt in office, the British government continued to show immense vitality and aggression. War was finally declared on Spain on 4 January 1762, and two days later George III was expressing his satisfaction to Lord Bute, by then secretary of state for the Northern Department, that the cabinet had agreed to launch expeditions against Louisiana and two Spanish targets: Havana, capital of Cuba, and Manila, the great port city and emporium for the China trade in the Philippines.[7] The capture of Havana was an astonishing feat of arms. Probably, the framework of the campaign was the product of Admiral Anson's mind, with technical help on the military side from his equally distinguished opposite number Field Marshal Ligonier, but fortune favoured the brave, for the fort commanding the entrance to Havana harbour, known as El Morro, was considered by the Spaniards to be the strongest in America. Nor was the crucial preliminary memorandum by Lieutenant Colonel Patrick Mackellar, the British chief engineer for the campaign, at all clear about the construction of the defences of Havana, the nature of the soil which the British engineers would have to work with, or even the exact number of forts.[8] The siege was an outstanding example of the way the credit of the British government could still finance major initiatives at the end of a long war in a way the French could not match, but it was also a race against bad weather and the disease which struck British regulars and American provincial units alike. Though the latter complained about the usual very unfair distribution of the fabulous prize money of over £737,000 – much of which went to the three members of the Keppel family who were respectively the land commander, his second in command, and a major general – the capture of Havana, and indeed of Manila in due course, placed formidable bargaining counters in British hands. To recover Havana, lynchpin of its Caribbean naval system, Spain had to cede at the peace the whole of mainland Florida, evacuating its colonists.

Though each new British victory made a moderate peace more difficult of attainment, there had been awareness at the highest levels of government in Britain that the choices facing even a triumphant Britain were not straightforward. Some influential voices consulted by the ministry were simplistic in their views. Thus Alderman Sir William Baker, a City magnate with lucrative and extensive involvement in the trade with colonial British North

America, not to mention American partners, was emphatic that the war had been fought to give security to the colonies, and that the only sure guarantee of that desirable end was the taking of all New France, preferably with an exclusive British control of the Newfoundland fisheries as well. He regarded the sugar island of Guadeloupe as expendable. That was roughly the position adopted by Pitt, though he added to the list of demands Senegal, Goree, and Minorca. Lord Chesterfield was of a similar mind. The ardently francophile Duke of Bedford was at the opposite extreme, at one point as unrealistic as Pitt in his own way when he deprecated virtually any territorial gains, but perceptive in his awareness that the elimination of French power in what was to be Canada would alter in a very dangerous way the balance of power between Westminster and the provincial governments in British North America. The Earl of Morton advised Lord North and Lord Chancellor Hardwicke in 1760 that there was much to be said simply for a frontier of maximum military security which would push back New France to the northern side of the Great Lakes and cut decisively its direct links with Louisiana. He feared that if the French were to be driven out of the north entirely they might concentrate their power in the south, making Louisiana a dangerous threat to the southern British colonies.[9] Morton preferred a divided, weakened French North America, or the total elimination of the French from north and south. He was remarkably shrewd, considering that the southern Anglo–French frontier had never, though at times by a very narrow margin, become a seat of war between the European powers.

The French advanced post, Fort Toulouse, established in 1717 at the junction of the Coosa and Tallapoosa rivers at the head of the Alabama River complex, had always been prominent in an endless Anglo–French cold war, in which the main prize was the alliance or at least the neutrality of the nearby Indian peoples. James Adair, who published a *History of the American Indians* in London in 1775, referred to Fort Toulouse as 'the dangerous Alebahma garrison'. Until the later 1750s there is no doubt that this military–diplomatic post more than held its own against British Georgia and the traders out of Charles Town. The latter had thoroughly penetrated the Creek villages, but the French managed to keep seven villages of Alabama Indians to the west of Fort Toulouse firmly within their sphere of influence until the shortage of trade goods due to British naval superiority in American waters undermined the French position from 1759. By late 1762 Choiseul was clear that Louisiana had been yet another net drain on the resources of the French Crown and he had decided to hand it over to the Spain he had so cynically used, as a sweetener.[10] East of the Mississippi, French territorial claims went to Britain, whose subjects also had to have a guarantee of freedom of navigation on the Mississippi to make these lands a viable economic prospect. However, from the French point of view ceding what was left of Louisiana to Spain made sense, for Spanish good will had to be somehow preserved to keep the option of a Bourbon alliance against the British in the war of revenge. For the unconquered and very French colonists of Louisiana, the cession of their territory to Spain by the Treaty of Fontainebleau was simply unbelievable. Given the relentless propaganda pumped out by both church and state about the unbreakable, sacramental bonds of fatherly concern, honour and religion binding the Most Christian King to such loyal subjects, confusion was understandable, and the bloodless rising by which the colonists saw off their first Spanish governor, the scholarly and amiable but ineffective Antonio de Ulloa, in 1768 was partly inspired by hope of countenance from Louis XV or the nearby British in Pensacola. The French government never flinched in its resolve to be rid of a fiscal liability. Apart from the secretary of the treasury, the Spanish government was equally determined to reassert authority over what it regarded as a vital outer bastion for Mexico. A strong expedition was swiftly despatched under another adventurer from County Meath, Alexander O'Reilly, who, unlike Admiral Peter Warren, had gone to work for a Catholic monarchy and had risen to inspector general of the Spanish army. Decisive and utterly ruthless, if not in the longer run a successful field commander, O'Reilly occupied the colony, tried the ringleaders of the rebellion, and put five prominent colonists to death by firing squad. Spain was clear that it needed to demonstrate its will to rule and that the danger of alienating the colonists was of no consequence compared with the danger of allowing them to think they might get away with a similar ploy in the future. Louisiana did indeed become, under firm Spanish rule, something of the menace to the south-western British colonies Morton had feared. In practice his preference for a weakened French presence, as he himself acknowledged, proved impractical as the British government took the fatally popular decision to fall into every trap Choiseul set for it. Choiseul believed there was a real possibility the British North American colonies would break into rebellion after 1763. Most informed outsiders shared his view. The Spanish ambassador, in discussions in London with that irascible Ulsterman Secretary of State Lord Hillsborough made it clear that Spain meant to enforce her authority in Louisiana. He told Hillsborough to his face that the French colonists had drawn bad lessons from the subversive behaviour of the British American colonists and that 'the citizens of New Orleans had anticipated what the English colonies were ready to undertake'. It was a fair comment.[11]

Though the future importance of the United States was to ensure that the late colonial history of British North America has been studied as an end in itself by generations of historians trying to excavate the pre-history of modern American identity, in the 1760s it has to be seen in the broader global context of the British monarchy to which the American colonies were attached, albeit very loosely in the majority of cases. In that context what becomes clear is that even before the war ended in 1763 there were severe struggles going on for the control of the vast gains of the war, and that these were primarily between elements within the British world, or closely allied to it. The conquest of Manila in 1762, for example, was mired in argument before it even happened. It was bound to be, because the elements of the small but effective force that achieved a surprise victory over a Spanish administration in the Philippines which was not aware of the outbreak of war until under attack – and which was being run, due to the death of the regular governor, by the unwarlike Archbishop Manuel Antonio Rojo – was a composite one. It was drawn not only from regular army units and the Royal Navy East India squadron, but also from the military forces of the EIC, from whose Madras base the expedition was mounted. The fortress city of Manila was in bad shape to resist an assault. Fields of fire were obscured by solid buildings which offered cover to assaulting troops and batteries, and the stone ramparts generated lethal splinters when under fire to the point of making gun positions on them untenable.[12] Though the British occupation of 1762–64 was constricted by guerrilla warfare in the hinterland of the city, the seizure of Manila by forces too small to mount a regular siege was remarkable; a tribute to navy–army cooperation in supplies, landings, and fire support; and an intrepid performance bearing in mind that good contemporary charts of the approach to the island of Luzon, on whose south-west coast Manila was situated, were not available and the British forces were operating on experience and seamanship rather than detailed knowledge much of the time.[13] It will not, however, do to see the squabbles which surrounded the conquest merely as evidence that the EIC was 'corrupt' and 'unreformed', for both descriptions fit the Westminster government just as well.

There were serious issues at stake. The EIC was unhappy about the expedition, on several grounds. It threatened to withdraw vitally necessary resources from the EIC's military and commercial operations at a time when both were under acute pressure. Though there was interest in EIC circles in establishing a trading post in the Philippines, everyone knew that Manila could not possibly be retained at a peace settlement. Alexander Dalrymple of the Madras presidency of the EIC, who ended up provisional governor of British-occupied Manila, had hopes of establishing an EIC post at Balambangan in Sulu, perhaps not far enough away from Manila to rival the large illegal trade which the British had long conducted with the Spanish colonists, a trade that yielded important amounts of the Mexican silver with which the Spanish Crown had to subsidise its loss-making colony in the Philippines. The expedition really served no useful purpose except, as its commanders told the Manila authorities when they appeared before the place in September 1762, to show the Spaniards that even their most remote dominions were not safe from the power of the forces of George III, nor from the reach of his just resentment.[14] On the other hand, the EIC held that the Crown should not establish direct rule within the area covered by its own chartered monopoly of British dealings with Asia. The Crown argued it could legally take and hold territory from European enemies in Asia (which rather conceded the point that it could not take and hold from Asians), but avoided legal squabbling by saying it would transfer any conquest *ex gratia* to the EIC. So the only thing truly worth arguing about was the distribution of any loot. Predictably the EIC thought it had an agreement for an even split with Crown forces, but the commanders of those forces, who believed the EIC had cheated them over distribution of French loot in India, reneged on that understanding and insisted on two-thirds for themselves.[15] Add to this the lack of enthusiasm of EIC officers for pressure to collect the absurdly inflated ransom of four million Spanish dollars which the greed of Vice Admiral Sir Samuel Cornish made him impose on Manila, and you had the makings of endless rows between Westminster, the EIC, and the Spaniards – rows that went on for years after the British, with no little physical difficulty due to lack of shipping and shipping mishaps, managed to evacuate Manila in 1764. All this was deep rooted in the very structure of the polycentric British monarchy. It was no accident.

Whether one looks at Asia or America, the pattern is the same: the fight to control the future share-out of power, assets, and prospects started before the war had finished. The Cherokee Indian peoples, for example, had more or less inclined to the British rather than the French side in the fluid diplomacy of the earlier eighteenth century. They had fought in expeditions against Spanish Florida, some of them had fought on the British side in the Tuscarora War, and in the desperate days of 1715–16 – when it had seemed that if the Yamassee Indians could widen their alliances, they might just be able to wipe out the struggling colony of South Carolina – the news that the Cherokee had moved against Creek emissaries trying to coordinate a wider Indian rising had been greeted in Charles Town as a crucial breakthrough for the colony. The Creeks were deeply tied into the British Indian trade. Access to the Creek townships was aggressively contested between Virginia and South Carolina traders, though conditions after the Yamassee War gave the Carolinians a clear edge. Between 1743 and 1756 the long reign of Governor James Glen saw an intensification of Carolinian expansionism; attempts to mediate Creek–Cherokee conflicts which were ill received by the Cherokee; a conference with them at Saluda in 1755 which saw some very ambiguous rhetoric capable in the minds of some colonial officials of being twisted into a Cherokee cession of all their land, rather than the gesture of politeness intended; and fort-building in the west in the shape of Fort Keowee in 1753 and an agreement to begin building Fort Loudon in 1756. The Cherokee population was falling. They were hit by a terrible smallpox epidemic in 1739, and there were perhaps only eight thousand Cherokee by the 1750s. Meantime fresh streams of white settlers were pressing down from the north, many from Pennsylvania. There was a substantial German element in the immigration. The newcomers had an important economic niche to fill in the hitherto plantation-dominated economy of South Carolina, for they grew and milled food grains in large quantities. Incidents of violence between traders and settlers and the Cherokee led Governor William Henry Lyttelton, Glen's ambitious successor, to try to assert paramountcy in the debated territories by invading them with a colonial army of 1200 fighting men plus slaves, camp followers, and wagon drivers in 1759. The expedition failed because it was unable to find appropriate targets and, with poetic justice, it was struck by smallpox, but it did mark the parting of the ways with old allies, for its aims were disingenuously touted as being 'to repel the invasion of and humble the Cherokee'.[16]

It may be doubted whether the Westminster government displayed much judgement in responding to furious colonial lobbying and despatching 1300 regular troops, including 400 Highlanders, with Colonel Archibald Montgomery in command, from the victorious northern war front to assist the South Carolinians in 1760. There can have been few causes which Montgomery and his Highlanders had less need to die for than that of the greed of the colonists. Typically, the best modern American historian of the ineptly named Cherokee Wars (which were truly settler wars), though meticulous about Indian tribal groups, does not seem to be able to distinguish between English and Scots nationalities, let alone use the term 'British' where appropriate. Gratitude was never a very strong colonial trait, and Montgomery's performance did not encourage it. The British army had, in fact, developed its techniques for wilderness fighting to an impressive degree, not just by aggressive patrolling using light infantry units, but also by modifying the accoutrements and tactics of the line infantry so that they were trained to fight from behind tree cover and even to aim at individual opponents. Montgomery did inflict considerable damage on Cherokee villages and crops, but as he entered the mountainous core of Cherokee Appalachia, despite the presence of colonial Ranger units and his own experience in Canada, he was caught at a disadvantage in a narrow pass. Making use of rifled weapons which outranged British muskets, the Indians inflicted significant casualties before the punitive column fought itself clear. Finding that he had only enough pack horses to carry either supplies or his wounded, but not both, Montgomery sensibly retreated, thereby boosting Cherokee morale.[17]

More frantic lobbying by the South Carolinians for additional military effort by the Crown was assisted by the success of the Cherokee in forcing the garrison of Fort Loudon to surrender because of exhaustion of their food supplies in August 1760. The garrison, a mixture of regular and provincial troops, was offered safe conduct, but suffered the same fate as the garrison of Fort William Henry after their surrender to a Franco–Indian army in 1757. The latter has been much the best remembered of a whole series of similar episodes which demonstrated that, whatever their commander agreed to, Indians regarded captives and scalps as an essential part of victory. In the Fort Loudon case, it was not the twisting of the event to support convenient myths, such as the ineradicable savagery of Indians, to support subsequent policies of Indian removal,[18] so much as the immediate response of the C-in-C North America, General Amherst, which mattered. To redeem the dishonour of the first formal surrender of British regulars to Indians, he sent Major James Grant with a substantial force of Highland troops which were then reinforced by provincial Rangers, and numerous allied Indians such as Mohawks, Chickasaws, and Catawbas – the last named being like so many Indian 'nations' a polyglot collection of fragments of peoples devastated by disease and war which had coalesced round a strategy of accommodation with more numerous surrounding white settlers. Grant was aware that the isolated Cherokee wanted peace. He also shared the views of James Adair, subsequently bluntly stated as 'we forced the Cherrake to become our bitter enemies, by a long train of wrong measures'.[19] Grant, a Scot who later became Governor Grant of East Florida, thought the settlers were the real villains of the piece. Adair believed that the Cherokee failed to hold Grant off almost entirely because of a crucial shortage of ammunition, but the upshot was that in under five weeks Grant brought the war to an end by destroying 15 townships and some 1400 acres of Cherokee cornfields. However, the appointment of John Stuart, the sole officer survivor of the Fort Loudon killings, as superintendent of Indian Affairs for the southern district of North America in 1762 offered hope to the Cherokee of some attempt to hold a balance between conflicting allies and subjects of the Crown.

One of the few influences inclining the colonial governments to behave with moderation and decency in dealing with Indian peoples was the cost of war with them. Lieutenant Governor William Bull plaintively listed, for the benefit of William Pitt in 1760, the expenses which confrontation with the Cherokee had already laid upon South Carolina. Like other provinces of British North America, South Carolina did not rely on the antiquated militia system for its striking forces but raised paid units for frontier service. Early in the wars it had raised a force of 525 Rangers whose pay rapidly rose from £15 to £20 a month. Bounties for Cherokee scalps offered by the colonial government went up even more dramatically in a short time, from £25 to £100. By August 1760 the South Carolina legislature passed an Act authorising the raising of an infantry regiment of 1000 men, 'the pay to privates Seven shillings and Six pence per day, and Five Pounds to the Officer for each Man enlisted'. The reason why men were so costly was that they were hard to recruit. Bull complained to Pitt that the regiment was in fact at half strength, and 'many of these raised in North Carolina'.[20] Semi-professional armies were what many colonial governments raised to fight the French or the Indians, so they acquired the same techniques as the Westminster government for raising troops, moderated only by the com-pulsive parsimony of their constituents. Regular British forces tended to compensate for the latter factor, tipping the military balance in the direc-tion of the colonials, as the Indian peoples rapidly spotted in the aftermath of French defeat in 1760. This seismic event deeply worried all Indian peoples on the frontiers of white settlement.

The argument that French Indian policy was more favourable to the Indians than British policy has a history which can be traced to British officials like Edmond Atkin, the Charles Town merchant who was appointed the first superintendent of the southern Indians in 1756. Between 1750 and 1754 he had been in London, where he wrote two important papers. One was a history of the bloody revolt of a section of the Choctaw nation against their long-standing relationship with French Louisiana, a revolt which led to a Choctaw civil war and in which the Choctaws – supporting a move towards a closer relationship with the British – first were encouraged by colonial authorities like Governor James Glen of South Carolina and then left in the lurch. In a second paper, which was submitted to the Board of Trade, Atkin lavishly praised French methods of Indian control as a way of advocating a similar British scheme which was to be entirely under the control of the imperial authorities and which would offer the Indians a controlled and fair trade at reasonable prices based on a network of forts – where the demon rum would not be allowed to dominate the proceedings, with all the baneful consequences which usually followed for the Indians.[21] Now Atkin, rhetorical strategy apart, clearly knew how ruthless the French could be with rebellious satellites like the Choctaw, let alone with declared enemies like the Chickasaw. In what is now central Wisconsin the Fox or Mesquakie Indians – who had resisted the expansion of the French fur trade and the intellectual and military empire of New France which always followed the fur traders – had experienced the full depths of treachery and genocide from Charles de Beauharnois, governor general of New France. He offered the Fox insincere peace as a cover for unleashing a war of annihilation in which the Indians, male and female, fought with extra-ordinary courage – especially in the climacteric battle and siege of a Fox fort on the Illinois Grande Prairie in 1730. Courage availed them little. After the inevitable massacre the surviving Foxes had to seek refuge with the Sac Indians.[22]

Nevertheless, especially among the northern Indian peoples who had not directly opposed major French policy objectives, there was a clear perception that the French had been far more generous patrons of their Indian associates than the newly ascendant British. Sir William Johnson was told by one informant in May 1763 that 'An Indian King named Nobaumigate had recently complained that the French had been far more reliable sources of firearms, gunpowder, and hard liquor than their successors, the British.'[23] Indian complaints ran much deeper than that. Apart from the appalled realisation that the diplomatic game of balancing between rival European powers was now gone for ever, Indians had specific grievances, starting with the continuing occupation by the British of old forts deep in Indian country, many formerly French, when the general Indian understanding had been that these positions would be evacuated at the end of the war. In that same month of May 1763 an Onondaga speaker, bearing three strings of wampum to convey the seriousness of his message, had formally complained to Johnson on behalf of the Six Nations of the Iroquois that not only were posts which the British military had told them would be maintained only temporarily to secure the peace still being occupied, but also that there were developments round them which were frightening. That traders there were cheating Indians after plying them with alcohol was hardly surprising. Despite the complaints of clerical moralists, brandy had been as pervasive a part of the French fur trade as rum had been and was of the British. General Sir Jeffrey Amherst had tried hard to ban the rum trade during the war, less out of sympathy with the Indians than from a desire to make them less feckless and therefore less of a charge on the accounts of the Westminster government. Some British officers, like Major Robert Rogers, former commander at the post at Michilmackinac between Lakes Huron and Michigan, argued that the rum trade was essential. Others pointed out that the southern Indians could and did obtain rum from the Spaniards anyway. Johnson was against the trade in theory, but ambiguous in practice. In fact there was no consensus, least of all at the level of those serving the Westminster government. Despite dissenting voices, there was a clear colonial consensus: they had spent a long time exploiting the Indians and they were not going to change now.[24] What really alarmed the Iroquois was the clearing of large fields around the British posts and the unmistakable signs of large-scale white immigration.[25]

It was not the Iroquois who led the most effective Indian response to the crisis, though the most French-influenced of them, the Senecas, participated. Indeed, despite the dramatic over-simplifications of the nineteenth-century

American historian Francis Parkman, it would appear that nobody 'led' the rising in the sense more or less required by the European 'great man' theory of history. In 1763 Indian peoples in the central region south of the Great Lakes, from the Senecas as far west as the Illinois, and from the Chippewas in the north to the Delawares in the south, rose to attack the British garrisons in their lands, capturing all of them except Forts Niagara, Detroit, and Pitt. General Amherst had contributed mightily to the creation of the loose confederation of peoples who rose. He was mean minded about the system of official gifts which the Indians regarded as the essential cement of any relationship with Europeans, and he deliberately tried to keep the Indians short of vital powder and shot. He was also rampantly racist, unlike many other servants of the Crown, who tended to be much less so than the average American colonist, and he made a bad job of concealing his contempt for the native American peoples. He wanted no help from friendly Indians at the crisis of the rising, describing the Christianised Mohicans of the missionary township of Stockbridge as 'a Worthless Tribe', and saying that all he wanted from the Canadian Indians was that they should 'Remain Quiet'.[26] He was openly genocidal in his response to what he saw as 'the Folly and Ingratitude of those who had Commenced Hostilities against us'. Extirpation was his preferred solution, if necessary assisted by conscious attempts to infect his Indian enemies with the smallpox which had broken out in Fort Pitt. Fortunately, he was no more capable of extirpation than the Indians were, due to lack of artillery, of capturing a fort they could neither surprise nor starve out.[27] The Indians' own ideal solution, which had been articulated by a series of religious prophets calling for a sharp breach with corrosive European influences and a return to a steadfast nativism, underlined by resolute opposition to any further British expansion, proved equally impractical.[28] It was a viewpoint publicly endorsed by the best-known Indian leader, the Ottawa chief Pontiac. He was influenced by the Delaware prophet Neolin who, like many other contemporary Indian seers, took elements of Christianity and blended them with native beliefs to create an 'Indian path' distinct from that of the whites. By implication this was a creed which might inspire a widespread Indian attempt to block white expansion west of the Appalachians, and Neolin did talk about negotiations followed by war.

War proved the correct option. It was not even necessary for the Indians to win it, though they could not afford to lose. Amherst's recall in November 1763, with his policies condemned by his London superiors, was a major Indian victory. Thereafter the war became a military stalemate. Pontiac's own protracted siege of Detroit failed and, in relieving Fort Pitt, which it was feared might be starved out, Colonel Henry Bouquet won on 5–6 August 1763 in the upper Ohio valley the only big field action of the war at Bushy Run. His force included light infantry from two Highland units, the 42nd and the 77th Foot, but how the battle was fought in detail remains obscure. Bouquet was conscious of the need to avoid sudden ambush. Once the hostile Indians were engaged, tree cover and the slow rate of fire of muskets made it possible to drive them back with a combination of musketry and short bayonet charges, but since they could retreat indefinitely, Bouquet only won on the second day by luring his opponents into an attack on an apparently fleeing British line, which then caught the Indians in a pre-arranged British ambush. Amherst's successor, General Sir Thomas Gage, was much more interested in conciliating than in conquering the Indians, with the help of advice from William Johnson. As serious negotiations were mounted from 1764, Johnson was emphatic that the very concept of making the Indians truly subject to the Crown was dangerous, and offensive to fiercely independent peoples. By 1765 the British were trying to build up Pontiac, hitherto primarily a war leader, into a great mediating chief with whom they could negotiate a settlement, but the Indians remained divided. Ironically, a murderous attack by a war party from the Wabash Indian villages on a British party led by the Irish trader George Croghan proved decisive, for it killed three Shawnee chiefs in Croghan's party and faced Indian militants with the certainty of revenge attacks by the Shawnee, Illinois, and Delawares, with British backing. War was certain to be unprofitable if it continued, so in 1765-66 a very reasonable settlement was reached in which the Indians acknowledged the British right to the old French posts, but the British tacitly accepted the need to try to uphold the territorial situation which obtained at the outbreak of hostilities. Pontiac, who had come to believe in the British image of himself, was assassinated in 1769 by one of the Algonquin Indians who had been the backbone of the rising, but who would never accept the highly manipulative British concept of chieftainship. Between 1763 and 1766 a protracted negotiation by force had sorted out, quite sensibly, some of the problems between the elements competing for the ambiguous heritage of British victory over New France.[29]

The Peace of Paris of 1763 had left the British global community with a dangerous plethora of apparently lucrative prospects, and no political structure capable of securing an agreed order at the various troughs. Elites in the American colonies had long been dominated by an entrepreneurial outlook which combined physical with market force to create opportunities for spectacular self-enrichment, but after the massive deployment of metropolitan forces and finances by the Westminster government in the recent war, many figures in metropolitan elite circles had the knowledge and the desire to share in the game, especially with reference to the recently acquired territories. As was ever the case, from the Elizabethan court culture up to the very different metropolitan public space of later eighteenth-century Britain, it tended to be the marginal figures who were hungriest and most unscrupulous, precisely because they needed quick gains to propel themselves securely into the privileged, propertied social and political elite. Hungry North Britons featured prominently in this category, and of these as good an example as any is furnished by the case of David Wedderburn, a brother of Alexander Wedderburn – himself an extreme case of the *arriviste* Scot at Westminster, though one who arrived and stuck in higher places than most. Alexander had opposed Lord North's regime as late as 1770, with the classic aim of being bought off with office, which he was in 1771, when he became solicitor general. In 1778 he became attorney general and then in 1780, by brazenly exploiting the desperately weak position of a government battered by adversity, he secured the position of chief justice of Common Pleas, which he coveted because he could not, once in it, be fired. He was to become lord chancellor in 1793 before retiring in 1801 as Baron Loughborough and Earl of Rosslyn. By any standards he was one of the most successful political whores of his time and his considerable talents and silver tongue had often enough given real satisfaction to those who hired them.

His brother David Wedderburn was a career soldier who stayed on the Army List until 1773, when he went on half-pay and died soon afterwards. In June 1764 he wrote to Alexander to signal his arrival in Antigua as lieutenant colonel in command of a regiment of troop replacements for the West Indian garrisons. Like his brother, he was professionally very sharp. His comments on the inadequacy of a standard 74-gun ship of the line with its lower tier of guns removed 'to contain a Regiment with the Women allowed' were shrewd, as well as a reminder that considerable numbers of women were a feature of even the acknowledged establishment of an eighteenth-century British regiment. Wedderburn had, in fact, lost only two men on his crossing, but he had no intention of remaining in the Leewards. He had started to network politically as soon as he landed and his aim was to get to New York to attach himself to the centre of military patronage in the 'family' of the C-in-C North America, General Gage, at the first opportunity.[30] He did indeed seize the first chance to sail for North America in the gap between the end of the hurricane season and the period before the prevailing north-west winds set in on the North American coasts, rejecting an option to stay for a period in Martinique on the typical grounds that it might be 'attended with much expence, and probably with little profit'. Profit was to be sought on a global frame of reference. David Wedderburn took his passage to New York in company with a Captain Pitman 'who had been in the East Indies, in Africa, in N. America, in France and in Flanders'. Having reached Antigua 'from a tour round the French and our new Islands. He had some business in New York.' Wedderburn was delighted at the respect accorded to his rank in the West Indies, adding that he would now 'never be able to endure being quartered in Great Britain, or submit, to the intolerable, and insolent familiarity, of your English men of fortune'. Though he meant to base himself in New York with Gage, he was intending to go to Pensacola at the first opportunity in the spring, meanwhile begging his brother Alexander to obtain for him a grant of lands in one of the two provinces into which the British government had divided Florida. Of his prospective lands he said he might 'on the spot find some means of turning them to advantage, if not it is only forfeiting the grant'. In other words, it was the classic 'venture' capitalist no-loss gamble of using political clout to secure public assets for very little or nothing with only the obligation to settle and develop them. But then development was the necessary step towards huge capital gains. Wedderburn was clearly too smart to sink his own money or credit into the development process. Other people were to make him rich.[31]

David Wedderburn was a fortune hunter in every sense of the word, even to the point of scouting round every foot of a 13-year-old heiress's father's plantation, just in case this marginal woman might become an asset to the Wedderburns. However, he was soon frantic to get to Pensacola on hearing that Governor Johnson was to send a large force against the Illinois Indians, who had rebuffed a small one the year before. As the only lieutenant colonel in West Florida, Wedderburn had hopes of the command of the expedition and with it entry into the decision-taking elite in West Florida. He admitted he was gambling, but said he thought that his business was 'to risk a great deal, in hopes of a little; *tentanda via est si me quoque possim tollere humo*'. It was, as the Latin suggested, a case of trying everything, as long as he could take the strain, in the hope that one of his lines would lead to a big payoff. It was not the valour of the old Spanish Conquistadores that he primarily admired, but their fantastic profits or, as he put it so neatly: 'In the present Situation of my affairs it would be much more convenient for me to go upon the Conquest of Mexico, or Peru, than to go to reduce a parcel of Lousy, warlike Savages, but I cannot chuse, and I must therefore take what offers, to make the best of it.'[32]

David Wedderburn's ambitions were laced with a knowledge of the unpredictability of the game he was playing. He lobbied for a land grant in East Florida from Governor Grant, yet another part of the Scottish mafia in the Floridas, and was disappointed when it appeared to go astray in the mails. However, he had the consolation that another fellow countryman, Governor Johnson, had told him he would grant him any lands he wanted which had not yet been given away. Wedderburn had his eye on land 'on the east side of Mobile'. To reach this position he had been useful militarily to Johnson, not by commanding the expedition against the Illinois, which had in any case been scaled down, but by taking over the command of the troops in the colony from an officer Johnson was determined to court-martial for insubordination. Wedderburn showed no ethnic hostility to Indians in the sense that he deemed their sports, especially lacrosse, 'manly', and was extremely interested in the idea of leaving a pestilential Mobile for the country of the Choctaws, where he hoped to learn their language. He had met Choctaw and Chickasaw Indians at a great congress in Mobile designed to secure agreed territorial boundaries and did not hesitate to describe one of the chiefs as 'a very particular and intimate friend of mine'. Nor was he averse to social intercourse with the Indians, on the grounds that they were gentle in manner and that he could entertain fifty of their warriors with no trouble, which was more than he would expect of a similar number of warriors from any other nation. Wedderburn was greedy, but not racist. Had he stayed with the Choctaw as he thought he might, he would no doubt have contributed to the early stages of the evolution of that extraordinary Scoto–Indian mestizo class of chiefs who were the nearest the British ever came to the Spanish genetic heritage in the Americas. What he did increasingly appreciate was that there was not enough capital available for serious development in West Florida, and that the key to present gain was to open an (illegal) direct trade with the Spanish colonies.[33]

The chance of stabilising a situation with so many selfish rogues loose in it was not great, but the London government had every incentive to try because stability would reduce cost. The Seven Years' War had cost some £160 million, possibly as much as twice the gross national product of Great Britain in 1760. State debt for which Westminster was responsible had climbed by nearly £60 million during the war, leaving the notorious post-war burden of £141 million in funded liabilities, which ate up, at the rate of £5 million per annum, half Great Britain's annual peacetime revenue. In 1765 there was an army of 10,000 regular king's troops on the frontiers of British America, costing £360,000 each year. The propertied fiscal conservatives who dominated Westminster had set their faces against higher direct taxation, indeed had reduced it. Attempts to extract fiscal contributions from the American colonies like George Grenville's Stamp Act of 1765 provoked colonial embargoes on trade with Britain and hostile political mobilisation in America. It was repealed by the Rockingham Whigs in 1766, a gesture which showed that economic considerations merely compounded basic fiscal and political dilemmas. Even Grenville had not expected it to raise more than £100,000 a year, if it had run smoothly, which it never did.[34] Long before that crisis, the Crown had moved in the obvious direction of trying to separate the white settler tide from the still formidable western Indians. Superintendents Johnson and Stuart reckoned that in their respective Northern and Southern Departments there were 26,000 Indian fighting men, divided between 12,000 in the north and 14,000 in the south.

Major conflict with Indians was still in progress in 1763 when a Proclamation Line was announced as the basic future principle of frontier administration. It was not meant to be an impermeable barrier to settler expansion, but it was meant to control it. In 1764 more precise definition of the line by negotiation was launched with an Indian congress at Atlanta, and between then and 1773 by treaty and purchase a continuous line from Florida to Fort Stanwix (now Rome, New York) was created. Johnson had linked the two parts of the line by the Treaty of Fort Stanwix with 'his' Indians in 1768. Johnson was a crook and his settlement was not approved by the British government because of its outrageous concessions to colonial land speculators, of which he was one. In particular, he handed to cronies the Wyoming valley between the Forks of the Susquehanna River, despite the fact that it had been promised to the Delaware Indians by negotiated agreements made at Easton in the later 1750s.[35]

In the Southern Indian Department, especially after the appointment of John Stuart, the son of an Inverness merchant of Jacobite sympathies, to the superintendency in 1762, there was more and more solidly based trust between the Indian peoples and the Crown's officers. Stuart and the commissaries who were his deputies sent to live with the Indians were well aware that it was the threat to their lands which above all disturbed the tribes. They gained Indian support by stressing their genuine anxiety to control abuses by traders and seizure of land by unscrupulous settlers. Stuart's policy of supporting designated and decorated 'medal chiefs' in specific tribes as mediators and instruments of Crown control – much as the French had before him – could breed resentment and turmoil. There was civil war among both the Chickasaws and the Choctaws in the 1760s. Nevertheless, Stuart did establish in the long run good relations with both, which in the case of the traditionally anti-British Choctaws was no mean achievement, as was Stuart's building of a bond of trust with the Cherokees. They, wisely, refused to cooperate with the South Carolinians in defining the Proclamation Line more precisely in 1765 until Stuart was at hand to check the utterly predictable colonial attempt to cheat on the broad terms of the previous agreement made in 1763.[36] Valuable to the Crown as the fund of Indian good will which Stuart was building up was, his policy of control was undermined by the fiscal problems which had first moved the Crown towards conciliation on the frontier. In the north, Iroquois spokesmen were complaining bitterly in 1766 about the 'unhappy situation' their brethren were being placed in 'owing to the White People using every low and unfair method to deprive them of their Lands, and even of their Habitations and Planting Grounds',[37] at just the time the metropolitan British authorities were deciding that they might as well cut costs and give up a thankless task by abandoning most of the western posts and surrendering control of the

Indian trade to the individual colonies. It was a recipe for chaos, as many saw. Sir William Johnson may have regretted lost opportunities for graft as he deprecated the move, but his views were shared by well-informed colonial observers such as William Franklin – illegitimate son of the great panjandrum Ben and royal governor of New Jersey from 1762, who thought the abandonment of the posts dangerously destabilising[38] – and Cadwallader Colden, who shrewdly remarked in 1769 that in trying to cut and run from a political and military burden in the west the ruling ministry in Great Britain hoped to gain ease, 'but I mistake greatly if the method now taken do not in time give more trouble and create greater expence'.[39]

By and large the traders were not exponents of Indian removal. Indeed in the southern six colonies the network of Scottish traders operating out of Charles Town and Savannah, headed by John Gordon in the former and by the brothers John and James Graham in the latter, built bridges between Crown officials, often fellow Scots to whom they were politically linked; the Indian trade; and the tribes, especially the Creeks. Led by a trader-begotten mestizo elite, the Creeks in particular were recovering demographically and adopting selectively European agricultural and political techniques. They were not fading away. As a result, they threatened the hopes of a key colonial group – the land speculators. Even a few of the wealthiest traders had joined the speculators' ranks. John Gordon speculated in land which had formerly belonged to Spanish colonists in East Florida, but the two surviving partners of the great Augusta trading house of Brown, Rae and Company, John Rae and George Galphin, both Irishmen, went into partnership with Lachlan McGillivray – a Scots trader deeply involved with the Creeks, whose most remarkable chief of the next generation he fathered – to speculate in Georgia land, which they obtained by political influence, cloaked by what they unctuously described in 1765 as 'true Patriotism'. They knew that to turn dubious land claims into valuable assets, you needed immigration. As an Assemblyman, McGillivray helped secure in 1766 colonial legislation 'for encouraging settlers to come into the Province'. The partners reckoned that the way forward lay in encouraging Irish Protestants to immigrate. Rae, writing to his brother in County Down a letter which was reproduced in the local press there, talked about hard work yielding on the frontier good living with 'as plentiful a table as most gentlemen in Ireland'.[40] However, the partners were really after much more than good eating and drinking. If all had worked out, financial killings on real estate would have been their equivalent of the silver mines of Mexico and Peru.

Whatever the speculators said, cheating, killing, and dispossessing Indians was essential if they were to have any hope of the obscene profits they all hoped for (and a very few achieved). The surrender of Crown control in the west was followed by such predictable abuses that a frontier colony like

West Florida where the Indian peoples were still numerous and important, and the Spaniards a potential threat, faced terrible problems. Indians were discontented because the old system of regular presents from the British government was as much in ruins as many of the old fortified frontier posts. Early in 1770 a Mr Bradley's plantation at Natchez was attacked by a Choctaw Indian party complaining that he had failed to live up to his promises to give them presents. They plundered the horses and goods kept in a nearby, near ruinous fort before fleeing. After some fighting, the goods were recovered, but one report which reached the governor of West Florida and his council cited an informant as saying 'he believes that a good deal may be owing to the great Quantity of Rum sold to the Indians at the Natchez, among the Articles retook from them were 50 or 60 Keggs Rum'. General Alexander O'Reilly, the future conqueror of West Florida, knew all about the chaos in the British Indian country, for he met refugees from this episode at a Spanish frontier fort, where they had taken refuge.[41] Hardly surprisingly, West Florida – a colony where the Crown had some real authority, unlike elsewhere in North America – was passing in May 1770 legislation designed to ensure 'the better Regulation of the Indian Trade in the Province'. It stated, absolutely correctly, that 'a well regulated Indian Trade would be of the utmost advantage to the Commerce of Great Britain, and for the Benefit and Safety of the British Colonies in America'. In effect it tried to resurrect the regime which had been abandoned in 1768, with licences for traders, secured by bonds, and provision that 'no Indian Trader, Clerk, Factor or Packhorseman shall maltreat or abuse any Indian or Indians and that they shall pay a proper respect to the medal Chiefs and Captains bearing Commissions'. There were to be set prices for the main trade goods to prevent excessive exploitation of Indian customers, plus standard weights and measures, balanced by an attempt to limit the amount of powder and shot sold to Indians, as well as an attempt to keep rifled gun barrels out of their hands.[42] Best described as a triumph of hope over experience, the legislation was part of a package which included 'An Act for punishing all persons who may infringe any of the Treaties that are made with the Indians'. Penalties in the shape of fines and minimal prison sentences were to be enforced against offenders by all Crown officers, from justices of the peace upwards. In particular, violations of the Proclamation Line of 1763 were to be punished, and the territorial rights of the Choctaws, Chickasaws, and Upper and Lower Creeks were to be respected.[43]

By 1770 it was much too late to hope to keep a minimum of order in the British world, and to avoid a radical reordering of that world by violence. One problem was that not only were colonial individuals looking for the equivalent of another Mexican or Peruvian bonanza, but so was a British government obsessed with the national debt left after the last war. Charles

Townshend, who is often remembered only for the way some of his fiscal proposals exacerbated the Anglo-American crisis of the 1760s, spent a great deal of his time in 1767 worrying about whether there was a politically acceptable way of squeezing revenue out of the EIC, very much visualised as a sort of silver mine. One official document circulating at cabinet level that year blithely envisaged taking out of the official revenues of sub-Moghul Bengal enough for the military needs of the EIC, enough for its administrative costs, including salaries to its servants, and a steady dividend to stockholders, plus of course enough to fund the indispensable investment in Asiatic goods for the China market, before a further payment to 'the Public' at most not exceeding the investment.[44] This particular hope was snatched at by the Elder Pitt, now Lord Chatham, in his second ministry, as a way out of the financial mess his own wartime profligacy had created. Basically, he proposed to set up a hostile inquiry into the EIC as a prelude to a smash and grab raid which would take a million a year from the EIC for the Westminster government by statute, all under the very dubious cover of 'parliamentary sovereignty' – itself a slippery concept, if only because in law sovereignty belonged to the king alone. It was he who exercised some of his sovereignty through legislatures which were enhanced versions of himself, and that sovereignty was pledged by his coronation oath to be wielded subject to the laws, customs, and usages of the realm. Many MPs thought that those usages hardly extended to what could be seen as barefaced robbery by statute. The government itself was split, with Townshend and Henry Conway palpably unhappy, which handed to George Grenville in opposition an opportunity he capitalised on brilliantly to destroy the measure.[45] The EIC still had to buy off the politicians with an annual £400,000 it could not afford, and was effectively bankrupt by 1772, but there was no easy way out for the Westminster-based executive. Even some of Chatham's colleagues had doubts whether Westminster could legally claim outright sovereignty over all EIC holdings and operations in India.[46] It was no accident that Chatham himself took refuge in a major mental breakdown in 1767 after the failure of yet another attempt to find the crock of gold at the end of the political rainbow in the shape of a botched bid to extract from the Spanish the alleged substantial balance owing of the ransom for Manila. His acting successor, the Duke of Grafton, may have been idle and self-indulgent, but his preference for a cottage at Newmarket and Miss Nancy Parsons over impossible problems is excusable, though his failure to take one obvious and feasible foreign policy decision is not.

The EIC rapidly disqualified itself as a potential asset, mainly due to the mixture of rascality and incompetence characteristic of its Madras council. They had fought their part of the Seven Years' War largely with the funds of Nawab Muhammed Ali, ruler of the Carnatic. In 1766 he, as a result, still owed the EIC 1,365,104 pagodas[47] (reduced from the 2,225,373 he had owed them in 1761), but he also owed to private creditors, who included most of the Madras council, a sum far in excess of his 1761 debts to the EIC, and at rates of interest which had been reduced from a 30–36 per cent peak to a figure of 20 per cent mandated by Governor Palk to the still formidable 10 per cent laid down by the EIC in 1766. Because he represented the hopes and fantasies of the local EIC officials, he had the ability to manipulate them and could point out to them that only by supporting his territorial claims could they hope to have adequate land revenue assigned to pay their interest charges. Muhammed Ali's near neighbour in the kingdom of Mysore was the Muslim soldier Haidar Ali, a son of the commander of the fortress of Bangalore, who had built up his position as an outstanding Mysore general. As a member of the Strachey family reported to the governor and council of Madras, Haidar 'by paying and rewarding well soon collected a number of European and Topass Deserters who with the Country Sepoys he had procured made his force very formidable'. In short, he was a rival in the military market, very much into skill transference by market mechanisms, and he spotted the optimal next move for a successful frontier commander, as a result of which he 'marched to his Master's Capital', and reduced him to a puppet.[48] The trouble, as Strachey was aware, in 1766 was that an entrepreneurial military imperialist like Haidar, or Napoleon after him for that matter, had to keep going on a policy of continual expansion. In 1766 Strachey was comforted to think Haidar had never faced a strong enemy and had had the worst of a brush with the Marathas. Haidar had early expanded into the territories of the minor rulers on the Malabar Coast. He aspired to naval power based on cooperation with the Bombay presidency of the EIC, which offered him facilities to build warships in the Marine Yard at Bombay, where very remarkable local Parsee shipwrights were establishing a great tradition. Haidar offered an alliance based on mutual support, but Bombay went off the idea, and the Madras presidency blundered into an alliance with the nizam of Hyderabad, the Marathas, and the egregious Muhammed Ali, aimed straight at Mysore. General Joseph Smith led an EIC contingent which accompanied the nizam's invasion of Mysore, but the grand coalition rapidly fell apart before Haidar's diplomacy and bribes, leaving the Madras presidency to face the full brunt of a justly enraged Haidar Ali. Smith believed in 1767 that Haidar's army 'from the best Accounts' consisted of:

5,000 Grenadier Sepoys, 8,000 others arm'd with European Arms,
49 pieces Cannon large and small. A Battalion consisting of a thousand
Topases. A Troop of European Cavalry of 60 Men. About 150 European

Artillery Men. 4000 Matchlocks. A number of Rocket and Gingall Men. 8000 Mogul Horse, and 12,000 cavalry.[49]

Obviously, though there were large numbers of infantrymen in this army armed and disciplined according to European modes, there were also plenty who were not. In set-piece infantry battle, therefore, Smith could and a couple of times did defeat the Mysore forces. But he lost his war, because of the overwhelming Mysorean superiority in cavalry, not just in sub-Moghul troopers for hire, but also in the shape of disciplined regular cavalry, like Haidar's red-coated lancers. The EIC was chronically short of cavalry. In the marshy valley of the lower Ganges in Bengal this hardly mattered, for waterways obstructed cavalry-outflanking tactics. In the Mysore wars it was a different story. Smith's troops could hold the swarming Mysore horse at a distance with the threat of cannon fire, but they could not bring them to action, let alone stop them cutting off the vital supply convoys.[50] Even a special 'flying corps' of light infantry, cavalry, and horse artillery under Colonel Wood failed, to the point of being ambushed by its proposed prey. Shortage of cavalry meant that the terrible difficulties in logistics, which the relatively poor nature of the countryside made inevitable, became crippling. Grain ran out in the army bazaar. Relief food convoys from the coast were cut off or gravely impeded. When the British hoped to cut off Haidar's son and heir Tipu, the latter merely broke the cavalry he commanded into small groups which slipped easily through the hill passes to safety in Mysore.[51] Early in January 1768 Smith was explaining he had been unable to send in the usual November returns on troop numbers because 'the Roads were so much infested with the Enemy, that the fear of losing prevented my sending them'.[52] Peace had to be made on Haidar's terms, which included an alliance for mutual support.

When the scale of the EIC's failures in the field became known in London in the spring of 1769, there was a spectacular fall in the value of EIC stock. Peace allowed some commercial recovery, but the company was for retrenchment, not the creation of expensive cavalry regiments.[53] The EIC Madras presidency had at least lost its war without assistance from or involvement of the Crown. However, the directorate in London decided not only to send out a supervisory commission to try to discipline its local European servants, but also to call for a Royal Navy squadron lest the French be tempted to intervene. That enabled the nawab of the Carnatic, simultaneously financial prisoner of the presidency and fiscal jailer of its officers, to work through his London agent, the devious John MacPherson, to suggest to the Westminster government that it would be more appropriate for the princes of south India to deal direct with the Crown. Lord Weymouth, the new secretary of state for the Southern Department, was responsive but ended up institutionalising a situation where Crown and company pursued conflicting policies in India.[54] Political confusion in the Madras presidency reached incredible heights in 1770 with the arrival of a small Royal Naval squadron under Sir John Lindsay, who carried secret instructions from the Westminster government to intervene in the politics of the presidency, in ways which were neither wise nor strictly legal. Both he and his successor, Commodore Harland, for example, were militantly in favour of breaching treaty commitments to Haidar Ali. As elsewhere in the British world, the locus of power was an open question.[55]

Nor was there any obvious solution by violence, in the sense of uniting the incoherent and squabbling groups which acknowledged to a greater or lesser extent the sovereignty of George III by attacking a common external foe. The British monarchy was grossly over-extended. The last successful war had generated a dismal range of difficult problems. The best British hope was to exclude the hostile Bourbon powers from the inevitably messy processes through which the British peoples would have to move as they tried to resolve their often incompatible demands, ambitions, and points of view. Aggressive naval deterrence had been the key to British foreign policy after 1763. It was a workable option because even the great Choiseul had not been able to broaden the fiscal basis of French naval power. He had been able cynically to exploit public revulsion at the loss of a Canada he was glad to be rid of to scapegoat corrupt naval administrators and to secure a very large public donation to build ships for the king's navy. With those funds (the ships were often not built for years) and revenues he persuaded the royal council to ascribe to payment of naval debt interest charges, he revitalised naval credit. His naval reforms in themselves were not sweeping or unprecedented. Basic tax reform was unthinkable.[56] The French navy was not entirely ready to face up to its British rival in the early 1770s. British nerve and alertness against signs of joint Franco–Spanish revanchism had, however, shown signs of faltering over the Corsican crisis of 1768, when Grafton, presiding intermittently over a decaying government, had allowed the French to make a considerable addition to the strength of their Mediterranean naval position by buying out Genoese claims to the island of Corsica and then crushing the local resistance led by the anglophile Pasquale Paoli. It was a war made for superior British sea power and politically all the more feasible because of Paoli. Acquiescence in French aggrandisement predictably encouraged a joint Franco–Spanish testing of British nerve in 1770–71, using the Falkland Islands as the improbable occasion. The claims of Spain, France, and Britain to legal 'rights' over the archipelago were all as fatuous as most European prescriptive claims in the Americas. The British settlement at Port Egmont was a token challenge to Spanish claims of prescriptive monopoly in the Pacific, to which it was an ineffectual staging post. The French settlement was sold to Spain specifically to enable a united Bourbon challenge to British naval supremacy to be mounted. It failed. The Westminster government was reluctantly prepared to fight. France was not. Choiseul's career was terminated by the humiliation. There was a case from the British point of view for precipitating war when the Bourbons were not ready. The southern secretary of state, Lord Weymouth, was throughout intransigent and ready for war, though the elderly first lord of the Admiralty, Lord Anson, had been slow to get warships fit for service. When it became clear that, partly for fiscal reasons, North wanted a nego- tiated solution, Weymouth resigned on the grounds that he had been per- sistently over-ruled in his own department. The government wheeled in the sympathetic and sycophantic pamphleteering pen of Dr Samuel Johnson to head off mounting opposition criticism by stressing the irrelevant point that the Falklands were of little inherent value.[57]

The crisis had not really been about the islands. It had briefly stirred memories of the rampant chauvinism with which so many of the inhabit- ants of British North American colonies had greeted the War of Jenkins' Ear, as Guy Johnson – nephew of Sir William, his deputy for the Six Nations from 1762, and his successor as superintendent of the Northern Indian District after Sir William's death in 1774 – told Lord Adam Gordon in February 1771. After telling Lord Adam, a Scottish soldier and peer with American experience and interests, mainly real-estate ones, that New York's popular Governor Dunmore, another Scottish nobleman, was to be pro- moted to the governorship of Virginia, Guy added, 'What engages all our attention at present is the prospect of a War, which is more wished for in this Country than any where else.' He stressed that the near certainty of Spanish-inspired Indian trouble on the frontier did not dampen colonial enthusiasm.[58] Whether tentatively planned British attacks on the Spanish Caribbean as well as on the peninsular naval base of Ferrol would have been successful is an interesting but irrelevant question. What is fact is that, once the Falklands crisis was out of the way, the government of Lord North began a reappraisal of policy towards the conquered colony of Quebec, initially stimulated by the arguments of the returning Governor Carleton to the effect that Anglicisation was impractical and wrong and that the Roman Catholic Church and French civil law must be virtually established as the price of loyalty. Recent scholarship has concentrated on the religious issue and on the way a 1771 report by one of the law officers, Alexander Wedderburn, encapsulated his own Scottish Enlightenment background of belief in toleration, and appealed to the pragmatic willingness for flexibility on the part of many members of the English Establishment from the king down.[59] Power can educate. However, the dimension of the resulting Quebec Act of 1774 which such scholarship has neglected was just as important, and more shocking to anglophone colonists south of Quebec. The act moved the boundary of Quebec south to the Ohio and west to the Mississippi. Wedderburn had ruled out any assembly in Quebec, which was to be governed as it always had been by governor and council, a regime based on acquiescence, not participation. The colonial press exploded in fury, pounding the sectarian drum. Alexander Hamilton, future father of the American Republic, declared that George III preferred 'a superstitious, bigotted Canadian Papist, though ever so profligate' to a liberal, enlightened New England Dissenter. 'Well he might' was not an answer which would have amused Hamilton. The *Newport Mercury* suggested in November 1774 that Lord North would soon visit Rome with a view to perhaps a cardinal's hat as a sign of the Supreme Pontiff's gratitude. Men who spouted this nonsense were soon happy to ally with the Most Christian and very Catholic King of France. Newport, Rhode Island, was to see the arrival of a French expeditionary force under the comte de Rochambeau in 1780. In 1774 it was more to the point that the new boundaries ruined the hopes of many western land speculators, such as those involved in the proposed Vandalia colony. They included George Washington and Patrick Henry, as well as a group of Philadelphia merchants. All saw their stock become worthless. Propaganda which fed off the prejudices of American Protestants nevertheless at its core argued about control of the future of empire. When the *New York Journal* thundered in July 1775 that 'The finger of God points out a mighty empire to your sons: the Savages of the wilderness were never expelled to make room in this, the best part of the Continent, for idolators and slaves',[60] it was becoming clear that settler and metropolitan versions of imperialism in North America were so incompatible that only force could move the argument out of impasse. For a complex of reasons, civil war within the bosom of the English nation was, in fact, very close.

Notes and references

1. Kate Hotblack, *Chatham's Colonial Policy* (Porcupine Press reprint edn, Philadelphia, PA, 1980), pp. 32–41.

2. Jeremy Black, *Pitt the Elder* (Cambridge University Press, Cambridge, 1992), p. 212.

3. *Vide*, for example, Fournier to Maurepas, 15 January 1746, and the 'Memoire pour faire connoitre la situation actuelle du commerce', associated with Maurepas–Fournier discussions in 1745: Maurepas Papers, Cornell University (hereinafter MPCU), Lot 4, 2u, and Lot 21, 22u, resp.

4. 'Memoire' by Jean Baptiste Bonnet, Marseilles, 1745: MPCU, Lot 66, 4u.

5. 'Memoire: Trois points ... 3o La facon de luy procurer un certain fond, independamment de ceux que le Roy pourrois fournir', *c.* 1743: MPCU, Lot 44, 22u.

6. James Pritchard, *Louis XV's Navy 1748–1762* (McGill–Queen's University Press, Montreal, 1987), p. 9.

7. George III to Lord Bute, 6 January 1761, printed in David Syrett (ed.), *The Siege and Capture of Havana 1762* (Navy Records Society, Vol. 114, London, 1970), p. 3.

8. 'Thoughts upon the Siege of the Havana by Lieutenant-Colonel Patrick Mackellar', *ibid.*, pp. 151–58.

9. Sir Lewis Namier, *England in the Age of the American Revolution* (Macmillan, London, 2nd pbk edn, 1961), p. 277.

10. Daniel H. Thomas, *Fort Toulouse: The French outpost at the Alabamas on the Coosa* (University of Alabama Press, Tuscaloosa, AL, pbk edn with new intro, 1989), pp. 52–62.

11. Cited in John P. Moore, *Revolt in Louisiana: The Spanish occupation 1766–1770* (Louisiana State University Press, Baton Rouge, LA, 1976), p. 189.

12. These points are made by the chief engineer on the expedition, Captain William Stevenson, in his report to the Court of Directors of the EIC, 10 November 1762, printed in *Documents Illustrating the British Conquest of Manila 1762–1763*, ed. Nicholas P. Cushner, Camden 4th Series, Vol. 8 (Royal Historical Society, London, 1971), pp. 45–48.

13. Nicholas Tracy, *Manila Ransomed: The British assault on Manila in the Seven Years' War* (University of Exeter Press, Exeter, 1995) is an excellent military history.

14. Cornish and Draper to the Spanish authorities in Manila, 24 September 1762, in *Documents*, ed. Cushner, doc. 30, p. 59.

15. *Vide* the exchanges in the memoranda printed in the first part of *ibid.*

16. Tom Hatley, *The Dividing Paths: Cherokees and South Carolinians through the revolutionary era* (Oxford University Press, New York, 1995), p. 115.

17. Daniel J. Beattie, 'The Adaptation of the British Army to Wilderness Warfare, 1755–1763', in Martin Ultee (ed.), *Adapting to Conditions: War and society in the eighteenth century* (University of Alabama Press, Tuscaloosa, AL, 1986), p. 81.

18. Ian K. Steele, *Betrayals: Fort William Henry and the 'Massacre'* (Oxford University Press, New York, 1990), Chap. 7, 'Perceptions'.

19. James Adair, *The History of the American Indians* (Johnson Reprint Corp., New York, repr. edn, 1968), p. 251.

20. Lieutenant Governor Bull to Pitt, 28 April 1761, printed in *Correspondence of William Pitt when Secretary of State with Colonial Governors and Military and Naval Commissioners in America*, ed. Gertrude Selwyn Kimball (2 vols, Kraus Reprint edn, New York, 1969), pp. 2, 420–25.

21. Wilbur R. Jacobs, *Dispossessing the American Indian* (University of Oklahoma Press, Norman, OK, pbk edn, 1985), pp. 62–67.

22. R. David Edmunds and Joseph L. Peyser, *The Fox Wars: The Mesquakie challenge to New France* (University of Oklahoma Press, Norman, OK, 1993).

23. Letter from Jean-Baptiste de Couagne, 26 May 1763, *Papers of Sir William Johnson Vol. X*, ed. Milton W. Hamilton (University of the State of New York, Albany, NY, 1951), p. 684.

24. Peter C. Mancall, *Deadly Medicine: Indians and alcohol in early America* (Cornell University Press, Ithaca, NY, and London), p. 167.

25. Report on Onondaga speaker dated 28 May 1763, *Johnson Papers X*, p. 683.

26. General Sir Jeffrey Amherst to Sir William Johnson, 28 July 1763, *ibid.*, p. 761.

27. J.C. Long, *Lord Jeffrey Amherst: A soldier of the king* (Macmillan, New York, 1933), pp. 186–87.

28. Gregory E. Dowd, *A Spirited Resistance* (Johns Hopkins University Press, Baltimore, MD, 1993), Chaps. 1–2.

29. Richard White, *The Middle Ground: Indians, empire and republics in the Great Lakes region, 1650–1815* (Cambridge University Press, Cambridge, 1991), Chap. 7, 'Pontiac and the Restoration of the Middle Ground'.

30. David to Alexander Wedderburn, 3 June 1764, Wedderburn Papers, Clements Library, Ann Arbor, MI (herein after WPCL), Vol. 1, No. 2.

31. Same to same, 12 October 1764, *ibid.*, No. 3.

32. Same to same, last page with date missing but from context clearly early 1765, *ibid.*, No. 4.

33. Same to same, 14 April 1765, *ibid.*, No. 6.

34. Nancy F. Koehn, *The Power of Commerce* (Cornell University Press, Ithaca, NY, 1994), pp. 5 and 100–01.

35. Jacobs, *Dispossessing the American Indian*, pp. 95–100.

36. J. Russell Snapp, *John Stuart and the Struggle for Empire on the Southern Frontier* (Louisiana State University Press, Baton Rouge, LA, 1996).

37. Chiefs of the Mohawks in council to Sir William Johnson at Johnson Hall, 13 August 1766, *Johnson Papers XII*, p. 167.

38. William Franklin to Sir William Johnson, 23 May 1768, *ibid.*, pp. 511–13.

39. Cadwallader Colden to Sir William Johnson, 26 February 1769, *ibid.*, pp. 698–99.

40. Edward J. Cashin, *Lachlan McGillivray, Indian Trader* (University of Georgia Press, Athens, GA, 1992), pp. 233–36.

41. Copy 'Mr Fergy who arrived this afternoon from New Orleans gave the following Account to the Governor in Council, of an attack Mr. Bradley and others have had with some Indians at the Natchez', dated 6 February 1770, Gage Papers, William L. Clements Library, Ann Arbor, MI.

42. 'An Act for the better regulation of the Indian Trade in the Province of West Florida', passed to the House of Assembly the 16th Day of May 1770, copy, Gage Papers.

43. 'An Act for punishing all persons who may infringe any of the Treaties that are made with the Indians', passed by the House of Assembly, 16 May 1770, copy, Gage Papers.

44. The document is preserved in the Charles Townshend Papers in the Clements Library, 8/33/13, No. VII, printed, 'Outline of a Scheme, for separating the Commercial Affairs of the Company, from that Share of the Profits, arising from the Dewannee, which may be ceded to the Public, in such a Manner, as to remove the Supposed Necessity, of receiving the Public, into a Partnership in Trade'.

45. Philip Lawson, *George Grenville: A political life* (Clarendon Press, Oxford, 1984), pp. 232–34.

46. Philip Lawson, *The East India Company* (Longman, London, 1993), pp. 118–19.

47. The pagoda or hun was the standard coin of south India. Whereas Moghul India's currency was silver-based, Hindu south India had created a system based on the gold pagoda, whose subsidiary coins were the half-pagoda and the fanam. The pagoda was usually stamped with the image of Vishnu and weighed 53 grains to the fanam's 5. It was worth about 3.5 rupees – in sterling about 7s 6d.

48. 'Extract from a letter from Mr. John Stracey, to the Governor and Council of Bombay dated at Merjie the 31st October 1766', in Orme MSS, British Library, Oriental and India Office Collections (hereinafter OIOC), OV33, ff. 1–11.

49. Joseph Smith to Robert Orme, 5 November 1767, Orme MSS, OV10, f. 13r, OIOC.

50. *Ibid.*, f. 13r.

51. *Ibid.*, ff. 31–32.

52. Joseph Smith to Charles Bourchier, President . . . of Council at Fort St George, 8 January 1768, p. 7, Orme MSS, OV64, OIOC.

53. G.J. Bryant, 'The Cavalry Problem in the Early British Indian Army, 1750–1785', *War in History*, 2 (1995), pp. 1–21.

54. Hugh V. Bowen, *Revenue and Reform: The Indian problem in British politics 1757–1773* (Cambridge University Press, Cambridge, 1991), pp. 76–82.

55. H.H. Dodwell (ed.), *The Cambridge History of the British. Vol. IV: British India 1497–1858* (Cambridge University Press, Cambridge, 1929), pp. 277–79.

56. Pritchard, *Louis XV's Navy*, pp. 203–05 and 221–22.

57. Nicholas Tracy, *Navies, Deterrence, and American Independence: Britain and seapower in the 1760s and 1770s* (University of British Columbia Press, Vancouver, 1998), and Peter D.G. Thomas, *Lord North* (Allen Lane, London, pbk edn, 1976), pp. 46–50.

58. Guy Johnson to Lord Adam Gordon, 18 February 1771, *Johnson Papers XII*, p. 893.

59. Philip Lawson, *The Imperial Challenge: Quebec and Britain in the age of the American Revolution* (McGill–Queen's University Press, Montreal, 1989), belies its title by the narrowness of its focus.

60. John C. Miller, *Origins of the American Revolution* (Little, Brown and Company, Boston, MA, 1943), pp. 373–75.

CHAPTER SIX

War and the reformulation of English identities in the age of the American Revolution

English America's 'total defection'[1] and apparent victory to July 1776

If the civil wars over the potential inherent in the different regional complexes built up under the real or nominal sovereignty of the English and later the British monarchy were as inevitable as the French and Spanish governments thought they were by the 1760s, the experience of conflict was in every region painful, with significant elements of the disreputable or the savagely brutal, or of both. Successor regimes which emerged from the implosion of the British world of 1775 were therefore at pains to rewrite the record to imply a consistent note of nobility and inevitability to their parturition. The Westminster-based British government, which had pulled a house down on itself by a mixture of protracted appeasement of colonial defiance of metropolitan authority and an assertion of parliamentary sovereignty over regional empires never likely to bow to its will on the scale necessary to make that sovereignty meaningful, was one of those successor regimes. It did not fail to emerge from the general reshuffling of the territories and assets associated with the British Crown with a strong acquiescent core territory in the shape of the United Kingdom of Great Britain. To that had to be added the still extensive colonial dependencies of Britain; and by 1800 the continuing vitality of the regime had been expressed in the acquisition of effective control of the territories of the British East India Company, and the incorporation of the kingdom of Ireland, whose aristocratic elite had at one point gone a fair distance along the road travelled by the gentry of Virginia in defying Westminster, into the new United Kingdom of Great Britain and Ireland.

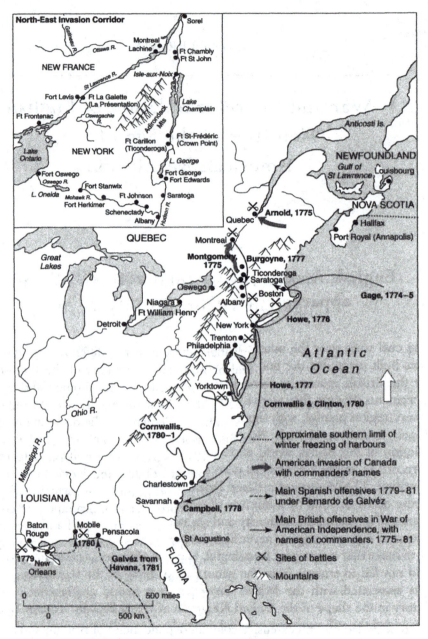

Map 8   The War of American Independence, 1775–81

However, it is the failure of the Westminster politicians – of whom the most important was, as he was meant to be, George III – to avoid disaster in America which has tended to ensure that the literature on the War of American Independence almost takes for granted the concept of 'The Fall of the First British Empire' as background. This whole rhetoric of shaking off imperial shackles receives short shrift in the best recent work on the historiography of the American Revolution. There were precious few to shake. By neglect and appeasement the Walpole and Pelham regimes of the first half of the eighteenth century had paved the way to disaster in the 1770s. Though colonial spokesmen repeatedly denounced ministers of the Crown for tyrannical innovations and demanded return to a mythical *status quo* of the era before 1763, the whole point is that there was no such thing. By *status quo* these spokesmen often meant the systematic neglect of long-established regulatory legislation. They also tended to regard the *status quo* as being on wheels, so that in the course of opposing every single attempt by the Crown to raise any kind of revenue in America – from the Stamp Act of 1765 to the Townshend duties on tea, paper, glass, red and white lead, and painters' colours of 1767; to the 1773 authorisation to the EIC to market its tea (still carrying a small 'Townshend' duty) in America through its own agencies – they ended up redefining acceptable regulatory activity by the metropolitan authorities as no activity. Nor was there any reason to believe that it would be possible to negotiate successfully with the colonies. The rhetoric of opposition leaders and groups like Chatham or the Rockingham Whigs suggested, quite dishonestly, that they had some sort of answer to the crisis. Edmund Burke, Rockingham's arch-propagandist, went on and on about the vast sums lost to the treasury by not returning to the system of requisitions, whereby the Westminster government asked colonies politely for appropriate contributions, to be voted by their assemblies. The system had never worked. It failed miserably in the newly independent United States after 1783. In Massachusetts there was no empire to collapse. The burning of the revenue schooner *Gaspee* in Narragansett Bay in June 1772 was not unprecedented; there had been a similar episode with a government sloop in 1769. Secretary of State Lord Dartmouth chose to appease in 1772, yet again.[2] There was no Crown government in Massachusetts, as the despairing Governor Thomas Hutchinson became increasingly aware.

The rhetoric of the articulate spokesmen for the colonies had for most of the period after 1763 made it very clear that there was little chance of any constructive response to the very real problems in the face of which successive London governments churned out their sequence of misguided or ineffective 'solutions'. The absolutely basic one of crippling war debt, mostly incurred by the United Kingdom in the course of a war it had hoped to avoid and which had in the last analysis been fought primarily to put an end for ever to the French threat to British North America, was shrugged off by Benjamin Franklin in the course of his examination before the House of Commons in 1766, when he was arguing for the repeal of the Stamp Act. Franklin insisted that it was a mistake even to suggest that the last war had been fought 'for the defense, or for the sake of the people in America'. There had been no essential American interest at stake in Acadia or the Ohio country. Braddock had marched to defend a selfish, purely British interest in the fur trade. The colonists, by way of contrast, had been 'in perfect peace with both French and Indians'. It had been 'really a British war'.[3] Franklin was, like all good representatives, lying abroad for the good of his public, in this case the colonies which employed him as their agent. The House of Commons was right to be both sceptical and offended by his lies, but they were self-serving ones and therefore widely believed in the American colonies. Old Dennys De Berdt – a Dissenter of Flemish extraction who served as agent in London for Massachusetts and Delaware, and died in 1770 – had been singing from the same hymnbook as Franklin years before. In 1765 he had written to Lord Dartmouth insisting that there was no case for the colonies helping with the debts incurred in the late war, since the debts were 'an expence which was cheifly occasioned by the supine neglect and timmid efforts of the Ministry of her Mother Country, which gave the French time to pour in Troops to the Continent of America'. De Berdt had protested violently against the Sugar Act of 1764, which had been essentially a modification of the Molasses Act of 1733, a piece of legislation that had been a dead letter. The 1764 Act both reduced the theoretically prohibitive tax laid on imported foreign molasses by the 1733 one to threepence per gallon and by implication accepted the inevitability of the import of sugars from the foreign West Indian islands, which had become an indispensable market for British North American colonial produce, especially the surplus agricultural commodities and fish of New England. Though various themes were exploited to denounce the Act there is no doubt that what was most objectionable about it was that it was clearly meant to be enforced. Although De Berdt harped on about the 'affectionate and warm attachment' of Massachusetts to the Mother Country, it was a theme interlaced with arguments for free trade with foreign countries and .scarcely veiled threats of social upheaval in Britain if the vital American trade were to be interrupted by adverse developments, economic or political. He even envisaged the unemployed might 'fall upon the Lands of the Nobility and Gentry'. Affection towards the Mother Country was something which increasingly, and not just in Massachusetts, was articulated as a prelude to a threat to withdraw it. A learned and ingenious book has been devoted to explaining the transition in eighteenth-century Massachusetts from a monarchical to a republican frame of mind, explaining the phenomenon by the fact that the province 'partook of monarchical culture, but lacked a monarchical society'. Given the colony's record of intermittent hostility to and evasion of, not to mention defiance of, the Crown since the day it was founded, it is difficult to see what needs to be explained. Continuity, not transition, is what is impressive. The man who told the Duke of Newcastle in 1740 that 'Massachusetts is a kind of commonwealth where the king is hardly a stadtholder', was correct.[4] The real problem was how long the Crown would tolerate a situation in which it was treated with more and more open contempt.

The point of no return for both parties came with the Boston Tea Party on the night of 16 December 1773, when in Boston harbour a radical-led group very nominally disguised as Mohawk Indians boarded three vessels which carried about 90,000 pounds of dutied tea worth some £9000, and threw the tea into the water. As with the former case of molasses, the duty represented a substantial cut in previous overall taxation levels but was doubly offensive to local opinion. Those who smuggled tea on a very large scale into the colonies from such sources as Amsterdam and the Dutch West Indies faced even more effective legitimate competition at a time when their own profit margins were being squeezed. Secondly, radicals like the Sons of Liberty were in the forefront of the widespread American hostility to paying the only surviving, and symbolically therefore very important, Townshend duty on the tea. Tea ships were turned away from Philadelphia and New York, and Virginia was to have its own much smaller 'tea party' early in the next year when Thomas Nelson – the dominant gentry figure in, ironically, the small port of Yorktown where the War of the Revolution was to end – threw a couple of tea chests into the York River.[5] However, Boston was where a mass of private property was wantonly destroyed in defiance of the King's Peace, literally under the guns of the Royal Navy. Admiral John Montague was an eyewitness. His squadron rode at anchor a few hundred yards offshore but, as he said in his report the next day, 'I could easily have prevented the Execution of this Plan, but must have endangered the Lives of many innocent People by firing upon the Town.'[6] Such an action would have delighted local radicals though their rhetoric of indignation would have known no bounds. In an attempt to whip up trouble after the collapse of the latest in a succession of non-importation agreements designed, usually successfully, to apply commercial coercion to Westminster, they had been passing annual motions about the 1770 'atrocity' laughably christened the Boston Massacre – in which royal troops were taunted and assaulted beyond endurance by a local mob which shouted its conviction that they dare not fire because they needed a magistrate's endorsement to do so. Everyone knew local magistrates were far too intimidated to give them that endorsement. Troops had previously seen comrades maimed, so after one of them was felled they fired without orders, killing five of their assailants. There was no specialised non-lethal anti-riot equipment available. Muskets and naval cannon killed if used.

America was an extreme case of a common British problem. In London and elsewhere in England similar situations were endemic. Pusillanimous magistrates and soldiers rightly afraid of legal prosecution if they did anything without a magistrate's sanction frequently allowed rioters to get completely out of hand, which could then lead to a snapping of military or magisterial temper and loss of life. In London alone loss of life amongst rioters ranged from the four weavers shot dead in 1763 to the hundreds of people shot down by troops in 1780, when one of the colonials' much lauded 'friends of America', John Wilkes, was to the fore as a magistrate authorising the most draconian measures in defence of order. In 1774 the secretary at war wrote despairingly to Lord Dartmouth, secretary of state for the colonies, asking for clear government directions to officers of units stationed in Massachusetts, Connecticut, Rhode Island, and New Hampshire as to when they could use force in provinces where no local magistrate was ever likely to authorise it. The law officers of the Crown were wheeled in, but the extraordinary fact remains that the government never gave clear guidance to officers of the British army as to how to behave when on riot duty. It preferred to preserve the option of scapegoating the military.[7]

The Boston Tea Party was the last in a succession of episodes which had demonstrated mounting contempt for royal authority. Radical Patriots like Boston's Sam Adams were unappeasable. There was no point in negotiating with people like him, and the so-called 'moderate' Patriots were simply the soft part of a 'hard man, soft man' act. They differed only in style, not substance. The response of the Westminster government, which took the form of the so-called Intolerable or Coercive Acts, was probably the minimum set of measures any regime could have taken to maintain any face of authority in the province, and by implication in most of North America, yet the militant colonists quite rightly judged that they had to fight at this point. The key was the modification of the Massachusetts Charter by Westminster statute. Lord North had been busy in 1773 with the passage of what is known as Lord North's Regulating Act, which was the first large-scale governmental intervention in the internal affairs of the EIC. The EIC was bankrupt, and needed a government loan to survive. Its servants in India were clearly out of hand. Charters were basically royal grants, and traditionally could only be challenged by a writ of *quo warranto* in the Court of the King's Bench. On such a writ the Virginia Company had, justly, lost its charter in the 1620s, and Massachusetts arguably deserved to lose its charter, for the second time, in the 1770s, on the basis on which it had lost it in the 1680s: sustained breach of the spirit and letter of a grant which presupposed that the recipient was a loyal subject of the Crown. In practice, most people accepted that charters had occasionally to be modified, and the Westminster legislature did it – though usually only after a genuine process of consultation and negotiation with the party concerned. Even so, the precedent was alarming, as the City of London said in a petition against the Bill which became North's Regulating Act in 1773, a petition which pointed out that its own local government, like those of most other municipalities in the kingdom, rested on a royal charter. The petitioners argued that if passed into law the Bill would 'prove of the most fatal consequences to the security of property in general, and particularly the franchises of every corporate body in this kingdom'.[8] They were right in principle, though it was not until the twentieth century that a British government abolished London, politically, for the grave sin of deeply annoying a prime minister. In 1774 it became clear that no colony's charter would be safe if that of Massachusetts were to be successfully modified. The closing of Boston's overseas trade by the Boston Port Act was a minimal response, and the only way anyone could see the town being persuaded to compensate the EIC for its losses. However, along with the Quebec Act, that measure was denounced, with three other measures as the Coercive or Intolerable Acts, and it was the other three which were decisive. The central one was the Massachusetts Government Act of May 1774, which altered that government so as to give the royal executive some real power, by terminating the election of the council, which was also the upper house of the legislature, by the House of Representatives. In future the governor was to nominate his council, which would hold office at his pleasure. He was also to nominate all judges, and there were to be restrictions on town meetings to deprive them of their role as the inner citadels of Massachusetts populist and democratic self-government. The other two Acts stiffened the ability of the executive to secure compliance by enabling the governor to move a case out of the provincial courts to another colony or Britain where he thought that politically motivated local juries would deny basic justice, as they had in the past, to Crown servants; and by compelling local authorities to find quarters for troops near the site of any trouble if barracks were not to hand. When the Continental Congress assembled in Philadelphia in September 1774 to coordinate resistance to the Coercive Acts, it became clear that the planter elites of Virginia and the Carolinas were as set on resistance as the populist demagogues of New England. When General Gage replaced the exhausted Thomas Hutchinson in 1774 as governor of Massachusetts, and the Royal Navy moved to enforce a blockade of the port, war was a clear likelihood, and both colonial protestors and royal officials knew that they had to be willing to fight to carry any weight at all, even in negotiation.

The interesting question is why so many colonial leaders were so willing to hazard war.

It has been demonstrated that they, whose material and intellectual culture was much more attuned to the rhythms and fashions of metropolitan British culture than had been the case in the mid-seventeenth century, had forged a political world view out of a highly selective version of metropolitan culture. They had established a consensus in America, based on the most radical elements in British political discourse, drawing heavily on the 'Commonwealth' tradition, whose leading ideologues had included Irishmen like Viscount Molesworth and Scots like Fletcher of Saltoun. From writers of the 1720s like John Trenchard and Thomas Gordon they had learned to articulate the view that liberty was under constant threat by the subversion of the public virtue which alone could sustain it, and that there was a widespread conspiracy so to undermine it on behalf of an incipient executive tyranny of monstrous dimensions. It was a very convenient creed, telling them they were the last best hope of mankind and endorsing all their main political objectives, but it was less significant as a trigger mechanism for war than it was to be as a shaper of their future polity. The ideology, for example, contained a very large element of passionate hostility to the very concept of standing armies, seen as the tools of a tyranny only kept at bay by the libertarian instincts of a virtuous citizen militia. Yet despite the sustained attempts by some radicals to manufacture trouble between colonists and royal troops, there was in fact very little friction between colonists and the twenty regular regiments of the post-1763 American Establishment.[9]

American colonial society was just not frightened by the prospect of war. It had been cradled in violence from the start. The earliest settlements had a defensive aspect, and once conflict broadened out to include European as well as native American peoples, wars fought with 'macabre intensity' were a regularly recurring theme in colonial history. Indian losers lost everything; European losers, a homeland. The free whites in the colonies were weapon-using people, and their belligerence steadily mounted as the crisis with the London government became more acute in the 1760s and early 1770s. False information that the Royal Navy had bombarded Boston in September 1774 was enough to set tens of thousands of armed men towards the town. An identical episode occurred around Philadelphia a few weeks later and John Adams recorded that 'the People seemed really disappointed when the news was contradicted'. He also thought that 'a Martial spirit has seized all the colonies'. He was clear that they were much more belligerent than they had been in the last war, which he felt would enable them to redeem themselves from corruption by displaying the 'great, manly and warlike virtues'. War was gendered. It was also purifying or redeeming, an illusion which was still alive and well in at least the early stages of the First World War 150 years later. Sam Adams, the Boston firebrand, thought that war would afford a 'golden opportunity of recovering the Virtue and reforming the Manner of our Country'.[10]

There is no doubt that George III and his Westminster governments were nervous at the prospect of what was bound to be a nasty civil war, with an obvious risk of foreign intervention. Nothing else can explain the lengths to which they had gone in their appeasement policies. Many colonials were positively enthusiastic about the idea of war. There were plenty of veterans around who had fought in the late French and Indian War, and who were sources of experience and advice. The advice could be supplemented by reading an extensive available military literature. Two of the more avid readers were a Rhode Island anchorsmith called Nathaniel Greene, who was to command the Patriot armies in the South for much of the coming war; and a Boston bookseller, Henry Knox, who also became a general and the 'father' of the American army's artillery tradition. An immense enthusiasm for military drill and practice, amounting to a *rage militaire*, swept the colonies in 1774–75. When ideology and military events appeared to coincide, the upshot was intoxicating, as when the by definition virtuous New England militia behind field defences proved more than capable of massacring exposed regulars at the Battle of Breed's or Bunker Hill. It is no accident that as the British army subsequently evacuated Boston, a thrill ran through all the rebellious colonies and Congress moved towards a declaration of independence in the early summer of 1776. It all looked as if it was going according to plan.[11] Even before the first shots had been fired, however, there were hard-nosed non-ideological reasons why leading Americans were confident that they would win any armed confrontation with George III and his London government.

Some of these were diplomatic. Part of the traditional self-congratulatory image of the origins of the United States of America created by generations of American scholars building on the rhetoric of the fathers of the republic themselves was the idea that Americans turned their backs on established European diplomatic methods, seen as 'a rotten, corrupt, and perfidious system of international dealings'.[12] Nothing could be further from the truth. The diplomacy of the revolution was European and conservative, and deeply influenced by the concept of the balance of power, which had been a colonial commonplace for decades. Of course, the precise interpretation given to that doctrine had varied as the circumstances of British North America changed. At every crisis with the French in the 1730s and 1740s Americans had preached to their fellow Britons in Europe that the American colonies were of inestimable value, the source of Britain's wealth and power, and the factor which gave Britain decisive weight in the European balance. In the 1750s this chorus rose to a crescendo. In 1754 Dr William Clarke of Boston wrote that the colonies were 'of such consequence to the Trade, Wealth, and Naval Power of Great-Britain' that their retention was the key to the maintenance of her 'Independency', not to mention 'her Superiority as a Maritime Power'. Should they be lost in the confrontation emerging with France in the Ohio country, the good doctor was sure that 'Great Britain herself must necessarily be reduced to an absolute subjection to the French Crown, to nothing more than a province of France'.

George III has been mocked for saying the same in the 1770s, but he was only saying what his now rebellious American subjects had been shouting in the period before 1760. Another obsessive theme of American colonial discourse was the destiny of white America, sustained by boundless land and surging population, to become the global seat of empire. Notoriously, Benjamin Franklin in his 1751 *Observations Concerning the Increase of Mankind* had predicted that if the colonies continued to double their population every twenty years in a land mass the size of North America, they would inevitably create an imperial colossus. In 1755 John Adams, the future first vice president and second president of the United States of America, responded to this sort of calculation by telling a friend that within a century America would be able to hold the mastery of the seas and give the law to all Europe. He did not change his views on America becoming the seat of empire at all before he left in 1778 to be a crucially important American commissioner at the court of Louis XVI. Franklin – who, incidentally, kept stealing the scene from Adams in Paris, to the latter's fury, by sly acting up to French expectations – had himself continued through the 1760s to trumpet America's imperial destiny. It was a colonial platitude. Sam Adams wrote in April 1774 that 'Providence will erect a mighty empire in America'. Arthur Lee in 1772 had forecast that 'America, in her turn will be the imperial mistress of the world', a situation which basically had come to pass by the end of the twentieth century.

It followed that the early tone of many members of the Continental Congress, especially after the British evacuation of Boston in March 1776, was one of swaggering arrogance, rather than fearful resolution. Beleaguered in Boston, General Gage spotted this temper, as indeed did thoughtful Patriots who worried, like John Joachim Zubly of Georgia, that too many were talking about 'presenting Law to a conquered People', rather than about defending themselves from a formidable power. Reinforcing this slightly irrational hubris was a very eighteenth-century calculation based on the concept of interest, which was basic to much contemporary political discourse in English. Both for commercial and for geopolitical reasons, Patriots reckoned that within a finite time the governments of both France and Spain would deem it in their interest to support the declared independence of the United States openly. So sure were the Patriots of this that they proposed, typically, to reward their helpers with very little indeed beyond the opening of American ports to their trade, in the full knowledge that for purely economic reasons Great Britain was likely to continue to dominate post-war American imports and exports.[13]

Militarily, the twelve colonies represented in the Continental Congress which defied the Crown in 1775 were a mixed bag, but they had in several cases an extensive experience of raising and deploying contract provincial armies. The most extensively studied province is predictably Massachusetts, where it has been shown that in the Seven Years' War the militia, which had decayed less in Massachusetts than in the rest of America, was used primarily as a source of recruits for a reasonably well-paid provincial army which took advantage of the fact that the nature of provincial society was such that it regularly made significant numbers of young males available for finite periods for military service. The army was contracted for a year, and its members were brutally business-like in regarding their job as one which either ended or had to be renegotiated on a set date. The collective military experience of veteran soldiers and administrators was still there in the 1770s as the imperial crisis came to a head, supplemented by a much higher level of political mobilisation and solidarity, even in townships which had showed the usual New England tendency to internal quarrels over local government decisions and especially over church matters. Everyone knew that the militia, because of its wide base (virtually all able-bodied men between 16 and 60 were theoretically in it), was incapable of a swift response. Minutemen companies had been formed of men enlisted with an obligation to stand to arms at a minute's notice, but with the guarantee of being paid reasonable wages for their time if called to serve outside the town they lived in. A place like Concord had been on a war footing for several months before it played its part in mauling the British column sent to destroy the cache of provincial weapons stored there. The colonists were far readier for the war they meant to fight than General Gage, who did not even have appropriate troops for the strike on Concord. John Howe, the spy who had alerted him to the Concord cache, had said specifically that only a quick-moving cavalry force of 500 had any hope of conducting what should have been a night operation before getting back safely into Gage's Boston lines. Gage had no cavalry. Not much wonder that few in Massachusetts expected a long war: a siege of Boston followed soon by an aggressive thrust into Canada would bring Westminster to terms.[14]

The attitudes of the metropolitan government towards the prospect of war were rather more complex. North basically felt cornered. The Stamp Act crisis had exhausted the sympathies for the American colonies of all but a tiny minority in the Westminster legislature.[15] The protracted struggle which had led to the repeal of all the Townshend duties except the one on tea turned out to be no long-term solution. The Declaratory Act of 1766 with its assertion of the ultimate sovereignty of the Westminster parliament had not only been a necessary tactical device to ensure the passage of the repeal of most of the Townshend duties by a reluctant House of Commons, but also a statement of the deepest convictions of the Rockingham Whigs – than whom there were few more outrageous exponents of the view that a simple majority in the Commons ought to entitle an administration to have its way. Even if the EIC tea had been free of duty when it reached America, it would not have been acceptable because, unless they were consignees, legitimate colonial tea traders as well as smugglers would have been under-cut, and the next American colonial absolute right asserted would have been freedom from monopoly.[16] Nor would it have been the last. Historians have been far too obsessed with the voluminous propaganda churned out by the presses in the course of the crisis between 1763 and 1776. The North government understood that propaganda had its place, especially in the mobilisation of support out of doors, which is why people as eminent as Sir John Dalrymple, Dr Samuel Johnson, and indeed John Wesley were encouraged to write in defence of the government's record and to denounce the demonisation of that government by American Patriots.[17] That most eminent American Thomas Hutchinson, the last civilian Loyalist gov-ernor of Massachusetts – himself demonised by fellow Americans whose leaders were often less moderate and tolerant, and always vastly more self-righteous, than he – found in his exile in Old England a ministry 'half-paralyzed with indecision and insecurity' and 'incapable of the art of making imaginative adjustments'.[18] Where imagination was needed was in conceptualising a war which, since it was quite unavoidable, short of unconditional surrender which contemporaries saw would have meant the end of anything which could rationally be called a British Empire, was potentially as much an opportunity as it was a danger.

There were influential people who grasped the need to invent a winnable war and appreciated that a straightforward attempt to conquer twelve or thirteen colonies which had only to a minimal degree ever been governed from London was the least promising approach. Lord Barrington, secretary at war from 1755 to 1761, and again from 1765 to 1778, had always been sceptical of what a dispersed British army could hope to achieve in North America. In 1766 he had produced a memo which seriously urged the withdrawal of troops from their western posts, which had proved of little value in the Indian wars of the 1760s; and from the seaboard of the middle colonies, where unsympathetic or intimidated magistrates were likely to make effective action against rioters virtually impossible. The army was to be concentrated in Nova Scotia, Canada, and the Floridas, whence it could possibly emerge to deal with an overt act of rebellion in a specific province. General Thomas Gage, writing to Barrington from New York in November 1776, pointed out that since troops in Canada were effectively ice-bound for six months in a year, Nova Scotia would be the sensible northern base for any force with a capacity to intervene further south, though the logistical limitations, especially availability of shipping, forced him to envisage that no more than 'Two or Three Regiments may be generally transported upon an Emergency'. Significantly, Gage also pointed out that in any colonial disturbance it would be difficult to ensure the safety of Crown ammunition and ordnance stores in places like New York.[19] Lethal opposition to Barrington's radical plan came from Amherst, who never acknowledged the folly of his own policy of small dispersed western garrisons; colonial lobbyists like Franklin, who were passionately hostile to Barrington's idea of a vast Indian reservation in the west where white settlement would be restricted; and from Lord Shelburne, the colonists' most predictable ally in government, who had supported plans for extensive development of settlements on traditionally Indian lands.[20] It is, however, easy to see why Barrington, who with George III ran the British army from day to day, contemplated a coming struggle with the principal American colonies with dread. He was well aware of the terrible logistical problems and the numerical inadequacies of any Crown forces likely to be deployed. Unsuccessfully, but wisely, he urged no serious military effort in rebel colonies, and a concentration upon naval blockade to bring the defiant colonists to the negotiating table.[21]

Reports reaching senior officers of the British army such as General Lord Amherst, by 1774 the lieutenant general of the ordnance and a privy councillor, made it clear even before Lexington that there was widespread support for the plight of Massachusetts in the other colonies. It was noted in the War Office that the bulk of opinion in Virginia was ardently supportive of the Continental Congress and that that Old Dominion had raised five thousand men to aid the Congress in its struggle with the Crown, which was five times the force the colony had been willing to raise in the late French and Indian War. Amherst was to become an adherent of the school which faced the fact that the Americans were likely to laugh at any proposals for serious political negotiations, and argued that naval blockade was the only way in which pressure could be placed on the rebellious colonies at an acceptable price.[22] There were optimistic fools like General James Grant, who was to serve in the coming war in North America, where he had already campaigned against the French. He stood up in the House of Commons to boast that with 5000 regulars he could march anywhere in the disaffected colonies. William Alexander of New Jersey, titular Earl of Stirling and a future American general, overheard the boast, which he repeated to his Maryland troops at the Battle of Brooklyn in 1776 to incite them to fight stoutly against the British left wing commanded by the same James Grant. So Grant's boast entered the mythic history of the revolution.[23]

Yet for every commentator who spoke like Grant, another can be found who stressed the enormous inherent strength of the colonists, often long before the revolution. Peter Williamson, a Scot kidnapped and shipped to America as a child, commented in his best-selling account of his adventures, which had reached a fifth edition by 1763, that Boston was in many ways as rich and sophisticated as any town in England, with merchants as rich as most London merchants and a formidable capacity to repel attack based on the fact that 'in 24 hours time 10,000 effective men, well arm'd might be available for their defence'.[24] A 1772 work on the current *State of the British Empire*, remarkable for its often cock-eyed optimism, simply took it for granted that the economic strength of the continental American colonies and their likely solidarity in any struggle with the British government would make it feasible, especially if Britain were mired in a European war, for them in the future to throw off allegiance to the Crown. This seemed not an immediate threat, when British naval supremacy still had the capacity to inflict terrible commercial loss on American rebels, but even at sea, the author stressed, the American colonists had shown formidable privateering capacities.[25] The odd British regular officer consoled himself with the thought that one 'smart campaign' by the professional forces of the Crown would sort out the American imbroglio even after Lexington, but by November 1775 London newspaper readers could read a warning from a Royal Navy officer in Boston that this was a dangerous delusion; the rebels meant business and fought hard. Vice Admiral Samuel Graves, the officer commanding the North American squadron of 30 ships scattered along several thousand miles of coast, was shrewd enough to see that the mere supplying of large regular armies would pose appalling problems. He stressed the case for an effective, hard-hitting coastal blockade, with no more pussy-footing, in the hope that the feelings of the totally intransigent New Englanders would not be hurt. Yet by 1776 he was gone and the Royal Navy's attempt at coastal blockade was already a failure due to lack of ships, which meant that the rebellious colonies had been able to export staple commodities on a big scale to finance the purchase of the arms and ammunition with which the early stages of the revolution were sustained.[26] Graves did manage to destroy the potential privateer nest of Falmouth to the accompaniment of howls of rage from the rebels, which indicated that this was indeed one way to hurt them, but he never had enough ships or the right ships for the job. He did not need reinforcements in the shape of the superb modern 74-gun ships of the line. They were for fleet actions against European navies. Graves needed schooners, sloops of war, and above all the obsolete 50-gun ships whose shallow draught made them ideal for coastal operations. In any case, he was soon being told to make his ships available for so many other purposes that he could achieve no decisive concentration of force, and was scapegoated and fired for failure to achieve the impossible.[27] Governor General Gage should have been fired for presiding over his subordinate Howe's tactical shambles at Bunker Hill and for lethargy in failing even to try to occupy and fortify the narrow necks of land which were the approaches to the heights commanding Boston, but he was in fact fired for telling Westminster the truth when he said that conquering New England was a concept beyond his reach unless he received 20,000 reinforcements at once. After that he had to go, but George III and his ministers never came up with a design for a war they could win. Gage had already told them that in the face of the 'vast numbers' of armed rebels in New England, they had to accept that its conquest would require not just 'Time and Perseverance' but also 'Strong Armys attacking it in various Quarters; and dividing their Forces'.[28]

Gage's successor, General Sir William Howe, found himself in command of about 12,000 troops blockaded by a colonial army of 16,000, of indifferent quality and poor discipline, but full of fight and holding naturally favourable defensive positions. There was a shortage of military muskets in the colonial militia around Boston, so troops were encouraged to bring along any shoulder arms they possessed. Consequently 'many were armed with hunting pieces such as the Hudson Valley and New England fowlers'.[29] After 17 June 1775, when the British regulars had been shocked and enraged by the slaughter of their ranks at the Battle of Bunker Hill, nobody doubted the lethal nature of the rebels' mixed collection of firearms. With the arrival of General George Washington as commander of the besieging force, its position became even stronger. Unlike the British regiments with their regular (and irregular) quotas of women, the colonial camp had no women in it, which meant it was singularly badly run, especially with respect to basic hygiene. Washington could not drill his troops in the more intricate manoeuvres of the eighteenth-century battlefield, but then he did not need to. Cashiering incompetent officers, flogging insubordinate soldiers, and insisting on adequate latrines and regular washing of clothes improved the health and discipline of an army which he sent out every morning after prayers to work on an increasingly effective system of fortifications.

Howe had been authorised to evacuate Boston, if he saw no alternative. Amazingly, he seriously considered another attempt to break out. By February 1776 Washington had been able to get rid of many of his worst troops and slightly strengthen his overall numbers to more than 17,000 men, thanks to reinforcements coming in from Pennsylvania, Maryland, Virginia, and other colonies from July 1775 onwards. His ammunition supplies had been increased significantly, as had his artillery. A wealthy young merchant and smuggler from New Haven, Connecticut, Benedict Arnold, had suggested that the cannon the rebel forces before Boston so badly needed might be seized, without too much difficulty, from Fort Ticonderoga (formerly the French Fort Carillon) which lay on the invasion route to Canada, between Lakes George and Champlain. If the New Englanders had been gearing up to fight the Crown for months, the Crown had done very little to prepare for serious war with New England. Its policy had been one of massive police actions with troops when exasperated, but they were always reactive, never pro-active. Ticonderoga should have been put in a good state of repair and reinforced, or abandoned and slighted after being cleared. Instead, its crumbling defences and inadequate garrison were simply swamped by a pre-dawn attack of local Partisans led by Ethan Allen and known as the Green Mountain Boys. Whether anyone could have commanded them may be doubted, but Arnold and Allen co-directed the coup.

Winter conditions made it possible for the enterprising Colonel Henry Knox to arrive before Boston on 24 January 1776 with sleighs, carts, and pack horses bearing forty-three cannon and sixteen mortars from Ticonderoga. Washington could now think of bombarding the town, which he did early in March to mask his seizure, by landing 2000 men, of Dorchester Heights, south-east of and overlooking Boston Neck, the narrow approach to the town. Inexcusably, Howe had not occupied this strategic position. His position was humiliating. He could not find enough shipping to evacuate his garrison. He dared not split it to evacuate in stages, or the vastly superior enemy would swarm over what was left of it. That a proposed night assault on 5 March on the rebel defences on Dorchester Heights was made impracticable by torrential rain was probably a blessing. There were twenty cannon in position to blow away assaulting British columns with canister fire, not to mention serried muskets. Howe was in a David and Goliath situation in which his poor bloody infantry had no chance of matching the performance of David's polished pebble. Howe had already worked out that even if he broke the besiegers' ring, he could go nowhere in pursuit of them as he had no transportation. On 17 March, in horribly crowded vessels and without waiting for promised shipping, he evacuated the city, destroying stores he could not carry and taking a thousand desperately upset Loyalists with him. That was a correct and humane decision, even if many children died on the voyage. These people could not be left to the tender mercies of their fellow countrymen.[30]

Howe could only head for Halifax, Nova Scotia, where food was as scarce and absurdly expensive as in besieged Boston, though firewood was more available. His troops had pulled down a significant proportion of Boston trying to avoid freezing to death. Through the spring of 1776 Howe had to stay in Halifax. The flag of the 'United Colonies' (thirteen red stripes, one for each colony, with a pre-1800 Union Flag of St George's and St Andrew's crosses in the upper left-hand corner) had flown over Washington's lines. Now it flew over Boston, but not for much longer. With Governor Dunmore summarily ejected from Virginia as ignominiously, if with less bloodshed, as the British garrison had been expelled from Boston, there seemed little doubt that the triumphant colonists had scored the sort of victory which the more militant of them had always assumed they had a God-given right to expect. If gentlemen in the House of Commons at Westminster said foolishly deprecatory words about American military spirit, they were amply matched by the hubris of American Whigs. 'With some exaggeration' the latter had depicted Lexington as the total rout of the fine flower of the British army. The British 'teeth are harmless, the claws are impotent, and this British Lion, who has frightened our children here will, we are persuaded, turn out nothing but a Scottish Ass from the Isle of Bute'. The Scotophobia which had greeted George III's first premier, the Earl of Bute, in the 1760s was still alive and kicking in English America in 1775.

Before the outbreak of serious fighting American Whigs had persuaded themselves that a hundred thousand colonists would instantly leap to arms, and some Whigs carried self-deception to the point of believing they would be joined by a host of faithful Indian allies bent on collecting British officers' scalps. Other colonial calculations had been a deal more realistic, such as that of the Bostonian who said in 1775, 'It is in vain, it is delirium, it is frenzy, to think of dragooning Three Millions of English People out of their Liberties, at the Distance of 3000 Miles.' Whigs were also convinced that they were so morally superior to their corrupt, effete opponents that 'the Glory of God is on our side and will fight for us, and this makes us bold as lions'. American Whig pre-war calculations that the sheer size of America would make them virtually unsubduable turned out to be sensible enough, as did their conviction that 'In the arts of the bush, and in skirmishing fight we stand unrivaled.' What was less sensible was the view that it was hardly worth opposing the landing of a British expeditionary force because, fighting 'with Roman intrepidity', of course, 'we can bush fight them and cut off their Offices very easily, and in this way we can subdue them with very little loss'. The hyping of the 'deadly' American rifle, which proved of limited utility during the war, pre-dated its outbreak.[31]

Franklin's calculations about the American birth rate and the astonishing growth potential it promised were all part of this pre-war or early war build-up of overweening self-confidence in Whig and Patriot circles. This sort of mentality was mainstream in much of colonial America. The Reverend Moses Mather (1719–1806), who came from a celebrated New England family of divines and who published in Hartford, Connecticut, in 1775 *America's Appeal to the Impartial World*, regarded the very earliest English settlements in America as 'the rudiments of a future empire, before in embryo'. He celebrated colonial feats of arms 'in a bloody and expensive, tho' successful war with the French and Indians', which the colonists 'have been almost continually engaged in' until the fall of French Canada. Mather was passionately opposed to negotiating with commissioners whom Lord North proposed (in a tactic Mather rightly saw as *divide et impera*) should talk with individual colonies, not the Continental Congress, about reconciliation. If British subjects could not emigrate and order their affairs 'independent of the king and kingdom', he asked, how could 'new empires' be founded?[32]

The decision to declare the thirteen states independent was therefore mainly an issue of prudence and timing. Without exception, committed Whigs and Patriots meant to take the substance of independence. They were not only confident they could defeat British armies, but also convinced that there were ways of bringing George III and his government to what they saw as a recognition of the inevitable. Two means were to hand. One was a quick stab into Canada to gather it into the rightful field of American expansion. Another was the formation of European alliances which would show Westminster that an American war was as dangerous as it was unwinnable. One of the first colonial moves in the conflict after the beleaguering of Boston had been an invasion of Canada in the winter of 1775–76. Their forces had been small, but General Guy Carleton, who was governor of Quebec and the garrison commander in Canada, had sent most of his best troops to Boston and only managed with difficulty to fend off the American assault with a garrison a mere 1800 strong and heavily dependent on militia, seamen, and recently recruited Scots immigrants rather than regulars.[33] Of the two American commanders, Richard Montgomery was killed and Benedict Arnold wounded in a desperate, unsuccessful assault launched on Quebec on 31 December in a blizzard. As usual, the Continental Congress had shown limitless appetite for territorial expansion, but much less ability to mobilise, pay for, and deliver the necessary means. Even so, its forces merely fell back on Montreal, with every hope 'that they would spend the summer of 1776 inside the walls of Quebec'.[34] Though reinforcements reached Carleton *via* the St Lawrence when the ice began to break up in May, he moved very cautiously, only decisively defeating a new American commander, General John Sullivan, on 8 June 1776. Even then, the Continental Congress was spared the full implications of the failure of the expedition. Between them, Carleton's army and the Royal Navy should have been able to pin down and destroy or capture the entire enemy force. Carleton did not want to do that. He let the Americans escape, as he reported to Secretary of State for the American Department Lord Germain, 'to convince all His Majesty's unhappy subjects, that the King's mercy and Benevolence were still open to them'. He did not grasp how little chance he had of modifying the American Whig mentality, when he had a very fair opportunity to modify Whig behaviour and expectation levels by exposing both to a stern dose of military realities. He only wanted to push the invaders out of Canada. He did, very slowly, pursue them, and in October finally defeated an American flotilla commanded by Benedict Arnold on Lake Champlain, but he had decided, before the battle, not to attack Fort Ticonderoga at the southern end of the lake. Subsequently, he pulled back into Canada.[35]

With the fall of Boston, and with Canada still in contention, the Congress understandably deemed it safe to come out into the open with a Declaration of Independence. Even Patrick Henry of Virginia, an irreconcilable if ever there was one, had had reservations about taking the step without assurance of foreign aid. Circumstances, rather than the pamphlet *Common Sense* published by the recent English immigrant Tom Paine, explain the dating of the Declaration for July 1776. Paine's brilliant oversimplifications and clarion call for a clean break helped shift the language of American republicanism away from the assertion of the rights of Englishmen towards the rhetoric of the Rights of Man, but even that was not at all new. Moses Mather had denied that Americans 'because they have the rights of British subjects, . . . are rendered incapable of enjoying the rights of men'. There was also widespread appreciation in the Congress of another of Paine's arguments: that if they wanted European allies they had to make it clear there would be no reconciliation with the British Crown. It must have seemed safe to make the Declaration to encourage the alliances rather than wait for the alliances before declaring independence. The snag was that shortly after the Declaration of Independence a huge armada of ships appeared carrying the army of 25,000 with which General Howe proposed to make a new start by invading Long Island.

The prolongation of the war as midwife to the conception and birth of a new nation from 1777

The decision to evacuate a beleaguered Boston and move the main British forces to New York in the summer of 1776 was strategically astute, for it was an escape from a prison, but it was part of an overall design which was based on several miscalculations and was never really executed with the drive that alone could have given it a chance of success. The design was in accord with the sanguine temperament and preference for seizing the

initiative which was characteristic of Lord George Germain, the able military administrator who became third secretary of state, with responsibility
for the conduct of the American war, in late 1775. He knew that outright
conquest was a naive concept, but believed that a sudden massive blow
aimed at the main body of rebel regulars, the Continental Line, would
discourage the disloyal and rally the considerable number of American
Loyalists believed, correctly, to be far more numerous in the central colonies than in New England. In the first place, Germain's wise opinion that
a protracted war made no sense, and that it was imperative to exert 'the
utmost force of the Kingdom to finish the rebellion in one campaign',[36] if
that could be done, presupposed an all-out offensive driven through with
maximum ruthlessness. Worse executants of such a policy could hardly
have been found than the two brothers appointed to head the Royal Navy
and the British army in the forthcoming campaign: Admiral Viscount Howe
and General Sir William Howe. They were respectively a great fighting
sailor and a competent light infantry specialist, but they had concealed
the depth of their lack of sympathy with the war to obtain high command.
Their insistence on being given powers as commissioners to negotiate with
the rebel colonies was criticised at the time, because both were grotesquely
inarticulate.

They were also stubborn as mules, and fought their own war at their
own increasingly glacial pace, interspersed with bouts of naive hope for real
negotiations when it was clear there could be none other than ones for
unconditional withdrawal until military or naval pressure had become
severe enough to change attitudes. General Howe's refusal to cooperate
with General John Burgoyne's thrust down the Hudson River in 1777 set
up the disaster which encouraged France to enter the war, though Burgoyne's
actual surrender at Saratoga was basically the result of his own self-serving
refusal to contemplate early enough the retreat and cutting of losses which
his brigadiers were urging on him as the correct military decision. A gambler
and active politician like Burgoyne preferred risking catastrophe to a
withdrawal which would have had the same effect on his career. When
to Burgoyne's irresponsibility is added the refusal of General Howe to act
aggressively from his Philadelphia base against General Washington's
forces in the winter of 1777–78 – Howe's senior officers were despairingly
pointing out that he could either act now, with some hope of success, or
retreat later – it becomes clear that a combination of rashness and half-
heartedness in the British high command in two different theatres had
guaranteed the long war that neither the colonists had expected, nor that
Germain wished to fight.[37]

It was this unexpected prolongation of the war after 1776 for another
five years that provided the context in which many of the founding legends

of the infant United States were laid down, and the nature of the options available for its future development debated. Such episodes as the suffering of Washington's army in Valley Forge in the severe winter of 1777–78 in Pennsylvania, when semi-starvation threatened a camp which was otherwise well sited and defensible, provided an appropriate example of heroic resolution in the face of long odds. The odds were mostly a problem about organising an adequate commissariat for the army without alienating political support by naked seizure of animals and grain from nearby farmers. Five hundred of Washington's horses died of lack of feed, and had to be replaced, but receipts were given for horses taken, the values being settled by a neutral evaluator.

Militarily the situation in the spring of 1778 was not at all threatening for Washington. General Henry Clinton replaced General Howe in command of the British army in Philadelphia in May, and by mid-June he was resigned to evacuating the city, taking with him, to his credit, 3000 Loyalists. His 10,000 troops were somewhat outnumbered by the enemy, but he was horribly exposed because of his horde of camp followers, the Loyalists, and a baggage train of 1500 wagons stretching for vulnerable miles across the countryside. Partly because the eccentric General Charles Lee, who was in command of the American advanced force, was opposed in principle to the risk of an all-out attack, the harassment of the retreating Clinton was poorly managed at the Battle of Monmouth Court House, but Clinton and Cornwallis mismanaged the British counter-attack and Clinton's army could only achieve its basic objective – retreat to New York.[38]

It is very difficult to see a point in the war where a decisive victory for Crown forces was truly possible. The Howes' sequence of tactical victories in New York and Pennsylvania in 1776 and 1777 gave metropolitan British government and opinion the impression that they were winning the war. Yet the massive commonsense of George Washington, and the clarity with which he grasped, despite his natural instinct for tactical aggression, the absolute strategic necessity to keep the Continental Army in being, meant that he would retreat out of disaster, every time. Apparent opportunities to cut him off turn out, on analysis, to be delusory. The classic case is the argument that if the Howe brothers had coordinated their actions better he and his army could have been trapped on Long Island in the 1776 summer campaign there. That presupposes the Royal Navy should have been able to dominate the narrow waters across which lay his lines of retreat. In practice, shallow water, deliberately sunken hulks and other built underwater obstacles, shore batteries, and fireships made the use of major fleet units quite impractical. Frigates, sloops, and brigs alone could think of trying to operate, but of these only the frigates were big enough to see off rebel sloops and brigs, and the frigates could not overcome the batteries and, above all, the row galleys which Washington deployed. These, ultimately with twin eighteen-pounder guns in the bows, had all the advantages which made the galley, from the sixteenth to the eighteenth centuries, a lethal enemy of the sailing ship in coastal waters. They were manoeuvrable, and by firing heavy guns on very low mountings they could hole an opponent 'between wind and water' and sink her. The Royal Navy could not close Washington's line of retreat.[39]

So the barren victories on the road to Philadelphia and the dispiriting retreat from it look not at all surprising in retrospect. Just possibly, if Howe had stepped up the pace and sharpened the bite of his thrusts, he could have done enough damage to the Continental Army to constitute a sort of 'victory'. Even then, it may be doubted if it would have been possible to negotiate any stable political peace. In any case Howe was for ideological reasons congenitally inclined to pull his punches, and so well connected politically that it required great determination and moral courage on the part of Lord George Germain to make the unanimous and long-overdue cabinet decision to sack General Howe stick, in the face of howls of protest from Establishment worthies ranging from Howe's mother to George III.[40] What made Howe's record all the more indefensible was the fact that the British were well aware of the looming danger of French intervention.

The hawks in Paris were led by the foreign minister, the comte de Vergennes, who was convinced after Bunker Hill that 'It will be in vain for the English to multiply their forces there . . . no longer can they bring that vast continent back to dependence by force of arms.'[41] Predominant opinion in Westminster did not agree. It thought the rebels could be daunted, though only if deprived of all hope of European succour. Signs of massive French rearmament became clear by the summer of 1775, when the Royal Navy was already under pressure due to the demands of North America. What the British government did not appreciate was that the resignation of Turgot, the main advocate of peace, retrenchment, and fiscal reform within the French government, in May 1776, signalled that France had taken a decision in principle for war. The British continued to hope that minimal deterrence, mainly by capital ship patrols in home waters and marginal preparation for a European war, would confine France to her well-known, clandestine support for the rebels. All of this meant that 'The great effort mounted in 1776 was in a sense a gamble on quick results to forestall and discourage the French.'[42]

The fact that the Howe brothers, with exceptional resources and so much riding on the achievement of battlefield victories, had shown an outrageous lack of drive and determination in two crucial campaign seasons in 1776-77 was common knowledge in England by the time they returned. In 1780 General Howe was defending his seat as MP for Nottingham, with the active help of his admiral brother Lord Howe. The general lost because he had alienated almost everyone. There was an embittered Dissenter interest, well entrenched in the corporation, which hated the British state (identified with Anglican ascendancy), and which itself identified with the American Patriots, on whom they projected their own frustrations and hopes. Everyone else in Nottingham blamed the Howes for wilful inaction in America and its consequences. So the brothers were damned both for going to America and for doing so little there.[43] There was much to be said for both points of view.

The final phase of British military operations in America was flawed from the start in ways which should have been apparent from experience of operations in Pennsylvania, New Jersey, and New York, which revealed quite early the extreme vulnerability of the local Loyalists, often referred to rather unfairly as Tories, to the terrorist tactics employed against them by the Whig or Patriot militias. These militias were employed as the principal means of internal control by the new state governments established in 1775–77. They may have had severe limitations in battle, but George Washington found them an indispensable supplement to his Continental regulars. Militia could free the regulars from the chore of defending coastal towns and exposed enclaves from British raids, for Bunker Hill had shown what militia could do behind defended fixed positions. They screened and could reinforce the Continental Line, to whom they were a vital source of intelligence. Above all they ruthlessly put down the Loyalists. In the words of the best study of these militiamen, 'Tories were hunted, apprehended, ousted or killed throughout the war'.[44] Indeed they were. The enduring hostility of New England to metropolitan control owed much to the predominant congregational religion of the region, but to argue that the American Revolution was in some sense a religious war is just not convincing.[45] It was a mass mobilisation which rapidly forged a self-righteous civic religion as its ideology, and one which in the name of liberty went in for ruthless populist suppression of dissenting voices. After Washington's surprise counter-offensive in the winter of 1776–77, and his victories at Trenton and Princeton – which forced Howe to pull back his lines and exposed New Jersey Loyalists who had rallied to the Crown to the full fury of their mortal enemies in the Whig militias – it should have been clear that Loyalist elements were most effective as conservative moderates within the new states, pointing out that a diet of spartan frugality and warlike republican virtue palled after a while. Instead, the Westminster government embarked after 1778 on its final fling in the shape of a southern option, heavily dependent on hopes of Loyalist support and truly impractical outside Georgia, where Loyalist government could be restored. A singularly vicious civil war, with abundant atrocities on both sides, was unleashed all over the South.

The American Department of the British metropolitan government had great faith in the new southern strategy. Georgia had been recovered for royal control by a small force in 1778. It was thought that the other colonies in the South would be vulnerable to piecemeal conquest, partly because of their large slave populations, and partly because their cash-crop economies made them dependent on imports for many necessities. Certainly Georgia had fallen quickly after its Patriot rulers had unwisely called attention to themselves by raiding into British East Florida and attacking settlements on the St John's River. Prodded by Germain, Clinton had diverted a force of just under 3000, mainly composed of Germans and American provincials, but led by a formidable scion of the Clan Diarmaid, Lieutenant Colonel Archibald Campbell, with his own 2-battalion regiment, the 71st Highlanders. Helped by a negro guide, he surprised and overwhelmed a rebel force to seize Savannah, which gave him a base from which he cleared Georgia. That the successful battle-group had included Americans, Germans, and Scots reflected accurately enough the complex ethnic structure of the Atlantic monarchy of George III.

Sir Henry Clinton, the British commander-in-chief North America, had led an unsuccessful attack on Charles Town, South Carolina, in 1776.[46] That may account for his less than enthusiastic adoption of the new strategy, though he did have a rational argument that moving British troops from New York would merely allow the Continental Congress to release powerful forces of its own from the middle colonies to checkmate British moves in the South. Nevertheless, he led a force of over eight thousand men south at the very end of 1779 in a huge convoy escorted by a squadron commanded by Admiral Arbuthnot. He had waited until it was known that the French fleet commanded by Admiral D'Estaing had left North American waters for France. After a dreadful passage, he put into friendly Savannah; despatched Brigadier James Patterson with five thousand men to launch a diversionary attack on Augusta, Georgia, which had fallen into enemy hands; re-embarked and sailed to launch an amphibious attack on Charles Town. By March 1780 he had it under close siege. The defenders made the mistake of thinking the town defensible even after the Royal Navy forced the bar to anchor in the harbour. In 1776 they had failed to pass the defending Fort Moultrie. When Charles Town surrendered on 5 May, 5500 American troops were captured as well as vast amounts of ordnance, arms, and ammunition. Over two hundred Loyalist inhabitants presented a congratulatory address to Clinton and Arbuthnot 'on the restoration of this capital and province to their political connection with the Crown and government of Great Britain'.[47] It was, and was seen in London as, a great feat of arms. By the time Clinton left in the summer of 1780, turning over command of the royal forces in the South to Lord

Cornwallis, most of South Carolina seemed to be in British hands. It was a deceptive situation.

The Loyalists were clearly a minority. The Patriot militants may also have been a minority but were clearly more numerous, and the key group was that very large one in the middle, full of people with shifting allegiances whose twin ambitions were to be on the right side of the apparently winning side, and to be left alone. Many were willing to take an oath of allegiance to George III, but when the king's representatives went further, trying to force these people to take up arms, often against kinsmen, they undermined the acquiescence on which (rather than on positive support) the Crown regime was built. As in Virginia, where Lord Dunmore had tried to broaden the narrow base of indigenous loyalism – largely confined to office-holders and the mercantile communities in Norfolk, Portsmouth, and the Eastern Shore[48] – by offering freedom to negro slaves who would fight for the Crown, the royal government of South Carolina reached out to the negro community for labour and soldiers. It was a double-edged sword, for it enraged white colonists who saw it as subversion and theft of property. When the British evacuation fleet left Charleston in December 1782, 5000 of the 9127 civilians aboard were negroes who had been promised their freedom. The total number of negroes fleeing Charles Town in 1782 may have been as high as 6000, compared with 4000 from Savannah and 4000 from New York. Ironically, most of the freed slaves leaving South Carolina as Loyalists were sent to East Florida, that designated Loyalist refuge, and plunged into fresh crisis when the colony was unexpectedly handed over to Spain in the peace settlement. Some were forced to return to South Carolina.[49]

The fundamental problem facing royal government was military: it never could control the combined threat of attacks by Continental troops and Patriot partisans. That fact undermined the essential role of the Loyalists in the British strategy for the South. They were supposed to run and control the province in order to free the royal army to move north in a rolling ride of conquest. Instead, South Carolina, like North Carolina after it, plunged into bloody civil war. At least one Whig luminary in Pennsylvania, Chief Justice Thomas McKean, had been prepared to rule in 1781 that during the War of the American Revolution, 'Pennsylvania was not a nation at war with another nation, but a country in a state of *civil war*; and there is no precedent in the books to show what might be done in that case'. That was generous and true. There had been thousands of Loyalists in Pennsylvania. The last active ones, the Doan Gang, who like the Whig Green Mountain Boys before them combined political and criminal motivation, were only driven out of the state in 1784. In 1777 a Whig legislature defined active loyalism as treason, and state coercive power fined, forfeited, imprisoned, and occasionally executed Loyalists.[50] However, the threat of a mutual bloodbath clearly restrained both sides' use of the extreme penalty in alleged treason cases. The odd Pennsylvania Loyalist who was executed by the state was usually, disingenuously, convicted of a pure felony – such as burglary, forgery, or theft at a certain level – with the political motivation conveniently ignored.

After the successful British offensive, the Carolinas were not playing legal games in a civil war. They were fighting a civil war with no inhibitions. The role of Continental troops in the South was absolutely fundamental, for they forced the royal troops to concentrate to oppose them, and thereby to surrender control of the countryside to swarms of Patriot (Whig is perhaps not a defensible term in the South) guerrillas. It was Patriot militia which in North Carolina separated the advancing Cornwallis from his outlying militia forces, thus setting the scene for their victory over Loyalist American militia at the Battle of King's Mountain. They terrorised Loyalists, reinforced the Continental Army's ranks in battles, and helped above all to secure the defeat of Cornwallis' hardest-driving subordinate, the arrogant and extremely brutal Colonel Banastre Tarleton at Cowpens, just after the far more humane Patrick Ferguson had been killed at King's Mountain. Tarleton's dreaded battle-group of mixed cavalry and infantry, the British Legion, was an American Loyalist one raised originally in Philadelphia in 1778.[51]

Sir James Wright, the Loyalist governor of Georgia, could see perfectly clearly the disastrous implications of Cornwallis' relentless and profitless drive northwards. His province needed modest but essential construction of forts, and adequate garrisons to protect it against rebel raids. Even given the renewed cooperation of the Indians, who had every reason to detest the vociferously Patriot American frontiersmen who were pressing on their lands, the 800 men Cornwallis assigned to garrison Georgia, approximately 500 in Savannah, with a notional 300 (in practice much less) in Augusta, were absurdly inadequate. Sir James told Germain in January 1781, on the eve of Cornwallis' march north to the drawn and costly battle at Guildford Courthouse in North Carolina on 15 March 1781, that:

> I cannot think this Province and South Carolina in a State of Security, and if Lord Cornwallis Penetrates far into North Carolina I shall expect a Rebel Army will come in behind him and throw us into the utmost confusion and danger – For This Province is still left in a Defenceless State.[52]

Seldom has eighteenth-century use of capital letters on key words conveyed a sharper, or more justified, sense of disquiet. The Loyalist people were an instrument to Cornwallis, not a firm obligation, and they were an inadequate instrument for the purposes of his lethally unrealistic plans.

It is true that as late as early 1781 there seemed a chance of the anti-British alliance cracking from within. The stresses of a long war had reduced the United States which acknowledged the leadership of the Continental Congress to an economic, political, and military state which shocked the officers commanding the French expeditionary force that had landed in Rhode Island. In 1780 Spain had frightened the French by holding separate, tentative peace talks with the United Kingdom of Great Britain, and had offered mediation, which would certainly have given the British better terms in North America than they eventually obtained, had the process acquired any momentum at all. There was already talk of an Austrian–Russian mediation (which the Westminster government very unwisely turned down in June 1781). Germain was full of fight in October 1781 just as French artillery began to pound Cornwallis' untenable defences at Yorktown.[53] Yet even if Vergennes, who was for fiscal reasons keen to get out of the war, had cynically abandoned his American allies in peace negotiations, which he or any other French minister was more than capable of doing, the British were further from being able to control twelve of the thirteen provinces which had revolted in 1775 than ever. No negotiation could now alter that fact. Nor did the position of the main British field army in America make any long-term sense, though the static positions they held were, with one possible exception, the right ones.

Even if they had gone for a blockade-based attrition, it would have been essential for the British to capture major seaports like New York, both as bases and to deny them to the enemy. The 1779 decision to evacuate Newport, Rhode Island, after the defeat in 1778 of an attacking American army and a superior French naval squadron – the latter action, in foul weather, showing the undoubted technical brilliance of Admiral Howe at its best – was very debatable. In the limited arena of a coastal siege, Crown forces at least knew where the enemy was or had to come. In the successful British siege of Charleston in 1779–80, the Hessian troops so mercilessly caricatured as blundering incompetents out of place in America proved themselves the good professional soldiers they were, by regularly and effectively ambushing American cavalry trying to probe the British landward lines as a prelude to an attempt to break up the siege.[54] In the other important southern port, Savannah, Crown forces commanded by General Prevost – vitally reinforced by a great Scottish soldier of the King, John Maitland, who died shortly afterwards – decisively defeated an all-out Franco–American assault in October 1779, serving their assailants much as the British had been served at Bunker Hill.[55]

Instead of restricting formal operations to these manageable killing fields and the very successful disruptive amphibious raids mounted on the Chesapeake, as well as entrenching the Loyalist regime in Georgia – which indeed was basely abandoned in 1782 – Cornwallis' determined plunge deeper and deeper into hostile territory in search of the will-o'-the-wisp of decisive victory offered Franco–American forces the ideal target of a small isolated British field army, whose eventual surrender at Yorktown in Virginia in 1781 destroyed Westminster's will to fight, ending the American war. At an early stage critics of the London government had pointed out that if all the colonies resisted seriously and France and Spain came in, disaster might loom. Though, as has been seen, the government was not unaware of the French threat, the official answer had been that resistance might well prove shallow and crumble before disciplined troops, and that the war was 'to the trade and navigation of the kingdom essential'.[56] It was soon clear that both points were false. By the end of the war British peace policy was based on the correct calculation that the war would make comparatively little difference to the commercial relationship between Great Britain and the eastern seaboard of North America. What was missing was a timely reconstruction of long-term politico–military strategy in the light of the truths which had become apparent or mentionable in the course of the early clashes of two adversaries who had both grossly underestimated the other's determination. There were winnable regional wars in North America, theatres where it would have been possible to concentrate enough force to make it clear to all involved that within those limits the royal troops were unbeatable. Instead, a protracted but ill-thought-out British effort had generated maximum shearing stress for all parties involved and fundamentally affected the changing patterns of identities in the North Atlantic world.

Only within regions, which were a fraction of the rebellious colonies, perhaps confined to Georgia and Charleston and the Carolina rice country, could Loyalists afford to come into the open – and, indeed, they needed to be concentrated there, as they were in East Florida, which was designated for that purpose. West Florida should have been eminently defensible against Spain if troops and ships had not been overly committed elsewhere. The remaining colonies could at best be sealed off enough to preclude effective European intervention while being pounded on their land and sea frontiers with a view to inducing not reconciliation, which was a futile hope, but war weariness based on loss. As early as February 1778 the fact that this was the likeliest attainable outcome to the war was recognised in official British circles. There is a famous memorandum by the Scottish moral philosopher and political economist Adam Smith circulating at the highest level which admitted as much. Smith had no significant influence on policy, except in so far as he articulated views which were already acceptable to his influential hearers. That was the key to the sales of his *Wealth of Nations*. He admitted in his American memo that his own preferred solution, which was American representation at Westminster as part of a negotiated union (a natural preference for a Scottish unionist), was by 1778 impractical and desired by virtually nobody who mattered in Britain or America. However, he was passionately hostile to the idea of fighting to preserve what could be preserved. He wailed about the cost of defending a south-west frontier against Spain, and forecast horrible defence costs against the independent colonies, as if the purpose of operations would not have been to discourage future aggression on the part of either Spaniards or Americans permanently. It would not pay, was his bottom line, reinforced by a long ramble on the theme that Spain would have acquired a natural ally against France had it had the wit to acknowledge the whole of the Netherlands as independent in the sixteenth century instead of resisting their rebellion. Grotesquely unrealistic as his views were on the world of the Counter-Reformation – where the redemption of part of the Netherlands for a Catholic future was essential for the Spanish monarchy, which only then could consider, mistakenly to reject, washing its hands of the heretic north – Smith seems to have struck a sympathetic chord in his opposition to limited objectives in the American war. He would clearly, like his friend David Hume whose fear of taxation he fully shared, have preferred no aims at all, but he must have reinforced an all or nothing bias in British policy.[57] By gambling to the very end on overall military victory, the London government, whose political core was the Westminster parliament, guaranteed decisive defeat in America, though not in the by then much wider war, which they won.

The substance of independence for a dozen or so colonies was probably inevitable by 1760; the shape of that independence and its territorial limits were largely the result of the ideological and tactical inflexibility of the Westminster system. It was after 1781 more consonant with Westminster's invincible conceit of itself as an institution to accept, in a sense, the emerging official American story about the inevitable birth of a new 'nation' rather than to remember the complexities of a vicious, bloody civil war in which Westminster ultimately had betrayed some of its most devoted supporters and had, too late, offered concessions which underlined the inadequacy of its own frequently reiterated political theology which reserved for it a mystical seamless sovereignty, however evasively defined. There were moral reprobates, like the loser at Saratoga, 'Gentleman Johnny' Burgoyne. He had immediately abandoned his captive soldiers for a life of comfort and self-justification in London, and ended his life a convert to the mantras of American nationalism and an exponent of nonsense about the British war effort being 'part of a general design levelled against the constitution of this country, and the general rights of mankind'. So he had lost to the inevitable, not thrown away an army by selfish incompetence. The former Loyalists were early scapegoats for a British political class trying to restore the credibility of institutions which had so clearly failed.

Francis Rawdon-Hastings, second Earl of Moira, an Irish peer and politician of Whiggish disposition, had fought through the American war from Bunker Hill to the summer of 1781. No tougher or more tactically talented officer faced the American rebels. Cornwallis described his defeat of General Greene's superior forces at Hobkirk's Hill as 'by far the most splendid of this war'. As the young Lord Francis Rawdon, he had been heavily involved with Loyalists, raising in Philadelphia a corps called the Volunteers of Ireland which did distinguished if erratic service. He was a ferocious critic of the state of Ireland in the late 1790s, using his membership of the British House of Lords in 1798 to insist that he, a former member of the Irish parliament, had seen in Ireland, as a result of the policies of the British executive, 'the most absurd, as well as the most disgusting tyranny that any nation ever groaned under'. An early and vocal opponent of the union of Britain and Ireland in 1800, he gave up opposing a measure so formidably supported by the British political establishment. Married from 1804 to Flora Campbell, Countess of Loudon in her own right, and therefore linked with a major Scottish political connection, Moira went on to be an extraordinarily popular commander-in-chief Scotland, and from 1813 an extremely important governor general of British India.[58] At some point after 1781 Moira wrote a passionate memorandum denouncing the rubbishing of the Loyalist role in the American war which was becoming prevalent in London just at the time when the Loyalists' triumphant opponents in America were persecuting them, demonising them, and writing them out of the record of their native land. He started by saying that 'It has been the fashion to say, that the Loyalists were few in number; or that their activity in our cause was never such as ought to have a claim upon our gratitude.' He then pointed out that whole battalions on the provincial establishment in the northern provinces were composed of men who had left their settlements, 'rather than take a part against Britain', and went on to draw on his own experiences, which had been primarily in the southern district, to stress how numerous and how committed the Loyalists had been. Five thousand white Loyalists alone had left Charleston when the British army finally evacuated that unconquered stronghold, and very many Loyalists chose to brave the wrath of their triumphant enemies rather than leave. Moira stoutly and rightly insisted that 'the number of our adherents was far beyond what the temper of the day is willing to admit'. He knew full well that the forces under Major Patrick Ferguson of the 71st Highlanders, who were defeated in October 1780 in the violent action at King's Mountain in North Carolina as they endeavoured to contain the activity of Patriot partisans, were composed entirely of provincial regulars from the northern provinces, and Carolina militia. Ferguson was the only non-American present at a battle of fundamental importance for Cornwallis' attempt to subdue opposition in the Carolinas. Moira rightly emphasised the sheer savagery of the Partisan war and the way their opponents systematically terrorised the Loyalists, not least at King's Mountain where they had shot down men trying to surrender and hanged opponents after capture. When the British high command might have 'called our friends together' Moira pointed out that there was usually 'no positive object against which to use them', and yet dispersed they were exposed to brutal attack by small parties of the enemy who could penetrate the Carolinas at will 'without the necessity of them ever touching on a public road'. This was one of the factors which had persuaded Cornwallis that a defensive war on the frontier of the Carolinas was impractical. The wiser conclusion might have been that only Georgia and possibly Charleston and the rice country of South Carolina were within the capacity of British power, and that to protect Loyalists they needed to be concentrated there while the striking power of the field forces was used systematically to destroy the economic base of the areas from which murderous hostile raids could be mounted. Instead, Cornwallis plunged on to Virginia and disaster. Nevertheless, Moira was emphatic that in view of the 'zeal and fidelity of the Loyalists', not to mention the atrocious sufferings of so many of them, 'it will be difficult for any sophistry to extenuate the inhuman disregard with which they have been repaid'.[59]

Notes and references

1. These words are taken from John Welsey's *A Calm Address to Our American Colonies* (London, 1775), which accused 'artful men' in England of conspiring to overthrow the credit of the British government, and eventually that government, by precipitating 'the total defection of North America from England'.

2. Robert W. Tucker and David C. Hendrickson, *The Fall of the First British Empire* (Johns Hopkins University Press, Baltimore, MD, 1982), pp. 305–06.

3. Quoted in *ibid.*, pp. 57–58.

4. Richard L. Bushman, *King and People in Provincial Massachusetts* (University of North Carolina Press, Chapel Hill, NC, 1985), pp. 83–85.

5. Bruce P. Lenman, 'Tea and Circumstances: Tempers came to a boil in 1774 when Thomas Nelson took matters into his own hands', *Colonial Williamsburg Journal*, Spring 1996, pp. 42–51.

6. Cited in Benjamin W. Labaree, *The Boston Tea Party* (Oxford University Press, London, pbk edn, 1966), p. 145.

7. Tony Hayter, *The Army and the Crowd in Mid-Georgian England* (Macmillan, London, 1978), p. 31.

8. 'The Petition of the City of London against Lord North's Regulating Act, 28 May 1773', printed in Peter J. Marshall, *Problems of Empire: Britain and India 1757–1813* (George Allen and Unwin, London, 1968), p. 107.

9. The classic study is John Shy, *Toward Lexington: The role of the British army in the coming of the American Revolution* (Princeton University Press, Princeton, NJ, 1965).

10. John E. Ferling, *A Wilderness of Miseries: War and warriors in early America* (Greenwood Press, Westport, CT, 1980), pp. 22 and 165–67.

11. John M. Dedderer, *War in America to 1775* (New York University Press, New York, 1990), pp. 142–43 and 206–09.

12. Samuel F. Bemis, *The Diplomacy of the American Revolution* (Oliver and Boyd, Edinburgh, 1957), p. 13.

13. James H. Hutson, *John Adams and the Diplomacy of the American Revolution* (The University Press of Kentucky, Lexington, KY, 1980), Chaps. 1–2. For all its slim bulk this is a work of extraordinary academic distinction.

14. Robert A. Gross, *The Minutemen and their World* (Hill and Wang, New York, pbk edn, 1976), pp. 111–12 and 133.

15. Peter D.G. Thomas, *British Politics and the Stamp Act Crisis* (Clarendon Press, Oxford, 1975), p. 371.

16. *Idem, The Townshend Duties Crisis* (Clarendon Press, Oxford, 1987), pp. 256–57.

17. *Idem, Tea Party to Independence* (Clarendon Press, Oxford, 1991), pp. 333–34.

18. Bernard Bailyn, *The Ordeal of Thomas Hutchinson* (Allen Lane, London, 1974), p. 313.

19. Gage to Barrington, 10 November 1766, *The Correspondence of General Thomas Gage 1763–1775. Vol. 2*, ed. Clarence E. Carter (Yale University Press, New Haven, CT, 1933), pp. 391–92.

20. John Shy, *A People Numerous and Armed* (University of Michigan Press, Ann Arbor, MI, rev. pbk edn, 1990), pp. 95–96.

21. *An Eighteenth Century Secretary At War. The papers of William Viscount Barrington*, ed. Tony Hayter (The Bodley Head for the Army Records Society, 1988), pp. 13–14.

22. J.C. Long, *Lord Jeffrey Amherst: A soldier of the King* (Macmillan, New York, 1933), pp. 224–25 and 257.

23. John G. Gallagher, *The Battle of Brooklyn 1776* (Sarpedon, New York, 1995), p. 14.

24. *French and Indian Cruelty Exemplified in the Life and Various Vicissitudes of Fortune of Peter Williamson* (Peter Williamson, Edinburgh, 5th edn, 1762), pp. 33–35.

25. *Political Essays Concerning the Present State of the British Empire* (W. Strahan and T. Cadell, London, 1772), pp. 416–23.

26. David Syrett, *The Royal Navy in American Waters 1775–1783* (Scolar Press, Aldershot, 1989), pp. 10 and 57.

27. John A. Tilley, *The British Navy and the American Revolution* (University of South Carolina Press, Columbia, SC, 1987), Chap. 4, 'The Scapegoat'.

28. Gage to Dartmouth, 25 June 1775, *Correspondence of Gage, Vol. 1*, p. 407.

29. *1776: The British story of the American Revolution* (National Maritime Museum, Greenwich, London, 1976), p. 51.

30. Christopher Hibbert, *Redcoats and Rebels: The war for America 1770–1781* (HarperCollins, London, 1992), pp. 39–41, 70–75.

31. These quotations are all cited in John C. Miller, *Origins of the American Revolution* (Little, Brown and Company, Boston, MA, 1943), pp. 428–34.

32. Moses Mather, *America's Appeal to the Impartial World* (Hartford, CT, 1775) is reprinted in *Political Sermons of the American Founding Era 1730–1805*, ed. Ellis Samdoz (Liberty Press, Indianapolis, IN, 1991), pp. 441–92.

33. Stephen Conway, *The War of American Independence 1775–1783* (Edward Arnold, London, pbk edn, 1995), p. 77.

34. Robert Middlekauff, *The Glorious Cause: The American Revolution 1763–1789* (Oxford University Press, New York, 1982), p. 308.

35. Paul D. Nelson, 'Guy Carleton versus Benedict Arnold: The campaign of 1776 in Canada and Lake Champlain', in Peter S. Onuf (ed.), *The New American Nation 1775–1820. Vol. 2: Patriots, Redcoats and Loyalists* (Garland Publishing, New York, 1991), pp. 227–54.

36. Cited in Piers Mackesy, *The War for America 1775–1783* (Longman, London, 1964), p. 55.

37. The exposure of the Howes' insubordinate, foot-dragging, and systematically self-deceiving performance in Ira D. Gruber's classic *The Howe Brothers and the American Revolution* (University of North Carolina Press, Chapel Hill, NC, 1972), has never been properly built into the general history of the revolution.

38. Middlekauff, *The Glorious Cause*, pp. 412–28.

39. William L. Calderhead, 'British Naval Failure at Long Island: A lost opportunity in the American Revolution', reprinted in Onuf (ed.), *The New American Nation, Vol. 2*, pp. 209–26.

40. Ira D. Gruber, 'Lord Howe and Lord George Germain: British politics and the winning of American independence', *ibid.*, pp. 189–207.

41. Nicholas Tracy, *Navies, Deterrence, and American Independence: Britain and seapower in the 1760s and 1770s* (University of British Columbia Press, Vancouver, 1988), p. 122.

42. Piers Mackesy, 'British Strategy in the War of American Independence', in Onuf (ed.), *The New American Nation. Vol. 2*, p. 103.

43. Ian R. Christie, *The End of North's Ministry 1780–1782* (Macmillan, London, 1958), pp. 145–46.

44. Mark V. Kwasny, *Washington's Partisan War 1775–83* (Kent State University Press, Kent, OH, 1996).

45. Jonathan C.D. Clark, *The Language of Liberty 1660–1832* (Cambridge University Press, Cambridge, 1994), carries this line about as far as learning and brilliance of argument can.

46. This was the original and official name in the colonial era, but it was often written 'Charlestown'. In 1783, when the city was incorporated, the modern form, Charleston, was officially adopted.

47. George Smith McCowen Jr, *The British Occupation of Charleston 1780–82* (University of South Carolina Press, Columbia, SC, 1972), p. 10.

48. Warren M. Billings, John E. Selby, and Thad W. Tate, *Colonial Virginia: A history* (KTO Press, White Plains, NY, 1986), pp. 348–49.

49. McCowen, *op. cit.*, p. 109.

50. Henry J. Young, 'Treason and its Punishment in Revolutionary Pennsylvania', in Onuf (ed.), *The New American Nation. Vol. 2*, pp. 351–77.

51. Hugh F. Rankin, 'Cowpens: Prelude to Yorktown', *ibid.*, pp. 256–93.

52. Heard Robertson, 'The Second British Occupation of Augusta, 1780–1781', *ibid.*, pp. 294–318.

53. Mackesy, 'British Strategy', p. 110.

54. This is clear from a reading of the Hessian narratives assembled in *The Siege of Charleston*, ed. Bernard A. Ulhendorf (University of Michigan Press, Ann Arbor, MI, 1938).

55. Alexander A. Lawrence, *Storm Over Savannah* (3rd edn, Tara Press, Savannah, GA, 1979).

56. Alexander Wedderburn, *Notes for a Speech in Parliament on American Affairs*, undated but clearly very early in the war, WPCL, Vol. 2, No. 1.

57. *Ibid.*, Vol. 3, No. 2. The document is reprinted in G.H. Guttridge (ed.), 'Adam Smith on the American Revolution: An unpublished memorial', *American Historical Review*, 38 (1943), pp. 714–20.

58. A major modern biography of Moira is scandalously overdue, but the *DNB* entry in Vol. IX provides a handy overview.

59. Memo, undated but post-1781, by Lord Moira, on the attitude of the Loyalists during the war, especially in the South, in WPCL, Vol. 1, No. 46.

The whirlwind of events and
the plasticity of identities

The American colonists were not just humble farmers striving for self-government. They were rampant imperialists stretching out for empire on a continental scale. It may be doubted whether France was wise to enter the war in alliance with these rebellious colonists in 1778. Her political leaders had thought it likely for a long time not only that the British American colonies would revolt, but also that they were in so strong a position that the British government would find it virtually impossible to suppress that revolt. Indeed, a protracted and indecisive struggle would have suited the main French objective of sapping an over-mighty Britain better, and would have avoided the financial collapse of the Bourbon monarchy which the costs of the war produced, precipitating the early stages of the French Revolution. To their American allies, the alliance was all gain, and it super-charged their already frightening appetite for further territorial aggrandise-ment. Even the cautious George Washington began to plan another invasion of Canada, with the keen support of his prominent French collaborator the marquis de Lafayette. American politicians began to think of bullying a cowed Britain into surrendering every object of American ambition under threat of the displeasure of the United States.

William Ellery of Rhode Island told a friend that Britain should, with French assistance, be deprived of 'every foot upon this Continent' and that 'we should be possessed of Canada, Nova Scotia, and the Floridas'. John Adams, a future president of the United States, chorused that as long as Britain retained any of those territories she would be 'the enemy of the United States, let her disguise it as much as she will'.[1] His was a conveni-ently self-serving view, but that was the American way, and the principal potential victims were the Indian peoples beyond the Appalachians, predes-tined prey for an imperial republic. In key states such as Massachusetts,

New York, Pennsylvania, Virginia, and South Carolina the opposition to British control had been led by elite groups fervently committed for reasons of both idealism and self-interest to rapid territorial growth at Indian expense. Pro-British non-expansionists in these states were rapidly marginalised to the point where one of them, William Byrd III of Virginia, complained mournfully in 1775 that 'The moderate are awed into silence, and have no opportunity to show their allegiance.' On New Year's Day 1777, Byrd shot himself dead.[2]

Whole peoples were faced with the fate Byrd chose in this swirling, uncertain era. Others invented or reinvented their identities. The white Anglo-Saxon leadership of the revolution had had a radical Whig version of English identity, as well as their regional identities, close to their hearts. Sam Adams saw himself as securing 'that true old English liberty, which gives a relish to every other enjoyment'. Josiah Quincy Jr, an important ideologue of the revolution, died in 1775 on his way back from a trip to England where the reluctance of many to swallow his highly tendentious and convenient reading of history persuaded him that Englishmen had lost their 'divine enthusiasm' for the liberties bequeathed by 'our Saxon ancestors'. Expansionist Patriots usually had a vested interest in immigration, without which huge land grants would not appreciate in value, so they did envisage various ethnic groups in America entering into the heritage they claimed, but it was an English heritage. In Pennsylvania John Dickinson, the future principal penman of the First Continental Congress, claimed that colonists were entitled to resist the Stamp Act precisely because they were Englishmen and entitled to the Englishman's privilege of not being taxed without consent.[3] Defying the Crown necessarily involved a reformulation of identity on a wider American basis, for any fool could see the colonies in revolt would hang separately if they did not hang together, and the alliance with France made it imperative to convert English into universal rights and consciously embrace an American identity which, unlike the equally valid American identity of the Loyalists, did not have a British component – though it had plenty of other complexities under its surface and remained politically fragile for a long time. What, however, did this necessary transition imply for the interests of many colonial American peoples who were white, but consciously non-English?

For some it was relatively straightforward, because their own interests, objectives, and culture fitted smoothly with the interests and objectives of those groups leading the revolution. The best example here is that distinct group of Irishmen known as Scotch–Irish, Protestant Ulstermen who were moving into America in large numbers in the decades before the revolution. They immigrated into New York, though that flow slowed when access to new land became more difficult; South Carolina, where they seem to have been greatly encouraged by bounties offered to white immigrants by the colony; and above all into Pennsylvania, where they moved to the western frontier or flowed south down into areas like the Shenandoah valley between the Allegheny Mountains and the Blue Ridge of Virginia. Colonial population in general was rising fast, increasing from 753,721 in 1740 to 1,689,583 in 1770, but behind this near 125 per cent increase lurked far faster growth rates in frontier areas. White populations in the same period grew by nearly 228 per cent in the Carolinas and Georgia, by more than 160 per cent in Pennsylvania and by nearly 150 per cent in New York and New Jersey.[4] Expansion was in the air and a royal governor doomed to desecration in the mythology of the revolution like Governor Lord Dunmore of Virginia was in fact quite popular (except with some frontiersmen who objected to his eventually making peace with the Indians) as late as 1774 when he had led a thousand Virginia militia against the Shawnee Indians of Western Virginia and the Ohio territory. The only battle of Lord Dunmore's War was fought and won at Point Pleasant, where the Kanawha River joins the Ohio, by more frontier militia under the Scotch–Irish Colonel Andrew Lewis, whose family was from what is now Northern Ireland, and whose cousin Meriwether was thirty years later to conduct with William Clark a famous reconnaissance for American imperialism at the behest of President Jefferson.[5]

The latter, whose political support depended heavily on small farmers worried by the ever-increasing domination of big slave-run estates in the tidewater areas of the Chesapeake and therefore hungry for new land for family farms, was always obsessed with grabbing Indian land in the west. Indeed as wartime governor of Virginia his policies showed the centrality of western lands to his politics. They also endangered the independence of Virginia and the United States. The state government collapsed disgracefully in the face of sudden British raids led by men like the American Benedict Arnold and the violent and ruthless – but militarily very effective – English Green Dragoon, Banastre Tarleton. Nor could Virginia offer much effective aid to the Carolinas when Cornwallis invaded them in 1780. The explanation for this lamentable situation was that Jefferson had invested Virginia's military assets in a drive to conquer British posts in Indian country north of the Ohio, a campaign led by George Rogers Clark, who had fought with Andrew Lewis at Point Pleasant in Lord Dunmore's War.[6] The Scotch–Irish, a tough, armed, frontier people, with a visceral and well-founded distrust of the Westminster government as strong as that of their Ulster Loyalist descendants in the late nineteenth and twentieth centuries, and for the same reason – they rightly thought that government deemed them expendable in Ireland – were well suited to the world of the revolution and Mr Jefferson. Though in the competitive ethnic politics of the

United States every group with a plausible claim to have had significant participation in the revolution, and indeed many who have not, hype their ancestors' or alleged ancestors' role in that episode, it really does seem that the Scotch–Irish – though no more totally solid in their views than any other group – were probably the most solidly and belligerently pro-revolution of all.[7] The Scots, only a hyphen and a word away, were a different proposition.

They had a complex history of relating to their union of 1707 with England, one in which the Atlantic world had played a role even before the union, when they had tried to establish a Scottish emporium on the Isthmus of Panama and failed. As late as the 1715 Jacobite rebellion in Scotland it seems clear that there was a substantial consensus among both the aristocracy which had once wished the union on a reluctant Scottish nation, and the bulk of the population, probably Lowland as well as Highland, that the union should be broken. This was not so by the time of the 1745 rising, which did draw strength from Scottish nationalist sentiment, but was pretty clearly a minority coup from the start. There always were strongly unionist elements in Scotland after 1707, and by 1750, as Scottish economic and intellectual life began to achieve unprecedented levels of vitality, a British and a British Atlantic framework of opportunity beckoned, as well as the old-established Scottish and European ones, which it has to be said remained very important to Scots. The way the Scots subsequently pushed out into every corner of the British Atlantic world roused resentment as well as appreciation. They were disliked by many in America for the reasons that made them disliked by many in England: they were aggressive, too successful, and owed too much of their success to an overly close relationship with the royal government. In the Chesapeake colonies, where the hard-driving Glasgow merchant houses had penetrated the piedmont and secured a very large proportion of the tobacco trade, they were cordially detested by the planters who were so heavily indebted to them. After 1763 they had become far more prominent in the Crown's military and civil establishments in the Americas, not to mention in the Crown's land grants, than Scotland's modest population would have led anyone to expect.[8] Like all other people in America they had complex identities, but the bulk of them were strongly Loyalist at the revolution. Old Jacobites who had left immediately after a rising were liable to continue their hostility to the Hanoverian regime in London by becoming Patriot in politics. Hugh Mercer, a veteran of Culloden and a doctor who had joined Prince Charles' Jacobite army as a surgeon's mate and fled to Philadelphia in 1746 or 1747, is a good example. He became a member of the same masonic lodge as George Washington, a Patriot militia colonel in Virginia, and was elected brigadier general by the Continental Congress. Eventually, he was killed in 1777 in the hour of victory at Princeton.[9] New immigrants closely identified with the more theologically conservative and passionately evangelical currents in Scottish church life – like John Witherspoon, the president of the College of New Jersey (later Princeton) – were also more liable to turn out Patriot in affiliation, but the most recent Highland immigrants notoriously marched in kilt and plaid to fight unsuccessfully for King George at Moore's Creek Bridge in North Carolina in 1776.

It has been said that Loyalists were drawn disproportionately from 'cultural minorities' and that this was partly because they felt the need of protection from the Crown against the majority. This certainly would explain why the German and Dutch communities produced significant numbers of Loyalists. Germans were in fact the main group of non-British immigrant Loyalists, protected from Anglicisation by their numbers, language, extensive networks, and leadership.[10] In practice many pietist German sects were pacifists and they, with the indifferent and Patriot factions, were a clear majority of Germans. Nevertheless, Germans and Dutch were Loyalists often because they were not Anglicised, and New Rochelle, the one area where immigrant French Calvinists still widely spoke French, was one of the few areas of extensive Huguenot loyalism.[11] Colonial British America was dominated by an English culture, different from that of Old England in outlook, but then there were several different kinds of Irishness, of which the Scotch–Irish represented one only. There were two major divisions in Scottishness, Highland and Lowland, but neither was English though both could add Britishness to their multiple identities, something most American English colonists never really did. That was the problem. The Virginian William Lee thought in 1774 that to use the term 'Britain', a national unit, rather than 'Great Britain', a geographical term, was to be guilty of an innovative Scotticism, and the increasingly pluralistic nature of the religious and ethnic composition of the dominions of King George III worried him, especially when he thought he saw the Westminster government trying to mobilise this motley crew against freedom-loving American Englishmen.[12]

Fraser's Highlanders, the 71st Regiment of Foot, had been on the Heights of Abraham with General Wolfe when he defeated the marquis de Montcalm in 1759. Their colonel, Simon Fraser, had raised them as part of his campaign to reinstate himself in the British ruling elite after his father Lord Lovat had been executed for high treason in the 1745 rebellion, and he himself had had an uncomfortable spell in the Tower of London. The 71st were also at Yorktown in 1781, piling their arms when the British army came out to surrender. In between those two dates Simon Fraser had recovered the estates forfeited by his father for treason, and had risen to be a general (he was not at Yorktown). Other ex-Jacobite Highland families had raised regiments to fight in the War of the American Revolution for

King George on such a scale that in 1784 they had their forfeited estates returned to them by a disannexing act designed to reward their loyalty.[13] Scots, both humble and great, were in the forefront of those who saw in a more coherent and powerful British global monarchy their own empire of opportunity. This did not mean they were losing their own identity or indeed the will to pursue limited nationalist objectives. Henry Dundas, later first Viscount Melville, a hard-liner in the War of the American Revolution, was to become the second most powerful man in the United Kingdom under the long political ascendancy of the Younger Pitt in the late eighteenth century. In cooperation with an Irish aristocrat, Governor General the Marquis of Wellesley, he did more than any other British politician to create an Indian empire which replaced North America as the necessary continental component in British great-power status. Yet Dundas was a Scots patriot who meant to keep the Scottish institutions guaranteed by the Act of Union 'intact and firmly under indigenous control'. He rolled back the frontiers of English dominance in Scotland by seeing that natives were appointed to such senior positions as the Barons of the Court of Exchequer and the commander-in-chief in Scotland, posts which had invariably been held by Englishmen since the union.[14]

There are records of one fascinating case where we can see the process of choice of allegiance during the American war, all the more fascinating because it is the exception which proves the rule – a Scots merchant in Virginia who chose the Patriot camp to the amazement of English-American Virginians, who to his annoyance could never quite believe what he had done. His name was Edward Johnson and he operated out of Manchester, a small settlement on the James River, opposite to and just south of Richmond (which was to become the state capital in 1780). He ran a typical general agent's firm, importing manufactured goods, from iron bars to textiles, and dealing in a vast range of consumer items ranging from stoves and grindstones to bellows. Right up to the eve of the revolution, he was importing and selling indentured servants, who tended to be skilled and included at least one doctor who had escaped from personal troubles by emigrating.[15] His main customers were the settlers in the expanding piedmont areas and the Shenandoah valley, so he was harassed by the sorts of problems one might expect, such as the difficulty at times of securing reliable wagon transportation for goods for his customers along the network of roads which were being developed to make interior settlements viable, shortage of cash, counterfeiting, and above all collecting debt.[16] As the final crisis with Britain became acute, he could show annoyance about the fact that the militant Patriot militia colonels, often big landowners, who were insistent that the merchants sign non-importation agreements in order to put pressure on Britain, were not exactly falling over themselves to offer financial help to the merchants whose businesses they were thereby at least partially closing down. The colonels were, of course, avoiding further increases in their own debts, which in any case they were beginning to feel it was almost a patriotic duty to evade.[17] Yet planters and merchants were bound together indissolubly and Johnson was the product of a process whereby, despite the dominance of expatriate firms in the export–import trade of the Chesapeake, an indigenous merchant community was emerging as part of accelerating diversification of the regional economy – which led observers to believe that merchants had done more in a brief span of years to change regional society than planters in a century.[18] The crucial fact about Johnson, however, was that he was married to the sister of the man through whom a large proportion of his business was arranged: Colonel William Preston, born in 1729 in Newton Limavaddy, County Londonderry, in Ulster, and by the 1770s the leading man of the Scotch–Irish on the north-west frontiers of Virginia.[19]

The Indian troubles of 1774 gave Johnson cause to worry about his frontier relatives.[20] William Preston, a surveyor and land speculator, had an agreement with Lord Dunmore to survey Ohio lands, an agreement he was anxious to transfer under the authority of the new state government, of which he was an active supporter, after the revolution broke out.[21] His view was that he and his people were reliving their great days at the time of the Glorious Revolution, when the Prentice Boys had shouted defiance to James II from the walls of Derry, and the Enniskillen men had sallied out to seek safety in attack. He and Johnson discussed during the revolution the need to drive pro-British Indians out of Kentucky, which was to become a major objective for land-hungry Virginians after the revolution.[22] Obviously, someone like Johnson was a major source of the powder and shot needed by the Scotch–Irish to fight Indians or British regulars. One of the problems created by the revolution was a shortage of gunpowder, which in America – like salt, which also soared in price after 1775 – was almost entirely imported.[23] Cordage for the infant states and federal navies might have been a problem but for the fact that hemp, which at times Johnson was less than keen to accept in exchange for the goods he imported for sale,[24] became briefly the main cash crop of the Scotch–Irish settlers in the Shenandoah valley.[25] Unlike most recent immigrant Scots, Johnson supported the cause of the revolution. It might have cost him his marriage, and would certainly have cost him his business to do otherwise. In any case, he may not have thought that he was risking more than a temporary trauma.

It was a platitude among commercial agents on the Chesapeake once the revolution had broken out that France would come to the aid of the revolting colonies, especially if it began to look as if their revolt was in trouble. Colonel William Aylett came from an old well-connected Virginia landed family, but he ran a business very similar to that of Edward Johnson, as well as exploiting agricultural land and timber. In April 1776, as a Patriot militia colonel, he had said that the only problem about defending 'the Land of Liberty' lay in securing adequate supplies of arms and ammunition. In August 1777, Richard Harrison, another commercial agent, wrote to him saying that:

> I verily believe that they [the French] will begin to act openly against England next Spring if no sooner especially if our Affairs should take a disastrous turn in America which Heaven avert! At all events their navy will be of infinite service to us as it will protect our trade from the Depredations of the Pirates that infest most other [West Indian] Islands.[26]

Johnson's problem was therefore not fear of ultimate defeat so much as identification with those likely to be defeated, for so many Scots were Loyalists that every time he opened his mouth and gave vent to a good Scots tongue, he was liable to be harassed by over-zealous militant Patriots. It was therefore not wise for him to go to Norfolk to negotiate payment of British treasury bills due to him at a time when that town was garrisoned by British regulars and under desultory siege by Patriot forces. He had a pass of sorts to take him through the lines, but ended up in front of the Virginia Committee of Safety on a charge of high treason to the American cause. Preston urged him to stress his innocence and political 'soundness', with humility. That and Johnson's argument that he would surely be crazy to defect to the Crown forces, leaving his 'wife, child, and whole estate' in Patriot hands, seems to have put an end to charges of crypto-loyalism and threats to seize his property.[27] Johnson's calculation as to where his long-term advantage lay was typical of the Patriot alliance. The revolting colonies were not socially particularly united. That was one reason their leaders had to talk so much about their being so. Many were riven with religious disputes. There were hordes of unassimilated foreigners in the middle colonies, and the back country in the larger colonies was forever defying the colonial government. However, most Americans, like Johnson, could see where their opportunity and interest lay in the imperial crisis of the 1770s.

Elsewhere in the British global sprawl, it was much more difficult to have a sense of what was likely to be the final outcome of the crisis, especially after France entered the war. The struggle against France and Spain hinged mainly on naval power, and informed observers like Admiral Augustus Keppel were doubtful whether all the dominions of the Crown outside North America could be defended after 1778. In the end they were all secured, if by narrow margins. The Earl of Sandwich, first lord of the Admiralty, proved an able, assiduous administrator, and backed bold strategic moves in desperate circumstance – such as the decision to declare war on the Dutch in December 1780, to deprive the French and Spaniards, not to mention the American rebels, of their services as purveyors of war supplies. He could not impose a rational naval strategy on his colleagues, which would have involved early concentration on home waters with a view to decisive action, so the naval war was fought too much in peripheral seas like the Caribbean, to the advantage of the Bourbon powers. However, with luck and an emergency drive to sheath British warship hulls with copper bottoms to increase their speed and length of seaworthiness, the margin for victory was found.[28] In India a great French fighting admiral, the Bailli de Suffren, fought the Royal Navy to a standstill on the Malabar Coast, but never quite established total maritime ascendancy.[29] Such was the in-depth strength of the British naval lead that the United Kingdom did not need continental allies. The sinews of her sea power were capable of 'overcoming the "unrestrained" naval efforts of the united house of Bourbon'.[30]

That still left the first governor general of the EIC's Indian Empire – or rather three regional ascendancies – in a desperate situation, for he had wars in his home presidency of Bengal which were then vastly complicated by the shambles into which the other two presidencies managed to plunge. The Bombay presidency launched an unsuccessful campaign against the formidable and closely adjacent Hindu power of the Marathas; while the villains who controlled the Madras presidency were by the summer of 1780 busy losing, not for the first time, a war against the remarkable Haider Ali, a Muslim soldier who had seized control of Mysore and embarked on a most ambitious modernisation of its economy and armed forces. On top of these woes, Hastings faced a most intelligent, if fortunately limited, French intervention, which like French intervention in North America was not designed to launch France back on what her leaders deemed the profitless game of overseas territorial conquest, but to destabilise British interests and possessions in India.[31] It is easy to see why John Robinson, the secretary to the treasury, advised his colleagues in the Westminster government in 1778 that they should not try openly to grab control of the EIC and its territories when they already had on their hands 'a rebellion in our colonies, a foreign war, and many other difficulties'. Besides, he thought it better that blame for mistakes which were bound to occur in the management of such extensive possessions so far away should 'fall upon the Directors of the Company', rather than upon 'the ministers of the King' who in the mess they were already in 'can hardly now retain a sufficient degree of authority and respect for the government of this country'. He recommended a covert take-over of the EIC from within which would give politicians their equivalent of heaven – power without responsibility and built-in scapegoats in the shape of the directors of an emasculated EIC.[32] In the end Hastings managed to mobilise enough resources, mainly from Bengal and Bihar, to save the day, a feat dependent on 'Indian soldiers, Indian taxes (Bengal in 1765 immediately yielded a public revenue one quarter of that of metropolitan Britain), on Indian financiers, and on a strengthened system of Indian commercial regulation'.[33] However, the cynicism and the instrumental view of that part of the British world which was the EIC was deeply typical of the attitude which the Westminster politicians were developing as they began to search the limits of where they might safely establish an ascendancy, based on acquiescence and convenience – their convenience.

Arguments of an ingenious but unconvincing kind have been advanced to the effect that the period 1750 to about 1830 saw the emergence and flowering of 'English nationalism'. Unfortunately the principal exponent of this view seems to have no conception of the complex relationships between British, English, Welsh, Irish, American, and Scottish identities, let alone of the fact that it was normal to have several of these coexisting within the average human psyche in the eighteenth century, and later.[34] The English national community, wildly polarised though it had become politically, remained at least nominally under the same British allegiance until 1775, but then it has to be said that the English underwent the second great schism in their corporate identity. When in 1774 imported tea and an effigy of Lord North went into the public bonfire along with the traditional effigies of the pope and the devil in New England on 5 November, Pope Day, it was clear that even the uses of the common calendar of ritual celebration were diverging fatally between Old and New England.[35] Yet a new American national identity was forged relatively slowly after the revolution rather than before it, when all colonial Englishmen had been perforce aware of the fact that they were American, but also of the fact that colonial American Englishmen came in even more different varieties than Irishmen or Scotsmen. Unity was therefore largely symbolic and achieved in an incorrigibly complex society with symbols which began to be forged in the furnace of revolution.[36] Many of those symbols were drawn from the classical heritage which was a pervasive influence on the thought of the Founding Fathers of the United States, especially the heritage of ancient Rome. When George Washington repudiated peace proposals from Burgoyne in 1777 he told him that the American armies fought for that liberty which was the spirit behind 'the arms of Rome in the days of her glory, and the same object was the reward of Roman valour'.[37] By definition, successful conquest and expansion was one of the hallmarks of a vigorous and virile republican people. The United States was meant to be an empire from the start. The Boston Congregational clergyman Jedediah Morse justified his 1789 work *American Geography* on the grounds that his compatriots should not rely on European geographers now that the United States 'have risen into Empire'. Washington looked forward in 1786 to the day when the United States would acquire 'some weight in the scale of Empires'. These terms were used without embarrassment until the era of the American Civil War, when they were replaced by a stress on nation and 'manifest destiny' rather than federal union or empire and expansion. The substance did not change, for the Civil War confirmed that the American federal union was an imperial state which crushed secession much more ruthlessly and effectively than the monarchy of George III.[38] Indeed, that monarchy was possessed neither of the will nor of the physical force needed to conquer the rebel American colonies. The charge against Lord North which stands the test of time is not that he 'lost' America, but that after he found himself in a war he did not want, he showed neither stomach nor talent for it, something which he himself, with characteristic modesty, admitted when he said repeatedly that he was 'totally unfit' to cope with the crisis.[39] The rebel colonies disposed of resources which made conquering them very difficult, and their expectations verged on the limitless. It was worth the effort of creating and defending a new identity to assert independent participation in control of both those resources and those prospects.

Two groups paid a grim price for the white settler's confidence and optimism, and neither derived any long-term comfort from the policies of the British government. One group was the black slaves whose physical efforts generated the cash crops from the southern colonies which went so far to fund the rebel war effort. Governor Lord Dunmore was right to see the Chesapeake as a key area in the early stages of the revolution, but he received little help from London, so he tried to supplement his risibly small forces by an Emancipation Proclamation in November 1775, promising freedom to any black slave who joined him to fight for King George. This confirmed the bitter hostility of the Virginia planter elite towards him. One planter, Edmund Pendleton, hoped that stories of slaves flocking to the governor were false. George Washington was for crushing 'that arch traitor' Dunmore, for fear that 'like a snowball rolling, his army will get size'. Dunmore had one thousand negroes with him at one point, but they were hit by smallpox and the governor so mismanaged his small campaign that he was rapidly driven off. Any army – British, American, or French – offered a bold slave a chance of freedom, and more slaves joined the British when they returned to the Chesapeake in 1777 and 1781,[40] but in the last analysis black bondage remained a fact of life throughout the revolution and deep into the next century.

The other group whose victim status was not altered, but rather on the contrary confirmed by the war, was the Indian peoples. They had contrived at least to partially control the pace of their own expropriation by a mixture of negotiation and force applied to the British government. In the War of the American Revolution, it is clear that almost all of them would have preferred to stay neutral in what was essentially a white man's quarrel. However, in the last analysis, their prospects were infinitely better if the Crown survived as a moderating force between them and the ever-increasing flows of settlers. In both the Northern and Southern Indian Departments royal officials such as Guy Johnson – nephew, son-in-law, and successor to Sir William Johnson – and until his death in 1779 John Stuart, could draw on a fund of some good will to try to build the Indians into a western front of Loyalists, Indians, and British regulars, capable of not just holding but also intimidating the rebel colonists. Peoples like the Cherokee and Iroquois were on the receiving end of settler imperialism in 1775–76 on a scale which made them not unwilling to attack settlements that threatened the long-term survival of their peoples. By 1779 massive American strikes against Cherokee townships and fields had confirmed the bitterness of the Indians towards the emergent United States, but also shown that there were limits to the Indians' capacity to cripple the American war effort when they were so vulnerable themselves.[41] Similar American tactics were used on the pro-British Iroquois. Fiercely destructive American punitive strikes led the Iroquois to name George Washington 'Town Destroyer', which is still the Iroquois name for the president of the United States.[42] These Indian peoples were allies rather than subjects of the British Crown but, whatever way the relationship is viewed, their abandonment in the peace settlement was an extraordinary act of betrayal by Westminster, especially on the north-west frontier of the United States where the Americans had just not won the ground militarily during the war. Immediately after the formation of the new and consciously imperial federal government in 1787, President Washington was to embark on a vicious and bitter war of conquest in the north-west, in which the Indian peoples put up a remarkable resistance. They had some ambiguous support from British agents based on Detroit, until they went down before the Legion Army commanded by the hardest of professional military hard-liners in America's emerging federalist elite, General Anthony Wayne, at the Battle of Fallen Timbers in 1794.[43] Indians who had fought on the Patriot side in the War of the American Revolution ultimately fared no better at the hands of an incorrigibly racist republic, as the fate of the Catawbas of the Carolina piedmont or the long-Christianised Stockbridge Mohicans of Massachusetts showed,[44] but that was small consolation to the formerly Loyalist-inclined Indian peoples.

In general, Loyalists were systematically betrayed at the peace settlement. Even Dean Tucker – the eccentric Anglican polemicist and political economist, who was opposed to the war with the American colonists because he thought them profitless, Dissenter-dominated appendages to the

Crown whose trade would be secured to Great Britain anyway by the laws of economics – simply took it for granted that the Loyalists would have to be looked after by the provision and securing for them of territorial asylums in parts of New York, the Carolinas, and, most obviously, Georgia.[45] On the contrary, even East Florida – an unconquered, designated Loyalist refuge into which Loyalist refugees had poured – was handed over to Spain in 1783, despite embittered protests from the Loyalists who had fought for the Crown, and who now would have to face unattractive options for relocation, since the Catholic King of Spain was not keen on Protestant subjects.[46] Alexander McGillivray – Creek chief, son of Clan Chattan, American of course, and in his own way a great one, Briton and Loyalist – was left after 1783 juggling his multiple identities between the new United States, whose general officer's commission he at one point held, and imperial Spain, which he hoped would save him from the cannibal 'friendship' of President Washington. Meantime Spanish officials debated with him and themselves where his ultimate loyalties lay. He was in fact a mestizo Creek and old-fashioned British American. It will not do to call this literate scion of the Scottish Enlightenment an English American. George Washington had been that; Alexander McGillivray, never.[47]

Thomas Pownall, former American colonial governor in Massachusetts and the British politician most systematically articulate on the problems of imperial government, had hoped for a 'rational, sound' reconsideration of the issues involved in the relationship between Britain and her settlement colonies. In 1776 he admitted in print in a comment on what he saw as the extremely over-simplified dogmatism of Adam Smith's *Wealth of Nations* on the American question, that the hazards of war would decide all and that 'I am afraid we are reasoning here about things which once were, and were most dear, and are no more.'[48] The hazards of peace proved just as alarming. Contemporaries could see that the resolutions in the Commons which declared the 'North American War impolitic, Grievous and impracticable' and those advocating its continuation 'enemies to their king and country' were likely to have alarming effects on 'the Congress and the Peoples of North America', at the least vastly sharpening the appetite and increasing the expectations of the former. The British negotiating position was seriously compromised by the resolutions' extreme language, which boded ill for the future. One observer shrewdly argued it would be better if 'others contrary to them [the movers of the resolutions] be appointed to bring about peace with those Colonies'.[49]

Britishness experienced a massive surge of official promotion and popular support in the late eighteenth and early nineteenth centuries in the face of a visceral threat both to the traditional hierarchical social order and to the structure of Westminster government from revolutionary and then

Napoleonic France. The government really had no choice but to try to incite mass British patriotism, despite the fact that doing so was politically to open a 'Pandora's box', because it needed participation in vastly expanded militia and regular military units. Military mass mobilisation inevitably accelerated a measure of mass politicisation.[50] Success in those wars was followed by an unprecedented era of economic expansion in the industrialised parts of the United Kingdom of Great Britain and Ireland, with which went the expansion of frontiers of European settlement and primary product production on a global scale. Nevertheless, the UK remained multi-national, as did its overseas dependencies and eventually self-governing colonies. Even the English had to be satisfied with a sense of dominance over and metropolitan proximity to what eighteenth-century people called the Great Engines of State. British patriotism was real, but the officially approved versions of it were defined by institutions like the monarchy and the Westminster parliament and Whitehall bureaucracy. France, towards alliance with whom the logic of European politics should have been moving Britain by the 1780s, was rather appalled at the scale of British concessions to the United States in the peace of 1783, for these clearly indicated lack of will to try to limit the bullying potential of what was likely to become the juggernaut of the Atlantic world. The sacrifices of British peoples and allies which Shelburne made to settle quickly with the United States, and which went well beyond what most Americans expected, contributed to the fact that he was the only eighteenth-century British minister defeated in the legislature over the terms of a peace settlement.[51] As it happened, the Fox–North ministry which succeeded to power was obsessed with a life or death struggle with George III, and chose simply to go along with Shelburne's terms.

So the war's end game handed the United States unparalleled, and to some extent unearned, future opportunities for territorial aggression, both against the native peoples of North America and against surviving European power on their borders. Imperial Spain had, rightly, refused formal alliance with American settler communities whose rebellion boded ill for monarchical authority in the Americas, and whose will to seize Spanish territories never really abated, even when Spain was fighting by their side. The unexpected prolongation of the war after 1776 had supplied the infant American republic with many of its founding legends, yet in many ways the key decisions about independence, and fundamental expectations of a future of expansion, had been in place long before the Declaration of Independence – which became an icon in retrospect, but at the time it was signed was seen as the far from convincing public relations exercise large parts of it were.

It is to be expected that it was received in Britain 'by many as arrant hogwash'. That was perhaps a shade unkind, but not entirely unjustified.

The *Gentleman's Magazine* was quite right to point out the philosophical superficiality, and debatable relevance, of some if its more sweeping generalisations, pointing out that 'All men it is true, are equally created, but what is this to the purpose? It certainly is no reason why Americans should turn rebels.' The 60 per cent or so of the Declaration which is a list of charges against George III was mostly wildly over-stated, and read unconvincingly even after some of the more extreme expressions of American-English prejudice and paranoia had been eliminated in draft.[52] Jefferson's original version read that King George had resolved 'to send over not only soldiers of our common blood, but Scotch and foreign mercenaries to invade and destroy us'. After editing, the 'Scotch' disappeared.[53] Though full of abstractions, such as the claim that any large body of resolved people may rightly choose to erect a separate government if dissatisfied with their existing one (an idea instantly repudiated by the United States government when it became a reality in the South in 1860), the Declaration is very much the complaints of exasperated colonial Englishmen who felt that their king had ignored their petitions for redress of grievance. President Lincoln's mystical reinvention of the Declaration during the Civil War has obscured its role as a *pièce d'occasion* in 1776.[54]

In fact, the Act of Independence had been passed two days before 4 July by the states' delegations, and there had been no serious dissent. A few delegates were apprehensive over the speed of separation from Great Britain, but their reservations were purely tactical. They differed only in emphasis, not in matters of substance. The cult of the Signers is in many ways as unhistorical as the myth of the Liberty Bell, which seems to have been invented in the mid-nineteenth century. Even Jefferson, who had drafted it, said, in a bad temper admittedly, that 'at least it would serve as a justification for what we have wrought'. It was not entirely plausible in that capacity. What sanctified it was successful war, just as a long-standing conviction that a war against King George was winnable accounts for its very existence. American colonists had for decades also held they could crush the Indian peoples and prey successfully on the Spaniards. The War of Independence became a longer, rockier road than many rebel colonists had expected, but their three military assumptions proved, ultimately, correct. These were the triple pillars on which the shaping, incorporating ideas of a new republic and nationality were to be raised, just as the success of British arms elsewhere from the Caribbean to the Coromandel Coast of India confirmed the survival of Westminster as another vigorous imperial power, albeit one which did not have the same potential for the integration of its peoples into one coherent body politic. Englishness survived its seismic rupture of 1775 as it had the much older rupture with the Old English of Ireland. It became the core group identity within a Westminster-ruled

British state. The communities ruled by that state had, like most human groups, complex identities of which the British element was important but not exclusive of other national or provincial loyalties. The fate of the Loyalists, however, served notice that to Westminster outlying British peoples could be like outlying provinces to the Austrian Habsburgs: expendable.

Notes and references

1. Richard W. Van Alstyne, *Empire and Independence: The international history of the American Revolution* (John Wiley, New York, 1967), p. 162.

2. Marc Egnal, *A Mighty Empire: The origins of the American Revolution* (Cornell University Press, Ithaca, NY, pbk edn, 1988), p. 310.

3. Trevor Colbourn, *The Lamp of Experience: Whig history and the intellectual origins of the American Revolution* (Liberty Fund reprint, Indianapolis, IN, 1998), pp. 94–99 and 133.

4. Jack P. Greene, *The Intellectual Construction of America: Exceptionalism and identity from 1492 to 1800* (University of North Carolina Press, Chapel Hill, NC, 1993), p. 83.

5. Edwards Park, 'A Little War for His Lordship', *Colonial Williamsburg Journal*, Autumn 1990, pp. 24–33.

6. Stephen E. Ambrose, *Undaunted Courage: Meriwether Lewis, Thomas Jefferson, and the opening of the American West* (Simon and Schuster, New York, Touchstone pbk edn, 1996), p. 57.

7. R.J. Dickson, *Ulster Emigration to Colonial America 1718–1775* (new edn, with introduction by G.E. Kirkham, Ulster Historical Foundation, Belfast, 1988); and Wayland F. Dunaway, *The Scotch–Irish of Colonial Pennsylvania* (University of North Carolina Press, Chapel Hill, NC, 1944), esp. Chap. 8.

8. Eric Richards, 'Scotland and the Uses of the Atlantic Empire', in Bernard Bailyn and Philip D. Morgan (eds.), *Strangers within the Realm* (University of North Carolina Press, Chapel Hill, NC, 1991), pp. 67–114.

9. *Dictionary of American Biography Vol. XII* (Scribner, New York, 1933), pp. 541–42.

10. A.G. Roeber, ' "The Origin of Whatever is not English among Us": The Dutch-speaking and the German-speaking peoples of colonial British America', in Bailyn and Morgan (eds.), *Strangers within the Realm*, pp. 220–83.

11. Wallace Brown, *The Good Americans: The Loyalists in the American Revolution* (William Morrow, New York, 1969), p. 47.

12. Peter J. Marshall, 'A Nation Defined by Empire, 1755–1776', in Alexander Grant and Keith J. Stringer (eds.), *Uniting the Kingdom?: The making of British history* (Routledge and Kegan Paul, London, 1995), pp. 221–22.

13. Bruce P. Lenman, *The Jacobite Clans of the Great Glen 1650–1784* (Scottish Cultural Press, pbk edn, 1995), Chaps. 9–10.

14. Michael Fry, *The Dundas Despotism* (Edinburgh University Press, Edinburgh, 1992), p. 236.

15. The Johnson material is in the Preston MSS in the collections of the Virginia Historical Society (hereafter PMVHS). For his retail trade *vide* letters between Johnson and William Preston from October 1769 to 1774 in PMVHS, 1P9267fFA2.

16. Edward Johnson to William Preston, 23 January 1773; 28 July 1773; ? January 1774, and 8 April 1774, *ibid.*, items 734, 749, 785, and 804.

17. Same to same, 2 July 1774, *ibid.*, item 826.

18. The best survey of this is Robert P. Thomson, 'The Merchant in Virginia 1700–1775' (unpublished University of Wisconsin PhD thesis, 1955). This is available through University Microfilms, Ann Arbor, MI.

19. Patricia G. Johnson, *William Preston and the Allegheny Patriots* (B.D. Smith, Pulaski, VA, 1976), is a good survey of his life.

20. Edward Johnson to William Preston, 2 August 1774, PMVHS, 1P9267fFA2, item 836.

21. Copy of transcription of a petition from William Preston to the Virginia Convention, 18 July 1775, *ibid.*, item 889.

22. Edward Johnson to William Preston, 2 September 1777, *ibid.*, item 967.

23. Bills for powder and lead to William Thompson and William Thomson, dated 5 November 1774, *ibid.*, item 848.

24. Edward Johnson to William Preston, 2 November 1777, *ibid.*, item 969.

25. George M. Herndon, 'The Story of Hemp in Colonial Virginia' (unpublished University of Virginia PhD thesis, 1959).

26. Cited in Charles K. Hatch, 'Colonel William Aylett: A revolutionary merchant of Virginia' (unpublished University of Virginia PhD thesis, 1936), p. 71.

27. Edward Johnson to William Preston, 24 August 1775, 16 December 1775, 23 December 1775, 1 June 1776, 31 July 1776, PMVHS, items 893, 908, 909, 930, and 937, recount the tragi-comic saga.

28. N.A.M. Rodger, *The Insatiable Earl: A life of John Montagu, 4th Earl of Sandwich* (HarperCollins, London, 1993), Chaps. 13–15.

29. Roderick Cavaliero, *Admiral Satan: The life and campaigns of Suffren* (I.B. Tauris, London, 1994).

30. Daniel A. Baugh, 'Why Did Britain Lose Command of the Sea During the War for America?', in Jeremy Black and Philip Woodfine (eds.), *The British Navy and the Use of Naval Power in the Eighteenth Century* (Leicester University Press, Leicester, 1988), p. 163.

31. Sudipta Das, *Myths and Realities of French Imperialism in India, 1763–1783* (Peter Lang, New York, 1992).

32. 'John Robinson's "Considerations on East India Affairs, 1778"', printed in Peter J. Marshall, *Problems of Empire: Britain and India 1757–1813* (George Allen and Unwin, London, 1968), pp. 117–19.

33. Peter J. Marshall, 'Britain and the World in the Eighteenth Century. I: Reshaping the Empire', *Transactions of the Royal Historical Society*, 6th Series, 8 (1998), p. 17.

34. Gerald Newman, *The Rise of English Nationalism: A cultural history 1740–1830* (Weidenfeld and Nicolson, London, 1987).

35. David Cressy, *Bonfires and Bells* (Weidenfeld and Nicolson, London, 1989), p. 206.

36. Michael Zuckerman, 'Identity in British America: Unease in Eden', in Nicholas Canny and Anthony Pagden (eds.), *Colonial Identity in the Atlantic World 1500–1800* (Princeton University Press, Princeton, NJ, pbk edn, 1987), p. 157.

37. Carl J. Richard, *The Founders and the Classics* (Harvard University Press, Harvard, MA, 1994), p. 84.

38. Richard W. Van Alstyne, *The American Empire: Its historical pattern and evolution* (Historical Association, London, 1960), pp. 9–10.

39. John Cannon, *Lord North: The noble lord in the blue ribbon* (Historical Association, London, 1970), p. 25.

40. Herald W. Mullin, *Flight and Rebellion: Slave resistance in eighteenth-century Virginia* (Oxford University Press, Oxford, 1972), Chap. 4.

41. J. Russell Snapp, *John Stuart and the Struggle for Empire on the Southern Frontier* (Louisiana State University Press, Baton Rouge, LA, 1996), Chap. 7.

42. Barbara Greymount, *The Iroquois in the American Revolution* (Syracuse University Press, Syracuse, NY, pbk edn, 1972), p. 221.

43. Wiley Sword, *President Washington's Indian War* (University of Oklahoma Press, Norman, OK, 1985), and Paul D. Nelson, *Anthony Wayne: Soldier of the Early Republic* (Indiana University Press, Bloomington, IN, 1985).

44. James H. Merrell, *The Indians' New World* (University of North Carolina Press, Chapel Hill, NC, 1989), Chaps. 5–6; and Patrick Frazier, *The Mohicans of Stockbridge* (University of Nebraska Press, Lincoln, NB, 1992).

45. George Shelton, *Dean Tucker* (Macmillan, London, 1981), pp. 212–13.

46. Carol W. Troxler, 'Refuge, Resistance, and Reward: The southern loyalists' claim on East Florida', *Journal of Southern History*, 55 (1989), pp. 563–95.

47. *Vide* the remarkable letters from the years 1788–89 published in John Walton Caughey, *McGillivray of the Creeks* (University of Oklahoma Press, Norman, OK, 1938), pp. 185–225.

48. Thomas Pownall, *A Letter from Governor Pownall to Adam Smith* (J. Almond, London, 1776), p. 48.

49. Letter from Messrs Rawlinson, Chorley, and Grierson of Liverpool to Mr William Feeles, Aux Caix, Hispaniola, 6 March 1782, printed in *The Spanish Town Papers*, ed. E. Arnot Robertson (Cresset Press, London, 1959).

50. Linda Colley, 'The Reach of the State', in Lawrence Stone (ed.), *An Imperial State at War: Britain from 1689 to 1815* (Routledge, London, 1994), pp. 165–84.

51. H.M. Scott, 'Britain as a European Great Power in the Age of the American Revolution', in H.T. Dickinson (ed.), *Britain and the American Revolution* (Addison Wesley Longman, Harlow, 1998), pp. 180–204.

52. Bill Bryson, *Made in America* (Secker and Warburg, London, Minerva pbk edn, 1995), pp. 52–53.

53. Andrew Hook, *Scotland and America 1750–1835* (Blackie, Glasgow, 1975), p. 51.

54. Garry Wills, *Inventing America: Jefferson's Declaration of Independence* (Random House, New York, Vintage pbk edn, 1979), Prologue.

Tides of empire and fortunes of war

The Declaration of Independence hardly proclaimed the birth of a new-minted nation. It claimed, to be precise, 'That these United Colonies are, and of Right ought to be Free and Independent States'. The culture of those states in 1775, for all the very large non-British immigrant communities in several of them, was predominantly English, both intellectually and in material terms. So shot through with classical republican rhetoric and with strident emphasis on the peculiar virtues of English liberty was even the official culture of Georgian England, that American Englishmen who resisted what they saw as the tyranny of George III did not feel they were repudiating their English heritage. On the contrary, they could move into the revolution believing that they were only behaving the way good Englishmen should. Their versions of English society were provincial and lacked the upper levels of the complex social hierarchy of Old England, but to interact with those levels they could move to the supreme metropolis, London. Benjamin Franklin did, and only in the 1760s did he finally decide that his future lay back in America. Just how identities would have evolved in thirteen loosely allied independent North American states if they had, as many of them expected, won their war and had their independence accepted as an irreversible fact of life in 1776 is impossible to guess. No doubt, the inherent dynamic potential for growth and change in their regional economies would have generated many of the social changes which it is rather too easy to ascribe to the revolution as such.[1]

However, the crucible of American national identity was the 'slow and torturing labor' of 'the winning of independence'. Only in 1781 did the final turning points come. In March the states finally ratified the Articles of Confederation 'after five years of wrangling shot through with high purpose and low motives'. In October a Franco-American army forced Cornwallis to surrender at Yorktown. The year 1781 and the date of the agreement of the Articles of Confederation in particular has a much better claim as the birthday of a new nation, at least in embryo, than 1776. The long delay in agreeing the Articles was largely due to bitter squabbling over the future of western lands.

Spain had originally tried to compel the American states to agree that Spanish authority should stretch east of the Mississippi as far as the Alleghenies, and that its future American allies should surrender all rights to navigation on the Mississippi. It was a fairly typical Spanish opening bid in the Americas, and proved unsustainable. Much more difficult was the clash between states like Virginia and Massachusetts, which had vast notional claims to western extension; and landlocked states like Rhode Island, Connecticut, Delaware, and Maryland, which had none. The landless states demanded that the expansionist ones surrender their claims to a new American nation. Eventually the landed states agreed so to surrender their claims, but Virginia, not unreasonably, asked that the claims of the usual collection of crooks and speculators organised as land companies with vast notional 'rights' be liquidated before her cession became final. The United States was born in a squabble about future empire. Indeed, it was the solution to that squabble, among other things.[2]

Of course, the identity of the new nation, quaintly nameless but expressed politically as the United States of America (and annexing 'American' as the national adjective in defiance of Latin America), was both fluid and uncertain. Those predominantly conservative elites, later mostly known as Federalists, who both consolidated what had been achieved and carried out a very partial counter-revolution in the shape of the new constitution of 1787, had a vision of a sober, conservative body politic which would be a classical republic like pre-imperial Rome, or like the Ancient Greek city states, cultivating elitist virtue as the bedrock of public integrity. By the 1830s it was clear that whatever the United States was to be, it was not to be like that. One result was that 'all the major revolutionary leaders died less than happy with the results of the Revolution'. The conclusions which can be drawn from this vary. One is that the founding fathers were alienated, not because the revolution had failed, but because 'it had succeeded . . . only too well'.[3] Another, which spares them the condescension of posterity, would be that they knew what they were saying and that the evolution of American life towards a populist, democratic, materialistic pattern, with very strong currents of evangelical religion running through it, was an evolution towards a national culture with which most of them could not comfortably identify.

'National' cultures are complex phenomena, partly the product of deliberate engineering, and always so in communities with several different traditions, one of which is trying to gain the upper hand and write the others out of the country's past as well as its future. In British North America the War of Independence was also a bitter civil war in which the Loyalists quite early on lost all control over the structures of government in the provinces revolting against the authority of George III. It proved impossible in the course of the war to restore them to effective control of more than Georgia. Though many assumed that the British government had both the obligation and means to provide them with an adequate territorial refuge in the south-east at the conclusion of hostilities, they ended up with none, and had to become refugees in Canada (i.e. what was left of British North America, and was so called until Canadian confederation in 1867), or Britain, or the British West Indies, or had to return to what was now their native state and come to terms with the new regime. They were lucky in that the regime's nationalism was not even interested in suppressing their language, which was its own, and that there was no basic sectarian thrust lurking, as sectarianism so easily does, behind a nominally secular rhetoric of nationalism. Reconciled Loyalists merely had to swallow, apart from material losses, an institutionalised demonisation of their past politics – often a demonisation based on parody, for the pre-war politics of many Loyalists, on all but the British connection, were very close to those of Patriots and Whigs.

The factious and irresponsible demand of the Rockingham Whig politician Charles James Fox that the British government acknowledge the independence of the United States before the peace negotiations started – thus depriving British delegates of one of the few levers they had to construct serious negotiations, as distinct from endlessly mounting and outrageous demands from the American side – was firmly rebuffed by Lord Shelburne, the principal architect of the peace settlement on the British side. However, Shelburne's approach to the settlement was to prove extremely controversial. He was known as 'the Jesuit of Berkeley Square', an accusation of hypocrisy and duplicity. Up to a point, the quip was unfair to both Jesuits and Berkeley. As anyone taught by them knows, Jesuits suffer from being more sophisticated and intelligent than most people to a point which makes them as disturbing to many Roman Catholics as they are to some Protestants. The case for Shelburne is much the same: that he simply had a sophisticated, liberal, enlightened policy which others found disturbing. As for hypocrisy, there is always Douglas Hurd's dictum that 'Very few politicians are hypocrites, because the first people whom they persuade with their arguments are themselves.'[4]

On the other hand, it is clear that Shelburne was compulsively secretive and utterly determined to control the nature of the settlement. Since he had little support in the Commons, and was wrestling with repeated attempts by his Rockingham Whig rival Charles James Fox to intrude into the negotiations, usually disruptively, Shelburne did his business privately in his house in Berkeley Square or in his country house outside London, often putting very little down on paper to make it impossible for cabinet colleagues to find out what he was doing by calling for papers. It has to be stressed that because historians have tended to look at these negotiations through the lens of nineteenth- and twentieth-century developments, they have exaggerated the significance of American and imperial issues and underestimated the central importance attached by both the British and the French to the European balance of power. Shelburne rapidly persuaded himself he had a rapport with his French opposite number Vergennes (who was solidly backed by Louis XVI), and began to think in terms of a Franco–British *entente* which would give the law to Europe. There was a very strong case for Anglo–French cooperation on a whole range of issues, but the whole concept of laying down the law to Europe was the sort of self-deceiving rhetoric which politicians are addicted to, and tend to believe after repeating it to themselves frequently.[5]

Shelburne ensured that he was not contradicted by sharing his programme with very few other than trusted agents. He was an idealist, but he was also anxious to rush through a settlement to strengthen his own hand, before parliament, with its disagreeable potential for argument and criticism, met in November. His idea was to pre-empt serious discussion by presenting parliament with a *fait accompli* achieved by executive use of royal prerogative. He was anxious to reach an unsigned but firm agreement with the United States first. This was perfectly feasible, since the American negotiators were anxious to terminate the war and just as cynical and unscrupulous (though deeply self-righteous) as the French ally they would effectively be abandoning by agreeing informally to a separate settlement with Britain. Shelburne was not prepared to give the Americans everything they wanted. Equally, in their hurry to make peace first the Americans surrendered more than they absolutely needed to surrender. These are but the *minutiae* of any negotiation process. Political calculation, much of it with a future commercial vision of the United States as a vast market for British goods, dominated Shelburne's approach. There was pressure on British ministers from mercantile pressure groups but absolutely no direct influence by such groups on the final settlement.

Shelburne was by 1782 a convinced free trader who hoped to create a new political world by a series of commercial treaties with the United States, Ireland, and France, but at the beginning he seriously hoped 'to preserve a union with America, on a basis of equal partnership at the imperial level'. To him a complete separation was unnatural, and he 'mistakenly believed that memories of his opposition to coercion gave him a personal position to wean the Americans back from secession'.[6] Benjamin

Franklin, who negotiated discreetly with Shelburne's agent, Richard Oswald, in Paris, rapidly disabused his lordship of the latter illusion, but strung him along by concealing the depth of his own acquired anglophobia whilst trying to maximise the returns from a mutation of it into a profound sense of self-righteousness as he suggested that the least the British government could offer was considerably more than it possibly could and survive. Modern British historians operating within a liberal consensus have tended to identify with what they see as the enlightened cleverness of Shelburne without looking at the very cogent criticisms advanced at the time.[7]

In so far as the United States remained within the commercial empire of the United Kingdom after 1783, it did so because of the convenience and cheapness of British manufactured goods and the need for British markets to earn the wherewithal to pay for them. Shelburne's Nonconformist client the Reverend Dr Richard Price foresaw in one of his post-war pamphlets, *Observations on the Importance of the American Revolution* (London and Boston, MA, 1784), that there were forces and pressures which might well drive an independent America towards high protective duties against imports.[8] Shelburne was right in believing that sharp political divisions made nonsense of human realities in the old British Atlantic world, but he was less good at striking a favourable balance with and commanding respect from forces he did not fully understand. He could be naive as well as subtle, and he was not given to exposing his ideas to criticism. Himself a member of the Irish House of Lords, he was shaken to discover that when he agreed to the repeal of the 1720 Declaratory Act in 1782, on the understanding that there would be a parallel treaty confirming the 'permanent connection' between the two kingdoms, Henry Grattan, the Irish leader, simply could not get such a treaty through his legislature. Yet Grattan's loyalty to the British Crown was absolute. Indeed the Irish peerage, to which Shelburne belonged, was a classic illustration of the extreme complexity of the reality of British nationalities in the eighteenth century. The nineteenth and early twentieth centuries saw historians create an image of an eighteenth-century Ireland polarised between a new, rapacious, 'English' landed elite and a cowering Roman Catholic, Gaelic peasantry. In fact intermarriage had long made a nonsense of the sharp division between 'native' and 'colonist' at the level of the peerage. Two-thirds of Irish peers regularly attended the Irish parliament in the eighteenth century and of these 95 per cent had ancestry reaching back beyond the Cromwellian and Williamite land confiscations. The Irish peers were a genetic mix derived from Gaelic, Norman-French, English, and Scottish stock.[9]

Britishness in the strict sense of the word has to be a post Anglo–Scottish union of 1707 phenomenon, but of course the term had been around much longer. James VI and I titled himself by proclamation king of Great Britain.

In practice, there does not seem to have been a lot of emotional mileage in that until quite late. The accession of George III in 1760, and his selection of a Scottish first minister, the Earl of Bute, provoked what Linda Colley has described as 'Runaway Scottophobia'. She is quite right to point out that this phenomenon did not reflect so much traditional antipathy between the two peoples as a response to a more recent development, artfully fanned by that devil John Wilkes, who managed to identify himself with the defence of traditional English values menaced by sycophantic non-freedom-loving Scots. It is no accident that Wilkes was a hero to Patriot American Englishmen, or that they also had occasional spasms of Runaway Scottophobia. It was really only after the second great schism in the Englishry had become irreversible in 1783 that the way was clear for the first great waves of mobilisation of opinion within the dominions of George III on the theme of being British, as an examination of Colley's book *Britons* shows pretty clearly.[10]

The book has been criticised for reflecting the 'Social Democratic' values of the period when it was published, whatever that may mean. In fact it holds up very well. If there is a criticism, it is one as valid when it was published as later: it does not allow enough for the massive Irish contribution to the construction of British identity, which long antedates the heyday of Arthur Wellesley, Duke of Wellington, the greatest British soldier of the Napoleonic wars, or Robert Stewart, Viscount Castlereagh, the man who more than any other held together the coalition which finally brought Napoleon down. To dismiss them as 'Anglo-Irish' is a mere sectarian slur. Wellesley came from what he called 'dear Dublin'. Castlereagh was very much an Ulsterman, albeit when the American ambassador Richard Rush went to his first official dinner at Lord Castlereagh's London town house in 1818, he was astonished to find the entire company conversing in French. Needless to say, the ambassador referred to his hosts as 'the English'.[11] Though there is earlier material in *Britons* – as befits its dates, which go from 1707 to 1837 – the vast bulk of the book is about the period after 1783 when Colley sees the sustained rise in the popularity of George III and therefore in his importance as a British icon, as well as the mass mobilisation of men and opinion necessary to prepare for massive resistance to real threats of invasion during the French revolutionary and Napoleonic wars. In the longer conspectus Colley regards war as vitally important in forging a sense of identity. Protestantism helped do that, but Protestants differed and belonged to three kingdoms and four nations. War could meld with a vague general sense of Protestantism because; 'success, above all success in war, was what the men who governed Great Britain were able to hold out as a legitimisation of their rule to the millions below them', and war was often against Roman Catholic powers. It will not, however, really do, before 1783, to argue, certainly in a colonial context, that apart from 'one, telling débâcle' (i.e. the War of American Independence) 'there was victory'.[12]

There were plenty of debacles, especially on the peripheries of the British monarchy. Some wars were exhausting draws, others went badly wrong. In India wars were being lost in the Carnatic in the 1760s and 1780s. Between August 1767 and April 1769 the Madras presidency of the EIC had fought a war with Hyder Ali and, despite tactical victories due to superior infantry, had suffered decisive strategic defeat due to Hyder's intelligent use of his vastly more numerous cavalry. In 1780 the inept and corrupt leadership of the presidency blundered into the Second Mysore War, in which Hyder Ali virtually wiped out a substantial EIC force in a battle at Pollilur. With his formidable son Tipu commanding his cavalry, and much improved infantry, Hyder was able to press Madras so hard that it only survived by calling in reinforcements under the veteran hand of Sir Eyre Coote from Bengal. Coote won tactical victories, but could not command much out-with Madras, his encampment, and the range of his field guns. With his departure due to illness and the arrival of French troops under the marquis de Bussy, sent to attack the British position in the Carnatic, the war went far from well for the EIC. The Mysoreans were even able to keep up their effort through the delicate transition to Tipu after the death of Hyder in 1782. The French were pushing the EIC forces hard and Mangalore fell to Tipu in January 1784.

What saved the British position was the general peace with France in 1783, which contained provisions to encourage allies of the contracting parties to accede to it. After having much the worse of the war, the EIC was lucky to secure a standstill peace.[13] The First Mysore War had caused a spectacular plunge in the value of EIC stock, and the Second was part of a general crisis of the EIC regional empires in India which saw their survival as a matter of some doubt. Warren Hastings, the governor general, who by a narrow margin saved existing positions, talked about 'establishing the sovereignty of the British people' over Bengal,[14] but the contemporary political crisis in Westminster over the implications of the emergence of the EIC as a considerable power in the sub-continent made it very clear that the crux of the Westminster debate lay in devising a system of control which would keep Indian patronage out of the British political system, out of the hands of the Crown, and above all out of the hands of predatory power-hungry politicians like Charles James Fox. British India was beginning to move towards a system of control at arms' length which transferred huge amounts of power and considerable freedom of action to those very few members of the Westminster elite prepared to take an interest in the sub-continent.

It is very debatable whether the experience of colonial wars between 1689 and 1783 can be described as a triumphalist experience, taken as a whole, for the British peoples. War was a very important and shaping experience, but often peripheral areas found themselves abandoned or poorly supported because of metropolitan obsessions with Europe. The state was more important after 1689, but its assault on the Spanish Empire after 1739 was a failure. The triumphs of the Seven Years' War proved evanescent. Essentially private initiatives in the style that had been dominant in the sixteenth and seventeenth centuries still employed entrepreneurial violence in the eighteenth century on Asian peripheries, but two wars developed catastrophically in the Carnatic after 1767. The whole concept of the Britishness which this very chequered record is supposed by some writers to have fuelled remained inherently ambiguous and contested. As John Brewer has indicated, 'British culture was never a monolith but was viewed differently by groups from different perspectives'. He also adds that in the eighteenth century, and one could say much later, 'its content and boundaries' were 'a persistent source of dispute'.[15] One of the factors which made the Madras presidency over-confident in 1780 was the recent arrival of reinforcements in the shape of Lord MacLeod's Regiment of Highlanders. The army commanded by Colonel William Baillie which fought Hyder at Pollilur was at one stage being directed in Scots Gaelic to compensate for the scandalous absence of usable EIC military codes for secure communication. The Highland and Irish mafias within the EIC military and civil services had ambiguous identities which matched the ambiguities of the EIC's relationship with Westminster, and indeed the general ambiguity of British identity.

In fact, the whole assumption that official British culture in the period 1688–1783 was stamped by a particularly imperialist outlook is itself very dubious. The inhabitants of the trendier frontiers of English departments, especially in the United States, who have an increasing tendency to try to marry literature and history in an interdisciplinary exercise which too often means no mental discipline at all, have a tendency to deal with this problem by just ignoring it. As good post-modernists, their approach to evidence is not so much selective as arbitrary and creative. The fact that no evidence is perfect does not mean that some is not better than other evidence, and historical activity is crucially linked to evidence assessment and to the search for wider categories of evidence. These, if they can be found and interpreted or reinterpreted, may indeed allow the voices of those suppressed or ignored by traditional history to be heard. However, if there is no evidence, they must remain mute, except by limited inference. Unfortunately the post-structuralism and anti-humanism associated with the immensely influential (and profoundly confused) French thinker Michel Foucault does reach the point of overtly arguing from philosophical positions deeply influenced by Foucault's German mentors Martin Heidegger and Friedrich Nietzsche – that all history is essential fiction. When this approach is applied to the deconstruction of imperial history, the upshot can be a weird 'meditation on the absent other' derived largely from linguistic theory and a self-flagellatory approach to mainstream western culture, when evidence of the racism and atrocities perpetrated by that culture on, say, Australian aborigines can be found abundantly in the much despised traditional sources, as soon as their relevance and importance is grasped.[16]

It is not surprising, therefore, though it is depressing, that the role of imperialism in eighteenth-century English culture can be taken for granted in a recent study which tries 'to evoke the ways in which the literature of the eighteenth century served the purpose of empire, and also the ways in which a radical critique might recruit that literature to uncover the operations of imperialism in the eighteenth century and to help put a stop to empire in the twentieth'.[17] The wonderful fusion of Marxism, feminism, and post-modernist radical discourse which such an interpretation of Jonathan Swift's *Gulliver's Travels* allows can be followed in statements about 'the fundamental implication of Swift's misogyny with mercantile capitalism', from which the reader moves to 'the ideological status of women in Swift's writing and the connection of the representation of women with capitalist expansion to the historical problem of colonialism', and finally to 'the mutual interaction of race and gender in Swift's major satire'.[18] What Dean Swift, Church of Ireland clergyman and Tory propagandist, would make of this is an interesting but unanswerable question. The early eighteenth-century imperialist framework is simply assumed. In such works it has to be. Few who write them know much history.

It is interesting that James Bruce of Kinnaird, the Scots laird who arrived back in London in 1774 after five years of residence and travel in Abyssinia in search of the source of the Blue Nile, congratulated George III in the first volume of five he published on *Travels to Discover the Source of the Nile* (1790) on being the first monarch to encourage the exploration of the world without aiming at military conquest or colonisation. Yes: there were plenty of racist prejudices around in the anglophone world, but Bruce was clear 'not that all men are equal, but that they are all brethren',[19] and his life in Abyssinia showed as little refusal to accept local habits as the behaviour of the EIC servant in India in the eighteenth century undergoing circumcision to allow for the sexual assumptions and preferences of his Muslim 'bibi' or resident lady friend.[20]

In the last analysis, the security of the essentially defensive imperial monarchy of George III after 1763 depended on the maintenance of naval superiority over not just any European rival, but also over any likely

257

combination of rivals, notably France and Spain. The British were anxious to uphold that superiority. They were not even willing to encourage naval building programmes in allies. They wanted to do it themselves. They had some built-in advantages. They had more dry-docks than their rivals, which enabled them to turn over ships undergoing essential periodical refit faster than their opponents. In 1774–83 Portsmouth and Plymouth alone coped, in 161 dockings, with 87 per cent of the crucially important 74-gun ships. They could contract out large proportions of an emergency building programme to a big and efficient shipbuilding industry. They usually had superior access to vital naval supplies from the Baltic and North America. Their range of overseas bases from Gibraltar (taken in 1704) to Minorca (acquired in 1708 but lost in both 1756 and 1782), with its great harbour at Port Mahon; to Bombay, where the EIC built a dry-dock in 1750; to Port Royal in Jamaica and English Harbour in Antigua; not to mention Halifax in Nova Scotia, developed from 1749 onwards. They also had a large pool of skilled seamen to draw on in their merchant marine, though manning in war was always a nightmare.[21]

These advantages were crucial, not for expansion but for bare survival, because in the period 1763–80 the British government entirely failed to sustain a safe margin of advantage over the Bourbon powers. Allied to a new anti-British Spanish king, Charles III, the French started a naval build-up in parallel to a reduction in European commitment before the peace of 1763. They only coordinated with any degree of efficiency with the Spaniards by the period 1766 to 1770, when the British wartime programme was over and Bourbon warship launches gave them an edge by the latter date when France and Spain had a combined naval tonnage of 380,000 tons to Britain's 350,000. The naval race was even more traumatic than it sounds from tonnage figures. The British had had an unsustainable 375,000-ton navy in 1760–65 – the greatest in history – but it still contained many elements which as early as the 1739–48 war had been recognised as obsolete. Broadly, British battleships were too small, and the 3-gundeck 80-gun ship, which was the largest type, could hardly use its lower tier of guns in any seaway. By the 1770s the Royal Navy was much more like the French or Spanish navies, with a line of battle dominated by 2-gundeck 74s – mounting 32-pounders on the lower gundeck and 18-pounders on the upper – all set rather higher than before, supplemented by a cruising navy of large single-gundeck frigates, with 12- or 9-pounder guns. French 74s were rather bigger with 36- and 18-pounders. After a lull in the construction race in 1771–75, there was a frenzy of launching. From 1776 to 1780, the belligerent powers launched about 300,000 tons of warships, and in the next five years 400,000. By huge effort the British cut the percentage superiority of the Bourbon fleets, but slowly. It was 20 per cent in 1775, 25 in 1780, but only 7 per cent by 1785. Still, Britannia hardly ruled the waves as she had in 1763.

In 1779 a combined Franco–Spanish fleet of 66 ships commanded the Channel, facing a British fleet only two-thirds in number of ships and possibly half in tonnage. That the Bourbon edge did not turn into naval disaster for Britain was due to factors mentioned, incorporation of captures into the Royal Navy, and excellent overall operational performance. The Bourbons, it may be added, never had the overwhelming advantage which virtually guarantees victory. They still continued the race after 1783 and by 1790 were rather more than 20 per cent stronger than Britain at sea. George III's Britain was far from being a maritime hegemon between 1765 and 1790, though the Royal Navy was clearly the best single fighting fleet.[22] The British monarchy after 1763 was unstable and loosely articulated. John Adams, Patriot lawyer from Massachusetts, correctly denied that 'the British Empire' was a legal entity under Common Law.[23] All there was was a global conglomeration with huge internal political problems and a central political structure such that its flexibility was extremely limited. It was still a monarchy, but one with heavy republican elements in which George III could only be an effective king by operating as the monarchical tier in a parliamentary complex based in Westminster, where coherence was difficult to achieve, even with a deep inter-penetration between the executive and the legislature. Those who dominated Westminster absolutely refused constructive incorporation to elements they feared they could not control.

Once the Crown started to move to impose more coherence, interstitial violence between units of the monarchy was always on the cards, if only because of the complete lack of agreement on the nature of political legitimacy within it. The EIC, for example, argued, probably correctly, that most of its post-1757 holdings in India were legally Moghul, not British. Most modern successor nationalisms are also thinly veiled forms of imperialism, bent on at least committing cultural genocide on variant identities within a given area, on linguistic, racial, or sectarian grounds; so the inhabitants of British North America were blessed in not having developed a coherent 'modern' sense of nationalism by 1775: 'Americans were still very far from being a people bonded by a shared sense of purpose or identity by the third quarter of the eighteenth century.' They were too divided, and when they did create, slowly, a new nation, it was rabidly territorially imperialist, but with a minimal and very civilised civic religion deep rooted in the English heritage of the thirteen colonies.[24]

War, war decisively heightened by foreign intervention and unexpectedly prolonged, had set them on that path. In studying British overseas expansion before 1783, the historian serves the temple of Clio, as all historians should, but he has to also sacrifice to Mars. Other deities, Pallas Athene of the arts and sciences, and Mercury for commerce, were acknowledged by seventeenth-century humanists as important in determining the development and character of human communities.[25] Nobody would suggest that war was the only determinant of the history of the English and then British globally spread communities before 1783, but it was a very important one and, as far as colonial identities and attitudes went, a very shaping one. Above all, the historian has to recognise that triumphalist narratives of British colonial wars in the 'long' nineteenth century from 1792 to 1914 are singularly bad models for a deeper understanding of colonial wars before that date. Between 1689 and 1783 the impact of colonial war on the frontiers of the English and British was heavily dependent on contingency. Luck and skill mattered. Little was predetermined. Intelligent adaptation to changing circumstances was the key to success or, often, mere survival. Therein lies much of the fascination of these wars.

At a deeper level, they also display the connections between the use of force and the formation and manipulation of group identities, many of which by the seventeenth and eighteenth centuries were laying claim to 'national' status. By the late nineteenth century, it had become intellectually fashionable to contrast 'nationalism' with 'imperialism'. The usual context for this was a situation in which a 'nation' claimed to be struggling rightly against 'imperialism'. Much before the end of the nineteenth century it is in fact difficult to find any sustained usage of the term 'British Empire', for the very good reason that the obvious political incoherence of the global sprawl of territories associated, in wildly different ways, with the Crown of the United Kingdom was generally recognised. Edmund Burke's aspirations to define empire as many states under one common head 'had left no lasting mark on the public mind after they had been defeated by separation in the case of America'.[26]

But the concept of 'nation', before the terrible simplifiers of the nineteenth and twentieth centuries started to play with it, was as complex and evasive as its imperial counterpart, from which, in practice, most rampant nationalisms cannot be separated. There have been a very few cases where a national identity has been based on a sense of civic solidarity within a plural society. Since the rise of the confessional state from the sixteenth century onwards, such identities have been scarce indeed in Christendom. Most nationalisms have since then been the product of circumstance and artifice, shaped by the needs – political, sectarian, linguistic, or racial – of a particular group or groups, and almost always implying cultural genocide and territorial claims against contiguous or coexisting elements. Often these are not peripheral elements in the shaping of a nationalistic agenda: they are core values which give it its support and bite. Corollaries, such as the usual nationalist attempt to hi-jack history to provide exclusive validation for the group in control of the nationalistic bandwagon, are therefore almost automatic.

When extended early-modern monarchies broke up, the firm control of adequate physical force – whether to check metropolitan pretensions or to terrorise and intimidate, dominate, or drive out domestic rivals – was always one of the key determinants of which identities could hope to achieve long-term viability. In Mexico the conservative Creoles who, with the Roman Catholic Church, eventually made independence viable, were precisely the people who had hitherto crushed independence movements whose social radicalism and widespread Indian support made Creoles fear for their own interests. As was said at the time, independence was 'accomplished by the same people who until then had been opposing it'.[27] In the North America of the late eighteenth century, two successor identities, both comparatively fragile coalition constructs, were able to emerge. The British North American one was defensive, largely defined in negative terms by the fact that refugee Loyalists and French Canadians were not like the people running the newly independent United States. Those states had their own problems of coherence, but were unanimous in destining for oblivion not just the Loyalist tradition, but those contiguous 'nations' left in the lurch by Shelburne.

The mestizo leaders of the southern Indian peoples are a fascinating and tragic example of a group of men trying to sustain a viable identity or group of identities in the face of odds they knew to be long. They could and did tell imperial Spain that it had to keep their alliance, not least by servicing their trading system, because they were fellow pre-destined victims of American expansionism. They addressed to the Spanish Crown a dignified, indignant, and moving repudiation of George III's presumption in 'ceding' to the United States the lands of Indian nations (they used that common term for themselves) who had been his independent allies, not his subjects.[28] They and their largely Scottish trading partners tried to create, within the structure of a Spanish alliance, salaried positions for mediator-agent figures like 'a gentleman of the name of John McIntosh who lives in the Chickasaws and has considerable stock of Horses and Cattle there'.[29] In retrospect, we know there was no future for gentlemen like John McIntosh, but unless historians abandon rational reconstruction of the past for mere sycophancy to victors, they must recognise the complexity of choices and the plasticity of events and identities. Losers have as valid identities as, and sometimes more honourable ones than, the often savage and always arrogantly self-righteous identity which breaks them by force before burying their memory under propaganda.

It was the misfortune of the American Loyalists to be subjects of a monarchy whose political structures were not only globally incoherent but also especially after 1760 ferociously factional in its core state, the United Kingdom of Great Britain. The condescending liberal myth, propagated assiduously by Victorian intellectuals like the Utilitarian philosopher John Stuart Mill, that Englishmen were and are characterised by a 'sheer inability to comprehend general ideas on the subject of government or anything else' is and always was nonsense. Obviously 'the British people of the Hanoverian era not only had a state but, in some sense, also knew that they had one'. The concept was freely available to them.[30] That core state was one of the units of governance in a British world that went into flux from Bombay to the Chesapeake in the crisis years from 1764 to 1784. In this political hurricane the priority of the elites in the various regional polities was to keep control of such state systems as they could dominate, at almost any cost. Thus, the Virginia gentry, once seen as leading a united people to independence, were under threat from two directions. Their attempts to manipulate the Westminster government's imperial policies foundered on the opposition of more successful lobbyists like the London merchants and the Indian allies of the Crown. Internally, the Virginia elite faced potential challenges from slave populations and from debt-burdened farmers whose restiveness was sharpened by economic crisis and the threat of recession. By the spring of 1776 the gentry believed that they had to take Virginia out of the dominions of George III if they were to regain control of their lower orders.[31]

The deceptive triumphs of the 1763 peace settlement had raised the level of interest in the Crown's overseas dominions to unusual heights in the United Kingdom. That was one of the reasons for the consensus behind the government's view that by 1775 continuation of a policy of endless appeasement of American colonial demands was pointless and self-defeating. Nevertheless, the identity of the realm and of its rulers remained primarily European. Attempts by modern writers with manipulative ulterior agendas to argue that 'the United Kingdom was established to serve the purposes of Empire'[32] are unhistorical and utterly unconvincing. The Union of 1707 that created the United Kingdom of Great Britain was an episode in a great European war – the War of the Spanish Succession. Its overriding purpose was to safeguard the northern frontier of England from the Franco–Jacobite threat. It is no accident that an excellent recent collection of essays on the Union of 1707, though it has the 'E' word in the title, contains little on overseas colonies as such.[33] They hardly featured in the contemporary debate. The Scottish city which traded most with America, Glasgow, was as hostile to the Union of 1707 as Dublin was to be to the further Act of Union of 1800, itself primarily the product of security worries in another great cycle of European wars – those with Revolutionary and Napoleonic France. George III and his ministers arguably fought from start to finish between 1775 and 1783 to uphold the United Kingdom in the front rank of the European great powers.

They succeeded eventually better than they knew, but not everyone in the political nation wished them well. Despite the consensus behind the government in 1775, the highly factional nature of Westminster politics ensured that there were elements in the 'formed' opposition (i.e. politicians habitually out of office but hungry for it) who hoped for military defeat. They had the brains to see that if the administration lost the war and could be depicted as losing it badly, their own chances of 'storming the closet' by imposing themselves on the monarch after North's fall would be greatly enhanced. The small, uninfluential radical groups (often Nonconformist in religion) who sympathised, or indeed identified with the American rebellion were genuinely committed to preserving what they saw as one Atlantic nation through conciliation. This made them notably obtuse about American Patriot motives and objectives in 1775–76.[34] Charles James Fox shared some of the radicals' ideology but tactical calculation also loomed large with him. When he taunted North in late 1775 with being a 'blundering pilot' who had 'lost a whole continent' he reinforced the dangerous illusion that Westminster had ever effectively ruled most of North America.[35] His subsequent undisguised distress at the news of British victories was connected with his fear that they would strengthen the hand of his arch-opponent George III. Defeat at Yorktown gave Fox and his leader Lord Rockingham their chance. It is hardly surprising that after censuring Shelburne's sell-out peace, the House of Commons lost interest in anything except the savage battle between the monarch and aristocratic factions. It was a fight for the control of a state-structure in Great Britain that had become temporarily as unstable in its central organs as Virginia had been a decade before.

The war with the United States was far from a hopeless cause in terms of fighting for advantageous peace terms that left other parties, including the new United States, with a healthy respect for British strength. In the 1940s Admiral Richmond, discussing the strategic application of sea power, cited a contemporary American observer of the War of the American Revolution who said that the privation caused by the cessation of commerce 'would probably have caused that war to end differently but for French aid'.[36] We now know from detailed research that the impact of the Royal Navy's blockade of the east coast of North America, on top of the other stresses of war, was extremely damaging. It did not matter that a complete blockade of several thousand miles of coast was impossible. Huge additional costs could be imposed, particularly on the crucial bulk commodity export trades. Sea-borne commerce could be massively depressed and insurance rates made to soar by the existence of a finite risk factor beyond the ordinary hazards of the sea. The near collapse of large parts of the American economy was relieved by a temporary revival on the Chesapeake in particular in 1780–81, which by a narrow margin made the Franco–American victory at Yorktown feasible. The revival proved temporary and long after French intervention the Royal Navy went on tightening aspects of its blockade. For example, it first imposed a reasonably effective form of blockade on Delaware as late as 1782.[37]

The eventual emergence of the beginnings of an expansionist national American identity was greatly assisted by the overall mismanagement of the war in North America by the British Crown. North was, as he admitted, a dreadful war minister. No sensible, coherent strategic vision was ever developed. The record of the Earl of Sandwich in managing the navy under desperately difficult circumstances may be defended. Lord George Germain's record is a different matter, if only because of the disastrous consequences from Saratoga to Yorktown of his chronic inability to establish coherent, functional chains of command. Above all, however, it was the decision of the hard-pressed British after 1781 to relegate North America to its pre-1754 marginal status that goes far to explain the eventual outcome. Most colonial wars from 1689 had been peripheral consequences of European conflict. That was as true of the EIC in Madras in 1744 as of New England in 1689 or 1702. Even the Seven Years' War had started in 1754 as a botched attempt by a deterrent strike to prevent obscure scuffles in the Ohio valley from being escalated to the point where they might provoke a European crisis. Colonial wars did help shape English, British, and American identities, but erratically, because very often these colonial conflicts were not of central importance in the minds of those who ran the British core state in Europe.

Notes and references

1. Gordon S. Wood, *The Radicalism of the American Revolution* (Alfred A. Knopf, New York, 1993), Parts 1 and 2.

2. Merrill Jensen, *The New Nation: A history of the United States during the Confederation 1781–1789* (Northeastern University Press, Classics edn, Boston, MA, 1981), pp. 3–12.

3. Wood, *Radicalism of the American Revolution*, p. 368.

4. The Rt Hon. Lord Hurd of Westwell CH, CBE [sic], 'Can Peace and Justice be Reconciled', *The Eagle* (St John's College, Cambridge, 1999).

5. *Vide* Andrew P. Stockley, 'Britain, France and the Peace of 1783' (unpublished University of Cambridge PhD thesis, 1995). I am grateful to Dr H.M. Scott for drawing the important conclusions of this work to my attention.

6. Peter Brown, *The Chathamites* (Macmillan, London, 1967), p. 90.

7. The classic example is the uncritical encomium in Vincent T. Harlow, *The Founding of the Second British Empire 1763–1793 Vol. I Discovery and Revolution* (Longman, London, 1952), Chap. 6.

8. Brown, *op. cit.*, p. 166.

9. Francis G. James, *Lords of the Ascendancy: The Irish House of Lords and its members, 1600–1800* (Catholic University of America Press, 1995), p. 104.

10. Linda Colley, *Britons: Forging the nation 1707–1837* (Yale University Press, New Haven, CT, 1992).

11. *Ibid.*, p. 165.

12. *Ibid.*, pp. 52–53.

13. For good brief accounts of the First and Second Mysore Wars see H.H. Dodwell, 'The Carnatic, 1761–84; in *idem.*, the *Cambridge History of the British Empire. Vol. V: British India 1497–1858* (Cambridge University Press, Cambridge, 1929), pp. 273–94.

14. Abdul Majed Khan, *The Transition in Bengal 1756–1775: A study of Saiyid Muhammed Reza Khan* (Cambridge University Press, Cambridge, 1969), p. 339.

15. John Brewer, *The Pleasures of the Imagination: English culture in the eighteenth century* (HarperCollins, London, 1997), Introduction, p. xxx.

16. Keith Windschuttle, *The Killing of History* (The Free Press, Sydney, 1997), Chaps. 4 and 5.

17. Laura Brown, *Ends of Empire: Women and ideology in early eighteenth-century English literature* (Cornell University Press, Ithaca, NY, 1993), p. 1.

18. *Ibid.*, p. 182.

19. J.M. Reid, *Traveller Extraordinary: The life of James Bruce of Kinnaird* (Eyre and Spottiswoode, London, 1968), pp. 304–05.

20. Roger Hyam, *Empire and Sexuality: The British experience* (Manchester University Press, Manchester, pbk edn, 1991), pp. 25–26.

21. Daniel A. Baugh, 'The Eighteenth Century Navy as a National Institution 1690–1815', in J.R. Hill (ed.), *The Oxford Illustrated History of the Royal Navy* (Oxford University Press, Oxford, 1995).

22. Jan Glete, *Navies and Nations: Warships, navies and state-building in Europe and America, 1500–1860* (2 vols., Historiska Institutionen, Stockholms Universitet, Stockholm, 1993), Vol. I, pp. 262–84.

23. Michael Zuckerman, 'Identity in British America: Unease in Eden', in Nicholas Canny and Anthony Pagden (eds.), *Colonial Identity in the Atlantic World 1500–1800* (Princeton University Press, Princeton, NJ, pbk edn, 1987), p. 157.

24. Richard Koebner, *Empire* (Cambridge University Press, Cambridge, 1961), p. 211.

25. Charles R. Boxer, *The Dutch Seaborne Empire 1600–1800* (Hutchinson, London, 1965), Chap. 6, 'Pallas and Mercury'.

26. Koebner, *Empire*, p. 296.

27. John Lynch, *The Spanish-American Revolutions 1808–1826* (Weidenfeld and Nicolson, London, 1937), p. 320.

28. Alejandor McGillivray A su Excelencia El Gobernador O'Reilly, 24 February 1785, and enclosed address from 'nosotros los Gefes y Guerreros de las Naciones Indias Crikes, o Talapuches, Chicacha, Cherokies', Archivos Nacionales de Cuba (hereafter ANC), Habana, Floridas, Legajo número 10, Signatura 54, 3r–5r.

29. William Panton Al Capitán General, Pensacola, 4 July 1790, correspondencia de Señor William Panton 1785–1799, ANC, Legajo número 1, Signatura 5, 166v.

30. J.A.W. Gunn, 'Eighteenth-Century Britain: In search of the state and finding the Quarter Sessions', in John Brewer and Eckhart Hellmuth (eds.), *Rethinking Leviathan: The eighteenth-century state in Britain and Germany* (The German Historical Institute and Oxford University Press, Oxford, 1999), pp. 99–125. The quotations are on pp. 125 and 99 resp.

31. Woody Holton, *Forced Founders: Indians, debtors, slaves, and the making of the American Revolution in Virginia* (University of North Carolina Press, Chapel Hill, NC, 1999).

32. Norman Davies, *The Isles: A history* (Macmillan, London, 1999), p. 1053.

33. John Robertson (ed.), *A Union for Empire* (Cambridge University Press, Cambridge, 1995).

34. Colin Bonwick, *English Radicals and the American Revolution 1773–1776* (University of North Carolina Press, Chapel Hill, NC, 1977).

35. Peter D.G. Thomas, *Tea Party to Independence: The third phase of the American Revolution 1773–1776* (Clarendon Press, Oxford, 1991), p. 279.

36. Admiral Sir Herbert Richmond, *Statesmen and Sea Power* (Clarendon Press, Oxford, 1946, reprinted (with corrections) 1947), p. 147.

37. Richard Buell Jr, *In Irons: Britain's Naval Supremacy and the American Revolutionary Economy* (Yale University Press, Cambridge, MA, 1999).

The scale of writing on colonial wars between 1688 and 1783 means that no comprehensive bibliography is feasible. What is here offered is a selection, mostly of books rather than articles. Most of the books offer the interested reader who wants to pursue themes the assistance of excellent bibliographies of their fields.

Imperial context

J.H. Parry, *Trade and Dominion: The European overseas empires in the eighteenth century* (Weidenfeld and Nicolson, London, 1971), surveys all Europe's empires. P.J. Marshall (ed.), *The Oxford History of the British Empire. Vol. II: The Eighteenth Century* (Oxford University Press, Oxford, 1998), provides an excellent modern overview. V.T. Harlow's two-volume study of *The Founding of the Second British Empire 1763–1793* (Longman, London, *Vol. 1 Discovery and Revolution*, 1952 and *Vol. 2 New Continents and Changing Values*, 1964) is important, but the 'swing to the East' thesis which is so central to its structure has not held up well to subsequent scrutiny, and it is in places, particularly in its discussion of Shelburne, so relentlessly Whig in interpretation as to obscure contemporary alternatives to or critics of policies followed. The earlier part of A.N. Porter (ed.), *Atlas of British Overseas Expansion* (Routledge, London, 1991), is useful for the period to 1783.

Roots of power

John Brewer, *The Sinews of Power: War, money and the english state 1688–1783* (Alfred A. Knopf, New York, 1989), and Lawrence Stone (ed.), *An Imperial State at War: Britain from 1689 to 1815* (Routledge, London, 1994) are important.

Military background

Christopher Duffy, *The Military Experience in the Age of Reason* (Routledge and Kegan Paul, London, 1987) is Eurocentric but gives a graphic sense of battlefield realities. Chapter 9 of the same author's *The Fortress in the Age of Vauban and Frederick the Great 1660–1789. Vol. II: Siege Warfare* (Routledge and Kegan Paul, London, 1985), covers colonial campaigns. Jeremy Black (ed.), *War in the Early Modern World 1450–1815* (UCL Press, London, 1999) tries to offer global coverage in a slim volume. Also useful are Maarten Ultee (ed.), *Adapting to Conditions: War and society in the eighteenth century* (University of Alabama Press, AL, n.p., 1986); Jeremy Black (ed.), *The Origins of War in Early Modern Europe* (John Donald, Edinburgh, 1987); and the second and third chapters in Michael Duffy, *The Military Revolution and the State 1500–1800* (Exeter Studies in History, No. 1, University of Exeter, 1980).

Naval background

Nicholas Rodger, *The Wooden World: An anatomy of the Georgian navy* (Collins, London, 1986) is fundamental. Peter Padfield, *Tide of Empires: Decisive naval campaigns in the rise of the west. Vol. 2: 1654–1763* (Routledge, London, 1982), provides a general survey. Jeremy Black and Philip Woodfine (eds.), *The British Navy and the Use of Naval Power in the Eighteenth Century* (Leicester University Press, Leicester, 1988), contains several relevant chapters. Privateering is less well covered than regular navies. Carl E. Swanson, *Predators and Prizes: American privateering and imperial warfare, 1739–1748* (University of South Carolina Press, Charleston, SC, 1991) is an exception. Two essays by John S. Bromley, 'Outlaws at Sea, 1660–1720', and 'Colonies at War', both reprinted in his collected essays *Corsairs and Navies 1660–1760* (Hambledon Press, London, 1987), pp. 1–20 and 21–28 respectively, are useful; while Patrick Crowhurst, *The Defence of British Trade 1689–1815* (Dawson, Folkestone, 1977) surveys measures taken to defend the colonial trades. Richard Pares, *Colonial Blockade and Neutral Rights 1739–1763* (Clarendon Press, Oxford, 1938; reprinted Porcupine Press, Philadelphia, 1975), is a technical study which does much to illuminate what was at stake in colonial war.

Regional studies

The Indian sub-continent

James P. Lawford, *Britain's Army in India from its Origins to the Conquest of Bengal* (George Allen and Unwin, London, 1978); Michael Edwardes, *The Battle of Plassey and the Conquest of Bengal* (Macmillan, London, 1961); Kirk H.A. Kolff, *Naukar, Rajput and Sepoy: The ethnohistory of the military labour market in Hindustan, 1450–1850* (Cambridge University Press, Cambridge, 1990); G.J. Bryant, 'Pacification in the Early British Raj, 1755–86', in the *Journal of Imperial and Commonwealth History*, 14 (1985), pp. 3–19; I. Bruce Watson, 'Fortifications and the "Idea" of Force in Early English East Indian Relations with India', *Past and Present*, 88 (1980), pp. 70–87.

North America in the colonial era

As a work of reference, Alan Gallay (ed.), *Colonial Wars of North America, 1512–1763: An encyclopedia* (Garland, New York, 1996), may be recommended. Douglas E. Leach, *Arms for Empire: A military history of the British colonies in North America, 1607–1763* (Macmillan, New York, 1973), is to be preferred to the same author's flawed *Roots of Conflict: British armed forces and colonial Americans, 1677–1763* (University of North Carolina Press, Chapel Hill, NC, 1986). Howard H. Peckham, *The Colonial Wars, 1689–1762* (University of Chicago Press, Chicago, IL, 1964), remains a useful, compact introduction, but the outstanding modern work is now Ian K. Steele, *Warpaths: Invasions of North America* (Oxford University Press, New York, 1994). The same author's *Betrayals: Fort William Henry and the 'Massacre'* (Oxford University Press, New York, 1990) is an excellent microstudy. James Titus, *The Old Dominion at War: Society, politics and warfare in late colonial Virginia* (University of South Carolina Press, Columbia, SC, 1991); Fred Anderson, *A People's Army: Massachusetts soldiers and society in the Seven Years' War* (University of North Carolina Press, Chapel Hill, NC, 1984); and Richard I. Melvoin, *New England Outpost: War and society in colonial Deerfield* (W.W. Norton, New York, pbk edn, 1989), are good modern regional studies. The best modern study of the Elder Pitt is now Marie Peters, *The Elder Pitt* (Addison Wesley Longman, London, 1998).

The West Indies

Apart from Richard Harding, *Amphibious Warfare in the Eighteenth Century* (Royal Historical Society Studies in History 62, Boydell and Brewer,

Woodbridge, 1991), which is really confined to the British West Indian campaign of 1740–42, the classic work by Richard Pares, *War and Trade in the West Indies, 1739–1763* (Clarendon Press, Oxford, 1936, reprinted Frank Cass, London, 1963), deservedly dominates the field.

The American Revolution

By far the best study of the war from the Westminster point of view is Piers Mackesy, *The War for America 1775–1783* (Longman, London, 1964). There is a University of Nebraska Press, Bison Book Edition, Lincoln and London, 1993, with an interesting introduction by John W. Shy. Mackesy sees the war as 'the last great war of the *ancien régime*'. Stephen Conway's *The War of American Independence 1775–1783* (Edward Arnold, London, pbk edn, 1995) sees it rather as the first 'people's war', on both sides. Robert Middlekauff, *The Glorious Cause: The American Revoluton 1763–1789* (Oxford University Press, New York, 1982), provides an up-to-date coverage of the military history set in an old-fashioned frame. There is a great deal of important military and naval material conveniently arranged in the National Maritime Museum catalogue 1776: *The British story of the American Revolution* (Greenwich, London, 1976). American scholars have produced whole libraries on different aspects of the conflict, but Robert A. Gross, *The Minutemen and their World* (Hill and Wang, New York, pbk edn, 1976) is a brilliant display of the ability of what Michael Zuckerman has called 'the new local history' to illuminate the opening clashes of the war. Ira D. Gruber, *The Howe Brothers and the American Revolution* (University of North Carolina Press, Chapel Hill, NC, 1972) is fundamental. Mark V. Kwasny, *Washington's Partisan War 1775–1783* (Kent State University Press, Ohio, OH, 1996) is an important recent study.

The naval side of the war may be followed in several excellent studies. Nicholas Tracy, *Navies, Deterrence and American Independence: Britain and seapower in the 1760s and 1770s* (University of British Columbia Press, Vancouver, 1988), is essential for the period from the 1760s to French intervention. David Syrett, *Shipping and the American War 1775–83* (Athlone Press, London, 1970), studies the increasingly insoluble logistical problems faced by the British government and his *The Royal Navy in American Waters 1775–1783* (Scolar Press, Aldershot, 1989) is an admirable overview, as is John A. Tilley, *The British Navy and the American Revolution* (University of South Carolina Press, Columbia, SC, 1987).

Imperial ideology

In this perhaps overstressed field, where many of the modern monographs are marred by an absence of historical knowledge, let alone context, the following may be recommended as solid pieces of scholarship: Richard Koebner, *Empire* (Cambridge University Press, Cambridge, 1961); Peter N. Miller, *Defining the Common Good: Empire, religion and philosophy in eighteenth-century Britain* (Cambridge University Press, Cambridge, 1994); and Kathleen Wilson, *The Sense of the People: Politics, culture and imperialism in England, 1715–1785* (Cambridge University Press, Cambridge, 1995).

INDEX

Abercrombie, Major General James 137, 141, 142, 143–4, 145
Abyssinia, Bruce's travels in 257
Act of Settlement (1714) 47
Act of Union (1707) 1–2, 36, 38, 53, 253, 262
Act of Union (1800) 262
Adair, James 169, 174
Adams, John 202, 204, 230, 259
Adams, Sam 200, 203, 204, 231
Africa, West African trading posts 165–6
Aix-la-Chapelle, Peace of (1748) 74, 95–6, 114, 132
Alberoni, Cardinal Julio 53, 54
Alexander of New Jersey, William 207–8
Allen, Ethan 210
American Civil War 154, 240
American identity 231, 239–40, 249–51, 259
American War of Independence 69, 146, 153, 195–225, 230–8, 240–5, 263–4
  and American identity 231, 249–51
  and the Articles of Confederation 249–50
  attitudes of colonial leaders 202–3
  and black slaves 240
  and the Boston Tea Party 199, 200
  and the British army 206–8
  British evacuation of Boston 204, 209–11
  and the Coercive or Intolerable Acts 200, 201
  Continental Congress 201, 204–5, 207, 212, 221
  Declaration of Independence 70, 213, 243–4, 249
  and English identity 231
  and France 204–5, 221, 222, 230, 231, 237, 238, 243

  and the Indian peoples 240–1, 244, 261
  Loyalists 234–5, 237, 241, 242, 245, 251, 261–2
  and the modification of the Massachusetts Charter 200–1
  and naval warfare 208–9, 215–16, 237–8, 263–4
  New England militia 203, 205
  Patriots 233–4, 235–7, 241, 251, 263
  peace settlement 239–40, 241–2, 243, 251–2
  and Spain 204–5, 221, 222, 223, 237, 238, 250
  see also North American colonies; United States of America
Amherst, Colonel Jeffrey 142–3, 151, 152, 174, 176, 177, 207
Andros, Sir Edmund, Governor of New England 15
Anglo–Dutch wars 5, 86
Anne, Queen 13, 29, 34, 47
  and the Act of Union 38
  and European issues 2
  and Roman Catholicism 29
Anson, Admiral George 66, 67, 68, 149, 168, 189
Antigua 147–8, 179, 258
Anwar-ud-din, Nawab 93, 97, 98
Arbuthnot, Admiral 218
Argyll, Duke of 52, 65
aristocracy
  and City financial interests 4, 6
  Irish 253
  Scottish 27–8, 51, 59, 233
Arnold, Benedict 210, 212, 213, 232
artillery, and Anglo-French wars in India 98–9, 101
Atkin, Edmund 134–5, 141, 145, 175
Aungier, Gerald 88, 90
Aurangzeb, Emperor of India 88